AF656730

# Bhagavad-Gītā

A New Exposition in a Broader Spectrum

# Bhagavad-Gītā

## A New Exposition in a Broader Spectrum

N.C. Panda

D.K. Printworld (P) Ltd.
New Delhi

**Cataloging in Publication Data — DK**
[Courtesy: D.K. Agencies (P) Ltd. <docinfo@dkagencies.com>]

**Panda, N. C. (Nursingh Charan),** 1929-
Bhagavad-gītā : a new exposition in a broader spectrum / N.C. Panda.
p. cm.
Includes bibliographical references.
ISBN 13: 9788124605257 (Hb)
ISBN 10: 8124605254 (Hb)

1. Bhagavadgītā — Criticism, interpretation, etc. 2. Yoga. 3. Philosophy, Hindu. I. Title.

DDC 294.5924046 22

© Author

*First published in India, 2009*

ISBN 13: 978-81-246-0525-7 (Hb) ISBN 10: 81-246-0525-4
ISBN 13: 978-81-246-0526-4 (Pb) ISBN 10: 81-246-0526-2

All rights reserved. No part of this publication may be reproduced or transmitted in any form or by any means, electronic or mechanical, including photocopying, recording, or any information storage or retrieval system, without prior written permission of the copyright holder, indicated above, and the publishers.

*Published and printed by:*
D.K. Printworld (P) Ltd.
*Regd. office* : *'Srikunj,'* F-52, Bali Nagar
Ramesh Nagar Metro Station
New Delhi – 110 015
*Phones* : (011) 2545 3975; 2546 6019; *Fax* : (011) 2546 5926
*E-mail*: dkprintworld@vsnl.net
*Web*: www.dkprintworld.com

*Dedicated to*

*late Revered* ***Aldous Huxley***

*one of the great thinkers*
*of the modern world*

The *Geeta* is one of the clearest and most comprehensive summaries of the Perennial Philosophy ever to have been done. Hence its enduring value, not only for Indians, but for all mankind. . . . The *Bhagavadgeeta* is perhaps the most systematic spiritual statement of the Perennial Philosophy.

— Aldous Huxley

# Prologue

THE *Bhagavad-Gītā* (*BG*) contains divine songs, the songs sung by God Himself. It is part of the *Mahābhārata*, the greatest and the best epic of the world. Chronologically speaking, it is the second ancient epic, the *Rāmāyaṇa* being the first one. How ancient is this epic is occasionally debated. It must not be post-Buddhistic (not later than 600 BCE), since it has no allusion to Gautama Buddha and the religion preached by him. Buddhism had a gigantic socio-religious movement in India and Asia. A great epic like the *Mahābhārata* could hardly ignore such a movement of great significance. We propose a tentative date as the fifteenth century BCE in which this epic might have been written. Some scholars, basing on their astronomical research, date the *Mahābhārata* era as the fifth or the fourth millennium BCE. We adhere to the idea that the Mahābhārata-War could not predate the Haṛappan civilization whose period has been ascertained by carbon-dating. Moreover, we have to consider comparative philology with reference to the language used in the Vedas, the Brāhmaṇas, the Āraṇyakas, the Upaniṣads and the Epics.

Some scholars claim that the *BG* is a later insertion in the *Mahābhārata* epic. They try to substantiate their opinion by the argument that such a long dialogue like the *BG* could not possibly be held in a battlefield. Such an argument in favour of credibility in the context of place and time would seem to be plausible for the common folk, but not for God. If all possibilities are cast into a common die, it would be a mechanical reductionism. A big volume of a book can be copied by a computer in an instantaneous flash. When Lord Vāsudeva desired to know the perplexity of Arjuna and communicated with the latter with a view to bringing him to the right path, He must have done it within a few minutes through mental flashes. Secondly, the conversation between Lord Vāsudeva and Arjuna was not electronically recorded. Vyāsa wrote the epic after the War was over. The subject matter of this epic was based on fact rather than fiction. Even if it was a fact, we have to bear in mind that Vyāsa, the great poet, must have given his poetic touch to his narration of facts. After all, a poet, in all ages, is not a scribe. The dialogue between Lord Vāsudeva and Arjuna, as depicted in the *BG*, has become a superb, literary excellence. The writer of this dialogue was Vyāsa, and not Lord Vāsudeva. This poet was a great seer (*draṣṭā*) and a great creator (*sraṣṭā*). He dictated the *Mahābhārata* to Lord Gaṇeśa. The past events of the War were revealed to him. He dictated whatever was revealed to him. "He who could grant the power of divine vision (clairvoyance, *divya-dṛṣṭi*) and divine audition (clairaudience, *divya-śravaṇa*) to Sañjaya to narrate the happenings of the War to the blind king, Dhṛtarāṣṭra, could not get the power of revelation to write the epic." Such an idea is ludicrous. To place Vyāsa on par with the common folk is outrageous.

Let us accept the fact that truth could be revealed to Vyāsa. What is the certainty that he recorded the truth? Vyāsa, the great seer, was not only a genius of rare talent, but also a person of the highest standard of morality and integrity. He was committed to truth (*satya-niṣṭha*). His father was Ṛṣi Parāśara and mother was Kālī (later renamed as Satyavatī). Kālī was born in a fisherman's family. Her father was a *dāsa* chieftain whose tribe was living on the bank of the Yamunā River. Kālī was ferrying a boat on which Parāśara was to cross the river. It happened to be a boat-trip of two persons only, Parāśara and Kālī. The seer fell in love with the black beauty who was still unmarried. They had consensual intercourse. Thus was Vyāsa born of Kālī and Parāśara. The child was a racial hybrid, 50 per cent aboriginal and 50 per cent *Ārya*. Who, other than Vyāsa, could reveal this fact about his parenthood? The quality and importance of the *Mahābhārata* could not be diminished at all, had Vyāsa suppressed this truth about his birth and lineage.

And what did Vyāsa write in his epic? He narrated the incidences of his sons and grandsons. King Vicitravīrya was the son of Śāntanu and Satyavatī. Vicitravīrya had a premature death, leaving his two widow-queens childless. There was an old custom of *niyoga*. Satyavatī, by getting advice from Bhīṣma (son of Śāntanu and Gaṅgā), requested her son, Vyāsa, for temporary sex-relation with the widow-queens to get two successors to the royal family. Ambikā and Ambālikā were the widow queens who became the mothers of Dhṛtarāṣṭra and Pāṇḍu, respectively. The queens were averse to the black colour and ugly face of Vyāsa. The eldest son was born blind and the other was jaundiced. Circumstantially, due to the repulsion of the queens, Vyāsa had intercourse with the royal maid who became the mother of Vidura, a learned person of high morality. All the Kauravas and the Pāṇḍavas were the grandsons of Vyāsa. Did the seer eulogise the actions of all his sons and grandsons? Seer Vyāsa was not an ordinary human being. To measure such a rare Great Man with a common yardstick is the greatest folly and blunder. India still dabbles in casteism. This great nation is yet to learn that Indian wisdom could hardly be living with lustre and brilliance, by the exhibition of definite proofs, in the hypothetical absence of the original and compilatory work of Vyāsa. (In this regard, we pay our obeisance to Ṛṣi Vālmīki too).

It would not seem to be an over-simplification if one says that reading other scriptures after the *svādhyāya* of the *BG* is redundant. Such a statement may not be the whole truth; but, in essence, it is not totally untrue. We get the quintessence of the Vedas, the Upaniṣads, the Sāṅkhya, the Yoga, all the systems of Indian philosophy and many other scriptures in the *BG*. In addition, it has its own synthetic, holistic philosophy, based on a strong foundation. It provides solutions to all types of human problems. After all, the *BG* has its birth from human predicament, dilemma, agony and dejection. The long dialogues in eighteen chapters of this scripture are mainly meant for providing solutions to the problems of life.

If the *BG* is considered as a religious book, it has a special feature. It does not contain commandments. It does not say "Do this" and "Don't do that." It advocates for free will. Towards the end of the last chapter of the *BG*, Lord Vāsudeva says to Arjuna:

"After intense deliberation on the knowledge you have gained, take your own decision and do as you like." Earlier in the *BG*, the Lord has said to Arjuna: "Question and cross-question me to clarify your doubts." In fact, the *BG* is not a religious book. It is a philosophy on spirituality. In the language of Aldous Huxley, it is a Perennial Philosophy given to mankind.

Many commentaries on the *BG* are already available. One may question: "Is there any need for another commentary?" Had the answer to this question been negative rather than affirmative, this book would not have been written. The Vedas say: "Truth is verily one only. The wise talk about it in different ways" (*satyamekaṁ viprā bahudhā vadanti*). By virtue of the inscrutability of Truth, light thrown on it again and again is not likely to be futile. Every time Truth retold would show some of its newer facets.

The present exposition on the *BG* is an updated one on the basis of modern thoughts in general and newer scientific discoveries in particular. As the title indicates, interpretation has been done in a newer vision in a broader spectrum.

The *BG* is universal in character. It does not belong to any particular religion or sect. It does not preach any specific philosophy too. In spite of this cosmic nature of this scripture, many commentetors have tried to drag it to their own fold to explain their own doctrine at the exclusion of others. Some others have seen the *BG* in the light of their own ideologies. As for example, Mahatma Gandhi and Lokamanya Bal Gangadhar Tilak interpreted the *Gītā* in favour of *karma-yoga* (the *yoga* of action). The *ācārya*s of the Vaiṣṇava sects presented sectarian interpretations, basing on their religious philosophical systems. They favoured the system of dualism and vehemently rejected any non-dualistic interpretation. Ācārya Śaṅkara rigidly adhered to his own school of non-dualism. Further, being influenced by his grand-teacher, Gauḍapāda, he did not extricate himself from illusionism, although mostly he is not an illusionist. Dr S. Radhakrishnan's commentary seems to be inadequate. Sri Aurobindo's book, *Essays on the Gita*, is not a systematic commentary. It comprises a number of essays and presents the reflections of the learned author on the *Gītā* philosophy *vis-à-vis* his own philosophy. Many others have written very good commentaries on the *BG*. In a prologue like this, we have no scope to exhaustively mention their names and their works. We have mentioned a few of them in the bibliography.

Every author has his own subjectivity. There is nothing like full objectivity in philosophy, literature and some other subjects. It is rather a fact that there is nothing like full objectivity in any subject with any individual. The present author is a great admirer of Śaṅkarācārya. In spite of this fact, on certain philosophical topics, he does not agree with the *ācārya*. Notwithstanding this fact, his reverence for the *ācārya* is not diminished at all. In general, he is reluctant to blindly deify anybody whosoever he may be.

The present exposition has some special characteristics. It has eighteen chapters in conformity with those of the *BG*. A varying number of essays have been written on each chapter. A few essays clarify some philosophical concepts or some special features of the *BG*, without any direct allusion to any verse. Nothing has been written on a very few verses of the *BG*. They serve in the scripture as links or possess less significance. Most verses of the *BG* have been commented upon in the essays. In addition, the reflections of the author have been presented on the flowing subject matter of the *BG*. The exposition on the *BG* does not contain the original Sanskrit text, although it does contain the English rendering of the verses.

The original Sanskrit text, with Roman transliteration, has been appended to the English text of the book at the end. This has been done, keeping in view the probable need of some readers who may be interested in a critical study of the original text and the author's English rendering.

The *BG* is not parochial and sectarian. It is not a book for any single religion. In fact, it is not a religious book at all. It is a book on spirituality of the highest order. With the rapidly changing vision of humankind, the whole universe is very soon ("soon" in the cosmic scale of time) going to be a family. The ancient Indian seers chanted a maxim: *vasudhaiva kuṭumbakam* (the world is verily a family). The Sanskrit word *vasudhā* refers to the "earth." The English word "world" generally means the "earth," with rare reference to the "universe." The Sanskrit word *jagat* (one in motion or change) or *viśva* (all) and the English word "universe" are synonyms. With the rapidly changing concepts on the cosmos, we dream to update the maxim by saying: *jagadeva kuṭumbakam* (the universe is verily one family). We don't think that we are day-dreaming in a domain of Utopia. We indulge in practical optimism. The cosmic citizen of tomorrow will read the *BG* to sequentially elevate himself from the state of animality to that of humanity, from the state of humanity to that of divinity, and finally from the state of divinity to that of *Brahman*-hood. Then only will the declaration of Aldous Huxley that the Gītā is the Perennial Philosophy of mankind be translated into action. Religions saved man from barbarism and savageness. It is unfortunate that religions have created problems too, and are still creating. It is time for man to transcend religions and adopt spirituality. It is only the spiritual man who would make attempts and would succeed to attain to the summit state of *Brahman*-hood. We are not speaking of the total transformation of *Homo sapiens* to *Brahman* or Gnostic Beings (*Brahmans*). We visualize a spiritual state in which more and more persons would elevate themselves to *Brahman*-hood, with the continuation of the cyclic *saṁsāra* or metempsychosis.

We hope this book would help the process of humanization and divinization. Our source is One. Our goal is One and That One which is our source. In the vast Ocean of Cosmic Consciousness (Pure and Fundamental), we are virtual bubbles, foams, surfs, ripples and waves. Nevertheless, it is also a fact that the bubble is not essentially different from the original Ocean. How can there be phenomena without the underlying noumena? The Upaniṣadic statement, *aham brahmāsmi* (I am *Brahman*) is the hub of the non-dualistic philosophy.

# Acknowledgement

I AM a lover of books and a lifelong voracious reader. Perhaps due to overuse of the eyes, without adequate rest, I lost my full vision twice in life, once in 1967 and a second time in 1996. In 1967, my retinas in both eyes were detached, the left one with seven holes and ruptures. At that time I was a Ph.D. student in the University of Missouri, Columbia, USA. I got a doctor (Prof. Dr Carl H. Ide) as a godsend. He was a free surgeon for me. He also spent dollars for my hospitalization and related expenditure. By surgical reattachment of the retinas, I regained some vision in my right eye and lost full vision in the left one during the long period between 1967 and 1996. I lost my full vision in my right eye in 1996 for the second time in my life. This happened due to retinal detachment again as a consequence of a faulty surgery of cataract. The left eye which was non-functional since 1967 became functional in 1996 after the surgery of a recently developed cataract. It regained about 20 per cent vision. But that amount of vision saved me from total blindness. For this, I am grateful to Dr Lingam Gopal and Dr (Mrs) Prema Padmanabhan of Sankara Netralayam of Chennai. If God closes one door, He opens another. At that time, I realized the purport of the provision of two eyes, two ears, two lungs, two kidneys and such other organs and limbs by Providence. Now I have developed corneal opacity in my right eye and open-angle glaucoma (high intra-ocular pressure) in both eyes. The little vision which I have regained in my left eye is dwindling now due to the degeneration of the optic nerve. During the last twelve years (1996-2008), it has been impossible for me to read and write. With great difficulty, I recognize known faces of friends and relatives. Sometimes I fail to recognize them too. In such a state of bad eyesight, it is still possible for me to continue my writing career. How has it been possible? I get the help of my family and my disciples. I make use of some recently invented gadgets for my writing. But, in spite of all sorts of human and mechanical help, I am not able to do my writing work in some special aspects peculiar to my books. Really speaking, I continue to be a writer by getting divine grace. This much I reveal here and shall not elaborate further. Let the mysticism be deeply buried in the thickest darkness. Being a scientist myself, I must be the watchdog of scientific temper. I must not irk the rationalists. However, I would submit that spirituality is also part of rationality. The tip of an iceberg is detected by empirical means whereas major portion of the iceberg remains undetected unless the latter is scanned by divine experience. We applaud experience gained through mediation (*parokṣānubhūti*); we have a tendency to discard a person's experience gained through immediate means (*aparokṣānubhūti*). On this issue, the golden maxim is: Let us agree to disagree.

I am glad to express my gratitude for Dr Bhabendra Putatunda, M.D., practising doctor in the USA, for his kind donation for the production of the manuscript of this book and some more books to be published in the near future. In different ways, my disciples have helped me in the production of my manuscript. My sincere thanks are due to Shakuntala Dash, Abhinna Chandra Sahu, Minati Dash, Sanjukta Sahu, Gobardhan Sahu, Amitava Sahu, Smita Sahu, Shambhunath Sahu, Kahnu Charan Sahu, Sujata Priyadarshini, Amita Sahu, Pradeep Kumar Das and Vishvadev Dash.

Without the dedicated support of my sons and daughters-in-law — Prakash, Bikash, Bibhas, Smita, Snigdha and Arati, an almost blind person could not have continued his writing career. I thank and bless them. I, with blessings, acknowledge the support of Shephali, my daughter, and Sudhir, my son-in-law.

When I perform penances (*tapasyā*) as a writer, I have to give less time to my wife, Manorama. She ungrudgingly bears with me and, with all sincerity, looks after my comforts. I am grateful to her for her love, affection and personal care.

As a senile and ailing author, I am in physical agony and mental ecstasy. My geriatric problems, due to senile degeneration, are too serious. My old age diseases (*jarā-vyādhis*) like blindness, deafness, cardiac ailments including bradycardia (pulse-rate 42 to 50), serious hypertension, osteoporosis and osteoarthrosis, obstinate, chronic constipation and insomnia make my life painful. I have made a truce with my senility. The source of my ecstasy is God, the Almighty. My love for my grandchildren — Nivedita (Nita), Madhusmita (Mita), Lopamudra (Lopa), Arpita (Soma), Anwesha (Lisha), Divyasha (Disha) and my only one grandson, Siddhartha (Munu/Manuraja) — and their love for me inactivate my physical suffering. I am a householder and not a recluse. My grandchildren provide the sap to the stem of my life. Without their love, I would have been simply the bagasse, a dry sugar cane plant, devoid of juice.

Last but not the least, I am grateful to Sri Susheel Kumar Mittal, the Director of the prestigious publishing house, D.K. Printworld, for publishing my books.

**Nrusingh Charan Panda**
(Ācārya Śaktipāda)

*Agastya Bhavan*
*712, Shahid Nagar*
*Khanduali Mandir Road*
*Bhubaneswar - 751 007 (Orissa)*
Rāmanavamī, vs 2066 (April 3, 2009)

# Contents

# Abbreviations

| | |
|---|---|
| *AĀ* | *Aitareya Āraṇyaka* |
| *ĀBrā* | *Aitareya Brāhmaṇa* |
| *ĀL* | *Ānanda-Laharī* of Śaṅkarācārya |
| *AU* | *Aitareya Upaniṣad* |
| *AV* | *Atharvaveda* |
| *BDP* | *Brahmāṇḍa Purāṇa* |
| *BG* | *Bhagavad-Gītā* |
| *Bhā* | *Bhāgavatam* |
| *BP* | *Brahma Purāṇa* |
| *BS* | *Brahma-Sūtram* |
| *BU* | *Bṛhadāraṇyaka Upaniṣad* |
| *CU* | *Chāndogya Upaniṣad* |
| *DBhā* | *Devī-Bhāgavatam* |
| *GMK* | *Māṇḍūkya-Kārikā* of Gauḍapāda |
| *GP* | *Garuḍa Purāṇa* |
| *HV* | *Harivaṁśa* |
| *ĪU* | *Īśopaniṣad* |
| *KP* | *Kūrma Purāṇa* |
| *KTU* | *Kaṭhopaniṣad* |
| *MAU* | *Māṇḍūkyopaniṣad* |
| *MBh* | *Mahābhārata* |
| *MP* | *Matsya Purāṇa* |
| *MS* | *Manu-Smṛti* |
| *MTU* | *Maitrī Upaniṣad* |
| *MUU* | *Muṇḍaka Upaniṣad* |
| *PD* | *Pañcadaśī* |
| *PP* | *Padma Purāṇa* |
| *PU* | *Praśnopaniṣad* |
| *PYD* | *Pātañjala Yoga-Darśanam* |
| *ṚV* | *Ṛgveda* |
| *ŚB* | *Śāṅkara Bhāṣyam* |

| | |
|---|---|
| *ŚBrā* | *Śatapatha Brāhmaṇa* |
| *SK* | *Sāṅkhya-Kārikā* |
| *SL* | *Saundarya-Laharī* of Śaṅkarācārya |
| *SPS* | *Sāṅkhya-Pravacana-Sūtram* |
| *ŚU* | *Śvetāśvatara Upaniṣad* |
| *TĀ* | *Taittirīya Āraṇyaka* |
| *TBrā* | *Taittirīya Brāhmaṇa* |
| *TS* | *Taittirīya Saṁhitā* |
| *TU* | *Taittirīya Upaniṣad* |
| *VāP* | *Vāyu Purāṇa* |
| *VC* | *Vivekacūḍāmaṇi* |
| *VP* | *Viṣṇu Purāṇa* |
| *VPDA* | *Vedānta-Paribhāṣā* of Dharmarāja Adhvarīndra |
| *VS* | *Vedānta-Sāra* of Sadānanda |
| *YS* | *Yājñavalkya-Saṁhitā* |
| *YV* | *Yajurveda* |

# 1

## Arjuna-Viṣāda-Yogaḥ
## The Agony and Dejection
## (The Despondency of Arjuna)

### 1.01 : Prelude to the Bhagavad-Gītā

THE *Bhagavad-Gītā* (*BG*) is part of the Indian epic, the *Mahābhārata,* written by Vyāsa, not later than the sixth century BCE. (The probable period may be 1500 BCE). There was a dispute over the right on the kingdom of Hastinā among the members of one family. Dhṛtarāṣṭra and Pāṇḍu were brothers, the former being the elder one. The Pāṇḍavas were the five sons of deceased Pāṇḍu. The Kauravas were the one hundred sons of Dhṛtarāṣṭra, a born-blind person who was seated on the throne after the demise of his younger brother, Pāṇḍu. Duryodhana, the eldest prince, was the *de facto* ruler on behalf of his father. He, at the behest of his maternal uncle, Śakuni, deprived the Pāṇḍavas of the kingdom or even part of it. Lord Śrīkṛṣṇa did not leave any stone unturned to settle the dispute amicably and peacefully. He approached the Kauravas and begged only five villages for the Pāṇḍavas. But, Duryodhana, the most wicked Kaurava, getting the evil advice of Śakuni, turned down the request of the Lord, with arrogance, obstinacy and bad behaviour. All negotiations failed. Finally, both parties prepared themselves for a war.

Bhīṣma was the first commander-in-chief of the Kaurava army. He got a boon from his father that nobody could kill him and that he would die if and when he wished. He was defeated (rather he gladly consented to be defeated). He lay on a bed of arrows, awaiting the advent of *uttarāyaṇa* (the summer solstice) for quitting his body. Sañjaya, the companion and counsellor of Dhṛtarāṣṭra, conveyed the news of Bhīṣma's arrow-bed to the king. This news was very much shocking to the blind king. He was perturbed and he lost his heart. He wished to hear a detailed account of the war-events from the beginning. Vyāsa offered divine vision to the king so that he could see, while sitting on his throne, all the war-events at a distance. But the king was horrified to see the death of his sons in the war. He wanted to hear the narration of the war-events from Sañjaya. And so did Vyāsa confer divine vision on Sañjaya for a period up to the end of the war. Thus, commenced the first chapter of the *BG*. It consists of 18 chapters and forms the 25th chapter of the "Bhīṣma-Parva" of the *Mahābhārata*.

If we consider one aspect of the *BG*, we may admit that it is unique in the world. In the language of Aldous Huxley, the *BG* is the perennial philosophy of the world. That a theistic philosophy, the best of its kind in the world, was born in the battlefield of Kurukṣetra[1] is very much intriguing. This intrigue is, however, apparent. Its real meaning is very deep and has cosmic significance.

The Mahābhārata War was fought during a period of 18 days only. On the first day of the War, Arjuna requested Śrīkṛṣṇa to place the chariot, known as Kapidhvaja, in between the Pāṇḍava and the Kaurava armies.[2] Śrīkṛṣṇa did what Arjuna desired. A fierce battle was about to begin. Pitāmaha (the grandfather) Bhīṣma was heading the Kaurava army. In the core of his heart, he had a soft corner for Arjuna in particular and the Pāṇḍavas in general, although he was sincerely and faithfully fighting for the Kauravas. He had high admiration for the personality, valour and qualities of Arjuna. The Pāṇḍavas were nurtured and trained by the grandfather. Arjuna cherished a high degree of reverence for the grandfather, the dearest and the most respectable person for all the Pāṇḍavas. Both were the best archers, although Arjuna was not strictly comparable with Bhīṣma. In spite of this fact, Arjuna

1. *BG*, I.1.

2. *BG*, I.21.

had no trace of timidity in his heart and was not afraid of Bhīṣma. The former was a great hero, with unparalleled valour. He had a spotless personality, as transparent as the whitest crystal. Nevertheless, Arjuna, the great hero, succumbed to delusion (*moha*), one of the greatest foes of the common human beings. He gave up the idea of fighting, set aside his bow (with the name "Gāṇḍīva") and arrows and declined to fight.[3]

Arjuna expressed the agony and dejection of his heart before Lord Śrīkṛṣṇa. The first chapter of the *Gītā* contains a number of verses, depicting this agony (*viṣāda*).[4]

In the battlefield, Pārtha (the son of Pṛthā or Kuntī; Pārtha is a name of Arjuna) saw all the persons with whom he was going to fight. They were the paternal uncles, grandfathers, teachers and preceptors, maternal uncles, cousins, nephews, grandsons, friends and companions. Realizing that he was going to kill his kinsfolk, he was seized with grief and agony. He was despirited and was overpowered with desperations. His limbs gave way; his mouth dried; his entire body shivered and his body-hairs stood on end. His Gāṇḍīva dropped down from his hand. (This Gāṇḍīva was a celestial bow. Varuṇa presented it to Arjuna at the instance of Agni, the fire-god, who was pleased with Arjuna). His skin was burning all over. His head reeled. He could not stand with steadiness. He saw bad omens. He did not find any virtue in killing his kinsmen.

Arjuna did not see any justification in killing his revered persons, kinsmen and relatives. "What for are the victory, the gain of kingdom, the worldly enjoyments and even the life, if I kill my own people, so near and dear and so honourable and respectful?" This was the question asked by Arjuna to Śrīkṛṣṇa.[5] He posed a number of further issues too.[6]

---

3. *BG*, I.47.

4. *BG*, I.28-46.

5. *BG*, I.31-37.

6. *BG*, I.38-45.

> By slaying the sons of Dhṛtarāṣṭra, we shall not get pleasure at all. We rather commit sins thereby. No person can be happy by killing his own kinsfolk.
>
> With the extinction of our family in this war, our righteous traditions would die away. With our family virtues got lost, unrighteousness (vice) would overpower us. Such an unholy situation would corrupt our women, resulting in the birth of *varṇa-saṅkara*s (racial and cultural hybrids). It is decidedly better to avoid fighting and slaying the kinsmen and thereby preserve the *kula-dharma* (family traditions of virtues and righteousness).

Finally Arjuna conveyed his last decision to Śrīkṛṣṇa:

> Let me not oppose the sons of Dhṛtarāṣṭra. Let me not harm them by my Gāṇḍīva. Let them rather slay me. That would confer greater felicity on me.[7]

So saying, being overwhelmed with sorrow in the battlefield, Arjuna abandoned his bow and arrows and sat on the seat of his chariot.[8]

### 1.02 : The Bhagavad-Gītā, the Supreme Scripture on Yoga

The *BG* is a unique type of Yoga-scripture (*Yoga-Śāstra*). This Yoga, instead of being secular, is theistic, and is still not restricted to any particular religion. Its import and application are universal. The Sanskrit word *yoga* has been derived from the verb-root *yuj*, meaning "to unite." By practising *yoga*, as prescribed by the *BG*, one can bring about communion between one's self and the Supreme Self, finally leading to liberation (*mokṣa*).

The *BG* has a broad range of liberalism. It does not pinpoint any single system only to attain the goal. A person liberates himself by practising *jñāna-yoga* (the *yoga* of knowledge on *Brahman*), *karma-yoga* (the *yoga* of detached action), *dhyāna-yoga* or *samādhi-yoga* (the *yoga* of one-pointed concentration on God), *bhakti-yoga* (the *yoga* of devotion) and by following other spiritual paths. Paths

---

7. *BG*, I.46.

8. *BG*, I.47.

are many; but the goal is one only. One may adopt a single system or multiple systems to reach the summit, the state of *Brahman*-hood.

Each chapter of the *BG* has been named as *yoga*, preceded by a specific attribute. The word *yoga* has a general meaning in the chapter-headings. It means "the way." By the adoption of the way(s), one can ascend the ladder from animality (*paśutva*) to humanity (*mānavatva*), from humanity to divinity (*devatva*) and from divinity to *Brahman*-hood (*brahmatva*).

The *BG* is a synthetic scripture. It synthesizes the wisdom of the Vedas, the Vedānta, the Sāṅkhya, the Yoga and many other spiritual scriptures. It is not an exclusive system. The ocean is one, although differently named. Rivers are many. They flow from different directions, follow straight paths for some distance and tortuous paths more frequently. But finally they all meet the ocean. There are many roads to a single destination. This truth is hardly realized by some persons, seized with narrow parochialism.

The attributive terms that precede Yoga in the eighteen chapter-headings of the *BG* are listed as follows:

1. Yoga of Despondency or the Yoga of Dejection (*Viṣāda-Yoga*);
2. Yoga of Knowledge (*Sāṅkhya-Yoga*);
3. the Yoga of Detached Action (*Karma-Yoga*);
4. Yoga of Renunciation of Action in Knowledge (*Jñāna-Karma-Saṁnyāsa-Yoga*);
5. Yoga of Renunciation of Action (*Karma-Saṁnyāsa-Yoga*);
6. Yoga of Meditation (*Dhyāna-Yoga*);
7. Yoga of Knowledge with Brahma-Realization (*Jñāna-Vijñāna-Yoga*);
8. Yoga of Concentration (*Dhāraṇā-Yoga*; *Abhyāsa-Yoga*; *Akṣara-Parabrahma-Yoga*);
9. Yoga of the Royal Science of the Royal Mystery (*Rājavidyā-Rājaguhya-Yoga*);

10. Yoga of Divine, Glorious manifestations (*Vibhūti-Yoga*);
11. Yoga of the Vision of the Cosmic Form (*Viśva-Rūpa-Darśana Yoga*);
12. Yoga of Devotion (*Bhakti-Yoga*);
13. Yoga of the Field and the Field-Knower (*Kṣetra-Kṣetrajña-Yoga; Prakṛti-Puruṣa-Viveka-Yoga*);
14. Yoga of Discriminating the Three *Guṇa*s or the *Yoga* of the Three Constituents (*Guṇa-Traya-Vibhāga-Yoga*);
15. Yoga of the Supreme Spirit (*Puruṣottama-Yoga*);
16. Yoga of Division of Attributes, Divine and Demoniac (*Devāsura-Sampad-Vibhāga-Yoga*);
17. Yoga of Threefold Faith (*Śraddhātraya-Vibhāga-Yoga*); and
18. Yoga of Liberation and Renunciation (*Mokṣa-Saṁnyāsa-Yoga*).

We may consider the chapters of the *BG* as a spiritual ladder. The lowest rung in the ladder is the despondency or dejection (*viṣāda*) of Arjuna, a representative of the human species. The highest rung in the ladder is liberation and renunciation. Barring a few exceptions of highly evolved persons, most of us ascend the spiritual ladder from the base rung of agony in life.

We start with agony in life. But, we should not continue to stay in the state of agony. We should make all efforts to prevent the halt in the ascent on the spiritual ladder. This ascent is the spiritual evolution. The full success may be attained in one life or in multiple lives. Everybody is potentially divine. It is not impossible for anyone (even the most ignoble sinner) to reach the summit of Godhead.

### 1.03 : The Cosmic Battlefield

Kurukṣetra was the battlefield in the Mahābhārata War. If it is regarded as symbolic, the entire universe is a battlefield for the whole humanity. It is rather a fact that every created entity, macro or micro, inanimate or animate, struggles for existence from the very moment of its inception till its end. And, in this struggle, the entire universe is considered as a mega battlefield. Why is it so? Cannot war be avoidable? Is continual struggle unavoidable and inevitable?

Discovery in physics in the twentieth century has revealed that the creation of micro-particles and energy-quanta occurred in the super-heated cosmic soup in pairs, each one in the pair being equal and opposite to its partner. This cosmic soup, referred to here, is the super-heated *Ākāśa* in the nascent universe.[9] What has been discovered in modern physics has already been given in the Upaniṣads.[10] Soon after the birth of the paired particles, they vigorously dance, collide against one another and die. This type of collision, conflict and destruction has been clearly described in the Vedas.[11] If we consider the mathematics of this twin production, we have to recognize that the precursor material of the universe is zero. A vast (how vast?) universe has been produced out of nothing. How is it possible? Does it not contradict the sacrosanct law of the conservation of matter and energy? The *BG* itself adheres to the law of conservation of Being.[12] The Sāṅkhya also certifies that something cannot be produced out of nothing and nothing cannot be converted into something. Only something can be transformed into something else. This *sat-kārya-vāda* of the Sāṅkhya is equally applicable to *pradhāna* and the manifested universe since the latter is only a transformation of the former. The Advaita Vedānta rejects the doctrine of transformation of the Unmanifested *Prakṛti* into the universe. It does posit the transformation of matter and energy in the universe subject to the condition of virtual changes and no real changes. The *Mūla-*

---

9. *R̥V*, X.72; I.89.10; X.90.6-10; X.129.3; X.130.1-2; 4-6; *ŚBrā*, XIII.1-5; *BU*, I.1.1-2; I.2.6-7; *CU*, I.9.1; VII.12.1; *MTU*, VI.6; *MUU*, I.1.8; *PU*, I.4; *TU*, II.1.1; II.6.1; III.1.1; III.2.1; III.3.1; III.4.1; III.5.1.

10. *BU*, I.3.1; I.4.4; *PU*, I.4-5.

11. *R̥V*, X.72.6.

12. *BG*, II.16.

*Prakṛti* or *Māyā*, under the Chairpersonship of *Parameśvara*, stages a magical show in which the universe illusorily appears as a reflection from the source of *Brahman*. Thus, the illusory universe has no precursor material.

What do we derive from the foregoing paragraph? The virtual universe has an in-built contradiction. Without a single exception, every entity of matter and energy of the universe has an equal and opposite entity. This being a fact, strifes and conflicts are bound to be unavoidable and inevitable. So do we claim that the universe is a mega-battlefield.

Coming back to the issue of the inevitability of the struggle for existence, we cannot afford to ignore the prominent role played by the *ahaṅkāra* in working for the "I" and against the "non-I." It is a meaningful evolute for the existence and survival of every created entity. But, unless it is controlled by the rein of spirituality, it may play a brutal and demoniac role.

It is the *ahaṅkāra* of the *antaḥkaraṇa* (the *buddhi, ahaṅkāra* and *manas* are the three principal components of the *antaḥkaraṇa*). that has the propensity to work for the "I" and against the "non-I," to struggle for the survival of the "I," to do all possible things for getting all sorts of comforts and pleasure (including sexual pleasure) at the cost of others and even by inflicting pain on others, for acquiring power and self-dominance by subjugating others and for possession of more and more wealth by exploiting others. These inherent traits of the *ahaṅkāra* generate six instinctual attributes, namely, strong desire (*kāma),* anger (*krodha),* covetousness (greed or *lobha),* delusion with strong attachment (*moha*), pride with arrogance (*mada)* and envy or malice (*mātsarya).* The "I" craves for these six attributes, without realizing that they are the enemies (*ripu*s). Out of passion (*rāga*), it works for those that are pleasant and develops dispassion or aversion (*dveṣa*) for those which are painful. It works for self-defence and self-protection. It tenaciously works for "life-instinct" (for the perpetual continuation of its own life, *abhiniveśa* in Patañjali's language), and, in this attempt, it commits aggression on others for their death. It is terribly afraid of its death (*maraṇa-trāsa).* This fear of death further stimulates the aggressive instinct against others and the development of the instinct of selfish interest for its own sake. The *ahaṅkāra* plays a role of double standards. Its life-instinct is very dominant for its own sake; but its death-instinct works brutally against others. There are exceptions, of course. Traits like love and hatred, friendship and enmity, selfishness and altruism, compassion and cruelty are also generated in opposite pairs. One levitates and the other one gravitates. Personal endeavour (*puruṣārtha*) helps one ascend the spiritual ladder. There is death of demoniac qualities with the constant rise of spirituality and divinity. Through spiritual uplift, man is not doomed to fall a victim to the pairs of opposites. The spiritual ladder finally leads to the summit, the state of *Brahman*-hood that is bereft of opposites (*nirdvandva*) and a state of Pure Consciousness.

In the present context, it is hardly possible to omit the primary cause of evil in the created universe. *Avidyā* (nescience) is the fundamental cause of evil. It may further be said that acquisition of informational knowledge, without realization of the identity of the self and the Supreme Self and of the noumenal, all-pervasive character of the Self and of the phenomenality of the universe, does not help remove nescience. The Cosmic Sportive Play (*jāgatika līlā*) of *Parameśvara* (God) and *Parameśvarī* (Goddess) is not possible in the hypothetical total absence of nescience in the created entities. *Vidyā* (sentience, knowledge) and *avidyā* (insentience, ignorance) are also opposite attributes, in-built in the *sṛṣṭā Prakṛti* (created Nature). They result from opposite attributes, *vidyā* from *sattva* and *avidyā* from *tamas*. It is the individual *puruṣārtha* (personal endeavour with determination), exhibited through the medium of *buddhi* (the subtle organ of individual intellect, located in the subtle body), with the help of the reflected light of the consciousness of the self (*ātmā*), that can dispel the darkness of *avidyā*. *Vidyā* dispels *avidyā* in the analogy of light dispelling darkness. The removal of *avidyā* is total in the *jīvanmukta* (liberated albeit still living) only. In others, it qualitatively and quantitatively varies in a wide range. The speculation of the total removal of *avidyā* from the total universe at a particular time or for all time to come contravenes the Vedāntic concept of the *līlā* doctrine.[13] Such a speculative hypothesis of the total absence of *avidyā* must recognize only the existence of *Saccidānanda* or *Saccidānanda*s, ever remaining as such, without further cycles of the universe, and inevitably without further *līlā*. To pinpoint our factor for the inevitability of the mundane struggle, we focus on *avidyā* as the source of evil. Derivatively, we emphasize it as a causal factor of perpetual mundane struggle.

We have described three factors that are responsible for the inevitability of perpetual struggle and conflict, including occasional battles and wars. One is the original genesis of micro-particles in pairs, equal and opposite in quality and quantity. All things of the micro and macro-universe, both non-living and living, are constituted of these particles. Each one of us, living or non-living, is a mixture of contradictions. The second one is the evolution of *ahaṅkāra* from *buddhi*. The inevitability of conflicts is universal and perpetual in every cosmic cycle, unless and until an individual evolves himself to higher and higher levels of spirituality, the ascent finally leading to complete annihilation of the "I" and the "my" (until he attains to *Brahman*-hood when he becomes I-less and my-less). A person can attain such a state of a complete void of the three strings — *sattva, rajas* and *tamas* (a state of *nistraiguṇya*). If and when he does it, he becomes *Brahman,* irrespective of the fact of the possession of the present body in this life or after the death of the present body at the termination of this life. The third factor is the differential presence of *avidyā* in created entities, with the exception of *jīvanmukta*s who are rare in number and infrequent in time. We rule out any hypothesis of total elimination of *avidyā* from all entities in any particular period.

Some thinkers dream and speculate on the total ascent of all human beings on the earth to *Brahman*-hood at the end of a spiritual

---

13. *BS*, II.1.32-3.

evolution and the transformation of the earth into an eternal heaven. According to their speculation, there will come a time when everybody will be a gnostic being, like *Brahman,* with separate individual existence. These gnostic beings will be separate *Saccidānandas*. If this idea is accepted *ex hypothesi,* we cannot simultaneously accept the perpetuation of struggle, conflicts, fighting and wars. In our opinion, this speculation would never come to be true. Moreover, the earth has a limited lifespan, with a birth and a death. For details of our justification, we request our readers to refer to our book *Cyclic Universe.*[14]

We rule out the concept of mass liberation. We cannot accept the concept of an eternal earth. Our solar system has a limited span of life. No galaxy, no star and no planet can live eternally. Our whole universe cannot stay eternally. Whatever has a beginning has an end.[15] Further, we assert that good and evil co-exist in the manifested universe. The *Mahābhārata* of Vyāsa is a unique classic in the whole world. Its characters, both good and bad, are universal since they transcend time, space and individuality. Characters like Dhṛtarāṣṭra, Duryodhana, Duḥśāsana and Śakuni were living in the past, are living at present and will be living in the future. Similarly, characters like Yudhiṣṭhira, Vidura and Bhīṣma, although less in number, were, are and will be existing in all the cycles of the manifested universe. If we accept evil as a fact of inevitability in the universe, we have to accept the existence of the cosmic battlefield.

In the Mahābhārata War between the Kauravas and the Pāṇḍavas, Kurukṣetra was the battlefield. This battlefield may be symbolically considered as a representative of the cosmic battlefield. Anything created or anybody born in the universe must be a soldier like Arjuna to fight the life-war or the survival-war.

Let us focus our discussion on the human species, living on

---

14. N.C. Panda, 2002.

15. *TUŚB*, Intr. (*na hi nityaṁ kiñcidārabhyate, loke yadārabdhaṁ tadanityam*).

the earth. Man has to fight against natural adversities and calamities. Nature is generally indifferent to the happiness and sorrows of man. The primitive, savage man was helplessly fighting for his survival. The modern man of the twenty-first century has controlled and harnessed Nature for his advantage to a major extent through scientific and technological developments. But, it cannot be said that still he is not a victim of natural adversities and calamities such as earhquakes, tsunami, cyclones, floods, famines, epidemics, accidents, et cetera. Further, it is a pity that the modern man creates problems for the human species, animal species, plant species and for the entire globe by dehumanizing himself and by wrongly applying the technology of science for creating misery for himself and for the extinction of the global civilization. The primitive savage, relatively speaking, was benign in comparison with the malignancy of the modern man. From these premisses, we have to deduce that the struggle is now going on and will continue in the future in changed ways and manners.

Our physical and mental traits are modulated by three *guṇa*s (strings that shape attributes), namely, *sattva, rajas* and *tamas*. Although the strings are three only, their vibrational blends of notes are innumerable due to varying proportions by different permutations and combinations. An individual person of pure *sattva* only is generally rare. Such a person is a lover of non-violence. He does not commit aggression. He is altruistic. He dedicates himself to the establishment of universal peace. A person, free from all the three strings, is liberated and, if he lives after being liberated, he does not become a normal worldly person. A person, with dominance of *rajas,* is full of activity. He is fond of dominating others. He has a general tendency of aggressiveness. A person, with dominance of *tamas,* is ignorant and has the tendency of considering vices as virtues. Persons, with dominance of both *rajas* and *tamas,* are dangerous in the society. Duryodhana was a man of this type. There is no guarantee that a person, with preponderance of *sattva,* will not be victimized by persons who indulge in vices. We get the character of Yudhiṣṭhira, a person of virtues, who became a victim of injustice. A good man should fight for his right. If he does fight, he performs his duty. If he passively tolerates injustice, he fails to perform his duty. Not only should he fight against injustice done to him, but also he should fight against injustice done to others in the society. Fighting for all noble causes, without considering gain or loss and personal interests is the duty of a good person. If he tolerates injustice meekly, mildly and timidly, he commits sins. It is almost impossible to say that, in the cosmic battlefield, necessity would not arise at all to become an Arjuna, with a Gāṇḍīva, to fight a fierce battle, a battle for justice, rights and righteousness. Yudhiṣṭhira, the eldest one among the five Pāṇḍava brothers, was a person of *sattva* attribute. Still he had to fight the Mahābhārata War. Mahatma Gandhi, one of the greatest and rarest noble souls in the history of humankind, had to fight a non-violent war for the freedom of India. There were, are and shall be occasions, even for virtuous persons, to fight for noble causes and to re-establish righteousness in the world.

What has been said here on the inevitability of the survival-war may not be misunderstood. We are not preaching for the doomsday. Optimism rather than pessimism should be the dream of man who should always strive for establishing peace. Man has descended from *Sat* (Existence), *Cit* (Consciousness) and *Ānanda* (Bliss). He is intrinsically blissful and not agonized. The ancient Indian *ṛṣi*s (seers) were daily praying for peace (*oṁ śāntiḥ, oṁ śāntiḥ, oṁ śāntiḥ*). At the outset, Lord Kṛṣṇa did not opt for war. He exhausted all ways and means for a peaceful settlement. He personally approached the Kauravas and begged for only five villages for the Pāṇḍavas. He sincerely made all attempts to avoid the war. But Dhṛtarāṣṭra, at the behest of Duryodhana and Śakuni, bluntly rejected the peace proposal. Unfortunately, it so happened that Duryodhana tried to imprison Lord Kṛṣṇa. Of course, it was his vain and foolish attempt. The practical world is different from the ideal one in which "ought" cannot be derived from "is." All attempts should always be made by all good persons to promote peace. But, success, in all cases, cannot be ensured. And, hence, is the unavoidability of fighting.

*Brahman*, the source of all of us, is Pure Bliss. Although peace and bliss are inseparable, we have both agony and ecstasy in our lives. For many of us, the ecstatic moments are relatively rare, and the agony is dominantly oppressive. The Holy *Gītā* starts from the agony of Arjuna. Its first chapter is known as *viṣāda-yoga* (*viṣāda* meaning "agony"). Thus, there is contradiction between the noumena and the phenomena, between the Absolute Being and the virtual universe. The Absolute Being is devoid of all the three *guṇa*s whereas the virtual entities are seized by blends of the three *guṇa*s. Constant efforts should be made for peace and for avoiding conflicts. But the intrinsic nature of the universe is such that conflicts and struggles cannot everywhere and always be avoided. It seems good and evil are in-built in the universe and they are concomitant from $t_0$ (the beginning of time, the time of the appearance of the cosmic egg) to $t_m$ (the maximum time, the time of the dissolution of the universe in *Māyā* or the *Mūla-Prakṛti*). Hence, love and hatred, peace and war, and ecstasy and agony are pepetual and universal in all the world-cycles.

The battlefield "Kurukṣetra" is an algebraic X. So also is Arjuna. The former is a miniature representation of the cosmic battlefield. The latter represents every human being in the world.

### 1.04: The Sacred Battlefield

Vyāsa, the author of the *Mahābhārata*, has qualified the Kurukṣetra battlefield as *dharmakṣetra*.[16] Here we have rendered this word into English as "a sacred field." However, such a translation is not strictly correct. The Sanskrit word *pavitra* is equivalent to the English word "sacred." The word *kṣetra* means "a field." But the word *dharma* has no exact equivalent in English.

Likewise, the word "religion" has no exact equivalent in Sanskrit and modern Indian languages. Prior to the sixth century

16. *BG*, I.1.

BCE, there were no religions in ancient India, although *sanātana dharma* had been in vogue. To do what should be done is *dharma* (*dhṛ* + *man*). *Dharma* is in conformity with *ṛta* (cosmic order) and *satya* (truth). The verb-root *dhṛ* literally means "to hold." Every created entity of the universe, non-living or living, has its own properties, by performing which the concerned entity does its duties for its own good and for the good of the entire creation. The universe works smoothly and progresses normally if all created entities function as they should with reference to the duties assigned to them in accordance with their inherent properties.

With the evolution of induced consciousness and the emergence of man, there was ascent of the freedom of will. This free will could induce subjectivity in the performance of duties and, thus, could refine duties in quality and ruin duties through abuse. Hence, the concepts of *puṇya* (virtues) and *pāpa* (vices, sins), in relation to the observance of duties, had their origin.

There was no attempt among the ancient Indian *ṛṣi*s (saints and seers) to fix a set of rigid conducts and rules to make a regimented religion. Religious scriptures in ancient India were many and voluminous too. Their authors were many. Nobody has founded the Hindu religion, as we name it today. The prescriptions were liberal, diverse and sometimes contradictory. It was a cafetaria-type of religion. Of course, mostly, the prescriptions and proscriptions were based on Vedic and Vedāntic ethics, humanitarianism, altruism and centred around a metaphysics of one formless, all-pervasive God, without the dichotomy of subject and object. There was no need of naming this religion prior to the birth of Buddhism and Jainism in the sixth century BCE. But surprisingly, the Vedic religion had no name until the eighth century CE. The Arabic invaders named the country where the Sindhu flows as Hind and the inhabitants of that country as "Hindus." The ancient name of this country was Bhārata where *dharma* was eternal and timeless (*sanātana*). It was a culturally cohesive country, but not politically.

This background had to be given to dispel the doubt that the compound-word *dharma-kṣetra,* given in the opening verse of the *BG,* has no relation at all with the modern concept of religion.

A religion has three main facets, namely, a set of metaphysical doctrines, a set of rituals and a set of ethics. Religions, in general, have different metaphysics, with sharp differences in many respects and a little commonality in restricted fields. Religious rituals are generally different. Religious ethics have many common aspects, although some sharp differences cannot be overlooked.

Many readers of the *BG,* from whom even some modern Hindus can hardly be excluded, discover the concept of *jihād* in the first verse of the first chapter of the *BG*. During the time of the *Mahābhārata,* Buddhism, Jainism, Judaism, Christianity, Islam and other religions were not born. In this historical background, there was no occasion for the people of one religion to fight against those of another religion. Secondly, the two rival parties in the Mahābhārata War were first cousins, belonging to a single royal family. If the word "religion" would be applied for that time, both the opponent parties were the followers of one religion only. Hence, it is irrelevant to say that they indulged in *jihād.* The distinction between *dharma* (righteousness) and *adharma* (*a* = not) was important for them. The Pāṇḍavas were on the righteous path; the Kauravas were on the unrighteous path.

Now we would come to the core question. How could the battlefield of Kurukṣetra be a *dharmakṣetra?*

It has already been said that the universe is a cosmic battlefield and that the life of every individual is a battlefield for himself. Having accepted these concepts, should we generalize that every individual has to involve himself in constant fighting and the concomitant violence and cruel bloodshed? Should he differentiate his "I" from the "non-I" and engage himself in the annihilation of all others other than his "I"? Can a sacred and holy scripture like the *BG* preach such an unholy doctrine as *dharma?* A clarification is necessary in order to dispel doubts on the moot points with regard to the concept of *dharmakṣetra,* given in the *Gītā.* It is baffling for any intellectual to designate a battlefield as a sacred field.

The life of every individual person is a battlefield in the cosmic mega-battlefield. But the battlefield of any single person is not divinely designed to cause violence and bloodshed. Peace (*śānti*) is the *mantra* of life. The prayer of life is *oṁ śāntiḥ.* Daily the Vedic seers were praying: "Let all be happy. Let all be free from diseases. Let all see everything good. Let not anybody suffer." (*sarve bhavantu sukhinaḥ. sarve santu nirāmayāḥ. sarve bhadrāṇi paśyantu. mā kaścid duḥkhabhāg bhavet*). Love, compassion, forgiveness, universal brotherhood and sisterhood, altruism and helping persons in need and distress are the noble attributes of life. A good person should shun hatred, cruelty and violence. The benevolent qualities of being humane are contradictory to what happens in a battlefield. How do we solve the anomaly then?

Every human being should acquire virtues and give up vices. He should do his duties and thereby do *dharma.* The whole life should be dedicated to *dharma.* The human species on the earth should make all possible efforts to abolish war from the world for all time to come. Man, the most intelligent being on the earth (may not be in the whole iniverse), should learn to live in peace, universal peace, and should have the determination to banish hatred and violence on a global level, and preferably on the cosmic level. A life with indulgence in hatred and violence is not worth living.

In spite of what has been said in the foregoing paragraphs, occasions do arise in life to fight against injustice. Let us refer to the *Mahābhārata* story in particular. An unholy conspiracy was made by arranging a deceitful, treacherous gambling in the play of dice in which Śakuni played the pivotal role. The Pāṇḍavas lost their kingdom. Their queen, Draupadī, was humiliated by the savage attempt to undress her in the *rāja-sabhā* (Royal Assembly). They were banished from the kingdom (both Hastinā and Indraprastha) for a period of 12 years. They were made to live incognito for a period of one year. Lord Śrīkṛṣṇa came to Hastināpura, requested Dhṛtarāṣṭra and Duryodhana to peacefully solve the family dispute. He begged for five villages only on behalf of the Pāṇḍavas. Duryodhana bluntly said NO to the request of the Lord, and not knowing who He was, made a vain attempt to put Him inside the prison. This was an occasion for the Members of the Royal Assembly to see the World-Image of the Lord. But, alas!, wicked Duryodhana and his friends took it as a black magic.

It was not a fact that no attempt was made to bring a peaceful solution of the dispute. But all attempts failed. Duryodhana, with the evil advice of his maternal uncle Śakuni, was adamant to torture the Pāṇḍavas in the most brutal manner.

Should one tolerate all types of injustice without protest and without taking action for remedy? If one does not fight for justice and meekly tolerates injustice, one fails to discharge one's duties and thereby one does *adharma.* Timidity and toleration of injustice, without a tough fight for the just right, can never be eulogized as *dharma.* Under such circumstances, fighting becomes inevitable. Such fighting is *dharma-yuddha* and the battlefield where fighting is done is a *dharma-kṣetra.* As a fact, every person's life is a battlefield. However, it would be desirable if it is rendered a sacred battlefield.

Some thinkers speculate that the earth is heading to be a heaven, an eternal heaven, that every person on the earth would be transformed into an immortal gnostic being, something like God, and that all these gnostic beings would permanently live with individual identities. It is hard for us to accept such speculation or Utopia. Every becoming entity is seized by *sattva, rajas* and *tamas,* in different proportions, of course. We do expect persons like Yudhiṣṭhira, albeit rare numerically, persons like Arjuna and Bhīma and also persons like Duryodhana, Duḥśāsana and Śakuni. That a large number of persons or all people would be devoid of the three *guṇa*s (*nistraiguṇya*) is a speculation that is not likely to materialize at any time. Emancipation (*mokṣa*) of individuals is a fact; but total liberation to a state of individual Godhead is a fiction, never attainable. Moreover, our earth will not be a permanent celestial being. Our sun, other suns in our galaxy, other galaxies and the entire universe have birth, sustenance and death. It is universal that anything with a beginning must meet an end. The universe has a beginning and shall have an end. The cosmic cycles had no beginning in the past and shall have no end in the future. Only *Brahman* (*Īśvara* and *Māyā* or *Mūla-Prakṛti* being not a second and a third separate entity, but being one *Brahman* only, without violating non-dualism) being unborn (*aja*) and without a beginning (*anādi*) is without an end (*ananta*).

The emanation (manifestation), maintenance or sustenance and dissolution of the universe are the triple aspects of the *līlā* (sportive play) of God and His *Śakti* (Power or Consort). Ignorance (*ajñānam, avidyā*) of the created entities is a prerequisite condition for the *līlā*. Ignorance and a state of freedom from conflicts and battle are incompatible. That all human beings will be completely free from ignorance at any particular time, that all will have *Brahman*-realization and that all will become *Brahman* with persistence of individuality at any particular time would never be a fact.

There is no life without struggle (*saṅgharṣa*) for existence. It is a universal statement. One may fight a war or a battle. One may fight against foes to commit aggression or to defend oneself. One may fight for acquiring power, name, fame, wealth or sex. One may struggle against natural calamities such as earthquakes, tsunami, flood, drought, pestilence or such other adversity. One may struggle for getting rid of diseases, poverty, lack of education, environmental pollution and social injustice and inequality. Once some older problems are taken care of, other newer problems will emerge. There would be no end to problems. And so also would there be no end to struggle.

The *BG* teaches how to convert a struggle into a non-violent struggle. If that is done, the life would be a sacred battlefield. Violence germinates in the mind. That is mental violence. It is expressed through speech and action. The former is vocal violence and the latter is physical violence. *Sāttvika guṇa* predominated in Yudhiṣṭhira. He fought a war in which physical violence was unavoidable. But he had neither mental nor vocal violence. Even with regard to physical violence, the Pāṇḍavas exhibited some noble behaviour, unprecedented in the annals of the history of the world. In the beginning of fighting with revered persons like Bhīṣma and Droṇa, Arjuna paid his obeisance to his *gurus* by throwing his arrow from his Gāṇḍīva-bow to fall at the lotus-feet of the *guru*. In return, the *guru* was blessing Arjuna in *āśīrmudrā* (blessing gesture) by saying *"vijayī bhava* (Be victorious)."All these were not formal. They meant what they did or said. Another occasion of the Mahābhārata War may be cited here. Ācārya Droṇa was the commander of the Kaurava army. While fighting was going on, people shouted: "Aśvatthāmā, either human or elephant, has been killed." Aśvatthāmā was the only son of Droṇa. On hearing this bad news, the Ācārya lost his heart. He wanted to ascertain the fact whether the elephant or his son was killed. "Who will speak the truth? Who will give the correct information?" Droṇa pondered over these questions. He was convinced with the idea that Yudhiṣṭhira was the person to speak the truth and nothing but truth. And so did he approach Yudhiṣṭhira to know the condition of his son, Aśvatthāmā. Can anybody think of such high morale as depicted in the *Mahābhārata*? This is an instance of *dharma-yuddha,* not fighting of one religion against another.

In the modern world, two World Wars were fought in the twentieth century. But in the same century, Mahatma Gandhi fought a non-violent war for the freedom of India. In his thought, words and actions, there was no trace of violence. He had love for the British rather than hatred. He was a soldier in a sacred battlefield.

The Holy *Gītā*, in which Arjuna was instructed by Lord Vāsudeva on righteousness *versus* unrighteousness, cannot be interpreted as preaching violence. We have to analyse the first verse of the first chapter of this sacred book and have to find out the contextual meaning. The whole cosmos is a cosmic battlefield. Life is full of struggles and is a battlefield for every individual. It is up to him to make it a sacred battlefield.

### 1.05 : The Blind King

Dhṛtarāṣṭra, the Kaurava king of the *Mahābhārata* of Vyāsa was born-blind. Due to being physically handicapped, he was feeling helpless and he developed an inferiority complex. We accept the narration of Vyāsa regarding the fact that the king was born-blind. In addition, we are presenting a different interpretation that has universal significance rather than personal and individual.

Dhṛtarāṣṭra was deprived of vision since his birth. He had some *sattva* to recognize what is good. But his *putra-moha* (delusion for his son, Duryodhana) and *moha* for the *siṁhāsana* (delusion for the throne) were so strong that his conscience (*viveka*) became non-functional. He lost the ability to discriminate right from wrong, virtues from vices, and righteousness (*dharma*) from unrighteousness (*adharma*). He was always suffering from internal conflicts, oscillating between extreme opposites (*dvandva*). For this reason, he was an unhappy person. A person, lacking in *viveka*, is blind (*andha*) even though he possesses good and powerful visual organs to see things.

Vyāsa has named many characters of the *Mahābhārata* epic according to their mental traits and physical functions. Some such names are Dhṛtarāṣṭra, Duryodhana, Duḥśāsana, Yudhiṣṭhira, Bhīma, Arjuna, Bhīṣma, Vidura and others. It is doubtful if the name Dhṛtarāṣṭra was given to the king by his parents. Vyāsa gave the name to this character in his epic since the blind king had the inborn propensity of being deluded (*mohagrasta*). He had delusion (*moha*) for the throne and the kingdom. He was getting extreme pleasure in tenaciously holding the kingdom. He had *moha* for his sons, especially the eldest one, Duryodhana. Selfish interest and delusion were responsible for his blind and unjust judgements.

Dhṛtarāṣṭra was not totally ignorant. On some occasions, he was conscious of the fact that his royal verdict was wrong. He was internally perturbed by his mental conflicts. But *moha* (delusion) was dominantly suppressing his intrinsic goodness. Delusion rather than conscience was the deciding factor for the actions which he was taking.

Was the king feeling helpless because he was handicapped? Did he suffer from inferiority complex because he was blind? Was he afraid of his wicked son, Duryodhana? Was he apprehensive of any probability of being dethroned by Duryodhana?

At least one thing was certain. Duryodhana or anybody else could not have dethroned the king. Bhīṣma (His original name was Devavrata), the greatest warrior of that age and the person dedicated to moral and principled life had taken the terrible oath to protect the Hastinā throne. Had the king given the slightest hint to Bhīṣma, Duryodhana, Duḥśāsana or any other wicked person could have been exterminated in no time.

It was the *pravṛtti* (intrinsic propensity) of Dhṛtarāṣṭra to have *rāṣṭra-moha* (delusion for the kingdom), *putra-moha* (delusion for the sons) and other types of *moha*. His unhappy life was due to his *moha*, but not due to his blindness or helplessness. The *BG* refers to *moha* a number of times.[17]

Dhṛtarāṣṭra represents most individuals of the human species. There are many Dhṛtarāṣṭras now in various fields in the modern world. The number soars in politics. In the name of democracy, dynastic rule works due to *moha* for the son, daughter, wife, husband and relatives, even if the persons concerned have no merit, no service and no sacrifice.

Vyāsa's Dhṛtarāṣṭra and many other characters of his epic transcend time, place and individuality. His classic characters were in the past, are in the present and will be in the future.

---

17. *BG*, II.52; III.2; IV.16 & 35; VII.13; XI.1; XIV.8, 13, 22; XVI.10, 16; XVIII. 7, 25,39, 60,73.

A person, with good physical vision, is still blind, if he is deluded (becomes *mohagrasta*), if he lacks in conscience or *viveka* (discrimination between right and wrong) and his judgement is based solely on selfish interest. Can humankind consciously beware of Dhṛtarāṣṭras and fight hard to get rid of this trait from the society in a non-violent manner?

### 1.06 : Afraid of Divine Vision

Dhṛtarāṣṭra, the blind king of Hastinā, was deprived of physical vision. He was a born-blind person. He gave his consent for the Mahābhārata War between cousins, the Kauravas and the Pāṇḍavas. He did foresee the horrors of the War, the cruel bloodshed and death of heroes of both sides. He could perhaps bear the sight of the death of his nephews; but, the death of his sons in the battlefield was terrible for him.

Vyāsa was willing to give divine vision (*divya-dṛṣṭi*) to Dhṛtarāṣṭra so that the latter could see the events of the War. The thought of seeing the death of his sons in the battle agonized the blind king. He requested Vyāsa for an alternative favour : "I am unable to directly see the carnage. I would request you to please grant the divine vision to Sañjaya who would narrate the War incidences so that I would know the events by hearing only." Sañjaya was the companion and counsellor of Dhṛtarāṣṭra. Vyāsa agreed to the proposal of the king and did what the latter desired.

This is the difference between a seer (*ṛṣi*) and another person who is severely affected with *moha* (delusion), the clinging to the "I" and "my" and the aversion for those other than the "I." Dhṛtarāṣṭra, being born-blind, was deprived of vision since his birth. Vyāsa was glad to bestow vision on him during the period of the War. If he could not tolerate to see his sons being killed in the battle, he could have avoided the War by giving the rightful share to the Pāṇḍavas. A person, devoid of conscience or *viveka* (the power of discrimination between good and bad, right and wrong) has the tendency of becoming egocentric.

Vyāsa was the biological father of Dhr̥tarāṣṭra, Pāṇḍu and Vidura. A question pops up here. How could not the genetic inheritance of the great sage favourably influence the personality and mental traits of Dhr̥tarāṣṭra? In reality, it is not only the genotype that determines the traits of a person. The genes one inherits from the father and the mother constitute the genotype. They do determine our physical and mental traits. But it is part of the story. The genes interact with the environment for producing the effects. By environment we mean the physical environment, the cultural environment, the religious, areligious or irreligious environment, the geographical environment, the political environment, the planetary environment and the environment of education and training. Last but not the least, there is a third factor that decides the types of the two factors already mentioned. It is the *karma-saṁskāra* of every individual, accumulated through previous births and stored in the *karmāśaya*, located in the *buddhi*, the intellectual instrument of the internal instrument (*antaḥkaraṇa*). It is neither inherited nor acquired. It is earned by an individual by dint of actions or *karma*. It is carried by the person himself or herself in the causal body in which the subtle body is dissolved. The *saṁskāra*s of Dhr̥tarāṣṭra and Vyāsa were totally different.

Here we would like to write a few words about the transcendental knowledge of Vyāsa, one of the few greatest seers and geniuses of the world. The great foundation of Indian culture and Indianness would not have existed without Vyāsa. (R̥ṣi Vālmīki is the second one who is prominent in contributing humaneness to the humanity at large). Vyāsa compiled the Vedas and many great scriptures of Indian wisdom. He wrote the great epic, the *Mahābhārata*. He incorporated the *Bhagavad-Gītā* in the *Mahābhārata*, forming the 25th chapter of the Bhīṣma-Parva of the latter. He also wrote the *Bhāgavatam*.

Vyāsa was not simply an author. He was a great hermit, sage and saint. He was able to see by his gross eyes as others do. In addition, he could see by his third eye. By austerities, penances and *yoga-sādhanā*, he had the power of clairvoyance (*divya-dr̥ṣṭi*), clairaudience (*divya-śravaṇa*) and many other *siddhis* (supernormal power of performance). He had also the power of bestowing any of the *siddhis* upon any person whom he selected.

Ṛṣi Patañjali has mentioned a number of *siddhis* in his book, *Yoga-Darśanam.*[18] Without the *siddhis* and the penetrating power of the rays of his third eye into the entire cosmos and without linking his mind with the Fundamental Being without becoming, he could not have contributed what he has done to the entire humanity. He was a great seer (*draṣṭā*) who could see the past, present and future and see what is here, there and everywhere beyond normal sensory contact. He was a great creator (*sraṣṭā*). He could create ideas and characters that transcend space, time and individuals.

The birth of this great seer is interesting and intriguing too. His father was Ṛṣi Parāśara and mother was Kālī. (The name Kālī was changed to Satyavatī after she married Śāntanu.) Kālī was a fisher-girl, the daughter of a *dāsa* chieftain of fishermen who lived on the bank of the Yamunā River. The fisher chieftain was engaged in the work of ferrying people across the river. Kālī, in the absence of her father, used to ply the boat between the two banks of the Yamunā. She was otherwise known as Matsyagandhī because of the fishy odour emanating from her body. Although dark-complexioned, she was exquisitely beautiful and sexy.

One day Ṛṣi Parāśara had to cross the river, Yamunā. On that day, Kālī was in charge of ferrying. While she was ferrying the hermit across the river, her boat passed by the side of an island in the middle of the river. In that romantic, environmental setting, Parāśara fell in love with Kālī. He created an artificial fog. In that foggy atmosphere, he had consensual, sexual intercourse with Kālī. From that very moment, Kālī who was Matsyagandhī became Kastūrīgandhī (one from whose body the odour of musk emanated). Kālī became pregnant and, without the normal gestation period, delivered instantly. Having blessed the fisher-

18. *PYD*, III.18-55.

girl that she would not lose her virginity, Parāśara left the place.

Vyāsa was dark in complexion and, hence, was known by the name Kṛṣṇa (meaning "black"); he was ugly-looking; he was born in a *dvīpa* (island) and, hence, the Hindus call him, by reverence, *Bhagavān* (God) Kṛṣṇa Dvaipāyana.

The birth story of Vyāsa is not directly relevant to the present topic. Why is this narration then? Even Indians hardly realize that the main source of Indian wisdom was Vyāsa who was born out of wedlock and whose mother was unmarried and a non-Aryan *dāsa* girl and father was an Aryan *ṛṣi*. The importance of the *Mahābhārata* could not be reduced at all, if Vyāsa would not have revealed the story of his birth. The saint was committed to truth (*satyaniṣṭha*) and so did he reveal it. Basing upon the birth-story of Vyāsa, the caste and racial conflicts that have persisted to be stigmatic to the human species on the earth would have vanished by this time. Vyāsa was a gifted prodigy. He was a genius of extraordinary merit and a hermit with many *siddhi*s. He was glad to bestow divine vision on Dhṛtarāṣṭra. But the blind king was not ready to receive it. He was rather afraid of it; because by gaining that, he could see the death of his sons in the battlefield. Hearing was less dreadful for him than seeing.

Dhṛtarāṣṭra was sitting on a rung of spirituality and divinity at a very low level in the ladder, much lower than the base rung. A person, devoid of conscience, afflicted with delusion (*moha*) and very much attached to his "I" and "my" with strong aversion to "non-I" and "non-my" became afraid of divine vision. Had he been assured of the protection of his sons, he could have perhaps rejoiced by seeing the death of the Pāṇḍavas and the Pāṇḍava army. But he was terribly afraid of the divine vision by which he could have seen the death of his sons and his army in the battle. Persons, afflicted with delusion (*moha*), maintain this type of double standard, one for their own and another for others. Had the king been benevolent, he could have been just to the Pāṇḍavas and avoided the Mahābhārata War.

**1.07 : Arjuna, the Algebraic X**

The whole universe is a usable, virtual existence (*vyāvahārika satya*), whereas *Brahman* alone is an Absolute Existence (*pāramārthika satya*). *Brahman* is Pure Consciousness (*viśuddha Cit*) and Bliss (*Ānanda*). This *Ānanda* is not joyfulness. *Brahman* is attributeless (*nirguṇa*) whereas joyfulness is an attribute. With reference to *Brahman*, *Ānanda* is a neutral state, free from joyfulness and sorrowfulness.

We are reflections of *Brahman*, albeit not transformations. Our source is Pure Consciousness and Pure Bliss. But, our consciousness, which is an induced one, is mixed with varying degrees of ignorance (*avidyā* or *ajñānam*). We are joyful sometimes; but we are afflicted with agony (*viṣāda*) very often.

The common man's life has ecstasy (*āhlāda*) and agony (*viṣāda*). This ecstasy is not bliss in the sense of *ānanda* with reference to *Brahman*. It is joy, resulting from sensuous pleasure, mostly of *rājasika* or *tāmasika* origin. The joyful life is very often interspersed with pain and agony. This agony is also due to the contact of our senses with objects, our attachment to the fruits of our actions and our frustration due to failure. Our pain is more burdensome to our life than our pleasure. We are more affected by our agony than by our ecstasy. In the whole universe (not only on our earth), we cannot find a single life, with *ānanda* only, without the admixture of *viṣāda*. (Of course, the lives of the *jīvanmukta*s, that is, of persons liberated, although still living, are exceptions. They experience pure *ānanda*, without the admixture of *viṣāda*). The Sanskrit word *viṣāda*, without being exactly equivalent, may be approximately expressed by the English terms "drooping state," "languor," "lassitude," "dejection," "depression," "despondency," "agony," "mental anguish," and "extreme mental or physical suffering."

The *BG* starts from the *viṣāda* of Arjuna. The first chapter of the *Gītā* is known as Arjuna-Viṣāda-Yoga. If we study the *Mahābhārata*, most of the main characters in the epic have been afflicted with *viṣāda*. Dhṛtarāṣṭra, Gāndhārī, Duryodhana, Karṇa,

Kuntī, the Pāṇḍava brothers, Draupadī, Bhīṣma, Droṇa, Vidura and many others more or less suffered the pangs of agony of life. Of course, the agony of characters such as Bhīṣma and Vidura was due to reasons other than personal interests. They were moralists and persons of high ethical profiles. They were very unhappy with the events that were happening.

The *BG* has used the word *viṣāda* and allied expressions in a number of places.[19] The common man, in general, is an agonized being. His agony is due to his incessant desire and insatiable lust, wrath, covetousness, delusion, egoistic arrogance and malice. The clinging to I-ness and my-ness is the main driving force of delusion (*moha*). And a deluded man cannot escape from *viṣāda* (agony).

When we interpret the first chapter of the *BG*, we feel that Vyāsa's Arjuna was an algebraic *X*. As *X* is a representative symbol in algebra, so does Arjuna represent all the common members of humankind. Every common person, in his life, is afflicted with *viṣāda* some time or other.

There are ways for getting rid of *viṣāda*. Our source is *Ānanda*, without any trace of *viṣāda*. We are in *viṣāda* only when we are alienated from our source. Lord Vāsudeva instructed Arjuna how to get rid of *viṣāda*. The latter followed God's instructions and fully surrendered to Him. What happened with Arjuna can happen with everybody in the universe. Agonized Arjuna is an algebraic *X*. Arjuna, free from agony, is also an algebraic *X*. There is no need for despair. Darkness is not a real entity. The absence of light is darkness. If we search for light, we get it and certainly get it. God is the source of light, Pure Consciousness. He is everywhere, within us and outside us, within the universe and outside the universe, omnipresent and all-pervasive. In the analogy of Arjuna, we are to get rid of agony and stay in *Brahman*, the Pure Bliss (*brāhmī-sthiti*).

---

19. *BG*, I.28; II.1 & 10; XVIII. 28 & 35.

**1.08 : God, the Charioteer**

In the Mahābhārata War, Lord Śrīkr̥ṣṇa offered his services to become the charioteer (*sārathi*) of Arjuna. The word *ratha* means "a chariot" and *sa* means "with." The word *sārathi* means "a charioteer," "a driver of a car," "a coachman." In the days of the *Mahābhārata, sārathis* belonged to a mixed caste, commonly called *Sārthī*, supposed to have sprung from a kṣatriya father and a brāhmaṇa mother. The other meanings of the word *sārathi* are "any leader or guide," "a helper or assistant."

We may ignore the social position of a *sārathi*, basing on the mixed nature of the caste. Nevertheless, a *sārathi* does not do an exalted job (a respectful service) by becoming a driver or a coachman. In spite of these hard facts, Śrīkr̥ṣṇa, the Lord of the universe, offered himself to be the servant of Arjuna.

Here we may mention a story of Śrīkr̥ṣṇa and Sudāmā, as described in the *Bhāgavatam*. Of course, Sudāmā's name occurs everywhere in the *Bhāgavatam* as Kucela. Sudāmā and Śrīkr̥ṣṇa were thick friends in their boyhood. Sudāmā (brāhmaṇa by caste) was a classmate of Śrīkr̥ṣṇa at the *āśrama* of sage, Sāndīpani. After their education was over, these two bosom friends went their different ways in life. Śrīkr̥ṣṇa became the Lord of Dvārakā. Sudāmā became a poor householder with many children. Starvation gripped the family. At the instance of his wife, Sudāmā left for Dvārakā to visit Kr̥ṣṇa, with the hope that he would get some financial help. He took a packet of parched broken rice (rice flakes) as a present to his friend. Śrīkr̥ṣṇa cordially received Sudāmā with love and affection, washed his feet and wiped them with clean towels, did all types of services for his comforts, ate one handful of rice flakes from the packet and enjoyed it.

After spending some days most happily with the old friend, Sudāmā started homewards. On his way back, he was thoughtful about what he would say to his wife as he did not receive any monetary help from Kr̥ṣṇa. When he reached home, he was amazed at what he saw. His old dilapidated house had converted itself into a mansion, with plenty of wealth. Inscrutable are the ways of the actions of God![20]

We have come across references where God is treated as a father, a mother, a friend, a playmate, a companion and such other relations. Here is a case where God serves the devotee (Arjuna) as a servant. God, merciful and compassionate, can play any role to help his devotee.

The Upaniṣads allude to the *ratha* (chariot) and *rathī* (the Lord of the chariot) in a different context, of course. The *Kaṭhopaniṣad* presents a parable of the chariot. "Know the Self as the Lord of the chariot and the body, verily, as the chariot."[21] The *Bṛhadāraṇyaka Upaniṣad* uses the simile of the chariot in the sense of the virtual and ephemeral nature of the universe that is a projected one. "There are no chariots; neither are animals yoked to them; nor are roads. He projects from Himself (from His *Śakti* or Power) chariots, animals and roads. There are no joys, pleasures and delights. He creates (through His *Māyā-Śakti*) joys, pleasures and delights. Without the real existence of tanks, lotus-pools and rivers, He (His *Māyā-Śakti*) creates (projects) tanks, lotus-pools and rivers. He (His *Māyā-Śakti*), indeed, is the agent.[22]

Ācārya Śaṅkara discards the idea that God is the agent (*sa hi kartā*). He says that the agency attributed to the Self (God) is only figurative. "The light of the Self is Pure Consciousness *(Viśuddha Cit)*. It, being reflected on the *antaḥkaraṇa* (the internal instrument), illumines the latter, which, in turn, induces the organs of the body to perform their functions."[23]

Śaṅkara's interpretation is correct with reference to the activities of all created entities. But, in the present context, he does not seem to be correct. This Upaniṣadic statement refers to

20. *Bhā*, 10th *Skandha*.

21. *KTU*, I.3.3.

22. *BU*, IV.3.10.

23. *BUŚB*, IV.3.10.

the cosmic activities that are performed by *Māyā*. She creates an illusory, virtual universe at the instance of God Who Himself is really the non-doer (*akartā*).

What has Śaṅkara said on the topic of God being a non-doer is true for Arjuna and has a fundamental relevance to the universe at large. Śrīkr̥ṣṇa, being God Himself, could have killed the one hundred sons of Dhr̥tarāṣṭra and the Kaurava army within a moment. Then, what was the need for a War of eighteen days? God Himself could have been the archer rather than the charioteer.

The cover-page art of this book and most *Gītā* books in general conveys a universal message. Everyone of us has to work as God's agent. God extends His hand and points out by His fingers to do the right duty. He is the *silent* guide, advisor, director and prompter. It is up to us to listen to his promptings. We may pay heed to what He silently indicates: We have the freedom (limited, of course) to ignore His promptings too. We may even ignore the existence of God. Our denial of God's existence and disregard of His promptings lead us to our peril. But God is not affected by what we do. His Power (the *Māyā-Śakti*) takes appropriate actions at appropriate times to protect His creation. The Pure Consciousness, all-pervading, illumines all, including the *Māyā-Śakti*, and thereby induces the Primordial Nature and the created Nature to function. There is a condition for receiving the illumination, of course. For the proper illumination and induction, the mirror is to be transparent rather than opaque. The intellect (*budahi*) of the *antaḥkaraṇa* (*buddhi* + *ahaṅkāra* + *manas*) of a human being may be transparent, translucent or opaque. The degree of opacity may also vary. We need a clean mirror to receive the illumination. In order that our *buddhi* becomes fully transparent, we have to make sincere efforts, in this life and the lives to come, through right actions, right knowledge, unwavering steadfast devotion, constant yoking of our mind to God and full surrender to Him.

We have already said that we could ignore the existence of God and that we could be callous to the invisible, inaudible, imperceptible (but detectable through our third eye) promptings of God. That freedom we have. However, we cannot disturb the cosmic balance in a major way for a long duration of time. And we cannot escape from the fruits of our actions in this life or the lives to come. We seemingly present two anomalous conditions. We say that a person has the freedom to embrace atheism and do what he likes. Simultaneously we say that no person can disturb cosmic balance and cannot escape from the fruits of his actions. We reiterate with emphasis that God is not the direct agent of the events in the universe where chaos and cosmos function simultaneously, the net result being cosmos. God's executive is His *Māyā-Śakti*. The light of Consciousness of God is reflected on *Māyā*. As a result, the insentient *Māyā* is rendered superconscious and plays the executive role in accordance with the desire of God. She also does not intervene, in each and every minute, in all events of the universe. She has laid down the laws of Nature, according to which events happen as causes and effects. Cosmic and individual events happen naturally under the executive supervision of the Primordial Nature (*Mūla-Prakṛti* or *Māyā-Śakti*) and the Chairpersonship of God (*Īśvara, Puruṣa*). When somebody or something tries to upset the cosmic balance, the *Māyā-Śakti* does not become an inert onlooker and immediately intervenes to restore order.

God is the Supreme Controller (*Parmeśvara*) through the agency of His *Śakti* (Power), Mother Goddess. Although a non-doer, He is not an inactive spectactor. No person or no non-living entity can become a potent danger to the law (*satya*) and order (*ṛta*) of the cosmos. Divine interference does become a necessity in perilous situations. Even such casual interference is done through *Māyā* under the Chairpersonship of God. In usual situations, the created nature operates through laws made by the Power of God. Even if God takes a form as an incarnation, He does not violate the natural laws in spite of His omnipotence.

Now we sum up the main emphasis of this topic. God serves as a charioteer not only for Arjuna, but also for everybody. Universally speaking, each one's body is a chariot and God sitting in the body is a charioteer. Each one of us gets the inner divine prompting. We may wisely act according to the prompting, or foolishly ignore the divine prompting due to the covering of dirt on the mirror of our intellect. The word "arjuna" literally means "white," "free from dirt or blemishes." All of us should make hard and sustained efforts to make our intellect transparent to receive the reflections of the light of God. The posture of the right hand of Śrīkr̥ṣṇa on the cover-page art of this book is very much meaningful and profoundly significant. If we receive the divine promptings, we shall not be afflicted with agony and our life will certainly be ecstatic in the absence or presence of pain in life.

# 2

# Sāṅkhya-Yogaḥ
## (The Way of Knowledge)

### 2.01: The Utmost Priority on Knowledge

THE second chapter of the *BG* is on *Sāṅkhya-Yoga*, the *yoga* of knowledge (*jñāna-yoga*). In this context, the word Sāṅkhya has no relevance to the Sāṅkhya school of philosophy and the word "knowledge" does not refer to erudition in anyone or more disciplines and the scholarly activities of a pundit. A person with plenty of informational knowledge, with memorizing and reproducing power, may be *ācārahīna* (unethical, immoral and unscrupulous in practices) and may be a menace to the society. Such a person cannot be called a *jñāna-yogī*.

What is the meaning of *jñāna* (knowledge) in the *BG* then? It means *Brahma-jñāna* (knowledge on *Brahman*) along with *Brahmopalabdhi* (realization of *Brahman*) and *Brahmānubhūti* (experience of *Brahman*). The knower of *Brahman* verily becomes *Brahman* (*brahmavid brahmaiva bhavati*). Topic 2.14 has been added to the second chapter in order to throw light on "knowledge," as conceived in the *BG*, and to dispel the confusion created by the inter-mingling of Kapila's Sāṅkhya school of philosophy and Śaṅkara's Advaita Vedānta.

A number of fundamental questions have been boggling the mind of common people since time immemorial. "Who am I? Wherefrom did I come? Am I a material product of sexual activity and nothing else other than my body, grown and nourished by the food I take? Where am I going? Is death the end of life (a permanent full stop)? Is the universe created? Is it uncreated and eternal? If the universe has a beginning, is it self-created as a result of vacuum-genesis? If the universe has an end, would it be finally nothing? Has the universe been created by God? Who is God? What is *Brahman?* Has the empirical and phenomenal universe a substratum, a rock-bottom foundation? Is that foundation the Absolute Reality (*pāramārthika satya*)? Is the universe an empirical reality (*vyāvahārika satya*)? What is the purpose of the creation of the universe? Is the universe accidental, a mere product of chance (*yadṛcchā*) only? What is the purpose of life? Is it for a painful existence? Am I the body or have I the body? Am I the self in the body-vehicle? What is the relation between my self and the Cosmic Self (God/*Brahman)?* What is *Māyā* or the *Mūla-Prakṛti* (Primordial Nature)? What is the relation between *Prakṛti* (the unmanifested Primordial Nature) and *Puruṣa* (the Supreme Person or God)? Is the self/Self birthless and deathless?" These and many other sundry questions have been baffling humankind. We get answers to these questions in *jñāna-yoga.*

The *BG* deals with *jñāna-yoga* (the *yoga* of knowledge), *karma-yoga* (the *yoga* of detached actions), *samādhi-yoga* or *dhyāna-yoga* (the *yoga* of meditation), *bhakti-yoga* (the *yoga* of devotion) and others. The question is: Why has the *jñāna-yoga* been described first of all? All the other types of *yoga* may end in superstitions without a basic background of the *yoga* of knowledge. And, hence, is the priority on the second chapter of the *BG*, with the title "the *Sāṅkhya-Yoga.*"

### 2.02: Brahman, Īśvara and the Jīvātmā

We have already said that the second chapter of the *BG* is on Sāṅkhya-Yoga that is not related to Kapila's Sāṅkhya philosophical system. Here "Sāṅkhya-Yoga" means "the Way of Knowledge (*Jñāna-Yoga*)." It has further been said that *jñāna-yoga* does not deal with informational knowledge, erudite scholarship, or knowledge on art and science. The contextual meaning of *jñāna* in the second chapter of the *BG* is *Brahma-jñāna* (knowledge on *Brahman*) and *Brahmopalabdhi* (realization of *Brahman*).

We interpret the whole *Gītā* on the basic foundation of non-dualism (*advaita-vāda*). When the second chapter of the *BG* is on *Brahma-jñāna,* we feel the necessity of presenting the topic of the absolute identity of *Brahman, Īśvara* (God) and the *jīvātmā*s (individual selves) and their empirical differences too.

*Brahman* is Existence (*Sat,* derived from the verb-root *as,* meaning "is," "to exist"), Pure Consciousness (*Cit*) and Pure Bliss (*Ānanda,* a state free from joyfulness and sorrowfulness).

Bertrand Russell says that "existence" is not an attribute. We agree with him. The Sanskrit statement *yadasti tatsatyam* (Whatever exists is Existence) is an identity statement like *A* = *A*. It is certainly true. Nobody except a nihilist can say "Nothing exists." Nevertheless, the nihilist has at least to be a solipsist since he cannot deny his own existence. The second Sanskrit statement *yatsatyam tadbrahma* (Whatever is Existence is *Brahman*) is a process of nomenclature. Here the question of truth and falsity of the statement does not arise.

The whole created universe and all its constituents, both inanimate and animate, are conscious. Of course, the quality and quantity of their consciousness vary in a wide range, depending upon their evolved mental apparatuses. This type of consciousness is empirical or induced. The world of matter and energy is intrinsically insentient. *Brahman,* the Pure Consciousness, reflected on matter and energy, renders the latter empirically conscious. We may say: "Man has consciousness." "The electron has consciousness." But we cannot say: "*Brahman* has consciousness." *Brahman* is not a material substance. It is *avastu,* that is, it is non-material. The statement "*Brahman* is Consciousness and Pure Consciousness" is correct. Here "Pure" means "unrelated and unconnected with anything and anybody."

The cosmic cycles are repeated *ad infinitum.* There was no universe as such before the appearance of the Cosmic Egg. The Cosmic Egg stayed for a time and then exploded (Big-Bang explosion). The evolution of energy-quanta, fundamental forces, quarks, micro-particles, hydrogen atom, stars, other elements inside stars, planets, satellites, planetary atmosphere and hydrosphere gradually and sequentially occurred through aeons. Inorganic evolution was followed by organic evolution, RNA and DNA evolution, leading to the evolution of living organisms. For all these things to happen, omniscience or super-intelligence was necessary. Moreover, the Big-Bang explosion was fine-tuned, and in the evolution of the universe, perfect co-ordination was maintained. Matter, including energy, is basically insentient. We cannot explain the origin, evolution, sustenance and dissolution of the universe in cycles without the guidance of a Super-Intelligent Being. Intelligent becomings, without a Super-Conscious Being, is not imaginable. A Super-Conscious Being has to be necessarily inferred, and that Being is *Brahman,* the infinitely Great (*Bṛhat*) Being.

Very soon we shall discuss that *Brahman* is attributeless (*nirguṇa*). If we say "*Brahman* is Blissful," we use a predicative adjective and, hence, we end in self-contradiction. If we consider the contextual meaning of bliss and do conceptual analysis, we do not really meet a situation of self-contradiction. The word *Ānanda* (Bliss) in the statement "*Brahman* is Pure Bliss" means a neutral state free from joyfulness and sorrowfulness.

*Brahman* is homogeneous (not corpuscular) and an unbroken whole (*akhaṇḍa*). It is all-pervasive (*sarva-vyāpī*). With reference to the universe, it is both immanent and transcendent.

*Brahman* is Being, without becoming. It has no precedent or precursor state. Neither has it a subsequent or succeeding state. If *Brahman* is designated as *B*, it continues to be *B* as Pure Consciousness. Hence, it is beginningless (*anādi*) and endless (*ananta*). In other words, it is birthless and deathless. It is changeless and unmodifiable (*avikriya*). It is never transformed into anything else. With reference to *Brahman* and the manifestation or creation of the universe, the Advaita Vedānta discards the doctrine of transformation (*pariṇāma-vāda*). *Brahman* is motionless (*acalam*), formless (*arūpam*), attributeless (*nirguṇam*), functionless (*niṣkriyam*), non-relational (*asambandhi*), spaceless (*anākāśam*) and timeless (*akālam*). It is *avastu* (not a substance made up of matter and energy). It is constant (*dhruva*). If any of these statements is violated, *Brahman* cannot be eternal and timeless. The expenditure of energy is involved to maintain a form, to exhibit some attribute, to perform some function, to make any movement and to undergo modifications. Wherever there is expenditure of energy, there must arise some entropy (some unutilizable heat energy). Absolute permanence is not possible for an entity that changes and undergoes modifications. Whatever has a beginning has an end. Only that which is beginningless is endless.

The power (*śakti*) of *Brahman* is *Māyā*, which is not an entity second to *Brahman*. As the power of the President of a country is not physically identifiable, but is inferable from the effects (*kāryānumeyā*), so is the case with the *śaktimān* (one who possesses power) and the *śakti* (power), both being co-eternal. *Māyā* herself is insentient, but the light of *Brahman*-Consciousness being reflected on her, She is rendered conscious. She is the Primeval Nature (*Mūla-Prakṛti*). Some Vedāntists confusingly identify this Unmanifest *Mūla-Prakṛti* with the manifested *prakṛti* (the totality of matter and energy in the universe, with diversified forms, properties and functions). The former is the Mother Creatrix whereas the latter is the product of creation.

*Māyā* is not an illusion. She can produce illusion by her concealing power (*āvaraṇa-śakti*) and projecting power (*vikṣepa-śakti*). She is the Mother of the universe and the Executive Power of God. In our mundane language, we say that She is the Spouse of God.

*Brahman*, with *Māyā* as the *upādhi* (limiting adjunct; an empirical container that can seemingly confine some *X* which is homogeneously all-pervasive), is *Īśvara* (God). Whereas the former is attributeless, the latter is associated with attributes (*saguṇa*). They are not two separate Beings. The word *Paramātmā* (the Supreme Self, Self, *Ātmā*) refers to both *Brahman* and *Īśvara*, both being one only. *Īśvara* is the Father and *Māyā* is the Mother of the universe. The former is the Chairperson (*adhyakṣa*) and the latter is the Executive Agent. The creation, sustenance and dissolution of the universe is done by *Māyā* under the Chairpersonship of *Īśvara*.

We have so far presented the Vedāntic metaphysics of One Being only, without becoming, seemingly three in number, but really a non-dual One only.

When God desires to have a universe (*jagat*), Mother Goddess (*Parameśvarī*), under the Chairpersonship of God (*Parameśvara*), creates one for the sportive play (*līlā*) of both. She herself is not transformed into the universe, unlike the concept in Sāṅkhya. She creates an empirical universe that is not nothing. It is something which is empirically true (*vyāvahārika satya*), but not absolutely true (*pāramārthika satya*). *Brahman* is never changeable or modifiable and never in motion, whereas everything in the universe is ever changeable and always in motion. No particle and micro-particle can live for a moment without motion or change. The universe is ephemeral and transient. For its existence and functioning, it depends upon *Brahman*, the underlying (*adhiṣṭhāna*) Reality; but the reverse is not true. We may take a simile, a poor one, of course. Without the hard disc in the computer, we cannot see anything on the desktop of its monitor. Still what we see on the desktop is not an illusory phantasy. *Brahman*, the Supreme Reality, has neither beginning nor end. On the other hand, every entity of the micro-universe has a beginning and an end every trillionth of a second or even earlier. The total universe, both micro and macro, has also a beginning and an end. The first half of its life is an expanding phase; the second half of its life is a contracting phase. Finally, at the termination of the contracting phase, it becomes a *bindu* (point, singularity) that contains the *Virāḍ* (the Cosmic Mind) that ultimately dissolves in *Māyā*, the *Mūla-Prakṛti*. *Virāḍ* or *Buddhi* is the hard disc of the universe, the disc that contains all the memory of the immediately preceding *para* (the Cosmic Period between the beginning of Time and the end of Time; the span of life of Brahmā, 100 years in His Time-Scale).

*Brahman*, the Self or *Ātmā* is all-pervading. When a created (manifested) entity serves as the *upādhi* of the pervasive *Brahman*, we name the embodied spirit as *ātmā*, self, or the individual self (*bhūtātmā* in a non-living entity and *jīvātmā* in a living entity).

The non-living entity has no developed mental apparatus like the *karmāśaya* to store *karma-saṁskāras*. Hence, inanimate entities have no re-incarnations. The living beings have evolved subtle, internal-instruments (*antaḥkaraṇa*) and gross nervous systems of different grades. *Homo sapiens* (the human species) on the earth has the best evolved mind and brain (the latter being the apparatus of the former). Man has a free will to do good or bad. For the possession of the free will, he is responsible for his actions and cannot escape from accountability. His self (*jīvātmā*) becomes bound to his *karma-saṁskāras* like chemical bonding in a methane molecule ($CH_4$) or in other chemical compounds. This process is known as *karma-bandhana*. Due to this bondage, the self acquires a body (we call it "birth") and discards the body (we call it "death"). Rebirths are chances like supplementary examinations to get rid of the bondage and, thus, to be liberated (to get *mokṣa*). Liberation or *mokṣa* is attained only when the self is fully released from bondage. A liberated self no longer retains its individuality; it fully merges in *Brahman* and becomes *Brahman* or the Self (*Ātmā, Paramātmā*).

Every individual (even the worst sinner) is potentially divine. He must have home-coming one day or the other. A birth means a chance for self-correction, self-purification. It is up to the individual person to make himself pure and purer or dirty and dirtier. *Mokṣa* is possible in the present life, in some future life, in this *kalpa* or some future *kalpa*, and in this *para* or some future *para*.

Every *ātmā* (individual self) is *Brahman*, provided it is free from the *karma-bandhana*. Chemically speaking, a water molecule is $H_2O$. Water, comprising many molecules of $H_2O$, evaporates from the ocean. The water-vapour condenses to become rain-water and falls on the earth. Water on the ground may be clear like spring-water, dirty sewarage water, water in blood, urine or pus. It may be scented, being mixed with sandalwood paste. It may acquire foul smell by being mixed with faecal matter. It may be deadly poisonous and fatal by being contaminated with pathogens or poisons. All such possibilities do exist. In spite of these possibilities, water has also the possibility of becoming pure $H_2O$. Distil and re-distil water several times to bring back to its original state of pure $H_2O$. The impurities do not belong to $H_2O$; they are adventitious, external substances that mix with $H_2O$.

Who will distil and re-distil the self? Nobody else will do this job. One oneself has to do it. To ascend the rungs leading to liberation is a process of self-purification. It may be done through the knowledge and realization of the Supreme Self, detached actions, meditation or devotion. The way may be a single one, or a combination of two or three, or all the ones. The Lord shows the way to Arjuna who represents all individuals of the human species. The ways are many; the goal is one. One may miss the way if one is unaware of the goal. The second chapter of the *BG* is introduction to knowledge on the Self (*Brahman/Parameśvara*), the Supreme Reality, the final goal.

### 2.03: The Meaning of Death

The Self or the Cosmic Self (*Paramātmā* or God) is non-corporeal, devoid of a body. But the individual self (*jīvātmā*) is embodied. It acquires a gross body at the time of conception in the mother's womb. It leaves the gross body at the time of death. Subsequent to death, the body, made up of matter and energy, is decomposed and transformed into other material forms. Nevertheless, it is not converted to nothing even after death. It loses its form and undergoes changes. The five great material states (*pañca mahābhūta*s — solids, liquids, gases, energy, *ākāśa*) undergo mutual transformations. Even in the death of the body, the self does not change at all. It is unmodifiable (*avikārya*), non-decayable (*avyaya*) and imperishable (*akṣaya*).

In death, the embodied self (*dehī*) gets rid of the gross body, but is still embodied. The subtle body (*sūkṣma* or *liṅga śarīra*) continues to serve as the *upādhi* (a limiting adjunct, an empirical container) of the self unless and until full freedom from bondage is obtained. The empirical bonding of the self and the *karma-saṁskāras* (stored in the *karmāśaya* in the *buddhi* of the *antaḥkaraṇa*) is the cause of rebirth.

The Supreme Self (*Brahman*/God) and the individual selves are identical, except for the empirical bonding of the latter. But for this bondage (*bandhana*), the individual selves are not many, even not more than one. Any self, free from bondage, is the Supreme Self. When God Himself is incarnated, he takes a form by virtue of the action of His *Māyā* and His birth has no connection with *karma-bandhana*. Thus, God-incarnate has a *māyā-śarīra* (an illusory body) unlike our bodies, gross, subtle, or causal.

Through the following verses, Śrīkr̥ṣṇa conveyed an important cosmic message to Arjuna. Bodies come to exist and they cease to exist. But a body is not the Self/self. The Self and the selves are identical and one. There is nothing like a plurality of selves. As one Self only, we are eternal in all the three periods of time (past, present and future) and timeless in the absence of time. (Time and Space, subsequent to the total dissolution of the universe and prior to its next creation or emanation, are non-existent. We are, however, sorry to express our thoughts by the use of temporal words, "subsequent to" and "prior to," for a timeless or *sanātana* state). The English versions of the Lord's message are stated below:

> There was never a time when I did not exist, nor you, nor these rulers of people. And never in the future, shall we all cease to be.[1]
>
> Just as the embodied Self (*dehī*) has, in the body, childhood, youth and old age, so does it get another body. A wise man is not bewildered by it.[2]
>
> O son of Kuntī (Arjuna), contacts of senses with their objects produce (the experiences of) cold and heat, pleasure and pain.

1. *BG*, II.12.
2. *BG*, II.13.

> They come and go. They are impermanent. O Bhārata (scion of Bharata's family), endure them patiently.[3]

Any born individual has a gross body and a subtle body. The five subtle sensory organs (*indriyas* or *karaṇas* for vision, audition, olfaction, gustation and tactility) are in the subtle body and they have their corresponding gross organs in the gross body (eyes, ears, nose, taste-buds on the tongue and the walls of the buccal cavity and touch-receptors on the skin). These senses come in contact with their objects (such as forms, sounds, odours, etc). and thereby produce the sensation of cold and heat, pleasure and pain. These sensations and experiences are fleeting in nature. Being born, one has to bear them patiently.

In a nutshell, death means "the self leaving the gross, material body." The self, not different from the Supreme Self, is eternally and timelessly permanent, whereas the material body and the experience of pleasure and pain due to the contacts of the senses with their objects are impermanent. The former is immortal; and the latter mortal. Knowing this hard truth, one should not be perturbed, perplexed and bewildered at all.

Lord Vāsudeva has given a good simile to explain the nature of death, likened to the action of discarding old clothes and putting on new ones.

> Just as a person discards worn-out clothes and puts on others that are new, so does the embodied self, discarding worn-out bodies, enters into others that are new.[4]

The man with spiritual knowledge and realization of *Brahman* is really wise. He comprehends the nature and meaning of death. Such a person remains unaffected with pain and pleasure. He does not exult in pleasure; nor does he feel dejected in pain. He patiently bears the pairs of opposites. He is able to attain immortality. Here we quote the language of the Lord:

---

3. *BG*, II.14.

4. *BG*, II.22.

> O great among men (Arjuna), the wise man whom these (pairs of opposites) cannot agitate, who remains the same in pain and pleasure, is fit indeed for attaining immortality.[5]

## 2.04: The Law of Conservation of Being

On the topic of the law of conservation of Being, we shall refer to only one verse of the *BG*. The said verse is quoted below:

> Nothing cannot be something. Something cannot be nothing. The truth about both these has been perceived by the seers of Reality.[6]

We have gone through the interpretation of this verse, made by many erudite and wise scholars. But nowhere have we found the meaning as stated here. Let us do the language and grammatical analysis of the verse, especially of the first half.

The word *sat* (*as* + *śatr̥*) has been derived from the Sanskrit verb-root *as*, meaning "to exist." The word *sataḥ* means "of that which exists." The word *asataḥ* means "of that which does not exist." The word *bhāvaḥ* (*bhū* + *ghañ*) has been derived from the verb-root *bhū*, meaning "to become." In the present context, the word *bhāvaḥ* means "becoming something" and *abhāvaḥ* means "becoming nothing." The sentences *asataḥ bhāvaḥ na vidyate* and *sataḥ abhāvaḥ na vidyate* are contradictory to each other. "Something cannot appear from nothing"; in other words, "Nothing cannot generate something." This is the meaning of the first sentence. "If there is something X, it can never be nothing." This is the meaning of the second sentence.

This theory of the *BG* contradicts *creatio ex nihilo* (creation out of nothing) and the general doctrine of nihilism. Does it contradict transformation of matter and energy too? No, it doesn't. It rather supports it. Every created entity of the universe and the universe as a whole are always in motion and modification. As a fact, the Sanskrit word *jagat* (*gam* + *kvip*), an equivalent of the English word

5. *BG*, II.15.

6. *BG*, II.16.

"universe," literally means "that which is in motion" or "that which always undergoes changes and modifications." An existing *X* can cease to be *X* and can become *Y* or *Z*. The product *Y* or *Z* can again become *X*. Transformations are natural phenomena that cannot be denied.

The Vedānta, however, discards the metaphysical doctrine of transformation (*pariṇāma-vāda*) of the Sāṅkhya. According to the latter, *Prakṛti* (the Primordial Nature) is transformed into the material and mental entities of the universe. The non-dualistic Vedānta rejects the doctrine of transformation. According to this school of philosophy, neither the *Puruṣa* (*Brahman/Īśvara*) nor the *Prakṛti* (*Māyā, Mūla-Prakṛti,* the Primordial Nature, the Power of *Brahman/Īśvara*) is transformed into the universe which is an empirical reality (*vyāvahārika satya*), but not an Absolute Reality (*Pāramārthika Satya*).

The real significance of this verse (II.16) in chapter 2 of the *BG* has a direct reference to the Absolute Reality (the Supreme Self = *Brahman*) which is unmodifiable. The Self is an eternal and timeless Existence (*Satya* = *as* + *kyap*). It has not come into existence from nothing. It shall never become nothing. It has no precedent (precursor) and subsequent states. This Existence (*Satya* = Reality) has neither a beginning nor an end.

Next, we would like to discuss the conservation laws of science. In the age of Newtonian science, before the twentieth century, the universe was considered to be eternal and uncreated. There were two laws of conservation, namely, (1) the law of conservation of matter and (2) the law of conservation of energy. The first law says: Matter cannot be created; nor can it be destroyed; there can be transformation only from one form to another form of matter. The second law says: Energy cannot be created; nor can it be destroyed; there can be transformation only from one form to another form of energy. These two laws were considered to be inviolable and sacrosanct in science. In 1905, Albert Einstein discovered the Special Theory of Relativity, according to which matter and energy are interconvertible (the equation is: $E = mc^2$). This discovery falsified the two conservation laws, when considered separately. Subsequently, scientists salvaged the laws by amalgamating the two laws into one only. The combined law said:

> Matter and energy, taken together, cannot be created or destroyed; however, there can be transformation of one form of matter into another form, one form of energy into another form and matter into energy and vice versa.

In the twentieth century, especially in its second half, quantum mechanics was developed. The quantum physicists saw the *tāṇḍava* dance of Śiva in the micro-universe. Micro-particles bounce up out of the vacuum, vigorously dance, multiply in number, add new mass, subtract mass too, clash among themselves and finally dip into the vacuum. This discovery of quantum physics appeared to give a deathblow to the law of conservation of matter and energy and established (?) the concept of nothing -> something -> nothing.

The concept of the void is alien to the Vedānta that accepts *ākāśa* as a subtle state of matter. However, the ancient Greek philosophy erred by equating Space and Void (Absolute Nothing). Later, the Bible presented the *ex nihilo* theory of creation. (God created the universe out of nothing in its finished form during a period of six days only). Both the philosophical and the religious concepts of the ancient West on the subject of the void (vacuum) exerted a tremendous influence on the minds of the Western scientists and philosophers for two millennia or more. There are still a number of cosmologists who are working in the field of vacuum-genesis (vacuum-fluctuation).

In the latter half of the twentieth century, cosmology became an important subject in science. The first half of the century prepared the ground for the development of cosmology. George Gamow conceived of a Big-Bang for the creation of the universe. In the 1970s, the Big-Bang explosion of the cosmic egg and the subsequent expansion of the universe received support from data of accidental (not planned), experimental observations. It could also be known that superheated space (*ākāśa*) is not a void, but is the source of myriads of micro-particles and is a beehive of activity. It was also known that particles appear from space and that they disappear into space.

These discoveries of cosmology and particle-physics in science discarded the old concept of the uncreated, eternal universe. It is a fact that the universe had a beginning. Is it also a fact that the universe has a creator? The scientist, being a human being, is not free from biases. His bias and age-old theophobia induce him to think of vacuum-genesis. Some scientists still think that the universe is an accidental product of vacuum-fluctuation.

We may mathematically express the statement "Nothing becomes something" as "nothing = something" or "not-$X$ = $X$." This is a self-contradictory statement. And all self-contradictory statements are certainly false and nonsensical.

All these discussions drive us to one conclusion. Being is existence, irrespective of its sense-perceptibility or sense-imperceptibility. The law of conservation of Being is inviolable, whatever the conditions may be. There is neither creation nor destruction of Being. It is undecayable. The concept of a void is erroneous. The concept of the plenum (*pūrṇa*) rather than a void or a vacuum (*śūnya*) is a fact. So does the Vedāntic seer chant:

> That is full; this is full.
> The full comes out of the full.
> Taking the full from the full, the full itself remains.
> *Aum*, peace, peace, peace.[7]

### 2.05: The Indestructible Self

We use the word "self," with a small s, when we refer to the individual self (*jīvātmā*). We use the same word, with a capital S, when we refer to the Supreme Self (*Paramātmā*).

---

7. *IU*, Invocation

The English word "soul" and the Sanskrit word *ātmā* (self) are not synonyms. According to the Bible, God creates a soul out of nothing in the mother's womb at the time of conception. Thus, the soul has a birth. But it is deathless. It continues to exist in the buried dead body. On the Day of Judgement, God sends the good souls to heaven for eternal bliss and the bad souls to hell for eternal damnation. Thus, the soul has birth, but no death. Having a single birth only, it is not reborn for self-correction and final redemption. The soul is different from God. The former is an object and the latter is the subject, in the analogy of a chair and a carpenter, respectively.

The Self and the self are identical and different. This statement is apparently self-contradictory. This seeming contradiction will be resolved in the next section. In this section, we will analyse and elaborate the concept of the Self.

*Brahman* is the Self. It is Existence (*Sat*), Consciousness (*Cit*) and Bliss (*Ānanda*), all these three words being neither attributive nor predicative adjectives. Whatever exists is existent (*yadasti tatsatyam*). The word *sat* has been derived from the verb-root *as*, meaning "is," "to exist." *Brahman* is pure and fundamental Consciousness. It is not correct to say that *Brahman* has consciousness or is conscious. The correct statement is: *Brahman* is Consciousness. The word *Ānanda* (Bliss) has a special connotation with reference to *Brahman*. It is neither joyfulness nor sorrowfulness. It is a neutral state, free from joy and sorrow. The statements or propositions, used for *Brahman*, are analytical rather than synthetic; or, else, they are like definitions. Being self-evidenced (*svataḥsiddha*), they do not need empirical proofs to be validated by sense-experience.

*Brahman* is changeless, unmodifiable (*avikārya*). If it is designated as *B*, this *B* remains as *B* eternally and timelessly. Any precursor entity, *A*, does not become *B*; and *B* does not become *C*, *D*, *E*, et cetera. When we accept this constant (*dhruva*) *B*, we have to accept the fact that *Brahman* is timeless (*akāla*). The past, the present and the future have no relevance to *Brahman*. It is eternnal (*nitya*) and eternal-cum-timeless (*sanātana*). It has no beginning. No *A* has become *B*. Thus, it is beginningless (*anādi*) and birthless (*aja*). It never changes to *C, D, E,* or anything else. It is deathless (*amara*) and endless (*ananta*).

Anything that is a product from a precursor substance and that is converted into other products cannot be beginningless, endless and eternal. Anything that has forms (*rūpa*), attributes (*guṇa*) and functions (*karma*) cannot be eternal. Anything that is relational (*sambandhi*) cannot be eternal. Anything that has motion (*gati*) and modifications or changes (*vikāra*) cannot be eternal. Anything that is material (matter and energy = *vastu*) cannot be eternal. Anything that has a beginning (*ādi*) must have an end.[8] What is the scientific explanation for all these statements in this paragraph? Without the expenditure of energy, none of these states, attributes and functions can be possible. With the expenditure of energy, the utilizable energy becomes less and less and entropy, the waste heat, becomes more and more. In due course of time, the entropy becomes maximum and the utilizable energy becomes zero. Although the quantity of energy in the universe is enormously vast, it is not inexhaustible. For this reason, the universe, as a whole, has a birth and a death. Its creation, sustenance and dissolution follow a cyclic path. An individual body has birth, growth, decay and death. Without exception, any material substance cannot be eternal. In contrast, *Brahman* (Self) is birthless, deathless, eternal (*nitya*) during the existence of time ($t_0$ to $t_m$, from the time of the creation to that of the dissolution of the universe) and is still Existence after the total dissolution of the universe and before its subsequent creation. This type of Existence of *Brahman* is called *sanātana* (existence in both the presence and absence of time).

With this much background information, we wish to quote the *BG* with reference to the indestructibility of the Self. Lord

8. *TUŚB*, Intr.

Śrīkṛṣṇa says to Arjuna:

> On the contrary, know That, by which all this is pervaded, to be indestructible. None can destroy this Immutable.[9]
>
> These bodies of the embodied Self — the Eternal, the Indestructible, the Indeterminable — are said to have an end. Therefore, fight, O descendant of Bharata.[10]
>
> Both he who takes It (the Self) for the slayer and he who takes It to be the slain know not (the truth). It neither slays nor is slain.[11]
>
> This (Self) is never born; nor does it ever die. Having been, it never again ceases to be. It is unborn, eternal, everlasting and ancient (primeval). It is not slain when the body is slain.[12]
>
> O son of Pṛthā (Arjuna), how can a man who knows It (the Self) to be indestructible, eternal, unborn and undecaying (immutable) cause anyone to be slain and whom does he slay?[13]
>
> As a person puts on fresh clothes after discarding worn-out ones, so does the embodied Self discard worn-out bodies and proceed to take new ones.[14]
>
> Weapons do not cut It; fire does not burn It. Neither does water wet It; nor does the wind dry It.[15]

Anything that is matter and that has parts can be cut, burnt, moistened and dried. The Self is not material and is impartite (partless). Hence, weapons cut not; fire burns not; water wets not; and wind dries not this Self.

> This (Self) cannot be cut, burnt, wetted or dried. It is eternal (*nitya*), all-pervasive (*sarvagata*), stable (*sthāṇu*), immovable (*acala*) and everlasting cum timeless (*sanātana*).[16]

---

9. *BG*, II.17.
10. *BG*, II.18.
11. *BG*, II.19.
12. *BG*, II.20.
13. *BG*, II.21.
14. *BG*, II.22.
15. *BG*, II.23.
16. *BG*, II.24.

> This Self is said to be unmanifested (*avyakta*), unthinkable (imponderable, *acintya*) and immutable (unmodifiable; not transformable; *avikārya*). Therefore, knowing It to be such, you ought not to mourn.[17]

The above-quoted paragraph needs some further explanation. The Self is beyond the ken of all the sense-organs; that is, It is sense-imperceptible. What is sense-perceptible (*indriya-gocara*) directly or indirectly, is manifested (*vyakta*) for us. It is, however, not the case with the Self due to its extreme subtlety. We can think of something that is sense-perceptible. Otherwise, even if something exists, we cannot think of it if it is beyond our sense-perceptibility. The Self is neither matter nor energy. It is impartite too. In other words, it is homogeneous, without being corposcular. It is partless and an Unbroken Whole (*akhaṇḍa*). *Brahman* (*B*) and the Self being identical, A does not become *B* and *B* is not transformed into *C*, *D*, *E*, or anything else. It continues to remain as *B* when the universe exists and when it does not exist. (The mental concept of time is meaningful after the beginning of creation and before the total dissolution of the universe. Time, as a mental construct, has relevance to the Cosmic Supermind or the human mind after the occurrence of events). Anything that has a body (*avayava*) is transformed or modified (*vikārya*). Anything that is partless (*niravayava*) is immutable. The Advaita Vedānta does not accept the doctrine of transformation (*pariṇāma-vāda*) for the Self, although it does accept it for the created becomings.

> O descendant of Bharata (Arjuna), this embodied Self (dwelling) in the bodies of all, is eternally indestructible. Therefore, you ought not to grieve for all beings.[18]

The Self dwells in the bodies of all. The indwelling Self is the *dehī* and the body in which the Self dwells is the *deha*. All bodies have beginnings; they change; and finally they die. But the Self (self) does not die. It is *avadhya* (cannot be killed).

---

17. *BG*, II.25.

18. *BG*, II.30.

The knowledge on the indestructibility of the Self (self) is an essential prerequisite for a *jñāna-yogī* (a person adept in the *yoga* of knowledge). Not only should he know this fact, but also should he have a full realization.

### 2.06: Unmanifest -> Manifest -> Unmanifest

The second chapter of the *BG* contains a verse whose essence is "unmanifest -> manifest -> unmanifest." Arjuna is despondent. He is stricken with grief. He does not want to fight with his kins and respectable superiors and to kill them in the war. In order to impart knowledge to Arjuna, Lord Śrīkr̥ṣṇa elaborates the Sāṅkhya-Yoga. Let us focus on the verse: unmanifest -> manifest -> unmanifest:

> O Bhārata (descendant of Bharata = Arjuna), beings are unmanifest in their beginning, manifest in their middle state and unmanifest again in their end. What is there then to lament?[19]

In the aforesaid verse, the meaning of "beginning," "middle state" and "end" are "before their birth," "during the period after their birth and before their death" and "after their death," respectively.

There is a need to elaborate the concept of unperceived -> perceived -> unperceived. The self (*ātmā*) is too subtle to be perceived by our five sensory organs. It has neither birth nor death. It is both eternal and timeless. It is unmodifiable. It never undergoes changes. It is formless, functionless and attributeless. It has no beginning, middle and final states. This birthless and deathless *ātmā* can never be perceived by our senses. It is eternally and timelessly immortal. It cannot be killed.

If the *ātmā* is *avyakta* (unmanifested), what is that which becomes *vyakta* (manifested) then? This is a pertinent question which has to be answered.

Each created being has a body in addition to the self (*ātmā*).

---

19. *BG*, II.28.

The body is the *deha* and the self is the *dehī* (embodied). Each one of us has three types of body, namely, the gross body (*sthūla śarīra*), the subtle body (*sūkṣma śarīra*) and the causal body (*kāraṇa śarīra*). The subtle and the causal bodies continue to stay until the individual self is liberated (gets *mokṣa*). Because of their subtlety, they cannot be perceived. The gross body, however, is perceived. It may be mentioned here that the subtle body is dissolved in the causal body when the gross body is abandoned.

The *buddhi*, an important component of the *antaḥkaraṇa* of the subtle body, contains our *karmāśaya* (reservoir of karmic *saṁskāras*). In the absence of these karmic traces, the self is liberated and there is no rebirth. So long as the karmic traces stay, the self is born and reborn again and again. It is the gross body that has birth and death. One gets a manifested state during the period between a birth and the subsequent death.

Beginning from the time of conception in the mother's womb, a micro-body is formed by the fusion of an ovum, coming from the mother, and a sperm, coming from the father. The process is called fertilization and the resulting unicellular micro-body is called a zygote. Simultaneous with the formation of the zygote, a *jīvātmā,* seated in its subtle and causal body, comes and dwells in the zygote. The selection of an appropriate womb and the placement of the self is done by God through the agency of His Power, *Māyā.* This placement is not arbitrary, however. The *karma* of the individual in the previous births is the criterion for the selection of an appropriate womb.

The zygote multiplies by cell-division. An embryo is formed in the mother's uterus. It develops into a foetus that becomes connected with the mother through an umbilical cord. This cord carries the mother's blood that is circulated in the foetal body. Thus the foetus gets nutrients to grow in the intra-uterine life. In the postnatal life, the baby grows by suckling the mother's breast and later by eating other foods. Throughout the life, both anabolism and catabolism are operative in the body-cells. The former is a constructive or building up process whereas the latter is a destructive or breaking up process. The incorporation of external matter into the body continues from the time of conception till that of death. The body is material and gross. It is sense-perceptible either directly or indirectly (through the aid of instrumentation such as microscopes and other devices). Even the brain is material and corporeal and can be perceived. But the inner mental apparatus (*antaḥkaraṇa*) cannot be perceived due to its subtlety. The self (*ātmā*) and the Self (*Paramātmā*), sitting in the body, like two birds on a tree (one eating the fruits and the other simply sitting), are not material. They are too subtle to be sense-perceptible.

When the self, associated with an *antaḥkaraṇa* in which *saṁskāra*s are installed, acquires a gross body, a person becomes *vyakta* (manifest) due to the perceptibility of the gross body. When the self leaves the gross body, the former becomes *avyakta* (unmanifest) as it is always so. The gross body dies. It means: The self leaves the gross body that is reconverted into the five states of matter and energy, that is, solids, liquids, gases, energy and *ākāśa* (*ākāśa* being the subtlest state of material existence). Nevertheless, the gross body is not converted into nothing. Something being completely annihilated and becoming nothing is a nihilistic concept which is rejected by the Vedānta. A thing, *X*, becomes something else, *Y*. This process is known as modification or transformation. The self or the Self is birthless, deathless and unmodifiable (*avikārya*). It never undergoes changes or any type of transformation.

The process of *avyakta* -> *vyakta* -> *avyakta* is not limited to human beings only. It is also applied to animals and plants. And it is applied to non-living matter of particles, micro-particles, quanta and quarks, especially in the micro-world. As a matter of fact, it is applied to the whole universe that undergoes a cyclic process of creation (manifestation, emanation from some existing source), sustenance and dissolution. Many particle-physicists and quantum-physicists observe (not through the naked eye) the cosmic dance in the micro-world. Particles appear from nowhere; they dance vigorously; they disappear (wrongly interpreted as their becoming nothing). The total universe has a similar fate. A Cosmic Egg appears from nowhere. It explodes as a Big-Bang. It evolves, exists and functions for many billion years. Finally, it undergoes a total dissolution. In this case too, many scientists explain this process as nothing -> something -> nothing. The concept of vacuum-genesis is popular among some cosmologists.

The *BG* discards the concept of nothing -> something -> nothing. This topic is discussed separately in this book. The *BG* favours the concept of unmanifest -> manifest -> unmanifest. This is a universal concept with reference to the total universe and each and every entity of the universe, both non-living and living. What is unmanifest is not necessarily nothing. What is manifest is not necessarily something as it appears in its apparent form. Rigorous logical analysis confirms the truth that something X becomes something Y, irrespective of our sense-cognizability.

### 2.07: Death is a Certainty for Anyone Born

The *BG* unambiguously declares that anybody who is born must die (*jātasya hi dhruvo mṛtyuḥ*) and that anybody who dies must be born (*dhruvaṁ janma mṛtasya ca*). Both birth and death are certainties (*dhruva*). They are unavoidable (*aparihārya; anivārya*). Here we quote the relevant verse of the *BG*.

> The death of one who is born is indeed certain. The birth of one who is dead is certain too. Therefore, you ought not to grieve over this unavoidable affair.[20]

Let us analyse what has been said in the foregoing paragraph. The verse contains two statements over birth and death. Both these statements are not analytical such as (1) $A = A$, (2) A man is a man, (3) Water is aqua, and (4) A triangle is a geometrical figure with three angles. These statements where the subject and the predicate are identical or synonymous are analytical and certainly

20. *BG*, II.27.

true. They do not furnish any additional information. All analytical statements are certainly true. Unlike a synthetic statement such as "A cow is a quadruped animal" that needs empirical verification through our sense-experience, analytical statements are self-evident (*svataḥ-siddha*).

Why did the *BG* declare that death is a certainty for anybody who is born? This statement is not deductive, but is inductive. We have been observing this fact. So far there has been no exception. A question arises: If there has been no exception in the past and there is no exception in the present, can there be any surety of no exception in the future? How can we be certain of the impossibility of the emergence of an immortal man (immortal *Homo sapiens*) in the future?

We cannot logically solve this controversy. We would try to dissolve it on the basis of facts outside the domain of logic. We should not whisk away the inductive observations. Any person who has been born has died. Lord Śrīrāma, Śrīkr̥ṣṇa, Gautama Buddha, Jesus Christ and many others, considered by their devotees as God or God-Incarnate, have died (left their bodies). All persons, superhuman or human, being born, have been dying. So far death has been an observational certainty on the earth.

In Hindu religious scriptures, the existence of gods and goddesses or *devatā*s (apart from one God) has been mentioned. They are incorporeal. They do not die during the life-period of a universe (*para* = the time between the creation and the total dissolution of a universe). But they are born after the creation of the universe and they die at the time of the total dissolution of the universe.

The material body has a beginning. It has a period of growth. Finally, it decays and degenerates. Whatever has a beginning has an end. Growth is generally followed by decay. Decay and degeneration generally end in death. All material bodies undergo changes and modifications. They function. They are in constant motion at least for their own existence. There is no created being, micro or macro, inanimate or animate, which is in absolute rest. (*Brahman* alone is in absolute rest). Functions and motions imply the expenditure of utilizable energy and the production of entropy (roughly speaking, waste heat). These facts having been accepted, we cannot reject the inevitability of death.

Death is a necessity. If birth is a continual process, death becomes an unavoidable necessity. We may take the example of the earth. There would be no standing place, no food, no water, no air, and no other necessities and amenities of life in the hypothetical case of the continuation of births and the cessation of deaths.

Death is a final outcome of birth. The process of wear and tear of every organ, tissue and cell that constantly function during life is unavoidable. The final state is old age, with or without invalidity. Old age, for many persons, is more painful than any specific disease. Death becomes welcome when painful old age and painful diseases cannot be tolerably confronted with.

The universe is not anthropocentric. It is not meant for man only. Lions, tigers, snakes, bacteria, viruses, protozoa, mosquitoes, flies and many other organisms are born. The chain of food and food-eater is operative. Pathogenic micro-organisms attack the human body and cause diseases. Our own genes mutate and declare sovereignty. They rebel and cause cancerous growths. Mosquitoes, bacteria, viruses, protozoa and malarial parasites mutate their genes for their struggle for existence and for being the fittest for survival. Newer and newer pathogens such as the HIV virus evolve and attack the human species. Natural calamities such as floods, droughts, earthquakes, tsunami and volcanoes cannot be altogether prevented. Deaths due to accidents cannot be totally eliminated. The prevention of the death of man seems to be impossible. Death can be postponed for some years. The span of life has been increased and can be further increased by the use of advanced medical science and technology, by improved economic standards, social welfare schemes, spread of education and health-consciousness.

The possibility of man himself causing the extinction of the human species on the earth cannot be ruled out. We believe that there will never come a time when all persons on the earth will be perfectly flawless and good. Knowledge-explosion will continue. But knowledge without wisdom is a liability rather than an asset. The misuse of technological knowledge for wiping out the human species from the earth is a probability, against which there is no guarantee of safeguard. A war-free, non-violent, peaceful earth should be our cherished goal. But there exists a wide gap between "is" and "ought."

Not only do living beings die, but also do non-living things too. The earth has been born and will die. Our sun has been born and will die. The whole universe has been created and shall have an end. In the macro-world, stars are dying in old places and appearing in new places. In the micro-world, particles and micro-particles are being born every moment and are dying every moment. Their birth and death are in continual flux. Death is a universal certainty for all, inanimate and animate, that have been created.

In our opinion, total uplift of *Homo sapiens* on the earth to a supramental status of Gnostic Beings would ever remain an unfulfilled dream and Utopia. Individual liberation has been going on and will be a continued phenomenon. But the ascent of the human species on the earth to the status of Godhood and separate, individual Godhood is not a valid proposition. In dualistic religious philosophy, the eternal stay of released *jīva*s in heaven (the abode of God), with eternal bliss, is a concept. But non-dualism cannot accommodate this concept, without ending in self-contradiction.

A self, in order to merge in *Brahman* or become *Brahman,* has to free itself from the three *guṇa*s (has to be *nistraiguṇya*). Even *sattva,* the best among the three *guṇa*s, cannot make one self liberated. There is no manifested universe when all the three strings of the *vīṇā* of Mother Sarasvatī are equipoised. The state of equipoise must be disturbed by Her alone by the inequal vibrations of the three strings. Every created entity, inanimate or animate, has preponderance (dominance) of one of the *guṇa*s. Even gods and goddesses are not exceptions to this rule. Hence, we cannot find any justification of the eternal existence of the universe and the eternal existence of separate individual Gnostic Beings.

Every created entity, living or non-living, has ego (*ahaṅkāra*). Ego and individuality necessarily go together. It generates six foes (*ripus*), namely, desire for sexual and sensual pleasure, power, material possession and comforts (*kāma*), anger (*krodha*), covetousness (*lobha*), delusion (*moha*), pride with arrogance (*mada*) and malice or envy (*mātsarya*). Ego is antagonistic to altruism. It works for itself at the cost of others. It is tagged to both the life-instinct and the death-instinct, the former for itself and the latter for others. Violence and exploitation are two manifestations of the six *ripus*. Only a few individual persons who have ascended the spiritual ladder to a very high level can subdue the ego, and those who have climbed to the summit can be I-less and my-less (*nirahaṅkāra* or *niraham* and *nirmama*). Such rare persons only can shun violence in their thoughts, speeches and actions. Absolute non-violence in the whole universe in a total scale would never be practicable. And violence is a cause for death. The total absence of ego and the *ripus* is an unattainable dream and Utopia.

Here we have put forth our arguments in favour of the inevitability of death of somebody or something that is born. Next, we come to the second proposition, given in the quoted verse of the *BG*. Whosoever or whatsoever dies will be certainly reborn.

We have no way to substantiate this statement by our observational facts, nor can we do it by logical analysis. We accept the scriptural evidence (*śāstra-pramāṇam*). We have written a sizeable chapter under the caption "The Potter's Wheel" in our book *Mind and Supermind*.[21] We do not want to repeat it here. We request our readers to go through this chapter for getting convincing evidences in favour of rebirth.

---

21. N.C. Panda, 1996, Chapter 3, *The Potter's Wheel*.

There is an exception to what has been said in the second proposition. After being liberated, the self (*jīvātmā*) is no longer reborn. There are two principal concepts on this issue in Indian philosophy. The non-dualists say that the individual self merges in the Universal Self (*Brahman*) by losing its separate identity in the analogy of the river-water merging in the ocean-water. The dualists hold that the self can never be the Self and that, on being liberated, the former goes to the Vaikuṇṭha (heaven, the abode of Nārāyaṇa) to be eternally sheltered at the feet of the Lord and to enjoy pure bliss.

Lastly, we conclude this topic by presenting a psychological anomaly. When we discard a worn-out cloth and put on a new one, we remain in a joyful mood. It is just the reverse in the case of death. Highly spiritual persons, albeit rare, are exceptions, however. The common individual, even though educated, is terribly afraid of death. We do not plead for inviting death. We do recommend to prevent or postpone death due to diseases, natural calamities and senility, as far as possible. We condemn man-made death by our strongest language. The body is a vehicle for doing meritorious work and for engaging oneself for social uplift. Each birth is a supplementary chance for ascending the spiritual ladder, leading finally to the summit of Godhead. But we are sure of the fact that death (departing from the body) is a certainty one day or the other. If we realize the significance of the relevant verse, given in the *BG*, on which this section elaborates, we would be glad to leave this worn-out body and get a new one.

### 2.08: The Identity of the Supreme Self and All Individual Selves

We have already quoted verse 2.30 of the *BG* in section 2.05 of this book. There we have focussed on the indestructibility of the Self. The body can be slain, but not the Self/self. This section is based on the same verse, but its focus is different. It lays emphasis on the identity of all the individual selves with the Supreme Self and the oneness of the Self. It does not limit the self to human beings only. The all-pervading Self resides in all living beings, including animals and plants, and all non-living objects — macro and micro. The verse is quoted again.

> O descendant of Bharata, the embodied Self (dwelling) in the bodies of all, is eternally indestructible. Therefore, you ought not to grieve for all beings.[22]

In this quoted verse, the Self and the self are indistinguishable. It contradicts dualism, that is, the difference between the *Paramātmā* (the Supreme Self) and the *jīvātmā*s (the innumerable individual selves). It unambiguously establishes the existence of one Self only and the identity of the Self and the seemingly numerous selves in individual bodies. The Self is impartite (*niravayava*), unchangeable and ever-lasting. It dwells in the bodies of all. Because of Its omnipresence and all-pervasiveness, It abides in all immobile and mobile bodies. Even when the bodies of all creatures are slain, the Self remains unslain (*avadhyaḥ*). If one realizes this fact, one is not perturbed even when all creatures are slain. There is no need of mourning for the dead.

One is likely to misunderstand this verse and the whole *BG* if one misinterprets this verse and some other similar ones as preaching for violence and genocide. One may distort the meaning of this verse by pleading that Śrīkr̥ṣṇa instigates Arjuna to commit cruelty and violence. One is to comprehend the background and the context of the *BG* in the Mahābhārata War. The Kauravas, under the leadership of Duryodhana and his mentor, Śakuni, committed injustice and sins. To meekly tolerate all sorts of injustice without resistance, protests and war (if unavoidable) is the worst type of sin. If cowardice is the yardstick of piousness and righteousness, the distinction of *dharma* (righteousness) and *adharma* (unrighteousness) is totally obliterated and our judgement performs a somersault.

We consider another issue in this context. Respectable persons

---

22. *BG*, II.30.

like Bhīṣma and Droṇa, revered by Arjuna from the core of his heart, were to be killed in the War. They were not sinners. They did not do any injustice. They were noble and ideal persons. But, circumstantially, they were fighting for Duryodhana against their dear Pāṇḍavas. Arjuna was mourning for the would-be death of these great men. The Lord advised him:

> You cannot slay Me (the Self). You cannot slay Bhīṣma, Droṇa and others because their selves are not different from the Self. Their bodies are to be slain since they fight for the sinner and against the virtuous, even if they are compelled by circumstances to do so. You can slay their bodies. And, for this, you ought not to grieve.

Another point is to be noted in connection with the interpretation of the quoted verse. Buddhism accepts the doctrine of no-self (*nairātmya-vāda, anātma-vāda*). Christianity recognizes the soul, the concept of which is different from that of the self (*ātmā*). Secondly, in Christianity, God and the soul are in the analogy of the subject and the object, the maker and the made. Thirdly, the Christian souls dwell in the human beings only. Animals, birds, fishes, snakes, plants, bacteria, viruses, protozoa, planets, stars, molecules, atoms, sub-atomic particles, micro-particles, quarks and quanta are soulless. In contrast, Advaita Vedānta holds that the Self is the indwelling Spirit in all created beings, both inanimate and animate and both micro and macro. In lifeless entities, it is called the *bhūtātmā*, whereas, in living beings, it is called the *jīvātmā*. The Self, being Pure Consciousness, everything of the universe is rendered conscious due to the reflection of the Self on all beings. The reflected or induced consciousness of created beings varies in degrees due to the variation in the evolution of the mental apparatus and due to the variation of the degree of *avidyā* (nescience, ignorance, the opaqueness of the *buddhi* or intellect).

### 2.09: Mental Equanimity for Opposite Results

Even though the second chapter of the *BG* is titled as Sāṅkhya-Yoga, it is really *Jñāna-Yoga* (the Yoga of knowledge on *Brahman*).

A *jñāna-yogī* does not forsake *karma-yoga* altogether, at least in the initial stage. Whenever and wherever is *karma* performed, then and there is the probability of opposite results. In such conditions, one should work without attachment to the results. The mind of the worker should be neutral to *rāga* (passion; vehement desire) and *dveṣa* (aversion; hostility; hatred; dislike). The development of a mental attitude of equanimity toward contradictory results, favourable or unfavourable, pleasure or pain, in the performance of work is a necessary condition for the realization of the ultimate Reality. It is also the best means for getting peace in life that cannot avoid the opposites and contradictions that are inbuilt in the world.

It is the nature of persons, other than an enlightened *yogī*, to do what gives pleasure (*sukha*) and not to do what gives pain (*duḥkha*). He weighs gain (*lābha*) and loss (*alābha*), victory (*jaya*) and defeat (*ajaya*). He selects the path that gives gain and victory. He does not consider the question of ought (*ucita*) and ought not (*anucita*), duty (*kartavya*) and contrary duty (*akartavya*), and righteousness (*dharma*) and unrighteousness (*adharma*). He opts for actions that give sensual pleasure, material gains and benefits, power, name and fame and victory over others.

The Lord advises Arjuna to maintain mental equanimity in discharging one's duties.

> Treating alike pleasure and pain, gain and loss, victory and defeat, strive to fight. Thus done, shall you incur no sin.[23]

To do one's duty is a virtue. To do something that is not one's duty is a vice. In the performance of *dharma* (righteousness), if one disregards the calculation of pleasure and pain, profit and loss, and victory and defeat, and performs duties for the sake of duty only, one's actions can never be contaminated with sins.

What should one do then? The answer has already been given in the quoted verse. Ponder over the issue of your duty. What is righteousness and what is unrighteousness? What is pious and

23. *BG*, II.38.

what is impious? What should you do and what should you not do? Don't base your judgement on the merit of pleasure, gain and victory. The foundation of your judgement should be your duty only. If you follow this principle in deciding the line of your action and if you act accordingly, you do not incur any sin.

### 2.10: Jñāna-Yoga versus Ritualism for Fulfilment of Desires

In chapter 2 of the *BG* (Sāṅkhya-Yoga = Jñāna-Yoga = the Yoga of Knowledge on the Supreme Reality), there are a few verses that apparently condemn the Vedas. The lovers of the Vedas are very much aggrieved for this reason. What has been told in the *BG*, in the verses to be quoted, is critical of the Vedic *karma-kāṇḍa* (ritualism done for the fulfilment of desires such as getting more wealth, power, comforts and many other worldly gains or other-worldly gains such as stay in heaven). The disapproval of hankering after wordly gains, with tenacious attachment to material prosperity, has been done with a purpose to lay emphasis on liberation (*mokṣa*). The *BG* is based on the Vedas and the Vedānta. It cannot afford, without involving in self-contradiction, to condemn the Vedas in general.

It is commonly believed that the Vedas deal with *karma-kāṇḍa* only and that the Upaniṣads are the scriptures on *jñāna-kāṇḍa* (subjects pertaining to knowledge). Of course, there is some truth in it. But such an exclusive division is not fully correct. The Vedic Saṁhitās (compilations of the Vedic hymns) hardly deal with ritualism. They constitute the principal portion of the Vedas. They contain hymns for prayer to God, for the guidance of human activities, on cosmolgy and cosmogony and on knowledge on the creation and the creator. The word *veda* itself means "knowledge." Books on the *karma-kāṇḍa* came later. Every religion has some ritual practices and so also does the Vedic religion.

The *BG* perhaps refers to those who conform to the Pūrva-Mīmāṁsā school. They discard other spiritual methods and perform Vedic rituals only, with the expectation of getting rewards, both this-worldly and other-worldly, such as getting progeny, wealth and impermanent or permanent residence in heaven.

Ritualism, either more or less, is part of every religion. It is not bad unless one gives undue emphasis on it, becomes a ritual fanatic, and performs ritualism only, while neglecting the other nobler aspects of spirituality.

Ritualism for worldly desires and gains is not compatible with the *yoga* of knowledge that leads to *brahma-nirvāṇa* (*mokṣa* or liberation by becoming *Brahman*). This liberation is unlike the latent existence of salt in the ocean-water, a process known as solution of a solute in a solvent. It is analogous to the process of the river-water flowing into the ocean to merge in the ocean-water and to become the ocean-water at the loss of individuality.

Now we quote the relevant verses of the *BG*:

> O son of Pṛthā (Arjuna), the unwise utter these flowery speeches. They revel in the letter of the Vedas. They declare that there is nothing else.[24]
>
> They hanker after desires. They regard heaven as their highest goal. What they do leads to rebirths for getting fruits of actions. They prescribe exuberantly many specific rites, expected to yield enjoyments and power.[25]
>
> They are deeply attached to pleasures and power. Their thinking minds have been carried away by the words of the Vedas (the *karma-kāṇḍa* portion). Being attached to pleasures and power, they have no conviction of a resolute intellect that can merge in the Self (that can attain the state of *samādhi*).[26]
>
> The Vedic *karma-kāṇḍa* deals with the three attributes (*guṇas*), namely, *sattva* (goodness and purity), *rajas* (passionate activity) and *tamas* (darkness, inertia, vigour). O Arjuna, become free from the triad of the *guṇas* (Be *nistraiguṇyaḥ*); free yourself from the

24. *BG*, II.42.
25. *BG*, II.43.
26. *BG*, II.44.

> pairs of opposites (Be *nirdvandvaḥ*); always resort to the *sattva* constituent; do not be anxious about new acquisitions (Be *niryogaḥ*) or about the preservation of already acquired ones (Be *niḥkṣemaḥ*). Master the self (Be *ātmavān* and be vigilant), that is, do not yield to the objects of the senses.[27]
>
> For a knower of *Brahman*, with the realization of the Self, there is as much use in all the (*karma-kāṇḍa* of) Vedas as there is use from a reservoir when all around there is an inundation.[28]

We conclude this topic by balancing the views of two contradictory groups, the Veda-lovers and the *Gītā*-lovers. The Vedas as such are not condemned in the *BG* and should not be condemned by any scripture. The Vedic rituals and all forms of religious rituals are meaningful for those who have not been able to attain to the state of a *jñāna-yogī*. Limited happiness is securable by performing rituals. But, for a *jñāna-yogī*, rituals have very little meaning and use. One who has the realization of *Brahman* (*Brahmānubhūti*) is a *jñāna-yogī*. And a knower of *Brahman* verily becomes *Brahman* (*brahmavid brahmaiva bhavati*).

For us, this is the right section where we can express our opinion on the claim that the Vedas are the words of God Himself, that they are eternal, incorrigible and inviolable, and that they are not authored by man. The advocates of this notion assert that the seers are not *sraṣṭā*s (creators) and that they are mere *draṣṭā*s (seers, persons to whom the divine truth has been revealed). We do not agree to such a view. We think that God is not the author of any scripture (not only the Vedas). When we allot the authorship of scriptures to human beings who are apt to err, we cannot afford to say that scriptures are infallible. As far as human knowledge is concerned, there is no last word, there is nothing like "the truth," and there is nothing like infallibility and incorrigibility. Notwithstanding what we have said here, we do recognize revelation. Most basic truths have been revealed to humankind.

27. *BG*, II.45.

28. *BG*, II.46.

Reality (we may give a name *Brahman* or some other word) is Pure, Fundamental Consciousness (Pure *Vidyā* or *Cit*). It is the source of Knowledge, Intelligence, Goodness, Virtues and Righteousness. This Fundamental Existence is eternal (*nityam*) and timeless (*sanātana*). The word *veda* and *vidyā* have been derived from the Sanskrit verb-root *vid*, meaning "to know." If we analyse the statement "The Vedas are eternal" in a wider context, as given here, we have a full agreement. There is no Fundamental Intelligence and Consciousness other than *Brahman*. There is no *vidyā* other than *Brahma-vidyā*. If true *vidyā* and *veda* are considered to be equivalent, that must come from the source of *Brahman*. Such knowledge is to be revealed to humankind. It cannot be experimental; neither can it come from sense-experience.

Can we accept anything said or written by anybody, howsoever esteemed he may be, to be true and nothing but true? Can it be one hundred per cent infallible and incorrigible? The *Brahma-Sūtram* has two aphorisms in this connection. The first one (*BS*, I.1.3) says: *śāstra-yonitvāt* (from its being the source of Scriptures). The second one (I.1.4) says: *tattu samanvayāt* (but that is the result of the harmony). The reception of the revealed truth by a seer might not have been accurate. Each statement of any scripture, howsoever sacred it may be, must be scrutinized on the basis of knowledge obtained through all methods available to humankind. Knowledge must be updated and it should be a continuous process. "All scriptural statements are inviolable and their corrections and updating are tantamount to blashphemy and sacrilege." Such a rigid notion stalls the progress of humankind and is fatally detrimental to human rights.

We conclude this section by saying that truth is told and retold by seers throughout the ages. Man can invent something; cannot create anything. Man can remove the cover of ignorance, and, thus, can discover something that has already been there. If any seer is telling anything new that is not present in *Brahman* in a figurative sense, knowingly or unknowingly he is not telling the truth. If somebody is telling the truth, he is not telling anything anew. That being so, Vyāsa could not give any new truth to us without getting it from the source (the Vedas) of *Brahman*. A wise seer like Vyāsa did not condemn the Vedas. He was critical of the Mīmāṁsakas, the ritualistic *karmakāṇḍīs*.

## 2.11: The Way of Detached Action for a Jñāna-Yogī

The second chapter of the *BG* is titled as Sāṅkhya-Yoga which here really means *jñāna-yoga*. We get some verses in this chapter on the way of action (*karma-yoga*). Such an inclusion may be confusing for some persons. Hence arises the necessity of giving a clarification first.

The *yogī*, pursuing the *yoga* of knowledge, does not and should not renounce all actions. Being totally detached, he performs actions for the sake of his duty only. Let us elucidate an important verse of the *BG*, given in the second chapter:

> Your right is to work alone; but never to the fruits thereof. Be you not impelled by the fruits of actions. Neither let your attachment be for inaction.[29]

Many economists may be sceptical of this verse. Work is usually done for getting fruits. Projects are planned and executed for getting results. Sincere and hard work is not possible without incentives. And incentives do involve attachment to fruits. How can there be economic progress of a society or a country if this verse of the *BG* is adopted as an ideal?

We have already mentioned that the way of action, as described in the relevant verse, is mainly intended for a *yogī* who pursues the way of knowledge. He cannot get *Brahma-nirvāṇa* unless he renounces desires for sense-objects and attachment to the fruits of actions. Everybody in the world cannot be a *jñāna-yogī* forthwith. He has the potentiality of becoming one in this life or in any one of the forthcoming lives. The common man works for profitable actions. Common people are in a competitive rat-race for getting more and more. They are motivated by their

29. *BG*, II.47.

insatiable greed. They are extremely attached to the fruits of their actions. The more the material gain, the more jubilant they become. But actions do not necessarily bear desirable fruits qualitatively and/or quantitatively. There arise sorrow, agony and frustration. On the contrary, action without attachment does not engender frustration.

One misinterpretation of the verse is to be highlighted here. The verse nowhere says to renounce the fruits of actions. It lays emphasis on actions without attachment to the fruits thereof. It disfavours any thirst (*tṛṣṇā, tanhā*) for the fruits of actions. It does not advise to reject fruits, the products of detached actions. It also denounces inaction. A *jñāna-yogī* must not renounce actions; but detached actions should be his *mantra*. Only when a *jñāna-yogī* becomes *jīvan-mukta* (released albeit still living), he stops doing actions except the minimum for living.

One cannot get liberation if one is attached to inaction. One cannot get liberation if one has thirst for the fruits of actions. In order to attain *Brahma-nirvāṇa*, one should perform actions for the sake of duty only, and this action too should be detached (*anāsakta*).

### 2.12: Buddhi-Yoga, the Way of Equanimity of the Intellect

This topic is on *karma-yoga*, the way of action, which is dealt with in the third chapter of the *BG*. Still it is discussed in the second chapter that is on *jñāna-yoga*, the way of knowledge. A *jñāna-yogī* must not be attached to inaction. At the same time, he must not have thirst for the fruits of action. If action is not to be performed, being prompted by its result, how should it be done then? Lord Śrīkṛṣṇa advises Arjuna on this topic.

> O Dhanañjaya (Arjuna), perform actions, with your intellect linked to God, abandoning attachment, and with evenness of mind in success and failure. This equanimity is Yoga.[30]

---

30 *BG*, II.48.

The word *buddhi* means "intellect." It is not an exactly correct rendering into English, since its concept does not exist in Western psychology. It is a subtle psychic organ, one of the three principal components, namely, *buddhi, ahaṅkāra* and *manas,* of the *antaḥkaraṇa* (the inner instrument; the internal mental apparatus). The *jñāna-yogī* does not cease to be a *karma-yogī* until he reaches a higher state in the spiritual ladder that is not too far from becoming a *jīvan-mukta* (liberated albeit still living). In order that he performs right actions, he has to be a *buddhi-yogī*. The term *buddhi-yoga* has been used by the *BG* only. Its special characteristics are: (1) While working, or at least before starting the work, unite your intellect with God (Be *yogasthaḥ*). (2) Dedicate your actions to God. Work for Him; in other words, work for the welfare of His creation. (3) Abandon attachment (*saṅga* or *āsakti*) to the fruits of actions. (4) The consequence of an action may meet with success or failure (*siddhi* or *asiddhi*). If you have performed detached actions, you will maintain mental composure. Your intellect will not be perturbed at all. Success and failure are equal to a *buddhi-yogī*. (5) Evenness (equanimity) of mind, in both success and failure, is known as *buddhi-yoga*. This *buddhi-yoga* is a branch of *jñāna-yoga*, with special reference to performance of actions.

> Work (impelled by the desire for fruits) is far inferior to that performed with evenness of intellect. O Dhanañjaya (Arjuna), seek refuge in the equanimity of the intellect. Miserable (wretched, pitiful) are they who are impelled by the desire for the fruits of works.[31]

> Endued with the equanimity of intellect, one discards here (in this world) both good and evil works (both *puṇya* and *pāpa*, the merits and demerits of works). Therefore, devote yourself to this *yoga* (*buddhi-yoga*). Yoga is skill in action.[32]

The last proposition in this verse (Yoga is skill in action). is very often misinterpreted. It is wrongly interpreted by reversing the

---

31. *BG*, II.49.

32. *BG*, II.50.

subject and the predicate of the statement (Skill in action is Yoga). A skilful mechanic, with the utmost efficiency and proficiency in his work, is not a *yogī*. This principle holds good for any profession and vocation. As a specimen, we may take two statements: (1) Man is an animal. (2) An animal is a man. The subject and the predicate have been interchanged in these two statements. As a result, the meanings have been changed. The first statement is meaningful, whereas the second one is absurd.

There is no guarantee that every work of a *yogī* must be virtuous and free from demerits. After all, to err is human. But a *buddhi-yogī*, with equanimity of intellect, working for the sake of own duty (*svadharma*) only, and dedicating the work to *Īśvara* (God), casts off here (in this world) both virtues and vices.

The question is: What is the *modus operandi* of casting off the merits and demerits of *karma*? Actions, dedicated to God, performed with equanimity of intellect and without attachment to the fruits thereof, do not create any *karma-saṁskāra* in the *buddhi*. Without accumulation of *karma-saṁskāra*s in the *antaḥkaraṇa*, the question of *puṇya* (merits) and *pāpa* (demerits) becomes irrelevant. Hence, it is said: Yoga (*buddhi-yoga*) is skill in works (*yogaḥ karmasu kauśalam*).

> Wise men (*jñāna-yogī*s), endued with the way of equanimity of intellect, discard, indeed, the fruits of work. They are liberated from the fetter (bondage) of birth. They attain the status which is free from all sufferings (they attain *mokṣa).*[33]
>
> When your intellect goes beyond the mist of delusion, then shall you attain to indifference, regarding what is to be heard and what has been heard.[34]

Two clarifications are necessary with reference to verse 2.52. (1) What is the contextual meaning of delusion here? (2) What are those yet to be heard and already heard?

The mist of non-discrimination is the problem. Delusion

33. *BG*, II.51.

34. *BG*, II.52.

obscures the distinction between the Self and the non-Self. When the intellect crosses the mire of delusion and goes beyond, it attains to the state of purity.

For a pure intellect, both knowledge already gained and that which remains to be gained will be understood to be of no value except the realization of the Self.

> You will attain to the state of the supreme Yoga when your intellect, bewildered by the Vedic texts regarding *pravṛtti* (activity) and *nivṛtti* (abstention from activity), becomes motionless and unwavering in concentration (in other words, your intellect is firmly established in the Self).[35]

This is the final state of *jñāna-yoga,* including the *buddhi-yoga.* The *yogī*'s intellect is fully established and absorbed in the Self (*Ātmā* = *Brahman*).

### 2.13: Sthitaprajña, the Man of Stable Wisdom

The Sanskrit word *prajñā* means "wisdom." It is not exactly "knowledge." It is qualitatively more than that. A person of stable wisdom is called *sthitaprajña.* When a *sthitaprajña* is anchored in *Brahman* in his concentration, he is *samādhistha* (in the state of being merged or absorbed in *Brahman*) *sthitaprajña.* When a person has the realization "I am *Brahman*" (*aham brahmāsmi*), he becomes a *sthitaprajña.* Arjuna wanted to know the distinctive marks of a *sthitaprajña* from Lord Śrīkṛṣṇa.[36]

The Lord answers to the question of Arjuna in a number of verses.

> O Pārtha (the son of Pṛthā = Arjuna), when one wholly discards all the desires of the mind and becomes exclusively content with the Self alone, one is called a *sthitaprajña.*[37]
>
> The silent sage (*muni*) is said to be *sthitadhīḥ* (*sthitaprajñaḥ* = a

---

35. *BG,* II.53.
36. *BG,* II.54.
37. *BG,* II.55.

> person of steady wisdom) when sufferings do not perturb his mind, when he ceases to crave for pleasures, and when he is rid of attachment, fear and wrath.[38]

Adversities are of three kinds: *ādhyātmika* (arising in the body such as fever, jaundice, hypertension), *ādhibhautika* (arising from external agents such as tigers, serpents, floods, cyclones), and *ādhidaivika* (arising from the acts of gods, planets, *prārabdha karma* or initiated karmic *saṁskāras*). The mind of the sage of stable wisdom is not afflicted at all by these adversities. Here we should make a note of an important fact. The Lord does not say that adversities do not befall a sage of stable wisdom. Even if they befall the *muni* (the sage who practises silence), he bears them without a trace of mental perturbation.

> He, who is everywhere unattached, not delighted by getting anything good nor vexed at meeting with anything evil, has stable wisdom.[39]
>
> As a tortoise withdraws its limbs from all sides, so does the *muni* withdraw his senses (*indriyas*) from the sense-objects. Then only does he become a *sthitaprajña*.[40]
>
> For an abstinent person, the sense-objects fall off. He does not feed on them. But the longing for the taste of sensuous objects is still retained. When he realizes the Supreme Reality as "I am verily That (*ahameva tat*)," even that longing for the taste wanes.[41]
>
> O son of Kuntī (Arjuna), the turbulent senses (*indriyas*) do forcibly snatch away the mind of even a striving learned man.[42]
>
> Controlling them (the senses) all, one should remain steadfast, exclusively united with Me. He who has brought his senses under control has verily stable wisdom.[43]

---

38. *BG*, II. 56.
39. *BG*, II.57.
40. *BG*, II.58.
41. *BG*, II. 59.
42. *BG*, II.60.
43. *BG*, II.61.

If a person does the contrary with regard to the senses and sense-objects in contravention of what has already been said, calamities befall him. All types of disasters germinate when one fails in one's efforts for self-control.

> Attachment to sense-objects is born when one thinks about them. Longing (*kāmaḥ*) arises from attachment (*saṅgaḥ*); and wrath (*krodhaḥ*) arises from longing.[44]

One may long for pleasure that may or may not be obtained. Even if a desire (*kāmanā*) is satisfied, it does not stop there. It shoots up spirally to end at no height. One desire, after being satisfied, clears the path for another desire. All desires cannot be satisfied. Thus, arises frustration. This frustration is the source of anger.

> From anger arises delusion; from delusion, loss of memory. Due to the failure of memory, intelligence perishes; total destruction is the outcome from the loss of intelligence.[45]

Delusion (*sammoha*) is the lack of discrimination between what ought and what ought not to be done. It arises from wrath. *Buddhi-nāśa* (the loss of intelligence) is the incapacity of the inner mental apparatus (*antaḥkaraṇa*). The *antaḥkaraṇa* is the inner faculty, capable of discriminating between right and wrong.

A *jñāna-yogī* (a *sthitaprajña*) does not long for sense-objects. The focus of his thought, speech and actions is liberation (*mokṣa*) only.

> The person who has controlled his mind approaches objects with senses free from attachment (*rāga*) and aversion (*dveṣa*). He brings the sense-objects under his own control. He attains to serenity (tranquillity, composure, repose).[46]

It is not always possible to avoid all sense-objects (*viṣayāḥ*). The *sthitaprajña* approaches unavoidable sense-objects by means of his

---

44. *BG*, II.62.
45. *BG*, II.63.
46. *BG*, II.64.

senses that are under the sway of his disciplined mind. Moreover, his senses are free from attachment and aversion.

> In tranquillity, all sufferings come to an end. The intellect of the person, whose mind is serene, soon becomes steadfast. The inner mental apparatus (*antaḥkaraṇa*) of a tranquil-minded person is composed.[47]
>
> One whose mind is not yoked to the Supreme Reality (Self) has no wisdom; nor can such a one have yearning for the knowledge of the Self. One can have no peace without this yearning. How can one get happiness without peace?[48]
>
> The wind drifts the boat away from its course on water in a sea. Just like that, the mind that conforms to the wandering senses robs one of wisdom (*prajñā*).[49]
>
> Therefore, O mighty-armed (Arjuna), one has stable wisdom when one's senses are fully restrained from sense-objects.[50]
>
> The self-controlled sage is awake in what is night for all beings. That in which all beings are awake is night for the silent sage (*muni*) who perceives the Supreme Reality.[51]

In the present context, night stands for darkness (*tamas*) or nescience (*avidyā*). Beings, without realization of the Supreme Reality, are sunk in the sleep of nescience in which they get the dream of the plurality of subjects and objects. But, different is the case with the enlightened sage who perceives the Supreme Reality.

It is not possible for a person to attain liberation (*mokṣa*) as long as he does not abandon desires and does not renounce longing for objects of desires. The Lord expounds further:

> As waters flow into a full, stable and still sea, so do all desires enter into the mind of a person of stable wisdom (*sthitaprajña*)

---

47. *BG*, II.65.
48. *BG*, II.66.
49. *BG*, II.67.
50. *BG*, II.68.
51. *BG*, II.69.

who attains peace. But he who yearns after objects of desire does not get peace.[52]

The desires, instead of affecting his mind, enter into the Ocean of the Self. He attains peace that leads to liberation. But any other person who hankers after objects of enjoyment (who habitually yearns after objects of desires) never attains peace (and liberation).

The person (*sthitaprajña*), who moves about, giving up all desires, devoid of longing and seeking nothing, being my-less (*nirmamaḥ*) and I-less (*nirahaṅkāraḥ*) attains peace.[53]

The person of stable wisdom (*sthitaprajña*) is a knower of *Brahman.* He attains the supreme peace, characterized by the cessation of all forms of transmigratory sufferings, the miseries of *saṁsāra* (metempsychosis). This is the state of final liberation. This is *Brahma-nirvāṇa,* a process in which the *sthitaprajña* becomes one with *Brahman;* he attains to the state of final liberation (*mokṣa*).

Now the *BG* presents the last verse, characterizing a *sthitaprajña.* It uses the term *Brāhmīsthitiḥ* (the state of *Brahman,* stay in *Brahman* by becoming one with It). A *Brahmacārī* (one who follows the path of *Brahman*) remains anchored in *Brahman* throughout his life. He attains the state of *Brahman*-hood, the state of Super-Consciousness, the state of Pure Consciousness (*Viśuddha Cit, Śuddha-Caitanyam*). On the topic of the *jñāna-yoga,* the Lord finally advises Arjuna in the verse to follow:

O Pārtha (Arjuna), this is the state of *Brahman.* After attaining to it, none gets deluded. Stationing oneself in It, even in the final stage of life (at the hour of death), one gains *Brahma-nirvāṇa* (one is assimilated in *Brahman;* one becomes *Brahman*).[54]

### 2.14: Vedānta and Sāṅkhya Compared and Contrasted

The *BG* uses a number of terms that are common to the Vedānta

---

52. *BG,* II.70.

53. *BG,* II.71.

54. *BG,* II.72.

and the Sāṅkhya. Such a use is common to many ancient Indian scriptures. Some interpreters of Indian philosophy of the past and of even the present wear spectacles of the Vedānta to see the Sāṅkhya or vice versa and thereby they are very much confused by a wrong notion that these two schools of philosophy are mostly in agreement. Unfortunately, it is a fallacy of a serious nature. This intermingling has resulted in utter confusion. To the best of our knowledge, any serious attempt has hardly been made to logically analyse the sharp differences of the two systems. Hence, we feel the necessity of presenting a separate section for comparing and contrasting the fundamental notions of the Vedānta and the Sāṅkhya. We find it convenient to place this section at the end of the second chapter of the *BG*, in which Sāṅkhya-Yoga has been identified with Jñāna-Yoga, without any reference to Kapila's Sāṅkhya. The purport of this section is twofold: It would eliminate Sāṅkhya-contamination from the Advaita Vedānta. It would also avoid many repetitions in the chapters to follow in clarifying the commonness and differences between the Vedānta and the Sāṅkhya. Secondly, it would present the main features of Vedāntic *jñāna-yoga*, as outlined in the *BG*.

*Brahman* is the hub of the Advaita Vedānta. It has been vividly described so in the Upaniṣads and the *Brahma-Sūtram*. The Vedas do emphasize the fact that *Brahman* or the *Puruṣa* or God is the non-dual Reality and that the manifested universe and the Unmanifested *Puruṣa* are two aspects of the same Reality.[55] One aspect is the Fundamental Reality, the Real Reality. The second aspect is the virtual reality, a usable reflection of the Fundamental One. *Brahman*, the fundamental Reality, is formless, functionless, attributeless, non-relational, unconditioned, immutable, timeless, eternal, spaceless, Pure Existence, Pure Consciousness and Pure Bliss. Here the word "Pure" means "unconnected with any entity other than the Immutable Being (*Brahman*) itself." It is the non-dual one, the only Absolute Reality (*Pāramārthika Satyam*) that is

55. *R̥V*, X.90 (Puruṣa-Sūktam); X.121 (Hiraṇyagarbha-Sūktam); *AV*, X.7 (Skambha-Sūktam); XI.7 (Ucchiṣṭa-Brahma-Sūktam); XIII.4.12-21.

the Existence (*sanmātram hi brahma*).[56] Here is no diversity whatsoever (*neha nānāsti kiñcana*).[57]

The Power (*Śakti*) of *Brahman/Īśvara* is *Māyā*.[58] She is otherwise known as *Prakṛti* or the *Mūla-Prakṛti*[59] (the Primordial Nature). She is undifferentiated (*avyākṛtā*), homogeneous and is the Seminal Power (*Bīja-Śakti*) of *Brahman*.[60] She is not second to the latter, both the Possessor of Power (*Śaktimān*) and the Power (*Śakti*) being one and the same in the analogy of fire and its heat. In this regard, we may present an illustration. The President of a country has constitutional power. The existence of the President can be empirically verified, but not his power that is inferable from his actions (from his excercise of power). This simile cannot be literally considered. *Brahman* cannot be empirically verified. *Māyā* also cannot be empirically verified since She is unmanifested (*avyakta*).[61] But the existence of *Māyā* can be inferable (*kāryānumeyā*) from the cosmic effects. *Māyā* is *svabhūtā* (own being) or *ātmabhūtā* (self-being) and, thus, is not different from *Brahman* or *Īśvara*.[62] She is *asvatantrā* (not independent); She is under the control of God (*īśvarādhīnā*) and is fully dependent upon God (*īśvarāśrayā*,

---

56. *BSŚB*, II.3.9 (*sanmātraṁ hi brahma*).

57. *BU*, IV.4.19 (*neha nānāsti kiñcana*); *KTU*, II.1.11.

58. *BSŚB*, I.2.22; II.1.14; II.1.24; *ŚU*, I.3 (*devātmaśakti*); IV.1; *ŚUŚB*, I.3 (*devasya dyotanādi-yuktasya parameśvarasya paramātmanaḥ ātmabhūtāṁ asvatantrāṁ na sāṅkhya-parikalpita-pradhānādivat pṛthagbhūtāṁ svatantrāṁ śaktim*); *BGŚB*, Intr. (Viṣṇu-*śaktiḥ*); IV,6 (*vaiṣṇavī*); XIV, 3; XV, 1 & 16; VC, I.10; VP, I.3.1-3.

59. *ŚU*, IV.10 (*māyāṁ tu prakṛtiṁ viddhi māyinaṁ tu maheśvaram*); *BSŚB*, I.4.8; I.4.11; *BGŚB*, Intr. (*sa ca bhagavān . . . triguṇātmikāṁ vaiṣṇavīṁ svāṁ māyāṁ mūlaprakṛtiṁ vaśīkṛtya ajaḥ avyayo bhūtānām īśvaro nityaśuddhabuddhamuktasvabhāvaḥ api san svamāyayā dehavān iva jāta iva ca lokānugrahaṁ kurvan iva lakṣyate*.)

60. *BSŚB*, I.2.22; I.4.2-3; *BGŚB*, XIII.5; *BU*, I.4.7.

61. *BSŚB*, I.2.22; I.4.2-3; *KTUŚB*, I.3.11: *BG*, VIII.18; VIII.20; *BGŚB*, Intr.; XIII.5; VC, I10.

62. *ŚUŚB*, I.3; *BGŚB*, XIV.3.

*parameśvarāśrayā*).[63] Both the Possessor of Power (*Śaktimān*) and the Power (*Śakti*) are inseparable, being one and the same.

The Vedāntic concept of *upādhi*,[64] otherwise known as *avaccheda-vāda* (the doctrine of limiting adjunct), is vitally important for a comprehension of the cosmos and its diversification. *Brahman* is *sarva-vyāpī*[65] (all-pervasive, omnipresent, ubiquitous), being homogeneous and not corpuscular. Due to its omnipresence, it is present inside all manifested entities and also in *Māyā* that is never manifested. In order to concretize this abstract concept of *upādhi*, we use two analogies here. Great Space (*mahākāśa*), limited within pots, becomes many separate spaces (*ghaṭākāśa*s) inside the pots. On breaking the pots, the *ghaṭākāśa*s disappear and continuous *mahākāśa* is restored. Similarly, we may visualize the oceanic water-mass and many aquatic animals in the ocean. Different animals in the ocean contain the ocean-water inside their bodies, and, thus, they function as limiting adjuncts of the same water. In the two examples cited here, the pots are the *upādhi*s of Space and the aquatic animals are the *upādhi*s of the ocean-water. *Brahman* itself is devoid of *upādhi*s (It is *nirupādhikam*).[66] With *Māyā* as the *upādhi*,

63. *BS*, I.4.3; *BSŚB*, I.2.22; I.4.3 (*parameśvarāśrayā*); I.4.9; *ŚU*, IV.10; *ŚUŚB*, I.3 (*asvatantrā*); *BGŚB*, IV.6.

64. *YS*, III.144; *BSŚB*, I.1.11; I.2.22; II.1.14; *GMK*, III.3-5; III.7.

The Vedāntic concept of *avaccheda-vāda* (the doctrine of limiting adjunct) uses the word *upādhi* in a technical sense. The concept of *upādhi* is better clarified by the illustration of *mahākāśa* (Universal or Great Space) and *ghaṭākāśa* (space limited in a pot). *Mahākāśa* is the container of pots and still the latter are the containers of the former. On breaking the pots, the *ghaṭākāśa*s disappear, with the restoration of the *Mahākāśa*. Each unbroken pot serves as an *upādhi* of the *Mahākāśa*.

Space or *Ākāśa* is not the blue sky which is not a real entity. It is the subtle substance (the so-called void or *śūnyam*) through which we move our hands and fingers. (See *ABrā*, III.4.2.1, and *ŚBrā*, III.3.2.19 on the nature of *Ākāśa*.)

65. *ŚU*, I.16; III.11; VI.11; *BG*, V.15; X.12; *BSŚB*, I.1.11; *BUŚB*, III.18.12; *KTU*, I.2.22; II.1.4; *MTU*, VI.7; *MUU*, I.1.6; *GMK*, I.1; I.28.

66. *BSŚB*, I.1.11; *BUŚB*, III.18.12.

it is *Īśvara* (God); with a lifeless entity as the *upādhi*, it is a *bhūtātmā*; and with a living entity as the *upādhi*, it is a *jīvātmā*.[67] This doctrine of *upādhi* (also known as *avaccheda-vāda*) establishes the oneness of *Brahman*, *Īśvara* and the seemingly multiple *jīvātmā*s. We translate the word *upādhi* into English as "limiting adjunct." The concept is better apprehended by the examples we have given. If *Māyā* is the *ādhāra* (container; holder), *Brahman* inside *Māyā* is the *ādheya* (content, an entity that is held). Since *Brahman* is omnipresent and all-pervasive, the apparent limitation is to be well conceived of in the analogy of many pots existing in Space and still holding the latter inside them. All apparently diverse entities are in *Brahman* and still the former serve as the limiting adjuncts of the latter. That *Brahman* is both inside and outside everything and that it is both immanent and transcendent would be clear after grasping the concept of *upādhi*.[68]

The concept of *upādhi* is helpful in understanding the concept of *devatā* (god). The Vedas and the *Prasthāna-Traya* (the Upaniṣads, the *Brahma-Sūtram* and the *Bhagavad-Gītā*) unequivocally declare that God (*Īśvara*) is one only.[69] At the same time, these scriptures mention the names of many gods (*devatā*s). Any created macro-structure or micro-structure, gross or subtle, of cosmic importance is a *devatā*. The sun-god (*sūrya-devatā*) is one example. *Īśvara*, abiding in our sun and presiding over it that serves as a limiting adjunct, is a *devatā*.[70] All gods are born after the initial creation of the

67. *BSŚB*, I.1.11; I.2.20; II.1.21; *BUŚB*, III.18.12; *VPDA*, ch. 1 & 7; *VC*, 245; *VS*, 38.

68. *MUU*, II.1.2 (*bāhyābhyantaraḥ*).

69. *ṚV*, I.84.7; VI.36.4; X.81.3; X.90; X.121; X.129; AV, II.2.1-2; X.7; XIII.4.15-18;XIII.4.21.

70. *BSŚB*, II.1.5 (*abhimāninyaḥ cetanāḥ devatāḥ*); II.3.13.

*Brahman*, being all-pervading, exists in all created entities, micro or macro. It becomes *Īśvara* or God by acquiring *Māyā* as an *upādhi*. *Īśvara* is called a *devatā* (god, not God) when it presides over an entity of cosmic importance. The entity may be gross like our sun; it may be subtle like the subtle Cosmic Plasma (*Āpaḥ*) where the presiding deity

→

universe.[71] Some gods like the *Āpaḥ*, the *Vāyu*, the *Agni*, the *Prāṇa* and many others perform vitally important cosmic functions.

There is a doctrine of reflection (*ābhāsa-vāda* or *pratibimba-vāda*)[72] in Advaita Vedānta. *Brahman*, the non-dual Reality, is Pure Consciousness. Uncreated *Māyā*, co-eternal with *Brahman*, and all the virtual entities created by *Māyā* in the universe are insentient (*jaḍa, acetana*). Having accepted these two facts, we have to explain the functional ability of both *Māyā* and the created entities of the universe. Any agent of any action, especially when the action is meaningful and co-ordinated, is necessarily to be sentient. *Brahman*, the Fundamental Consciousness, is reflected on *Māyā* and all created beings and, thus, makes the latter conscious. There is nothing in the virtual universe, either living or non-living, which is devoid of consciousness,[73] although the nature and degree of consciousness vary, depending on the evolution of the mental apparatus. This reflected consciousness is otherwise known as induced consciousness, to be distinguished from the Fundamental Consciousness. Induced consciousness is limited in nature and varies in a broad spectrum whereas the Fundamental Consciousness is Omniscience. *Māyā* is intrinsically *avidyā*[74] (insentient); but, due to the reflection of *Brahman* on Her, She is

→ is named as Varuṇa. Whereas God (*Parameśvara*) is One and only One for the entire universe, identified as *Brahman* with *Māyā* as the *upādhi*, a god or a *devatā* has limited potency. A *devatā* is not omnipotent unlike God. No *devatā* is the Supreme Lord and the Ruler of the universe. Neither is he the creator, the sustainer and the annihilator of the universe.

71. *ṚV*, X.129.6.

72. *BS*, II.3.50 (*ābhāsa eva ca*); III.2.18; *BSŚB*, II.3.50; *BU*, IV.4.18; *BUŚB*, IV.3.10; IV.4.18 (*svataḥ kāṣṭha-loṣṭa-samāni hi tāni caityanyātma-jyotiś-śūnyāni); KTU*, II.2.15; *MUU*, II.2.10-11; *ŚU*, VI.14 (*na tatra sūryo bhāti, na candratārakam; nemā vidyuto bhānti, kuto'yamagniḥ. tameva bhāntamanubhāti sarvam; tasya bhāsā sarvamidaṁ vibhāti.*); *BG*, XV, 6 & 12; *BGŚB*, XV.7; *YS*, III.14.3.4; III.144.

73. *CUŚB*, VI.11.2 (*cetanāvantaḥ sthāvarāḥ*).

74. *BSŚB*, I.4.3 (*avidyālakṣaṇā hi bījasaktiravyaktaśabdanirdeśyā parameśvarāśrayā māyāmayī mahāsuptiḥ .... avidyā hyavyaktam*).

eternally and timelessly superconscious. Functionally speaking, *Māyā* is never unconscious. She, being the *Śakti*, shares the omniscience of the *Śaktimān*.

The Advaita Vedānta has a doctrine of induction (*preraṇā-vāda; pravartana-vāda*).[75] Before we discuss this doctrine, we should better be acquainted with two processes in science. Electromagnetism is induced in a revolving coil placed between two magnets. Iron-filings are magnetized when they are present in the proximity of a magnet. *Brahman* is all-pervasive and motionless. On the contrary, cosmic entities, created by *Māyā*, are in constant motion. (No entity of the universe, living or non-living, micro or macro, can exist for a moment without motion). In the analogy of a revolving wheel between two magnets producing hydro-electricity, entities, created by *Māyā*, become induced to generate consciousness. Next, we elaborate on the second example of induction due to proximity (*sānnidhya-vāda* = doctrine of vicinity or proximity). *Māyā*, the Power of *Brahman*, is not a separate entity and, hence, cannot be away from the latter. *Brahman* is inside and outside all created entities that are bound to be in proximity due to the homogeneity and pervasiveness of the former. Through this mechanism of the presence of the Fundamental Consciousness in the vicinity, Cosmic Intellect (Supermind, *Virāḍ, Buddhi*) is inducted in *Māyā*. Also through the same mechanism, the induction of an individual intellect (*buddhi*) does take place in each created entity, both inanimate and animate. *Brahman* is mindless[76] albeit Pure Consciousness; but the induced mind of *Māyā* is *Virāḍ* or *Buddhi* (the Cosmic Mind, the Supermind, the *samaṣṭi-buddhi* or the Collective Intellect). This description makes it clear that *Virāḍ* is not a real entity, second or third to *Brahman*. For the first time, the word *virāḍ* and its genesis have been mentioned in the *Ṛgveda*[77]

75. *BSŚB*, II.2.2 (*yathā 'yaskānto maṇiḥ svayaṁ pravṛttirahito 'pyayasaḥ pravartako bhavati*); *MUUŚB*, III.1.1 (*paśyatveva kevalam, darśanamātreṇa hi tasya prerayitṛtvaṁ rājavat*).

76. *BU*, III.8.8 (*amanāḥ*); *MUU*, II.1.2 (*amanāḥ*).

77. *ṚV*, X.90.5 (*tasmādvirāḷajāyata virājo adhi pūruṣaḥ*).

(X.90.5: *tasmād virāḷajāyata virājo adhi pūruṣaḥ*). It is an usable mega-entity, the Cosmic Mind or the Supermind. Both *Māyā* and *Virāḍ* (*Buddhi* of *Māyā*) are ubiquitous. The concept of *Virāḍ* or *Virāṭ*, as given by us, is different from that of others. It is not the totality of the world-stuff. Neither is it the Great Cosmic Person (*Puruṣa*). It is not the *Mahat* of the Sāṅkhya. *Mahat* is the first evolute of the *Pradhāna* or the *Prakṛti* of the Sāṅkhya. In this process, *Prakṛti* is transformed or modified into *Mahat*. *Hiraṇyagarbha* or Brahmā of the Vedas[78] is not the same as *Virāḍ*. The word *Hiraṇyagarbha* (golden embryo) has two meanings in use. One refers to the superheated Cosmic Egg of golden hue. The other refers to God, presiding over *Virāḍ*. He is *Virāḍātmā* who is Brahmā, the Creator. Very often, *Virāḍ* and *Virāḍātmā* are mistakenly made equivocal.

The philosophy of non-dualistic Vedānta strictly adheres to non-dualism; but, it still explains the apparent presence of the universe in diversity. It says: *Brahman*, the non-dual Reality, is Existence, Consciousness and Bliss. If it is designated as *B*, then *B* remains as *B* without changes whatsoever. In other words, *Brahman* is eternally and timelessly *avyaya*. This *B* is the Absolute Reality (*pāramārthika satya*). Advaita Vedānta does not say that the universe (*jagat* = *gam* + *kvip*; that which is in motion or which is constantly changeable) of matter and energy does not exist. The famous verse of Ācārya Śaṅkara (*brahma satyaṁ jaganmithyā; jīvo brahmaiva nāparaḥ*) is most often misunderstood. The *jagat* is *mithyā*; but is not *asatya*. The words *satya* and *asatya* are contradictory terms; but the words *satya* and *mithyā* are contrary ones. The *jagat* is an usable *vivartta* reality (*vyāvahārika satya*). *Brahman* is Real whereas the universe is virtual. The virtual universe is a diverse appearance of the non-dual *Brahman*. It changes from moment to moment; it is impermanent; its appearance depends upon the permanently and timelessly existent *Brahman* that is the substratum as well as the indwelling spirit (*adhiṣṭhāna*). *Brahman* appears as $J_1, J_2, J_3, \ldots J_n$, (*J* stands for the *jagat*). This is the doctrine of superimposition (*adhyāsa-vāda*). Ācārya Śaṅkara expresses this

78. ṚV, X.121 (Hiraṇyagarbha-sūktam).

doctrine by a short sentence: *atasmiṁstadbuddhiḥ*.[79] (One thing is apprehended as some other thing). Algebraically speaking, *B* appears as non-*B*, and not as *B*. The post-Śaṅkarite non-dualists renamed this doctrine as *vivartta-vāda*, which is illustrated by the illusory appearance of a rope as a snake. Here it should be noted that the doctrine of superimposition speaks of illusion rather than hallucination. The surface variegated appearance is the multiplicity of the visible and invisible universe whereas the underlying substratum is the rockbottom foundation which is *Brahman*.

Why do we see *B* as non-*B*? Why don't we see *B* as *B*? What is the cause of the non-dual Being appearing as manifold entities? This question has been answered by many Vedāntic interpreters by using a single word *avidyā* which means "nescience" or "ignorance." Some equate *Māyā* with *avidyā*. We reject this idea. Being reflected by *Brahman*, *Māyā* is super-intelligent and super-conscious. Albeit intrinsically insentient, being reflected by the light of the Consciousness of *Brahman*, She is eternally and timelessly super-conscious. Thus, practically speaking, there is not a single moment when *Māyā* is insentient. *Parameśvara* (God) is the Father of the universe and *Parameśvarī* (*Māyā*, the Mother Divine) is the Mother of the universe. For the sportive play (*līlā*)[80] of the Divine Couple, the Mother creates the virtual universe under the Chairpersonship (*adhyakṣatā*)[81] of God. The universe is a supramental construct of the Mother Creatrix. With the hypothetical case of omniscient created beings, without ignorance at all, no *līlā* of the Divine Couple would be a feasible proposition. And, hence, *Māyā*, the Mother Creatrix, creates illusion in the created beings by Her concealing power (*āvaraṇa-śakti*)[82] and

---

79. *BSŚB*, Intr., *Adhyāsa-Bhāṣyam* (*atasmiṁstadbuddhiḥ*).
80. *BS*, II.1.32 (*na prayojanavattvāt*); II.1.33 (*lokavattu līlā kaivalyam*).
81. *ṚV*, X.129.7 (*yo asyādhykṣaḥ parame vyoman*); *BG*, IX.10 (*mayādhyakṣeṇa prakṛtiḥ sūyate sacarācaram; hetunānena kaunteya jagadviparivartate.*); *ŚU*, VI,11 (*eko devas sarvabhūteṣu gūḍhas sarvavyāpī sarvabhūtāntarātmā; karmādhyakṣas sarvabhūtādhivasas; sākṣī cetā kevalo nirguṇaśca.*).
82. *VC*, 115; VSS, 51-4; *BGŚ*B, VII.25; *ŚU*, VI.10; *ŚUŚB*, VI.10.

projecting power (*vikṣepa-śakti*).[83] It is up to the individual to exercise his/her *puruṣārtha* (individual effort and determination) to remove the veil of ignorance or, reversibly, to render the darkness of ignorance denser and densest. *Karma-saṁskāra*s of evil type render the *buddhi* opaque; those of benign type render the *buddhi* transparent; and those of intermediate type render the *buddhi* translucent. The more hazy is the *buddhi* of a person, the more ignorant is he. It is the individual effort (*puruṣārtha*) that can remove the opacity of the *buddhi* and make it transparent.

Ācārya Śaṅkara, while interpreting the *Prasthāna-Traya* (the *Brahma-Sūtram,* the Upaniṣads, and the *Bhagavad-Gītā*), has clearly mentioned the creation, the sustenance and the dissolution of the universe.[84] If he negates the universe, he cannot accept the *sṛṣṭi, sthiti* and *laya* of the universe, without the involvement of self-contradiction. In this context, he also mentions the names of Brahmā, Viṣṇu and Rudra (Śiva) as one God playing the roles of the Creator, the Sustainer and the Destroyer of the universe, respectively.

*Brahman,* being Pure Existence, Consciousness and Bliss, is actionless, attributeless, non-relational and devoid of *upādhi.* The same *Brahman,* with *Māyā* as the *upādhi,* is *Parameśvara* (God) Who is associated with the three strings of *Māyā* and, hence, is *saguṇa* (related with the cosmic strings). He is a non-doer (*akarttā*),[85] but is the Chairperson (*Adhyakṣa*) of all cosmic functions. His Executive Agent is *Māyā* or the *Mūla-Prakṛti* (the Unmanifested Primordial Nature).[86] The principal cosmic functions, that is, creation (*sṛṣṭi*), sustenance and preservation (*pālana, sthiti*) and annihilation

83. *VC,* 113 & 117; *VSS,* 51 & 54.

84. *BS,* I.1.2; *BSŚB,* I.1.2; I.1.4 (*brahma sarvajñaṁ sarvaśakti jagadutpatti-sthiti-laya-kāraṇam*); I.1.5; I.1.11; II.1.1; II.1.14.

85. *BG,* IV.13; XIII.29; *ŚU,* VI.12 (*eko vaśī niṣkriyāṇāṁ bahūnām ekaṁ bījaṁ bahudhā yaḥ karoti . . .*); *ŚUŚB,* VI.12 (*sarvā hi kriyā nātmani samavetāḥ kintu dehendriyeṣu; ātmā tu niṣkriyo nirguṇaḥ*).

86. *BS,* I.4.3; *BSŚB,* I.4.3; II.1.14; *BGŚB,* VII.16; XIII.19; ŚU, I.3; ; VI.10; *ŚUŚB,* I.3; *SL,* 1-2; *DBhā,* I.2.5.

(*saṁhāra, vilaya*), are executed by God through *Māyā*. She also intervenes and corrects all cosmic disorders of a major nature to avoid destabilization of the cosmos. Actions of individual created entities of the universe, both inanimate and animate and micro or macro, are done by their respective *antaḥkaraṇa*s that are also reflected by the light of the Consciousness of *Brahman*.

On this issue of *Īśvara* (God) being *akarttā* (a non-doer), there is utter misunderstanding and confusion. The *Bṛhadāraṇyaka Upaniṣad* declares: *sa hi karttā* (He is really the doer).[87] In the same text, the scripture gives a vivid description of the virtual nature of the universe. Scriptural evidences are many to testify the fact that God who is one and only one is the Supreme Ruler of the universe.[88] There is no real contradiction if we try to understand the totality in a holistic way with a meditative mood. The Cosmic Chairperson gets things done through the agency of His Power. The individual created entities do also exercise their own free will in discharging their functions. We can say: "God is a doer." We can also say: "God is a non-doer." Both these statements are true in their appropriate contexts.

The two words *Parmeśvara* and *Parameśvarī* mean "the Supreme Controller" in the masculine and the feminine gender, respectively. God dwells in everything, animate and inanimate, and He is the indwelling Controller (*antaryāmī*).[89] He controls the entire universe (*viśva-niyantā*). How can He be a non-doer? He is a non-doer, because He does not act directly; He functions as a Chairperson. His Executive Agent is *Māyā*, the Power of God (*Īśvara-Śakti*). He superintends the activities of *Māyā*. A king does not directly act for his kingdom. Subjects and officers work on his behalf. So does

87. *BU*, IV.3.10 (*na tatra rathāḥ, na ratha-yogāḥ, na panthāno bhavanti; atha rathān ratha-yogān pathaḥ sṛjate; na tatrānandaḥ mudaḥ pramudo bhavanti; athānandān mudaḥ pramudaḥ* sṛjate; *na tatra veśāntāḥ puṣkariṇyaḥ sravantyo bhavanti; atha veśāntān puṣkariṇīḥ sravantīḥ sṛjate. sa hi kartā.*)

88. *BS*, I.2.18; I.3.10-11; I.3.43; *BSŚB*, I.2.18; I.3.11; II.3.23; BU, III.3.7-III.7.23; III.8.7-9; IV.4.22; *BUŚB*, III.8.9; *MAU*, 6; *ŚU*, II.17; III.1-2; III.4; III.17-8; VI.12; VI.17; *TU*, II.8.1; *BG*, IV.6; VIII.9.

89. *YV*, XXXII.11-2; *BU*, III.7.3-III.7.23; *BUŚB*, II.3.13; *MAU*, 6; *TU*, II.6.1.

God work and does not work. In one sense, He is *karttā* (doer). In another sense, He is *akarttā* (non-doer). It is the *antaḥkaraṇa* in general and the *ahaṅkāra* in particular that function inside a created entity, only by being enlightened by the light of the consciousness of the self (*ātmā*).[90] Each individual being is the doer of his/her/its own actions. But without getting the reflection of the Divine Being, it is not possible for the *antaḥkaraṇa* to function. In this sense, the individual is the doer and God is the non-doer.

*Māyā* is neither matter nor energy. She is the Power (*Śakti*; not energy or *ūrjā*) of *Brahman/Īśvara*. She creates the universe of energy (matter and energy being the same; matter being a packet of energy); but She Herself is not energy. She is co-eternal with *Brahman/Īśvara*, omnipresent and homogeneous (*avyākṛtā*) like the latter. She is not constituted of constituent components. The three *guṇas* (strings; not attributes in the present context) are not Her constituent components. She supramentally constructs these three strings that are virtual.[91] These ideas are alien to many Vedāntic interpreters.

According to the Advaita Vedānta, the Cosmic Cycles are repetitive, without a beginning and an end.[92] In every cycle, the virtual universe evolves in a definite sequence (in Śaṅkara's language, *krameṇa, na yugapat*)[93] and undergoes involution in the reverse sequence.[94]At the termination of the involution, the *bindu* or the singularity dissolves in the *Buddhi* or the *Virāḍ* that, in turn,

90. *BUŚB*, IV.3.10 (*yac caitanyātmajyotiṣāntakaraṇadvāreṇāvabhāsayati kāryakaraṇāni .... tatra kartṛtvamupacayata ātmanaḥ.*); *ŚUŚB*, VI.12 (*sarvā hi kriyā nātmani samavetāḥ, kintu dehendriyeṣu, ātmā tu niṣkriyo nirguṇaḥ.*); *BG*, IV.13; XIII.29; XIII.31.

91. *ŚU*, IV.5 (*ajāmekāṁ lohita-śukla-kṛṣṇāṁ bahvīḥ prajāḥ sṛjamānaṁ sarūpāḥ. ajo hyeko juṣamāṇo 'nuśete; jahātyenāṁ bhuktabhogāmajo 'nyaḥ*).

92. *ṚV*, X.72.2; X.130.1-2; X.190.3; *BU*, II.1.20; *MTU*, VI.22; *MUU*, I.1.7; *ŚU*, I.6; VI.1.

93. *BUŚB*, II.3.6 (*sraṣṭā tyekopi krameṇānekaṁ sraṣṭavyaṁ sṛjet . . . arthāttu kramo'vagamyate*); *MUUŚB*, I.1.8 (*krameṇa, na yugapat*)).

94. *BS*, II.3.14 (*viparyayeṇa tu kramo 'ta upapadyate ca*); *BUŚB*, II.3.14; *CUŚB*, III.14.1.

merges in *Māyā* in the analogy of salt in the ocean-water. It is the total dissolution[95] of the universe at the end of a *para* (the total period of a Cosmic Cycle).[96] At the beginning of the next *para, Virāḍ* re-crystallizes from *Māyā*. When the Advaita Vedānta declares that *Māyā* is the precursor state of the universe (*jagataḥ prāgavasthā*),[97] it compares *Māyā* as a solvent and the potential universe as a solute. However, it does not commit any process of transformation or modification of *Māyā* into the universe of matter and energy. *Virāḍ* serves as the cosmic-mega-compact-disc that zips the whole universe and stores it in a potential state. The subsequent phase of evolution of the universe starts when God desires.[98] Advaita Vedānta discards the concept of the eternality of the universe, while accepting the eternality of the revolving

---

95. The process of continual dissolution is aptly described in *BU*, I.2.5 (*sa yad yad evāsr̥jata tat tad attum adhriyata. sarvaṁ vā attīti tad aditer adititvam.*).

    Total dissolution takes place at the termination of a *para*, the Cosmic Period from the birth of the universe to its death. For this purpose, refer to the following sources: *BS*, I.2.9; II.3.14; *BSŚB*, I.1.2; I.1.4-5; I.1.11; I.2.2; I.2.9; I.3.30; II.2.1 (*prasāritasya ca jagataḥ punaḥ svātmanyevopasaṁhārakāraṇam*); *CUŚB*, III.14.1; *ŚUŚB*, I.3; *TU*, III.1.1; *BG*, XIII.16; *MBhā*, XII.339.29.

    The creation, sustenance and dissolution of the universe are executed by the Mother Divine: *SL*, 1; *ĀL*, I.1; *DBhā*, I.2.5 (*sr̥ṣṭvākhilaṁ jagadidaṁ sadasat svarūpam, śaktyā svayā triguṇayā paripāti viśvam. saṁhr̥tya kalpa-samaye ramate tathaikā, tāṁ sarva-viśva-jananīṁ manasā smarāmi.*).

96. Brahmā's lifetime is called a *para*. It is one hundred years of his own measure. One-half of a *para* is a *parārdha* (*ardha* meaning one-half). One *para* = 311,040 billion or 311.04 trillion human or earth years. One *parārdha* = 155,520 billion or 155.52 trillion human or earth years. One billion = $1\times10^9$; one trillion = $1\times10^{12}$.

    For further details, see the *Viṣṇu-Purāṇa*, I.3.5; I.3.16; I.3.20-2; III.2.50; VI.3.10-12; VI.4.9; the *Kūrma-Purāṇa*, Ch.V; *Bhā*, XIII.4.3-4; *BG*, VIII.17-9.

97. *BSŚB*, I.2.22 (*bhūtasūkṣma*); I.4.2-3 (*prāgavasthā jagataḥ*); *KTU*, I.3.11.

98. *R̥V*, X.129.4 (*kāmastatagre samavartādhi manso retaḥ prathamam yadāsīt*); *BU*, II.5.19; IV.3.13; *CU*, VI.2.3 (*tadaikṣata bahu syāṁ prajāyeyeti*); *CU*,

→

cycles of the universe.

An acosmic period prevails after a total dissolution. We cannot logically use any temporal and spatial language in the absence of a universe. Time is a mental construct that arises only when events occur. Space is part of the universe and does not exist in the absence of a universe. *Brahman* is spaceless (*anākāśam*) and timeless (*akālam*).[99] In spite of these facts, we use temporal language out of compulsion. When God desires a universe, *Māyā* initiates its virtual creation. She plays Her *vīṇā* with three strings. She disturbs the equipoise (*sāmyāvasthā*) of the vibrations of these strings. As a result, *nāda-brahma* is generated. (Specific amplitudes and frequencies of subtle *oṁkāra-dhvani*, produced by the vibrations of the strings, are called *nāda-brahma* which is not the sound we perceive. *Nada-brahma*, echoed by the created entities of the universe, is the unbeaten sound or the *anāhata-dhvani*). This initial symphony brings about the manifestation of the dissolved *Virāḍ* out of the Mother Creatrix. So does the Vedānta say that *Virāḍ* is the first evolute from *Māyā*, the primordial evolvent which is not an evolute. It is more appropriate to say that *Māyā* is the primordial solvent and *Virāḍ* is the solute. Next, the frequencies change for the generation of *Āpaḥ* from *Virāḍ* or *Buddhi*.[100] This subtle primordial Cosmic Fluid is not water ($H_2O$). It is a super-condensed, subtlest state of a Primordial Fluid that appears as a dimensionless point (*bindu* or singularity) which is otherwise known as the Cosmic Egg.[101]

---

→ VI.2.4; *MTU*, II.6; *MUU*, II.1.5; *ŚU*, IV.5; V.12; VI.12; *TU*, II.6.1 (*sc 'kāmayata bahu syāṁ prajāyeyeti*).

99. *BU*, III.8.8 (*anākāśamamanaḥ aprāṇam*); *MTU*, VI.14 (*dve vāva brahmaṇo rūpe kālaścākālaśca*); *MUU*, II.1.2 (*aprāṇo hyamanāḥ*).

100. *Ṛ̥V*, VI.50.7; X.17.10; X.82.5-6; X.121.7-8; X.90.5 (*tato virāḷajāyata*); X.129.3 (*apraketaṁ salilaṁ sarvamā idam*); *AV*, I.4.1-4; IV.2.6 & 8; *YV*, XIII.2-4; XXVII.25-6; *BU*, I.2.1 (*tan mano 'kuruta . . . āpo 'jāyanta*); V.5.1; *CU*, IV.10.4; *KTU*, II.1.6; *TĀ*, X.22; *MS*, I.8; *VāP*, VI.1-11.

101. *BGŚB*, Intr. (*nārāyaṇaḥ paro 'vyaktādaṇḍamavyakta-smbhavam*); *Ṛ̥V*, X.82.5-6;YV, XXXI.19; *CU*, III.19.1; *ŚBrā*, VI.1.2-3; XI.1.6.1 (*Sṛṣṭi-Brāhmaṇam*): *āpo ha vā 'idamagre salilamevāsa. sā tapo 'tapyanta. tāsu tapastapyamānāsu hiraṇyamayamāṇḍaṁ sambabhūva. ajato ha tarhi samvatsara* →

*Prāṇa* evolves from *Āpaḥ* inside the Cosmic Egg[102] and vigorously vibrates (*spandanam* or *kampanam*)[103] inside the Egg. Heat and pressure develop due to the vibrations of *Prāṇa*. As a consequence, the Egg explodes with a gigantic force.[104] This explosion is known as the Big-Bang. Simultaneous with the explosion of the Cosmic Egg, *Ākāśa* or Space evolves from *Prāṇa*.[105] This nascent universe of *Āpaḥ, Prāṇa* and *Ākāśa* is a super-heated soup. The Vedas and the Upaniṣads symbolically describe this extreme heat as *tapaḥ, yajña* and such other words.[106] In this super-heated state, micro-particles and particles are born from *Ākāśa*. The super-heated, boiling soup, present in the nascent *Ākāśa* that puffs out and reabsorbs micro-particles is known as Aditi in the Vedas.[107]Aditi gives birth to these particles in pairs, each member of each pair being equal and opposite to each other in every respect.[108] Thus, the precursor material of the vast universe is zero, the *tucchya* of the *R̥gveda*.[109] The particles vigorously dance in the hot cosmic

→ *āsa. tadidaṁ hiraṇmayamāṇḍaṁ yāvatsamvatsarasya velā tāvatparyaplavata.*) *tataḥ samvatsare puruṣaḥ samabhavat, sa prajāpatiḥ; MBhā*, XII.299.3; *MS*, I.9; *BP*, I.1.39; *GP*, I.4.6-11; *HV*, I.1.36-8; *KP*, I.4.40-1; *MP*, II.25-30; *PP*, III.3.31; *VP*, I.2.54-60; *BDP*, I.1.3.24-7; *Vāp*, IV.76-9; *Bhā*, II.6.6; II.6.21.

102. *AV*, XI.4; *BS*, I.1.23; II.4.1; II.4.7-8; II.4.17; *BU*, I.2.6; II.1.20; III.9.9; *CU*, V.1.1; *MUU*, II.1.3; *PU*, VI.4.

103. *BS*, I.3.39; *KTU*, II.3.2.

104. *R̥V*, X.81-2; *TBrā*, II.8.9.6; *CU*, III.19.1(*asad evedam agra āsīt. tat sadāsīt. tat samabhavat. tat samvatsarasya mātrāmaśayata. tan nirabhidyata. te āṇḍakapāle rajatañca suvarṇañca abhavatām.*); *BGŚB*, Intr.; *MS*, I.9; I.12; *Bhā*, II.2.21; III.6.6; *PU*, I.4-5.

105. *KTU*, II.1.7; *MUU*, II.1.3; *PU*, VI.4; *TU*, II.1.

106. *R̥V*, I.89.10; X.90.6-10; X.129.3; X.130.1-2; 4-6; *BU*, I.2.6-7; *PU*, I.4; *MTU*, VI.6; *MUU*, I.1.8; *TU*, II.6.1; III.1.1; III.2.1; III.3.1; III.4.1; III.5.1.

107. *R̥V*, I.89.10; X.90.6-10; X.129.3; X.130.1-2; 4-6; *ŚBrā*, XIII.1-5; BU, I.1.1-2; I.2.6; *MTU*, VI.6; *MUU*, I.1.8; *PU*, I.4; *TU*, II.6.1; III.1.1; III.2.1; III.3.1; III.4.1; III.5.1.

108. *BU*, I.3.1; I.4.4; *BUŚB*, I.1.2; *PU*, I.4-5.

109. *R̥V*, X.129.3 (*tama āsīt tamasā gūḷhamagre apraketaṁ salilaṁ sarvamā idam. tucchyenāmbapihitaṁ yadāsīt tapasastanmahināјāyataikam.*).

soup, collide against one another, disappear and reappear.[110] With the gradual decline of the cosmic temperature, the four fundamental forces sequentially separate (first, gravitational force; second, strong nuclear force; third, weak nuclear force; the last remaining one, the electro-magnetic force). *Ākāśa* expands[111] rapidly after the Big-Bang and is still expanding, although at an ever-decelerated rate. There would come a time when the expansion of the universe would stop and then a contracting phase (Big Crunch) would begin. Cosmic evolution takes place during the phase of expansion. Cosmic involution takes place during the phase of contraction. Involution would be the reverse process of evolution.[112] The Vedas and the Upaniṣads describe these phases by the shuttle model and the spider model.[113] All the energy and matter of the universe sequentially evolve from *Ākāśa* during the first phase and sequentially return to *Ākāśa* in the terminal phase.[114] At the concluding stage of the Big Crunch, *Ākāśa* becomes *Prāṇa*, *Prāṇa* becomes *Āpaḥ*, *Āpaḥ*, as singularity, merges in *Virāḍ* and finally *Virāḍ* dissolves in *Māyā*. One Cosmic Cycle begins with the appearance of *Virāḍ* and closes with the disappearance of *Virāḍ*. Here, "appearance" means "manifestation from an unmanifest state" and "disappearance" means "going from a manifested to an unmanifested state." The source of *Virāḍ* is *Māyā* and the final receptacle of *Virāḍ* is *Māyā*.

Here we have briefly described physical cosmology and cosmogony. It does not say anything on the evolution of mind. The Vedic and Vedāntic evolution of mind takes a different course, rather a lateral branch. The Vedic mind is different from the

---

110. *ṚV*, X.72.6 (*atrā vo nṛtyatāmiva tīvro reṇṇurapāyata*).

111. *ṚV*, X.129.5; *MUU*, I.1.8 (*tapasā cīyate brahma*).

112. *BS*, II.3.14 (*viparyayeṇa tu kramo 'ta upapadyate ca*); *BSŚB*, II.3.14; *BUŚB*, II.3.14; *CUŚB*, III.14.1.

113. *ṚV*, X.72.2; X.130.1-2; X.190.3; *BU*, II.1.20; *MTU*, VI.22; *MUU*, I.1.7 (*yathorṇanābhiḥ sṛjate gṛhṇate ca*); *ŚU*, I.6; VI.1; VI.10.

114. *ABrā*, III.4.2.1; *ŚBrā*, III.3.2.19; *CU*, I.9.1; VII.12.1.

material brain. The former uses the latter as an apparatus. The mental pathway of evolution is as follows.

The Vedāntic evolution of mind takes a path, different from that of the material evolution. *Virāḍ* or *Buddhi* becomes *buddhi* (individual intellect) in a created entity, either inanimate or animate, that serves as an *upādhi*. Egoity (*ahaṅkāra*) evolves from *buddhi*. Eleven evolutes arise from *ahaṅkāra*. They are: *manas,* the five subtle sensory instruments for cognition and the five subtle motor instruments for action. These ten instrumental organs are specific to the human species. The type and number of these instrumental organs vary in plants, animals and inanimate entities. In particles and micro-particles, they may be totally absent. But it is to be mentioned here that no created entity, even if lifeless, is devoid of *manas* and *ahaṅkāra*. This dual scheme of physical and mental evolution differs from that of the Sāṅkhya system. Further, it may be mentioned here that, in the Sāṅkhya system of evolution, *ahaṅkāra* is the evolvent of sixteen evolutes. Five subtle fields (*tanmātras*), the precursor of matter and energy, are the additional evolutes. This concept of Sāṅkhya cannot be accepted in the modern concept of scientific evolution; neither can it be accepted in the Vedic and Vedāntic concept of evolution. An inanimate universe of matter and energy had evolved before life appeared. The evolution of living species on the earth (here we are not speaking of extra-terrestrial evolution of life for the purpose of simplification) is comparatively recent if we consider the age of the present universe and that of our solar system and our earth. How can the *ahaṅkāra* (which is a subtle psycho-organ of an individual) generate the whole universe, albeit in sequence or generate an individual body of matter and energy, with super-intelligently designed, complex organs?

The gradual evolution of micro-particles, particles, elements, compounds, inorganic matter, organic matter, plants, animals and human beings takes many long eras. We get glimpses of species evolution on our earth. We do not exactly know how many Galaxies exist in the universe. We do not know the nunber of solar systems in our Milky Way Galaxy and the number of habitable planets in all the solar systems. At the present stage, we have little knowledge on exobiology. Elsewhere in the universe, civilizations, less and more advanced in comparison with ours, do probably exist. In principle, we do accept evolution in cosmology and cosmogony. But we reject the Darwinian mechanistic evolution and evolution of any type that is atheistic and materialistic. On this ground, we reject the evolution given in the Sāṅkhya system too. The Sāṅkhya evolution is atheistic, although not materialistic due to the acceptance of the infinite number of conscious *puruṣa*s. Moreover, the universe is eternal and beginningless in the Sāṅkhya and, hence, does not evolve. Its evolution is restricted to that of each human being. The absurdity in this evolution is that matter and energy are the last evolutes.

In our Vedic and Vedāntic concept of evolution, the virtual universe which is not real but which is not nothing is designed and operated by the Father Divine and the Mother Divine. The whole universe has been planned, designed[115] and executed by only one Father of the universe and only one Mother of the universe, the latter being the Power of the former and the Executive Agent of the former. The Cosmos cannot exist and cosmic activities are not feasible without omnipresence, omniscience and omnipotence of which God only is in possession.

In addition to the initial creation and the final, total dissolution, creation, sustenance and destruction are continual activities throughout a *para*. Only one God (*Parmeśvara*) is known as Brahmā, Viṣṇu and Rudra (Śiva) with reference to cosmic creation, maintenance and destruction, respectively. The respective Powers (*Śakti*s) are Sarasvatī, Lakṣmī and Kālī, respectively. Only one Mother Divine (*Parameśvarī*) becomes three for functional purpose only. The Vedāntic triad of three Gods as one God only and three Goddesses as one Goddess only has been clearly mentioned in

115. *BS*, II.2.1 (*racanānupapatteśca nānumānam*).

the scriptures.[116] In order to dispel any doubt, a clarification is necessary over the issue of one God becoming three Gods and one Goddess becoming three Goddesses. For this purpose, we take the help of an analogy. The Governor of a state is the Vice-Chancellor of a university and the Chairperson of a Red-Cross society. He does not become three persons by virtue of his three roles. Moreover, it is the Vedic tradition to designate one God by many names on the basis of *guṇa* (attribute) and *karma* (action) described contextually.

We strictly adhere to non-dualism. *Brahman*, the Absolute Reality (*Pāramārthika Satya*) is non-dual. Simultaneously, we assert the virtual existence of the illusory universe which is reality in use (*vyāvahārika satya*). Some Vedic and Vedāntic interpreters find cosmic realism in these scriptures and vehemently criticise the concept of the magical nature of the universe. But the Vedas and the Upaniṣads clearly mention that the universe is a magic show and that God is a magician who himself is not affected by His Magic.[117] In this context, one statement of Śaṅkara is worth mentioning: "Both one and many are true (*ata ekatvaṁ nānātvaṁ cobhayamapi satyameva*)."[118]

Now we would like to present the concepts of *bandha* (bondage) and *mokṣa* (release, liberation) of the individual self (*jīvātmā*). A subtle organ known as *karmāśaya* (the karmic reservoir) exists in the *buddhi* (the psycho-organ of intellect of the internal instrument or the *antaḥkaraṇa*, located in the subtle body or the *sūkṣma śarīra*). All karmic impressions are recorded in the *karmāśaya*

116. *ŚUŚB*, I.3 (*devasya parameśvarasya ātmabhūtāṁ brahmaviṣṇuśivātmikām*); *ŚU*, VI.18; *BSŚB*, I.3.30; *MTU*, V.1 (*tvaṁ brahmā tvaṁ ca vai viṣṇustvaṁ rudrastvaṁ prajāpatiḥ*); *MTU*, V.2; VI.5; *ŚL*, 1 (*śivaḥ śaktyā yukto yadi bhavati śaktaḥ prabhavituṁ, na cedevaṁ devo na khalu kuśalaḥ spanditumapi. atastvāmārādhyāṁ hariharaviriñcādibhirapi, praṇantuṁ stotuṁ vā kathamakṛtapuṇyaḥ prabhavati.*); *ŚL*, 2.

117. *ṚV*, VI.47.18; *BSŚB*, II.1.21; *BU*, II.5.19; *ŚU*, III.1; V.3; *VS*, 40; *BGŚB*, VII.25.

118. *BSŚB*, II.1.14 (*ata ekatvaṁ nānātvaṁ cobhayamapi satyameva.*).

in the analogy of text-data, audio-data and video-data being recorded on a CD. Since the self is the experiencer, it becomes virtually bound to the karmic *saṁskāras*. We may take an illustration from chemistry. A methane molecule has one carbon atom bonded to four hydrogen atoms. In all chemical compounds, atoms are bound to one another by different types of bonding. The bondings can be broken and the atoms may be set free. Similar are the binding and the release of the self. Karmic *saṁskāras* may be *sāttvika, rājasika* and *tāmasika*. All these three types of *saṁskāras* bind a self. So long as the *karmāśaya* is not fully erased, the self (*jīvātmā*), being alienated from the Self (*Paramātmā*), is subject to metempsychosis, the transmigratory course of the cycles of births and deaths. We may take another illustration. Pure water is chemically $H_2O$. Water in the blood, phlegm, urine, sewerage and factory effluent acquires extraneous substances, colours, odours, flavours and toxins. This impure water can be distilled and re-distilled to bring it back to its pure state of $H_2O$. This is the *mokṣa* (liberation) of water. The *jīvātmā* must get rid of the *karma-saṁskāras* to become *Paramātmā* or *Brahman*. It is *Brahma-Nirvāṇa* or the concept of liberation in the Advaita Vedānta.[119] Here it may be emphasized that the self loses its individual identity by attaining to liberation and becoming *Brahman*.

In rare cases, liberation is possible in one life only. It may take a number of lives for most of us. It may not be possible even in a *para*. In such a case, the bound *jīvātmās* are carried in the *Virāḍ* that is dissolved in *Māyā*. They are born and reborn in the next *para*, waiting for liberation in some life or the other. Every *jīva* is potentially Śiva. Every birth is a chance granted to the self to try for becoming *Brahman*. *Mokṣa* (liberation) is the final outcome for everybody. The worst sinner is intrinsically *Brahmaṇ* and shall become *Brahman* one day or the other. No other system of philosophy in the universe is so optimistic.

Incompatibility is observed in the concepts of liberation of

119. *BG*, II.72; V.24-6; *ŚU*, VI.10; *ŚUŚB*, VI.10; *TU*, II.1.1.

the Advaita Vedānta and the Sāṅkhya. The four Vedic dicta (*mahāvākyas*) of the former (*tattvamasi* = Thou art that,[120] *ayamātmā brahma* = This self is *Brahman*,[121] *Prajñānam brahma* = Consciousness is *Brahman*,[122] *aham brahmāsmi* = I am *Brahman*[123]) unambiguously identify the self and the Self. In each living being dwell both the self and the Self, like two birds sitting on the branch of a tree, one eating the fruits and the other sitting and watching indifferently.[124] This duality continues so long as the self is alienated from the Self due to the accumulation of *saṁskāras*. On being freed of this virtual bondage, the self becomes the Self by the simultaneous loss of individuality. It is impossible to accommodate this idea in the Sāṅkhya. The philosophy of Sāṅkhya rejects non-dualism.[125] It is a dualistic school, the fundamental realities being *Prakṛti* or *Pradhāna* and infinite number of *puruṣas*.[126] This dualism has an occult pluralism. Its *puruṣas*, belonging to a category, are infinite in number.[127] The products of its *Prakṛti* are also pluralistic and real too. Its universe has no creator, no controller, no designer and no co-ordinator. It has no *Brahman* and no *Īśvara*. Thus, the question of *Brahma-Nirvāṇa* does not arise in the Sāṅkhya.

Now we present a brief account of the Sāṅkhya metaphysics. *Prakṛti* and *puruṣas* of Sāṅkhya are uncreated and co-eternal. *Puruṣas* are neither evolutes nor evolvents whereas *Prakṛti* is not an evolute, but is an evolvent. *Pradhāna* is the primordial material principle. It is one only, although its products are many. It is active,

---

120. *CU*, VI.8.7; VI.9.4; VI.10.3; VI.12.3; VI.13.3; VI.14.3.

121. *BU*, II.5.19.

122. *AU*, V.3.

123. *BU*, I.4.10.

124. *ṚV*, I.164.20 (*dvā suparṇā sayujā sakhāyā samānaṁ vṛkṣaṁ pariṣasvajāte. tayoranyaḥ pippalaṁ svādvattyanaśnannanyo 'bhicākaśīti)*; *KTU*, I.3.1; *MUU*, III.1.1-2; *ŚU*, IV.6.

125. *SPS*, I.157; V.61-3.

126. *SPS*, I.67; V.72; I.157 (non-duality has been expressly rejucted by the Sāṅkhya); *SK*, 3 & 22.

127. *SPS*, I.67; I.76; I.149; I.152; I.154; VI.35-6; VI.45.

but intrinsically insentient.[128] In contrast, *puruṣa*s are inactive and indifferent, but are sentient.[129] *Prakṛti* is independent; it is not under the control of the *puruṣa*s.[130] Being reflected by the light of the consciousness of any *puruṣa* and due to the proximity of the *puruṣa*, *Prakṛti* becomes active. The former phenomenon is known as the doctrine of reflection (*ābhāsa-vāda*)[131] and the latter the doctrine of proximity (*sānnidhya-vāda*).[132] The Sāṅkhya presents the simile of the co-operation between a blind and a lame person in the context of its two realities.[133]

The Sāṅkhya *Prakṛti* spontaneously works, when conjoined with a *puruṣa*.[134] It works for the *puruṣa* only and not for itself.[135] When a specific *puruṣa* is released, it stops working for him. The released *puruṣa* stays in an isolated state in a higher realm in bliss. But the number of bound *puruṣa*s would never become zero. Hence, the activity of *Prakṛti* is eternal.[136]

*Mahat* or *Buddhi* is the direct evolute of *Prakṛti*.[137] *Ahaṅkāra* evolves from *buddhi* and the former becomes the evolvent of the *manas*, the five subtle instruments of cognition, the five subtle instruments of action and five fields (*tanmātra*s = that only). Each of the five *tanmātra*s becomes an evolvent of a gross material becoming (solids, liquid, gaseous, energy, Space or *Ākāśa*). These evolutionary steps have been furnished through a number of aphorisms in the Sāṅkhya philosophical scriptures.[138]

---

128. *SPS*, I.61; I.67; I.76; III.58-61; VI.32; VI.35-6.
129. *SPS*, I.15; I.19; I.49; I.52; I.54; I.61; I.143; I.162-3; VI.32-3; *SK*, 11 & 55.
130. *SPS*, I.96-7; I.99.
131. *SPS*, I.96-7; I.99; I.164; II.35; VI.27-8.
132. *SPS*, I.96-7; I.164; VI.27-8.
133. *SK*, 21.
134. *SPS*, III.47; III.58-63; *SK*, 56-8.
135. *SPS*, I.66; I.144; III.47; III.58; III.63.
136. *SPS*, I.158-9; III.63-4; III.66; VI.43; *PYD*, II.22.
137. *SPS*, I.67; I.71; II.13; *SK*, 3 & 22.
138. *SPS*, I.61; I.67; I.71-3; II.10; II.16-7; II.19-20; *SK*, 3 & 22.

*Mahat* and its direct or indirect products are the direct or indirect modifications of *Prakṛti* in the analogy of wood being transformed into a chair or gold being transformed into a necklace. Whereas Sāṅkhya sticks to its doctrine of transformation (*pariṇāma-vāda*),[139] the Advaita Vedānta rejects this doctrine and explains the multiplicity of the universe by its *adhyāsa-vāda* or *vivartta-vāda*. The Sāṅkhya system does not accept the *adhyāsa-vāda*.[140]

Most interpreters equate the Vedic *Virāḍ* and the Sāṅkhya *Mahat*. Such an interpretation, however, is not correct. *Pradhāna* is itself converted into *Mahat*. On the other hand, the Vedāntic *Māyā* or *Prakṛti* is never converted into anything. She illusorily projects a virtual universe which is a deceptive appearance of *Brahman* that serves as the substratum. Sāṅkhya does not recognize this doctrine of illusion. It is a system of realism. The universe is real for it. The Sāṅkhya holds that the universe is real and eternal,[141] that it has neither a beginning nor an end and that Space and time are real and eternal.[142] The doctrine of limiting adjunct (*avaccheda-vāda*) is an important concept in the Advaita Vedānta. But this doctrine is rejected by the Sāṅkhya.[143]

There is a general misconception that the Sāṅkhya is the oldest philosophical school to advocate the evolution of the universe. An eternal universe, without a beginning and an end, does not evolve at all with reference to cosmological and cosmogonical evolution in a total scale. But it is also a fact that it is the Sāṅkhya that speaks of evolution in an elaborate way for the first time in the world. Where does the anomaly lie then? The plan of evolution of the Sāṅkhya is confined to the human species only and that too for every individual human being separately. When one *puruṣa* is associated with *Prakṛti*, individual evolution ensues. When the

139. *SPS*, I.61; I.130; VI.32; *SK*, 16; *PYD*, IV.14.

140. *SPS*, II.5; V.53-4.

141. *SPS*, I.12-3; I.42; I.44; I.79; I.158-9; II.6; VI.52.

142. *SPS*, I.12-3.

143. *SPS*, I.51; I.150-1; VI.46; VI.59.

said *puruṣa* is dissociated from *Prakṛti*, the former is released.[144] This release is known as *kaivalya* in the Yoga of Patañjali.[145]

The Sāṅkhya *Prakṛti* is constituted of three *guṇa*s, namely, *sattva, rajas* and *tamas*.[146] These *guṇa*s are attributes. It is a fallacy to say that an entity, created or uncreated, is made up of attributes. We may take some examples. Sugar is not made up of sweetness and silver is not made up of whiteness. An attribute is a property exhibited by certain entity and cannot be the constituent of the latter. The products of *Pradhāna*, that is, all the evolved entities of the universe, are also made up of the same three *guṇa*s. The Sāṅkhya *Pradhāna* is both manifested and unmanifested. The evolved entities are not different from the original evolvent. *Pradhāna* or *Prakṛti* homogeneously pervades its manifested products. In contrast, *Māyā* or *Prakṛti* of the Advaita Vedānta remains always unmanifested. The virtual universe of matter and energy, illusorily created by *Māyā*, cannot be identified with the latter.

The Advaita Vedānta does use the word *guṇa* in three different senses. One of its meanings is "a string." The *vīṇā* of Mother Sarasvatī has three strings, with the names *sattva, rajas* and *tamas*. The virtual universe is created due to the vibrations of these strings. The vibrations of each string produce a group of attributes or properties in the created entities. These attributes also carry the name of the respective string that is responsible for generating. A third meaning of *guṇa* is the *svabhāva* (own nature) of a created entity, shaped and moulded by the *karma-saṁskāra*s. With reference to the use of the word *guṇa* in the Sāṅkhya and the Advaita Vedānta, utter confusion prevails due to intermingling.

144. *SPS*, I.16; I.19-23; I.52; I.85; III.47; III.63-5; III.68; III.70-5; VI.16-7.

145. *SPS*, I.144; *PYD*, IV.34 (*puruṣārthaśūnyānāṁ guṇānāṁ pratiprasavaḥ kaivalyaṁ svarūpapratiṣṭhā vā citiśakteriti*).

146. *SPS*, I.126; I.136; III.48-50; VI.39; VI.42 (The *sāmyāvasthā*, the equipoise or the equilibrium of the three attributes halts all creative activities. An *asāmyāvasthā* or a disturbance of the equipoise leads to creation.) *SK*, 11.

The Advaita Vedānta unambiguously rejects the idea of the transformation of the *Mūla-Prakṛti* into the universe (*Māyā-pariṇāma-vāda*), the transformation of God into the universe (*Īśvara-pariṇāma-vāda*) and the transformation of *Brahman* into the universe (*Brahma-pariṇāma-vāda*). It steadfastly adheres to its own doctrine, the *adhyāsa-vāda* or *vivartta-vāda*. It accepts the virtuality of the universe. The fact of virtuality is a practical event in physics and computer science. The Advaita Vedānta has a doctrine of imaging (*pratibimba-vāda*). Accordingly, the universe is a reflected image of *Brahman*, projected by *Yogamāyā*, the Mother of the universe and the Spouse of the Almighty. There is a difference, however, between the Advaita imaging and the mirror-imaging. The mirror-image is a replica of the source whereas the universe is a magical show of diversity, brought about by the projecting and concealing powers of *Māyā*, even though the *Brahman*-source is one only and devoid of forms and attributes.

The Primeval Person in the Vedas and the Vedānta is the *Puruṣa*[147] (*Brahman*/*Īśvara*). But these scriptures also describe the Cosmic Form[148] (*Viśva-Rūpa*) of the *Puruṣa*. The *Yajurveda*[149] categorically asserts that the Supreme Being has neither a form nor an icon. The Being is formless and the same Being has the Cosmic Form. Self-contradiction seems to be involved in it. But, in reality, there is no self-contradiction. One and only One is the Real Being. The apparent multiplicity is the variegated imaging. Some interpreters wrongly identify God and the universe. When the universe is a reflection of *Brahman* and a virtual creation done by its Power, the virtual universe cannot be an entity separate from the Primordial Being.

The Sāṅkhya is fundamentally incompatible with the Vedānta. The former does not mention *Brahman* or any equivalent word for it. It expressly says that it does not get any evidence for the

147. *ṚV*, X.90.

148. *ṚV*, X.81.3; X.90.1; *ŚU*, III.11-21; *BG*, XI; XIII.13.

149. *YV*, XIII.3 (*na tasya pratimā asti yasya nāma mahadyaśaḥ.*); *MUU*, II.1.2.

existence of God (*Īśvara*).[150] It rejects the doctrine of superimposition (*adhyāsa-vāda*) of the Advaita Vedānta. It also rejects the *avaccheda-vāda* (the doctrine of *upādhi*). It is against non-dualism and sticks to dualism in a guise of pluralism. It is a school of realism whereas the Advaita Vedānta is not. It has no concept of *Māyā*. Its *Mahat* is not the same as the *Virāḍ*. The *Mūla-Prakṛtri* of the Vedānta is not the *Pradhāna* or the *Prakṛti* of the Sāṅkhya. It has not a Supreme Ruler of the universe. Its *Pradhāna* or *Prakṛti* is not under the control of any *puruṣa*. It has multiple *puruṣa*s whereas the Advaita Vedānta has One *Puruṣa* only. Its evolution is not cosmic. It has no cosmology and cosmogony. It has no cosmic design and a cosmic designer. It is not understood why Indian philosophers have intermingled the Sāṅkhya and the Vedānta.

The tenth chapter of the *BG* has eulogized Kapila (*siddhānāṁ kapilo muniḥ*).[151] This short sentence is perhaps the cause of an age-old blunder. The lexicographic meaning of *kapila* is "fiery red." Kapila was a sage in ancient India long before Gautama Buddha and at the time of or before the *Mahābhārata* era. He was the founder of the Sāṅkhya philosophy. No scripture of Kapila is extant now. Similar is the situation with his direct disciples. The *Sāṅkhya-Pravacana-Sūtram* and the *Sāṅkhya-Kārikā*[152] were written many centuries after Kapila (some time after Buddha and before Jesus Christ). If the Sāṅkhya philosophy, as presented to us now, really descended from Kapila, we would be reluctant to accept the idea that Vyāsa, the author of the *Mahābhārata*, referred to the founder of the Sāṅkhya. The *Śvetāśvatara Upaniṣsad* has used the word *maharṣi* for God Rudra.[153] In the same place, reference has been made to Hiraṇyagarbha (Brahmā) of the *Ṛgveda*.[154] The same

150. *SPS*, I.92-3; I.96; V.2; V.6; V.10.

151. *BG*, X.26.

152. N. Sinha, 1979 (1st publ. 1915 by Panini Office, Allahabad), *The Sāṅkhya Philosophy*, New Delhi: Oriental Books Reprint Corpn.

153. *ŚU*, III.4.

154. *ṚV*, X.121.

Upaniṣad has described Brahmā, the *Hiraṇyagarbha* (Golden Embryo), as Kapila Ṛṣi (Seer Kapila).[155] In our opinion, the relevant statement of Vyāsa in *BG*, X.26 carries the connotation: "Among the seers who meditate by observing silence, I (Lord Kṛṣṇa) am Brahmā (Kapila with the radiance of molten gold)."

Lastly, we would focus on the philosophy of liberation, as described in the Advaita Vedānta and the Sāṅkhya. According to the former, the individual self (*jīvātmā*) which is not otherwise different from the Universal Self (*Paramātmā*) re-establishes its identity on being released from the bondage. What is this bondage? Since the self is the experiencer, it is bound to the karmic impressions (*karma-saṁskāras*) that are generated by the actions of the individual and stored in the karmic reservoir (*karmāśaya*)[156] located in the *buddhi* (the individual intellect, a subtle psycho-organ in the subtle body). With the erasure of all the karmic impressions from the *antaḥkaraṇa* (inner instrument), the self is no longer bound. This process is known as release from the bondage (*mokṣa*). A liberated self loses its own identity and becomes *Brahman*. All released selves become *Brahman* only.

The Yoga-system of Patañjali uses the word *kaivalya* (isolation from *Prakṛti*) for liberation. On the issue of liberation or emancipation of an individual *puruṣa*, both the Sāṅkhya and the Yoga are in agreement. The Sāṅkhya asserts that all *puruṣa*s are intrinsically free; their bondage is due to their feeling that they are associated with the *Prakṛti* or *Pradhāna*.[157] Once the *puruṣa* mentally severs its association with the *Prakṛti*, it becomes really isolated and lives by itself as a pure conscious spirit in a higher realm. Such liberated *puruṣa*s are infinite in number and they are different from one another. Bound or unliberated *puruṣa*s are also infinite in number. The Sāṅkhya says that there would never come a time when the number of bound *puruṣa*s would be zero.

---

155. *ŚU*, V.2.

156. *PYD*, II.12.

157. *SPS*, I.57-9; I.155; III.47; III.63-5; III.68.

The Advaita Vedānta has two types of *Prakṛti*, namely, Unmanifested (*Avyakta*) and manifested (*vyakta*). The former is the *Mūla-Prakṛti* (the Primordial Nature), not different from *Māyā*, the Mother Divine, the *Śakti* of *Brahman/Īśvara*. The latter is the universe of matter and energy, illusorily projected by *Māyā* as virtual appearances of *Brahman*. The virtual universe is not non-existent (it is *mithyā*, but not *asatya*); but it is not Absolute Reality (not *pāramārthika satya*) unlike *Brahman*. The universe is a usable, virtual reality (*vyāvahārika satya*). The Sāṅkhya rejects the *adhyāsa-vāda* of Advaita Vedānta. It hardly makes any discrimination between the Unmanifest *Prakṛti* and the manifest *Prakṛti*, the latter being the transformed products and the evolutes of the former. Both the unmanifested and the manifested *Prakṛti*s, in the Sāṅkhya, are made up of the three attributes, *sattva, rajas* and *tamas*.

In the Advaita Vedānta, the *Avyakta-Prakṛti* or *Māyā* is co-eternal with *Brahman/Īśvara*. Both the Possesser of Power (*Śaktimān*) and the Power (*Śakti*) are inseparable. They are non-dual rather than dual. The doership of *Īśvara* is due to the execution by *Māyā*. If we accept these fundamental concepts of the Advaita Vedānta, we have to reject the dissociation-concept of the Sāṅkhya. *Māyā* is the Mother Divine. We need Her grace. We cannot be dissociated or isolated from Her when *Brahman* or *Īśvara* is inseparable from Her. A released self becomes Self or *Brahman*. *Māyā* is never separated from *Brahman*. The attributeless *Brahman* becomes *Īśvara*, with attributes, by virtue of *Māyā* serving as the *upādhi* of *Īśvara*. Thus, a released self who has already become *Brahman* becomes devoid of *upādhi*. Nevertheless, *Brahman* is in possession of *Śakti* that is the *Prakṛti* (*Mūla-Prakṛti*).

Any question does not arise for the self not to get rid of the manifested *Prakṛti* for release from the bondage. Separation of the self from the gross body does occur in death. Lastly, we have one more *prakṛti* or *svabhāva* (the totality of the *karma-saṁskāra*s recorded and stored in the *antaḥkaraṇa*) which is to be erased and annihilated for attaining to *mokṣa*. The Sāṅkhya concept of liberation is at variance with this concept given here.

The *BG* has tried to get a grand synthesis of the chief streams of ancient Indian thoughts. It has been successful to make a confluence of many streams. In this process, some terms common to different systems have been used, with different contextual meanings. Some interpreters of the *BG* have missed the contextual meanings, have not made incisive analysis, have not made a thorough dissection and have, as a result, committed conceptual error in mixing up immiscible ideas. In order to guard against any such pitfalls, we have inserted this section here in the second chapter of the *BG* which has been named as the Sāṅkhya-Yoga, but which deals with Jñāna-Yoga. In addition to a comparison and contrast of the Sāṅkhya and the Advaita Vedānta, the Yoga of knowledge of the latter system has been briefly described in the present section. Further, Sāṅkhya and Advaita Vedānta are extremely incompatible philosophies, if considered fundamentally. Of course, there are some common elements in the field of psychology. It is rather a fact that the structures and functions of the *antaḥkaraṇa* (internal instrument) have been more elaborately described in the Sāṅkhya, Yoga and Tantra than in the Vedānta.[158] Caution must be exercised in order to correctly comprehend the *BG* which presents its own synthetic thesis on the basis of non-dualism.

The *BG* has used the word Yoga in a number of places. It is a fact that the discussions on Yoga made by the *BG* are so extensive, intensive and integral that it itself is a superb piece on Yoga literature. Any person interested in Yoga can hardly ignore the Yoga system of Patañjali. All Advaita-Vedāntins do respect Patañjali, the great seer in the world. But it is to be admitted that

158. *SK*, 33; 35 (Among the structures of the *antaḥkaraṇa, buddhi, ahaṅkāra* and *manas* are the principal ones); *SPS*, II.41 (Among the three principal structures of the *antaḥkaraṇa, buddhi* is the principal one.); *SPS*, II.42 (The *buddhi* is the receptacle of infinite number of *saṁskāras*.); *SPS*, II.43 (Recollection or *smṛti* is the action of *buddhi*.); *SPS*, I.99 (The *antaḥkaraṇa*, being lighted by the conscious *puruṣa*, is the actual agent of actions.); *SPS*, VI.54 & 64 (It is the *ahaṅkāra* that is the real *kartā* or agent; but not the *puruṣa*).

the non-dualists do adopt the Yoga-techniques of Patañjali even though they are not in agreement with the seer in his total philosophy. Patañjali has adopted the philosophy of the Sāṅkhya, with one exception. The Sāṅkhya is purely atheistic whereas Patañjali has aphorisms on *Īśvara*.[159] His *Īśvara* is a special *puruṣa* (*puruṣa-viśeṣaḥ*),[160] but is not a creator. According to his concept of *kaivalya* (liberation; the isolated blissful stay of the *jīva* in a higher realm of the universe), the *puruṣa* attains it by spiritual, yogic methods, resulting in the isolation of the *puruṣa* from the *Prakṛti*. The Advaita Vedānta does not accept this Sāṅkhya theory of liberation. Patañjali's universe is also eternal, without creation and total dissolution. We reject the concept of the eternality of the universe and accept that of the cyclic universe, with creation, sustenance and total dissolution. We have great regard for Ṛṣi Patañjali. We follow his theory and practical techniques. But we present our own philosophy of Yoga-Vedānta which is different from that of the seer.

Similar path we trod with regard to Tantra. We present our Tāntrik theory under the caption of Tantra-Vedānta. The *BG* has integrated some seminal concepts of Tantra and the Advaita Vedānta. To the best of our knowledge, this aspect has so far been ignored by interpreters of the *BG*. We strictly adhere to non-dualism and at the same time speak of the Mother Divine and the Father Divine. We regard *Māyā* as the Mother of the universe and as the *Śakti* and Spouse of *Parameśvara*. The Father Divine is the Chairperson and the Mother Divine is His Spouse and Executive. She plays prominent roles in the creation, sustenance and dissolution of the universe. This Mother Divine (*Māyā*), as depicted in the *BG*, does not strictly conform to the Śākta and the Tantra philosophy. We have a blend of non-dualism, Yoga and Tantra in our interpretation of the *BG*. We have not deviated from non-dualism in any of our other books too.

---

159. *PYD*, I.23-4; I.27-8.

160. *PYD*, I.24

# 3

## Karma-Yogaḥ
## (The Way of Detached Action)

### 3.01: What is Karma-Yoga?

THE third chapter of the *BG* describes *karma-yoga* (the way of detached action). Many persons use this compound-word in a literal sense and that is why they wrongly interpret it. One who does not idle away, who is busy in works throughout the life with sincerity and diligence and for whom work is worship is to be appreciated for his work-culture; nevertheless, he is not a *yogī* and a *karma-yogī*. A sincerely hard-working farm-labourer, factory-worker, business-executive, administrative officer, engineer, doctor or a politician does deserve credit for his work-culture. Still it would not be correct to say that he is a *karma-yogī*.

Who is a *karma-yogī* then? Action done without attachment to the fruits thereof (*nirāsakta karma*) is *karma-yoga*. Action done as duty for the sake of duty only is *karma-yoga*. Action done without gainful motive and selfish interest is *karma-yoga*.

In the second chapter of the *BG*, the Lord has indicated that the path of renunciation (*nivṛtti*) is better than the path of activity (*pravṛtti*). In other words, the Yoga of Knowledge (Sāṅkhya-Yoga) is superior to the Yoga of Action (Karma-Yoga). Having said this, the Lord still induces Arjuna to work. In such a situation, Arjuna is confused and his mind is agitated. He wants a clarification from the Lord.

> O Janārdana (Kṛṣṇa), if your view is that knowledge is superior to work, why do you, O Keśava, engage me in this terrible work?

> With perplexing words, you are, as it were, bewildering my understanding. Tell me, with certainty, that one by pursuing which I may attain the highest good.[1]

The Lord, in the beginning, promulgated a twofold discipline for mankind, namely, the discipline of knowledge (*jñāna-yoga*) and that of detached actions (*karma-yoga*). The former is mainly for the ascetics who have the discriminative knowledge between the Self and the non-Self, who practise celibacy and who have embraced the life of renunciation. The latter is meant for the householder, the performer of works.[2] It is also a fact that the *yoga* of knowledge is superior to that of works.

But it is also to be recognized that both these disciplines are not incompatible and that the latter is not practicable without any knowledge and application of the former. It is a natural tendency of man to work for the gratification of sensual pleasure, the acquisition of more and more wealth and power and all types of selfish interest. A person, without the least discriminatory knowledge of the Self and the not-Self and without a minimum realization of *Brahman*, cannot perform detached actions.

To expel the confusion of Arjuna, the Lord further explains:

> A person, by abstention from works, cannot become a *jñāna-yogī*. None attains perfection through the mere renunciation of works.[3]

To consider the issue from another angle, it is really the *karma-yoga* that prepares the seed-bed for the *jñāna-yoga*. Good works, performed in the present life or past lives, attenuate the sins already incurred and purify the mind. This process, by generating knowledge, gives a start to the *yoga* of knowledge. Without detached actions, the intellect (*buddhi*) cannot be purified. Without a purified intellect, the *yoga* of knowledge cannot be attained. It is hard to achieve renunciation without *karma-yoga*. And *saṁnyāsa*

1. *BG*, III.1-2.
2. *BG*, III.3.
3. *BG*, III.4.

(renunciation) is a prerequisite for the full practice of *jñāna-yoga*. Thus, both these disciplines of *yoga* are interactive and interdependent. They produce synergistic effect.

Let us sum up the topic. Simple action, howsoever sincere and hard, is not *karma-yoga*. Action, performed without attachment to the fruits thereof, is *karma-yoga*. This *yoga* is primarily meant for householders (*gṛhasthas*) whereas *jñāna-yoga* is for *saṁnyāsīs*. The latter is better than the former for attaining emancipation. Nevertheless, both are not exclusive of each other and are not contradictory to each other. Even the ascetic cannot abandon actions altogether. On the other hand, a *karma-yogī*, totally ignorant of *jñāna-yoga*, may be over-busy in types of actions which may be contrary to *yoga* itself.

### 3.02: Action is Better than Inaction

The Lord eulogizes *jñāna-yoga* and unambiguously says that it is at a much higher level than *karma-yoga*. At the same time, He does not denounce *karma-yoga*. He rather positively prescribes it even for a *jñāna-yogī*.

> None indeed, even for a moment, remains without performing action. All are made to work, helplessly, by the *guṇas* (attributes) born of *Prakṛti* (Nature).[4]

The *guṇas*, namely, *sattva, rajas* and *tamas,* born out of the Primordial Nature (*Mūla-Prakṛti* or *Māyā*), compel everyone (unless someone has already become a perfect *jñāna-yogī* or *jīvan-mukta*) to do work.

It may be noted here that the Vedānta philosophy and Yoga-Vedānta do not accept the doctrine of transformation (*pariṇāma-vāda*) of the Sāṅkhya. The three attributes or traits are the empirical productions of the vibrations of the three strings of *Māyā* in conformity with the *Adhyāsa-vāda* of Śaṅkara. The expression "born of" should not be literally understood as "giving birth to a child by a mother." The word *guṇa* has two meanings; one is "string" and the other one is "attribute." The first meaning is applicable to

4. *BG*, III.5.

the *Mūla-Prakṛti*. The second meaning is applied for the created entities of the universe, both inanimate and animate. *Māyā* or the *Mūla-Prakṛti* is the Unmanifest *Prakṛti;* the universe of matter and energy is the manifested *prakṛti*; the store of *karma-saṁskāras* in the *karmāśaya* located in the *buddhi* of an individual person is also his *prakṛti* or *svabhāva*. This third *prakṛti* is the agent that compels a person to be engaged in righteous or unrighteous activity.

> Restraining the organs of action, he who lets his confounded mind dwell on the objects of the senses is called a hypocrite.[5]

The Lord elaborates the correct way of becoming a *karma-yogī*.

> But he who, controlling the senses by the mind, commences the *yoga* of action with the organs of action, being unattached (*asaktaḥ*), is held to excel, O Arjuna.[6]

Two important points have been highlighted in the aforesaid verse. The mind of the *karma-yogī* must control his senses while performing actions. Secondly, his actions must be free from attachment.

It is unfortunate that many interpreters of the *BG* have misunderstood it when they say that *jñāna-yoga* is to be practised by the illumined (wise) person and that *karma-yoga* by the un-illumined (*ajñaḥ* = ignorant) person. Many religious teachers and ascetics still now preach for the renunciation of the world and worldly actions. This has perhaps gone against the work-culture of some people. In all the eighteen chapters of the *BG*, Lord Śrīkṛṣṇa has persuaded Arjuna to work. Arjuna placed his bow on the ground, saying that he would not fight. The Lord instructed him to renounce inaction. Nowhere has he said that the way of action is to be followed by the ignorant. His emphasis was on detached action.The word *anāsakta* (unattached) is a key-word in *karma-yoga*.

---

5. *BG*, III.6.
6. *BG*, III.7.

The next verse of the *BG* is very clear on what we have said here.

> Perform prescribed work. Action is superior to inaction. Indeed, even the bare maintenance of your body would not be possible by inaction.[7]

The expression *niyataṁ karma* means "bounden or obligatory action." Bathing, eating, sleeping, urination, defecation and such other actions that are necessary for the maintenance and health of the body must be performed. Such actions are *niyataṁ karma*. Even if someone is a *jñāna-yogī* and a *saṁnyāsī*, he should perform the obligatory actions for the proper maintenance, health and nourishment of the body which is the vehicle through which journey is to be conducted to reach the goal of life.

> Except for works other than those done for sacrifice (*yajña*), this world is bound by *karma-saṁskāra*s. O son of Kuntī (Arjuna), being free from attachment, do work for That (*Yajña*).[8]

The *Taittirīya Saṁhitā* says: "Sacrifice (*Yajña*) is indeed Viṣṇu (God)."[9] Thus, the contextual meaning of *Yajña* in this verse of the *BG* is "God." Any action performed, with attachment to the fruits thereof, causes bondage. Even fire-sacrifice, that is, oblation (*homa*), performed, with attachment to fruits, creates bondage. In the said verse, emphasis has been laid on two conditions: (1) Perform actions without attachment to the fruits thereof. (2) Work for God. Clarification is necessary for the second condition. God does not need any services for Him. What is the meaning of "Work for God" then? A *karma-yogī* works for the welfare of the universe created by God. Detached work for God's creation should be the motto of a *karma-yogī*.

We sum up this topic by saying: Action is better than inaction. Our work should be devoid of attachment. We should work for the welfare of the creation of God.

7. *BG*, III.8.
8. *BG*, III.9.
9. *TS*, I.7.4.

### 3.03: The Work-Culture

In the third chapter of the *BG* on *karma-yoga*, the Lord says that a *jñāna-yogī* has no duty to perform. The relevant verse may be quoted here.

> But, for a person who delights solely in the Self, who is content with the Self and who finds satisfaction alone in the Self, for him there is no duty to perform.[10]

What has been said in this verse applies to an accomplished *jñāna-yogī*. Such a person delights only in the Self (*Brahman/Īśvara*), and not in the objects of the senses. He is not satisfied with food, drink, et cetera, although he eats for the sake of living; he is satisfied with the Self alone. Unlike most persons who are contented with material possession, power and fame and sensual gratification, the *jñāna-yogī* disregards such acquisition and is content with the Self alone. Such a *saṁnyāsī* is completely bereft of desires. There is nothing to do for such a person who has already realized the Self.

The Lord wants to convey that Arjuna has not yet attained the state of perfect knowledge and *Brahma*-realization. In his present state, he should not renounce his duties. Next, the Lord says:

> Therefore, without attachment, always perform the action that should be done; because, a person attains to the highest by performing action without attachment.[11]

Two conditions have been attached to the said verse. (1) Perform actions, without being attached (*anāsaktaḥ*). (2) Do that deed which ought to be done (*kāryaṁ karma samācara*). In other words, do not do any type of actions that should not be done.

Arjuna belongs to the warrior-class (kṣatriya). Past kings like Janaka, Aśvapati and others, being kṣatriya, through action alone, did abide in perfection (attained liberation, *mokṣa*). They engaged

10. *BG*, III.17.
11. *BG*, III.19.

themselves in action as a result of their *prārabdha karma* (the *karma* which was the cause of the present birth and had to be worked out in this life alone). They directed their actions for the welfare of the world (*lokasaṁgrahārtham*). Doing right actions, without attachment, is the means for mental purification (*sattva-śuddhi*). And no liberation is possible without mental purification.[12]

> The best of men should not renounce work for the guidance of the world (*lokasaṁgraha*). Others follow whatever is done by him. The world conforms to the standard set by him.[13]

The Lord puts a question to Arjuna: Can't you observe Me? Don't you see me always engaged in work?

> I engage myself in action although I have no duty whatsoever to discharge in all the three worlds. For Me, there is nothing unattained and nothing remains to be won. Still I ceaselessly work.[14]
>
> O Pārtha (Arjuna), were I not at all to engage myself in tireless action, persons will tread My path in all possible ways.[15]
>
> The worlds will perish, if I do not work. I may ruin My created beings by causing confusion due to abandonment of work.[16]

In verse 17 of this chapter, the Lord says that a *jñāna-yogī* (who has reached his life's goal of being the knower of the Self and who has become the Self) has no duty to perform. The present verse (*BG*, 3.24) dispels any misunderstanding by saying that still a *jīvan-mukta* (liberated even though living) should work to promote others' well-being.

The work-culture, prescribed by the *BG*, has two standards, one for the enlightened and the other for the un-enlightened. The following verse is clear on this dual aspect.

---

12. *BG*, III.20.
13. *BG*, III.21.
14. *BG*, III.22.
15. *BG*, III.23.
16. *BG*, III.24.

> O descendant of Bharata, as the un-enlightened act, being attached to the work, so should the enlightened act without attachment, desirous of the welfare of the world.[17]

Doing duty for the sake of duty, without all desires and attachment to the fruits of actions, is an exalted ideal to be practised by the enlightened. But the un-enlightened cannot practise this ideal *karma-yoga*. Let them work for getting fruits. Let them work to fulfil their benign desires. After all, action is better than inaction. The mind of the common men should not be bewildered by imposing the higher ideals on them. The ideal actions of the wise man should induce the common men to be imitated. So does the Lord say:

> The wise man should not generate disturbance in the mind of the ignorant persons who are attached to action. He should induce the others (the un-enlightened) in all activities by performing his own work persistently and precisely.[18]

### 3.04: The Doership of the Guṇas of Prakṛti

At the outset, it would be better to clarify the distinction between the created *prakṛti* (the universe) and the *Mūla-Prakṛti*. *Māyā*, the Power (*Śakti*) of *Brahman/Īśvara*, is the *Mūla-Prakṛti* or the Primordial Nature. She is always Unmanifest (*Avyakta*) and is the Mother of the manifested (*vyakta*) universe (Nature or *prakṛti*). In the Vedānta philosophy, by the word *Prakṛti*, is generally meant the *Mūla-Prakṛti*, with reference to the *Puruṣa* who is One only, the Supreme Lord. The former is the Mother Divine and the latter the Father Divine. We do not find any difference between the *Māyā* and the *Mūla-Prakṛti*. For details, reference may be made to section 2.14 of this *BG*.

Confusion has been confounded due to mixing up the Vedāntic *Prakṛti* and the Sāṅkhya *Prakṛti*. Most interpreters of the *BG* have committed this mistake. In this section, by the expression "the

---

17. *BG*, III.25.

18. *BG*, III.26.

*guṇas* of *Prakṛti*," we mean the three strands or strings of the *vīṇā* of *Prakṛti*, and not the attributes of the manifested universe. The three strings of the *vīṇā* are named as *sattva, rajas* and *tamas*. Their vibrations create the whole universe as manifold appearances of the all-pervading *Brahman*. These vibrations also create three main types of attributes, namely, *sattva, rajas* and *tamas*. There are innumerable blends of these attributes in different combinations and permutations. These attributes belong to the created *prakṛti* (created by *Māyā*). But the strings, *vivartta* in nature, are handled by the *Mūla-Prakṛti*, the Mother Divine. Here we consciously avoided the word "empirical" and used the Vedāntic word *vivartta*. "Empiricism" and "phenomenalism" are words used in Western philosophy with reference to sense-experience, sense-data, phenomenal knowledge gained through experimental observation and sense-experience. The concept of *vivartta* is alien to Western philosophy. It is a special concept and a very important one in Advaita Vedānta. According to it, *Brahman* (*Īśvara* and *Māyā* are inclusive without violating the non-duality) is the only non-dual reality (*pāramārthika satya*). There is no diversity whatsoever.[19] But the Advaita Vedānta does accept a separate type of existence of usable entities (*vyāvahārika satya*). The *vivartta* evolutes belong to this second class. The divine *vīṇā*, its three strings (*sattva, rajas, tamas*) and all entities of the created universe, both inanimate and animate, are *vivartta*s. Whereas the Sāṅkhya evolutes are real products (*utpāda*s) of *Prakṛti* or *Pradhāna*, the Vedāntic evolutes are usable *vivartta*s, conjured mentally and magically by *Māyā*. Unlike the Vedāntic *Prakṛti*, the Sāṅkhya *Prakṛti* is transformed into the products of the universe. The divine *vīṇā* and its three strings are also *vivartta*s. All *vivartta*s are diversified appearances of *Brahman* in the analogy of a rope as a snake. It is not a fact that nothing appears as something. It is *Brahman* that appears as the manifold universe. And this type of creation is brought about by *Māyā*.

---

19. *BU*, IV.4.19: *neha nānāsti kiñcana*.

With this much introductory note, we proceed to interpret the verses of the *BG* with special reference to *karma-yoga*.

> In all ways, actions are performed by the *guṇa*s of *Prakṛti*. But the person whose mind is deluded by egoism thinks, "I am the doer."[20]

This verse is very often misinterpreted by importing the Sāṅkhya ideas. In the Sāṅkhya, both *Prakṛti* and the products of *Prakṛti* are in possession of three attributes, *sattva, rajas tamas*, that perform all actions; they are the causal agents of all activities. We do not agree to this idea. Conceptual analysis will convince us that attributes cannot perform actions. A person, X, is kind or cruel. His kindness or cruelty does not perform his kind or cruel actions. Having accepted this analysis, we have to explain the meaning of this verse. The explanation follows the next verse:

> But, O mighty-armed (hero, Arjuna), the knower of the truth of the distinction between the *guṇa*s of *Prakṛti* and their operations does not attach himself to works, being convinced that *guṇa*s operate amid *guṇa*s.[21]

The three strings or strands of *Prakṛti*, through their vibratory effects on the *antaḥkaraṇa*, make the subtle sensory and subtle motor organs (*indriya*s) act on objects (*viṣaya*s) of the senses. In contrast, the self (*ātmā*) does not function at all. One who realizes this is a truth-knower and does not get attached to works and the fruits thereof. The *antaḥkaraṇa* is subjected to influences from two sources, namely, the vibrations of the three strings of the *vīṇā* of the *Mūla-Prakṛti* (*Māyā*) and the *karma-saṁskāra*s stored in the *karmāśaya* located in the *buddhi* of the individual person. This second source is also known as the *prakṛti* or the *svabhāva* of the individual. The *karma-saṁskāra*s impel the *antaḥkaraṇa* to do work in one way or the other.

Persons, deluded by the *guṇa*s of *Prakṛti*, cling to the works of

---

20. *BG*, III.27.

21. *BG*, III.28.

> these *guṇa*s. The knower of the whole (the knower of the whole truth) ought not to destabilize those of partial knowledge and of dull wit.[22]

In the said verse, the person of perfect knowledge or the knower of the whole (*kṛtsnavit*) means "the knower of the Self." In contrast, the dull-witted person of partial knowledge thinks that he works for the fruits of actions. He is attached; he clings to the fruits of actions.

Verse 3.29 has a similarity with verse 3.26. Let the common man work for fruits and for fulfilling his desires with attachment. After all, action is superior to inaction. The person, with perfect knowledge on the Self, should not destabilize the un-enlightened one. There is no harm in performing work with attachment, if we consider the plight of the un-enlightened. He will gradually evolve through many births to reach a state in which he will perform detached actions. One message this verse conveys: The enlightened should set examples by detached actions, so that the common men may imitate them.

Lastly, we summarize this topic. The self or the Self (both being identical in the Advaita Vedānta, with apparent and fictitious differences, of course) does not work. Who is the executive agent then? It is the *Prakṛti*, by playing Her *vīṇā* with three strings or strands (*guṇa*s), that works through vibrations and production of divine musical notes. Again, it is the individual *prakṛti* (*svabhāva* or store of *karma-saṁskāra*s) that works, being associated with the cosmic vibrations. Persons, deluded by the *guṇa*s of *Prakṛti* and their *svabhāva*s, attribute the doership to themselves. They act for the fruits of works. Such persons of dull wit and imperfect knowledge cling to work. They are neither *jñāna-yogī*s nor *karma-yogī*s.

A further clarification is necessary on the question of the agency of work. The vibrations of the three strands or strings of the Unmanifest *Prakṛti* make the whole universe and every entity of

22. *BG*, III.29.

the universe work. Thus, the *Avyakta Prakṛti*, under the Chairpersonship of God (*Parameśvara*), is the Executive Agent for all cosmic events. She functions through the vibrations of the three *guṇa*s of Her *vīṇā*. It may, however, be noted that every entity of the *vyakta prakṛti* (the manifested universe) plays the role of an agent for the functions of its own. It is the *antaḥkaraṇa* (*buddhi, ahaṅkāra* and *manas* being the three principal components) that is the agent, being rendered conscious by the light of the Consciousness of the Self/self. Mother Divine (*Prakṛti, Māyā*) is not responsible for the good or bad actions of individuals.

### 3.05: Surrender All Works to God Alone

All persons who work and ought to work are not *jñāna-yogī*s. When they become attached to works and the fruits thereof, they are also not *karma-yogī*s. There must be some method to convert *karma* to *karma-yoga* (the *yoga* of action). The Lord discloses this clue to Arjuna.

> Surrender all works to Me in a spiritual frame of mind (with the mind centred on the Self). Crave naught (Be a *nirāśī*). Be my-less, that is, be free from all sense of selfish possessions. Fight with unconcern (*vigatajvaraḥ*), being free from (mental) fever.[23]

Part of the Sanskrit text in the verse says: "*sarvāṇi karmāṇi mayi saṁnyasya* (Renouncing all actions in Me)." We have already said that the *BG* proscribes renunciation of actions. The contextual meaning of "renunciation" in this verse is "surrendering or offering all actions to God." The *karma-yogī* offers all his actions to Vāsudeva, the Supreme Lord and Self of all, while thinking that he works for the Lord (for the creation of the Lord) as His service-person. While working, his mind is centred on the Self. The Lord prescribes three more conditions for the *karma-yogī*. (1) He should be a *nirāśī*. He should give up all expectations of getting returns from his works. (2) He should be my-less (*nirmama*), that is, free from all sense of selfish possessions or ownership. (3) He should

23. *BG*, III.30.

be *vigatajvaraḥ* (*vigatasantāpaḥ, vigataśokaḥ*) while discharging his duties. The word *jvara* literally means "fever." Here it contextually means "sorrow" or "worry."

> Those men who constantly conform to this doctrine of Mine, being faithfully respectful and unenvious, are liberated from the bondage of work too.[24]

This verse contains a word *śraddhā*. It means "faith mixed with love and respect." The *karma-yogī* should consider Lord Vāsudeva (God) as his Supreme *Guru* (*guru* = spiritual preceptor). With strong faith in God, with devotional respect for God and without cavilling and envy, one should work, conforming to the doctrine, given in verse 3.30. If done so, one liberates oneself from the bondage of work. The word *asūyā* means "envy." Here it contextually means "finding fault with." One having *śraddhā* in God ought not to find fault with Him too.

Clarification is necessary on the point of the bondage of work. Merits (*dharma*) and demerits (*adharma*), virtues (*puṇya*) and vices or sin (*pāpa*) are associated with work, since work may be good or evil. Works are not free from these contradictions. To get rid of these contradictions and to convert work into *karma-yoga*, one has to follow the instructions given in verses 3.30-31 of the *BG*.

The Lord asserts that this doctrine, based on scriptural authority, that work must be done remains valid. Persons who violate this doctrine are ruined. So does the Lord caution in the following verse:

> But know those who, deluded in all knowledge and devoid of discrimination, carp at this teaching of Mine and refuse to conform to it, to be ruined.[25]

Every diligent worker is a hard worker, but not a *karma-yogī*. Every sincere worker, attached to the fruits of work, is a good worker, but not a *karma-yogī*. One should learn and practise the

---

24. *BG*, III.31.

25. *BG*, III.32.

art of converting work into *karma-yoga*. Lord Vāsudeva has taught this art to Arjuna. Through Arjuna, the Lord has taught this art to all of us, since Arjuna is an algebraic *X*.

### 3.06: The Compulsive Action of the Common Man and the Way to Get Over It

All men, wise or unwise, act in conformity with their own nature, shaped in accordance with their *saṁskāra*s (karmic impressions arising out of their actions done in past lives and manifested at the commencement of the present birth). This idea is expressed in the following verse.

> Even a person of knowledge behaves in conformity with his own nature. All living beings conform to nature. What can repression (restraint) do?[26]

Verse 3.35 of the *BG* may be quoted here on contextual ground:

> Superior is the law of one's own nature (*svadharma*), albeit lacking in merits, to that of another even though well discharged. Better is death in one's *dharma*; the *dharma* of another is full of fear.[27]

In this verse, *dharma* does not mean "religion." The Sanskrit language has no exact equivalent for the English word "religion" and the English language has no exact equivalent for *dharma*. The law of one's own nature is one's *dharma*. Arjuna was born with a warrior's nature. In the battlefield, he preferred to be a recluse. So did the Lord become critical of the vacillation of Arjuna.

The word *prakṛti* (nature) has been used in verse 3.33 of the *BG* in a different sense. Here "nature" means impressions of work, righteous and unrighteous, already done in past lives, manifested in the beginning of the present life. (In Śaṅkara's language, *prakṛtiḥ nāma pūrvakṛtadharmādharma saṁskāraḥ vartamānajanmādau abhivyaktaḥ, sā prakṛtiḥ*). Every living being — even one with

26. *BG*, III.33.

27. *BG*, III.35.

knowledge — behaves in conformity to his own nature. That being so, what will prohibition (*nigrahaḥ = niṣedharūpaḥ*) by Lord Vāsudeva or scriptures do to change the course of nature (the functioning of the *prārabdha karma*)?

We are in agreement with Śaṅkara's interpretation of the said verse of the *BG*. Having agreed, we are confronted with a serious problem. If all living beings work in accordance with their *prārabdha karma,* there remains no scope for individual initiative (*puruṣakāraḥ*) and all scriptures are simply futile.

Lord Vāsudeva gives a satisfactory solution to this intricate problem. One has to control the senses (*indriyas*) and know the Self (*Ātmā = Brahman*). Then only will the actions be those of a *karma-yogī*.

> Senses have attachment (passion = *rāga*) and aversion (*dveṣa*) in respect of their respective objects. None should come under their sway. They indeed are obstacles in one's path.[28]

The person who is a non-*yogī* has a liking for that action which gives sensual pleasure. This tendency is known as *rāga* (attachment, passion). Such a person is repelled from actions that are unpleasant or painful. This tendency is known as *dveṣa* (aversion). The average man is guided by these two fundamental principles of behavioural psychology. But, in order to convert *karma* into *karma-yoga,* one should not submit to attachment and aversion. These two are the stumbling blocks on the path to spiritual betterment. A *karma-yogī* uses his individual initiative (*puruṣakāra*) to subdue these tendencies.

Attachment leads to unending desires. Failure in getting the desires fulfilled generates frustration and anger (angst). Unpleasant and painful experiences give rise to wrathful behaviour. The Lord elaborates on the origin of these two foes.

> It is craving (*kāma*), it is wrath (*krodha*), born of the string of *rajas*.

---

28. *BG,* III.34.

> It is all-devouring and all-sinful. Know it as the foe here (on earth).[29]

It is craving that changes to wrath, when impeded by someone or something. A person works, being incited by *rajas*. He works to fulfil his desires. But all desires are never fulfilled. One fulfilled desire leads to a new one or more of the same. The second desire leads to a third one and so on. The string of *rajas* impels the person to crave voraciously. At some point in the chain, there is a block and, thus, craving is transformed into frustration, finally generating wrath. Craving is the worst foe in the empirical life.

> As fire is enveloped by smoke, a mirror by dirt, and a foetus by the placental membranes, so is knowledge by craving.[30]
>
> O son of Kuntī, knowledge is covered by the insatiable fire of desire, the constant enemy of the wise.[31]

Craving is a persistent foe for a man of knowledge (not for a man of *Brahman*-realization). His knowledge is obscured by this foe. The man of knowledge is already conscious of the fact that he suffers because of his craving. But, for the obscuring effect of craving on knowledge, he is flung into the trouble due to his inability to abandon the former, which acts as an insatiable fire. The situation is totally different for the ignorant, however. Albeit in the grip of craving, the ignorant man looks upon it as a friend.

> The senses (*indriyas*), the mind (*manas*) and the intellect (*buddhi*) are said to be the abode of craving. By means of these, it (craving) obscures knowledge and deludes the embodied spirit.[32]

What have been said in the foregoing paragraphs are facts and, hence, cannot be gainsaid. What is the solution then?

---

29. *BG*, III.37.
30. *BG*, III.38.
31. *BG*, III.39.
32. *BG*, III.40.

> Therefore, O best of Bhāratas, first control the senses and thereby slay this wicked (sinful) craving that destroys knowledge and realization.[33]

> It is said that the subtle senses are noble; that nobler than the senses is mind; that intellect is even nobler than the mind. What is nobler than even the intellect is He, the Supreme Self.[34]

The Supreme Self is the beholder of the intellect (*buddhi*). The *buddhi* itself is insentient. It becomes sentient by being reflected by the Self. Without getting the light of the Self, the *buddhi* has no consciousness of itself.

> Thus, O mighty-armed (Arjuna), knowing Him (the Self) as nobler than the intellect, and restraining the self by the Self, destroy the enemy in the form of craving, so hard to conquer.[35]

Thus, a *karma-yogī* is he who devotes himself to actions, without being attached to the fruits thereof. He works for God, that is, for the welfare of the creation of God. Craving for sensual enjoyment is the main foe. The *yogī* offers his work to God. He controls his subtle senses, mind and intellect through his devotion to God. Then only is *karma* (action) rendered to *karma-yoga*.

---

33. *BG*, III.41.

34. *BG*, III.42.

35. *BG*, III.43.

# 4

# Jñāna-Karma-Saṁnyāsa-Yogaḥ
## (Way of Renunciation of Action in Knowledge)

### 4.01: The Ancient Tradition of Yoga

THE European historians and Vedic scholars unknowingly (or with motive and bias) distorted historical facts on Vedic India. In their opinion, the Haṛappan civilization was Draviḍian; the Aryans migrated from the area near the Caspian sea; they entered into the Indus Valley through Mesopotamia and Iran; they attacked the Draviḍians, killed many of them and drove them away to the South. Further, they say that the Yoga culture originally belonged to the non-Aryan Indians. They got some archaeological materials on which some yogic postures were inscribed. From these Haṛappan archaeological findings, they deduced the non-Aryan origin of Yoga.

The deduction of the European scholars was a fiction (a malicious fiction) rather than a fact. The Vedic Aryans were extra-terrestrial in origin. They came to the Indus Valley from the *Deva-Loka* (which was definitely outside our solar system, but probably inside our Milky Way galaxy) by their spaceship and landed on the Arvāvat and the Sārasvat seas (now the Rajasthan desert). They settled on the Indus Valley. They were the builders of the Haṛappan civilization. They later migrated to other parts of undivided India, Iran, Egypt, Mesopotamia, Greece and the mainland of Europe.

In pre-Vedic India, a large number of non-Aryan tribes were living in different regions. The Tāmils (Trāmila = Drāmila = Drāviḍa) were the only Drāviḍians who lived in the farthest South and could not come in contact with the Vedic Aryans for some millennia. There was no occasion for a clash between the Vedic Aryans and the Drāviḍians of present Tamil Nadu.

Aryan and non-Aryan clashes did occur especially in the beginning stage. But, in course of time, there was more of cultural co-operation, synthesis, coexistence and compromise than of conflict and struggle. The present Indian culture is a great river that is the outcome of the confluence of many streams, tributaries and rivers. It is not purely Vedic nor purely non-Vedic, neither purely Aryan nor purely non-Aryan.

Too many non-Aryan tribes (although to some extent racially mixed now) are still extant in India. One can verify even now and see that Yoga is not part of their own culture.

Now let us know what the *BG* says on this topic:

> I told this immutable Yoga to Vivasvān who declared it to Manu. Manu told it to Ikṣvāku.[1]

Yoga is immutable or imperishable. This statement has a special meaning here. The fruit of Yoga, namely, right perception leading to emancipation (*mokṣa*) is unfailing. God imparted knowledge on Yoga to Vivasvān who ruled the *Deva-loka* (outside our planet earth; perhaps outside our solar system in our Milky Way galaxy). Vivasvān declared it to his son, Manu. This Manu (most probably not the author of the *Manu-Saṁhitā*) declared it to his son, Ikṣvāku. Manu was the king of *Deva-loka*. Consequent upon a devastating deluge in the extraterrestrial homeland of the Aryans, he, heading a team of the Aryans, used a spaceship to fly to the Indus Valley of the earth. Ikṣvāku, the son of Manu, succeeded his father for ruling the new Aryan kingdom. The ancient Indus Valley civilization was built by the descendants of Manu.

> Thus, traditionally transmitted, royal sages (*rājarṣis*) knew this Yoga. Due to long lapse of time, Yoga has been lost here.[2]

---

1. *BG*, IV.1.
2. *BG*, IV.2.

With this allusion to the ancient Yoga, Lord Vāsudeva says that he is instructing him the same ancient Yoga.[3]

Arjuna was puzzled by listening to what the Lord said. Vivasvān had been born earlier than Lord Vāsudeva. Then, how could it be possible for the Lord to impart knowledge to Vivasvān?[4]

The Lord removes the puzzlement of Arjuna by declaring the doctrine of reincarnation (*punarjanma-vāda*).

> Many births of Mine as well as yours have already taken place.
> O Arjuna, I know them all; but you do not know.[5]

The *BG* unambiguously declares the doctrine of reincarnation. A person is born and reborn again and again until he/she attains liberation. The gross body (*sthūla śarīra*) dies and is transformed into other forms of matter and energy. But as long as the subtle body (*sūkṣma śarīra*) and the causal body (*kāraṇa-śarīra*), with the internal mental apparatus (*antaḥkaraṇa*), containing the karmic reservoir (*karmāśaya*), continue to exist, rebirth becomes inevitable. The self, intrinsically ever free, is usably bound to the karmic impresses (*saṁskāras*) in the *karmāśaya*. This bondage (*bandhana*) is to be severed by performing Yoga, as prescribed by Lord Vāsudeva in the *BG*. Emancipation is the same as becoming free from bondage that automatically ends in *Brahma-nirvāṇa* (becoming *Brahman*).

### 4.02: The Doctrine of Avatāra

The word *avatāra* means "God born as an individual of any living species, human or sub-human." In the Hindu mythology, God has been embodied as an *avatāra* in the form of a man, half human and half lion, fish, tortoise, etc.

The word *avatāra* has the prefix *ava* (meaning "down") and is derived from the verb-root *tṛ*. The word literally means "descent."

---

3. *BG*, IV.3.
4. *BG*, IV.4.
5. *BG*, IV.5.

By taking a form, God apparently descends from the Supreme Level to a little lower one in the cosmic rung. Very soon it would be clear that God, as an *avatāra*, does not really descend.

A person is reborn only when his *antaḥkaraṇa* (internal apparatus of the mind-complex) contains karmic impressions of *dharma* (righteousness) and *adharma* (unrighteousness). With the *antaḥkaraṇa* devoid of mental impressions (*karma-saṁskāra*s), mind does not exist. In the absence of a mind, birth does not take place. God is eternal, timeless and birthless (*aja*). No *karma-saṁskāra*s accumulate in Him since He does not perform *karma* and has no mind. The words *dharma* and *adharma* are not relevant to Him. If we accept these facts, we cannot get a satisfactory explanation for the birth of God in a human form or a sub-human form.

In order to dispel the doubt from the mind of Arjuna, Lord Vāsudeva says:

> Although I am unborn (*ajaḥ*), the immutable Self (*avyayātmā*) and the Ruler of all created beings, yet, subjugating My *Prakṛti*, I take birth through My *Māyā*.[6]
>
> O scion of Bharata (Arjuna), whenever righteousness declines and unrighteousness rises, then I create a form for Me.[7]

The body of an *avatāra* is not *karmaja* or *saṁskāraja*, that is, it is not born of the karmic impressions unlike ours. It is an empirical form, created by *Māyā*, as desired by God. The self of an individual human being or animal is embodied and it is bound to the karmic impressions. However, God, the Supreme Self, is always free. He pervades all. Not only is He within the empirical body of the *avatāra*, He is also simultaneously pervasive in the whole universe. He is within and outside the *avatāra*; He is within and outside the universe. Hence, in the concept of the *avatāra-vāda*, it would be wrong to conceive the limitation of the Supreme Self within the empirical body of the *avatāra*.

---

6. *BG*, IV.6.
7. *BG*, IV.7.

God, being a non-doer (*akarttā*), does everything through His Power (*Śakti*). This Divine Power (*Īśvara-Śakti*) is *Māyā*. God and *Māyā* are known as *Puruṣa* and *Prakṛti*, respectively. The former is the Possessor of Power (*Śaktimān*) and the latter is the Power (*Śakti*), both being inseparable like fire and its heat. Many philosophers have committed a blunder by equating *Māyā* with illusion. Really, She is not illusion. The Mother Creatrix, the Consort of God, cannot be illusion. She can create illusion if She likes and needs. She has the concealing and projecting power (*āvaraṇa* and *vikṣepa śakti*).

After this diversion, we would go back to the *BG* to know more about the function of the *avatāra*. An *avatāra* performs specific functions. On this point, the Lord speaks further.

> For the protection of the virtuous, the destruction of the wicked and to secure establishment of righteousness, I take birth in every age.[8]

We do not find this *avatāra-vāda* (*vāda* = doctrine) in religions other than Hinduism. There is nothing wrong in the doctrine itself. "God, the Omnipotent Lord, the Creator of the universe, cannot create a living form for Himself." Such a statement does not seem to be sensible. But we interpret the *avatāra-vāda* in a different way. An *avatāra* does not descend from heaven to the earth, from an upper locality to a lower one. In a cosmic sense, there is neither upper nor lower. These are relative terms, depending upon the gravitational force, with special reference to the location of the observer. God who is omnipresent, omnipotent and omniscient can assume a form anywhere and at any time to become an *avatāra*. Of course, only He decides the full potency or a partial potency of the Divinity of the *avatāra*, depending upon the need of the divine mission.

In Hinduism, the *avatāra-vāda* has more misuse than use. Now many *bābā*s (a Hindu monk, *guru*, religious instructor or preceptor, *yoga-guru*) claim that they are *avatāra*s and each one is a full God.

8. *BG*, IV.8

At a particular historical time, especially in the modern age, the number of living Gods in Hinduism swell up to hundreds or more. Many Hindu religious sects do not worship God; they worship the founder of the sect and/or the spouse as God/Goddess. The *guru-vāda* has also multiplied the number of Gods and pushed the real God (One and only One) into oblivion. In our opinion, this seems to be an unholy augury. The misuse of the *avatāra-vāda* has drifted some Hindus away from the most ancient and noblest traditions of the Vedas, the Upaniṣads, the *Brahma-Sūtram* and the *BG*.

The birth and action of an *avatāra* are to be qualified in order to distinguish them from those of other living beings. In this regard, the Lord says:

> He who thus truthfully knows My divine birth and action is not reborn on leaving the body. He reaches Me (He is liberated.), O Arjuna.[9]

Here we quote Śaṅkara's language: *tat janma māyārūpaṁ, karma ca sādhūnāṁ paritrāṇādi mama divyam aprākṛtam aiśvaram*. (That birth has the nature of an appearance. In other words, it is a birth of an illusory form. The body is not material. It is not *karmaja*, not the product of *karma-saṁskāra*s, but it is *māyāja*, an illusory form produced by *Māyā*, the Power of God. The divine work is the protection of the virtuous, etc.)

## 4.03: A Way of Getting Liberation

Lord Vāsudeva teaches Arjuna a way of getting liberation. The ways are many. It is one of them. The Lord says:

> Freed from passion, fear and wrath, being fully absorbed in Me, purified by the austerity of knowledge, many have attained My status.[10]

---

9. *BG*, IV.9.
10. *BG*, IV.10.

Attraction for pleasure is passion (*rāga*). The senses (*indriyas*) have attraction for their objects (*viṣayas*). Just the reverse is the case with aversion (*dveṣa*). When the senses have repulsion from their objects, we call this phenomenon *dveṣa*. The senses seek pleasure in *rāga*; they repel from pain in *dveṣa*. Both *rāga* and *dveṣa* are normal psychological phenomena. There is nothing wrong with them in usual situations. When indulgence in pleasure for the gratification of the senses becomes a strong habitual urge, it becomes a passion. This passion is undesirable. The avoidance of pain is also undesirable when one has to work in a painstaking situation for the benefit of oneself, the family, the society and the world.

One has to work fearlessly. Passion, self-interest, the hope of getting favour, the apprehension of being punished and the thought of death generate fear. Fear makes a mind morbid and purges peace out of the latter.

Anger is a potent and terrible enemy of man. It deranges the normal working of the mind. It kills the human faculty when it operates with its full force. It must be shunned in order to be a good man.

The *jñāna-yogī* is a knower of *Brahman*. He realizes his non-difference (identity) with *Brahman/Īśvara* (God). With such a realization, he is fully absorbed in God. He takes refuge in the Supreme Lord (*Parameśvara*). There are two statements in this paragraph. 1. The *yogī* should establish his identity with God and should be fully absorbed in God. 2. The *yogī* should take refuge in God (sheltered in Me = *māmupāśritāḥ*). The first statement refers to *jñāna-yoga* (the *yoga* of knowledge) and the second one to *bhakti-yoga* (the *yoga* of devotion).

Such *yogīs* should purify themselves by the fire of knowledge (*jñānatapasā pūtāḥ*). This is the best way for *citta-śuddhi* (the purification of the *antaḥkaraṇa*). Once they do *citta-śuddhi* through the austerity of knowledge, they attain the status of God. This is their final emancipation, which is non-dualistic in nature.

**4.04: Many Ways to the Same Destination**

Religious persons have mostly the tendency to hold that their own religion is the only one that can give salvation. Basing on such a pseudo-concept, the words *mleccha*, *kāfir*, heathen and *jihād* have been in usage and have been creating problems in the long history of humankind. The followers of these religions regard persons following other faiths as infidels.

The Vedas are exceptions to what has been said in the foregoing paragraph. "Reality is One only. The wise men express It in many ways."[11] The same idea has been expressed in the same Veda in the *mantra*s belonging to other *sūkta*s too.[12]

The whole universe, irrespective of many religions, has one God only. The concept of one Hindu God, a Christian God, a Judaic God, an Islamic God, and so on, is absurd. Again, we are speaking of the earth, not of the whole universe. Our earth is an insignificant point in the immeasurably vast universe. There may be many planets in the different galaxies of the universe where living beings may be inhabiting. Their civilizations may be varying in a wide range. In the modern world of scientific advancement, it is not unreasonable to speculate the existence of exobiology with advanced civilizations and different sorts of religions. It is our firm conviction that all religious scriptures have been written by men, and not by God. The primitive man had the divine inspiration to think of the idea of God. Some gifted individuals could link up their minds with God and thereby divine knowledge could be revealed to them. This has happened not only in religions, but also in other fields such as arts and science. The transmitter has transmitted correctly and accurately. But there can be no guarantee as to the correct reception of the receiver. Had there been a guarantee, all revelations would have been one and the same. But contrary is the fact. Some Hindus claim that the Vedic words are eternal and that God is the author of what has been

11. *Ṛ̥V*, I.164.46.

12. *Ṛ̥V*, X.82.3; X.114.5; X.121.1.

said in the Vedas. They steadfastly hold that the Vedas are incorrigible. Similar is the trend with some persons of other religions. God nowhere leaves His footprints or fingerprints. His sportive play would not be a feasibility had there been no ignorance at all in His created beings. We don't think there is any incorrigible and infallible final truth in any scripture. The intellect of a person, however gifted he may be, may not be one hundred per cent transparent. It may be translucent; it may have varying degrees of opacity. The truth revealed may be received by the intellect in a distorted form. The seer may not be able to link up with the Lord with the utmost perfection. "The whole truth has been revealed; it is incorrigible and infallible; any correction to it is profane." This idea is the worst enemy of humankind. It has done and is doing the greatest damage to humanity.

For the sake of argument, we may accept that all religious scriptures contain the revealed truth. God for the whole universe is one, and, hence, the source is one. That being the fact, all revelations should have been identical. But that is not the case. We may say that the scripture of a particular religion only has been revealed and that others are not. There is no way to justify such a claim.

The *Brahma-Sūtra* has two aphorisms in this regard. (1) The (original religious) scripture springs from the source (God).[13] (2) But (its correctness is tested by) co-ordination or agreement (with observed facts, logical analysis and inferences).[14]

If we accept the revelation theory literally in its entirety, we end in trouble. Science has discovered many facts that are at variance with the so-called revealed scriptures. Human reason also finds flaws in many scriptural injunctions.

Some lovers of the Vedas claim that only the Vedic words are eternal and that they are the words of God. They say that these words were revealed to the Vedic seers while they were in

13. *BS*, I.1.3 (*śāstra-yonitvāt*).

14. *BS*, I.1.4 (*tattu samanvayāt*).

meditation. Such a claim is unfounded, if scientifically analysed. Words are vibrations of sound in a medium of air. Before the Cosmic Egg appeared and after the singularity disappeared, that is, before the creation and after the dissolution of the total universe, there is no question of the existence of air, vibrations of the vocal organs, reception by the auditory organs and sound-recognition by the auditory centre in the brain. The human species appeared long after the earth was formed. All these conditions could not be fulfilled for words to be eternal. New words are coined. Some old words go into oblivion. The same word carries different meanings in different contexts. It has also happened in the Vedas. Words as such do not carry eternal intrinsic meanings. We give meanings to words, and that too in use. Basing on these considerations, we cannot accept the claim that the Vedic words are eternal.

A number of Hindus hold the opinion that all religions are one and the same, preaching, in principle, similar ideologies. Such an opinion is uncritical and simplistic. Every religion has some metaphysics, some ethics and some rituals. The metaphysics and the rituals are not common at all. In the sphere of ethics, there is some degree of commonness; but there are sharp differences too. Each religion is fundamentally different from the other.

Secular people are against religions. But secularism (atheism) may be the beliefs of a few individuals. It would never replace religions. Spirituality should be our goal. If that goal is ever attained in the future, all religions, like different rivers, would merge in the ocean of spirituality. But that is a noble dream, at least for the present. What is the solution then?

We hope the human species will not stagnate at the present religious level. Spirituality is expected to evolve and religions would fade away. Even at the present religious level, we have a solution. The only practicable method is religious tolerance, co-existence and social harmony. The seminal principle of this method is the recognition of the fact that many roads lead to one and the same destination and that many rivers flow into one and the same ocean. In the garden of religions, let a thousand flowers blossom. It is up to the individual person to choose one or the other flower of one or any other colour and of one or any other fragrance.

The *BG* has a permanent solution of this problem. The following verse gives that solution.

> Whatsoever the way in which they approach Me, in the same way do I resort to them. O son of Pṛthā (Arjuna), in all ways, men tread paths leading to Me.[15]

Someone may misunderstand this verse by taking a wrong meaning of the word "Me." Lord Vāsudeva (Śrīkṛṣṇa) says it. Vāsudeva is not a Hindu God only. He is God and the only God of the entire universe. There is nothing like a Hindu God, a Muslim God, a Christian God, a Judaic God and the like. People of other religions may address God by other names. Different names of God do not change the oneness of God.

The essence of the quoted verse is this: There may be many paths to tread; but the destination is one only. God is the only one goal to be reached.

Religious tolerance, religious co-existence and respect for the other person's faith should be the civilized behaviour of humankind.

### 4.05: Types of Persons in Conformity with Their Innate Nature Resulting from Their Works Done in Their Past Lives

A number of persons in the world, desiring quick success of their works, worship deities (*devatā*s) like Indra, Agni and so forth. They think that these gods are different from *Parameśvara* (the Supreme Lord, one and only one God). In this context, reference may be made to the *Bṛhadāraṇyaka Upaniṣad*.[16] Being prompted by their intense desire for quick success, they offer *yajña*s (oblations)

---

15. *BG*, IV.11.

16. BU, I.4.10.

to alien deities. On this point, the Lord says in the following verse:

> Here people worship gods, desiring the success of their works. For, in this human world, quick is the success born of works.[17]

The expression *karmajā siddhi* means "success born of works." It is not a fact that no fruits accrue to a person who worships deities other than God. It is only God who receives the offering of oblations or any other type of worship. The Lord points out the misconception of the common devotee who alienates the many gods from God, one and only one.

Depending upon the works done in the past lives, *saṁskāra*s are formed and stored in the *karmāśaya* (the reservoir of karmic impressions) of the *buddhi*. The karmic impressions of the past lives mould the innate nature (*svabhāva*) of an individual in the present life. Accordingly, his traits (*guṇa*) and actions (*karma*) conform to a type in the present life. There are four major types, as described in the next verse.

> Depending on the trait-type (*guṇa*) and *karma-saṁskāra*s (of the past lives), the fourfold type-system has been ordained by Me. Even though I am the ordainer, know Me as the immutable non-agent.[18]

The word *cāturvarṇya* in the verse has been interpreted as the four castes in the Hindu religion. The Sanskrit word for "caste" is *jāti* and for "colour" is *varṇa*. Each one of the four castes among the Hindus hasn't a specific colour. Moreover, God, one and only one for the whole universe, has not created four castes in all the religions of the world. Caste-system among the Hindus was a social evolution in the prevailing circumstances of the ancient age. In the present social context, it has become obsolete, although still extant, being propped by political interest and group interest. The word *varṇya* literally means "shades of colour" and contextually means "types."

---

17. *BG*, IV.12.

18. *BG*, IV.13.

The innate tendencies (*svabhāvas*) of persons belong to four major types, namely, brāhmaṇa, kṣatriya, vaiśya and śūdra. A person, with spiritual innate tendencies for acquiring, augmenting and spreading knowledge, is a brāhmaṇa; one, with innate tendencies to rule and fight against injustice, is a kṣatriya; one, with commercial attitude to produce more wealth, is a vaiśya; one, with an attitude to do manual labour and serve the society, is a śūdra.

The four trait-types, as described here, are universal and not confined to Hinduism only. They are operative at all times — past, present and future. It would be wrong to associate this verse or the verse in the Puruṣa-Sūkta of the *R̥gveda*[19] to any caste-system based on the birth of a person in a particular family.

Verse 4.13 of the *BG* says that God is the ordainer and still is the non-agent (*akarttā*). Here we quote Śaṅkara's language: *yeṣāṁ tu karmaṇāṁ karttāraṁ manyase, paramārthataḥ teṣām akarttā eva aham* (Metaphysically, I am not the agent of those works of which you deem Me the agent). The Lord further explains this point.

> Works do not taint Me. I do not desire their fruits. One who knows Me to be such is not bound by works.[20]

Works do not originate a body for God. He does not yearn for the fruits of works. In the absence of both these, works taint Him not. Persons who know God to be the Self of all and a non-agent without yearning for the fruits of works become free from bondage too. Works do not originate psycho-physical organisms for them.

Ancient sages did work after realizing this fact. Without renouncing work, they were seekers after liberation. The Lord mentions this point.

> Knowing thus was work done by the ancients (ancient sages)

19. R̥V, X.90.12.

20. *BG*, IV.14.

> who were seekers after liberation. Therefore you do only work, as was done by the ancients in bygone days.[21]

The Lord instructs Arjuna to do work and not to renounce it. He advises to imitate the ancient sages (like Janaka and such others) who sought liberation by working without yearning for the fruits of works. For mind's purification (*ātmaśuddhyartham, cittaśuddhyartham*), work should be done for the wellbeing of the world (*lokasaṁgrahārtham*). Without the purification of the mind, one is ignorant of the Self (*anātmajñaḥ*). And one who is ignorant of the Self cannot be liberated.

Irrespective of the family in which one is born, one should make efforts to elevate oneself through the transmigratory cycles of life. It is possible for everybody to become a knower of *Brahman* (*brahmavit*) and to be liberated (to become *Brahman*).

### 4.06: Inscrutable is the Nature of Action

In the previous section, Lord Vāsudeva has instructed Arjuna to do work and not to renounce it. But inscrutable is the nature of action. Work should be done, but only good work should be done. The Lord has used three words, nan.ely, *karma* (action), *akarma* (inaction) and *vikarma* (bad action) to classify works. He elucidates the nature of these three types of works.

> What is action? What is inaction? In deciding this issue, even the sages are deluded. Therefore, I shall elucidate the nature of action, by knowing which you will be freed from evil.[22]

Lord Vāsudeva poses these questions and assures Arjuna to furnish proper clarification. He further says:

> The nature of action is to be known. The nature of bad action and, besides that of inaction are to be known. Inscrutable is the nature of action (*gahanā karmaṇo gatiḥ*).[23]

21. *BG*, IV.15.
22. *BG*, IV.16.
23. *BG*, IV.17.

> He who can see inaction in action and action in anaction is intelligent among men. Being a doer of all actions, he is in union with God.[24]

"The perception of non-action in action and vice versa" seems to be a contradictory proposition in Aristotelian logic. It is, however, not contradictory if one contextually analyses the words *karma* and *akarma* in the verse. Many interpreters of the *BG* have presented their views that are not acceptable to us. Our interpretation is something different. If one performs works without attachment, while being united with God, he does works for the welfare of the world. This work is *karma* (action) that is sanctioned by scriptures. This *karma* is not binding in nature. If somebody relinquishes the usual worldly works and spends his whole time for the realization of God leading to liberation, he also performs work, but that is inaction (*akarma*). Both *karma* and *akarma* are prescribed, depending upon the spiritual status of a person.

> He whose all undertakings (*samārambhāḥ*) are devoid of desires for results and planned gains and whose actions are burnt by the fire of knowledge is called by the wise (the knowers of *Brahman*) as a learned person (*paṇḍita*) with discrimination between the good and the bad.[25]

> Giving up attachment to the fruits of actions, eternally contented, dependent on nothing, though engaged in action, he does nothing at all.[26]

In this verse and the previous one, the Lord emphasizes a few points to explain inaction in action. Actions without attachment to the results thereof, actions burnt by the fire of *Brahma-jñāna* (knowledge on *Brahman*), eternal contentment and seeking no support, depending on which one seeks to achieve an end in life (the *Gītā*'s word is *nirāśraya*) are the means of inaction, even if one engages oneself in action.

---

24. *BG*, IV.18.

25. *BG*, IV.19.

26. *BG*, IV.20.

The Lord continues the topic of inaction in action :

> Free from expectations (*nirāśī*), controlling the mind and the self, relinquishing all possessions, one who performs actions exclusively for the body incurs no sin.[27]

In this verse, the word *citta* means "the internal apparatus of the mind (*antaḥkaraṇa*)" and the word *ātmā* means "the external psycho-physical organism as a whole." Both these are to be controlled in order to attain inaction in action.

> Content with what is randomly gained, having transcended the pairs of opposites, free from envy, equanimous in success and failure, he is not bound even though he acts.[28]

While instructing Arjuna, the Lord always emphasizes the non-renunciation of actions. But he qualifies actions so that actions do not bind the self. How does one achieve this end? If a person burns his *karma* (actions) in knowledge (*jñāna*, really *Brahma-jñāna*), he is not at all bound by his actions.

### 4.07: Perform All Actions as Sacrifices for God

The Sanskrit word *yajña* is usually rendered into English as "sacrifice." The rendering is not accurate; but in the absence of a proper English word, we try to manage with it. The Vedic Aryans were doing *yajña* and thereby paying homage to God by oblation in the fire. This type of religious action was known as *homa* or *yajña*. The general meaning of *yajña*, however, is "sacrificing the self-interest for the benefit of others." In the present context, any benefit for God does not carry any meaning. Here we use this word to mean "offering to God as a mark of respect" or "offering to God for the benefit of his creation."

If we dedicate our actions to God, if we work for God, that is, for the welfare of the creation of God, we thereby sacrifice our actions for God.

---

27. *BG*, IV.21.

28. *BG*, IV.22.

> He whose attachment has vanished, who has been liberated, whose mind has been established in knowledge, and who performs work for sacrifice alone, gets all his *karma* dissolved.[29]

The word *karma* in this verse refers to *kriyamāṇa karma* (the karmic impressions being imprinted in the present life). Because, for a person who is already liberated (whose all bondage due to righteousness or *dharma* and unrighteousness or *adharma* having fallen off), and who is attached to nothing whatsoever, he has no cumulative karmic impressions (*sañcita karma*) in his karmic ledger.

Now the Lord presents a non-dualistic picture perceived by the knower of *Brahman*.

> The means of the sacrificial offering is *Brahman*. The oblation is *Brahman*. The oblation is offered by *Brahman* in the fire of *Brahman*. The sacrificer (the *Brahma-jñānī karma-yogī*), being absorbed in *Brahman*, reaches *Brahman* alone.[30]

The process or the means (the word *arpaṇa* has been used) is the sacrificial ladle. The *jñāna-yogī*, while doing *agni-hotra* (fire-sacrifice), sees *Brahman* only. The instrument of oblation, the oblation itself, the doer of offering oblation are all *Brahman*. The *yogī* remains in a state of *samādhi*; he is fully absorbed in *Brahman*. Such a *yogī* reaches *Brahman* alone. The idea given in this verse is purely non-dualistic. If one can attain to this state, one's action becomes inaction.

The Lord continues his instructions on different types of *yajña* (sacrifice) to be free from bondage due to actions.

> Other *yogī*s perform sacrifices to *deva*s (gods or deities) only. Others offer the self as sacrifice by the Self Itself in the fire of *Brahman*.[31]

In reality, the self (*jīvātmā*) and the Self (*Paramātmā/Brahman*) are identical. When the Self or Supreme *Brahman* is conjoined to

---

29. *BG*, IV.23.
30. *BG*, IV.24.
31. *BG*, IV.25.

adjuncts like the intellect (*buddhi*), the attributes of all these adjuncts are superimposed on the Self inside the limiting adjunct (*upādhi*). In this superimposed state, the Self is known as the self. The Supreme Self or *Brahman*, however, is formless, functionless, attributeless, non-relational, spaceless, timeless, and is neither matter nor energy. It is pure Existence, pure Consciousness and pure Bliss. It is directly experiential, without any mediation. Through its mediation alone, everything else is experienced. The word "pure" as a qualifying term for "Existence," "Consciousness" and "Bliss" means "non-relational" or "unconditioned."

Sacrifices (*yajñas*) are many in types. The Lord gives some more examples.

> Others sacrifice the subtle sense-organs (*indriyas*) in the fires of restraints; yet others sacrifice the objects (*viṣayas*) of the senses in the fires of the senses.[32]
>
> Others sacrifice all sense-activities and the activities of *prāṇa* in the fire of self-restraint, kindled by the knowledge of *Brahman*.[33]
>
> Ascetics, subjecting themselves to severe disciplines and rigid vows, perform sacrifices in a number of ways. Some perform *dravya-yajña* (*dravya* = material things or cash) by giving away their wealth or material possessions (as sacrifice in holy places and to worthy persons). Others perform *tapoyajña* (*tapaḥ* = penances) by sacrificing the results of their penances. Some others perform *yoga-yajña* by sacrificing the results of their yogic activities. Others perform *svādhyāya-yajña* by sacrificing the results of their study of scriptures and knowledge on *Brahman*.[34]
>
> Some constantly practise the regulation of the Prāṇic energy by blocking the movement of the in-breath and out-breath. They sacrifice the in-breath in the out-breath, and, similarly, the out-breath in the in-breath.[35]

---

32. *BG*, IV.26.
33. *BG*, IV.27.
34. *BG*, IV.28.
35. *BG*, IV.29.

In the process of *prāṇāyāma*, the intake of the Prāṇic energy is *pūraka*; its retention is *kumbhaka*; and its outgo is *recaka*. In this verse, the in-breath (inward force) is *prāṇa* and the out-breath (outward force) is *apāna*. When inhalations and exhalations are done through both the nostrils in equal durations, with or without a short *kumbhaka* after inhalations and exhalations, the *prāṇāyāma* is known as *ujjayī*. If accompanied by a mental *mantra-japa*, it may be *śvāsa-mantra-sama-tāna* (both inhalations and exhalations should be slow and deep, with synchronization of the *mantra-japa*). The *mantra* may be *om* while inhaling and the same *om* while exhaling. Alternatively, it may be the *ajapā-japa* (*so 'ham*), *so* while inhaling and *ham* while exhaling.

The above-mentioned verse also refers to alternate breathing in equal durations through the left and the right nostrils. After an exhalation through the left nostril (this step is not inclusive of the *prāṇāyāma*), inhalation is done through the left nostril, exhalation through the right nostril, inhalation through the right nostril, and then exhalation through the left nostril. This completes one cycle. The cycles are repeated. The durations of inhalations and exhalations are maintained almost the same. Optionally, a short *kumbhaka* may follow every inhalation and exhalation. In the final step, a long, deep inhalation through the left nostril is recommended. This last step is also not inclusive of the *prāṇāyāma*-cycles. This type is known as *kumbhaka-rahita-nāḍī-śodhana-prāṇāyāma* (*kumbhaka-rahita* means "without retention of breath").

> Yet others, with strictly regulated diets, sacrifice the Prāṇic breaths in the Prāṇic breaths. All of them, being conversant with sacrifice, destroy their sins by acts of sacrifice.[36]
>
> They take the ambrosial remains of these sacrifices and go to the timeless *Brahman*. The non-performer of sacrifices does not own even this world. How then, O the best of the Kuru princes, can he win the other world?[37]

36. *BG*, IV.30.

37. *BG*, IV.31.

> Thus have many sacrifices been spread out in the pages of the Vedas. Know them all to be born of action. Thus knowing, you shall be liberated.[38]

In this section, *yajñas*, in various forms, have been described. All of them are born of action. The *karma* (action) can be rendered into *akarma* (inaction) by offering the *karma* to *Brahman* (*brahmārpaṇam*). In the present context, "inaction" does not mean "renunciation of action" which is discouraged by the *BG*. Actions will be purged from their blemishes if the doer has knowledge on *Brahman*, realizes *Brahman* and offers his actions to *Brahman* (works for the welfare of the creation).

### 4.08: The Greatness of Knowledge on Brahman

Lord Vāsudeva has narrated varieties of *yajñas* for the guidance of Arjuna. Lastly he gives topmost importance to *jñāna-yoga* or *Brahma-jñāna* (knowledge on *Brahman*).

> O scourge of foes, *jñāna-yajña* (the sacrifice of knowledge on *Brahman*) is superior to that of materials. O son of Pṛthā (Arjuna), all actions, in entirety, culminate in knowledge.[39]

It may be mentioned here that material sacrifice (*dravya-yajña*) engenders fruits whereas *jñāna-yajña* does not. All other sacrifices, in entirety, undisputedly, culminate in knowledge on *Brahman*, which is the sole means to liberation (*mokṣa*).

The next questions are: How does one get *Brahma-jñāna*? Who will impart it? The Lord answers to these questions:

> Know that by obeisance, exhaustive questionings and services (to the *guru*, the spiritual preceptor). The wise who have realized the truth will impart that knowledge to you.[40]

*Gurus* (*ācāryas*) who have realized *Brahman* (who have *Brahmopalabdhi*) are *jñāna-yogīs*; they are the *sad-gurus* (genuine

---

38. *BG*, IV.32.
39. *BG*, IV.33.
40. *BG*, IV.34.

*gurus* of high spiritual order). Lowly prostrate your whole body before your *guru*. This is obeisance. Attend to your *guru* and please him by your sincere services. Ask questions to your *guru* again and again on nescience, bondage, knowledge, *Brahman*, liberation and others that arise in your mind.

By getting knowledge from the *brahma-jñānī guru*, one dispels one's delusion and becomes a seer of all (*sarva-darśī*). The Lord elaborates this point.

> Knowing which, you will not, O Pāṇḍava (Arjuna), again get deluded like this; and by which you will behold all beings in (your) self and then in Me.[41]

This verse establishes the identity of the *jīvātmā* (individual self) and the *Paramātmā* (Supreme Self or God) in the non-dualistic manner.

> Even if you are the worst among all sinners, by the raft of *Brahma*-knowledge alone, you will swim across all sins.[42]
>
> As blazing fire reduces all fuel to ashes, so, Arjuna, does the fire of *Brahma*-knowledge reduce all *karma* to ashes.[43]
>
> Verily, nothing exists here as purifying as *Brahma*-knowledge. Being perfected in Yoga (*karma-yoga* and *samādhi-yoga*), one attains to *Brahma*-knowledge in one's self after the lapse of a long time.[44]

There are some conditions and qualifying terms that must be fulfilled in order to gain *Brahma*-knowledge.

> The man of faith, intent on gaining *Brahma-jñāna*, and having mastered his senses, attains it. Once he has attained *Brahma-jñāna*, without delay, he goes to the state of supreme peace.[45]

---

41. *BG*, IV.35.
42. *BG*, IV.36.
43. *BG*, IV.37.
44. *BG*, IV.38.
45 *BG*, IV.39.

Three conditions have been mentioned in the aforesaid verse. 1. The person must have unwavering faith in God and in his *guru*. (The *guru* should be a *sadguru*, a spiritual preceptor with high, spiritual enlightenment, moral values and *Brahma*-realization). 2. He should be devoted to his *guru* and should strictly follow the instructions of the latter so that he can ascend the spiritual ladder at a speedy rate. 3. He should subdue his senses (*indriyas*) by withdrawing them from their objects.

> The person with ignorance and without faith and the doubting self perish. This world, the next world and happiness do not accrue to the doubter.[46]

Here "doubter" does not refer to a person who has doubts in issues on the empirical life and the empirical universe. On such issues, doubt (*saṁśaya*) is a boon. The average man accepts everything without questioning. Inquisitiveness has been blunted in him. It is the genius who does not accept anything without scrutinization. Doubt is the mother of discoveries and inventions.

Irrespective of the rating of intelligence, below average, average, above average, or exceptionally genius, agnostics, atheists, nihilists and sceptics whirl in the transmigratory world, full of agony. The situation, however, is totally different for a God-believer. It is not a fact that he has no doubts and questions. Even with *śraddhā* in God, he may have many doubts and questions on the empirical universe and on spiritual matters. His strong faith in God and his spiritual quest gradually lead him to the light of knowledge. Finally he becomes a knower of *Brahman*. The context of doubt must be well comprehended in order to get the correct meaning of the term used in the *BG*. The issue raised here is clarified by the verse to follow.

> O Dhanañjaya (winner of wealth, Arjuna), he who has renounced work through Yoga (*Brahma-jñāna*), who has slain

---

46. *BG*, IV.40.

> doubts with knowledge on *Brahman* and who is poised in the self is not bound by actions.[47]
>
> Therefore, O scion of Bharata (Arjuna), with the sword of knowledge slay the doubt in (your) heart born of nescience. Take refuge in Yoga (*jñāna-yoga*) and stand up.[48]

By this, we close the fourth chapter of the *BG*. The Lord repeatedly advises Arjuna to become a *karma-yogī.* At the same time, He says that *karma* has binding effect. To get rid of this binding effect, He has prescribed an antidote, and that is *jñāna-yoga* (the *yoga* of knowledge and realization of *Brahman*).

---

47. *BG*, IV.41.

48. *BG*, IV.42.

# 5

## Karma-Saṁnyāsa-Yogaḥ
## (The Way of Renunciation of Action)

### 5.01: Arjuna's Dilemma

AT the outset, let us remove a general confusion on the contextual use of the words "Sāṅkhya" and "Yoga" in the *BG*. In both the second and the fifth chapters of the *BG*, the word "Sāṅkhya" has no relation with Kapila's Sāṅkhya system of philosophy. It means *jñāna-yoga* (the *yoga* of knowledge and the realization of *Brahman*). Similarly, the word *yoga* contextually means *karma-yoga* (the *yoga* of performance of detached action without clinging to the fruits thereof).

We have repeatedly said that the *BG* teaches work-culture and does not favour the renunciation of work. It is a unique *yoga-śāstra* (sacred scripture on Yoga) in the annals of the history of humankind. It was born in a battlefield and a sacred battlefield. If one has a full comprehension of the background of the *BG*, one must realize that the book is on work-culture, with some conditions, of course. If the conditions are fulfilled, work is rendered into *karma-yoga*.

Being confused and bewildered, Arjuna asks the Lord:

> O Kṛṣṇa, you praise the renunciation of actions; and again their performance you praise. Tell me for certain which of the two is better.[1]

---

1. *BG*, V.1.

The Lord replies to Arjuna's question through a number of verses:

> Both renunciation of work (*karma-saṁnyāsa*) and performance of work (*karma-yoga*) promote the supreme good. But, of the two, *karma-yoga* is superior to the renunciation of actions.[2]
>
> O mighty-armed (Arjuna), he who neither shuns nor seeks should be known as a perpetual *saṁnyāsī* (renouncer). Because he is free from the pairs of opposites (*nirdvandva*), he is easily liberated from bondage.[3]

In this verse, the Lord does not maintain any distinction between a *karma-yogī* and a *karma-saṁnyāsī*. While working, the former neither shuns nor seeks anything and he is indifferent to pairs of opposites such as pleasure and pain, success and failure, and profit and loss.

The Lord also affirms the non-difference between *jñāna-yoga* (Sāṅkhya) and *karma-yoga* (Yoga). Equality of vision is common to both.

> Children (the ignorant ones), not the wise, affirm the difference between *jñāna-yoga* and *karma-yoga*. Even if one properly resorts to either one of them, one gains the fruit of both.[4]
>
> The status won by Sāṅkhya (*jñāna-yoga*) is also attained by *karma-yoga*. He who perceives Sāṅkhya and Yoga (*karma-yoga*) as one understands correctly.[5]
>
> But renunciation of action, without *karma-yoga*, O Mighty-Armed (Arjuna), is hard to be attained. With *karma-yoga*, the silent sage (*muni*) attains *Brahman* with no delay.[6]

Thus, the Lord tried to convince Arjuna that *karma-yoga* should never be neglected and that it should be the means to the attainment of *jñāna-yoga* and *karma-saṁnyāsa* (renunciation of action).

---

2. *BG*, V.2.
3. *BG*, V.3.
4. *BG*, V.4.
5. *BG*, V.5.
6. *BG*, V.6.

## 5.02: The Art of Converting Action into Non-Action

Through a number of verses, Lord Vāsudeva explains how the *yoga* of action serves as a means to the attainment of the *yoga* of knowledge.

> With mind united with God through *karma-yoga*, the *yogī* purifies his *citta* (the *antaḥkaraṇa*, the internal instrument, with three major components, namely, the *buddhi*, the *ahaṅkāra* and the *manas*) and controls his ego and senses. Then his self becomes the Self of all beings. At this state, he is not tainted even though he works.[7]
>
> The knower of the Reality, with mind united with God, thinks "I work not at all" even when he sees, hears, touches, smells, eats, walks, sleeps, breathes, talks, evacuates, holds, opens and closes the eyes, knowing that the senses move among sense-objects.[8]
>
> Reposing all actions in *Brahman*, forsaking attachment, the *karma-yogī* works. He is not stained by sin as water does not moisten the lotus-leaf.[9]
>
> With mere body, mind, intellect and senses, the *karma-yogī* performs actions, forsaking attachment for self-purification (*sattva-śuddhi* or *citta-śuddhi*).[10]
>
> The *karma-yogī*, giving up the fruits of actions, attains peace, born of steadfastness. The non-*yogī* worker, attached to the fruits by the force of cravings, is bound.[11]
>
> The embodied being, self-controlled (one who has conquered his senses), mentally renouncing all works, happily sits in the nine-gated city, neither working or causing others to work.[12]

The expression "All works" in this verse refers to the obligatory, occasional, desire-prompted and forbidden works. The nine gates

---

7. *BG*, V.7.
8. *BG*, V.8-9.
9. *BG*, V.10.
10. *BG*, V.11.
11. *BG*, V.12.
12. *BG*, V.13.

of the body are: The seven openings in the head (the two eyes, two ears, two nostrils and the mouth), the anus and the urethra. The self (*jīvātmā*) resides in the city of the body, having given up all works.

This topic presents the art or skill in converting action into inaction. Even though the body works, the self is not subjected to bondage like a lotus-leaf floating on water.

### 5.03: The Non-Doer Self

The Self (*Paramātmā*) and the self (*jīvātmā*) are identical except for one difference. *Brahman*, with *Māyā* as the *upādhi* (limiting adjunct), is *Īśvara* (God, Self), whereas *Brahman*, with an individual living being as the *upādhi*, is the self (*jīvātmā*). Advaita Vedānta holds that *Brahman* is formless, attributeless, functionless, non-relational, spaceless, timeless and eternally and timelessly immutable. *Brahman*, the Self and the self being identical, the *BG* re-affirms the truth that the Self or the self is a non-doer (*akarttā*). Many religious scriptures describe God as the doer of cosmic and individual actions and also as the agent who induces all living and non-living beings to work. But contrary is the opinion of the *BG*.

> The Lord creates neither agency nor objects (to act upon) for the world; nor does He unite the fruit with the action. It is *svabhāva* that acts.[13]

The word *svabhāva* literally means "own state." It is otherwise known as the *prakṛti* of a person. The *svabhāva* or the *prakṛti* of an individual person is his innate tendency, born of the karmic impressions (*karma-saṁskāras*) accumulated in the subtle and the causal bodies during the previous births. Śaṅkara has equated *svabhāva* with *Māyā* (the Power of God/*Brahman*) or the *Mūla-Prakṛti* (the Primordial Nature) that remains always Unmanifested (*Avyakta*). On the point of the identity of *svabhāva* and *Māyā*, as conceived by Śaṅkara, we do not agree with him, with reference

13. *BG*, V.14.

to the present verse. He is, of course, right if he identifies Cosmic *Svabhāva* and *Māyā*. But, in the present context, the verse of the *BG* speaks of the individual *svabhāva*. We make a further clarification on the individual *svabhāva*. For all practical purposes, it is the *antaḥkaraṇa* that is the *svabhāva* that works. Neither God (the *Puruṣa*) nor *Māyā* (the *Prakṛti*) works for any individual, either living or non-living entity.

> The omnipresent Lord accepts nobody's sin or merit. Knowledge is shrouded in ignorance. Hence, do living beings get deluded.[14]

The edifices of religions would collapse if doership of the actions of individual beings is ascribed to God. In that case, any individual would not be responsible for his good or bad actions. The statement that God is Truth (*Satya*), Benign or Benevolent (*Śiva*) and Beautiful (*Sundara*) would be meaningless if He makes the murderer to commit murder and the rapist to commit rape. Moreover, the noble-hearted, saintly person would not deserve any credit for his righteousness. Religion and spirituality could be topsy-turvy if God becomes the agent of the actions of individual entities, either living beings or lifeless things — micro or macro. Even *Māyā*, the Power or Consort of God, is not the agent of the actions of individual entities. She is God's executive agent for actions at a cosmic level, creation, sustenance and dissolution. The maintenance of Cosmic Order is an important activity of sustenance. *Māyā* does intervene in the activities of individuals if and when those activities disturb the Cosmic Order. She also prompts some individuals to act on Her behalf for the restoration of Cosmic Order.

Duryodhana, the wicked Kaurava prince, disowned his responsibility and threw it on the shoulders of God, Lord Hṛṣīkeśa (Vāsudeva) when death was imminent for the former. He presented his plea like this: "I know what righteousness is. I do not have a tendency (a propensity) to adopt it. I know what unrighteousness is. I do not have a tendency to refrain myself

14. *BG*, V.15.

from it. O Hṛṣīkeśa, dwelling in my heart, you prompt me to work, and I act in whatever way you engage me.[15]

Some religious scriptures assert that it is God who acts and makes every entity of the universe and the whole universe act in whatever way He wills. The *BG* does not agree to this sort of claim. God is the Chairperson (*Adhyakṣa*) of the cosmic activities. The Power of God (*Īśvara-Śakti* or *Māyā*) is His executive agent for the creation, maintenance and dissolution of the universe. God rules and controls the universe through His Power, the *Māyā-Śakti*. But it is to be recognized that each and every created entity has the ability to function and does function. This freedom of action is limited, however. Whenever anything or anybody tries to upset the Cosmic Order, divine intervention sets in, through the agency of *Māyā*, to restore the order.

We may support what we said by citing an incidence from the *Mahābhārata*. Lord Vāsudeva did not engage Duryodhana and Duḥśāsana to make the barbarous attempt to undress Draupadī in the Royal Assembly (*Rāja-Sabhā*). Had there been no grace of the Lord, these culprits would have been successful in stripping the Pāṇḍava queen of her clothes. The Lord approached the Kauravas to beg for five villages only on behalf of the Pāṇḍavas. It was a humble begging and a sincere attempt to avert the terrible War. Duryodhana, at the behest of his maternal uncle, Śakuni, bluntly rejected the request and vainly attempted to put the Lord into prison. No persuasion and advice made by his parents and superiors could prevent Duryodhana from ill-treating the Lord. All persons present in the Royal Assembly had the vision of the world-image (*viśva-rūpa*) of the Lord. Even the blind king Dhṛtarāṣṭra had the vision. The Lord blessed the blind king and gave him temporary vision to get a glimpse of the world-image of the Lord. Dhṛtarāṣṭra, being intensely delighted, devotedly prayed to the Lord: "O God, after seeing your world-image, I have nothing else to see. Please make me blind again." The Lord

15. Quoted from *The Pāṇḍava-Gītā*.

did what the blind king desired. But Duryodhana could not be moved. Śakuni and Duryodhana were responsible for the massacre and cruel bloodshed in the Mahābhārata War. God was, of course, sitting in their hearts. But He did not give the ill advice to them to opt for the War.

Having accepted the teaching of the *BG* that God is non-doer (*akarttā*), we have to explain the fact that insentient beings are able to work. *Māyā* is insentient (*jaḍa*). The created universe of matter and energy is insentient. *Virāḍ* or *Mahat* is insentient. The *antaḥkaraṇa* or the internal mind-complex is insentient. Only *Brahman/Īśvara* is sentient and omniscient. Is it possible for an entity to function meaningfully in the absence of consciousness? It is a valid question and it has a valid answer too. Only *Brahman* is the fundamental and pure Consciousness. It is non-functional. Consciousnness is a prerequisite for an entity to be functional. The light of Consciousness of all-pervasive *Brahman*, being reflected on *Māyā* and the entities created by Her, renders the latter conscious due to induction of consciousness. Thus, everything in the universe, micro or macro, lifeless or living, is conscious. Of course, the quantity and quality of consciousness vary depending upon the level of evolution of the mental apparatus in the subtle body and the nervous system in the gross body. The human being has five sheaths, namely, the *annamaya kośa* (the material sheath), the *prāṇamaya kośa* (the vital sheath), the *manomaya kośa* (the mental sheath), the *vijñānamaya kośa* (the intellectual sheath) and the *ānandamaya kośa* (the blissful sheath). Particles or micro-particles like the proton, electron, photon or neutrino have the first three sheaths on the lower rungs of the evolutionary ladder. But they are not in possession of the higher two sheaths. It may be mentioned here that *Prāṇa* is not life (*jīvana*) and that it is the super-unified force, without which work is not possible. All the four fundamental forces are the offspring of *Prāṇa*.

The title of this topic is "The Non-Doer Self." God is the ruler and controller of the entire universe. He is the creator, sustainer and destroyer of the entire universe. In spite of the recognition of these facts, the *BG* gives the idea of the non-doer Self. One has to comprehend the metaphysics of the Vedānta in order to dispel any misunderstanding of apparent contradictions.

**5.04: Brahma-Jñāna Begets Brahma-Nirvāṇa**

In this topic and elsewhere in the *BG*, we come across words like knowledge (*jñāna*), ignorance or nescience (*ajñāna, avidyā*), a wise man (*paṇḍita*, pundit) and *Brahma-nirvāṇa* (merging in *Brahman* and becoming *Brahman*, by losing individual identity). First we should elucidate the meaning in use of these terms.

The literal meaning of *jñāna* is "knowledge," without any qualification. The contextual meaning of this term in the *BG* is "knowledge on *Brahman*, with full realization." This word, in the Vedānta, does not refer to any informational knowledge on the material universe or any atheistic ideas and doctrines. *Vidyā* is a synonym of *jñāna*. The lack of *vidyā* is *avidyā*. The lack of *jñāna* is *ajñāna*. These word-pairs are contradictory terms. We use the English words "ignorance" or "nescience" for the Sanskrit word *avidyā* or *ajñānam*. In the Vedānta in general and in the *BG* in particular, a wise man is he who has known and realized *Brahman*. He is otherwise known as a *jñānī, prajñāvān* or *paṇḍita*. The Sanskrit word *nirvāṇa* literally means "the act of being extinguished." It is an important concept in the Buddhist philosophy which cherishes the doctrine of no-self (*anātma-vāda*) and uses the word *nirvāṇa* for the reduction of an individual mental complex to nihility. Its lexicographic meaning is: "perfect bliss and release from *karma*, attained by the extinction of individuality." Buddhism holds the doctrine of flush and does not accept the existence of any immutable Reality such as *Brahman*, permanently existing in an unchangeable state. It adheres to the doctrine of nihilism (*śūnya-vāda*) whereas the Vedānta steadfastly adheres to *pūrṇa-vāda* (the doctrine of plenum or fullness). The compound word *Brahma-nirvāṇa*, used in the *BG*, has the Vedāntic relevance. It accepts the Vedāntic maxim "The knower of *Brahman* becomes *Brahman* (*brahmavid brahmaiva bhavati*). The self of one who attains *Brahma-*

*nirvāṇa* loses its separate identity and characteristics after becoming the Self or *Brahman*. It is to be noted that Vedāntic *Brahma-nirvāṇa* discards the concept of being extinguished and being reduced to nihility (nothingness).

Now we quote a number of verses from the *BG* to elucidate the topic:

> But, for them whose ignorance is destroyed by knowledge of the Self, their knowledge reveals the Supreme, like the sun (revealing objects).[16]
>
> Those whose self is That (the Supreme *Brahman*), who have their intellect absorbed in That, who steadfastly make That as their supreme abode and who are devoted to That, having cleansed their impurities by knowledge, proceed to the status (of *Brahman*) whence there is no return.[17]

When a person becomes a *Brahma-jñānī* (knower of *Brahman*), *Brahmānubhavī* (a realizer of *Brahman*), a *Brahma-darśī* (a seer of *Brahman*, that is, he sees everything in *Brahman* and sees *Brahman* in everything), he becomes a *sama-darśī* (he sees the same Supreme Self everywhere and in everything).

> The wise become *sama-darśī* (have equality of vision). They perceive the same in a *brāhmaṇa*, endowed with knowledge and humility, a cow, an elephant, a dog and a dog-eater. (In all, he sees *Brahman* and nothing else.)[18]

A *Brahma-darśī* who is a *sama-darśī* is not required to wait for his liberation subsequent to his death. He is emancipated even in this life in this world.

> Even here is birth vanquished by them whose minds abide in equality. Hence, they rest in *Brahman* that is flawless indeed and is the same homogeneously.[19]

---

16. *BG*, V.16.
17. *BG*, V.17.
18. *BG*, V.18.
19. *BG*, V.19.

Once the sage abides in *Brahman* and, being a *sama-darśī*, sees *Brahman* everywhere and in everything, he becomes free from delusion and is not affected by the empirical contradictoriness.

When a person fixes his mind in *Brahman*, is united with *Brahman* (becomes *Brahma-yukta*), sees everything in *Brahman* and sees *Brahman* in everything, he attains to *Brahma-nirvāṇa* and becomes a *karma-saṁnyāsa-yogī*. He renounces actions although he still works for the welfare of the creation of God, with no attachment to the fruits thereof.

### 5.05: The Peace and Bliss of a Brahma-Jñānī

It has already been said that a *jñāna-yogī* is one who is a knower of *Brahman* and a realizer of *Brahman*. He is not affected by opposites such as pleasure and pain.

> He who knows *Brahman* and abides in *Brahman*, with a steady intellect and being undeluded, should not be elated when gaining the pleasant and should not grieve on obtaining the unpleasant.[20]
>
> With the inner sense (*antaḥkaraṇa*) unattached to external contacts, he realizes bliss that is in the Self (*Brahman*). His self, being united with *Brahman*, he enjoys inexhaustible bliss.[21]
>
> Since enjoyments, born of objective contacts, generate pain only, O son of Kuntī (Arjuna), they have a beginning and an end. The wise man does not delight in them.[22]
>
> He who can withstand even here (in this life) — before the fall of his body — the urge of lust and wrath, being united (with *Brahman*), is happy.[23]
>
> He who is joyful within, who sports within and is lighted within is a *yogī* who becomes *Brahman* and attains to the bliss of *Brahman*.[24]

20. *BG*, V.20.
21. *BG*, V.21.
22. *BG*, V.22.
23. *BG*, V.23.
24. *BG*, V.24.

In this verse, "within" means "within the Self." The word *Brahma-nirvāṇa* in this verse, in the verse to follow and elsewhere in the *BG* unambiguously supports the philosophy of the non-dualistic Vedānta. After the self (*jīvātmā*) gets liberation (*mokṣa*), it loses its own identity and becomes one with *Brahman*.

> The seers, gaining identity with *Brahman* (liberated even though still living), having got their blemishes attenuated, doubts dispelled and their inner sense (*antaḥkaraṇa*) controlled, become busy for the promotion of the welfare of all beings.[25]
>
> The ascetics, free from lust and wrath, with the inner sense disciplined, having the right perception of the Self (*Brahman*), attain *Brahma-nirvāṇa* on both sides (gain the peace of *Brahman* both when they are alive and dead).[26]

In reality, this is the status of a *jīvanmukta* (a person liberated even though still living). An identity has already been established between the Self and his self. He is *Brahman* while living; he is *Brahman* after death. He gets the peace and bliss of *Brahman* on both sides of his death. It must be noted, however, that his material body is still subjected to growth, decay, diseases and death and that he cannot exercise the power of creation, sustenance and dissolution. After the death, a liberated self loses its identity, being merged in *Brahman*, and hence cannot separately function as God or a god.

> Having shut out external contacts, fixing the eyes between the eyebrows, equalizing the in-breath (*prāṇa*) and the out-breath (*apāna*) moving within the nostrils, controlling the senses, mind and intellect, getting rid of desire, fear and anger, the silent sage (*muni*), intent on liberation as the supreme goal, is eternally emancipated.[27]

In these two verses, the *BG* has briefly described the essential features of the *rāja-yoga* or the *samādhi-yoga*. For such a *yogī*,

---

25. *BG*, V.25.
26. *BG*,V.26.
27. *BG*, V.27-8.

liberation (*mokṣa*) is the final refuge and goal. And he gets it.

> Having known Me (God) as the partaker of sacrifices (*yajña*) and penances (*tapaḥ*), the Supreme Controller of the worlds (the whole universe) and the friend of all beings, he (the silent sage) attains peace.[28]

With this, we complete the fifth chapter of the *BG* on *karma-saṁnyāsa-yoga* (the way of renunciation of action). Nowhere does the Lord teach Arjuna to resort to inaction. Notwithstanding this fact, one should have a comprehension of the spiritual meaning of inaction.

28. *BG*, V.29.

# 6

# Dhyāna-Yogaḥ
## (The Way of Meditation)

### 6.01: The Simultaneous Practice of Saṁnyāsa and Yoga

It is a general belief of the common man that a *saṁnyāsī* must resort to renunciation of all actions. It has already been emphasized that the *BG* does not teach renunciation of all actions. One can (rather should) simultaneously be a *karma-yogī*, a *saṁnyāsī* (renouncer) and a *dhyāna-yogī* (one who has mental composure through mind's concentration). The *BG* starts the sixth chapter by the following verse:

> Without depending on the fruits of action, whosoever performs the work that ought to be done is a *saṁnyāsī* and a *yogī* (*karma-yogī*); but not he who is a non-worker and who has given up the household fire-rituals (*agnihotra*).[1]

Some elaboration is necessary for explaining some terms of this verse. One who plans and performs some work gets the benefit of the work for himself or for social welfare. There is nothing wrong in getting the benefit. But craving for the fruits of action is proscribed by the *Gītā*. For performing one's duty, one should not lean on or depend upon the fruits of action. In other words, one should be *anāśritaḥ*.

There is a second important expression in the verse. "Do the work that ought to be done (*kāryaṁ karma samācara*)." Never perform an *akāryaṁ karma* (any work that should not be done).

---

1. *BG*, VI.1.

A question may be asked: "What is the purpose of associating *dhyāna-yoga* with *karma-yoga* and *saṁnyāsa-yoga*?" Without mental composure attained through the practice of mind's concentration, and without uniting the self with the Supreme Self, it would be difficult to give up craving for the fruits of action. And, without renouncing craving for the fruits of action, *saṁnyāsa* (renunciation) is not possible. On this point, the *BG* says:

> O Pāṇḍava (Arjuna, the son of Pāṇḍu), know that which they call *saṁnyāsa* (renunciation) to be *yoga*; for none becomes a *yogī* without renouncing *saṅkalpa*.[2]

Renunciation is characterized by the rejection of all works and the craving for the fruits thereof. It seems to be contradictory to practise *karma-yoga* and *karma-saṁnyāsa* simultaneously. The solution lies in the rejection of *saṅkalpa*.

What is *saṅkalpa*? Should one reject *saṅkalpa* in all circumstances? The word *saṅkalpa* has a number of meanings: 1. Will, volition, mental resolve; 2. purpose, determination; 3. a solemn vow to perform an observance; 4. expectation of advantage from a holy voluntary act; and 5. craving desire for the fruits of action done. A *saṁnyāsī* should abandon the craving desire for the fruits of action. But he has also a *saṅkalpa* to ascend the ladder of spirituality and attain liberation. A firm determination to perform a good action must not be abandoned. Contextually speaking, here the *BG* prescribes rejection of *saṅkalpa*, that is, craving for the fruits of action.

*Karma-yoga*, devoid of attachment to the result, is an external aid to *dhyāna-yoga*. So does the Lord declare:

> For the silent sage (*muni*) who seeks to ascend the ladder of *yoga* to reach its peak, work (*karma-yoga*) is said to be the cause (of the ascension). For the very sage who has reached the summit, quiescence (*śama*) or inaction (*saṁnyāsa*) is said to be the cause (of *mokṣa*).[3]

---

2. *BG*, VI.2.

3. *BG*, VI.3.

Next, the Lord elaborates the traits of a *yogārūḍha* (one who has ascended the ladder of *yoga* and reached its peak) person.

> When the sage, being no longer attached to the objects of the senses, works, renouncing all *saṅkalpas*, he is said to have scaled the ladder of *yoga* and reached its peak (that is, he is a *yogārūḍha*).[4]

Desire springs from thought. Its root lies in *saṅkalpa*. Having renounced all *saṅkalpas*, one gives up all desires and all actions. Once a person becomes *yogārūḍha* (stationed on the summit of *yoga*), his self becomes lifted up by himself above the empirical turmoils of the worldly life.

### 6.02: You Can Be Your Own Friend or Foe

In topic 1 of chapter 6 of the *BG*, ascent to the summit of *yoga* (in other words, the gradual ascension to attain to the *yogārūḍha* state) has been prescribed. One becomes a *karma-yogī*, practises *dhyāna-yoga*, renounces all *saṅkalpas* and finally becomes *yogārūḍha* (reaches the peak of *yoga*). At the *yogārūḍha* state, the sage renounces all *saṅkalpas*, all desires and all actions. Thus, one lifts up by oneself from the worldly multitude of evils.

In attaining the *yogārūḍha* state, one has to lift oneself up. Instead of lifting up, one may also sink into the fathomless ocean of worldly turmoils. In the former case, one will be blissful; in the latter case, one will be sorrowful and agonized. Let us be acquainted with what the *BG* says on this topic.

> A person should elevate himself by himself; he should not sink (submerge) himself. He alone is his friend or his foe.[5]

This verse uses the term *ātmā* in a different sense. Here this word means neither "the individual self (*jīvātmā*)" nor "the Universal Self (*Paramātmā*)." It carries the ordinary sense of "self." A person himself does lift himself or sink himself by the actions of his *buddhi*, *ahaṅkāra* and *manas*.

4. *BG*, VI.4.
5. *BG*, VI.5.

> He who has verily conquered his self by his self has his own self as the friend. But the self alone verily operates as the foe of one who is not self-controlled.[6]

One conquers oneself (one is self-controlled) by subduing the aggregate of the body and the senses. One who cannot subdue one's body and senses by the activity of his *buddhi*, *ahaṅkāra* and *manas* is not self-controlled. The self-controlled person is his own friend. He who is not self-controlled is his own enemy. One who has already attained the *yogārūḍha* state is self-controlled.

> The Supreme Self exists as the immediate One (*sākṣāt ātmabhāvena vartate* = is directly experienced without any mediation) for him who is self-controlled and serene (whose *antaḥkaraṇa* or inner sense has been tranquillized). He is equanimous in opposite states like cold and heat, pleasure and pain, and honour and dishonour.[7]

> The *yogī* (the *yogārūḍha* sage), having subdued his senses, being content with wisdom (*jñāna*) and realization of the Self (*vijñāna* = *Brahmopalabdhi* = *Brahma-jñāna*), having attained the immutable (changeless) state, is said to be in communion with the Supreme Lord. To him, a lump of earth, a stone and a piece of gold are all alike.[8]

> He whose intellect is the same in respect of the well-wisher, the friend, the foe, the one who is indifferent or neutral, the arbitrator (arbiter), the hateful, the relative, also the righteous and the unrighteous, attains excellence.[9]

The *dhyāna-yogī* derives indirect (*parokṣa*) and direct (*aparokṣa*, *pratyakṣa*, *sākṣāt*) knowledge. Through the direct experience (*aparokṣānubhūti*) of *Brahman*, he gets the conviction that there is nothing more to be known or to be done. At this peak state of *yoga*, he becomes a *Brahma-vit* (knower of *Brahman*). And a knower of *Brahman* verily becomes *Brahman*. At this state, he is composed

6. *BG*, VI.6.
7. *BG*, VI.7.
8. *BG*, VI.8.
9. *BG*, VI.9.

and unshakable; he is devoid of elation, dejection, anger, desire and delusion. He is freed.

### 6.03: Conditions to Be Set for Meditation

The *BG* is a composite scripture that teaches how to lead a holistic life. Unlike the *Pātañjala Yoga Darśanaṁ*, it does not provide details on meditation (*dhyāna* or *samādhi yoga*). In spite of this fact, it does prescribe meditation in a synoptic way. In this regard, we would present here eight verses of the *BG* (6.10-17) to focus on the topic of meditation.

> Retiring into solitude, living alone, with controlled mind and body, free from cravings, owning nothing (without accumulation of property), the *yogī* ought to practise concentration of mind (*ātmā* = *antaḥkaraṇa*) incessantly.[10]

Now the *BG* describes some preliminary conditions preparatory to the practice of *dhyāna*.

> Setting one's own firm seat in a clean spot, neither too high nor too low, spreading *kuśa*-grass, a hide (of a deer or tiger) on the grass and a cloth on the hide, sitting on it, making the mind one-pointed and controlling the functions of the mind and senses, the *yogī* practises *dhyāna-yoga* for self-purification (the purification of the *antaḥkaraṇa* = *buddhi* + *ahaṅkāra* + *manas*).[11]

It may be mentioned here that the seat of a *yogī* must fulfil two conditions, namely, (1) the provision of a cushion (not too soft) for a comfortable sitting and (2) sufficient insulation to prevent the leakage of the Prāṇic energy to the ground. In the days of yore, the *yogī*s were using hides of dead animals (not hunted and killed animals) for their seats. On ecological grounds, the laws of many countries now do not allow the possession of the skins of wild animals. Hence, the use of skins or hides of animals for meditational purpose may be dispensed with in the present conditions.

---

10. *BG*, VI.10.
11. *BG*, VI.11-12.

> Holding the torso, neck and head in an erect, motionless and steady condition, gazing on one's nose-tip, without looking around, tranquillizing the inner sense (*antaḥkaraṇa*), forsaking all sorts of fear, being firm in the vow of a *brahmacārī*, controlling the mind, the integrated *yogī*, keeping his thoughts anchored in Me (God), deems Me (God) as the Supreme Reality.[12]
>
> Thus, keeping himself without interruption, disciplining the mind, the *yogī* attains peace abiding in Me (God), (finally) culminating in emancipation (*nirvāṇa, mokṣa*).[13]

The *yogī* has to regulate his food, sleep, rest and such other routine activities in order to maintain physical and mental health. In this regard, the Lord prescribes a middle path.

> O Arjuna, it is not *yoga* for him who eats too much or who does not eat at all; not for him who sleeps too much or who is (always) awake.[14]
>
> One who is moderate in eating and recreation, moderate in exertion in working, moderate in sleep and wakefulness (practises) *yoga* that destroys all pains.[15]

What has been said in this topic does not cover the techniques of meditation. The conditions that are conducive to successful meditation have been laid down. Under all circumstances, they are important means to success in meditation.

### 6.04: The Greatest Gain of the United

The Sanskrit word *yoga* is derived from the verb-root *yuj* which means "to unite," "to yoke," "to link," "to be merged." The *BG* lays more emphasis on the etymology of the word *yoga*, and, hence, its definition of *yoga* comprises two criteria, intense devotion and meditative, deep concentration. One who fulfils these two criteria is really united with God; his individual self is united with the

12. *BG*, VI.13-14.
13. *BG*, VI.15.
14. *BG*, VI.16.
15. *BG*, VI.17.

Universal (Supreme) Self; he is a *yogī*. This link cannot be established by mechanical concentration only. Devotional concentration is the means to the end of being united. The *BG* does not recognize anything like secular or atheistic *yoga*.

For the elaboration of this topic, we will take the help of six verses of the *BG* (6.18-23).

> The *yogī* completely controls his mind. He rests in the Self (God, *Paramātmā*) alone. He becomes neutral to longing for all worldly desires. When he fulfils these conditions, he is said to be united (*yukta*).[16]

> A lamp in a windless spot does not flicker. This is the simile for a *yogī* who has controlled his mind and practised one-pointed concentration.[17]

By nature, the mind is always in motion like a flickering lamp in a windy atmosphere. It stirs from moment to moment. All types of thoughts enter into it. This natural condition of the flickering mind is totally changed by the *yogī* through the practice of concentration. He fully merges his self (*ātmā*) in the Self (*Paramātmā*, God). It is the state of *samādhi*, an establishment of complete identity with the Supreme Self.

> When the motionless mind, withdrawing from objects by the practice of *yoga*, attains quietude, the *yogī* rejoices in the Self, beholding the Self by his inner sense (*antaḥkaraṇa*).[18]

> The *yogī*, after attaining the *samādhi* state, experiences infinite bliss, grasped only by the intellect (*buddhi*). This bliss (*atīndriyaṁ sukham*) is not generated by objects and, hence, transcends the sense-organs. Thus, having been anchored in the Self, the *yogī* does not move away from the Reality.[19]

> Having been anchored in the Self and having experienced the

16. *BG*, VI.18.
17. *BG*, VI.19.
18. *BG*, VI.20.
19. *BG*, VI.21.

> limitless bliss, the *yogī* deems no other gain greater. Being established in the Self, he is not shaken even by great sorrow and is not overpowered even by grievous pain.[20]

A person hankers after different types of gain such as more and more wealth, power, position, name and fame, dominance over others, sensual pleasure and so many other worldly profits (*lābha*). A *yogī*, however, after having been established in the Self, attains the supreme gain. For him, no other acquisition is superior to this spiritual gain.

It is not claimed that no calamity would befall a *yogī* who has established himself in the Self (Reality, Universal Self). But he is not shaken by any natural calamity or man-made inflictions and any type of grievous danger.

Doubts may arise in the minds of persons in the statement that an accomplished *yogī*, established in the Self through *dhyāna* (yogic concentration), is not disturbed at all by any grievous pain or dangerous situations. Our counsel is short and simple: "Do it and feel." You have to experiment and experience. So does the Lord say :

> Know the *yoga* as the disjunction from experienced pain or as the severence from the contact of pain. It has slowly and gradually got to be practised with conviction and an undejected mind.[21]

### 6.05: Infinite Bliss in Meditation through Communion with *Brahman*

This section deals with *samādhi*, the eighth and the highest limb of the *rāja-yoga* of Patañjali. (Patañjali lived in an era much later than that of the *Mahābhārata*. Still his system of *rāja-yoga* was as old as the Vedas). *Samādhi* is the climax state of meditative *yoga*, and, in this state, the *yogī*'s self completely merges in the Supreme Self and thereby he gets infinite bliss.

20. *BG*, VI.22.

21. *BG*, VI.23.

> Wholly abandoning all desires born of *saṅkalpa* and controlling, on all directions, the whole group of senses by the mind alone, by slow steps, one should withdraw with the help of the resolute intellect. Anchoring the mind in the Self, one should think of nothing whatsoever.[22]

The complete inactivity of the mind or the total absence of thoughts in the mind (*bhāvaśūnyāvasthā*) is an essential condition of successful *samādhi-yoga*, the peak of the meditational state. This state has been emphasized in this verse. Some *yoga* schools express this state by the use of the language *bhāvātīta dhyāna*. Such expression is not correct, however. There is a thought and a single thought, flowing uninterruptedly, in *dhyāna* (the seventh limb of *yoga*). *Samādhi* transcends the state of *dhyāna*. This transcendental state, the eighth and the summit state of *yoga*, has been classically named as *samādhi*.

"Think of nothing whatsoever" is a difficult task. By nature, the mind is always active, restless and wandering. On this point, the *BG* prescribes:

> Curbing the restless, unsteady mind wandering away from all causes whatever, one should bring it under the sole control of the Self.[23]

In our book, *Meditation: Science and Practice*,[24] we have prescribed Patañjali's technique for attaining to a thoughtless state. If one is initiated by a *guru*, one should silently do the *japa* of the *guru-mantra* for a couple of minutes, then should do the mental *japa* of *om* (or any other monosyllabic *mantra*) for two to three minutes. After the suspension of the *mantra-japa*, one should remain in a thoughtless state as long as possible (say, for five to twenty minutes). If thoughts, extraneous or endogenous, disturb the waveless state of the mind, one should resume the *japa* of *om* for a short while and again come back to the thoughtless state. Thus,

---

22. *BG*, VI.24-25.
23. *BG*, VI.26.
24. N.C. Panda, 2003a.

the monosyllabic *mantra* serves as a support (*ālambanam*) for the removal of thoughts. One may directly do the mental *japa* of *om* in the beginning before coming to the thoughtless state if one is not initiated. But it is to be noted that the initial mental *japa* of *om* is an indispensable prerequisite for attaining to the thoughtless state. Of course, for accomplished *yogīs*, any *japa* may not be necessary to abruptly come to the *samādhi* state.

A perfect *yogī* is fully absorbed in *Brahman* during the period of *samādhi*. His blissful state is described by the *BG* as follows:

> Verily, supreme bliss accrues to this sinless *yogī*, with tranquil mind and quieted passion, who has become *Brahman*.[25]
>
> Thus, uniting himself always (with God), the sinless *yogī* attains, with ease, to infinite bliss due to contact with *Brahman*.[26]

The *yogī*, after reaching this elevated state of *yoga*, becomes a *jīvan-mukta* (free or liberated albeit still living). He becomes *Brahman*.

### 6.06: God in All, All in God — A Yogic Vision

It has already been said that the Sanskrit word *yoga* has been derived from the verb-root *yuj*, meaning "to yoke," "to unite," "to add." When talking about *yoga*, the *Gītā* lays much importance on this meaning. Any practice, physical or mental, is not *yoga*, if it does not facilitate the yoking of the *ātmā* (the individual self) to the *Ātmā* (the Universal Self, *Brahman* or God). The same non-spiritual or secular, physical and mental techniques may be beneficial to the body and the mind. They may prevent and cure many diseases. They may improve the health of the body and the mind. But they do not find a place as *yoga* in the spiritual science, since they cannot link the *jīva* with God.

> He who unites his self with the Supreme Self through *yoga* gets equality of vision everywhere. He beholds the Supreme Self in all beings and all beings in the Supreme Self.[27]

---

25. *BG*, VI.27.

26. *BG*, VI.28.

27. *BG*, VI.29.

The *yogī*, constantly uniting his individual self with the Universal Self (*Brahman* or God), sees the same everywhere. Possessed by the cognition of the identity of *Brahman* and his own self, he beholds the Self, abiding in all beings, and all beings (both inanimate and animate, including even the Creator, Brahmā) in the Self. This state of the *yogī* is that of *samadarśana* (seeing the same everywhere, an equal vision of identity, without any distinction whatsoever in the whole cosmos).

> For him who beholds Me everywhere and beholds everything in Me, I am not lost to him; neither is he lost to Me.[28]

When a *yogī* becomes a *samadarśī* (seeing all in the Self and seeing the Self in all), as described in the foregoing paragraph, he gets plenary knowledge and cosmic vision. He sees God everywhere and sees all things (the whole aggregate of beings) in God. When it happens, God does not get lost for him, nor does he get lost for God.

The concept of God in everything and everything in God may not be misunderstood. The Western philosophy of monism, identifying God with the universe, is not stated in the verse referred to. The Advaita philosophy (Non-dualism) is different from monism. It does not equate the universe and God. It holds that God is both immanent and transcendent. *Brahman*, the underlying Reality (*adhiṣṭhāna*) appears as the phenomenal universe. Śaṅkara names it as *adhyāsa-vāda* (*atasmiṁstadbuddhiḥ*).[29] The post-Śaṅkara non-dualists rename it as *vivartta-vāda*[30] that says that the universe is an illusory appearance of *Brahman*, in the analogy of seeing a snake in the place of a rope. We do accept the illusory appearance of the universe on the substratum of *Brahman*; but we are not in favour of the extreme illusionism (in fact, the doctrine of hallucination) that asserts the nothingness of the

28. *BG*, VI.30.

29. *BSŚB*, Intr.

30. *Ṛ̥V*, X.129.3; *PD*, VI.130.

universe. The universe is not non-existent. It is transitory and changeable. It does not permanently stay as it is. The appearance of the universe, as experienced by our senses, is illusory. But *Brahman* which appears as the multiplicity of the universe is the Absolute Truth. How does B appear as non-B and many non-B's? *Brahman*, the unchangeable, unmodifiable, attributeless, functionless, formless and non-relational Reality functions as the substratum (*adhiṣṭhāna*) to appear as the empirical, phenomenal universe. It becomes a self-contradictory fallacy. Māyā, the Power of *Brahman* through Her projecting power (*vikṣepa-śakti*) and concealing power (*āvaraṇa-śakti*) spreads Her magical net. And so is the genesis of the universe which is usable and not nothing. It is not only usable for us. It is primarily meant for the sportive play (*līlā*) of *Puruṣa* and *Prakṛti*.[31]

The two verses of the *Gītā*, quoted here (6.29-30), go in favour of non-dualism rather than dualism. They unambiguously establish the identity of the individual self (*jīvātmā*) and the Universal Self (*Paramātmā*).

When the *yogī* reaches the state of *Brahma*-realization, as described in the two verses, he attains to the state of liberation (*mokṣa*). The next verse of the *Gītā* is clear on this point.

> He who, having been established in the Super-Unified Existence, adores Me dwelling in all beings, is the *yogī* who abides in Me, no matter how his mode of life is.[32]

When the self (*jīvātmā*) abides in Viṣṇu (*Paramātmā*, God), he attains the state of Godhead. That is his *mokṣa* (liberation).

What has been described in these three verses of the *BG* is the yogic *samadarśana* (equal vision), the vision of God in everything and that of everything in God.

---

31. *BS*, II.1.33.

32. *BG*, VI.31.

## 6.07: A Fundamental Basis of Moral Philosophy

Moral philosophy has immense importance for the human society. It is important in both religions and secularism. A person may be a believer in God, or he may be an atheist or agnostic. Irrespective of the difference in the personal philosophy, an ethical and a moral life improves the quality of man. Such a man gets mental peace in situation of affluence or poverty, prosperity or disaster.

In religious and/or spiritual life, morality is a seminal principle. Without moral practice, a person cannot ascend the rungs of the spiritual ladder that leads to Godhead or liberation of any type, non-dualistic or dualistic.

What is the fundamental basis of morality? Has it really a foundation? Is it based on social traditions, religious customs and scriptural prescriptions and proscriptions? Is it relative? What is immoral for an individual or a society is moral for another. Is it purely based on subjectivity? Is it not objective at all? These questions have been baffling humankind for ages.

The *BG* does not issue commandments of do's and don'ts. It does not specifically say what is moral and what is immoral. It furnishes the basis of morality. On this basis, the person himself will take a decision after judging the prons and cons of the specific issue. Lord Kṛṣṇa lays the foundation of the edifice of moral philosophy in the following language.

> O Arjuna, he who applies the same standard of pleasure or pain for all others as for himself is considered as the best *yogī*.[33]

Any action, physical (*kāyika*), verbal (*vācanika*) or mental (*mānasika*), may be pleasant or painful. If it is pleasant for me, it would be pleasant for others, provided circumstances are not different. If it is painful for me, it would be painful for others under equal conditions. I am agonized if someone tortures me physically, verbally or mentally. My behaviour should not inflict pain in others. I feel happy if someone's behaviour towards me is good. I should

33. *BG*, VI.32.

behave in such a manner so that other persons become happy. This is the fundamental principle of moral philosophy.

It is natural for everybody to seek pleasure and to avoid pain. We use the word "pleasure" in a *sāttvika* sense in the present context. We are not talking of carnal pleasure, bestial pleasure and sensuality. The same standard should be applied for others as for me. Maintaining a favourable standard for me and an unfavourable standard for others is not ethical. The idea that I am superior to others and hence deserve a special standard of pleasure and pain is egocentric and selfish. Even if I am superior to others in capability and intelligence, I should be prepared for self-sacrifice and feel happy in making others happy.

The *Gītā* uses the word *yoga* and *yogī* in a very broad sense. *Yoga* embraces everything that is good, benign, benevolent and humanitarian. A *yogī* maintains the same standard of pleasure and pain for others as for himself.

We have already said that this basic standard of morality, as given in the *BG*, is equally applicable for the theists, atheists and agnostics. A simply ritualistic person, even if he is a believer in God, may practise egocentricity by violating this basic principle of morality. A spiritual person, with realization of *Brahman*, does appreciate this fundamental principle and does practise it in action.

An agnostic, who does not get solid proof for the existence or non-existence of God, may also be a good moralist by adopting this basic principle. There is, however, a problem for him. Under usual circumstances, there is no difficulty for him to practise this standard. But there are unusual situations too. Sometimes a person faces grievous situations of moral crisis (*dharma-saṅkaṭa, nīti-saṅkaṭa*). At other times he falls a victim to his temptation for working in favour of his self-interest. It is difficult for him to consistently practise morality at the cost of his own interest by strictly adhering to the moral standard, given in the *BG*.

An atheist can hardly practise a uniform moral standard in all situations. The Russian novelist F.M. Dostoevsky has rightly said:

"Everything is permissible if there is no God." In a "God-less" universe, "Might is right"; egocentricity and self-gratification are the only guiding factors of all activities. An atheist generally ignores the issues of morality, amorality and immorality. Being an egocentric person, self-centredness and opportunism are the deciding factors for whatever he does.

Immanuel Kant, the famous German philosopher, re-stated the moral principle of the *BG*. We do not say that he copied the *BG*. All seers see alike and think alike. Kant enunciated his moral principle from his own thought. But it is unfortunate that the age-old moral principle of the *BG* has received scant attention of scholars.

### 6.08: The Transmigratory Ascension of the Yogī

Arjuna, after being taught by Śrīkr̥ṣṇa on *yoga*, felt that the equanimity of the mind is an important yogic characteristic. But the mind in reality is restless. It seems impossible to bring the restless, turbulent, strong and tough mind under control. "How is it possible to still and control the restless mind?" Here we may render Arjuna's question into English.

> O Madhusūdana (slayer of Madhu = Kr̥ṣṇa), of this *yoga* elucidated by You, as characterized by sameness (equanimity), I do not see its lasting endurance, owing to the restlessness (of the mind). O Kr̥ṣṇa, the mind is indeed fickle, a fomentor (one that foments the body and senses), strong and tough. I deem its control as extremely difficult as that of the wind.[34]

The Lord agreed with Arjuna on the fact that the mind is restless and difficult to be controlled. At the same time, he asserts that it is possible to bring the mind under control. The Lord reveals the clues.

> O mighty-armed, undoubtedly the mind is fickle and difficult to

34. *BG*, VI.33-34.

be controlled. But, O son of Kuntī, it may be held in check by means of practice (*abhyāsa*) and detachment (*vairāgya*).[35]

In my opinion, *yoga* is hard to be attained by one whose self is uncontrolled. But, by a striving one, the self can be controlled and *yoga* can be achieved by appropriate means.[36]

In this verse, the word *ātmā* does not mean the "individual self" (*jīvātmā*). It rather means the *antaḥkaraṇa* (*buddhi* + *ahaṅkāra* + *manas* + the ten subtle instruments or subtle *indriyas*), or simply the mind-complex.

Arjuna did accept the advice of Śrīkr̥ṣṇa. But he had still a doubt of another type. To clarify his doubt, he asked further questions through three verses.

One, endowed with *śraddhā* (faith mixed with sincerity and devotion) in *yoga*, may not strive in practice and may have the mind wandering away from *yoga*. What fate, O Kr̥ṣṇa, is in store for him who fails to gain perfection in *yoga?*[37]

Having fallen off from both (*karma-yoga* and *dhyāna-yoga*), unestablished (lacking a firm hold) and being confounded in the path leading to the attainment of *Brahman*, O Mighty-Armed, does he not perish like a scattered cloud?[38]

O Kr̥ṣṇa, You are to completely dispel this doubt of mine; for it could not be possible for anyone other than You to dispel this doubt.[39]

In responding to the request of Arjuna, the Lord dispelled the doubts, raised by the former, through a number of verses that are being quoted here:

O son of Pr̥thā (Arjuna), neither here (in this world) nor hereafter (in the world to be), shall surely be his ruination. For, O *tāta*

35. *BG*, VI.35.

36. *BG*, VI.36.

37. *BG*, VI.37.

38. *BG*, VI.38.

39. *BG*, VI.39.

> (literally meaning "father," affectionately used to address a son), no evil comes to the doer of good.[40]
>
> Having reached the worlds of the meritorious, and having dwelt there for long-lasting years, he who has slipped from *yoga* is born in a home of pure and prosperous householders.[41]
>
> Or else, he is indeed born in a family of wise *yogīs*. This sort of birth, however, is rarer in this world.[42]
>
> O son of the Kurus (Arjuna), there he is linked to the intellect relating to the previous body, and strives harder (more than what he did in the previous birth) to attain perfection.[43]

The *yogī* who ascends the path of *yoga* is very much influenced by his previous yogic practice in earlier births. His act of unrighteous nature (*adharma*) in the previous births enfeebles his *yogaja saṁskāras* (impress produced by the practice of *yoga*). On the other hand, his act of righteous nature (*dharma*) in the previous births fortifies his *yogaja saṁskāras*. Even in the former case, when the effect of *adharma* is exhausted, the *yogaja saṁskāra* begins to produce its effects. The *yogaja saṁskāra* remains inoperative for some time due to the antagonizing action or the unrighteous actions in the previous births, but does not get destroyed.

> By that very previous (in the past life) practice (of *yoga*), he is attracted towards it (in this life) even though he does not do it consciously by being under his control. Even he who desires to know about *yoga* goes beyond the sphere of Vedic injunctions.[44]

There is too much confusion about the compound-word *śabda-brahma*. Some regard all words used in all languages as *Brahman*. There is no trace of truth in such a concept. The contextual meaning of *śabda* in *śabda-brahman* is "the revealed words of the Vedas." According to Śaṅkara, *śabda-brahman* means *vedokta-karmānuṣṭhāna-*

40. *BG*, VI.40.
41. *BG*, VI.41.
42. *BG*, VI.42.
43. *BG*, VI.43.
44. *BG*, VI.44.

*phalam* (the fruits of actions performed in conformity with what has been said in the Vedas).

> The *yogī*, striving harder and harder (in the practice of *yoga*), cleansed of all sins, gains perfection (in *yoga*) in the course of many births, (finally leading) to the attainment of the supreme goal.[45]
>
> The *yogī* is regarded as superior to those who practise austerities and asceticism (*tapasyā*), also to those who have gained knowledge through the mastery of scriptures, and to those who do the Vedic rites (like the fire sacrifice). Therefore, O Arjuna, become a *yogī*.[46]
>
> Among even all *yogī*s, he who, full of faith, with the inner self merged in Me, devotes himself to Me, is deemed by Me as the most united one.[47]

The *yoga* on which discussion has been done in the sixth chapter of the *BG* is based on Yoga-Vedānta rather than the Yoga of Patañjali. We accept, with reverence, almost all the techniques of the latter system. There are subtle differences, however, between the details of the Yoga philosophy and that of the Advaita Vedānta. We don't find the concept of *Brahman* in Patañjali's Yoga. Secondly, his *Īśvara* (God) is a special self (*puruṣa-viśeṣaḥ*) who is not a creator. Thirdly, he accepts the doctrine of transformation (*pariṇāma-vāda*) of the Sāṅkhya. Fourthly, his concept of liberation (*kaivalya*) is the complete isolation of the self (*puruṣa*) from *Prakṛti*. His *puruṣa*s are innumerable and, on attaining salvation, they stay in a higher realm permanently in perfect peace. The Vedānta, especially the non-dualistic one, rejects all these philosophical concepts of Pātañjala Yoga. It accepts *Brahman* as the only non-dual Reality. The Supreme Self or God/*Brahman* and the individual selves of living beings (*jīvātmā*s) and those of lifeless entities (*bhūtātmā*s) are one and the same. The universe is not a transformation of

45. *BG*, VI.45.
46. *BG*, VI.46.
47. *BG*, VI.47.

*Prakṛti* or *Pradhāna*. It is a usable, phenomenal, illusory appearance whose substratum is *Brahman*. It is, however, not nothing. It is *Brahman* that appears multifariously. The Vedāntic explanation of the usable, phenomenal, *vivartta* universe is based on the *adhyāsa-vāda* (*atasmiṁstadbuddhiḥ* = perceiving one thing as something else; perceiving the substratum, *Brahman*, as the multiplicity of the universe). For liberation (*mokṣa*), the *BG* uses the term *Brahma-nirvāṇa*. In contradistinction with the Buddhist meaning of *nirvāṇa* as "becoming void (*śūnya*)" or "being extinguished," *Brahma-nirvāṇa* signifies "merging in *Brahman*, with the simultaneous loss of separate identity." The *BG* and the Advaita Vedānta emphasize the action of the complete absorption of the self in the Self in the process of doing *yoga*. That is why the word *yuktaḥ* (being united; merging in) has been repeatedly used. The Yoga system of Patañjali does not support the Buddhistic *nirvāṇa*. But neither does it support the merging of the individual self in the Supreme Self on attaining liberation. Thus, there are some conceptual differences in the philosophies of Patañjali's Yoga and Yoga-Vedānta. However, such a conceptual difference does not affect the practice of *yoga*.

# 7

## Jñāna-Vijñāna-Yogaḥ
## (The Way of Material Knowledge and Realized Divine Knowledge)

### 7.01: Two Types of Knowledge

THE title of the seventh chapter of the *BG* is *Jñāna-Vijñāna-Yogaḥ*. At the outset, it becomes necessary to define *jñāna* and *vijñāna* and to compare and contrast these two words.

The word *jñāna* has been derived from the Sanskrit verb-root *jñā* which means "to know." The English equivalent of *jñāna* is "knowledge." In the modern usage, *vijñāna* is "science."

The *BG* uses these two words, with different meanings, however. *Jñāna* is knowledge on the gross and subtle entities of the material universe. The entities may be sense-perceptible. They may be empirically verifiable directly or indirectly. They may also be sense-imperceptible. Their existence, properties and functions may be inferable indirectly from sense-perceptible events.

*Vijñāna* is knowledge on *Brahman*, the non-dual, absolute Reality. Of course, *vijñāna* is *Brahma-jñāna* (knowledge on *Brahman*) plus something else. What is that something else? It is realization of the Self (*svānubhūti*, *Brahmānubhūti*), immediate experience or realization (*aparokṣānubhūti*).

Persons who exhibit erudition in scriptural knowledge, speak eloquently on *Brahman*/God, and still are without firm faith (*śraddhā*), devotion, ethical practices and God-realization, have gained *jñāna* rather than *vijñāna*.

Atheists and agnostics are not rare in number. Some of them have acquired enough knowledge on the material universe; but they may have moral and spiritual illiteracy. They claim that they are rationalists and that their knowledge is based on scientific truth and logical analysis. In fact, they lack knowledge in both science and logic and firmly adhere to dogmas. We request them to refer to our books *Māyā in Physics,*[1] *The Vibrating Universe,*[2] *Mind and Supermind*[3] and *Cyclic Universe.*[4]

Some ancient Indian philosophers of great fame are the revered founders of the Vedānta. They hold the opinion that the existence of *Brahman*/God can be proved by scriptural evidence (*śāstra-pramāṇa*) and Vedic evidence (*śruti-pramāṇa*) only. They claim that logical analysis cannot definitely prove the existence of *Brahman,* since no language can be applied to *Brahman.* We do not outrightly reject such a claim. However, our opinion in this regard is somewhat different from this traditional claim. We have a conviction that we have provided logical and inferential evidences in favour of the existence of *Brahman*/God in our books, already mentioned. In the present section of the *BG,* we will know what the Lord says to Arjuna.

> O Pārtha (Arjuna), with the mind intent on Me, performing *yoga,* taking refuge in Me, listen to Me so that you will know Me fully, without any doubt whatsoever.[5]

Human endeavour (*puruṣārtha*) is necessary to acquire *Brahma-jñāna* (*vijñāna*). One has to set one's mind on God. One has to unite his self with the Supreme Self by the practice of *yoga.* One has to take refuge in God.

He who knows God's true Being becomes all-knowing. In

1. N.C. Panda, 2005.
2. N.C. Panda, 2000.
3. N.C. Panda, 1996.
4. N.C. Panda, 2002.
5. *BG,* VII.1.

this connection, the Lord says :

> I shall exhaustively tell you this *jñāna* together with *vijñāna*. Once you grasp it, you will have nothing more here again to be known.[6]

Most people do not know God's true Being. It is difficult to know and, to surmount the difficulty, there are hardly a few persons to strive. The Lord says:

> Hardly one among thousands of persons strive for perfection. Even among those who know and strive, only some rare one knows Me in reality.[7]

With this much introduction to *jñāna*, *vijñāna* and *Brahmānubhūti* (experience or realization of *Brahman*), we will proceed to the next topic on the two types of Nature, inferior and superior.

### 7.02: Two Types of Nature

Lord Vāsudeva instructs Arjuna on two types of *prakṛti* (nature), namely, lower or inferior and higher or superior.

> Earth, water, fire, air, *ākāśa*, mind (*manas*), intellect (*buddhi*) and ego-sense (*ahaṅkāra*) — thus, is this My distinctive eightfold nature.[8]
>
> O mighty-armed (Arjuna), this is the lower nature (*aparā prakṛti*). But know My higher nature (*parā prakṛti*) to be other than it. (My higher nature) is the field-knower (*jīvabhūtā kṣetrajñalakṣaṇā*) by which this universe is upheld.[9]

The *parā prakṛti* or the higher nature is the *jīvātmā* in living beings and the *bhūtātmā* in lifeless entities. It is the field-knower (*kṣetrajña*). The field (*kṣetra* or the manifested *aparā prakṛti*) cannot be sustained in the hypothetical absence of the field-knower (*kṣetrajña* or the *parā prakṛti*).

---

6. *BG*, VII.2.
7. *BG*, VII.3.
8. *BG*, VII.4.
9. *BG*, VII.5.

> Know all beings to be born of these (My dual nature — *aparā* and *parā*). I am the source of the entire universe which also dissolves into Me.[10]

In interpreting verse 7.6 of the *BG*, Ācārya Śaṅkara says:

> The birth and dissolution of the entire universe are due to Me. I, the omniscient Lord, am the cause of the universe through the medium of My two natures (*prakṛtidvayadvāreṇa ahaṁ sarvajñaḥ īśvaraḥ jagataḥ kāraṇam*).

What Śaṅkara says here is correct. But the concept needs further elaboration. The *jīvātmā* is the field-knower, not essentially different from the *Paramātmā* (the Supreme Self, God, *Puruṣa*). In no other scripture of the Vedānta is the *jīvātmā* (self) depicted as *prakṛti* (nature). Since the *jīva* is associated with the manifested nature (the lower nature), the *BG* names it as *prakṛti*, albeit the higher (*parā*) one.

The *Mūla-Prakṛti* (the Primordial Nature, *Māyā*, *Īśvara-Śakti* or the Power of God) is eternally and timelessly Unmanifest (*Avyakta*). She may not be confused as any one of the created *prakṛti*s or their totality. She is the Mother Creatrix of the manifested *aparā prakṛti* (the universe of matter and energy). In chapter 13 of the *BG*, *Māyā* has been described as the unmanifested *Aparā Prakṛti* (AP-UM) and the created universe as the manifested *aparā prakṛti* (AP-M). Unlike the concept in the Sāṅkhya, the Vedāntic *Avyakta Prakṛti* is not modified into the manifest universe. We have to be careful in avoiding confusion in the use of the word *prakṛti*. *Īśvara* is *Puruṣa* and *Māyā* is *Prakṛti*, both being Unmanifest and co-eternal. It is, however, to be emphasized that this *Avyakta Prakṛti* is the Mother of the *vyakta prakṛti*. At the time of the total dissolution, all entities of the manifested *aparā prakṛti* follow a reverse pathway to be finally dissolved in *Mahat* or *Virāḍ* or *Buddhi* that is the Supermind of *Māyā*. The Mother and the Father of the universe are *Māyā* and *Īśvara* (God), respectively.

---

10. *BG*, VII.6.

The birth, maintenance and dissolution of the universe are effected by the combined efforts of the *Puruṣa* (God) and the *Prakṛti* or *Māyā* (Goddess), the former being the Chairperson and the latter the Executive of the Chairperson.

The rest of the Vedāntic cosmology and cosmogony has been mentioned in brief in section 2.14 of this book. There is no need of repetition here.

### 7.03: God is the Eternal and Timeless Seminal Principle

In this topic, we shall discuss six verses (7.7-12) of the *BG*. Before we go to the proper subject matter, we shall explain the difference between two words — "eternal" and "timeless."

In Sanskrit, the word *nitya* or *śāśvata* means "eternal," and the word *sanātana* "eternal and timeless." We want to indicate how "eternal" is distinguished from "eternal and timeless."

Time has birth and death. It is born at the beginning of the creation of the universe. It dies when the total universe undergoes dissolution. It is not a created entity. It is a mental construct. The mind conceives of time when an event occurs. With the occurrence of more than one event, we refer to the mutual occurrences. Before the emergence of *Homo sapiens* (human species), the Supermind was conceiving of time. There must be a mind or a Supermind for constructing the concept of time.

When something continuously exists during a cosmic period ($t_0$ to $t_m$; from the beginning to the end of time), it is eternal (*nitya*).

After the total dissolution of the universe and before the subsequent creation, there are no events at all. The concept of time cannot arise at all without events. The eventless state is timeless. The word *sanātana* covers both the states, with and without time. Hence, it means "eternal and timeless."

God is the eternal and timeless seminal principle. Let us know what the *BG* speaks of this topic.

O Dhanañjaya (Arjuna), there is nought else beyond Me. All

> this (all entities of the whole universe) is strung on Me like gems on a thread.[11]
>
> O son of Kuntī (Arjuna), I am the sapidity in Waters (Subtle Cosmic Plasma). I am the radiance in the moon and the sun. I am the *Praṇava* (the sacred syllable, OM) in all the Vedas. I am the sound inherent in Space (*Ākāśa*). I am the manhood in mankind.[12]
>
> I am pure odour in the earth; brilliance in the fire; life in all beings; and austerity in ascetics.[13]
>
> O son of Pṛthā (Arjuna), know Me to be the eternal and timeless seed (seminal principle) of all beings; the intellect of all intellectual beings; and the splendour of all those who are splendorous.[14]
>
> Also of the mighty, I am the might, devoid of desire and attachment. O foremost Bhārata prince (Arjuna), in all beings, I am (their) desire, unopposed to righteousness.[15]

Verse 7.11 of the *BG* needs more elucidation and further clarification. God says: "I am the strength of the strong." Is He the strength of the wicked, immoral persons? If that is so, the fundamental concept of God is tainted. To avoid this misinterpretation, God adds two attributes of "strength" which must be devoid of desire (*kāma*) and attachment (*rāga*). If someone is strong and he uses his strength to fulfil his carnal desires of selfish interest and sensual gratification, he has brutal strength, opposed to divinity and all ethical standards. Strength should be used for all good purposes and not for evil ones. In the same verse, the Lord says: "I am desire in all beings who are unopposed to righteousness." All desires, as such, are not bad. A doctor desires to save the life of a patient. A statesman desires to remove poverty and illiteracy of his country. A spiritual person desires to

11. *BG*, VII.7.
12. *BG*, VII.8.
13. *BG*, VII.9.
14. *BG*, VII.10.
15. *BG*, VII.11.

be more and more divine and to finally attain liberation. With such a sense, God is the desire of righteous persons. The Lord further says :

> And whatever entities are *sāttvika, rājasika* and *tāmasika,* know them to proceed from Me alone. Nevertheless, I am not in them; (rather) they are in Me.[16]

All beings, living and non-living, are formed out of the vibrations of three strings. The vibrational product of each string acquires an attributive state, namely, *sattva, rajas* and *tamas.* These attributes are mostly combined in different proportions. Highly spiritually evolved beings are exceptions, however. They give up *rajas* and *tamas* and retain *sattva* only. Finally, they give up *sattva* and become devoid of all the three attributes. They are the *jīvanmukta*s (liberated albeit still living).

One important distinction between the *guṇa*s of the Unmanifest *Prakṛti* (*Māyā*) and the manifested *Prakṛti* (the created entities) has been hardly recognized by the interpreters of the Vedānta. With reference to the former, the three strings of the *vīṇā* of the Mother Creatrix are the *guṇa*s. With reference to the latter, three trait-types exhibited by the created entities are the *guṇa*s. The same word is used with two different meanings. One must be careful in distinguishing the meanings.

What decides the trait-type of an individual created entity? It is decided by two factors, namely, the divine vibrations and the *karma-saṁskāra*s of the individual entity. The amplitude, frequency and wavelength of the divine vibrations are tuned in accordance with the doctrine of *karma.*

## 7.04: Divine Illusion

In the previous section, it has been said that all created entities, formed of *sattva, rajas* and *tamas,* proceed from God alone (are born of the *Śakti* of God alone), and that they have been generated

16. *BG,* VII.12.

by their own karmic forces. Now we proceed to present the influence of Divine Illusion on the *jīvas*.

The meaning of *Māyā* is not one and only one everywhere in the Vedāntic scriptures. We commit blunders if we do not take the contextual meanings for our consideration. One important meaning of *Māyā* is "the Power of *Brahman/Īśvara*," that is the Primordial Nature (*Mūla Prakṛti*). She is eternally and timelessly unmanifested (*Avyakta*). The Possessor of Power and the Power, being bipolar, are co-eternal. She is the Mother of the universe, the Executive Agent under the Chairpersonship of God, the Father of the universe. Both constitute the bipolar non-dual Reality. *Māyā* has concealing power (*āvaraṇa-śakti*) and projecting power (*vikṣepa-śakti*). She herself is not illusion; but she creates illusion, a sort of magical phenomenon. Magic cannot create a magician. Had the Mother Creatrix been Herself illusion, She could not create the illusory universe. By the excercise of Her power, she creates the usable universe, ever-changeable and modifiable. Her power makes *B* (*Brahman*, the substratum or *adhiṣṭhāna* of the universe) appear as non-*B*. A second meaning of *māyā* is "illusion." The phenomenon of illusion may be illustrated as a rope appearing as a snake. A third meaning of *māyā* is delusion (*moha*), accompanied with attachment (*āsakti*). A fourth meaning of *māyā* is magical illusion (*māyā-jāla, indra-jāla*), indicating essentially nothing, although perceived apparently as something or many things. We now discuss the topic of divine illusion, as given in the seventh chapter of the *BG*.

> Being deluded by these threefold natures evolved from *guṇas* (of *Prakṛti*), this entire universe does not cognize Me, the immutable (Reality) beyond them (the three *guṇas*).[17]

A clarification is necessary about the three *guṇas* and their products. The Sāṅkhya says that *Prakṛti* is constituted of three attributes, namely, *sattva, rajas* and *tamas*. It further says that *Prakṛti* is tranformed into the material entities of the universe. Here

17. *BG*, VII.13.

"transformation" involves "modification," *A* being modified into *B*. The Vedānta rejects the doctrine of transformation (*pariṇāma-vāda*) with reference to *Brahman, Īśvara* and *Māyā*. We agree to what the Vedānta says. But we do not find any satisfactory Vedāntic explanation on the issue of these *guṇa*s and their evolutes in the Vedāntic scriptures.

We cannot accept the statement that *Prakṛti* (*Māyā* or *Mahāmāyā, Īśvara-Śakti*, the Power of *Brahman*/God) is made up of three attributes — *sattva, rajas, tamas*. Secondly, we cannot accept the concept of the three strings as attributes or qualities. In our opinion, these *guṇas* of the *Mūla-Prakṛti* are strings or strands of the divine *vīṇā* of Mother Sarasvatī who represents the *Mahāmāyā* or the Power of *Brahman*. When She plays Her *vīṇā*, vibrations, with innumerable musical notes, are produced. The vibrations of each string are characterized by a group of attributes. Thus, three groups of attributes, namely, *sattva, rajas, tamas*, are produced. The entities of the empirical and phenomenal universe are created out of the vibrations, incorporating blends of the attributes in different permutations and combinations. A specific created entity has the preponderance of one group of attributes, with, of course, the combination of the other two. Proportions of the three groups of attributes vary in different entities. Verse 7.13 of the *BG* mentions "threefold entities evolved from the three divine strings."

Now the Lord tells the way, by following which one can go beyond the divine illusion.

> Indeed this divine illusive power of Mine, in possession of these three strings, is hard to cross over. Those who surrender themselves to Me alone cross over this illusion.[18]

Verse 7.14 of the *BG* uses three words, namely, *daivī* (divine), *guṇamayī* (full of *guṇas*, in possession of *guṇa*s), *mama* (my), with reference to *Māyā*, the Power (*Śakti*) of God. *Māyā*, the Mother of the universe, is divine. In the analogy of fire and heat, She belongs

18. *BG*, VII.14.

to God and not different from Him. She is in possession of *guṇa*s (three strings of a divine musical instrument). Here our interpretation is special and unique. Other interpreters of the *BG* have accepted the Sāṅkhya view, according to which *Prakṛti* is made up of three *guṇa*s or attributes. We don't agree with them. The Vedāntic *Prakṛti* is homogeneous and impartite. *Sattva, rajas* and *tamas* are three divine strings in the possession of *Māyā*. When She plays Her *vīṇā*, with three strings, musical notes are produced as a result of vibrations. The compound-word *guṇamayī* is made up of two words, *guṇa* and *mayī*. The suffix *mayaṭ* means "full of." When one says "an area is *jalamaya*," one means thereby: "That area is full of water." "That area is constituted of water" is not the meaning. We would like to leave a note here that our interpretation of the Vedānta, Yoga and Tantra makes a meaningful and happy blend, a complete confluence. We also speak of Yoga-Vedānta and Tantra-Vedānta.

One point is to be emphasized here. Some interpreters of this verse and similar other verses of the *BG* say that the devotee shall have to exclusively surrender to Śrīkṛṣṇa alone. Such an idea is not correct. When Lord Śrīkṛṣṇa uses the first person words such as "I," "Me," "My," He means "God," "to God" and "God's," respectively. God has no name. We give names to Him, and call Him by thousands of names. The universe has been created by one God only, irrespective of the different names used by devotees of different religions. Only ignorance makes one think that every religion has a God, different from God of another religion. Even in the same religion, as for example, in Hinduism, persons belonging to different sects (such as some Śaivas and Vaiṣṇavas) commit this mistake.

We have so far been speaking about *Māyā* or *Prakṛti*, as stated in the first line of the verse. The second line of the verse also contains the same word, *māyā*. But the meaning, in the second case, is different. It is "divine illusion." Now we focus on the question of Arjuna.

Doubt arises in the mind of Arjuna. If one, by surrendering oneself to God, passes beyond the divine illusion, all can do that and thereby they can cross over this illusion. Why does it not happen? The Lord removes the doubt.

> The evil-doers, the deluded, the worst of men, robbed of knowledge by divine illusion, assuming a demoniac attitude, do not surrender to Me.[19]

The kind of illusion described in this section is divine in origin. However, it is not divine in quality. It is provided by Providence. What for does God do it? The sportive play (*līlā*) of the Father and the Mother of the universe is not possible in the hypothetical total absence of ignorance and illusion.

In spite of what has been said here, man is not as helpless as it seems. He has the *puruṣārtha* (power of personal effort) to tear the veil of ignorance and to fully surrender to God alone. If he does so, he can cross over the divine illusion.

### 7.05: Four Types of Devotees

The *BG* describes four types of devotees and specifies the best among the four. The Lord says :

> O Arjuna, four types of persons of righteous actions worship (resort to) Me. O Best of Bhāratas, they are the distressed, the seeker of knowledge, the seeker of wealth, and the wise.[20]

In the aforesaid verse, "knowledge" means "knowledge concerning the true nature of God." Majority of the devotees are the distressed (persons afflicted with calamities such as diseases, theft, robbery, suspension from service, unemployment, poverty, natural calamity, and the like) and the wealth-seekers. The latter category of persons worship God for various types of gains (not necessarily wealth only). They want more riches, power and position, awards and rewards, name and fame, children, comforts,

---

19. *BG*, VII.15.

20. *BG*, VII.16.

social prominence and all other types of gains.

> Of them all, the knower (of My true nature), ever united (with Me), with devotion of the One (Me alone), excels; for, exceedingly dear am I to the knower, and he is dear to Me.[21]

> Noble indeed are all these (four); but I deem the knower to be My very Self; for, uniting his self with Me, he is established in Me alone, the goal without parallel.[22]

In this verse and similar other ones, "in Me alone" should be properly interpreted. It does not carry a sectarian and communal meaning. Here "Me" means "the Supreme *Brahman*," "the One and only One God of the universe," irrespective of multiplicity of religions and faiths.

The knowers and realizers of *Brahman* are not too many in number. One takes many births and makes sincere efforts in all these births to attain to *Brahman*-hood. Once more the Lord extols the knower.

> At the end of many births, the man of knowledge takes refuge in Me, realizing that all this is Vāsudeva. Such a great self (soul) is extremely rare.[23]

In the Hindu mythology, the son of Vasudeva (and Devakī) is Vāsudeva. Lord Viṣṇu took birth in the womb of Devakī to rid vices and re-establish virtues in the society. The Hindu scriptures declare that such divine incarnations of God do take place as and when required for the welfare of the creation. But these scriptures recognize one and only one God for the whole universe. The idea of the existence of more than one God is outright rejected in Hinduism. Accordingly, Vāsudeva is not different from Jehovah, Allah or any other name of God. Of course, the metaphysical details of religions about God and His creation do differ among religions.

The sixth chapter of the *BG* is on Yoga. In the succeeding

---

21. *BG*, VII.17.

22. *BG*, VII.18.

23. *BG*, VII.19.

chapter, that is, in the seventh, verse 7.19 describes the state of the culmination of Yoga. The *yogī*, the knower of *Brahman*, sees everything of the universe as Lord Vāsudeva, the Supreme *Brahman*. Although rare are *yogī*s of this type, every individual person should make sincere efforts through one or many births to reach this supreme goal.

### 7.06: Worshipping God vis-à-vis Gods

Most people in the world hold a wrong notion that the Hindus worship many Gods. Even many Hindus cherish the same idea. No scripture of the world is older than the Vedas that unambiguously declare the oneness of God. The Vedānta says that *Brahman* is non-dual and that there is nothing else other than *Brahman*. The followers of the Vedic religion worship one God only, although they use different names for the same one God. The multiplicity of names becomes necessary for the description of God's attributes and functions.

Many Hindus worship gods too. These gods are too many in number. In Sanskrit language, they are known as *devatā*s. Both *deva*s (male deities) and *devī*s (female deities) are *devatā*s. No god or goddess is the Supreme Lord, the creator, sustainer and destroyer of the universe. No god is omnipresent, omniscient and omnipotent. All *devatā*s are born after the initial creation of the universe. They cease to exist consequent upon the total dissolution of the universe.

Lord Vāsudeva instructs Arjuna on the topic of worshipping God *vis-à-vis* gods.

> Deprived of knowledge by this and that desire, (people) resort to other deities. Being constrained by their inborn (innate) nature, they adopt this or that rite (this or that religious discipline).[24]
>
> I impart unswerving faith to each devotee who seeks to worship whatsoever form with *śraddhā*.[25]

---

24. *BG*, VII.20.

25. *BG*, VII.21.

> Endued with that faith, he engages himself in the worship of that form. From that divinity, he gains the objects of his desires; for, these are verily ordained by Me alone.[26]

> But the fruit accruing to those small-minded men comes to an end (is limited). The worshippers of gods go to the gods; My devotees come to Me.[27]

In verse 7.21, the word *tanu* (body) has been used. Lord Vāsudeva has taken a human form. People, lacking in knowledge and wisdom, may be thinking that Vāsudeva has manifested from an unmanifested entity like all living beings. But that is not the case with the Lord. On this point, He says:

> The unintelligent consider Me, becoming manifested from an unmanifested state, not knowing My supreme state, (the ever-present), the immutable.[28]

Living beings are born; they live; and they die. They undergo the cyclic process of unmanifest —> manifest —> unmanifest. They are born due to their karmic impressions on their *antaḥkaraṇa*. On being liberated, they are no longer born when their karmic traces are fully erased. When God takes a form, He does it through His *Yoga-Māyā*. This *Yoga-Māyā* is the Power of God, personified as a deity. She is not different from *Māyā*, the Power of God/*Brahman*. She assumes this name with reference to two conditions, namely, (1) when the divine Power is magical and illusory and (2) when God utilizes this Power in creating something, either empirical or illusory.

The body of the human being or any other living being is *karmaja* (born of *karma-saṁskāras*). But the body of God, born as a human being or any other living being, is not *karmaja*. It is *māyāja* (magical appearance) conjured by *Yoga-Māyā*, when and where God desires. We may take the example of Śrīkṛṣṇa. His human

26. *BG*, VII.22.
27. *BG*, VII.23.
28. *BG*, VII.24.

form is magically produced by *Yoga-Māyā*. God is all-pervading or omnipresent irrespective of the birth of an incarnation, either with full potency or with partial potency. When the Divine Potency is partial, the incarnation is called an *avatāra* (literally meaning "descent"). All-pervading God is not confined to the form of the incarnation, either full or partial. At the same time, the incarnation, with a form and full potency, has no reduced degree in His omnipresence, omnipotence and omniscience.

The Lord further elaborates the illusive power of *Yoga-Māyā*. He also indicates the means by which one can remove the veil of ignorance, can take refuge in God, and can get liberation.

> Veiled by the delusive power of My *Yoga-Māyā*, I am not revealed to all. This deluded world knows not Me, unborn and immutable.[29]
>
> O Arjuna, I know the beings of the whole past, the present and the future; but Me none knows.[30]
>
> O descendant of Bharata, scourge of foes, all beings, at the time of birth, get confounded due to the delusion of dualities, arising from attachment (desire) and aversion.[31]

This verse presents a fundamental principle of behavioural psychology. Pleasure and pain are the factors that play crucial roles on the behaviour of a person. Pleasure leads to desire for more and more; pain leads to aversion. The first one generates worldly love and the second one generates hatred.

Now the Lord shows the way of extricating oneself from the pairs of opposites.

> But those persons whose sins have come to an end, who act righteously, and who are freed from the delusion of dualities, worship Me with a firm resolve.[32]

---

29. *BG*, VII.25.
30. *BG*, VII.26.
31. *BG*, VII.27.
32. *BG*, VII.28.

> Taking refuge in Me, those who strive for release from old age and death come to know that *Brahman*, in its entirety, and also the reality of the inner self and all the works.[33]
>
> Those who know Me, with the *adhibhūta* (My manifestation in matter and energy), with the *adhidaiva* (My manifestation in divinities), and with the *adhiyajña* (My manifestation in worship, penances and sacrifices), uniting the mind with Me even at the time of departure (death), realize (experience, get *brahmānubhūti*) Me.[34]

For getting liberation (*mokṣa*), the *Gītā* lays much emphasis on the mind's concentration on *Īśvara* (God) at the time of death. It is a difficult job to merge the mind in God during the time immediately before death. But, with life-long devotional practice and steadfast concentration in God, it is possible to take refuge in God at the time of death. Mahātmā Gandhi did it when he was assassinated. And so did some others in the world.

33. *BG*, VII.29.

34. *BG*, VII.30.

# 8

# Tāraka-Brahma-Yogaḥ
## (Saving Knowledge of *Brahman*)

### 8.01: The Meanings of Some Metaphysical Terms

IN verses 7.29-30 of the *BG*, the Lord used some metaphysical terms, without elaboration of their meanings. In the beginning of the present chapter (verses 8.1-2), Arjuna questions the Lord to know what they stand for. The question of Arjuna is quoted here:

> O best of *puruṣas* (best of selves or spirits), what is that *Brahman?* What is *adhyātma?* What is *karma?* What is called *adhibhūta?* And what is said to be *adhidaiva?* O slayer of Madhu, who, in this body, operates the sacrifices (is *adhiyajña*) and how? And how art thou known, at the time of departure (death), by the self-controlled (*yogīs*)?[1]

Lord Vāsudeva answers the questions of Arjuna through a number of verses

> The imperishable is the Supreme *Brahman*. (Its) innate nature (the inner self) is called *adhyātma*. Work (*karma*) is the manifest creation, bringing forth beings into existence.[2]

What does not perish (never wanes) is *Akṣara* and that is the Supreme *Brahman*. If *Brahman* is designated as *B*, this *B* remains as *B* eternally and timelessly. It never decays. It never undergoes modifications. (It is changeless.) It has neither a precedent nor a subsequent state.

The same Supreme *Brahman* (*paraṁ brahma*), residing in each

1. *BG*, VIII.1-2.
2. *BG*, VIII.3.

body, is the inner self (*adhyātma*). *Brahman* is all-pervading (*sarva-vyāpī*). There is not a single entity, non-living or living, in which *Brahman* does not exist. This indwelling *Brahman* is the inner self (*pratyagātman*) that is the subjective spirit.

Any type of sacrificial act is called *yajña*. It involves austerities (*tapaḥ*, literally meaning "heat"). Here *yajña* means "creation that brings all beings, both inanimate and animate, into existence." This act is the *karma*. This act of the initial creation was performed in a superheated state. And so is it called *sṛṣṭi-yajña* (*sṛṣṭi* = creation, emanation = *visargaḥ*). Thus, referentially, *karma* here means "the act of creation by God"). In regard to our interpretation of *yajña* and *karma*, being a synthesis of ancient Indian wisdom and the cosmology of modern science, reference may be made to the *Bṛhadāraṇyaka Upaniṣad*.[3]

> The perishable existence is the *adhibhūta*; and the *Puruṣa* is *adhidaivata*. O best of the embodied (best of men = Arjuna), here in the body alone, I am the *adhiyajña*.[4]

Any existing entity, inanimate or animate, with origination, undergoes decaying process and finally perishes. Whatever perishes is *adhibhūta*. The etymological meaning of the word *puruṣa* is that by which all is filled (*pūrṇam anena sarvam iti*), or he who lies in the city (*puri śayanāt*). Here the word "city" means "the city of Virāṭ and all its evolutes." *Hiraṇyagarbha*, seated in the sun-god and all other gods (divinities = *devatā*s), is the *Antaryāmī* (the Inner Controller or Ruler). He is the *Adhidaivatam*, *Parameśvara*, the Supreme Ruler of the universe. The *Adhiyajña* is He who identifies Himself with all sacrifices. The *Taittirīya Saṁhitā* says: "Sacrifice is indeed Viṣṇu (*yajño vai viṣṇuḥ*)."[5] In the bodies of all creatures other than *devatā*s, Viṣṇu/Kṛṣṇa/God is the *Adhiyajña*.

The terms used in verses 8.3-4 of the *BG* carry special meanings

---

3. *BU*, I.1.1; I.2.1.
4. *BG*, VIII.4.
5. *TS*, I.7.4.

and hence their meanings in use have been elaborated in the present section.

### 8.02: Meditate on God at the Time of Departure

In the religious psychology of the Vedānta, much importance has been given on the unconscious. At the time of death, whatever idea is imprinted on the uppermost layer of the unconscious becomes the controlling factor of the psyche in the next life. This ancient Western word "psyche" is identified with "soul" which, in turn, is identified with "mind." Here we are using this word in the Vedāntic or Yogic sense. Accordingly, it is *antaḥkaraṇa*, different from the soul. An accomplished *yogī* or a highly spiritual person may be liberated, without further birth, if he can contemplate on God immediately before death. Let us know what the *BG* says on this topic.

> At the time of death, whoso, remembering Me alone, departs giving up his body, proceeds to My status. There is no doubt of this.[6]

The principle operating in what has been given in the aforesaid verse is universal. At the time of death, one may contemplate on something else other than God. The thought, at the last moment of life, divine or demoniac, influences the mental personality of the person in the next life.

> O son of Kuntī (Arjuna), remembering whatever being, one leaves the body at the end, that alone he reaches, having been constant in the thought of that being.[7]

At the time of the *Mahābhārata*, image/form/idol-worship of different gods was in vogue, in addition to the worship of one God alone. The verse says: Thinking of a particular god (*devatā*), at the time of death, determines the physical and mental traits of the person in the next life.

---

6. *BG*, VIII.5.
7. *BG*, VIII.6.

> Therefore, at all times, remember Me and fight. Dedicating mind and intellect to Me, you shall doubtless come to Me alone.[8]
>
> O son of Pṛthā (Arjuna), with mind, not moving towards anything else, with the practice of Yoga for uniting the intellect with God, constantly contemplating God, one goes to the Supreme, Divine Spirit (Supreme God).[9]

Now the Lord gives a description of the characteristics of the Resplendent *Puruṣa*.

> Whoso meditates on the Wise Seer, the Ancient (the birthless and the deathless one; eternal and timeless), the Over-Ruler (the Governor of the entire universe), the subtler than the subtlest (the minuter than the minutest), the Upholder of all, the imponderable of form, the resplendent like the sun and the one who is beyond darkness, (goes to Him).[10]
>
> At the time of departure, with the mind unmoving and with devotion and strength of Yoga, fixing the *Prāṇa* at the spot between the eyebrows (at the *ājñā-cakra*), he reaches the Supreme, Divine Lord.[11]

This verse refers to an advanced technique of Yoga, by which one raises the *Prāṇa* from the lotus of the heart (*hṛdaya-puṇḍarīka*) to the eyebrow centre through the central *suṣumṇā-nāḍī*. It also refers to a very advanced technique of *bhūta-jaya* (victory over the five material states).

A life-long practice of what has been said in this section enables a person to contemplate God at the time of death. Such a devotee has to live a pious and detached life so that thoughts on sensuality and depravity do not seige the mind at the time just before death. The divine thought on God erases the impresses on the conscious and the unconscious and becomes firmly stamped on the mind and the intellect. It would then be the only factor to shape the

8. *BG*, VIII.7.
9. *BG*, VIII.8.
10. *BG*, VIII.9.
11. *BG*, VIII.10.

next life or to attain to *mokṣa* (liberation) without further life.

**8.03: The Ultimate Goal of No Return**

In the Vedānta of the non-dualistic school, *mokṣa* (liberation) means "merging the self in the Supreme Self or *Brahman*." Once it happens, there is no longer any re-birth. To get *mokṣa* or to become *Brahman* is the final goal from which there is no return. This final state is that of *Saccidānanda* (Existence, Consciousness, Bliss). Let us know what the *BG* says on this topic:

> What the knowers of the Veda speak of as the Imperishable, what the self-controlled ascetics, freed from attachment, enter into, seeking which they live a life of continence, that goal I shall briefly declare unto you.[12]
>
> Controlling all gateways of the senses, and confining the mind in the heart, fixing own *Prāṇa* in the crown of the head, intent on the steadiness of Yoga, uttering the monosyllable *OM* (that designates *Brahman*), constantly remembering Me, whoso departs, leaving the body, attains the Supreme Goal.[13]

In the first one of the aforesaid two verses, the word *hṛt* means "the eyebrow centre" rather than the physical cardiac organ and the word *mūrdhan* means the *sahasrāra* (the thousand-petalled lotus), especially the *brahma-randhra*.

> O son of Pṛthā (Arjuna), to the *yogī* who is perpetually in communion, who remembers Me constantly and eternally, with the mind not thinking of anything else, I am easily attainable.[14]
>
> Having attained Me and winning supreme perfection, the great sages no longer get rebirth which is ephemeral and the abode of all sufferings.[15]

In the section to follow, the Lord describes two groups of worlds (*lokaḥ, bhuvanaḥ*). There is return of the self (rebirth) from anyone

---

12. *BG*, VIII.11.
13. *BG*, VIII.12-13.
14. *BG*, VIII.14.
15. *BG*, VIII.15.

of the realms, including that of *Brahmā*. There is no return when a self attains to God alone.

### 8.04: The Return and Non-Return of the Self

Before we discuss the proper topic, we would like to furnish some preliminary information to be necessary for understanding the subject matter.

The total universe (*viśva, jagat*) has seven constituent units, each one being called a *lokaḥ*. Each *lokaḥ* has a name. The names of the seven *loka*s are: *bhūḥ, bhuvaḥ, svaḥ, mahaḥ, janaḥ, tapaḥ,* and *satyam* or *Brahma*.

All interpreters have so far considered the *loka*s as horizontal regions, placed one over the other, arranged on a vertical axis, the *satya-loka* occupying the highest region and the *bhūrloka* occupying the bottom one. Accordingly, our earth is the *bhūrloka* in the total sphere of the universe. This interpretation is not scientifically correct. The concepts of "upper" and "lower" have relevance with reference to the gravitational force of a celestial body on which a person stands. Our earth is above and below many celestial bodies if we consider this aspect. If we deny this sense of relativity of ups and downs, based on gravitational force, we end in the final inference that there are no higher and lower realms.

We do not agree to this traditional interpretation. In our view, all the seven *loka*s are here, there and everywhere. Starting from the *bhūḥ*, they serially reduce their grossness and increase their subtlety. The *bhūḥ* has four dimensions (three for space and one for time). With the gradually increasing higher degree of subtlety, the number of dimensions continues to increase. The *satya-loka* or the *brahma-loka* has the highest number of dimensions and is the subtlest among the seven. All the seven *loka*s have time as the common dimension, although it is relative. After entering anyone of the seven *loka*s, one cannot stay there permanently and has to return to the transmigratory existence of life and death. But once one merges in *Īśvara/Brahman*, one never returns to the mortal world or any world. In order to enter the *svarloka* (the third one), one has to be body-less, matter-less and massless.

A thousand *catur-yuga*s make a day of 12 hours of Brahmā and the same period makes a night. Thus, two thousand *catur-yuga*s make a day of 24 hours for Brahmā. He lives one hundred years (each year having a duration of 360 days of His time).

The words *catuḥ* and *yuga* mean "four" and "aeon," respectively. The four *yuga*s are *kṛta* (*satya*), *tretā*, *dvāpara* and *kali*, having a duration of 1,728,000, 1,296,000, 864,000 and 432,000 earth-years, respectively. The four together make a *mahā-yuga*, comprising 4,320,000 or 4.32 million human (earth) years.

One day of Brahmā, excluding His night, is known as a *kalpa*. At the termination of a *kalpa*, the three *loka*s, namely, *bhūḥ*, *bhuvaḥ* and *svaḥ*, undergo dissolution. A *kalpa* is followed by a night of Brahmā. The said three *loka*s remain in a latent, dissolved state during the night. Brahmā goes to a state of sleep during the night. When Brahmā wakes at the termination of His night, the next *kalpa* begins and the said three *loka*s are created again. The other four *loka*s are not affected at all by the day and night of Brahmā.

One earth-year of 360 days is a divine day (day + night) in the *devaloka* (celestial realm). One divine year contains 360 divine days (including nights). There are four *yuga*s, namely, *kṛta* (*satya*), *tretā*, *dvāpara* and *kali*, consisting of 4800, 3600, 2400 and 1200 celestial years, respectively. A day (12 hours) of Brahmā has a duration of 1,000 *caturyuga*s or a *kalpa* (4.32 billion or $4.32 \times 10^9$ earth-years). One night of Brahmā also contains 4,320 million or 4.32 billion earth-years. Thus, 8.64 billion earth-years make one day and one night of Brahmā. This period, multiplied with 360, gives the duration of Brahmā's year, which is 3110.4 billion human years. Brahmā lives for a period of 100 years (His time) or 311.04 trillion (1 trillion = $1 \times 10^{12}$) human years. This period is known as one *para*. One-half of a *para* is a *parārdha* (*ardha*, meaning "a half"). The first *parārdha* is the expanding phase of the universe and the second *parārdha* is its contracting phase. Total dissolution of the whole universe (all the seven *lokas*) coincides with the termination of the second *parārdha* of each *para*.

Brahmā no longer stays after a *para*. It would be wrong to say that He dies after a *para*. Many Purāṇas have committed this blunder. Brahmā, Viṣṇu and Rudra constitute the Trinity of one Divine Being (*Parameśvara*) only. He has no birth and no death, if considered on the basis of metaphysical totality. However, the Purāṇas describe the birth and death of Brahmā to make the matter simple for the common folk. After the total dissolution of the universe, the three Divine Beings cease to be three and become One only. Again, at the beginning of the next *para*, with the manifestation of the universe, the One Being plays three roles as the Trinity.

There is a confusion in identifying *Hiraṇyagarbha* and *Virāṭ*. *Virāṭ* is the cosmic mind (*samaṣṭi-buddhi*). *Brahman*, the Pure Consciousness, being pervaded in *Māyā*, induces and impels an intellect. This mega-structure of consciousness for the whole universe is known as *Virāṭ* or *Virāḍ* which is the supermind of *Māyā*. This Vedāntic process is known as the doctrine of induction (*pravartana-vāda* or *preraṇa-vāda*). Unlike the traditional interpretation that mixes Sāṅkhya and Vedānta, *Virāṭ* is not an evolute and *Māyā* is not its evolvent. Neither is it the fact that *Māyā* or *Virāṭ* is transformed into the universe in the analogy of gold being modified into a necklace or wood into a chair. The Sāṅkhya is a philosophical school of realism and dualism that accepts the doctrine of transformation. In contrast, the Advaita Vedānta is a philosophical school of non-dualism that rejects the doctrine of transformation. Both schools accept the theory of evolution, without any identity in the concept of evolution, of course. This school of non-dualism rejects the concept of the transformation of *Brahman, Īśvara, Māyā* and *Virāṭ*. Its evolution has a definite sequence and the so-called products are mental constructs like the thought-processes of an artist or the dream-processes of a dreamer. Who is the artist or dreamer here? *Māyā* or the *Mūla-Prakṛti* is the divine artist who, under the Chairpersonship of *Īśvara*, conjures the universe and spreads Her magical net in the analogy of a spider. *Virāḍ* may be compared with the hard disc of a mega-computer and the universe with the window desktop of its monitor. This supermind of *Māyā* is the super-compacted cosmic hard disc. Without exception, all entities, created or uncreated, are pervaded by *Brahman*. Accordingly, *Māyā* and *Virāḍ* are pervaded by *Brahman*. The all-pervading *Brahman*, with *Māyā* as the *upādhi*, is *Īśvara* (God) and, with *Virāṭ* as the *upādhi*, is *Virāṭātmā*. *Āpaḥ* (the primordial subtle, cosmic plasma; not water) is the first manifested entity. A Cosmic Egg (*Aṇḍam*) is formed by the super-condensation of the *Āpaḥ*. *Prāṇa* (the Super-unified primordial force) evolved from *Āpaḥ*. A huge quantity of heat was produced as a result of the vibration of *Prāṇa*. The Cosmic Egg was superheated and acquired a golden hue. This was the Golden Embryo or *Hiraṇya-Garbha*. *Īśvara* who presided over this *Hiraṇya-Garbha* was *Hiraṇya-Garbhātmā* or Brahmā. The word *Hiraṇya-Garbha* is used in some scriptures inter-changeably for Brahmā and the Cosmic Egg.

*Virāṭ* or *Buddhi* of *Māyā* and the *buddhi* (intellect, a subtle psycho-organ in the subtle body of each created entity) play similar roles, the former in a cosmic scale and the latter in an individual scale. The individual *buddhi* contains a sub-organ known as *karmāśaya* (the reservoir of karmic impressions). So long as the karmic impressions are not totally erased and the *karmāśaya* is not empty, the cycles of birth and death would continue. One may stay in a higher realm, say, the *svarloka*, for a limited time; but one has to be reborn due to one's residual *karma*. The attainment of even the highest *loka* (*Brahma-loka*) does not lead to liberation and stay there is not permanent. Unless and until the *karmāśaya* is not fully emptied, one cannot merge in *Brahman* and become *Brahman*. An unliberated self continues to revolve in the cycles of birth and death.

An issue may be clarified here. Even at the termination of a *para* when the total universe is fully dissolved in the *Virāḍ*, the unliberated selves (*jīvātmās*) continue to potentially stay in their bound state in *Virāḍ*, the super-compacted cosmic hard disc. They again become embodied at the advent of the next creation. So the return of a self is a certainty so long as it is not liberated. There is no return when the self becomes the Supreme Self.

With this background information, let us proceed to know what the Lord says on the present topic.

> Worlds, up to and including the *Brahma-loka* or *satya-loka* (the seventh realm), are subject to returning again, O Arjuna. But, after attaining to Me, O son of Kuntī, there is no more rebirth.[16]

All the seven *loka*s are limited by Brahmā's Time (His day, night, year and span of life). Anything, limited by Time, undergoes cyclic processes, because Time or time itself is cyclic rather than linear.

> The day of Brahmā lasts for a thousand (*catuḥ* = four) *yuga*s (ages), and the night ends in a thousand (*catuḥ*) *yuga*s. There are men who know the day and night of Brahmā.[17]

The word *yuga*, in this verse, means *caturyuga* (four *yuga*s: *satya, tretā, dvāpara, kali*). Even Ācārya Śaṅkara has equated Prajāpati (Brahmā) and *Virāṭ* in his interpretation of this verse. We have a different opinion, however, and we have already expressed it in this chapter. Prajāpati or Brahmā presides over (becomes the *adhyakṣa* of) the manifested *Virāṭ* and the Cosmic Egg (*Hiraṇya-Garbha* = Golden Embryo) produced out of *Virāṭ*. But He Himself is not *Virāṭ*; neither is He the Golden Embryo. He is the creative aspect of God, One and only One God. Because of His Chairpersonship (*adhyakṣatā*) of the Golden Embryo, He is referred to as *Hiraṇyagarbha* in the Vedas and the Vedānta. He is really the *Hiraṇya-Garbhātmā*. He gets the universe created through His Consort or Power, Mother Sarasvatī who continues to play Her *vīṇā* (Her musical string-instrument).

---

16. *BG*, VIII.16.

17. *BG*, VIII.17.

> At the break of (Brahmā's) day, all manifestations are born of the Unmanifest (*Avyakta*). When (Brahmā's) night falls, they are dissolved there alone, in what is called the Unmanifest.[18]
>
> O son of Pṛthā, the very same host of beings, being born again and again, get helplessly dissolved at the time of (Brahmā's) nightfall and remanifest at (His) daybreak.[19]

The word *bhūtagrāmaḥ* means "the multitude of beings, both animate and inanimate." It has already been said that the duration of a day of Brahmā (excluding His night of equal duration) is a *kalpa* (4.32 billion = $4.32 \times 10^9$ earth years).

> But, distinct from that Unmanifest, is another eternal and timeless Unmanifest Being, that perishes not (even) when all beings perish.[20]

A clarification is necessary on the two *avyaktas* (unmanifest). The primordial nature (the power of *Brahman*, or *Māyā*) is *avyakta*. Everything of the gross universe and the entire gross universe (the three realms of *bhūḥ, bhuvaḥ* and *svaḥ*) undergo dissolution in *Māyā* at the nightfall of Brahmā. From a state of manifestation, they go to an unmanifested state. In the latter state, they merge in *Māyā*, the *avyakta* (unmanifest). At the daybreak of Brahmā, these empirical entities remanifest (become *vyakta*). Distinct from this *avyakta* (*Māyā*), *Brahman/Īśvara* is the Supreme Being that is Existence, Imperishable (*Akṣara*), and *Avyakta* (Unmanifested).

> The Unmanifest and the Imperishable (*Akṣara Brahman*) is said to be the supreme goal. My supreme abode is that, attaining which none returns.[21]
>
> O son of Pṛthā, that Supreme *Puruṣa* (Spirit) is attained by unswerving devotion. (He is) the *Puruṣa* in whom all beings dwell and by whom all this is pervaded.[22]

---

18. *BG*, VIII.18.
19. *BG*, VIII.19.
20. *BG*, VIII.20.
21. *BG*, VIII.21.
22. *BG*, VIII.22.

The Supreme Lord (*Parameśvara*, God) is known as *Puruṣa*, because He is *Pūrṇa* (Full, Infinite) and because He dwells in the *puri* (the city of the body of every inanimate and animate created entity). By unswerving devotion, one can attain Him, and, once attained, one is no longer reborn.

### 8.05: The Supreme Goal of the Dhyāna-Yogī

In verse 8.22 of the *BG*, it has already been said that the Supreme *Puruṣa* is attainable by unswerving devotion. Next, the Lord says that He may also be attained by yoga (*dhyāna-yoga*).

Although we accept the techniques of Pātañjala Yoga, we are not in agreement with Patañjali on his metaphysical doctrine. His insentient *Prakṛti* is one only, but his *puruṣa*s (sentient spirits) are many. God (*Īśvara*) is a special *puruṣa* (*puruṣa-viśeṣaḥ*), free from *karma* and *kleśa*s. His universe is eternal and his God is not a creator. In his concept of liberation (*kaivalya*), the *puruṣa* is disassociated from *Prakṛti* and remains in an isolated state, without further rebirth. Both Sāṅkhya and Pātañjala Yoga do not recognize *Brahman*, the Supreme Reality, the non-dual Being without becoming.

For our metaphysics, we adhere to Yoga-Vedānta. Our concept of *mokṣa* (liberation) involves the complete erasure of the *karma-saṁskāra*s imprinted in the *karmāśaya*, finally culminating in the merging of the self in the Supreme Self. We may express the contrast by saying that *kaivalya* is a process of subtraction whereas *mokṣa* is one of addition. In the process of addition, the self loses its individual identity and becomes the Supreme Self (*Brahman*). In the process of subtraction, the *puruṣa* is disassociated from the *Prakṛti* and lives eternally in bliss in an isolated state. In Yoga-Vedānta, the universe is created, sustained and dissolved in cyclic processes that were infinite in the past and will be infinite in the future. The yoga metaphysics does recognize the rebirths of the bound (*kaivalya*-unattained) *puruṣa*, but does not have a provision of the timeless existence of *Brahman*, the existence of a Creator God (*Saguṇa Brahman*), the total dissolution of the universe and the cyclic nature of the creation, sustenance and dissolution of the universe.

With this much background information, we may now go through the concluding verses of chapter 8 of the *BG*.

> O best of Bhārata princes, I shall tell you that time at which, if departed, the *yogī*s (engaged in meditation) do not return, and also the time at which, if departed, they return.[23]

> The knowers of *Brahman*, departing in time marked by Fire, Light, day-time, the bright fortnight, the six months of the northern passage of the sun, reach *Brahman*.[24]

In this verse, the word "Fire" (*Agni*) and "Light" (*Jyoti*) refer to the deities presiding over time. So also are the terms "the day-time," "the bright fortnight" and "the six months of the northern passage of the sun" that refer to the presiding deities.

> Passing away during time marked by smoke, night-time, the dark fortnight and the six months of the southern passage of the sun, the *yogī* reaches the lunar light and returns.[25]

In this verse too, the smoke, the night-time, the dark fortnight and the six months of the sun's southern course refer to the respective deities presiding over the respective time.

> These bright and dark paths of the universe are truly considered to be eternal. Going by the first (bright) one, man does not return; going by the other (dark), he returns again.[26]

The bright path is the path of knowledge and the dark one is the path of nescience. By treading the path of knowledge, one gets *mokṣa* (liberation). The path of nescience leads to *bandhana* (bondage). In interpreting verses 8.24-26, we take the meanings of the key-words in spirit, but not in letter.

---

23. *BG*, VIII.23.
24. *BG*, VIII.24.
25. *BG*, VIII.25.
26. *BG*, VIII.26.

> O son of Pṛthā, after knowing these paths, no *yogī* is deluded. Therefore, at all times, engage yourself in Yoga.[27]
>
> The *yogī*, by knowing this, transcends all the meritorious fruits of (learning) the Vedas and (actions of) sacrifices, penances and gifts, and he attains to the primeval, supreme abode.[28]

The main emphasis of this concluding section of this chapter is the transition of *dhyāna-yoga* (meditating on the monosyllable *OM*, *BG*, 8.13) to *jñāna-yoga* (the *yoga* of knowledge of *Brahman*). The word "bright (*śukla*)" stands for knowledge on *Brahman* and the realization thereof. The word "dark (*kṛṣṇa*)" stands for nescience (*avidyā, ajñānam*). The former leads to liberation, whereas the latter to bondage. The *yogī*, by constantly meditating on *OM*, becomes a *jñāna-yogī*. He knows *Brahman* and thereby becomes *Brahman* (*brahmavid brahmaiva bhavati*).

27. *BG*, VIII.27.

28. *BG*, VIII.28.

# 9

# Rājavidyā-Rājaguhya-Yogaḥ
## (The Yoga of Royal Knowledge and Royal Mystery)

### 9.01: God is Immanent and Transcendent

THE title of this section is intricate and intriguing. The Lord begins by saying:

> Now I shall reveal to you, who carp not, this most recondite knowledge, combined with its realization, having known which, you will be liberated from evil.[1]
>
> It is the sovereign science, the sovereign secret, the best of purifiers. It is directly (without any mediation) comprehensible, righteous, very easy to perform, and imperishable.[2]
>
> O scorcher of foes (Arjuna), persons, without faith in this spiritual law, return, without attaining Me, to the way of repeated deaths.[3]
>
> The entire universe has been pervaded by Me in My Unmanifested Form. All beings dwell in Me; but I do not dwell in them.[4]

*Brahman/Īśvara*, the sense-imperceptible Existence, does not dwell in a particular place like the heaven. God pervades the entire universe.

This verse rejects the Western philosophical concept of monism that holds that God is nothing other than the entire universe. The statement "All beings dwell in Me" emphasizes the fact that "No

1. *BG*, IX.1.
2. *BG*, IX.2.
3. *BG*, IX.3.
4. *BG*, IX.4.

being devoid of the Self can empirically exist (*na hi nirātmakaṁ kiñcit bhūtaṁ vyavahārāya avakalpate* — Śaṅkara). All beings exist with self-hood, with Me as the Self. Hence, it is said that they exist in Me."

The Lord further declares that He does not dwell in beings. Such seemingly contradictory statements are not really contradictory and need further clarification. God pervades all created beings, inanimate and animate, micro and macro. Still He does not dwell in them. What is the significance of such statements?

Objects, having forms, come in contact with one another. *Brahman* is not an object and has no form. It is unconnected with anything. Unlike the analogy of blood or water in the body, *Brahman* cannot be said to stay inside any created object, the latter serving as a receptacle. Nevertheless, It is the innermost Being of every entity, even the *ākāśa* which is subtle and formless. "*Brahman* does not dwell in beings." In the present context, this sentence means: "It has the absence of contact with phenomenal, usable beings."

> Neither do beings exist in Me; behold My Divine Yoga. My Self brings beings into existence and sustains them, yet does not dwell in them.[5]

In *BG*, 9.4, it has been said: "All beings exist in Me (*matsthāni sarvabhūtāni*)." In the said verse, it has also been said that God does not dwell in them, and that He pervades the entire universe. In the next verse (*BG*, 9.5), God said: "Neither do beings exist in Me." Apparently, these self-contradictory statements confuse us. This confusion disappears if we try to understand the sentence *paśya me yogamaiśvaram* (Behold My Divine Yoga). This Divine Yoga is *Yoga-Māyā*. *Brahman*/God is unmanifested (*avyakta*) whereas the phenomenal, usable universe is manifested (*vyakta*). Under the Chairpersonship of God, His *Yoga-Māyā* executes the manifestation of the universe which is an usable (*vyāvahārika*) reality only (not

5. *BG*, IX.5.

an Absolute Reality which is *Brahman* only). In the language of Advaita Vedānta, the universe is *vyāvahārika satya*, whereas *Brahman* is *pāramārthika satya*.

We present a poor simile or imagery to over-simplify the inscrutable twin-concept of the immanence and the transcendence of *Brahman/Īśvara*. Many aquatic living species have their abode in the ocean-water. Water is present inside the bodies of all the flora and fauna living in the ocean. All these living organisms live in the ocean. But the ocean does not live in any one of the living species.

> As wind, moving everywhere, eternally rests in *ākāśa* (space), know that so do all beings rest in Me.[6]

In this verse, the word *nityam* (eternally) should mean "during the lifetime of the universe." *Brahman* is *avastu* (not material) and non-relational (*asambandhi*). God's non-connection with anything and His lack of contact with everything are stressed upon in this verse.

## 9.02: The Primeval Nature is the Executive Agent

A fundamental Vedāntic concept must be clarified before we proceed to discuss this section. Reality is bipolar, one pole being *Puruṣa* and the other one *Prakṛti*. Both are co-eternal and unmanifested. We use the word "both," because we cannot express without using it. *Brahman* is non-dual; Its Power (*Śakti*) is not an entity, second to It and separate from It. They may be analogically understood as fire and heat. The *Śakti* is dependent upon the *Śaktimān* (Possessor of Power); but the reverse is not true.

*Brahman*, with *Māyā* as the *upādhi*, is God. Whereas the former is *nirguṇa* (unconnected with the three divine strings), God is *saguṇa* (connected with these strings). God is *Puruṣa* (the Supreme Spirit). *Māyā* is the unmanifest (*avyakta*) *Prakṛti* (primeval nature). Many persons confuse by equating this *avyakta Prakṛti* with the

6. *BG*, IX.6.

manifested nature, the universe of matter and energy. The former is the Mother Creatrix whereas the latter is the manifested nature, created by the former. *Māyā* is the primordial nature (*Mūla Prakṛti*), ever unmanifest and never manifest. The Vedānta discards the Sāṅkhya concept of the doctrine of transformation that holds that the unmanifest *Prakṛti* or *Pradhāna* is transformed into the manifest universe.

Both the Sāṅkhya and the Vedānta share the doctrine of reflection (*ābhāsa-vāda* or *pratibimba-vāda*). Accordingly, *Prakṛti*, intrinsically insentient, is rendered sentient due to the reflection of the consciousness of the *Puruṣa* (only one *Puruṣa* in the Vedānta; multiple *puruṣa*s in the Sāṅkhya). *Māyā* or *Prakṛti* is functionally sentient due to the reflection of the light of Consciousness (*Brahman*). Thus, for all practical purposes, *Māyā* is sentient and omniscient.

Śaṅkara, in his philosophy of non-dualism, mostly accepts *Māyā* as *avidyā* (nescience) and illusion. Although in his total philosophy, he has not erred in his concept of *Māyā*, he has been misled by Gauḍapāda's crypto-Buddhist doctrine of *śūnyavāda* (nihilism) and *māyāvāda* (illusionism). It may be mentioned here that Govindapāda was the spiritual preceptor of Śaṅkara and Gauḍapāda was the spiritual preceptor of Govindapāda. In reality, Śaṅkara was neither a crypto-Buddhist nor an illusionist. Gauḍapāda's influence on Śaṅkara was palpable and, hence, he has been more misunderstood than understood. We do recognize the phenomenal and ephemeral nature of the universe, in contrast with the absolute nature of *Brahman*. We also accept the fact that *Māyā* projects the universe as manifold appearances of the non-dual *Brahman* and that She conceals the absolute Reality. In spite of these facts, we recognize *Māyā* as a metaphysical Being, the feminine pole of the total bipolar Reality. The masculine pole is *Īśvara* (God) and the total, non-dual Reality is *Brahman*, the neutral One, without form, attributes, functions and relations, being Pure Consciousness only. *Māyā* is the Mother of the universe. In the anthropomorphic language, She is the spouse of God. She is *Parameśvarī*, the Supreme Goddess.

She Herself is not an illusion. She creates illusion by Her projecting power and concealing power. God is a non-doer (*akarttā*). Being the Chairperson and having full control on His Power (*Māyā*), He gets the universe created, sustained and nourished, and finally dissolved. God's Power (the *avyakta śakti*) is the Executive Agent.

With this much background information, now we proceed to know what the Lord says on this topic.

> O son of Kuntī, all beings go into My *Prakṛti* at the end of a *kalpa*. At the beginning of the (next) *kalpa*, I send them forth again (I create them again as in the previous *kalpas*).[7]

A *kalpa*, its duration, the manifestation of the universe from the Unmanifest *Prakṛti* and the dissolution of the universe (three *lokas* — *bhūḥ*, *bhuvaḥ* and *svaḥ*) have already been described in *BG*, 8.17-19. One day of Prajāpati Brahmā (excluding His night) is a *kalpa*. It consists of 1,000 *catur-yugas*, having a duration of 4,320 million (4.32 billion) human or earth years. One human year of 360 days is equal to a single day of Brahmā. His night has the same duration as that of His day. During His night, all beings of the universe, inanimate and animate, remain in an unmanifested state, being dissolved in the *avyakta Māyā* (unmanifest, primordial *Prakṛti*). Brahmā sleeps during His night. He lives 100 years of His time. His lifetime is a *para*. At the end of a *para*, all the seven *lokas* of the universe dissolve in *Māyā* or the unmanifest, primordial *Prakṛti*.

> Resorting to My *Prakṛti*, I get this entire multitude of bound beings emanated again and again. (These beings) are helpless under the sway of *Prakṛti*.[8]

Inequality prevails in the multitude of created beings. Can't we say that God, the Creator, is guilty of this inequality? Is He not kind to some and cruel to others? Can't He be charged for His favouritism and prejudices? The Lord answers to this question.

7. *BG*, IX.7.
8. *BG*, IX.8.

> O Arjuna, those actions bind Me not. Being unattached to those acts, I am, as it were, indifferent (neutral) (to them all).[9]

There is an apparent contradiction here. The Lord says, "I get this multitude of beings emanated from *Prakṛti*" (*BG*, 9.8) and again He says, "I am neutral or indifferent" (*BG*, 9.9). The anomaly is resolved in the next verse.

> With Me presiding, the Primordial Nature (*Mūla-Prakṛti* or *Māyā*) gives birth to the moving and the unmoving (beings). O son of Kuntī, for this reason, the universe undergoes evolution and involution.[10]

The concept of God's Chairpersonship has been given in the Vedas,[11] the Upaniṣads[12] and here in the *BG*. The *Mūla-Prakṛti* (*Māyā*) is the Executive Agent. But She cannot work without the Chairpersonship of God. Indian philosophical schools such as the Pūrva-Mīmāṁsā and Buddhism hold the concept of the eternality of the universe. The former upholds the notion of a steady-state universe. In all the Western religions, God has created the universe in a finished form within a short period (say, in six days) and the created universe, with a beginning, stays eternally. According to the Sāṅkhya, the universe has no Creator God; it has neither a beginning nor an end; and *Prakṛti* evolves in the process of transformation (*pariṇāma-vāda*). The Yoga philosophy of Patañjali accepts the main tenets of the Sāṅkhya, with the single exception that it does recognize the existence of God who is not a Creator. Thus, Yoga too holds the notion of the eternality of the universe. Śrī Aurobindo's system of evolution envisages the involution of *Brahman* into insentient matter (incontience) and the subsequent evolution of matter into life, mind, overmind and supermind. In his Utopia of evolutionary model, each human being would finally reach a summit state of a Gnostic Being on this Earth-Heaven.

---

9. *BG*, IX.9.
10. *BG*, IX.10.
11. *ṚV*, X.129.7.
12. *ŚU*, VI.11.

According to his speculation, each Gnostic Being would continue to preserve his/her individuality and gain emancipation and immortality. In other words, each emancipated Being would be a *Brahman*, without being merging in *Brahman*. Śrī Aurobindo's evolution is a linear one, without being cyclic and the cosmic processes permanently come to an end when the earth is transformed into heaven and all members of the human species become gods. In his system, physical evolution and species evolution stop at the human level, and then each mental man becomes a supramental being.

Darwinian evolution is atheistic, mechanical, chance-based (based on random mutation and natural selection of the fittest ones). His universe is also eternal, without a beginning and an end. His evolution is never-ending. The Aurovindites claim that Darwinian evolution terminates in the appearance of *Homo sapiens* (the human species). However, it is not a fact. Darwin has never committed that random mutations, natural selection and the consequent evolution would come to a standstill at a certain stage. In fact, Darwinian concept is fragmentary rather than holistic. It starts from living species, without any utterance on the cosmic evolution prior to the appearance of the living organisms. It does not commit anything on the liniarity or the circularity of the total cosmos.

The Vedāntic evolution is theistic and cyclic. In this system, neither *Brahman* nor the *Mūla-Prakṛti* (*Māyā*) undergoes evolution. Under the Chairpersonship of God (*Puruṣa*), *Prakṛti* (the unmanifest primordial nature) creates a phenomenal, usable (not real, not unreal) universe that undergoes continual evolution and destruction during the whole period of its sustenance. Its dissolution involves a sequential reversible retreat, finally leading to its merging in the unmanifest nature and remaining there in an unmanifested state until its next emanation. Its first evolute is the Supermind, the *Virāḍ* or the Aggregate (*Samaṣṭi*) *Buddhi*. All the subsequent evolutes are the serial manifestations from the cosmic intelligence (*Virāḍ*). In computer-analogy, evolution or creation or emanation is the display of what is stored in the hard disc on the desktop of the monitor; involution and dissolution follow the reverse pathway to finally disappear from the desktop and to be stored in the hard disc. *Virāḍ* or the Supermind serves as the super-compacted-cosmic-hard-disc, the Supermind or the *Buddhi* of the *avyakta Prakṛti*.

Neither *Puruṣa* nor *Prakṛti* is the efficient cause of the inequality in the created nature. The human species has evolved with highly evolved *antaḥkaraṇa* (internal instrument) and an evolved brain. Man has his freedom of will. His karmic *saṁskāra*s are imprinted in his *karmāśaya*. He himself is responsible for what he is and for his happiness and suffering. In a nutshell, this is the *karma-vāda* (the doctrine of *karma*). The *Puruṣa* or the *Prakṛti* is in no way responsible for the inequality in the universe.

*Puruṣa* is neither the efficient nor the material cause of the universe. He is a silent witness (*sākṣī*) and the Chairperson (*adhyakṣa*) whose power (*śakti*) is the Executive Agent. Under His Chairpersonship, *Prakṛti* is the efficient cause of all the cosmic events (creation, sustenance and dissolution; control and maintenance of order). But She is not the efficient cause of the individual actions of the created entities of the universe. The *svabhāva, prakṛti* or the *antaḥkaraṇa* of an entity is the doer of its actions. *Māyā* or *avyakta Prakṛti* is not the material cause of the universe too. She is not modified or transformed into the universe. She projects a universe out of Her Supermind. For this dreamy or magical projection, no materials (*upādāna*) are necessary. All newly created entities are produced in pairs, equal and opposite in all traits, their combinations resulting in zero. In the language of the *Ṛgveda* (X.129.3), the universe has been produced from *tucchya* (practically from nothing). It is unfortunate that, being wrongly influenced by the Sāṅkhya concepts, interpreters of the Vedānta have theorized that *Īśvara* is the efficient cause of the universe and that *Prakṛti* or *Māyā* is its material cause. This author has committed this blunder too in some of his previous publications.

### 9.03: One and Only One Supreme Lord

Lord Vāsudeva had a human form. God is eternal (*nitya*) and timeless (*sanātana*), Pure Consciousness (*Viśuddha Cit*), non-doer (*akarttā*) and unattached (*anāsakta*). It seems to be contradictory to assume a human form, to be immanent and transcendent, to be omnipresent and to become the Supreme Lord of all beings (*Maheśvara*). The Lord proceeds to resolve this apparent contradiction.

> Fools deride Me, who have assumed a human body. (They) are unaware of My higher state as the Supreme Lord of beings.[13]
>
> With futile hopes, futile works, futile knowledge and mindlessness, they have resorted to the delusive nature of monsters and demons.[14]
>
> But magnanimous persons, O son of Pṛthā, resorting to a divine nature, worship Me with a single mind, knowing Me as the imperishable source of beings.[15]
>
> Incessantly glorifying Me, striving with steadfast vows, bowing to Me, eternally united (with Me), they worship Me with devotion.[16]
>
> And others too worship Me with the sacrifice of knowledge (*jñāna-yajña*), (looking up to) Me with face turned everywhere, as one, as different, as manifold.[17]

There is only one God, not two, three or more. But some distinctly worship God as the sun, the moon and the others. Some worship God, the All-faced, who exist in all forms (*viśva-rūpa*) as manifold, with the idea that one God alone, with His face on all sides exists in all forms. Lord Vāsudeva confirms what the devotees do in the following verse:

> I am the *kratu*; I am the *yajña*; I am the *svadhā*; I am the *auṣadha*; I

---

13. *BG*, IX.11.
14. *BG*, IX.12.
15. *BG*, IX.13.
16. *BG*, IX.14.
17. *BG*, IX.15.

> am the *mantra*; I am the *ājyam*; I am the fire; I am the oblation.[18]

First we present Śaṅkara's interpretation of this verse. *Kratu* is a type of Vedic sacrificial rite. The word *yajña* here means "oblation or fire-sacrifice," enjoined by *Smṛti* (post-Vedic Hindu scriptures). In the present context, *svadhā* is the offering of food made to the ancestral spirits. Herbs on which living beings feed, including rice, wheat, barley, et cetera, are named as *auṣadha*. Alternatively, *svadhā* may denote the food of all living beings whereas *auṣadha* may mean healing herbs. The sacred text with which oblation is offered to the manes and gods is a *mantra* in the present verse. Melted and clarified butter used for oblation is *ājyam*.

Our interpretation does not essentially differ from that of Śaṅkara. However, there are differences in the meanings of some words. As Śaṅkara has said, *kratu* is a special type of complex Vedic sacrificial rite. *Yajñaḥ* carries the usual meaning of "worshipping God through the fire-sacrifice." *Svadhā*, in the present context, is "food or libation added to the fire in a fire-sacrifice as an offering." Here *auṣadha* means "dried herbs, in a powdered form, added to the fire in a fire-sacrifice." *Ājyam* is "the material made by melting and clarifying butter, used for oblation, or for pouring into the holy fire at the sacrifice." The word *mantra* means "a sacred text by chanting which one consecrates"; or it means "a sacred syllable or verse for chanting or silent utterance in the act of meditating on its meaning." *Hutam* is "oblation, the act of offering melted, clarified butter in the fire." Whatever may be the meanings of the words, used in the verse, they convey only a single essence that everything is God and there is nothing else other than God.

> I am the Father of this universe, (its) Mother, the Sustainer, the Grandfather. I am the holy, sacred One to be known. I am the monosyllable *OM* and also the Vedas — the *Ṛk*, *Sāman* and *Yajus*.[19]

---

18. *BG*, IX.16.

19. *BG*, IX.17.

> (I am) the Goal, the Sustainer, the Lord, the Witness, the Abode, the Refuge, the Well-wisher (Friend), the Source (from which all beings emanate), the Receiver in which all beings dissolve (in the final dissolution), the One in which all beings stay, the Storehouse (the deposit of *karmas* of beings in subtle forms) and the indestructible Seed.[20]

> I cause heat. I arrest and send forth rain. I am immortality and also death. O Arjuna, both being and non-being am I.[21]

Verse 9.19 of the *BG* uses two sets of self-contradictory words that are not permissible in Aristotelian logic. They are, however, standard uses in Vedāntic as well as quantum logic. God is immortality (*amṛtam*) and also death (*mṛtyuḥ*). God is being (*sat*) and also non-being (*asat*). When reference is made to two sets of conditions and two types of existences, this type of apparently self-contradictory words or statements are permissible. *Brahman*, the Absolute Being, is *amṛtam* (deathless) and *sat* (absolute Existence). The manifested universe of multiplicity and transitoriness, usably and phenomenally existent and functional, is death and non-being. The manifested universe is *Brahman* in one sense. Verses 9.16 to 18 clarify this concept.

Now the Lord speaks about the persons who perform Vedic rituals to go to heaven and, after the expiry of the effects of their meritorious actions, come back to the mortal world.

> The knowers of the three Vedas, drinking *soma*-juice, cleansed of sins, worship Me by fire-sacrifice (*yajña*) and pray for going to heaven. They reach the holy world of the Lord of the *devas* and enjoy the divine pleasures of the *devas* in heaven.[22]

Here the *BG* refers to the *karmakāṇḍa* (portions of ritual observances) of the three Vedas — *Ṛk*, *Yajuḥ* and *Sāman*. Some Vedic interpreters have misinterpreted the word *soma* as a kind of alcoholic drink. It is, however, far from truth. It is a herb, the

---

20. *BG*, IX.18.
21. *BG*, IX.19.
22. *BG*, IX.20.

juice of which is extracted, mixed with milk and honey for flavour, and the mixture is taken for imparting coolness to the body and mind and for giving vitality and vigour to the whole body-system. It is not a fermentation product; neither is it an intoxicating drink. It is offered to the *deva*s and God in the fire-sacrifice.

The holy world of the Lord of the *deva*s means "the abode of Indra" who had performed a hundred sacrifices.

> Having enjoyed the vast world of heaven, they enter the mortal world, on the exhaustion of their merit. Thus, conforming to the injunctions of the three Vedas, and desiring objects of pleasure, they go and come (go to heaven and return to the mortal world).[23]

Here two clarifications are necessary. In the religions of the West, the provision of rebirth is absent and those who go to heaven stay there eternally in bliss. The Vedic religion, however, does not provide an eternal abode for any human being. Secondly, we do not recognize the seven worlds as regions located one over the other, unlike the traditional concept in Hinduism. In our opinion, all the seven worlds (*lokāḥ*) are present here, there and everywhere. They differ in grossness and subtlety and possess varying number of dimensions. The first three *loka*s are *bhūḥ*, *bhuvaḥ* and *svaḥ*, the third one being heaven. In addition, there are four other worlds, namely, *mahaḥ*, *janaḥ*, *tapaḥ* and *satya*.

These two verses of the *BG* (9.20-21) are meant for persons who have desires to go to heaven and enjoy pleasures there. Next, the *BG* speaks about persons of right knowledge, who are devoid of desires.

> For persons who exclusively meditate on Me, wholeheartedly worship Me and are incessantly united with Me (through meditation), I bring prosperity and security to them.[24]

This verse begins with the word *ananyāścintayantaḥ*. The devotees, with true knowledge of *Brahman* and *Parameśvara* (Supreme God),

---

23. *BG*, IX.21.

24. *BG*, IX.22.

constantly meditate on Me, not separate from them. They have the full comprehension that the Supreme Lord is their very Self. The verse has two special words, namely, *yoga* and *kṣema*. The former word means "getting what is not already possessed." The latter word means "preservation of what comes into possession." Those devotees who realize non-separateness between themselves and God, who simply have God alone as their resort, and who never entertain any desire or concern even for their life or death are taken care of by God for their *yoga* (prosperity) and *kṣema* (security).

A doubt arises in the mind of Arjuna. Devotees who worship gods (*devatās*) should be considered as worshippers of God alone. On this issue, Arjuna requests Lord Vāsudeva to dispel the doubt.

> O son of Kuntī, even those devotees of other divinities (*devatās*), endowed with faith, worship Me alone too, but by the wrong method.[25]

There has been quite a confusion over the issue of one God or many Gods (gods) in the Hindu religion. The concept of monotheism was proclaimed in the Vedas unambiguously before the birth of all other religions of the world. The Vedānta spells out the concept of *Brahman* and that of non-dualism. These two concepts have not yet been assimilated by most persons in the world, even by many Hindus.

God is one only and gods are many in number. The gods have births and deaths. They are born after the initial creation, they merge in God, consequent to the total dissolution. Any major created entity, like our sun and moon, becomes an *upādhi* for God who pervades the entire universe. God who presides over such created entities becomes a god (*devatā*). He is the *Antaryāmī* (the Inner Controller). Every *devatā* or god is not different from God; but any god cannot be identified with God. A vessel, submerged in the ocean, contains water of the ocean. Notwithstanding this

25. *BG*, IX.23.

fact, water in the vessel, sitting at the bottom of the ocean, is not the entire water-mass of the ocean.

> I am indeed the Enjoyer and Master of all fire-sacrifices (*yajñas*). But they (the worshippers of gods) do not really know Me. Therefore, they lapse.[26]

Worshipping gods, in ignorance, even by the wrong methods, is not totally futile. The fruit of the sacrifice certainly accrues. How does it happen then?

> The devotees of gods go to the gods; those devoted to the manes go to the manes; the *Bhūta*-worshippers go to the *Bhūtas*; My worshippers too come unto Me.[27]

Ācārya Śaṅkara has given the contextual meaning of *Bhūtas* (*bhūtāni vināyakamātṛgaṇacaturbhaginyādīni*). They are the *Vināyakas*, the group of divine mothers, the four *Bhaginīs*, and the like.

How does a worshipper of gods (not God) get the fruit of his *yajña*? The real fruit is only *citta-śuddhi* (the purification of the mind), which qualifies the worshipper for the acquisition of *jñāna* (knowledge). But these worshippers become enjoyers of trifling results, whereas the staunch devotee of God attains liberation and is no longer reborn.

### 9.04: Offering Everything to God is the Easy Means to Worship

When the Vedic Aryans descended to Sapta-Sindhu (the land of seven rivers; the land of the Indus Valley) from the *Deva-loka* (an extra-terrestrial location outside our solar system, but inside our galaxy) under the leadership of Manu, they did not use forms, images, idols and statues as representative models for God and did not do *pūjā* (worship as in vogue at present). They were praying to one God only and offering oblation of dehydrated and clarified butter (*ghṛtam*) in the fire-sacrifice (*homa*).

---

26. *BG*, IX.24.
27. *BG*, IX.25.

At the time of the Mahābhārata War, form-worship and *pūjā* had already been adopted by the Aryans. The act of offering (*samarpaṇa*) is the essential feature of any *pūjā*. Lord Vāsudeva instructs Arjuna on the easy ways of doing *pūjā* that may be performed with or without form-worship. Material offering may be done. Mental offering may also be done without the use of material things. It is called *mānasa pūjā*. Let us know what the Lord says:

> Whoever, with devotion, offers Me a leaf, a flower, a fruit, or water, I enjoy that, the devout gift of the pure-hearted worshipper.[28]

A few things are to be noted with reference to this verse. Firstly, offering must be done with devotion (*bhakti*). Secondly, the cost or the kind of the material is not important. Thirdly, the mind of the worshipper must be pure. It must not be contaminated with bad will, malice, egoism and violence. Lastly, the offering may be done with elaborate ritualism, recital of *mantra*s and scriptural erudition. The offering may also be done, of course, with devotion, without ritualism, erudition and *mantra*-recital. While offering, the worshipper may use his own language, simple enough, crude or polished, flowery or bland (insipid); or he may not use any language at all and silently communicate with God for the act of his offering.

> Whatever you do, whatever you eat, whatever you sacrifice, whatever you offer as gift, whatever austerity you perform, O son of Kuntī, do all this as a dedication (*samarpaṇa*) to Me.[29]

It is a generalized advice of the Lord to His devotee. You may construct a house to live in. Before you live in, dedicate the house to God. As an author, you may write a book; but dedicate it to God. When you eat your meals, first offer the food to God. When you sacrifice (perform *yajña*), first offer the sacrifice to God. If

---

28. *BG*, IX.26.

29. *BG*, IX.27.

you practise penances, offer them to God. When you donate money, materials, food, clothes and anything else to learned, spiritual persons, or to illiterate, poor and distressed persons who are badly in need of them, offer your gift to God. When you marry and enjoy sex-play with your spouse, first offer your sex-life to God.

> Thus, will you be released from the bonds of actions, with their results, good and evil. Your self being united with the Self by the Yoga of renunciation, you will be liberated and come to Me.[30]

The *BG* does not preach renunciation of work. But actions themselves cause bondage and are productive of good and evil fruits. There is a remedy for ridding the bad effects of actions. The Yoga of renunciation, that is the act of offering everything to God, is the remedy. It will cleanse the *antaḥkaraṇa*. With the *antaḥkaraṇa* fully cleansed, the self shall go unto God when the body drops away. The non-dualistic Vedānta claims that, on being released, the self becomes the Self, with the concurrent loss of previous identity, albeit the separate identity had been apparent and usable only.

### 9.05: God's Devotee Has a Special Status

Doubt may arise in the mind of the common man (spiritually speaking, deluded Arjuna is still a common man) in the neutrality of God. Should God have affection and hatred, due to which He favours His devotees and not others? The Lord clears this doubt.

> Towards all beings I am the same. To Me there is none hateful or dear. But those who worship Me with devotion are in Me and I am in them too.[31]

If we analyse this verse, the question of God's showing favour to His devotees or special liking for His devotees does not arise. The actions and conduct of a true devotee are free from blemishes

30. *BG*, IX.28.

31. *BG*, IX.29.

and are dedicated to God. Such a devotee deserves love from the Lord.

> If someone, despite his extremely wicked conduct, worships Me with undivided devotion, he must indeed be deemed as good; for his resolution is right.[32]
>
> Soon he becomes a righteous person and attains to lasting peace. O son of Kuntī, know for certain (My) proclamation that My devotee never perishes.[33]

The word *pratijānīhi* means *niścitaṁ pratijñāṁ kuru* (be absolutely assured and proclaim). Although, in this verse, the Lord asks Arjuna to proclaim that God's devotee never perishes, it is Lord Vāsudeva Himself who really promises and proclaims that His devotee never perishes. As we understand this expression, God clearly expresses: Know My promise, My certain proclamation (*pratijñā*) that My devotee never perishes.

> The devotee's birth, in this or that family, as male or female, is not important. He/she, taking refuge in God, attains to the supreme goal.[34]
>
> It is a fact that the world is transient and joyless (*anityamasukha*). By worshipping God, everyone can attain the supreme goal (liberation). It becomes still easier for learned persons who are the knowers of *Brahman* and for kings who have attained to sainthood.[35]

The Lord advises Arjuna to be a devotee. Devotion and taking refuge in God will certainly lead to the attainment of liberation:

> Set your mind on Me; be My devotee; sacrifice unto Me; pay obeisance to Me. Being wholly intent on Me, thus uniting your self, you will surely come to Me, the Self.[36]

---

32. *BG*, IX.30.
33. *BG*, IX.31.
34. *BG*, IX.32.
35. *BG*, IX.33.
36. *BG*, IX.34.

God is the Self of all beings, both inanimate and animate. The difference between a self and the Self is added extrinsically; it is not inherent or innate; in other words, it is adventitious only. The Great Self (*Parameśvara*, God) is the Supreme Goal, the Supreme Destiny. Through steadfast devotion, one can reach the Supreme Self. And once reached, one becomes the Supreme Self. After attaining this final goal, one does not come back, that is, one is no longer reborn.

# 10

# Vibhūti-Yogaḥ
## (The Yoga of Divine Glory)

### 10.01: The Universe is the Empirical and Phenomenal Manifestation of God

We have already mentioned that the Vedānta does not accept the doctrine of transformation (*pariṇāma-vāda*) of the Sāṅkhya. Neither has the *Puruṣa* nor the *Prakṛti* been transformed into the universe. Śaṅkara, the great exponent of the non-dualistic Vedānta, enunciates his *adhyāsa-vāda* (*atasmiṁstadbuddhiḥ*). *Brahman*, being the substratum (*adhiṣṭhāna*), phenomenally manifests diversely. *Brahman* (*B*) appears as non-*B*, the non-*B* being $J_1$, $J_2$, $J_3$, . . ., $J_n$. Here *J* represents the *jagat* (*gam* + *kvip*); it is that which is in motion; the usable (*vyāvahārika*), phenomenal (*prātibhāsika*), transient, ever-changeable universe. This doctrine of *adhyāsa-vāda* does not whisk away the universe as nothing, mere hallucination. If a rope appears as a snake, *Brahman* is the former and the universe is the latter. The manifested universe is not nothing; it is a virtual existence (*vyāvahārika satya*), although not an absolute existence (*pāramārthika satya*). *Brahman*, the real existence, appears as the manifold virtual existences due to the magical activity of *Māyā*, the Power of *Brahman*.

Every entity of the universe — micro or macro, beautiful or ugly, benign or malignant — is a manifestation (*pariprakāśa*, *abhivyakti*) of God. But the expression of divine glory in the manifested entities is not uniform. Some are more glorious; some others are less glorious; and some are not glorious at all.

God is incomprehensible. Even the seers fail to know Him. He is Unmanifest (*Avyakta*). But His glory (*vibhūti*) is manifested in the created universe. Lord Vāsudeva hints at His incomprehensibility, inscrutability.

> The hosts of gods know not My origin; neither do great seers; because, in all respects, I am the source of gods and the great seers.[1]
>
> He who knows Me as birthless and beginningless and as the great Lord of the worlds is undeluded among mortals (men) and is freed from all sins.[2]

Śaṅkara gives the contextual meaning of the word *Maheśvaram* as *turīyam ajñānatatkāryavarjitam* (the Fourth or the Transcendent, devoid of nescience and its effects).

Lord Vāsudeva is the great Lord of the worlds for the following reasons too:

> Intellect, knowledge, non-delusion, forgiveness, truthfulness, self-restraint, calmness, pleasure, pain, birth, death, fear and fearlessness, non-violence, equanimity, contentment, austerity, charity, renown, ill-fame — (these) different kinds of dispositions of beings arise from Me alone.[3]

In verses 10.4-5, some contradictory dispositions have been listed. God does not whimsically create these dispositions of living beings, whose karmic *saṁskāra*s act as the determining factors.

> The seven great seers and the four ancient Manus, endowed with My powers, were born of (My) mind. These beings (creatures) are their progeny.[4]

In each *kalpa,* fourteen Manus appear and hold office in succession. The four Manus, referred to, are the Sāvarṇas, namely, Sāvarṇi, Dharma-Sāvarṇi, Dakṣa-Sāvarṇi and Sāvarṇa. The seven *ṛṣi*s are

1. *BG,* X.2.
2. *BG,* X.3.
3. *BG,* X.4-5.
4. *BG,* X.6.

Bhṛgu, Marīcī, Atri, Pulastya, Pulaha, Kratu and Vasiṣṭha.

> He who truly knows this glory and Yoga of Mine becomes established in the unshakable state of integration. There is no doubt about it.[5]

> I am the source of all. From Me everything evolves. Thus thinking, the wise, endowed with devotion to the Supreme Truth, adore Me.[6]

> With minds fixed on Me, *prāṇa*s absorbed in Me, mutually enlightening, and always speaking of Me, they rejoice and get satisfaction.[7]

The words *manaḥ* and *prāṇa*, used in the verse, carry their special Vedāntic meanings. The former one is not identified with the brain. It is a subtle organ in the subtle body. It comprises the *buddhi, ahaṅkāra* and *manas*, combinedly called the *antaḥkaraṇa*, and the additional subtle organs, five sensory and five motor, these ten being called *indriya*s in the Sanskrit language. *Prāṇa* has been traditionally translated into English as "life" and as "vital breath." It is an unfortunate serious mistake. *Āpaḥ* evolves from *Virāḍ* and *Prāṇa* evolves from *Āpaḥ*. *Prāṇa* is the primordial working entity of the universe, the super-unified force. It has no equivalent word in English. We may coin a new word and name it as "viton." All the four fundamental forces and all kinds of energy are unified to become *Prāṇa*. No created entity, either inanimate or animate, can do any work without *Prāṇa*. It is all-pervasive in the universe. It is the evolvent of the evolute, *Ākāśa* (Space). *Āpaḥ*, *Prāṇa* and *Ākāśa* can serve as the medium of transmission of energy-waves and forces. In Yoga and Kuṇḍalinī-Tantra, the control and regulation of *manaḥ* and *Prāṇa* are important useful techniques. The cosmic *Prāṇa* are resolved into five types of *prāṇa*s in the body. They are the *prāṇa, apāna, udāna, vyāna* and *samāna*.

I give that *buddhi-yoga* to them who are uninterruptedly united

---

5. *BG*, X.7.

6. *BG*, X.8.

7. *BG*, X.9.

> with Me and who lovingly adore Me. (By that *buddhi-yoga*), they draw nigh to Me.[8]

Here the compound word *buddhi-yoga* needs an explanation. It is a special term of the *BG*. *Brahman* is Pure Spirit or Pure Consciousness (*śuddha caitanyam*). It is attributeless and functionless. It does not directly destroy nescience (*avidyā, ajñānam, mithyā-jñānam*). The intellect of a devotee, through devotion and deep concentration on God by *dhāraṇā, dhyāna* and *samādhi*, receives a greater density of illumination from *Brahman*, the only source of the Light of Consciousness. As a result, the *antaḥkaraṇa* rids its opacity and translucency, and becomes transparent. Once nescience and illusory knowledge are destroyed, the *buddhi-yogī* comes unto God.

Although *Brahman* is attributeless and functionless, *Īśvara* (God) is not so. *Brahman*, with *Māyā* as the *upādhi*, is God who has attributes and functions through the executive agency of *Māyā*, the Power of God. The next verse throws more light on this issue.

> Out of mere compassion for them (devotees), I, dwelling in their internal instruments (*antaḥkaraṇa*), destroy the darkness (in them).[9]

Now Arjuna understands that the whole universe is a virtual manifestation of *Brahman*, that the self is liberated through devotion and meditation by which the devotee gains *buddhi-yoga* and gets divine compassion to destroy nescience and to realize the Supreme Truth. Arjuna has further doubts that he wants to be clarified. If everything is the virtual manifestation of God, there must be some glorious manifestations upon which he must meditate. When God, being formless (*arūpa*) and unmanifested (*avyakta*), cannot be directly perceived by senses, the devotee must feel the presence of God in some glorious manifestations (*vibhūti*s). He asks a pertinent question to the Lord: "What are the *vibhūti*s?" This question will be discussed in the next section.

---

8. *BG*, X.10.

9. *BG*, X.11.

**10.02: Arjuna Wants to Know the Divine Glory**

God is the source of everything in the universe. But everything is not a *vibhūti* (a glorious phenomenon). Arjuna wants to know the *vibhūti*s of God in detail.

> Thou art the Supreme *Brahman*, the Supreme Abode, the Supreme Purifier. (Thou art) the eternal, divine Spirit (*Puruṣa*), primordial God, unborn and all-pervading.[10]
>
> (Thus have) all seers — seer-god Nārada, also Asita, Devala and Vyāsa — hailed You. And to me yourself declare the same.[11]
>
> O Keśava (Kṛṣṇa), I deem as true all this that You tell me. O Lord, neither the gods nor the demons know Your manifestations.[12]
>
> O *Puruṣottama* (Supreme Spirit), O Source of all beings, O Lord of all beings, O God of the gods, O Lord of the universe, only You Yourself know the Self, by Yourself.[13]
>
> You ought indeed to speak, in their entirety, of Your divine glories, by means of which You abide, pervading all these worlds.[14]
>
> O Yogin, how shall I, ever meditating, know You? O God, in what several things am I to meditate on You?[15]
>
> O Janārdana (Kṛṣṇa), speak to me once again, in detail, Your yoga and glory; for, there is no satiety for me in listening to this ambrosial (account).[16]

Lord Vāsudeva answers to the question of Arjuna. He gives a sample list of His *vibhūtis* in which Arjuna may envision the divine manifestations.

---

10. *BG*, X.12.
11. *BG*, X.13.
12. *BG*, X.14.
13. *BG*, X.15.
14. *BG*, X.16.
15. *BG*, X.17.
16. *BG*, X.18.

**10.03: Glorious Manifestations of God**

God is formless (*arūpa*). To see a form (or forms) of formless God is a self-contradictory concept. God is non-material (*avastu*). To see God in matter is a self-contradictory concept. In spite of the self-contradictions in seeing God, one can experience sense-imperceptible God through one's five senses by the sense-perceptions of the divine glories manifested by God's creation. Let us go through the verses that describe a number of divine glories.

> Well, I shall speak to you now, O best of Kurus (Arjuna), of the more prominent of My divine glories; for, there is no end to a detailed account (of them all).[17]
>
> O Guḍākeśa (Master of sleep = Arjuna), I am the Self, resident in the hearts of all beings; and I am the beginning, and the middle, and also the end of all beings.[18]

The word *guḍākā* means "sleep" (*nidrā*), and *Īśaḥ* means "master." Arjuna is *jitanidraḥ* (one who has conquered sleep) and, hence, is addressed as *guḍākeśa*. God is the beginning — the cause or the source — of all beings. He is the middle of all beings. Here "middle" refers to the manifested (*vyakta*) state. He is the end of all beings. In the total dissolution (*mahā-pralaya*), the whole universe of matter and energy, of inanimate and animate beings dissolves in Him.

> I am Viṣṇu among the Ādityas; of the luminaries, the radiant sun; of the Maruts, I am Marīci; of the asterisms, I am the moon.[19]

The Ādityas, twelve in number, are the sons of Kaśyapa and Aditi. They are: Dhātā, Mitra, Aryamā, Indra, Varuṇa, Aṁśa, Bhaga, Vivasvān, Pūṣa, Savitā, Tvaṣṭā and Viṣṇu.

The Maruts, forty-nine in number, were born of Diti and Kaśyapa. They became the wind-gods and friends of Indra.

> Among the Vedas, I am the *Sāma-veda*; of the gods, I am Vāsava

17. *BG*, X.19.

18. *BG*, X.20.

19. *BG*, X.21.

> (Indra); among the senses, I am the mind; and of created beings (both inanimate and animate), I am consciousness (*cetanā*).[20]

The gods are thirty-three in number. They are the eight Vasus, the eleven Rudras, the twelve Ādityas, Indra and Prajāpati.

The five senses of perception (for seeing, hearing, smelling, tasting and touching), the five senses of action (for locomotion, prehension, phonation, reproduction and excretion) and mind are the eleven senses. All of them belong to the subtle body rather than the gross body.

When quantum mechanics of physics was discovered in the second half of the twentieth century, it could be known that the whole universe and every particle and micro-particle of the universe are conscious. The *BG* has given the concept of the conscious matter, including energy, in the remotest ancient age.

> And I am Śaṅkara among the Rudras. Of Yakṣas and demons, I am Kubera, the Lord of wealth. Of the Vasus, I am Pāvaka (the purifying fire) and among the mountains, I am Meru.[21]

The eleven Rudras are Hara, Bahurūpa, Tryambaka, Aparājita, Vṛṣākapi, Śambhu, Kapardī, Raivata, Mṛgavyādha, Śarva and Kapālī. In this verse, Śambhu has been referred to as Śaṅkara.

The eight Vasus are: Dhruva, Dhara, Soma, Aha, Anila, Anala, Pratyūṣa and Prabhāsa.

> O son of Pṛthā (Arjuna), know Me to be Bṛhaspati, the chief among the priests. Among the war-generals, I am Skanda. Among the reservoirs of water, I am the ocean.[22]
>
> I am Bhṛgu among the great seers; I am the monosyllable (*OM* that designates *Brahman*) among utterances; I am sacrifice of *japa* (repeating utterances of God's name and *mantras*) among sacrifices; and I am the Himālayas among immobile objects.[23]

---

20. *BG*, X.22.
21. *BG*, X.23.
22. *BG*, X.24.
23. *BG*, X.25.

> Among all trees, (I am) the peepul (*Ficus religiosa* = *Aśvattha* = *pippala*); among divine seers, (I am) Nārada; among divine minstrels, (I am) Citraratha; and among perfected sages, (I am) the sage, Kapila.[24]

All interpreters of the *BG* equate Kapila of this verse with Kapila, the founder of the Sāṅkhya philosophy. The latter was an atheist, albeit not a materialist. He recognized the insentient *Prakṛti* or *Pradhāna* and innumerable sentient *puruṣa*s (spirits). But he rejected the existence of *Brahman/Īśvara* (God). The non-dualistic Vedānta establishes the identity of the Supreme Self and the individual selves. The Sāṅkhya has no Supreme Self (no *Brahman*; no *Īśvara*) and regards the individual selves as distinct sentient entities. The *puruṣa*s are functionless whereas the *Prakṛti* is active. She acts for the *puruṣa*s none of whom has any control over the former. The Vedāntic cosmology is cyclic, with creation, sustenance and dissolution of the universe. The Sāṅkhya cosmology is linear, with the acceptance of the eternality of the uncreated universe. Of course, it does recognize the cyclic evolution of individual human beings until the attainment of *kaivalya* (the Sāṅkhya and the Yoga type of liberation, separation of the *puruṣa* from the *prakṛti*). The *mokṣa* (liberation) of the non-dualistic Vedānta is merging of the individual self in the Supreme Self, with the concomitant loss of individual identity. The Sāṅkhya accepts the doctrine of transformation (*pariṇāma-vāda*), according to which *Prakṛti* is modified into the universe. On the contrary, the Vedānta holds the doctrine of the appearance of *Brahman* as the multiplicity of the virtual, phenomenal universe. We find realism in Sāṅkhya and *vivartta-vāda* in Advaita Vedānta. The question is: With fundamental variances, how did the *BG* extol Kapila, the founder of the Sāṅkhya, as a glory of God?

The *Bhāgavatam*[25] has mentioned Kapila as an incarnation of Lord Viṣṇu. Vyāsa, the author of the *Mahābhārata* and also of the

---

24. *BG*, X.26.

25. *Bhā*, III.24.19.

*Bhāgavatam*, has praised Kapila who could not be an atheist. Is Vyāsa's Kapila someone different from the founder of the Sāṅkhya? Has the word *sāṅkhyācārya* been later inserted in the *Bhāgavatam* by others as an identity of the founder of Sāṅkhya? It may also be the fact that the disciples of Kapila have distorted the original philosophy of the Master. (No authoritative book of Kapila is extant).

Our interpretation is different from that of all others. "Kapila" (the literal meaning of this word is "fiery red") in the present verse refers to Brahmā, the God who presides over the Golden Embryo. (The Cosmic Egg had the colour of molten gold). We deduce our conclusion from a number of premises. The first premise is the *Hiraṇya-Garbha-Sūktam* of the *R̥gveda* (X.121). *Hiraṇya-Garbha* has two meanings. One is the "Golden Embryo" or the Cosmic Egg. The second one is the "Chairperson of the Cosmic Egg" (Brahmā, God who creates). One of the Purāṇic names of Viṣṇu is Padmanābha and of Brahmā is Svayambhū. Viṣṇu generated Himself inside His lotus-like umbilicus and thus was the birth of Brahmā who was to superintend the creation of the universe. Our second premise is the *Śvetāśvatara Upaniṣad*. One of its verses (III.4) describes Lord Rudra as *maharṣi* (the Great Seer). The same verse narrates the birth of *Hiraṇya-Garbha* (Lord Brahmā) from God. In another verse (V.2), this Upaniṣad directly states the birth of R̥ṣi Kapila, the one who is the first-born. We are to note the word *agre* (in the beginning) in both the *R̥gveda* and the *ŚU*. We present our dissenting view for the judgement of our readers. We better continue the presentation of the verses of the *BG*.

> Among horses, know Me to be Uccaiḥśrava, born of ambrosia; among lordly elephants, Airāvata; and among human beings, their king.[26]

The horse named Uccaiḥśrava was brought forth when the ocean was churned for the sake of getting *amr̥ta* (nectar). Irāvat is the name of the ocean. Like Uccaiḥśrava, Airāvata was produced as

26. *BG*, X.27.

the offspring of Irāvat when the ocean was churned.

> Among weapons, I am the thunderbolt; among cows, I am Kāmadhuk (wish-granting cow); I am Kandarpa, the progenitor; among serpents, I am Vāsuki.[27]

Indra fashioned his weapon, *vajra*, out of the bone of Dadhīci. Vasiṣṭha's cow, Kāmadhuk or Kāmadhenu, could yield all objects desired and could yield as much milk as desired. Kandarpa or Kāma is the god of love, the progenitor, the cause of progeny.

> And Ananta among the *nāga*-snakes am I; among the creatures in water, I am Varuṇa; among the manes, I am Aryamā; I am Yama among the controllers and subduers.[28]
>
> Among the demons (the progeny of Diti), I am Prahlāda; of reckoners, I am Time; of beasts, I am the lion, their king; of the birds, I am Garuḍa, the son of Vinatā.[29]
>
> Among the purifiers, I am the wind; among the bearers of weapons, I am Rāma; of fishes, I am the shark; among rivers, I am the Gaṅgā (Jāhnavī).[30]
>
> O Arjuna, of creations, I am the beginning, the end and the middle; of all knowledges, I am the knowledge of spirituality (of the Self); of disputants, I am the dialectic.[31]

*Adhyātma-vidyā* (spiritual knowledge, knowledge of *Brahman* or the Self) is the means to liberation (*mokṣa*). No other knowledge can be comparable with it. There are three kinds of disputations, namely, *vāda*, *jalpa* and *vitaṇḍā*. *Vāda* is the discussion, devoid of bias, with the sole object of arriving at the truth. Those, engaged in *jalpa*, make an assertion of their own opinion, while aggressively attempting to refute that of their adversary, irrespective of the argument being right or wrong. One who engages oneself in idle

27. *BG*, X.28.
28. *BG*, X.29.
29. *BG*, X.30.
30. *BG*, X.31.
31. *BG*, X.32.

carping at the arguments of one's opponent, without logical refutation of the opponent's viewpoint, does *vitaṇḍā*. Among the three, *vāda* is the best type of discussion.

> Among letters, I am *a* (the first letter); among their (grammatical) compounds, I am the additive one (*dvandva*); I am alone Time imperishable; I am the Dispenser, facing all directions.[32]

It is not a fact that time is imperishable. It is neither a physical nor a metaphysical entity. It is a mental construct only, with relation to either the mind or the Supermind. With the happening of more than one event, the concept of time arises in the mind or the Supermind. Time is born with the birth of the universe. Time is dead with the total dissolution of the universe. The present verse uses the language *akṣaya kālaḥ* with reference to the concept of *Brahman*, being *sanātana* (eternal as well as timeless). *Brahman* is Existence (*Satya*) when the universe exists. *Brahman* is also Existence when the universe does not exist.

There is also a second interpretation of the statement, "I am the Time imperishable (*ahameva akṣayaḥ kālaḥ*)." Śaṅkara says: "God is Rudra-Śiva, the reckoner or destroyer even of death (*parameśvaraḥ kālasyāpi kālaḥ*)."

God is *viśvatomukhaḥ dhātā*, the multifaced dispenser of the fruits of work of the entire universe.

> And I am Death, carrying all away; and, of things yet to be, I am (their) origin. I am the speech of women; I am Fame, Glory, Memory, Intelligence, Endurance and Forbearance.[33]

Interpreters of this verse, including Śaṅkara, have found different meanings of some terms. We interpret in a little different way. God is *Mṛtyuḥ* (Death). He seizes life or is the destroyer of life. He is *Sarvaharaḥ* (One who carries all away). In the process of dissolution (momentary, partial or total), He (His *Prakṛti*) receives all who dissolve in the analogy of salt in water. Future creation

---

32. *BG*, X.33.

33. *BG*, X.34.

(emanation or re-manifestation) is to follow dissolution. And God (His *Mūla-Prakṛti*) becomes the source (origin = *udbhavaḥ*) of all to be re-created. It is God who is the sweet feminine speech. Irrespective of gender, He is the Fame, Glory, Memory, Intelligence, Endurance and Forbearance.

> Also, among the Sāman-chants, I am the Bṛhat; among the Vedic metres, I am the Gāyatrī; among the months, I am the Mārgaśīrṣa; and among the seasons, I am the Spring, the abode of flowers.[34]
>
> Of the tricksters (of the fraudulent), I am gambling (such as the game of dice); of the vigorous, I am the vigour; I am victory (of the victorious); (of men of resolution), I am the resolve (*vyavasāyaḥ*); of men of virtue, I am the virtue.[35]

We use the word "virtue" for *sattva* in the verse. There is not a word in English to substitute the Sanskrit word *sattva*. Goodness, righteousness, dutifulness, light of knowledge, virtuousness and such other good qualities are combinedly expressed by the word *sattva*.

> Among the members of the Vṛṣṇi-clan, I am Vāsudeva; among the Pāṇḍavas, I am Dhanañjaya (Arjuna). Also, among the contemplative sages, I am Vyāsa; among the seers, I am the seer, Uśanāḥ (Śukrācārya).[36]
>
> Of those who chastise, I am the sceptre; of those who seek victory, I am the tactical policy; also, of secrets, I am silence; and of the learned, I am the knowledge.[37]

Punishers are of two kinds — those who punish others for their self-interest, pride and arrogance, egoticism and sadism; and those that chastise bad persons who go astray on the wrong path. Lord Vāsudeva refers to the second type of punishment.

The Lord says: "*ahaṁ jñānavatāṁ jñānam* = I am knowledge of

---

34. *BG*, X.35.

35. *BG*, X.36.

36. *BG*, X.37.

37. *BG*, X.38.

the learned." Here He does not refer to any informational knowledge. By "knowledge," He means *samyag-jñānam*, comprehensive, true knowledge on the Reality. It is *Brahma-jñānam* which arises on the ripening of *samādhi*.

> O Arjuna, and whatsoever is the seed of all beings, that also am I. That which is without Me, movable or immovable, exists not.[38]

*Brahman* is all-pervading. There is nothing in the universe, bereft of *Brahman*. That Self is the self of each created entity, living or non-living, mobile or immobile and micro or macro. No entity can exist in the hypothetical absence of the Self. All manifested entities are virtual, their existence being dependent on the Reality (Self). We may draw an analogy of the memory of the hard disc and the virtual memory of a computer to explain the *sadasat* (existence and non-existence) nature of the universe. To conclude the topic of the glories (*vibhūti*s) of God, Lord Vāsudeva says that He is the seed (*bīja*) of all beings.

### 10.04: The Universe is the Glorious Manifestation of a Quarter of the Lord

Man does not know how big the universe is. He does not know all its dimensions and extensions. He has infinitesimally limited knowledge on the micro- and the macro-universe. He is also not sure of the correctness of whatever he knows. In such a situation, Lord Vāsudeva mentioned a sample of His glories (*vibhūti*s) to Arjuna. The Lord summarily expresses it by the following verse:

> O scourge of foes (Arjuna), there is no end of My divine glories; but, this detailed description of My glory has been (partially) narrated by Me for the purpose of illustration only.[39]
>
> Whatever being is glorious, prosperous or powerful (energetic), that know you to have been born of part of My splendour.[40]

38. *BG*, X.39.
39. *BG*, X.40.
40. *BG*, X.41.

We interpret the word *śrī* as a symbol for prosperity. Śrī is Lakṣmī, the Power or Consort of Lord Viṣṇu. She is the personification of prosperity, affluence, lustre, beauty and auspiciousness.

> O, Arjuna, wherefore do you need to know the details of all these? Steadying and supporting this entire universe with a fragment of My Power, do I abide for ever.[41]

*Brahman* is partless (*akhaṇḍa*) and homogeneous (not corpuscular; is a continuous whole without component parts). The word *aṁśa* (part) in the verse is to be correctly interpreted without violating the concept of the Unbroken Whole which is the Reality. With reference to the universe, *Brahman* is both immanent and transcendent. The Western philosophy of monism, equating the universe with God, cannot be accepted by the Indian school of non-dualism. God pervades the universe. God transcends the universe. *Brahman* and the universe are not identical. The former appears as the multiplicity of the universe. The former is the Absolute Reality (*pāramārthika satya*) whereas the latter is the virtual and practical reality (*vyāvahārika satya*).

For a comprehension of the meaning of this verse, reference may be made to the *Ṛgveda*[42] and the *Taittirīya Āraṇyaka*.[43] The entire universe is but a quarter of Him. Three-quarters of the Reality (*Brahman*) transcend the universe.

In verse 10.17 of the *BG*, Arjuna asked questions to Lord Vāsudeva: "How shall I meditate on Thee? In what several things art Thou to be thought of?"

To answer the questions of Arjuna, the Lord narrated some of His divine glories. But His glories (*vibhūtis*) have no end. What the Lord did was a mere illustration of a sample. In verse 10.41 of the *BG*, the Lord summarized: Whatever being is energetic, powerful, potent and glorious is manifestation of My splendour.

---

41. *BG*, X.42.
42. *ṚV*, X.90.3.
43. *TĀ*, XXX.12.

God is formless (*arūpa*). How should the devotee visualize the form (*rūpa*) of the formless? The only way to do it is to feel the presence of God in the beings in which His splendour is manifested.

We see God in the rising sun. We see Him in the full moon. We see Him in the beauty of the flowers and feel Him in the fragrance therein. We see Him in the butterfly, the rainbow and anything and everything of His creation where His beauty, order, auspiciousness, glory, potency and splendour are manifested.

Most people of the world hardly know that the Vedas and the Vedānta, for the first itme in the history of mankind, gave the concept of *Brahman* that has not yet been assimilated so far. The universe has only one God who is formless, birthless, deathless, immanent and transcendent. He is omnipresent, omnipotent and omniscient. In one respect, He is both subject and object. In another respect, He is rid of subjectivity and objectivity. In spite of these fundamental, scriptural declarations, most people of the world think that Hinduism has many Gods in many forms. The pity is that most Hindus, not aquainted with scriptures, also think in the same way.

This author has been very often asked a question. "Have you seen God?" He has answered: "God cannot be seen, because He is formless. Anything I perceive through my senses is done through the medium of God only. But the senses cannot perceive Him. The formless cannot have a form. Man, for his easy visualization and conception, imagines forms for God. It may also happen that God may appear before the devotee in a form. But these forms of God are not real; they are imaginary and may conform to any sort of imagination. Such imaginary forms are useful too. But, if not properly understood, they create superstition." The tenth chapter of the *BG* clearly states that God may be perceived in His glorious manifestations in the universe. The eleventh chapter is titled as the "Vision of the World-Image (*viśva-rūpa-darśanam*)." There Arjuna does not see God in any one of the forms worshipped by the Hindus. He sees the universe and separate entities of the universe in God. What is important is the immediate experience (*aparokṣānubhūti*) of God.

What have been stated in the previous two paragraphs may not be misunderstood as the condemnation of image-worship by the Hindus. The Lord has approved it in the *BG* for most persons who cannot easily conceive of the formless Being. But an image should be a visual aid, an aid for perception, cognition and intellection. The map of India cannot be India. How can an image or an idol, conceived by man and made by man, be God, the Creator, the Sustainer and the Destroyer?

# 11

## Viśva-Rūpa-Darśana-Yogaḥ
## (The Yoga of the Vision of the Cosmic Form)

### 11.01: Arjuna's Supplication for the Vision of the Cosmic Form of God and God's Grant

ARJUNA listened to the divine glories manifested in the created beings — divine beauty, lustre, splendour, power, strength, valour, intelligence, wisdom, and so on. He accepted the advice of the Lord. Nonetheless, He wanted something more. He desired to directly behold the primordial and divine cosmic form of God. So did Arjuna address Lord Vāsudeva:

> By the words you have spoken, supreme, occult and spiritual, out of compassion towards me, this delusion of mine has gone.[1]
>
> O Lotus-eyed, about the origin and dissolution of beings, I have heard from You in detail, as also about Your inexhaustible grandeur.[2]
>
> O Supreme Lord, Highest Spirit, so is it as You have declared Yourself. Yet I would desire to see Your Lordly form.[3]
>
> If You, O Lord, think me capable of seeing it (Your Lordly form), O Lord of Yogas, then reveal to me Your immutable Self.[4]

Lod Vāsudeva was moved by the request of Arjuna. Finally, He decided to show His Cosmic Form (*viśva-rūpa*). The Lord says:

---

1. *BG*, XI.1.
2. *BG*, XI.2.
3. *BG*, XI.3.
4. *BG*, XI.4.

> O son of Pṛthā (Arjuna), behold, then, hundreds and thousands of My forms, diversified, divine, variously coloured and shaped.[5]
>
> Behold Ādityas, Vasus, Rudras, the two Aśvins and Maruts. Also behold, O Bhārata, many marvels hitherto unknown.[6]
>
> O Guḍākeśa (subduer of lethargy = Arjuna), here now behold the entire universe with moving and unmoving beings, extant in "one abode" in My body; and (behold) whatever else you desire to see.[7]
>
> You, however, are not capable of seeing Me merely with this eye of yours. I give you a divine eye. (With that divine eye), behold My Lordly Yoga.[8]

The literal meaning of the word *yoga* is "union." In this verse, *yogamaiśvaram* may mean the Yoga-Power or the Supreme Power (*yoga-śakti*) of God. The vision of the Cosmic Form leads to the entry into God, the union with Him.

None can see the Cosmic Form of God with the gross eyes. The third eye is needed for a divine vision. *Siddha yogī*s do develop the divine eye. Arjuna was not a *siddha yogī*. Lord Śrīkṛṣṇa was pleased with Arjuna and made him capable of beholding the Cosmic Form of God.

### 11.02: Arjuna Beheld the Cosmic Form of God

After giving divine eye to Arjuna, Lord Nārāyaṇa revealed His transcendent and cosmic form. Sañjaya gave a description of what Arjuna saw to king Dhṛtarāṣṭra:

> With numerous mouths and eyes, with many marvellous sights, with many divine ornaments, with many weapons, uplifted; wearing divine garlands and apparel, smeared with divine scents, full of marvels, boundless God, with faces on every side.[9]

---

5. *BG*, XI.5.
6. *BG*, XI.6.
7. *BG*, XI.7.
8. *BG*, XI.8.
9. *BG*, XI.10-11.

> If a thousand suns were to simultaneously rise up in the sky, their splendour would have a (somewhat) semblance to that of the Mighty Being.[10]

The verse does not equate the splendour of a thousand simultaneously rising suns and that of the Mighty Lord. The former would be somewhat comparable to the latter. The splendour of the Cosmic Form shall definitely surpass that of the hypothetical phenomenon (the simultaneous rising of a thousand suns).

> Then and there, the son of Pāṇḍu (Arjuna) beheld the entire universe, residing together in the body of God of gods, variegated in manifold ways.[11]

## 11.03: Arjuna Narrated His Vision of the Cosmic Form of God

Arjuna saw the Cosmic Form of God. He has been seeing Śrīkṛṣṇa during the last many years, starting from his childhood. He never realized who He was seeing. Suddenly he was stricken with awe and wonder.

> Then, filled with amazement and with hairs standing on end, Dhanañjaya (Arjuna), with his head bowing down and hands folded, spoke to the Lord.[12]
>
> O Lord, I see all gods in Your body, as also hosts of all grades of beings — the mighty Brahmā seated on the lotus, all the seers, and all the celestial serpents.[13]
>
> I behold You with many hands, bellies, faces and eyes, with a form boundless in all directions. O Lord of the universe, O Cosmic Form, no end, no middle and also no beginning of Yours do I see.[14]
>
> I see You with diadem, mace and discus. (I see) a mass of

10. *BG*, XI.12.
11. *BG*, XI.13.
12. *BG*, XI.14.
13. *BG*, XI.15.
14. *BG*, XI.16.

radiance, dazzling in all directions, very hard to look at. (I see You) blazing all around like burning fire and sun. (I see You) immeasurable.[15]

You are the Imperishable, the Supreme One, worthy to be known. You are the Supreme Abode of this universe. You, the immutable, are the Guardian of eternal righteousness. I deem You to be the eternal and timeless Spirit.[16]

I see You, without beginning, middle or end; with inexhaustible energy and numberless arms; with the sun and the moon as Your eyes; with blazing fire as Your mouth, scorching this whole universe with Your radiance.[17]

This space between the *bhūrloka* and the *svarloka*, as also all points of space have indeed been pervaded by You alone. O Magnanimous Being, beholding this marvellous awful form of Yours, the three worlds are trembling (terrified).[18]

We regard the seven *loka*s (worlds), present here, there and everywhere, as ones decreasing in grossness and increasing in subtlety, starting from *bhūḥ* and ending in *Satya* or *Brahma*. They also go on increasing their dimensions in the said order. The three *loka*s in this verse are *bhūḥ*, *bhuvaḥ* and *svaḥ*.

Verily these hosts of gods enter into You. Some, being frightened, extol with folded hands. Groups of eminent seers and perfected spirits, exclaiming "May it be well," praise You with hymns, complete in all respects.[19]

Rudras, Ādityas, Vasus, Sādhyas, Viśvedevas, the two Aśvins, Maruts, the ancestral spirits, hosts of celestial minstrels, Yakṣas, demons and perfected spirits gaze at You, all being amazed.[20]

O Mighty-armed, having seen Your immense form, with many mouths and eyes, with many arms, thighs and feet, with many

15. *BG*, XI.17.
16. *BG*, XI.18.
17. *BG*, XI.19.
18. *BG*, XI.20.
19. *BG*, XI.21.
20. *BG*, XI.22.

bellies, looking fearful with many tusks, the worlds are terrified, and so am I.[21]

On seeing You touching the sky, blazing, many-hued, with mouths wide-open and eyes distended and flaming, my inner self is deeply distressed. I have neither courage nor peace, O Viṣṇu.[22]

Having seen Your mouths, terrifying due to tusks, resembling *kālāgni* (glowing like the all-consuming fire of Time at the dissolution of the world), I fail to know the directions (like east, west, north, south, up and down); nor do I find peace. Be graceous, O God of gods, O Abode of the universe.[23]

All those sons of Dhr̥tarāṣṭra, together with hosts of monarchs, Bhīṣma, Droṇa, and that charioteer's son (Karṇa), as also the leading warriors on our side rushingly enter into Your awesome mouths, terrifying due to tusks. Some are observed sticking between the teeth, with their heads crushed.[24]

As the multitudinous torrents of rivers flow towards the sea alone, so do these heroes in the world of men enter Your blazing mouths.[25]

As moths, with accelerated speed, enter a blazing fire to perish, just so, to perish, do people too enter Your mouths with accelerated speed.[26]

(You) repeatedly lick, swallowing all the worlds on all sides with Your blazing mouths. O Viṣṇu, filling the entire universe with radiant energy, Your dreadful rays are burning (causing distress).[27]

Lord Śrīkr̥ṣṇa is Viṣṇu with a human body. The word *viṣṇu* has been derived from the Sanskrit verb root *viś*, meaning "to

21. *BG*, XI.23.
22. *BG*, XI.24.
23. *BG*, XI.25.
24. *BG*, XI.26-27.
25. *BG*, XI.28.
26. *BG*, XI.29.
27. *BG*, XI.30.

pervade," "to enter." Viṣṇu is the all-pervading Spirit, God Himself.

Having seen the terrible Cosmic Form of God, Arjuna is deadly frightened. He wants to know who the Lord is.

> Tell me who You are with Your awesome form. Salutation to You, O Supreme Spirit. Be graceous. I wish to know You, the Primeval Being; for, I understand not Your activity.[28]

Here ends Arjuna's vision of the Cosmic Form of God. In the next section, Lord Vāsudeva pacifies and consoles Arjuna who has been dreadfully terrified.

### 11.04: God's Consolation and Advice to Arjuna

Arjuna was very much distressed when he beheld the terrible Cosmic Form of God. The Lord consoled him and advised him about what he should do. The Lord said:

> I am the mighty world-destroying *Kāla*, here engaged in infolding the worlds. Even without you, all the warriors arranged in the opposing armies shall cease to be.[29]

The common, popular meaning of *kāla* is "time." In the present context, however, its meaning is different. *Kāla* is *Parameśvara* (the Supreme Lord = God) conditioned by the Power of Activity (*Kriyā-Śakti*).

The Lord has revealed His Cosmic Form (*Viśva-Rūpa*) in different forms to different persons. To Arjuna, He revealed Himself as Rudra, the Lord of Destruction (*saṁhāra-karttā*). To Mother Yaśodā, He revealed Himself as Viṣṇu, the Lord of Preservation (*sthiti-karttā, pālana-karttā*). To Brahmā, He revealed Himself as a combination of Brahmā, the Lord of Creation (*sṛṣṭi-karttā*) and Viṣṇu, the Lord of Preservation. To Duryodhana, He revealed Himself as a combination of Viṣṇu and Rudra (*pālaka* and *saṁharttā*, respectively).

---

28. *BG*, XI.31.
29. *BG*, XI.32.

The activity of destruction of Rudra is not tantamount to annihilation (reducing the created beings to nothing). It is the process of infolding or dissolution (*pralaya*). It is *samāhāra*, the process of reabsorption.

Even if Arjuna does not fight and kill the warriors — Bhīṣma, Droṇa, Karṇa and others, they shall cease to be. Such being the case, it would be wise for Arjuna to fight. Thus, does the Lord advise :

> Therefore, do you stand up and acquire fame. Conquering the enemies, enjoy the affluent kingdom. Verily by Myself, have they been already slain. O Savyasācin (Arjuna), merely be an apparent cause.[30]

In Indian philosophy, some causes are efficient (*nimitta-kāraṇa*) and some others are material (*upādāna-kāraṇa*). The doer of an action is the *nimitta-kāraṇa* whereas the precursor material of the present product is the material cause. In the present verse, the word *nimitta* is not used in the sense of an efficient cause. One meaning of *nimitta* is "for" or "on behalf of." The Lord says: "I have already slain. You merely play an apparent role for Me and be the apparent slayer." In another sense, the Lord instructs Arjuna: "Be simply a tool of Mine," "Work on my behalf."

We would like to revise the traditional interpretation of the Vedāntic concept of causation. God, because of His Chairpersonship and all-pervasive presence, is the *pracodaka kāraṇa* (impelling or inspiring cause) of cosmic events, although He is a non-doer (*akarttā*). *Māyā* or the *Mūla-Prakṛti*, being the doer of all cosmic events, is the *nimitta-kāraṇa* (a causal agent that executes on behalf of someone else; in this case, *Māyā* works on behalf of God). Any created entity, animate or inanimate, is the subjective cause of any action done by it. Such a statement of subjective cause is necessarily true, because every action has its own doer or every verb has its own subject, either expressed or understood. (In Śaṅkara's language, it is: *yatkāryaṁ tatsakartṛkam*). Actions

30. *BG*, XI.33.

involving modifications or transformations necessarily have material causes. The precursor material is the material cause (*upādāna-kāraṇa*) of the modified product. Unlike the Sāṅkhya, the Vedānta does not accept the *avyakta* or the *mūla-Prakṛti* as the material cause of the universe. The universe, being amaterial, virtual and apparent for all practical purposes (*vyāvahārika*), cannot have a material cause. All entities of the universe appear in pairs, opposite to each other in mass and properties. The sum of all the pairs is zero. *Brahman* appears as the manifold universe which is not a modification of the Being (*Brahman, Īśvara, Māyā*). This is all about the concept of causation in the Advaita Vedānta. Any discussion on the justifiability, rationality and universality of an effect preceding a cause does not come under the purview of the concept of causation in the Vedānta. *Māyā*, the Mother Creatrix, can create any magic which baffles human intellection and is totally inscrutable. Of course, the doctrine of transformation holds good in the manifested universe even in the Vedānta, in the anlogy of gold being transformed into a necklace.

The Lord continues his instruction to Arjuna in verse 11.33 and finally concludes in the next verse.

> You do kill Droṇa, Bhīṣma, Jayadratha, Karṇa and similarly other heroic warriors too who have been slain by Me. Don't worry. Fight; you shall conquer enemies in the war.[31]

In this verse, Lord Vāsudeva specifically mentions the names of some warriors of whom Arjuna was apprehensive to conquer. Droṇa was Arjuna's most venerable teacher. The former was master of the science of archery, and was in possession of celestial weapons. Bhīṣma was Arjuna's revered grandsire; was in possession of celestial weapons; and had death at his own free will. Jayadratha was the prince of the Sindhu kingdom and the son-in-law of Dhṛtarāṣṭra. He married the only Kaurava princess, Duḥśalā. Jayadratha's father Vṛddhakṣatra, the king of Sindhu, was engaged in a penance with the object that whosoever would

---

31. *BG*, XI.34.

cause his son's head to fall on the ground would immediately have the same fate too. (Arjuna killed Jayadratha on the fourteenth day of the war. He caused the head of Jayadratha fall on the lap of Vr̥ddhakṣatra, who, being unaware of the fact that it was his son's head, immediately threw it on the ground). Karṇa was in possession of celestial weapons. Indra gave him an unfailing *Śakti* (spear). He was the son of Sūrya, the sun-god.

It was natural for Arjuna to think of the impossibility of killing Droṇa, Bhīṣma, Karṇa, Jayadratha and similar other ones. After beholding the Cosmic Form of Śrīkr̥ṣṇa and getting the assurance from the Lord that He had already slain them, Arjuna gave up his apprehensions and became ready to obey the Lord's advice unconditionally.

### 11.05: Disillusioned Arjuna

> Having listened to that speech of Keśava (Kr̥ṣṇa), trembling, with folded hands, Arjuna (Kirīṭī) bowed down. Falling prostrate, overawed with fear, he again spoke to Kr̥ṣṇa falteringly.[32]

One name of Arjuna was Kirīṭī, literally meaning "the diademed one." Indra placed a diadem (*kirīṭa*), possessing the radiance of the sun, on the head of Arjuna who fought the *dānava*s (demons).

> It is indeed appropriate, O Hr̥ṣīkeśa (Kr̥ṣṇa), that the universe, in extolling You, should be delighted and gratified. The demons flee in fear to all directions. All the hosts of perfected *yogī*s bow down (to You).[33]
>
> O Great Being, why should they not bow to You, the pre-eminent, primal creator of even Brahmā? O Infinite Being, O Lord of gods, O Abode of the universe, You are the Imperishable, at once Being and Non-Being, and also what is beyond both.[34]
>
> You are the Primal Lord, the Ancient Spirit, the Supreme Abode of this universe. You are the Knower, the Knowable (the object to

32. *BG*, XI.35.
33. *BG*, XI.36.
34. *BG*, XI.37.

> be known) and the Supreme Abode. O Being of Infinite Forms, by You is the universe pervaded.[35]
>
> You are Vāyu, Yama, Agni, Varuṇa, the Moon, Prajāpati and the Great Grandfather. To You, salutations, salutations a thousand times. Again, repeatedly, salutations to You.[36]

The words Vāyu and Agni do not mean here the physical wind and fire, respectively. God, presiding in any mechanical force, is Vāyu. God, presiding in any form of energy, is Agni. They are gods, albeit not God who is one only. Yama is the god of death. Varuṇa is God presiding in the cosmic, primeval, subtle plasma (*Āpaḥ*, *Ka*, or *Nāra*). He is also a god. The moon, sun, or any other celestial star, planet or satellite is presided by the all-pervading *Brahman*. The presiding deity is a god. Prajāpati (the progenitor of creatures) is Brahmā. The Great Grandfather is the Father of even the Grandfather, Brahmā.

> O All, Salutations in front of You and behind You. Salutations be on all sides of Yours. Your power is infinite and Your energy unmeasured. You pervade all and so You are the All.[37]

God pervades the entire universe. There is nothing divorced from God. And, hence, He is the All.

> Being unaware of this majesty of Yours, deeming You a comrade, I have rashly (disrespectfully, forcibly) addressed You as Kṛṣṇa, Yādava (cowherd), friend, due to carelessness or love (affection).[38]
>
> In whatever way You have been disrespected, in fun, while walking, reposing (resting), sitting, or dining, in privacy or in public, O Acyuta (Kṛṣṇa), I beg You, Immeasurable One, to forgive all this.[39]

---

35. *BG*, XI.38.
36. *BG*, XI.39.
37. *BG*, XI.40.
38. *BG*, XI.41.
39. *BG*, XI.42.

> You are the Father of the world (*loka*) of beings, moving and unmoving. Being its pre-eminent Teacher, You are worthy of being worshipped by it. In the three worlds (*bhūḥ, bhuvaḥ, svaḥ*), there is none who is even equal to You. O You of incomparable power, how can there be one greater than You?[40]
>
> Therefore, saluting and prostrating my body, I crave Your grace, O Mighty Being, worthy of adoration. O Lord, You should bear with me, as a father does with his son, a friend with his friend and a lover with his beloved.[41]
>
> Overjoyed am I, having seen what has been hitherto unseen. Yet my mind is smitten with fear. Show me, O Lord, only that (familiar) form. Have mercy, O God of gods, O Abode of the universe.[42]
>
> I wish to see You like that diademed, bearing a mace and a discus in hand(s). Assume that same four-armed form, O thousand-armed Being, O Cosmic Form.[43]

Observing Arjuna terrified due to the vision of the Cosmic Form, Lord Vāsudeva withdrew that Form and consoled him with kind words.

## 11.06: Śrīkṛṣṇa Showed His Human Form and Pacified Arjuna

Arjuna could no longer bear to behold the Cosmic Form of God. On the request of Arjuna and knowing that he was fear-struck, Lord Vāsudeva withdrew His Cosmic Form and spoke affectionate words consolingly:

> By Me, being gracious to You, O Arjuna, by My Yogic Power, I have revealed to you this supreme form of Mine, resplendent, cosmic, infinite and primal, which has not been beheld before by anyone other than you.[44]

---

40. *BG*, XI.43.
41. *BG*, XI.44.
42. *BG*, XI.45.
43. *BG*, XI.46.
44. *BG*, XI.47.

> O great hero of the Kurus (Arjuna), not by the Vedas, not by sacrifices, not by studies, not by gifts, not by rituals, not by severe austerities, can I be beheld in this form by anyone other than you, in the world of men.[45]
>
> Don't be fear-stricken nor bewildered, having beheld this awesome form of Mine. Rid of fear and glad at heart, behold again that (the human) form of Mine.[46]
>
> Having thus spoken to Arjuna, Vāsudeva showed His own form (human form with two arms) again. Assuming His gentle form once more, the Mighty Being pacified him who had been terrified.[47]

According to the *Viṣṇu-Purāṇa*[48] and the *Bhāgavata*,[49] Śrīkṛṣṇa had four arms at the time of His birth. Immediately thereafter, He assumed the two-armed form.

After seeing the human form of the Lord, Arjuna became cheerful and said:

> O Janārdana (Śrīkṛṣṇa), seeing this, your gentle human form, now I have become composed in mind and have been restored to my own, normal nature.[50]

Lord Vāsudeva further consolidates the normalcy of the mental state of Arjuna by more soothing words:

> It is extremely hard to behold this form of Mine, which you have seen. Even the gods perpetually crave for seeing this form.[51]
>
> Not by the Vedas, nor by penance, nor by gifts, nor by fire-sacrifices, can I be seen in this way, as you have seen Me.[52]

---

45. *BG*, XI.48.
46. *BG*, XI.49.
47. *BG*, XI.50.
48. *VP*, V.3.8.
49. B*hā*, X.3.9.
50. *BG*, XI.51.
51. *BG*, XI.52.
52. *BG*, XI.53.

> But, O Arjuna, by undivided (undistracted) devotion, may I be known, seen in reality, and also entered into, O scourge of foes; for, I am of such a nature.[53]

> Whosoever does work for Me, makes Me his supreme goal, becomes devoted to Me, gets rid of attachments, and bears no enmity towards all beings, comes to Me, O son of Pāṇḍu (Arjuna).[54]

"Do work for Me." This advice has a special meaning. God does not need any service for Him. He does not need personal services, since He is not a person. The devotee has to work for God's creation. The devotee has to be the *nimitta* (a mere instrumental representative) for God.

This last verse of this chapter lays emphasis on devotion. The next chapter is a full discourse on the Yoga of Devotion.

After completing the eleventh chapter of the *BG* on the vision of the Cosmic Form of God, we feel the necessity of leaving a note of caution. One is likely to misunderstand this chapter by equating the Western philosophy of monism and the philosophy of the *BG*. In a number of places, the *BG* has clearly stated that God is immanent in the universe and transcendent to the universe. Arjuna has addressed the Lord as "O Abode of the universe" (*BG*, XI.45). Had the Lord and the universe been equated, such a language could not be used in the *BG*. This concept of the *BG* is in conformity with that given in the Puruṣa-Sūkta of the *Ṛgveda*.[55, 56] The Western monism is alien to Indian philosophy. The former equates God and the universe. No system of Indian philosophy deems the universe to be equivalent to God. The Advaita Vedānta holds that the universe is an illusory appearance of *Brahman*, that it is not nothing, that it is virtual, practical and apparent, and that *Brahman* is immanent in the universe and transcend to the universe.

53. *BG*, XI.54.

54. *BG*, XI.55.

55. *ṚV*, X.90.2: *puruṣa evedaṁ sarvam.*

56. *ṚV*, X.90.3: *pādo 'sya viśvā bhūtāni tripādasyāmṛtaṁ divi.*

If a rope appears as a snake, the illusory snake is not nothing, because it is the rope. What Arjuna saw in the Cosmic Form of God cannot be whisked away as a hallucination. He had a vision of the empirical truth underneath which lies the Absolute Truth as the rock-bottom. All what we observe in a monitor of a computer do exist in its hard disc, albeit not in the form as visible to us.

# 12

## Bhakti-Yogaḥ
## (The Yoga of Devotion)

### 12.01 : A Dilemma for Arjuna

GOD is formless, unmanifested and imperishable. One may meditate on Him to attain liberation. God expresses Himself in an infinite number of divine glory (*vibhūti*), as described in the tenth chapter of the *BG*. One may meditate on any divine glory to reach the same goal. The eleventh chapter of the *BG* gives a description of the Cosmic Form of God. Now, Arjuna has the doubt in his mind: Which way of God's worship, without form or with form, is better? The twelfth chapter, the way of devotion, begins with Arjuna's question.

> Of those devotees who, ever united, worship You thus elaborately, and also those who (meditate on) the Imperishable, the Unmanifest — who among them know Yoga best?[1]

The Lord answers to the question of Arjuna through a number of verses. And all these verses pertain to the Yoga of Devotion. We will present the contents of these verses in the following section. In the present section, we would like to dissolve a pertinent issue that is often raised by some scholars. The controversy is the issue of dualism versus non-dualism with reference to *jñāna-yoga* (the Yoga of Knowledge) and *bhakti-yoga* (the Yoga of Devotion). In interpreting the *BG*, we have leaned towards Śaṅkara's non-dualism. That being so, we have to explain the fundamental basis

1. *BG*, XII.1.

of *bhakti-yoga*. If "He (God) is I (*so 'ham*),"[2] "All this verily is *Brahman* (*sarvaṁ khalvidaṁ brahma*),"[3] "This self is *Brahman* (*ayamātmā brahma*),"[4] "Here there is no diversity whatsoever (*neha nānāsti kiñcana*),"[5] where is the question of devotion and worshipping? Who is devoted to whom? "I worship myself." "I am my devotee." Both these statements do not seem to be meaningful.

Non-dualism is metaphysically true and absolutely true. But dualism and pluralism are empirically true on the broad canvas of non-dualism.

The Upaniṣadic statement "Let me produce many, desired He (*so 'kāmayata, buhu syāṁ prajāyeyeti*)"[6] and Śaṅkara's statement, "Both oneness and multiplicity are true (*ata ekatvaṁ nānātvaṁ cobhayamapi satyameva*)"[7] cannot be whisked away to establish non-dualism. At the absolute (*pāramārthika*) level, non-dualism is true. At the practical and applied (*vyāvahārika*) level, non-dualism, dualism and pluralism are simultaneously true. After the total dissolution of the universe and before the next creation, dualism and pluralism carry no meaning.

Any created being, micro or macro, inanimate or animate, is pervaded by *Brahman* and is also pervaded by *Virāḍ* or *Buddhi* (the Cosmic Mind, the Supermind or the Cosmic Intellect). It is in the analogy of the ocean-water existing inside all sorts of oceanic plants and animals and inanimate oceanic materials. In the Vedāntic language, the pervaded being is the *upādhi* (limiting adjunct) of the pervading Being.

*Brahman*, pervading an inanimate object and presiding over it, is the *bhūtātmā*. *Brahman*, pervading an animate being and

2. *BU*, I.4.1; *CU*, IV.2.1.
3. *CU*, III.14.1.
4. *BU*, II.5.19.
5. *BU*, IV.4.19; *KTU*, II.1.11.
6. *CU*, VI.2.3-4; *TU*, II.6.1.
7. *BSŚB*, II.1.14.

presiding over it, is the *jīvātmā*. In both cases, the Self (*Ātmā*) becomes the self (*ātmā*).

The *Buddhi* (Cosmic Intellect), limited inside a created being, either inanimate or animate, becomes the *buddhi* (individual intellect) of each created entity. This *buddhi* evolves to become the *antaḥkaraṇa* (the internal instrument). In non-Sanskrit languages, the word has no exact equivalent. We may call it "mind-complex." It is a subtle organ rather than gross. It is a composite structure too. The gross brain, with its associated nervous structures, is the apparatus of the mind. The more evolved a created being, the more structurally complicated and functionally efficient is the *antaḥkaraṇa* due to the more evolved nature of its apparatus (mainly the cerebral structures). The principal components of the *antaḥkaraṇa* in the human being are the *buddhi*, *ahaṅkāra* and *manas*.

The *antaḥkaraṇa* has a free will, albeit not unlimited. The self is not the agent of actions. It is the *antaḥkaraṇa* that is the agent. Of course, it cannot function without being reflected by the light of the consciousness of the self.

Some actions of an individual being generate karmic impressions that leave subtle traces in the *buddhi*. In course of time, these traces accumulate to form the *karmāśaya* (reservoir of *karma*s). In the absolute sense, the self is ever free. In the usable sense, the self becomes bonded with the *karma*s in the analogy of chemical bonds in a molecule. This phenomenological binding is the cause of rebirth and the experience of pleasure and pain. A bound self becomes alienated from the Primal Self.

The foregoing description provides the basis of dualism and pluralism. For an individual, with a karmic reservoir, dualism is functionally meaningful. On the other hand, an individual whose karmic reservoir has been fully erased (who has been rid of the *karma-saṁskāra*s) attains liberation (*mokṣa*). His *ātmā* (individual self) becomes the *Ātmā* (the Universal Self). He is no longer a created being; he becomes *Brahman*, without being second to It. This is the state of non-dualism. At this state, he can exclaim like Śaṅkara, as quoted below:

> I am God (*Nārāyaṇa*). I can annihilate the hell. I can put an end to the three worlds (*Bhūḥ, Bhuvaḥ, Svaḥ*). I am the Supreme Spirit (*Puruṣa*). I am the Controlling Lord (*Īśaḥ*). I am the Unbroken Whole (*Akhaṇḍa*). I am the last Witness. I have no Controller (Nobody else controls Me.). I am I-less; I am My-less.[8]

So long as one does not reach the I-less and My-less state, one cannot become a non-dualist in the practical life. Almost all of us are dualists and pluralists. We should make all attempts to ascend the ladder and reach the summit, the state of *Brahman*-hood. That is the non-dual state.

In the dualistic state, we are impelled by the consideration of "I and non-I" and "My and non-My." The three grammatical persons — first, second and third (I, you and he) — are operative factors to decide our line of action.

The Yoga of Devotion is an indispensable means for attaining to the Yoga of Knowledge (the realization of "I am He" or "He is I"). And, thence, is the *mokṣa* (liberation), becoming *Brahman* in the absolute sense.

### 12.02 : Formless Worship and Form-Worship

Lord Vāsudeva did not decry anyone of the two methods to attain the goal. One may meditate on the Imperishable, the Unmanifested, Absolute *Brahman* which is attributeless, acosmic and impersonal. One may also worship a personal God, with attributes and functions and of a particular form or the cosmic Form. The Lord recommends the latter for most persons for whom the former may be difficult.

> Those who, fixing their minds on Me, being ever steadfast, and endowed with supreme faith, worship Me, are, in My opinion, (them do I deem as) the best in Yoga.[9]
>
> But those who sincerely worship the Imperishable, the

---

8. *VC*, 495: *nārāyaṇo 'haṁ narakāntako 'ham; purāntako 'haṁ puruṣo 'hamīśaḥ akhaṇḍabodho 'hamaśeṣasākṣī; nirīśvaro 'haṁ nirahṁ ca nirmamaḥ.*

9. *BG*, XII.2.

> Indefinable, the Unmanifest, the Omnipresent, the Unthinkable, the Unchangeable, the Immovable, the eternally Constant, having restrained all the sense-organs fully, being even-minded (equanimous) everywhere, being engaged in the welfare of all beings, verily (do they) come into Me.[10]

Verse 12.2 speaks in favour of worshipping God with form and attributes. Are both the ways of worship one and the same? The Lord gives a definite answer to this question in the next verse:

> Greater is the trouble of those whose minds are set on the Unmanifest; for, embodied beings find it hard to tread the path of the Unmanifest.[11]

In reality, it is not hard for the *Brahma-jñānī* (the person who has known and realized *Brahman*) to contemplate the Imperishable, Unmanifest, Formless *Brahman*. For such a *jñānī* who can realize "*ahaṁ brahmāsmi*[12] (I am *Brahman*)," the formless worship is quite good and satisfactory. It may rather be said that form-worship is not suitable for him, albeit not contradicted.

But different is the case for those (most persons) who have not ascended the ladder to the level of a *jñānī*. The ones who have attachment to the "I" and "my" and are not much enlightened to grasp the formless Reality find it difficult to do *nirguṇa* (attributeless) and *arūpa* (formless) worship.

### 12.03 : Devotion to God with Forms and Attributes

On this topic, we shall discuss seven verses (12.6-12) of the *BG*. They will provide a summary presentation of the Yoga of Devotion.

> But those who worship Me, renouncing all actions in Me, regarding Me as the Supreme Goal, meditating on Me with single-minded Yoga, and setting their minds on Me, for them, O Pārtha

10. *BG*, XII.3-4.
11. *BG*, XII.5.
12. *BU*, I.4.10.

> (Arjuna), very soon I become the deliverer from the sea of empirical life leading to death.[13]
>
> Fix your mind on Me alone; let your intellect dwell in Me; henceforth, undoubtedly, in Me alone will you dwell.[14]
>
> If you are not able to fix your mind steadfastly on Me, seek to reach out to Me, O Dhanañjaya (Arjuna), through *abhyāsa-yoga* (the *yoga* of repeated efforts).[15]

On the topic of *abhyāsa* (practice), reference has already been made vide verse 6.35 of the *BG*. Here the compound-term, *abhyāsa-yoga*, has been used in a special sense. As a first step, one may fix the mind on a single, gross object such as an image of a deity. This practice would lead to purity of mind (*sattva-śuddhi*), steadfastness (*sthiratā*) and finally to inward one-pointedness on the Cosmic Form of God.

> If you are unable even to practise *abhyāsa-yoga*, be you intent on doing actions for My sake. Even by doing actions for My sake, you will attain perfection.[16]

God is not like a human being, with a body, a family, and other worldly involvements. "Work for My sake" should mean "Do selfless work for My creation."

> If you are unable to do even this, with the self subdued (controlled), taking refuge in Me, abandon the fruits of all actions.[17]
>
> Knowledge is indeed superior to *abhyāsa*. Meditation is superior to knowledge. Renunciation of the fruits of actions is superior to meditation. Peace immediately follows renunciation.[18]

With reference to worshipping God with forms, we have a word

---

13. *BG*, XII.6-7.
14. *BG*, XII.8.
15. *BG*, XII.9.
16. *BG*, XII.10.
17. *BG*, XII.11.
18. *BG*, XII.12.

of caution. God is One and One only for the entire universe, irrespective of diversity of religious faiths. He is really formless, although He can assume multiple forms through His *Yoga-Māyā*. The topic of the Cosmic Form (*Viśva-Rūpa*) of God simply indicates that God is both immanent and transcendent and that the multiplicity of the empirical forms of the universe is contained in God. For the average embodied persons, form-worship becomes necessary to facilitate concentration on something concrete. But it is to be remembered that the map of India is not India and a model of a methane molecule, with a carbon atom at the centre and four hydrogen atoms at the periphery, is not the methane gas itself. In the latter case, a model of methane is a teaching aid only. Moreover, multiplicity of forms and names of God must not be construed as many Gods and many of their real forms. God is One only; God has no forms whatsoever.

### 12.04 : The Multitude of Attributes of the Saṁnyāsī Who Contemplates on the Akṣara Brahman

A devotee, with knowledge on the Self, who has renounced the world and who contemplates on the Imperishable (*Akṣara*), should acquire the following attributes in order to become a favourite devotee of the Lord.

> He who has no hatred to all beings, is friendly and compassionate, my-less and I-less (free from all sense of possession and egoism), even-minded in pain and pleasure, forbearing (unaffected even when abused and smitten), ever content, steady in meditation, self-controlled, possessed of firm conviction, with mind and intellect fixed on Me is My devotee who is dear to Me.[19]

> He by whom the world is not afflicted, and who is not afflicted by the world, who is free from elation, intolerance (intolerance of another's superiority = envy), anger and anxiety is dear to Me.[20]

---

19. *BG*, XII.13-14.

20. *BG*, XII.15.

> Dear to Me is My devotee who craves not (who does not expect anything from anybody), is pure (who has purity of his body, mind and speech), an adept (a competent person), unconcerned (indifferent, without taking the side of anybody), unworried, and who has renounced all selfish undertakings.[21]
>
> Dear to Me is the devotee who is not elated, who does not hate, grieve, or desire, and who renounces good and evil.[22]
>
> The man who, being full of devotion, is the same to the foe and the friend, and also in honour and dishonour, who, being free from attachment, is the same in cold and heat, in pleasure and pain, who treats blame and praise alike, who is silent, content with whatever accrues, who is homeless (having no fixed abode to dwell) and steady-minded is dear to Me.[23]
>
> The devotees who follow, indeed, the immortal virtues, as set forth above, endued with faith, deeming Me the Supreme Being, are exceedingly dear to Me.[24]

This verse concludes the chapter on the Yoga of Devotion. A person cannot ascend the spiritual ladder without devotion to God. Devotion is an indispensable aid to spiritual ascension for both the householder and the *saṁnyāsī*. It is also meaningful for a *jñāna-yogī* before his final liberation (before he becomes *Brahman*).

---

21. *BG*, XII.16.
22. *BG*, XII.17.
23. *BG*, XII.18-19.
24. *BG*, XII.20.

# 13

## Kṣetra-Kṣetrajña-Vibhāga-Yogaḥ
## (The Way of Discrimination of the Field and the Field-Knower)

### 13.01:Introductory Remarks on the Metaphysics of Chapter 13

WHILE going through chapter 13 of the *BG*, reference should be made to its chapter 7, where the superior or higher *prakṛti* (*parā prakṛti*) and the inferior or lower *prakṛti* (*aparā prakṛti*) of the Lord (*Īśvara*) have been compared and contrasted. Confusion prevails among the interpreters of the *BG* on the meanings of *Prakṛti,* and on the lower and the higher *prakṛti*s of the Lord. There is also confusion on the identification of the Field and the Field-Knower. On some finer points of this topic, we differ even from Śaṅkara.

The Father of the universe is God (*Parameśvara*). He is the Supreme Person (*Puruṣa*). The Mother of the universe is the Power (*Śakti*) of God. She is *Parameśvarī* (the Mother Creatrix, the Supreme Goddess). She is the primordial nature (*mūla-Prakṛti*). Both *Puruṣa* and *Prakṛti* are ever unmanifest (*avyakta*). Being co-eternal, they form the bipolar Reality. They are not two metaphysical Beings. They constitute a single, non-dual Being, the *Prakṛti* being the *śakti* of the *Puruṣa* (the *śaktimān*, the possessor of *śakti*). The *Puruṣa* is the chairperson (*adhyakṣa*) and the *Prakṛti* is the executive agent (*kartrī*). The *Puruṣa* is not the real doer (He is *akarttā*). But He is called the doer through His chairpersonship over His *śakti* (power) who is the real executive agent. Thus, *Prakṛti* or *Māyā* is the real doer of all cosmic events.

The primordial *Prakṛti* (the *mūla-Prakṛti*) has three constituent strings or strands (*guṇas*). These are the superstrings of the String Theory of modern physics. They are not attributes or qualities, unlike the translations made by many interpreters. Due to the *spanda* or *kampana* (vibrations) of these strings (*sattva, rajas* and *tamas*), the whole usable universe (micro and macro) of energy and matter, fields and particles, is manifested.

The totality of the usable universe is also known as *prakṛti.* But this created *prakṛti* is different from the *mūla-Prakṛti.* The latter creates the former. The created or manifested *prakṛti* is *vyakta,* whereas the *mūla-Prakṛti* is *avyakta* (unmanifest).

The *Mūla-Prakṛti* is otherwise known as *Māyā, Yoga-Māyā* or *Mahāmāyā.* In our mundane language, we may say that She is the Spouse of God (*Īśvara-Patnī*), although, in reality, She is the power of God (*Īśvara-śakti*).

Most interpreters have mixed up the metaphysics of the Sāṅkhya and that of the Vedānta. They say that the three "attributes (*guṇas*)" of *Prakṛti* have been transformed into the material universe. Such an idea is far from truth. The Vedānta, at least the non-dualistic Vedānta, rejects the doctrine of transformation (*pariṇāma-vāda*) of the Sāṅkhya. Śaṅkara's *adhyāsa-vāda* or the *vivartta-vāda* of the post-Śaṅkara non-dualists explains the virtual existence and practical functioning of the universe. The *adhyāsa* doctrine (*atasmiṁstadbuddhiḥ*[1]) explains the virtual universe as the appearance of *Brahman* (the substratum or *adhiṣṭhāna*) as the multitudinous universe in the analogy of a rope erroneously perceived as a snake. But Śaṅkara too has erred when he says that the three *guṇas* of *Prakṛti* are transformed into all kinds of effects (*prakṛti ca triguṇātmikā sarvakāryakāraṇaviṣayākāreṇa pariṇatā* . . .).[2]

The *mūla-Prakṛti* or *Māyā* is not Herself an illusion. Albeit

1. *BSŚB*, Intr. (*atasmiṁstadbuddhiḥ*).

2. *BGŚB*, XIII. Intr.

insentient, She acquires consciousness due to the reflection of the Fundamental Consciousness (*Brahman*) on Her. Had She been insentient, She could not be the executive agent and She could not create, sustain and dissolve the universe.

Many interpreters of the Vedānta wrongly equate the *mūla-Prakṛti* (*Māyā*) and the aggregate of the created energy of the universe. *Māyā* is the power (*śakti*) of *Brahman*/God. She is ever unmanifest (*avyakta*). She illusorily creates energy and matter of the universe. But She Herself is not the material energy (*ūrjā*).

Next, we come to the *Aparā Prakṛti* (Field) and *Parā Prakṛti* (Field-Knower) of God.

The first manifested entity is the Vedic *Virāḍ* (*Virāṭ*). It is the supermind or the cosmic *buddhi* (*samaṣṭi-buddhi*), the aggregate or collective intellect of the *mūla-Prakṛti*. From *Virāḍ*, does *Āpaḥ* (the primeval, subtle cosmic plasma) evolve. It super-condenses into a cosmic egg (*bindu, aṇḍa*). Inside the egg, *Prāṇa* evolves from *Āpaḥ*. *Prāṇa*, the super-unified force, vibrates. As a result of this vibration (*kampana, spandana*), the egg explodes. Synchronous with the explosion of the cosmic egg, *Ākāśa* (Space) evolves from *Prāṇa* and expands. Super-heated Space, in the newly born universe, produces quanta, micro-particles, particles and the four fundamental forces, separated serially from one super-unified force. Here we would not go further to trace the subsequent evolution of the universe. Our readers may refer to our book *The Cyclic Universe* for details of Vedic and Vedāntic cosmogony and cosmology.[3]

The supermind or the *samaṣṭi-buddhi* is ubiquitous. It pervades *Ākāśa* and all material entities evolved from *Ākāśa*. It pervades all inanimate and animate beings. *Buddhi* (the aggregate intellect) becomes *buddhi* (intellect in an individual, *vyaṣṭi-buddhi*) when it acquires a limiting adjunct (*upādhi*). Thus, every created (evolved) entity, acting as an *upādhi*, acquires *buddhi*. From *buddhi* (individual intellect), evolves *ahaṅkāra* (a subtle psycho-organ for ego, self-sense), and from the latter, evolves *manas* (mind). These three,

3. N.C. Panda, 2002.

that is, *buddhi, ahaṅkāra* and *manas,* constitute the principal components of the *antaḥkaraṇa* (the internal instrument in the subtle body).

We have differed from the scheme of evolution, given by the Sāṅkhya. Our scheme traverses two bifurcated paths. It has a main path for the material evolution. It has a branch from the main path for the mental evolution.

*Māyā,* the *avyakta mūla-Prakṛti,* the power of *Īśvara,* is the unmanifest *aparā Prakṛti.* The universe of matter and energy and the *antaḥkaraṇa*s, comprising the *buddhi, ahaṅkāra* and *manas,* are combinedly called the manifested (*vyakta*) *aparā prakṛti.* There should not be confusion over the use of the words *Prakṛti* and *prakṛti.* The former is *avyakta,* the Mother Creatrix, and the latter is *vyakta,* the created universe of matter and energy and the individual minds.

Next, we describe the *parā Prakṛti* (the higher or superior nature of God). The individual selves, both *bhūtātmā*s and *jīvātmā*s, are designated by the *BG* as the *parā Prakṛti.* The *bhūtātmā*s are the selves in the non-living entities and the *jīvātmā*s are the selves in the living entities. All these individual selves are not intrinsically different from the Universal Self (*Paramātmā).*

The embodied self becomes a *bhūtātmā* in an inanimate object and a *jīvātmā* (*jīva*) in an animate being. Thus, every created (evolved) entity contains a material body and a spirit (*bhūtātmā* or *jīvātmā*). This self dwelling in an inanimate being or an animate being is the spirit that is the superior nature (*parā Prakṛti*) of God. Nowhere else other than the *BG* has the self been designated as *Prakṛti.* And this *parā Prakṛti* is the *Kṣetrajña* (Knower of the Field).

Everything that is potentially insentient is rendered sentient due to the induction of consciousness, brought about by the all-pervading Fundamental Consciousness through reflection or proximity. Thus, the whole universe is conscious, the consciousness varying in quality and quantity, depending upon the evolution of the mental sheath (*manomaya-kośa*) of the created being. *Brahman* is Pure Consciousness (*Viśuddha Cit*) whereas the individual consciousness in a created being (*bhūta*) is its *cetanā*. And, hence, the Lord says: "I am consciousness in the created beings (*bhūtānāmasmi cetanā*)."[4]

With this much introduction, now we proceed to discuss the individual verses of the thirteenth chapter of the *BG*.

### 13.02: The Field and the Field-Knower

In the beginning of chapter 13 of the *BG*, Lord Vāsudeva makes a distinction between the Field and the Field-Knower. The Lord says:

> O son of Kuntī (Arjuna), this body is called the field. He who knows it is called the field-knower by the sages (by the knowers of the field-knower).[5]

After the discovery of quantum physics, science has recognized that the whole universe and all its constituents (micro or macro, inanimate or animate) are conscious. In this verse, the word, *śarīra* (body), should refer to the body of each and every entity of the universe — micro and macro, inanimate and animate. The body is the Field; the *bhūtātmā* or *jīvātmā* in the body is the Field-Knower.

> Know Me also, O Bhārata (Arjuna), as the Field-Knower, present in all fields. The knowledge of the Field and the Field-Knower is deemed by Me as the real knowledge.[6]

Please note the word, *api* (also), in verse 13.2 of the *BG*. God says that He is also the Field-Knower, present in all Fields. This statement unambiguously declares that the individual selves and the Great (Cosmic) Self are one and the same.

Can we say that all the individual selves are not different? In the case of inanimate objects, the *bhūtātmā* is merged in the *Paramātmā* (Supreme Self) consequent upon the disintegration of

4. *BG*, X.22.
5. *BG*, XIII.1.
6. *BG*, XIII.2.

the material body. The *bhūtātmā* has no bondage (*bandhana*). On the other hand, the *jīvātmā* becomes bound to *karma-saṁskāras*, stored in the *antaḥkaraṇa* (inner instrument). A bound *jīva* is practically and usably different from other *jīvas*. But once the *jīva* is free from bondage, it re-establishes its identity with the Supreme Self. And that is *mokṣa* (liberation).

> Listen to Me, in brief, what that field is, what it is like, what its modifications are, and whence is what; and also who He (the Field-Knower) is and what His powers are.[7]

It has been sung variously by seers in various distinctive chants, and also stated in passages, indicative of *Brahman,* full of reasoning and definitiveness.[8]

> The great becomings (fields), the ego, the intellect, and also the Unmanifest, the ten senses and one (mind) and the five objects of the senses (the states of material existence), desire, hatred, pleasure, pain, the fundamental forces, awareness, the inherent, intrinsic properties of matter — these are briefly said to be the field and its modifications.[9]

There are a few common aspects of the Vedāntic metaphysics and the Sāṅkhya metaphysics. But there are fundamental differences too. Many scriptures and many interpreters have created confusion by intermingling the two immiscible philosophies. We have to be very careful in distinguishing the meanings of many words common to these two systems of philosophy. We have already presented an analytical, comparative study of these two systems in section 2.14 of this book.

In verse 13.6 of the *BG,* four inherent attributes of the inner instrument (*antaḥkaraṇa*) have been listed. They are desire, hatred, pleasure and pain.

In this context, here we quote one aphorism of Patañjali. The

---

7. *BG,* XIII.3.

8. *BG,* XIII.4.

9. *BG,* XIII.5-6.

unconscious (*avidyā*), the I-centredness (*asmitā*), the thirst for pleasure (*rāgaḥ*), the antipathy or aversion to already experienced pain (*dveṣaḥ*) and the fear of death (*abhiniveśaḥ; maraṇatrāsaḥ;* tenacity of mundane existence) are the five *kleśa*s or afflictions (progenitors of grievous pain or distress in life).[10] The *saṁskāra*s, especially the *vāsanā-saṁskāra*s, are the imprints on the unconscious that are the causal factors of painful life. They unconsciously induce a person to do everything by any means to satisfy the *vāsanā*. Egocentricity or egotism (*asmitā*) induces a person to do everything for the comfort, prosperity and dominance of the "I" at the cost of others. *Rāga* is hankering after getting that which is pleasurable, agreeable, propitious, or soothing. Patañjali says: Thirst for pleasure is *rāga*.[11] To brood over the concept of pain is *dveṣaḥ*.[12] The fear of death is *abhiniveṣaḥ*.[13] These five attributes of the *antaḥkaraṇa* are the five pillars on which the superstructure of Indian behavioural psychology stands.

With reference to the words, *saṅghāta* and *dhṛti*, given in verse 13.6 of the *BG*, our interpretation is different from the traditional ones. The lexicographic meaning of *saṅghāta* is "compression," "condensation," "compactness," "aggregate," "collection," "cluster" or "heap." The traditional interpreters have accepted its meaning as "the aggregate or the combination of the body and the senses." In our opinion, *saṅghāta*, in the present context, means "the super-unified force (*Prāṇa*) and the four fundamental forces, serially separated from this super-force." These four are the gravitational force, the strong nuclear force, the weak nuclear force and the electro-magnetic force. No material body can remain in a condensed or compacted form in the hypothetical absence of these forces. Thus, *saṅghāta* is a field (*kṣetra*).

The word, *dhṛti*, has been traditionally interpreted as

10. *PYD*, II.3: *avidyāsmitārāgadveṣābhiniveśāḥ kleśāḥ.*

11. *PYD*, II.7: *sukhānuśayī rāgaḥ.*

12. *PYD*, II.8: *duḥkhānuśayī dveṣaḥ.*

13. *PYD*, II.9.

"fortitude" or "firmness." It has been derived from the Sanskrit verb-root, *dhṛ*, meaning "to hold," "to support." It contextually means "the properties inherent or intrinsic in a created being." The properties of a created entity support the latter. *Dhṛti* is a field (*kṣetra*). In this sense, *dhṛti* and *dharma* are not different. *Dhṛti* is the sustentation by which all components of the gross and subtle bodies are upheld.

The word, *cetanā*, as a field, needs some clarification. What is called *cetanā* is *ātma-caitanya-ābhāsa*, the light of the Fundamental Consciousness (*Cit*, *Ātmā*, Self, or *Brahman*) reflected on the insentient *Prakṛti* and Her virtual creations. The *kṣetra* or field is insentient (*jaḍa*). But usable, virtual awareness (*cetanā*) is induced in all entities of the *kṣetra* as a result of the reflection of the all-pervasive Consciousness (*Brahman*). According to this doctrine of the reflection of Consciousness, every entity of the universe, animate or inanimate, macro or micro, is conscious. Ācārya Śaṅkara, the great exponent of non-dualism, says: *cetanāvantaḥ sthāvarāḥ* (the immovable or the inanimate beings are conscious).[14]

What has been said in the foregoing paragraph is *cetanā* (awareness) as a field (*kṣetra*). In contrast, Lord Vāsudeva has declared in the *BG*: "I am awareness in the created beings (*bhūtānāmasmi cetanā*)."[15] From this declaration of the Lord, one should not infer that *cetanā* is the field-knower (*kṣetrajña*). The Lord's declaration is figurative only. One can comprehend the Lord's statement on the basis of the doctrine of reflection of Consciousness.

What has been said in verse 13.3 of the *BG* has been briefly described in verses 13.5-6. In comparison with verse 7.4, in which eight types of *Prakṛti* (*Aparā Prakṛti*) have been listed, the two verses (13.5-6) of the thirteenth chapter present a more elaborate list of the *kṣetra* by adding the modifications of *buddhi* and *ahaṅkāra*, and the properties and powers (*prabhāva*) of the *antaḥkaraṇa*. This

---

14. *CUŚB*, VI.11.2.

15. *BG*, X.22.

enlarged list also includes the unmanifest *Prakṛti* (*avyakta*) which is *Māyā* or *Īśvara-Śakti* (the power of God), considered as an *aparā Prakṛti*.

Before closing the section 13.02 on the field and the field-knower, we feel the necessity of updating the concepts of space and time. The seminal concepts of the field and the field-knower have been presented in the *BG* in chapter VII (7.4-6) and chapter XIII (13.5-6). In both the places, *kham* or *ākāśam* has been enlisted as one of the fields. Surprisingly, the *BG* does not consider *kāla* or time as a field. Among the philosophers and the scientists in the whole world, there has been utter confusion on these two items. Hence, a need arises to trace the historical background, make a comparative analysis and present our concepts on space and time.

For the ancient Greek philosophers of atomism, space was a void and an absolute void which served as a container of all material objects of the universe, the latter being the contents floating in the void. Democritus (460-370 BCE) gave the idea of empty space in which nothing exists and through which existing things can move. He conceived of the world made up of atoms and the void. The Democritean concept of void misguided the Western philosophers and scientists until the mid-twentieth century and some are not yet free from the puzzlement even in the twenty-first century. Till now some scientists are busy with "vacuum genesis" and "vacuum fluctuation."

Aristotle (384-322 BCE), the ancient Greek philosopher and naturalist, imagined a fifth element called ether, existing beyond the four shells (earth, water, air, fire) of the world. It filled the heavens. It was unearthly, unmoving and unchanging. In his view, nature abhors a vacuum and, thus, there is no room for emptiness.

Sir Isaac Newton (1642-1727) discovered the law of gravitation. According to him everything in the universe attracts everything else. The earth attracts the moon. The moon attracts the earth. How is the force of gravitation transmitted in space? Newton himself was puzzled. He thought of ether as a medium. He was not sure of this medium too.

It is worth referring to the classical Michelson-Morley experiment done in 1887. Its null results confirmed the non-existence of ether.

In 1905, Albert Einstein (1879-1955) published his Special Theory of Relativity. This theory proves that matter is a packet of energy and that both matter and energy are interconvertible. This theory also says that both space and time are relative, when considered with different frames of reference. Light that travels at the highest speed in nature may be transmitted either as particles or as waves. For the transmission of particles, a medium is not necessary whereas, in the latter case, a medium is needed. Thus, Einstein did not need an ether medium for the transmission of light (vide his discovery of photo-electric effect for which he received the Nobel Prize).

Einstein formulated his General Theory of Relativity in 1915 and published it in 1916. Newton viewed gravity as a force between bodies. But Einstein held gravity bound up with the shape of space itself. Thus, the General Theory of Relativity affirms that gravity is a property of space. The presence of mass curves space. A gravitational field is really a curving of space. The greater the mass, the larger the curvature of space in its vicinity. Mass distorts the "flatness" of the four-dimensional space-time continuum and produces "hollows" that give rise to the notion of curved space. The more massive the matter, the deeper the hollow.

We agree to the notion that time is relative. The seers of ancient India did recognize it. While interpreting some verses of the *BG*, we do refer to Brahmā's time, the earth-time and so on. But we assert that time is not a real entity and it is a mental construct only. With the occurrence of more than one event, the concept of time is born in the individual minds or the Supermind of *Māyā* (*Virāḍ*). Time is born with the appearance of the cosmic egg. Time dies with the dissolution of the singularity, the *bindu*, or the cosmic egg. We don't find any clarification of the concept of time in Einstein's Special Theory of Relativity. The Vedānta is clear on the topic that *Brahman* is *akālam* (timeless) and *anākāśam* (spaceless). It also refers to *kāla* for describing cosmic or common events. But it excludes *kāla* from the list of *kṣetra*s (fields). Some Indian scriptures and writers have an erroneous notion that time is eternal and that time is the original source and the final receptacle of everything and everybody. Such a notion is not correct, however.

Einstein's Special Theory of Relativity correctly describes the relativity of *dik*s (dimensions of length, breadth and height or thickness). *Dik*s are mental constructs rather than real. They are mere concepts in the mind on directional extensions. This theory does not say anything on the relativity of *Ākāśa* which really is not relative. There is no word in English or any Western language for the Sanskrit word *ākāśa*. Modern Indian philosophers, including even S. Radhakrishnan, have translated *ākāśa* as "ether". Of course, Radhakrishnan has admitted that space or ether is not the adequate equivalent for *ākāśa*. Ether is a fictitious concept that has no real existence. Of course, a chemical known as ether does exist. Aristotle's ether is not that chemical and it does not exist. People in general equate *Ākāśa* and the blue sky (*nīlaṁ gaganam*) which is really non-existent and an appearance only. What is this Vedāntic *Ākāśa* then? It is that through which we move our hands, that through which our spacecraft flies and that which holds all the celestial objects. *Ākāśa* is material, the subtlest matter among the five *mahābhūta*s and the most elastic one among these five. It is full rather than empty. The word *śūnyam* (void) is meaningless in the dictionary of the Vedānta. This philosophy recognizes the plenum (the *pūrṇam*) rather than the *śūnyam*. The great genius scientist, Albert Einstein, perhaps did not refer to *Ākāśa* as a form of matter in his Special Theory of Relativity. His equations referred to the three dimensions of space, and not to *Ākāśa* itself that is a created mega-entity (created immediately after the Big Bang explosion).

We agree with Einstein, the scientist genius, on his concept of the curvature of space in his General Theory of Relativity. This finding has later been experimentally proved by other scientists who observed the curving of light beams, coming from distant stars, towards the sun during a total eclipse. Here we add a finer concept to what has been said by Einstein. Matter pulls matter. The greater the mass, the bigger the pull. Is *Ākāśa* matter? To the best of our knowledge, Einstein has not specifically said anywhere that space is matter. If space is nothing, is an absolute void, can any celestial body, howsoever massive it may be, pull or attract space? What we emphasize is the fact that *Ākāśa* itself is matter and the most elastic matter. By virtue of this elastic property, a massive celestial object curves *Ākāśa* in its vicinity to a greater extent in proportion to its mass. We have observed a general satisfaction among physicists regarding the mechanism of action of gravitation. Did Einstein's revised version on the mechanism of gravitation really solve the problem? We have a feeling that we are still in search for a better solution. "*Ākāśa* serves as a medium for the transmission of gravitational force, electromagnetic force and the other forces. It also serves as a medium for the transmission of energy-waves." These two statements may not be whisked away as a figment of imagination of an ignorant non-physicist. Once this concept is experimentally proved to be true, the riddle of action-at-a-distance would finally evaporate.

With a special reference to Einstein's discoveries of the two laws of relativity, here we pose a few problems for conceptual analysis, although we totally agree to the two epoch-making discoveries that left landmarks in the annals of the history of science. If *Ākāśa* is an absolute void and is not a form of very subtle matter, we don't find any meaning of the statement, "A massive body, X, pulls space, Y, in its vicinity." "Something, X, pulls Y which is nothing." It is a meaningless statement. Secondly, pulling space by a massive body is the cause of pulled space being curved. In this case, curving is an effect of pulling. What is the science of pulling? Can an effect explain the mechanism of action of its cause? We seemingly solved the problem; but we really did not. Thirdly, in conformity with the universal law of matter-wave duality, light can travel as particles or as waves. Einstein himself was the discoverer of the photo-electric effect. For light-particles (photons) to travel, he did not need an ether medium or any medium at all. Our question is: Does not a massive body pull energy particles or waves? Our fourth question is: What is the nature of hollows created due to the curving of space? Are the hollows absolute voids? Are they not the same *Ākāśa* which is potentially full?

We have high reverence for Albert Einstein. We do admire his great discoveries. But, at the same time, we do realize that there is nothing like "the last word." The Vedāntic *Ākāśa*, as we have understood it, is a form of matter, the subtlest and the most elastic. It serves as a medium too. Once we recognize it, there is nothing like action-at-a-distance. Everything is connected with everything else.

We use the term *Ākāśa* for the totality of Cosmic Space, with the initial letter capital. We do that to distinguish the total Cosmic Space from any limited space and specific, definite space. However, we want to point out that *Ākāśa* is finite (although too vast); it is not infinite. Any created entity is bound to be finite. Einstein too has declared the finiteness of space.

Now we make a summary presentation of the early Vedāntic evolution. *Virāḍ* is the first evolute that manifests from *Māyā,* the Mother Creatrix. *Āpaḥ* (not the common water, but the subtlest, Cosmic Plasma) evolves from *Virāḍ*. It super-condenses to a point (*bindu*), the cosmic egg (*BGŚB*, Intro.; *MS*, I.9; *ṚV*, X.81-2). Inside the egg, *Prāṇa* (not life; it is the super-unified force) evolves from *Āpaḥ*. *Prāṇa* vigorously vibrates. As a result of its vigorous vibration, the cosmic egg explodes (*CU*, III.19.1). This explosion is known as the Big Bang (*Mahā-Rava* in *Śaiva* and *Tāntrika* philosophies). Simultaneous with the Big Bang, *Ākāśa* (*Kham*) evolves from *Prāṇa*. The nascent *Ākāśa* is a type of superheated soup, with a tremendously high temperature. The Vedas give the name Aditi to this nascent *Ākāśa* which is a beehive of activity. Micro-particles are produced from it and absorbed into it. And so does the *Ṛgveda* (I.89.9-10) describe the simultaneous behaviour of Aditi (a rapid process of flux) as both parents and offspring. The same Veda *(ṚV*, X.72.6) presents a vivid picture of the vigorous dance of particles or *reṇus*. The hot *Ākāśa* rapidly expanded in an accelerated rate and is still expanding, albeit the rate has been decelerated.

The *Brahma-sūtram* (I.1.22) says: "*Ākāśa* is a virtual manifestation of *Brahman*." In a real sense, it does not establish the identity of *Ākāśa* and *Brahman*. Virtual manifestation is the befitting expression for this purpose. The *Upaniṣad*s (*TU*, II.1.1; *CU*, IV.10.4-5; *BU*, V.1.1) also corroborate the idea that *Ākāśa* or *Kham* is a created entity, a virtual manifestation of *Brahman*. The *Chāndogya-Upaniṣad* further adds that, like *Kham*, *Kam* (*Āpaḥ*) and *Prāṇaḥ* are also virtual manifestations of *Brahman*. The *Bṛhadāraṇyaka-Upaniṣad* (already cited) puts emphasis on the absolute fullness of *Brahman* and the virtual fullness of *Ākāśa*. The concept of *śūnyam* does not exist in the Vedānta. Everything and every locality (even in the apparently empty *Ākāśa*) are pervaded by plenum (*pūrṇatā*) rather than absolute vacuum (*śūnyatā*). If, after all, *śūnyam* has a use in the Vedānta, it has a relative meaning in the *vyāvahārika jagat* (empirical, usable universe).

For the present purpose, let us start the cosmic evolution from *Ākāśa* and end the cosmic involution in *Ākāśa*. The *Upaniṣad*s (*CU*, I.9.1) say: "What is the final goal of this world?" The reply to this question is *Ākāśa*. For all these creatures are produced from *Ākāśa* and they return to *Ākāśa*. By the word "evolution" people, in general, mean Darwinian evolution which is limited to species evolution. Particle evolution, separation of the four fundamental forces, evolution of elements, inorganic evolution, organic evolution, evolution of stars, galaxies, planets, satellites, atmosphere, hydrosphere and so many other things precede the species evolution of Darwin. We do accommodate all these schemes of evolution in our Vedāntic evolution, with a condition, of course. Our Vedāntic evolution is not materialistic and chance-oriented. It is theistic, controlled and regulated by God as the Chairperson and executed by the Mother Creatrix who designs, harmonizes and co-ordinates under perfect control. The apparent chaos is a necessary phenomenon for the establishment of an orderly cosmos. We may quote the language of Ācārya Śaṅkara from his introduction to the BS: *satyānṛte mithunīkṛtya* (Order is established by coupling order and disorder). The Big Bang is followed by a Big Crunch, the latter being the reverse of the former (*BS*,II.3.14). In the process of involution, the whole universe of matter and energy finally becomes the *Ākāśa* which, in turn, serially and reversibly becomes *Prāṇa, Āpaḥ, Virāḍ,* the last one being dissolved in *Māyā,* the Power of God (*Īśvara-Śakti,* the Unmanifest *Prakṛti*). And so do revolve the cosmic cycles *ad infinitum.*

The origin of a concept in the mind precedes the coinage of a word for it. Alternatively, the discovery of an object necessitates a verbal symbol for it. Neither of these two happened in the West from the time of Democritus to the middle of the twentieth century. However, the situation changed in the last half of the said century when the particle-physicists, the quantum-physicists and the cosmologists made their discoveries that could revolutionize the earlier notions on the universe. Why could not Indians earlier speak of the revealed truths given in their ancient scriptures? Even today they are not speaking. Foreign political subjugation for a long period, its adverse impact on the national psyche in generating an inferiority complex and intellectual decadence in comparison with the Vedic age may be ascribed to as the probable factors.

### 13.03: Means of Obtaining True Knowledge on the Field and the Field-Knower

Book-learning is not enough to know the field and the field-knower. One has to acquire some qualities in order to be entitled to that knowledge. Here the Lord lays down the complete means to that knowledge:

> Humility, unpretentiousness (modesty), non-violence, forbearance (forgiveness), uprightness, respectful service to the *ācārya* (*guru* or teacher), purity (physical, mental and vocal), steadfastness, self-control, dispassion towards the objects of the senses (aversion to sense-objects), and also the absence of egoism, perception of evil in birth, death, old age, sickness and pain, non-attachment, non-identification of self with the son, wife, home and the like, and constant equanimity in the occurrence of the desirable and the undesirable, unswerving devotion to Me by the *yoga* of non-separation, resort to solitary spots, aversion to human crowds, constancy in cultivation of spiritual knowledge, perception of the end (final goal) of the knowledge of Truth — all this is declared to be Knowledge. What is other than this is ignorance.[16]

Dispositions, starting from humility in verse 13.7 and ending in perception of the content of philosophical knowledge, are called knowledge (*jñāna*), because they are conducive to the acquisition of true knowledge. On the other hand, dispositions counter to them such as vanity, self-esteem, violence, revengefulness, crookedness, indifference toward the teacher or even his humiliation, indulgence in sensual pleasure, egoism, longing for social prominence, dislike for sacred studies, lack of devotion to God, and such other attributes and activities are declared to be ignorance. It is impossible to know *Brahman* without cultivating the dispositions that are conducive to true knowledge.

### 13.04: Knowledge on Brahman

One becomes qualified to know *Brahman* after one acquires the favourable dispositions enlisted in verses 13.7-11. Now we shall quote seven verses of the *BG* (13.12-18) that throw light on knowledge on *Brahman*.

> I shall describe that which should be known, knowing which one attains to immortality. The Supreme *Brahman* is without a beginning. It is said to be neither existence nor non-existence.[17]

---

16. *BG*, XIII.7-11.
17. *BG*, XIII.12.

*Brahman* has neither birth nor death, neither beginning nor end. "Whatever has a beginning shall have an end." This statement is universally true. One who knows the immortal *Brahman,* that is, one who has realized It, becomes *Brahman* (*brahmavid brahmaiva bhavati*). After one becomes *Brahman,* the question of becoming mortal does not arise.

Reference may be made to verse 19 of chapter 9 of the *BG.* There it is said: "I am immortality and also death; I am *sat* (existence) and *asat* (non-existence)." In the present verse, the Lord says: "*Brahman* is neither existence nor non-existence." This seeming contradiction must be resolved.

*Brahman* is Absolute Existence and Absolute Consciousness. There is no question of *Brahman* being non-existence. But the virtual, usable universe (all created or manifested entities) is *sat* and *asat*. The existence of all manifested entities is dependent upon *Brahman* that acts as the substratum (*adhiṣṭhāna*) and appears as the plenitude of the universe. The multitudinous entities of the universe are ever changeable during their existence. Their existence itself is uncertain. Their virtual existence is also transient, but not eternal. They do not continue to stay in any constant form. They are mortal. In spite of what has been said about the manifested universe, the virtually existent universe cannot be said to be different from *Brahman*. There is nothing else other than *Brahman* that reveals itself and unfolds itself through the agency of its power (*śakti*) which is called *Māyā*. The apparent contradictions of both *sat* and *asat* and neither *sat* nor *asat* disappear when one comprehends the distinction between the Absolute Truth (*Pāramārthika Satya*) and the virtual, usable truth (*vyāvahārika satya*).

The sceptic argues: If *Brahman* is neither *sat* nor *asat,* if it is devoid of all characteristics, if it is beyond the reach of speech and thought, it must be a non-entity (*śūnya*). Such an idea comes to the mind due to lack of comprehension. The following verses dispel the doubt.

With hands and feet everywhere, with eyes, heads and mouths

> everywhere, with ears everywhere, That exists, enveloping all in the universe.[18]

The existence of the field-knower (*kṣetrajña*, self) is ascertained through the sense-organs of all beings. In this context, the sense-organs of all beings act as the *upādhis* (limiting adjuncts). The sense-organs and motor-organs are insentient. Even the internal instrument (*antaḥkaraṇa*) is insentient. Behind or underneath these insentient, subtle organs of the subtle body must there be a self-conscious principle which presides and directs. And that principle is the inner self, essentially not diffferent from *Īśvara/Brahman*.

*Brahman* is knowable, but is not directly cognizable through our five senses of perception. It is beyond all phenomena (*niṣprapañca*), whereas the virtual universe is phenomenal and illusory. To use any language for *Brahman*, we have no method other than superimposition (*adhyāropa*) and negation (*apavāda*). The latter activity is erroneous attribution and subsequent refutation thereof.

*Brahman* stands encompassing all things of the whole universe. It envelops everything. It completely pervades all in the universe. The power (*śakti*) of the all-pervasive Consciousness (*Brahman*) is *Māyā*, the *mūla-Prakṛti* (the primordial nature), the Mother of the universe. It is She who has the capacity of inducing the activity of the *buddhi*, *ahaṅkāra*, *manas*, and sensory as well as motor subtle organs.

Someone may think that *Brahman* is really in possession of the *upādhis*. It is not really a fact. To ward off this doubt, proceed the next verses.

> Shining by the functions of all the senses, yet without the senses; unattached and veritably sustaining all; devoid of attributes and yet the experiencer of attributes; without and within all beings; the unmoving and also the moving; because of Its subtlety, It is incomprehensible; It is far off as well as near; It is undivided and yet It seems to be divided in beings. That, the

18. *BG*, XIII.13.

> Knowable, is the sustainer of beings; their devourer and generator, too.[19]

In the aforesaid three verses, contradictory language has been used for *Brahman*. In Aristotelian logic, the use of contradictory language for a certain entity is nonsensical. What is seemingly self-contradictory is necessarily meaningless is not true with reference to the subtlest metaphysics in Vedāntic logic and also in quantum logic of modern physics. Perfect silence is most appropriate for *Brahman*. If one uses language for It, one has to use negative or contradictory language. With reference to the Absolute *Brahman*, no language can be correct, whereas with reference to *Brahman* with attributes (*Īśvara*) and the virtual universe (the virtual universe is not an entity second to *Brahman*), the apparently contradictory terms are very often correct. Any language, used for *Brahman*, must unavoidably be negative or contradictory.

> The Light even of lights, said to be beyond darkness, that is, the Knowable, the Knowledge and the Goal of Knowledge, seated in the hearts of all.[20]

Everything other than *Brahman* (the Pure Consciousness) is insentient. The word "everything" in this sentence encompasses the uncreated and created entities. The *mūla-Prakṛti* (primordial nature) or *Māyā* is uncreated and co-eternal with *Brahman*. She is insentient. The non-living created entities, both micro and macro such as the neutrino and the sun, are insentient. The *buddhi, ahaṅkāra* and *manas* of created living beings are insentient. All these are rendered sentient by being illuminated by the Fundamental Consciousness (*Brahman*). Our virtual consciousness is induced consciousness. The scriptures say: "Illumined by which Light, the sun shines."[21] "By Its light, all this shines."[22] "The light which

19. *BG*, XIII.14-16.
20. *BG*, XIII.17.
21. *TBrā*, III.12.9.
22. *KTU*, II.2.15.

residing in the sun illumines the whole world."[23]

The following verse concludes the topic on hand:

> Thus have the Field, Knowledge and the Knowable been briefly described. My devotee, on knowing this, becomes fit to enter into My state.[24]

The last part of the verse, "becoming fit to enter into My state," needs some further elucidation. Once the devotee knows and realizes what has been said in verses 13.13-18 of the *BG*, he attains the state of abidance as the Supreme Self (*paramātma-bhāva*). That is his attainment of *mokṣa* (liberation).

### 13.05: Prakṛti and Puruṣa — The Eternal Verities and Generator of All Beings

In the interpretation of chapters 7 and 13 of the *BG*, one should be very cautious in distinguishing the different contextual meanings of the word, *prakṛti*.

The Sāṅkhya *Pradhāna* or *Prakṛti* has one meaning only. It is transformed into material and mental modifications of individual living beings, especially the human species. The Sāṅkhya *puruṣa*s (spirits) are innumerable, each insentient individual body being associated with a sentient spirit. The Sāṅkhya has no *Puruṣa*, equivalent to *Brahman/Īśvara*.

The non-dualistic Vedānta uses the word, *Puruṣa*, for *Brahman/Īśvara*. It also uses the word, *puruṣa* for the individual self (*jīvātmā*). It uses the word, *Prakṛti* for the *Śakti* (Power) of *Brahman/Īśvara*. This *Prakṛti* is *Māyā* or the *avyakta* (the unmanifest, the *mūla-Prakṛti*). It also uses the word, *Prakṛti* for the totality of the manifested universe of matter and energy, including their subtle psycho-organs. This manifested *Prakṛti* is the *aparā-Prakṛti*. The individual body is also the *aparā-Prakṛti*. Even the *mūla-Prakṛti*, the *avyakta* or *Māyā* is the *aparā-Prakṛti*. The *BG* uses the compound-word, *parā-*

---

23. *BG*, XV.12.

24. *BG*, XIII.18.

*Prakṛti* for the individual self (*jīvātmā*) only. Here lies the confusion. In no other Vedāntic scripture, do we find the word, *prakṛti* for the inner self which is essentially not different from the Great Cosmic Self. Is such a use of the *BG* inappropriate? We do not consider this use to be inappropriate. But to establish its propriety, some clarification is necessary.

The individual self (*jīvātmā*) is bound to the *karma-saṁskāra*s in the *karmāśaya* of the *antaḥkaraṇa*. The self, albeit not different from the Supreme Self, is alienated so long as it is bound. Even after the death of the body, the self resides in the subtle and the causal bodies. This state of the self continues until it is released from bondage (until it attains liberation or *mokṣa*). If *mokṣa* is not attained within a *para* (a Cosmic Period, starting from the creation to the final dissolution of the total universe of seven *loka*s), the bound self, residing in the causal body, stays in the *Virāḍ* or Supermind that dissolves in *Māyā* or the *mūla-Prakṛti*. In the subsequent creation of the universe, the bound self, residing in the causal body, is reborn.

The bound self resides in the *aparā-Prakṛti*. When it is free from bondage, it is no longer *Prakṛti* by re-establishing its identity with the Supreme Self. The bound self in the *aparā-Prakṛti* is known as *parā-Prakṛti*. The *parā-Prakṛti*, on being liberated, becomes the *Puruṣa*.

Some analysis is necessary on the status of *Virāḍ*, *Buddhi*, or the Supermind. Is it a separate metaphysical entity? There is only one metaphysical entity and that is the non-dual *Brahman*, one without a second. *Māyā* or the *mūla-Prakṛti* is the power (*śakti*) of *Brahman*, without being second to the latter, the possessor of the power (*Śaktimān*). The *Śaktimān* and the *Śakti* are co-eternal, being not different from each other. *Brahman*, with *Māyā* as the *upādhi*, is *Īśvara* (God). The former is attributeless whereas the latter is with attributes. *Brahman*, with an inanimate and an animate entity as *upādhi*, is the *bhūtātmā* and the *jīvātmā*, respectively. *Brahman* is mindless (*amanāḥ*). *Brahman* (Pure Consciousness), being reflected on insetient *Māyā*, makes the latter super-conscious. This reflected Consciousness is the cosmic intellect (*samaṣṭi-buddhi* or *Buddhi*), otherwise known as *Virāḍ* or Supermind. *Māyā* works through this Supermind. It would be a gross expression if we say that the Mind of *Māyā* is the *Virāḍ, Buddhi, Mahat,* or the Supermind. And such an expression serves as a correct means of communication.

After this brief diversion, we would go back to the main topic to learn what the Lord says.

> Know that *Prakṛti* (the *Śakti* or Power of *Brahman/Īśvara*) and also *Puruṣa* (*Brahman/Īśvara,* the Supreme Spirit) are both beginningless; and know also that all evolutes and attributes (*guṇas* which appear in the evolutes such as pleasure, pain and delusion) are born of *Prakṛti*.[25]

The word, *Puruṣa* in this verse, stands for *Brahman*. Without violating the non-duality of *Brahman, Puruṣa* is invariably associated with Its *śakti* (power). The *Śaktimān* (possessor of power) and the *Śakti* constitute a bipolar Reality. To clarify the issue, we may consider a poor analogy. The President of a country has power. The former has physical existence whereas the latter, without possession of physical existence, is wholly dependent upon the former. The *śakti* of *Brahman* is *Māyā,* the Mother Creatrix. *Brahman,* the Absolute Being, without becoming, is attributeless (*nirguṇa*). The same *Brahman,* with *Māyā* as the *upādhi,* is *Īśvara* (God). Again, it may be emphasized that *Brahman* and *Īśvara* are not two separate Beings. *Īśvara* has attributes and, hence, is *saguṇa*. *Māyā* is *Brahma-Śakti* and *Īśvara-Śakti*. She is *avyakta* (unmanifest), *avyākṛtā* (undifferentiated), the *mūla-Prakṛti* (the primordial nature). *Īśvara* is the Father of the universe and *Māyā* is the Mother of the universe. The former is the chairperson and the latter is the executive agent for the former. Both are co-eternal. They are beginningless and endless.

Many scholars of the Vedānta have two major confusions with regard to *Īśvara-śakti,* the primordial nature (*Prakṛti*). They equate

25. *BG*, XIII.19.

*śakti* with energy. Matter is a packet of energy. Albert Einstein, in 1905, has already proved that matter and energy are not different. The universe of matter and energy is an evolute whose evolvent is the *Virāḍ, Buddhi, Mahat,* or the Supermind. *Māyā* or Mother Creatrix is the creator of this universe of matter and energy. The created universe is also called *prakṛti* (nature), but it is the nature, created by the primordial nature, the *Īśvara-śakti* or *Mūla-Prakṛti* or *avyakta-Māyā.* The energy of the universe is *vyakta* (manifested), irrespective of the fact of our ability to perceive or not. Moreover, *śakti* is translated as "power" and *ūrjā* as "energy." The material energy is *ūrjā.* It is an evolute by which work is done.

The second confusion of many scholars is equally serious. They translate *Māyā* as "illusion." But *Māyā* is not illusion. She is a metaphysical Being, the Mother of the universe. She is one pole (the feminine, spiritual principle) of the bipolar Reality, the other pole being *Īśvara* (the masculine, spiritual principle). *Parameśvarī* (the Supreme Mother-Deity of the universe) cannot be called an illusion. She creates illusion by Her projecting power (*vikṣepa-śakti*) and concealing power (*āvaraṇa-śakti*). With reference to the creation of illusion, *Māyā* is called *Yoga-Māyā.* Of course, in a few places in the Vedānta, the word *māyā* is used in the sense of illusion.

The universe, with all its constituents, is the manifested *aparā prakṛti* (inferior nature). It has beginning (birth) and end (dissolution, *pralaya*). It would be a travesty of truth if we say that the universe, with all its constituents, is beginningless. And anything that has a beginning shall have an end.[26]

Of course, the beginninglessness and endlessness of *saṁsāra* (metempsychosis) is to be accepted. How do we reconcile two contadictory concepts, namely, the birth and death of the unliberated living beings and the universe as a whole and the eternality of *saṁsāra*? *Buddhi* (the aggregate Cosmic Intellect, *Virāḍ, Mahat,* the Supermind or the Cosmic Mind) is the first manifested

---

26. *TUŚB,* Intr. (*na hi nityaṁ kiñcidārabhyate. loke yadārabdhaṁ tadanityam.*)

entity in a cosmic cycle of creation, sustenance and dissolution. The same *Buddhi* is also the last remaining, manifested entity in the cosmic cycle. All *vikṛtis* (evolutes), following a reversible pathway, finally merge in *Buddhi*. And this *Buddhi* dissolves in the *mūla-Prakṛti* or *Māyā*. In fact, *Buddhi* or *Virāḍ* or *Mahat* is the mind of *Māyā*. The dissolution of *Buddhi* in *Māyā* is known as *mahā-pralaya* (final, total dissolution). After a total dissolution and before the next creation (manifestation, emanation), only *Brahman/ Īśvara* and the *mūla-Prakṛti* (*Māyā*) continue to stay. *Īśvara*, the Father of the universe, is the last witness of the potential universe dissolved in the Mother. When *Īśvara* desires to see the latent, potential universe as an actual one (albeit virtual), then only, the Mother causes the dissolved *Buddhi* to re-manifest and evolve into a manifested universe. The evolutes of the material universe appear from *Buddhi* and it is not a fact that they appear from nothing. The crystals of salt (NaCl) appear from the seawater. But the salt was already dissolved in the seawater, although it was not visible to the eye. The manifestation of salt from an unmanifested state is not a process of *creatio ex nihilo*. Creation is a process of unfolding and dissolution is a process of infolding. If we consider this aspect of Vedāntic cosmology and cosmogony, we do have a comprehension of the eternally repeated *saṁsāra* (metempsychosis).

The second part of verse 13.19 of the *BG* says that evolutes and attributes are born of *Prakṛti*. On this statement, some interpreters have confusion too. We mix up the Sāṅkhya and the Vedānta which are immiscible. And, hence arises the confusion.

The *Īśvara-Śakti, Māyā, avyakta,* or *mūla-Prakṛti* is never transformed (modified) into the universe of matter and energy. It is not a process of gold being a necklace or wood being a chair. Neither is it a process of the food-starch being converted into body-fat. The Godhead of God is eternally and timelessly united with *Māyā*, the power of God. Through the executive agency of this power, God creates, sustains and dissolves the universe. These three activities are continuous and simultaneous during every cosmic cycle. A cosmic cycle begins with an origination and ends in a final dissolution. All these are the activities of *Māyā* (the Mother of the universe) under the chairpersonship of God (the Father of the universe).

Although the Sāṅkhya upholds the doctrine of transformation (*pariṇāma-vāda*) and the Vedānta rejects it, in interpreting verse 13.19 of the *BG*, Śaṅkara accepts the Sāṅkhya doctrine. He says: "Intellect, et cetera, up to the body and sense-organs, the *guṇas* such as the apprehension of pleasure, pain and delusion are born of *Prakṛti*. *Prakṛti* is God's causal power to produce transformations. The modifications and *guṇas* are the transformations of *Prakṛti*." (*vikārān buddhyādidehendriyān tān guṇān ca sukhaduḥkhamoha-pratyayākārapariṇatān viddhi jānīhi prakṛti-sambhavān; prakṛtiḥ īśvarasya vikāra-kāraṇa-śaktiḥ triguṇātmikā māyā; sā sambhavaḥ yeṣāṁ vikārāṇāṁ guṇānāṁ ca tān vikārān guṇān ca viddhi jānīhi prakṛti-sambhavān prakṛti-pariṇāmān*).[27]

We do not agree with Śaṅkara on this issue of the doctrine of transformation of the *mūla-Prakṛti* into the *vikṛtis*, that is, into the created universe. *Māyā* is never modified into the universe. Further, we do not agree to the view that *Māyā* is constituted of three *guṇas*, namely, *sattva, rajas* and *tamas*. There isn't anything that is made up of *guṇas* or attributes. A rose that is red in colour is not made of redness. Sugar that is sweet in taste is not made of sweetness. It is rather made of carbon, hydrogen and oxygen in a certain molecular configuration. A person who is kind or cruel is not constituted of kindness or cruelty. *Māyā* is both *sat* (existence) and *asat* (non-existence). It is existent as the power of the Lord. It is non-existent as a separate entity. Moreover, it is neither matter nor energy to be made up of constituent units.

Still we have to explain the Vedāntic statements, "*Māyā* is *guṇamayī*," "*Māyā* is *triguṇātmikā*" and "*Īśvara* is *saguṇa*." *Māyā* virtually produces three strings or strands (*guṇas*) — *sattva, rajas* and *tamas*. These are the three superstrings that are eternally and

27. *BGŚB*, XIII.19.

timelessly in possession of the power of the Lord. They are the strings of Her supramentally produced divine musical instrument known as *vīṇā*. She continuously plays the *vīṇā* in the presence or the absence of the universe. The vibrations of the strings of the *vīṇā* are equipoised in the absence of the universe. When She disturbs this equipoise, creation of the universe ensues. Disturbance involves the dominance of one of the three strings. The frequencies and the wavelengths of the vibrations of all the three strings are unequal throughout all cosmic periods. The vibrations of the strings generate all enities of the universe. Depending upon the dominant string and the proportions of all the three strings, the created entities of the universe possess trait-types or attribute-patterns. The *karma-saṁskāra*s of a living individual interact with the vibrations of the strings to give definite shapes to these types or patterns. Both *Īśvara* and *Māyā* (*Puruṣa* and *Prakṛti*) become associated with the attributes of the created entities, and so do they become *saguṇa* and *guṇamayī*, respectively. In contrast, *Brahman*, rid of the *upādhi* of *Māyā*, is *nirguṇa* or attributeless.

*Īśvara* or God, being one and one only, is named as three — Brahmā, Viṣṇu and Rudra — with reference to the activity of creation, sustenance and dissolution, respectively. They are also associated with *rajas, sattva* and *tamas,* respectively. The Power of God or *Māyā* is the Mother of the universe. She, being one and one only, is named as three — Sarasvatī (alternative names are Gāyatrī or Sāvitrī), Lakṣmī, Gaurī (or Kālī), respectively. Accordingly, Sarasvatī is the Mother Creatrix. She plays Her *vīṇā* with three strings — *sattva, rajas* and *tamas.* When these three strings are equipoised, there is no manifest universe. When God desires to have a universe, for the *līlā* (sportive play) of the Father and the Mother of the universe, Mother Sarasvatī disturbs the equipoised state (*sāmyāvasthā*) by playing Her *vīṇā,* with changes of vibrations (*spandana, kampana*) and consequent production of appropriate musical notes. As a result, the *vyakta* (manifest) *aparā Prakṛti,* already dissolved in the Cosmic Mind (Supermind, *Virāḍ, Buddhi, Mahat*) of *Māyā* manifests and starts evolving. This is the essence of creation. There is no transformation or modification of *Māyā* or *avyakta mūla-Prakṛti* in the process of creation. The creative magic and music of Mother Sarasvatī creates an apparent universe of multiplicity on the rock-bottom of *Brahman*, the non-dual Reality.

It is difficult for us to accept Śaṅkara's interpretation of verse 13.19 of the *BG*. For him, the *aparā-Prakṛti* (the lower *Prakṛti* of Īśvara) is the *Prakṛti* and the *parā-Prakṛti* (higher *Prakṛti*, that is, the *jīva* or the principle of consciousness) is the *Puruṣa*. For the *jīvātmā*s (the individual selves), the *BG* has used the word *parā-Prakṛti* in chapters 7 and 13. The contextual meaning of the word *Puruṣa* in verse 13.19 is *Īśvara* (God) and is not the *parā-Prakṛti* (*jīvātmā*). Here we may quote Śaṅkara's own language: *prakṛtiṁ puruṣaṁ ca eva īśvarasya prakṛtī; tau prakṛtipuruṣau ubhau api anādī viddhi . . . prakṛtidvayavattvam eva hi īśvarasya īśvaratvam, yābhyāṁ prakṛtibhyām īśvaraḥ jagadutpattisthitipralayahetuḥ.* (Know that both *Prakṛti* and *Puruṣa* are the modes of *Īśvara*, They are beginningless. . . . Indeed, the Godhead or the Lordship of *Īśvara* consists merely in His being possessed of the two *Prakṛti*s).

We do not agree with Śaṅkara's interpretation. In the said verse, *Prakṛti* is the *avyakta* (unmanifest) *Prakṛti* or *Māyā* or the *mūla-Prakṛti*, and *Puruṣa* is God (*Īśvara*) Himself. Both are beginningless, endless and co-eternal.

*Puruṣa* (the Supreme Self, *Brahman*, *Īśvara*) is neither the material nor the efficient cause of the evolution, involving modifications, of the universe. Neither are the modifications born of the individual selves that are not essentially different from the Supreme Self. In the language of the *BG*, the individual selves are the same as the *parā Prakṛti*. As a matter of fact, *vikāra* or *vikṛti* means "modification" in the Sāṅkhya that upholds the doctrine of transformation. In contrast, in the Advaita Vedānta, this word means "a virtual change in the sequential process of evolution." The expression "virtual change" that is in vogue in physics and computer science is almost synonymous with *vivartta* of the Advaita Vedānta.

To avoid terminological confusion, we would use PP (*parā-Prakṛti*) for the individual selves or the *jīvātmās*, AP-UM (*aparā-Prakṛti* — unmanifest) for the *mūla-Prakṛti* or *Māyā*, and AP-M (*aparā-Prakṛti* — manifest) for *Virāḍ* and the evolutes of *Virāḍ*, that is the entire universe of matter and energy.

The second line of the verse (*BG*, 13.19) states: "All evolutes and attributes are caused by *Prakṛti.*" Here *Prakṛti* refers to AP-UM or *Māyā*. Most interpreters have translated *prakṛti-sambhavān* as "born of *Prakṛti.*" For us, it is "caused by *Prakṛti*," "created by *Prakṛti*," "originated from the source of *Prakṛti.*" We do not accept the idea that the universe (AP-M) is a modification (*pariṇāma* or *utpāda*) of AP-UM or *Māyā*. Neither do we accept the idea of *Māyā* giving birth to the universe in the analogy of a mother giving birth to a baby. Thus, in our opinion, the *Avyakta Prakṛti* is the efficient cause (*nimitta kāraṇa*) of the universe so far as cosmic events are concerned. She is not the material cause (*upādāna kāraṇa*) of the universe which is the illusory appearance of *Brahman*, the Absolute, non-dual Reality. Of course, the *antaḥkaraṇa*, consisting of the *buddhi*, *ahaṅkāra* and *manas*, of every individual being of the created universe is his/its own executive cause of the individual actions.

Next, Lord Vāsudeva clarified the distinction between *parā Prakṛti* (indwelling *puruṣa* or the *jīvātmā)* and the *aparā prakṛti*. Henceforward in the present chapter, *puruṣa* means "the indwelling spirit in an individual body" and *prakṛti* means "an individual body." In Sanskrit language, the former is the *dehī* and the latter the *deha*.

> *Prakṛti* (*aparā prakṛti*, specially referred to *buddhi* here) is said to be the cause in the production of the effects (body) and the instruments (senses, *karaṇas*). *Puruṣa* (the *jīvātmā*, the *parā prakṛti*, the *kṣetrajña*, the *bhoktā* or experiencer) is said to be the cause in the experience of pleasure and pain.[28]

---

28. *BG*, XIII.20.

The *karaṇa*s (instruments) are of two types, namely, the subtle sense-organs of perceptions and the subtle motor organs of actions. In the former type are the five subtle sensory organs of vision, audition, olfaction, gustation, and tactility. In the latter type are the five subtle motor organs of locomotion, prehension, excretion, reproduction and phonation.

It may be emphasized here that *Ātman* (the Supreme Self, *Īśvara*) who is changeless (*avikriya*) and ever-free (*nitya-mukta*) cannot be subject to the *saṁsāra* (metempsychosis) and cannot be bound. Verse 13.20 of the *BG* uses the word *puruṣa* for the *parā-prakṛti, kṣetrajña*, or *jīvātmā* (the individual self).

Verse 13.20 of the *BG* mentions the causes and the effects. The traditional interpreters of the Vedānta describe two types of causes, namely, efficient cause (*nimitta kāraṇa*) and material cause (*upādāna kāraṇa*). They say that *Īśvara* is the efficient cause and that *Māyā* or the *Mūla-Prakṛti* is the material cause. Such a concept is not in conformity with the Vedāntic doctrine, according to which *Īśvara* is a non-doer and the universe is not a modified product of the *Avyakta-Prakṛti*. We have analysed the Vedāntic concept of causation and would like to briefly mention it here. The Advaita Vedānta has four types of causes, namely, the impelling or the inspiring cause (*pracodaka kāraṇa*), the representing, executive cause (*nimitta, nirvāhī kāraṇa*), the active cause (*kartṛka-kāraṇa*) and the material cause (*upādāna-kāraṇa*). *Īśvara* is not directly the cause of any action. But, because of His chairpersonship, He impels, inspires or induces His *śakti* (*mūla-Prakṛti* or *Māyā*) who acts on His behalf. *Māyā* or the *avyakta Prakṛti* executes all cosmic events as the power and representative of God. She is the *nimitta kāraṇa* (*nimitta* meaning "on behalf of"). Every entity of the manifested *aparā prakṛti* in the universe is the active cause (*kartṛka kāraṇa*) of its own actions. Every deed has a doer. Every verb has a subject, either expressed or understood. In Śaṅkara's language, *yatkāryaṁ tat sakartṛkam*. If there is a transformation or modification, the effect or the product has a precursor state. The preceding state of existence is the material cause of the consequent state. Something *X* is modified into *Y*. This *X* is the material cause of *Y*. Unlike the concept in the Sāṅkhya, *Māyā* is not modified into the universe. Hence, She cannot be the material cause of the universe. The use of the word "modification" is meaningful only after *Virāḍ* manifests and subsequent processes of evolution take place. The evolvent becomes the material cause and the evolute the effect. However, it may be noted here that all modifications in the cosmic evolution are phenomenal only. In the language of the Advaita Vedānta, an evolute, instead of being a modification, is a virtual entity, a usable *vivartta*.

### 13.06: The Transmigration of the Jīva

For the individual self (the *jīvātmā, kṣetrajña, parā prakṛti*), the word *puruṣa* has been used in the present section. For the purpose of this section, the *puruṣa* must not be confused with the *Paramātmā* (the Supreme Self, *Puruṣa, Īśvara* or God).

The Vedas, the Vedānta, the *Brahma-Sūtra*, the *Bhagavad-Gītā*, the Great Epics and the *Purāṇa*s support the doctrine of reincarnation of the *jīva*. Let us know what Lord Vāsudeva says about the transmigration of the self.

> *Puruṣa* (the individual self), indeed lodged in *prakṛti* (the manifested *aparā prakṛti*, the body) experiences the attributes born of *prakṛti*. Attachment to the attributes is the cause of his birth in good and evil wombs.[29]

In verse 13.21 of the *BG*, *puruṣa* refers to the *jīvātmā* and *prakṛti* to the manifested *aparā prakṛti* (the *śarīra, deha* or body). Here the body constitutes the gross, subtle and causal bodies. The subtle body, due to its minuteness, is not sense-perceptible. Among other structures, it contains the *antaḥkaraṇa* (internal instrument) and *karmāśaya* (reservoir of *saṁskāra*s, both *vāsanā-saṁskāra*s and non-*vāsanā-saṁskāra*s). The causal body contains both the gross and subtle bodies in a potential, latent state, suitable for being dissolved

---

29. *BG*, XIII.21.

in *Buddhi, Virāḍ,* or *Mahat*. The causal body is more minute than the subtle body.

The Supreme Self is not subject to transmigratory existence. He has no desire (*kāma*). He does not experience pleasure and pain. He is free from delusion. He has no nescience (*avidyā*). Hence, He is free from attachment to the attributes (*guṇa*s). He does not identify Himself with the attributes.

The Supreme Self (*Īśvara*), very infrequently when dire necessity arises, takes an illusory form (a body) and is known as an *avatāra*. The potency of an *avatāra* is a descent from one hundred per cent to a percentage lower than the full. Lord Vāsudeva is, however, an exception. With full omniscience, omnipotence and omnipresence, He is one hundred per cent *Parameśvara* (Supreme Lord). Irrespective of the full or partial Lordship, the form assumed by the Lord is always illusory. The Supreme Self resides inside and outside every individual body, but does not experience the pleasure and pain of the body.

A human body or a non-human living body cannot experience without being associated with an embodied self (*jīvātmā*). In this process of experience, the embodied self develops attachment to the attributes (*guṇa*s). And this attachment involves the identification of the *jīva* to the *guṇa*s.

The *karmāśaya* (reservoir of karmic *saṁskāra*s) is a subtle organ in the *antaḥkaraṇa* of the subtle body. All the *karma-saṁskāra*s are stored in this subtle organ. The *jīvātmā* becomes bound to these *saṁskāra*s. As long as this bondage persists, the *jīva* is to be born and reborn. With the complete erasure of the *karmāśaya,* does transmigration vanish, resulting in the merging of the self in the Supreme Self. That's what we call *mokṣa* (liberation) or *Brahma-nirvāṇa* (becoming one with *Brahman*, with the loss of individual identity).

Rebirth is an opportunity to the *jīva* for rectification, purification, self-distillation, sublimation and ascension on the spiritual ladder, finally leading to *Brahman*-hood. It is up to the alientated *jīva* to avail of the opportunity to ascend to the summit.

The *jīva* may descend too and descend to the abyss of the ocean of life. In the upward or downward journey in the transmigratory path, the *jīva* may be born in good wombs if the sojourn is upwards and in evil wombs if the sojourn is downwards.

This upward or downward journey is not limited to the human species only. A human self may be born in the womb of a tiger, a snake, or a worm. On the other hand, a human self may be born in the family of a saint and a seer.

Śrī Aurobindo, adhering to his concept of philosophical evolution, discards the downward journey of the *jīva*. Such a notion, however, has no sanction of the Hindu classical scriptures.

### 13.07: The Supreme Self in the Body

We have already cautioned that it would be a serious blunder to import the philosophy of Sāṅkhya into the Vedānta. This has unfortunately become the case with many Vedāntic interpreters. The *puruṣa*s (sentient spirits) of the Sāṅkhya are infinite in number. Each one is a *jīva*, either bound (*baddha*) or isolated and released (*kaivalya-prāpta*). The Sāṅkhya hasn't a Great or Supreme Self known as *Paramātmā* or *Parameśvara* (God). It has one *Prakṛti* or *Pradhāna* that undergoes transformation or modification in its serial steps of evolution. On the other hand, the non-dualistic Vedānta has *Brahman, Īśvara* (the Supreme Self) and innumerable individual selves, all being the non-dualistic One Self only. We have to be careful in distinguishing the different contextual meanings. The Vedāntic *Prakṛti* is not one. *Māyā*, the primordial nature (*mūla-Prakṛti*), *Brahma-śakti*, or *Īśvara-śakti* (the power of God) is co-eternal with God. Both of them constitute the bipolar Reality. *Māyā* is the executive agent of the Lord. She, ever remaining unmanifest (*avyakta*), is never converted into any product of the universe or any individual body. The original *aparā Prakṛti* (inferior nature) is the *mūla-Prakṛti* or *Māyā*, eternally and timelessly unmanifested. *Virāḍ* or *Buddhi* or *Mahat*, that had undergone dissolution in *Māyā* at the termination of the previous universe, manifests as the primal evolute at the beginning of the creation of the subsequent universe. *Buddhi* undergoes serial modifications, resulting in the universe of matter and energy, the internal instrument (*antaḥkaraṇa*) and the physical body with subtle and gross organs of cognition and action. All these, starting from the *Buddhi* and ending in the bodies, constitute the manifested *aparā prakṛti*. The one non-dualistic Supreme Self becomes many due to association with diverse *upādhi*s (limiting adjuncts). The embodied selves become bound. But they are the sentient beings. They are the selves (*jīvātmā*s), otherwise known as the field-knowers (*kṣetrajña*s) or the *parā prakṛti* (superior nature).

The *puruṣa*s, referred to in verses 13.20-21, are the individual selves. On the other hand, the *Puruṣa*, referred to in verse 13.22 of the *BG* in the present section, is the Supreme Self (*Maheśvara* or God Himself).

Before we interpret verse 13.22 of the *BG*, we would like to quote the *Ṛgveda* and some Upaniṣads with reference to the residing of the Supreme Self and the individual self in everything and everybody.

> Two birds, companions, always united, cling to the same tree. Of these two, the one eats the sweet fruit and the other looks on without eating.[30]

In interpreting the *Muṇḍaka Upaniṣad* (III.1.1), Śaṅkara says that *Īśvara* (the Supreme Self, God) permits the processes of the universe as the witness and thus impels the activities (*paśyateva kevalam; darśana-mātreṇa hi tasya prerayitṛtvaṁ rājavat*).

The Vaiṣṇava philosophers who are against non-dualism and who assert that God is different from the individual selves who are also different from one another use this quoted Vedic and

---

30. *ṚV*, I.164.20 ( *dvā suparṇā sayujā sakhāyā samānaṁ vṛkṣaṁ pariṣasvajāte. tayoranyaḥ pippalaṁ svādvattyanaśnannanyo 'bhicākaśīti*); *ŚU*, IV.6; *MUU*, III.1.1; *KTU*, I.3.1.

Vedāntic statement in their favour. But, in our opinion, they are not correct. How can they interpret the Puruṣa-Sūkta of the *Ṛgveda* in favour of dualism?[31] It clearly says that all this is verily *Puruṣa (Brahman/Īśvara)* by declaring *puruṣa evedaṁ sarvam.* Moreover, verse 13.2 of the *BG* clearly establishes the identity of the Supreme Self and the innumerable individual selves residing in all fields (bodies).

With this much background information, now we proceed to know what the Lord says about the *Paramātmā* (Supreme Self) and the *jīvātmā* (individual self) residing in the body.

> The onlooker, permitter, supporter, experiencer, the Supreme Ruler; and also spoken of as the Supreme Self; He is the Supreme *Puruṣa* in this body.[32]

God resides in the body as an *upadraṣṭā* (one who stays near and looks on without being engaged in any action). The prefix *upa* means "nearest" and the word *draṣṭā* means "seer." God is *anumantā*, that is, He gives assent or approval to actions by His mere presence. God is the supporter (*bharttā*), because He provides support to the *buddhi* (intellect), ego (*ahaṅkāra*), *manas* (mind), senses and instruments (*indriyas, karaṇas*) and the gross body for holding them in their respective forms and also in a combination. The body as a whole (gross, subtle and causal) is the reflection (*ābhāsa*) of the Pure Consciousness (*Śuddha Caitanya*). God is also the experiencer (*bhoktā*). In reality, the Supreme Self is not the experiencer. But He is said to be the experiencer, because due to Him alone, the mental states like pleasures, pains and delusions get intellectualized as it were.

### 13.08: The Jīvātmā, on Cognizing the Paramātmā, Becomes Brahman

In this section, we shall discuss verse 13.23 only. The English

31. *ṚV*, X.90.

32. *BG*, XIII.22.

rendering of this verse is as follows:

> He who thus knows the Spirit (*Puruṣa*) and (His) Power (*Prakṛti*) together with (Her) strings (*guṇas — sattva, rajas, tamas*) is not born again, in whatever way he may live.[33]

This verse conforms to what has been said in the *Muṇḍaka Upaniṣad*:[34] The knower of *Brahman* becomes *Brahman*.

On this issue, the antagonist raises objections. The *BG* teaches the absence of rebirth, subsequent to the dawn of *Brahma*-knowledge. But what happens to the *prārabdha-karma*s, *sañcita-karma*s and *āgāmī-karma*s? First, let us clarify these three types of *karma*s. The karmic traces that have already begun to yield their fruits in the current birth are *prārabdha* (already initiated). The heap of *karma* done in the present life and done even after the dawn of knowledge in the current life is called *āgāmī*. The cumulative *karma*s of the past several births, not yet come into force in the current birth, is called *sañcita* (saved). It may be mentioned here that the *karma*s, being done in the current life (*kriyamāṇa karma*) do not bear fruits in the current life and they are added to the cumulative *karma*. It may further be mentioned that all the *karma*s done in the past lives do not become the *prārabdha* in the current life and that only part of the past *karma*s becomes the *prārabdha*.

The opponent view may be summed up as follows. "It is unreasonable to presume the annihilation of all *karma*s unless and until they yield their results even subsequent to the dawn of *brahma-jñāna*. It is normally expected that the three types of *karma*s should give rise to at least three births. Alternatively, the three types of *karma*s combinedly may give rise to at least a single birth."

The scriptures,[35] however, declare that *Brahma-jñāna*, with realization, annihilates *sañcita-karma* and *āgāmī-karma* and leads to

33. *BG*, XIII.23.

34. *MUU*, III.2.9: *sa yo ha vai tat paramaṁ brahma veda brahmaiva bhavati.*

35. *MUU*, II.2.9; *CU*, V.24.3; *BG*, IV.37; *MBhā*, Vanaparva, 200.110.

no more births after the fruition of the *prārabdha-karma* of the current life. For the fruition of the *prārabdha*, there is delay only so long as the *jīvātmā* is not released from the body. The *Brahma-jñānī* is really a *jīvanmukta* (released albeit still living with a body).[36]

The *Pātañjala Yoga-Darśanam* enlists five afflictions (*kleśa*s), namely, *avidyā* (literally meaning "nescience," but here contextually meaning "the Unconscious"), *asmitā* (egoism), *rāga* (attachment), *dveṣa* (aversion) and *abhiniveśa* (*maraṇa-trāsa*; fear of death or clinging to life).[37] All these five *kleśa*s constitute the seeds of all evils. They occasion all acts of *dharma* and *adharma* and thus bring about future births.

The *jīvātmā*, on cognizing the Supreme *Brahman*, becomes a *jīvanmukta*. He comes to his real state, the state of *Brahman*-hood and thus he becomes *Brahman*. He is no longer affected by the five *kleśa*s during the remaining period of his current life. The *prārabdha-karma* continues to function and undergoes fruition until the death of the present body. It produces good and bad effects on the body; but the *Brahma-jñānī* (the *jīvanmukta*) is not at all affected by the body. It may, however, be noted that a *jīvanmukta*, before leaving the body, cannot exercise the powers of *Īśvara* (God).

In some rare, exceptional cases, even the *prārabdha-karma* is burnt out by *Brahma-jñāna*. Once an arrow leaves a bow with sufficient force toward a right target, the arrow must strike the target. But a spiritual force from the opposite direction, with potency much greater than the force of the arrow will impede the rushing arrow and crush it to pieces on the way, or burn it out on the way. This action, however, is not common and may be called a rare exception.

Some self-styled gods — godmen and godwomen — among the Hindus, claim the individual existence of a released self (*muktātmā*) as the Supreme Self (*Paramātmā, Īśvara*, God), while in

---

36. *CU*, VI.14.2.

37. *PYD*, II.3.

the body and after departing from the body. Logical and conceptual analysis cannot support such a claim. According to the Advaita Vedānta, a self, after being liberated, loses its individuality and separate identity. It merges in *Brahman* that is One only and the non-dual One, homogeneous, devoid of constituent parts. According to Vaiṣṇavic dualism, a *jīvātmā*, on being released, goes to *Vaikuṇṭha* (heaven) and stays in permanent bliss in the company of Nārāyaṇa (God) as the servant of the Lord. Any dualistic philosophy of religions does not confer omniscience, omnipotence and omnipresence on a released self that cannot create, sustain and annihilate the total universe or any part of it. Religious metaphysics would collapse and crumble if we accept many Gods and many *Brahmans*.

### 13.09: Several Alternative Paths to Self-Realization

The traditional fourfold classification of Yoga has been enumerated in verse 13.24-25 as alternative paths to Self-realization. Verse 13.24 recommends *dhyāna-yoga* (*rāja-yoga* of Patañjali), *jñāna-yoga* (the *yoga* of spiritual knowledge, with realization of *Brahman*) and *karma-yoga* (the *yoga* of detached action) to the aspirant (*sādhaka*). Verse 13.25 prescribes *bhakti-yoga* (the *yoga* of devotion). Anyone of these alternative paths may be followed to achieve the end. Alternatively, combination of any two, three or all four may be practised to realize the Self.

> By meditation, some behold the Self in the self by the self; others by Sāṅkhya-*yoga* (*jñāna-yoga*); and yet others by *karma-yoga*.[38]

"Beholding the Self" means "perceiving the *Paramātmā* (*Īśvara* or the Supreme Self)." The word "self" "in the self" and "by the self" refers to the *jīvātmā* (individual self).

Meditation is one-pointed concentration on *Brahman* after withdrawing the subtle sense-organs into the mind. It is an incessant thought (a single thought only) in an unbroken stream

38. *BG*, XIII.24.

in the analogy of a current of oil being poured from one higher pot to a lower one. This is what is called *dhyāna-yoga* or *rāja-yoga* of Patañjali. Due credit is given to Ṛṣi Patañjali who codified and streamlined the Yoga of meditation in a holistic and comprehensive way. But he is not the founder of Yoga. Had it been so, the *Mahābhārata*, much older than the *Yoga-Sūtra* of Patañjali, could not have dealt with it. The ancient Vedic seers used this technique for spiritual uplift and also for getting truth revealed.

The term "Sāṅkhya-yoga" has little relation with Kapila's philosophical school of Sāṅkhya. It is the Yoga of Knowledge, as described in the second chapter of the *BG*. A *jñāna-yogī* is to know *Brahman*, is to distinguish the Self from the non-Self and is to realize *Brahman*. For some interpreters, Sāṅkhya-yoga stands for the Sāṅkhya philosophy of Kapila. We do not agree with them.

When actions are performed without attachment to the fruits thereof, and performed as an offering to God, they form a class of *yoga*, the *karma-yoga*, as described in chapter 3 of the *BG*. This *yoga* is one of the paths to Self-realization.

> Still others, not knowing thus, worship as they have heard from others. They too go beyond (overcome) death indeed, by being devoted to what they have heard.[39]

Everybody hasn't the talent or the aptitude for practising *rāja-yoga*, *jñāna-yoga* or *karma-yoga*. They listen to instructions from their spiritual preceptors (*ācārya*s or *guru*s) and others who have realized the Self. They worship God and, thus, practise *bhakti-yoga* (the *yoga* of devotion). Such a person, solely by his *śraddhā* (faith) and *bhakti* (devotion) is liberated.

The *sādhaka* is to select anyone of these four types of *yoga* for getting liberation (*mokṣa*). In doing so, he has to estimate his *śraddhā*, mental aptitude and inclination and his own intellectual capacity. He may adopt anyone of these four systems of *yoga*. He may also combine more than one or all the four systems. No single system

---

39. *BG*, XIII.25.

can be claimed to be the only one through which *mokṣa* can be attained.

## 13.10: Enlightenment Gained by Realizing the Unity of the Spirit

In this section, we shall discuss three verses of the *BG* to establish the non-duality of the Self. Enlightenment ensues from the realization of this fact.

> Whatever being is born, either unmoving or moving, O best of the Bhāratas (Arjuna), know it to be due to the union of the field and the field-knower.[40]

Ācārya Śaṅkara, while interpreting this verse, leans more on the doctrine of illusionism (*māyā-vāda*). We do not agree with him. We base our interpretation of this verse on what has been plainly said in it. It is enough to interpret *sañjāyate* as "virtually produced or generated."

The words *sthāvara* (unmoving) and *jaṅgama* (moving) carry their usual meanings as they look in a gross (*sthūla*) state. In their subtle (*sūkṣma*) state, however, all created beings in the universe (*jagat* = *gam* + *kvip*) are constantly in motion. No created being can exist without motion. The perfectly motionless Being is *Brahman* only.

All beings, in the empirical universe, evolve from *Virāḍ* or *Mahat* or *Buddhi*, that is dissolved in *Māyā*, subsequent to a total dissolution and that evolves from *Māyā* as the first evolute at the time of a new creation (emanation). To use a common language with some inaccuracy in thought, *Virāḍ* (the cosmic mind or supermind) crystallizes and thus manifests as the first step in the creation of the universe. The sequential evolution (*vivartana*) of *Virāḍ* or *Buddhi* (cosmic intellect) results in the mundane field (*jāgatika kṣetra*). *Brahman* is Absolute Reality (*pāramārthika satya*) whereas the field is a virtual, usable reality (*vyāvahārika satya*). It

40. *BG*, XIII.26.

would not be correct to say that the field does not exist at all and that it is a mere phantasy. The field is not hallucinatory, but is illusory by virtue of the illusory appearance of *Brahman* (the substratum) as the virtual field. In the present context, the word "field" is not equivalent to the same word used in physics. It is the full creation, both field and particles and all sequential evolutes from the original evolute of *Virāḍ*.

*Brahman* is Pure *Cit* (*śuddha caitanyam*), the only sentient Being. Everythging other than *Brahman/Īśvara* is insentient (*jaḍa*). Accordingly, *Buddhi* or the cosmic intellect is insentient. But both the *mūla-Prakr̥ti* (*Māyā* = *Brahma-Śakti* = *Īśvara-Śakti* = AP-UM) and AP-M (the rest of the *aparā Prakr̥ti*) are practically sentient, albeit intrinsically insentient. Due to the reflection of the all-pervading Fundamental Consciousness (*Brahman*) on the *aparā Prakr̥ti* (both AP-UM and AP-M), consciousness is induced in *Māyā* and also the cosmic field or the universe. *Māyā* becomes superconscious and the entities of the universe are in possession of consciousness in varying degrees with regard to quality and quantity, depending upon the evolutionary state of their own mental apparatus.

No becoming is possible without consciousness (intelligence). The virtual, usable, illusory universe does exist, evolve and function. Although the Cosmos starts from Chaos, both are intelligently planned and designed for a fine-tuning.

Who plans and who designs? It is the AP-UM (*Avyakta Prakr̥ti*), under the chairpersonship of *Īśvara*, who plans, designs and executes the cosmic events. Inside an individual body or a field, action is possible by the union of the *parā prakr̥ti* (*jīvātmā*, *kṣetrajña*, self) and the field (*kṣetra*).

Advaita Vedānta does assert that the Supreme Self (*Paramātmā*) is identical with the individual selves. Hence, the Lord declares in verse 13.2 of the *BG* "Me do you also know to be the field-knower in all fields."

Now the meaning of verse 13.26 of the *BG* is clear. No evolution is possible without the union of the field and the field-knower.

Evolution is not chaotic, accidental, random and chance-based. What is apparently chaotic is really orderly (*ṛta*). Evolution is not based on the play of dice. Chance does not determine it, although the operation of instrumental chances cannot be whisked away. Evolution is guided by an Intelligent, Divine Being. And He is the chairperson (*adhyakṣa*) of the entire Cosmos.

### 13.11: The Supreme Lord — The Substratum of the Cosmic Ocean

*Brahman*, the Pure Consciousness (*Viśuddha Cit, Śuddha Caitanyam*) is the underlying Reality on which the virtual, usable universe appears in multitudinous forms and functions in manifold ways. It is the rock-bed of the illusory universe. It is the screen on which pictures of different shades appear and disappear. It is the beginningless, endless, permanently unmodifiable substratum (*adhiṣṭhāna*). The waves, the billows, the ripples, the tides, the breakers, the bubbles, the surf, the froth are ever-changeable appearances belonging to the cosmic ocean. A spiritually ignorant person takes the surface appearances to be real and ignores the underlying Reality, the eternal and timeless substratum. The *Brahma-jñānī*, however, cognizes the substratum as the non-dual Reality in the analogy of a canvas on which paintings of the phenomenal universe appear to exist. To use the language of Emmanuel Kant, the famous German philosopher, *Brahman* is the noumena and the universe is the phenomena.

The illusionists present just the opposite view. They assert that only *Brahman* exists and that the universe does not exist. It is a sheer misunderstanding of the difference between the noumena and the phenomena. We may take the example of a computer. One types a book in a computer. The text appears on the screen of the monitor. The appearance is phenomenal only. The Central Processing Unit is different from the window of the monitor. We cannot dismiss the phenomena on the monitor. The universe which is the empirical reality (*vyāvahārika satya*) is not non-existent (*asatya*), although it is *mithyā*. It is not the Absolute Truth (*pāramārthika satya*). Phenomena are ever-changeable and never constant. They cannot exist independently; they are reflections of some independent existence; we cannot think of an illusory snake in the absence of a rope. Now let us know what the Lord says on the topic of phenomena and noumena.

> He who sees the Supreme Lord, dwelling alike in all beings, the unperishing (Lord) in the perishing beings, alone does see.[41]

God, being all-pervasive and omnipresent, abides *equally* in all beings — good or evil, virtuous or sinner, inanimate or animate and micro or macro. All the beings have births, growth, decay and death. They cannot exist without motion, modifications and changes. Death is a certainty for all created beings, inanimate or animate. But God who *equally* resides in all created beings is changeless, unmodifiable and deathless. The Lord elaborates further.

> Since he beholds the Lord dwelling *alike* everywhere, he does not injure the Self by the self. Thus, he reaches God, the Supreme.[42]

Nobody can injure the Self (the Supreme Self or God). What is the meaning of injuring the Self by the self? Ignorant persons resort to the non-self and they repudiate the Self (Supreme Self). Such act of repudiation is expressed as "injuring the Self." The expression "by the self" does not mean "by the *jīvātmā*." It means "by the ego or *ahaṅkāra* or by the *antaḥkaraṇa* as a whole." "One reaches the Supreme Goal" means "One is liberated."

There is another meaning of the statement, "He does not injure the Self by the self." A *Brahma-jñānī* cannot injure anybody else — humans, animals, plants and others — once he realizes that the Supreme Lord *equally* resides in all beings. The Self and the selves are identical; the Self resides in all beings; and the Self is immortal. After realizing these facts, one cannot injure any created being in

41. *BG*, XIII.27.

42. *BG*, XIII.28.

the whole universe. To injure others is the same as injuring oneself. And it is a hard fact that the Self cannot be injured.

### 13.12: The Non-Doer and the Doer

The mixing of Sāṅkhya and Vedānta has created much confusion and has introduced error in Vedāntic interpretation. Even *Ācārya* Śaṅkara is not free from this contamination. Before we present this topic of "the non-doer and the doer," we would try to clarify some anomalies, especially with reference to *prakṛti, avidyā, kartā* and *akartā*.

*Prakṛti, Avyakta, Brahma-śakti* or *Īśvara-śakti* is not nescience (*avidyā*). In Tantra, the Mother Divine (śakti) is omniscient and the Father Divine is also omniscient. The Tāntrik philosophy does not recognize the reflection of the Śiva-Consciousness on the Śakti for rendering the latter conscious. *Advaita* Vedānta, however, has a different view. According to this view, *Brahman* is Pure Consciousness; but, the power of *Brahman* (*Māyā* or the *mūla-Prakṛti*) is insentient (*jaḍa*); the reflection of the *Brahma*-Consciousness on *Māyā* renders the latter conscious. We accept this concept of the *Advaita* Vedānta rather than that of the Tantra. But we cannot accept the erroneous concept that *Māyā* is functionally *avidyā* or nescience. *Māyā*, as a result of the reflection of *Brahman* on the former, is not functionally insentient. Due to this reflection, She not only becomes sentient, but also omniscient. An insentient Being cannot be an agent (*kartrī*). She casts a veil of ignorance on the created beings by virtue of Her concealing power (*āvaraṇa-śakti*) and projecting power (*vikṣepa-śakti*).

*Brahman* does not do anything and permanently stays as non-relational Fundamental Consciousness. The same *Brahman*, with *Māyā* as the *upādhi* (limiting adjunct), is *Īśvara* (God). God is the chairperson of all universal activities, but is not a direct agent of any action whatsoever. Under His chairpersonship, does *Īśvara-śakti* or *Māyā* function. Thus, the Mother Divine is the real agent (*kartrī*). She creates the universe as Mother Sarasvatī; sustains it as Mother Lakṣmī; and destroys it as Mother Kālī. She is the doer of these cosmic functions. But She is not the doer of the individual functions of individual created entities. The manifested *aparā-prakṛti* is the doer of individual functions. Whenever the Cosmos is disturbed and its balance is upset, Mother Divine intervenes to restore the balance. And She executes through Her Power which is beyond the laws of the material universe. This Power is Her *kriyā-śakti*. She corrects any disturbance in the universe by Her extra-cosmic Power. Inscrutable are the ways of Her actions.

Mother Divine (*avyakta* or the *mūla-Prakṛti*, the primordial nature) has a divine musical instrument known as the *vīṇā* with three divine strings (*guṇa*s). These are not attributes unlike the attributes (*guṇa*s) of the manifested *aparā-prakṛti*. The three strings are *sattva, rajas* and *tamas*. They are in an equipoised state (*sāmyāvasthā*) when there is no universe. In the absence of a universe, only Father Divine and Mother Divine stay. Both of them constitute the bipolar Reality. They are eternally and timelessly inseparable. They are beginningless and endless (without birth and death). They are co-eternal or co-timeless.

When Father Divine desires to have a universe for the sportive play (*līlā*) of the Divine Couple, one and only one God assumes the role of Brahmā (Creator God) and one and only one Goddess assumes the role of Sarasvatī (Mother Creatrix). She plays Her divine *vīṇā* with three strings (already described) and thereby disturbs the equipoised state. The vibrations (*spandana, kampana*) of the strings in different notes and combinations of notes create the virtual universe which is both unreal and real. The *oṅkāra-dhvani* (here *dvani* refers to the modes of the vibrations, but not to the sound-vibrations in the air), produced as a result of the vibrations of the strings of the *vīṇā,* crystallizes the *Virāḍ* (*Buddhi*, Cosmic Mind, Supermind), already dissolved in *Māyā*. *Virāḍ* is the primal evolvent from which sequential evolution takes place and continues to be in the creative process throughout a cosmic cycle.

The virtual universe as a whole and all entities of the virtual universe cannot be sustained without Mother Lakṣmī, the Power of Lord Viṣṇu. One and only one Goddess assumes the role of

Mother Lakṣmī. She plays the role for the sustenance (*paripālana*) of the universe. Continual creation and continual annihilation are two opposite processes that perpetually operate throughout every cosmic cycle. There are local annihilations and periodical annihilations. Even in every living being, at the micro level, annihilations are continual processes. All entities of the universe, micro and macro, inanimate and animate, undergo continual dissolution. Finally in a cosmic cycle, the total dissolution of the whole universe takes place. All types of dissolution are brought about by Mother Kālī, the Power of Lord Rudra. One and only one Goddess assumes the role of Mother Kālī for the purpose of dissolution. As one God assumes the role of three Gods (Brahmā, Viṣṇu, Rudra), so also does one Goddess assume the role of three Goddesses (Sarasvatī, Lakṣmī, Kālī). The three Mothers are the *Śakti*s of the three Fathers. Essentially, however, there is only one Father of the universe and there is only one Mother of the universe. The Father of the universe functions through the agency of the Mother of the universe. The Father is the chairperson; the Mother is the executive agent.

The Sāṅkhya says that *Prakṛti* or *Pradhāna* is transformed into the universe of matter and energy. This is the doctrine of transformation (*pariṇāma-vāda*). The Sāṅkhya does posit the existence of innumerable selves (*puruṣa*s); but it does not accept the existence of a Supreme Lord. For the first time in the world, it enunciates the theory of evolution. But its system of evolution is limited to the cyclic evolution of individual human beings. Like other atheistic systems of philosophy, it accepts a permanent universe, without a beginning and an end. It is not aspiritual, since it accepts the existence of *puruṣa*s. Notwithstanding this fact, it does not recognize the existence of God (*Parameśvara*). Its *Prakṛti* or *Pradhāna* has nothing to do with Mother Goddess (*Parameśvarī*, *Mahāmāyā*), the Power of God. The Advaita Vedānta rejects the doctrine of transformation and enunciates its *adhyāsa-vāda* or *vivartta-vāda*. Śaṅkara is the exponent of *adhyāsa-vāda*. In spite of this fact, he has succumbed to the influence of the Sāṅkhya and says that the universe is a modification of the three *guṇas* of *Prakṛti*.

In some of our previous publications, we have also toed the traditional contamination of the Vedānta with the Sāṅkhya against our will and repeated the two traditional slogans: (1) God is the efficient cause of the universe. (2) *Māyā* is the material cause of the universe. We want to correct ourselves at least in our last publication on the Vedānta. God (*Puruṣa*) may be deemed as the impelling, inspiring, or inducing cause of the universe by virtue of His chairpersonship (*adhyakṣatā*). Being a non-doer (*akarttā*), He cannot be called the *efficient cause*. But such a mistake has been traditionally continuing. *Māyā*, the *mūla-Prakṛti* or *Īśvara-Śakti* is really the representative, active cause (*nirvāhī, nimitta kāraṇa*) of all the overall phenomena of the cosmos. She is the executive agent of God. But She is not the material cause of the universe in the analogy of gold being converted into a necklace. The wrong concept of *Māyā* being the material cause of the universe has been perpetuated in the Vedāntic scriptures due to the influence of Sāṅkhya that upholds the doctrine of transformation. *Virāḍ, Buddhi, Mahat*, the Supermind, or the Cosmic Intellect, being the mind of the Primordial Nature, is also co-eternal and timeless with God. It is beginningless and endless. This Cosmic Intellect is really the evolvent of the universe. It dormantly stays in *Māyā* in the absence of a universe. It is the first manifested entity at the time of the creation of the universe. *Virāḍ* becomes manifest from its unmanifested condition. It did not become nothing when it dissolved in *Māyā* at the termination of the immediately previous cosmic cycle. In its latent, dissolved condition, it did contain all the nano-traces of the previous universe. In reality, the universe is a *buddhi-nirmāṇa* (mental construct) of *Māyā* or the *mūla-Prakṛti*. With all this background information, we now quote what the Lord said on the topic under discussion:

> He who sees all actions being performed everywhere by *Prakṛti* alone, and the Self as a non-doer, verily sees.[43]

43. *BG*, XIII.29.

We have already explained that *Prakṛti* (*Māyā* or *Īśvara-Śakti*)[44] performs all overall cosmic functions pertaining to the creation, sustenance and dissolution of the universe. She also sets the universe in order wherever and whenever utter disorder prevails. She executes actions desired by the Father Divine. These are the executive functions of the *mūla-Prakṛti,* the unmanifest *Māyā* (AP-UM).

*Māyā* or the Mother Divine, however, does not execute the activities of the manifested or created nature (AP-M), both inanimate and animate. The manifested *aparā-prakṛti* performs the functions of every created individual entity. It is the *antaḥkaraṇa* (*buddhi, ahaṅkāra* and *manas*) that guides the activities of all individual particles, cells, tissues and organs that work for themselves, whereas the *antaḥkaraṇa* holistically works for the individual system as a whole.

The *Puruṣa* or *Ātmā* (both the Supreme Self and the individual selves — *Paramātmā* and *jīvātmā*s or *bhūtātmā*s) is actionless. Notwithstanding this unambiguous statement, the universe cannot function without the chairpersonship of *Īśvara* (God) and the manifested *aparā prakṛti* cannot function without the chairpersonship of the *parā prakṛti* or the *jīvātmā.*

Now the Lord expounds the fundamental basis of altruism and the plenary existence of the virtual universe.

> When one realizes the separate existence of (all) beings as abiding in the One, and (all beings) proceeding from that One alone, one then attains to *Brahman* (becomes *Brahman*).[45]

When the One Self resides in every individual body and the One Self is not different from each individual self, one may think that the Self must be afflicted by the defects and demerits of the individual. The Lord clears this doubt.

---

44. ŚU, IV, 10.

45. *EG,* XIII.30.

> Being beginningless and free from attributes, this immutable Supreme Self, though dwelling in the body, O son of Kuntī, neither acts nor is tainted.[46]

Anything that has a beginning has an end. God has no beginning, and, hence, is imperishable. That which has a cause undergoes the processes of growth, decay and destruction. God, being uncaused, is immutable and imperishable. That which has attributes has functions. That which has functions is impermanent and is tainted. God, being attributeless, is functionless. It is said that *Brahman*, with attributes, is God. It is, however, a fact that God is free from attributes. He is the creator and controller of the universe that is in possession of attributes and, hence, He is indirectly associated with attributes. A functionless Existence as Pure Consciousness cannot be involved (*lipta*) in anything and, hence, cannot be tainted.

The Lord further elaborates the taintlessness of *Brahman*.

> As the all-pervasive *Ākāśa* (Space), due to its subtlety, is not tainted, so is the Self, present in the body everywhere, not tainted.[47]

> O Bhārata (Arjuna), just as the one sun illumines the entire world (solar system), so does the Lord of the field (*kṣetra*) illumine the whole field.[48]

> They who thus, with the eye of wisdom, perceive the distinction between the field and the field-knower and the way of release from the manifested *Prakṛti* go to the Supreme.[49]

In the last verse (13.34), the *BG* has used the expression *bhūtaprakṛtimokṣa* (release from the created or manifested *Prakṛti*). In this case, *bhūta* means "that which has become or has manifested." It has a reference to the manifested *aparā prakṛti*. The

46. *BG*, XIII.31.
47. *BG*, XIII.32.
48. *BG*, XIII.33.
49. *BG*, XIII.34.

first manifested *aparā-prakṛti* is *Virāḍ, Mahat, Buddhi,* the Cosmic Intellect or the Supermind. In the absence of the virtual universe, it stays as a solute in the solvent of *Māyā,* which is the unmanifest state (*avyakta*) of *aparā-prakṛti.* When a cosmic cycle begins, *Virāḍ* manifests and becomes the first evolvent of evolutes that sequentially evolve to form the universe. All evolutes in the cosmic evolution are the *vivartta*-products (direct or indirect) of *Virāḍ* or *Buddhi.* The body itself in which the self dwells is a component of the manifested *aparā prakṛti.* On getting diliverance from the manifested *aparā prakṛti,* coinciding with the erasure of the *karma-saṁskāras* from the *antaḥkaraṇa,* one goes to the Supreme, that is, one is liberated by becoming *Brahman.*

In Sāṅkhya and Pātañjala Yoga, the *puruṣa* is liberated or gets *kaivalya* on being separated from the *Prakṛti* (unmanifested and manifested *Prakṛti* are one and the same in Sāṅkhya and Yoga.). The Vedānta has been contaminated with this idea that the *parā prakṛti* or the self is liberated, when separated from the *avyakta Prakṛti* or *Māyā.* Such an interpretation is not correct. *Māyā* is the Mother Divine in Advaita Vedānta, Yoga-Vedānta and Tantra-Vedānta. *Īśvara* or the *Puruṣa* is inseparable from *Māyā,* and, hence, the question of separation does not arise. The Vedāntic *puruṣa* or the self (*ātmā*) is not to make efforts to get rid of the Mother Divine. The *mūla-Prakṛti* or the primordial nature does not bind the *puruṣa* to the *saṁsāra.* Thus, we conclude from this discussion that the word *prakṛti* in verse 13.34 of the *BG* means "the manifested *aparā prakṛti.*"

One who cognizes the distinction between the field and the field-knower and fully realizes the field-knower attains *Brahma-nirvāṇa* (completely merges in *Brahman,* with the loss of separate, individual identity).

# 14

## Guṇa-Traya-Vibhāga-Yogaḥ
## (The Yoga of the Division of the Three Guṇas)

### 14.01: Introduction to Guṇas

WHEN we interpret the Vedānta, we try to extricate it from the web of the Sāṅkhya. Much confusion has been created by intermingling two separate philosophical systems that have more differences and less commonality. The Advaita Vedānta is theistic and non-dualistic whereas the Sāṅkhya is atheistic and dualistic (in another sense, pluralistic).

*Māyā* is *Brahma-Śakti* or *Īśvara-Śakti*. The possessor of power (*śaktimān*) and the power (*śakti*) are inseparable like fire and heat, respectively. They form the bipolar Reality and the non-dual Reality too. *Īśvara* (God) is the Father Divine and *Māyā* (Goddess) is the Mother Divine (Mother Creatrix). In our mundane language, we designate *Māyā* as the Consort or Spouse of God. One is the spouse (*kalatra*) of the other. By saying this, we outright reject the claim of the illusionists that *Māyā* is Herself an illusion.

It has been traditionally said that *Māyā* or the *mūla-Prakṛti* is constituted of three *guṇa*s, namely, *sattva, rajas* and *tamas*. In some of our earlier publications, we have been guilty of committing this mistake by toeing this age-old tradition. These three *guṇa*s are three strings (the superstrings of the string-theory of modern physics), contained in the *Buddhi* (cosmic intellect, supermind, *Virāḍ, Mahat*) of *Māyā*. She mentally conjures these three strings and the *vīṇā* to which these strings are attached. *Virāḍ* or the cosmic intellect is induced by the reflection of the light of the fundamental

Consciousness. Since *Brahman* and *Māyā* are co-eternal, *Virāḍ* is beginningless and endless. The three divine strings, contained in *Virāḍ*, are beginningless and endless too. The Vedānta upholds the idea that *Māyā* is undifferentiated (*avyākṛtā*). That being so, the Vedāntic *Māyā* cannot be said to be constituted of these three *guṇa*s. The word *guṇa* has two meanings, namely, "string" and "attribute." In the present context of the Unmanifest Divine Being, the former meaning is appropriate and the latter meaning is not. Because *Māyā* is in possession of three strings as parts of Her musical string instrument (*vīṇā*), the Vedāntic scriptures use the word *guṇamayī* as an adjective for Her.[1]

Attributes like "good," "red," "sweet" cannot be the constituents of anything. They are exhibited properties. Analytically speaking, it is an absurd idea that something or somebody is made up of properties, exhibited by the former.

Two questions arise: Is *Buddhi* a metaphysical entity, separate from *Māyā?* Are the strings metaphysical entities, separate from *Buddhi?* The answers to both the questions are "No." The reflections of the fundamental Consciousness (*Brahman*) on its power, *Māyā*, induces consciousness in the latter. That reflection or the virtually induced entity is the cosmic intellect or the supermind or the *Buddhi*. *Māyā* can create all types of virtual entities by the use of Her *Buddhi*. The divine musical instrument, the *vīṇā*, and the three strings of this instrument are virtually conjured by *Māyā*.

*Brahman,* with *Māyā* as the *upādhi*, is *Īśvara* or God. Only one God is named as Brahmā, Viṣṇu and Rudra, depending upon the string with which He is associated. Brahmā is associated with *rajas;* Viṣṇu with *sattva;* and Rudra with *tamas*. God, being the chairperson, gets the cosmic activities executed by His power (*śakti*). One and only one *Śakti* of God, depending upon the cosmic role, assumes three different names. The same *Śakti* is called Sarasvatī, Lakṣmī and Kālī with reference to Brahmā, Viṣṇu and

1. *ĀL*, I.1; *DBhā*, I.2.5; *BG*, VII.14; *ŚU*, IV.10.

Rudra, respectively. The cosmic activities performed through the string of *rajas, sattva* and *tamas* are creation, sustenance and annihilation, respectively.

*Brahman* is attributeless (*nirguṇa*) and functionless (*niṣkriya*). It is immutable, pure consciousness (*viśuddha cit*), and existence (*sat*). It is unmodifiable, that is, it is eternally and timelessly without changes. The attributeless, functionless *Brahman* is *nirupādhikam;* in other words, it is devoid of limiting adjuncts. This fundamental Reality is not associated with the strings and the cosmic entities and events, resulting from the vibrations of the strings.

We differ from the traditional interpretation, borrowed from the Sāṅkhya philosophy of Kapila, and, hence, repeatedly stress the point that *Māyā,* the *Daivī Prakṛti,* does not undergo transformation or modification to become the universe of matter and energy. She is the unmanifest (*avyakta*) *aparā-prakṛti.* Neither do we accept the doctrine of *brahma-pariṇāma-vāda* (the transformation of *Brahman* into the universe). The doctrine of transformation of *Brahman, Īśvara* and *Māyā* into the universe has been clearly rejected by the Vedānta. What is the precursor material of the universe then? In other words, what is the material cause of the universe? Has it sprung up from nothing? The idea of something becoming nothing and nothing becoming something has already been rejected in verse 2.16 of the *BG*. Now we are enmeshed in a knot which has to be unfastened. The whole universe of matter and energy is immaterial. It is virtual and phenomenal only. *Brahman, B,* appears as the multitude of the universe. And this is brought about by *Māyā*. How does She do it? She has *kriyā-śakti* (acting power), *icchā-śakti* (desiring power), *bala-śakti* (power of force), *āvaraṇa-śakti* (concealing power) and *vikṣepa-śakti* (projecting power). By Her concealing power, She casts a veil of ignorance on the created entities that cannot perceive *B* (*Brahman*) as *B*. By Her projecting power, She projects manifold pictures of the universe, *B* appearing as non-*B*. In a nutshell, this is the doctrine of Śaṅkara's *adhyāsa-vāda* (*atasmiṁstadbuddhiḥ*). The *vivartta-vāda* of the later Vedāntins also expresses a similar doctrine, according to which a rope illusorily appears as a snake.

If the *adhyāsa-vāda* is accepted, the question of the material cause of the universe does not arise at all. The effect is not material and, hence, its precursor is not material. The effect is a supramental projection of the Supermind or the *Virāḍ* or the *Buddhi*. The unreal magic is born out of pairs that are equal and opposite to each other. The sum of all the cosmic tweens is zero (the *tucchya* of the *R̥gveda*, X.129.3). The traditional Vedāntic interpreters have erroneously declared the simile of gold being converted into a necklace or *Māyā* being converted into the universe. We have also wrongly imitated them in some of our previous publications. Here we assert that *Māyā* is not the material cause of the universe. She is, of course, the executive agent of *Īśvara* (God). When God desires to have a universe, *Māyā* creates it. God is the Chairperson (*Adhyakṣa*) and desires to have a universe for the sportive play (*līlā*) of the divine couple. His power, *Māyā*, creates the universe on behalf of God. In reality, *Māyā* is the executive cause of all cosmic events. Since God is the chairperson and *Māyā* works on behalf of God, the *nimitta kāraṇa* (the agent who causes something for somebody else) is applicable for Her. Traditionally, however, God who is a non-doer (*akarttā*) has been described as the *nimitta kāraṇa* and *Māyā*, the unmodifiable *avyakta*, has been said to be the *upādāna kāraṇa* (material cause). Of course, we are to cognize the fact that, without the reflection of *Brahman* on *Māyā*, the latter, being intrinsically insentient, cannot possess *Buddhi* and cannot be the executive agent.

All cosmic activities are supramental phenomena. The universe is a supramental construct. It is the product of the cosmic intellect, the supermind, the *Buddhi*, or the *Virāḍ*, belonging to *Māyā*. Creation or emanation is the evolutionary mental unfolding of the mental infolded. And dissolution is a process of gradual involution which is the mental infolding of the mental unfolded.

A cosmic cycle is constituted by an evolution followed by an involution. The cycles operate *ad infinitum.*

The total universe of matter and energy, after the Big Crunch and at the time of the final dissolution, dissolves in *Virāḍ*, and, in turn, *Virāḍ* dissolves in *Māyā.* The manifest universe becomes unmanifest. There is death of time and dissolution of space. Our concepts of time and space are different from those of traditional philosophies. Time is a mental construct rather than a real entity. There is no time in the absence of actions and events. However, the situation is different with regard to space. What Einstein thought of relative space was really the relativity of dimensions (*dik*s) of space. In contrast, the Vedāntic space or *Ākāśa* is not relative. Neither is it the Aristotelian void. It is the subtlest state of matter with the highest elasticity. In the phase of evolution, the superheated *Ākāśa* is the source of all the matter and energy of the universe. In the phase of involution, the other four states of matter (solid, liquid, gaseous and energy) sequentially dissolve in their respective precursor state to finally become *Ākāśa*. This ākāśic substance serially undergoes involution to become *Prāṇa, Āpaḥ* and *Virāḍ*. In the last step of the total dissolution of the universe, *Virāḍ* dissolves in *Māyā* like salt in water. When God (*Īśvara*) desires to have a universe, *Māyā* creates the universe under the chairpersonship of God. The unmanifest universe becomes manifest again. This emanation or manifestation is a gradual, evolutionary process. The first evolute is *Virāḍ* which becomes the direct or indirect evolvent of all entities of the whole universe. And so does the *Ṛgveda* say: *tasmādvirāḷajāyata virājo adhi pūruṣaḥ* (*Virāḍ* was born from Him, and from *Virāḍ*, arose the created beings in which the *Puruṣa* pervaded).[2]

Over the concept of *Ākāśa*, the Western world was too much confused by the Greek thought of a total void. This idea persisted for more than two and a half thousand years and misguided even the scientists. Only in the latter half of the twentieth century, did

---

2. *ṚV*, X.90.5.

cosmology, particle physics and quantum physics change this age-old concept. The solid, aqueous, gaseous and energy-universe could not evlolve without *Ākāśa* as the evolvent. It is a plenum, and not a void (*śūnyam*). It is the subtlest and the most elastic matter. The Newtonian puzzlement of action at a distance becomes a pseudo-problem if *Ākāśa* is known as a medium of the transmission of waves. Because of its extreme elasticity, it is more curved in the vicinity of a stellar body. Its curvature does not explain the mechanism of action of the gravitational force (vide Newton's theory of gravitation and Einstein's General Theory of Relativity). It is rather a gravitational force that pulls it and curves it. Indian philosophers have been translating *Ākāśa* as "ether," the Aristotelian ether that received a death-blow in 1887. We have to appreciate the Vedāntic cosmology and cosmogony and the place and role of *Ākāśa* in it. *Śūnyam* is a meaningless word in the Vedānta; *pūrṇa* (Full, plenum) is a key-word in the Vedānta. Here we had to spell out *Ākāśa* to dispel the confusion of the creation of something out of nothing.

After a diversion, we come back to the manifested *guṇa*s. The unmanifested *guṇa*s are the three strings of *Māyā*, namely, *sattva, rajas* and *tamas*. The manifested *guṇa*s are also three in number, with the same names. Why do we use the same names for the manifested and the unmanifested *guṇa*s? The vibrations of each of the three strings virtually produce cosmic entities with corresponding properties. Further, with reference to the created living entities with internal instruments (*antaḥkaraṇa*s), the corresponding properties are modulated by the past *karma-saṁskāras*. The vibrational types and the resulting properties of the created beings are the manifested *guṇas*, traditionally translated into English as "attributes." Both the unmanifested *guṇa* (string) and the manifested *guṇa* (attribute) are expressed by one Sanskrit word (*guṇa*) only, and that is the root of the utter confusion.

Classical Indian philosophy is rarely free from imageries. To express the primal, abstract state of the present seemingly concrete universe, abstraction becomes unavoidable, imagery becomes essential and, hence, is the necessity of imageries at a high cost of accuracy. This principle is also applied in modern physics in dealing with topics like early cosmology and quarks. Mother Sarasvatī plays the divine *vīṇā*. She strikes all the three strings differently to produce various musical notes of infinite number of combinations and permutations. Depending upon the characteristics of the vibrations (*spandana* or *kampana*) of the strings of the divine *vīṇā* and the dominance of one of the three strings, each evolved entity acquires the dominance of one of the three attributes. A string, with its vibrations, in the unmanifest state corresponds to a trait-type or an attribute-type in the manifest state. In general, no evolved entity is purely *sāttvika, rājasika,* or *tāmasika* with regard to the possession of attributes. Each one is a peculiar blend of the three attributes in different proportions, with the dominance of one of them.

With this much introduction to the *guṇa*s, we are now ready to discuss the individual verses of the present chapter.

### 14.02 : The Seed in the Womb

It has been said in verse 13.21 of the *BG* that the dwelling of the *puruṣa* in the *prakṛti* and his attachment to the *guṇa*s is the cause of his *saṁsāra* (metempsychosis). What are the *guṇa*s? This question has already been answered in topic 14.01. In what manner is the attachment? How do the *guṇa*s bind the self? What is the way for the self to be released from the binding to the *guṇa*s? What are the characteristics of a liberated person? Chapter 14 of the *BG* answers these questions. The present topic (14.02) is on the Seed-Giver and His womb. The Lord begins this chapter with the following verse.

> I shall again declare that supreme knowledge, the best of all forms of knowledge, by knowing which all the *muni*s (sages

who maintain silence) have passed from here (this virtual world) to the highest perfection.[3]

The *BG* is full of knowledge. But here the Lord extols the supreme knowledge that leads to liberation (*mokṣa*).

Resorting to this knowledge, they have achieved My own nature. They are not born at the time of creation (of the universe); nor are they destroyed at the time of (its) dissolution.[4]

"They have attained My own nature." This statement clearly carries the non-dualistic meaning. "They have identified with Myself, *Parameśvara*, the Supreme Lord." The *BG* does not countenance any distinction between the self (*jīvātmā*) and the Self (*Paramātmā*) and between the Self and *Brahman*.

My womb is the Great *Mahat* (*Virāḍ* or *Buddhi*). I cast the germ (seed) therein. Thence (from the act of impregnation), O Bhārata (the scion of Bharata = Arjuna), is the birth of all beings.[5]

There has been confusion among interpreters about the term *Mahadbrahma*. In the present context, *brahma* has no direct relevance to *Brahman*; neither has it any relevance to Brahmā, the Creator God. Here it means "great (*bṛhat*)" since *Mahat* is greater than any of its effects (evolutes). *Mahat, Virāḍ, Buddhi* (the cosmic intellect, the supermind) is the primal, manifested *aparā-prakṛti* and, being the great mind of *Māyā,* it is co-eternal with the Divine *Prakṛti* (*Māyā,* the Power of *Parameśvara*). In the initial step of creation, *Mahat* appears from *Māyā* and, thus, becomes manifest. In the process of total dissolution, *Mahat,* containing the latent traces of the entire universe, dissolves in *Māyā* and, thus, becomes unmanifest. In contrast, *Māyā,* the Divine Power of *Brahman*/God remains always unmanifested (*avyakta*). It may not, however, be misunderstood that *Mahat, Buddhi* or *Virāḍ* is an entity, separate from *Prakṛti* (*Māyā*), the power of God. *Mahat* or *Virāḍ* or *Buddhi* is

3. *BG,* XIV.1.

4. *BG,* XIV.2.

5. *BG,* XIV.3.

the mind of the Divine *Māyā*. It is the supermind. As a person's mind is not an entity, separate from the person himself, so is the *Mahat*. We can have a better comprehension of this metaphysics if we accept the virtual universe as a mental construct, a mental projection of *Māyā*, the *mūla-Prakṛti*. *Brahman*, the fundamental, pure *Cit* (Consciousness), with *Māyā* as the *upādhi*, makes its power conscious. And it is a fact that consciousness is associated with a mind or a supermind.

Swami Ranganathananda of Ramakrishna Mission has equated *Mahadbrahma* with Brahmā.[6] With all respect to this learned sage, we humbly differ from him. The Sāṅkhya *Mahat* or *Buddhi* is the Vedic *Virāḍ*. It is the first evolute manifested from *Māyā* or the *mūla-Prakṛti*. It cannot be equated with Brahmā, the Creator God, who is not different from the One and only One God of the universe.

The word *garbha* in verse 14.3 of the *BG* refers to *Hiraṇyagarbha* (the Golden Germ, the Golden Embryo, the Cosmic Egg in the Big-Bang cosmology of Modern Physics). The birth of all beings via the origination of *Hiraṇyagarbha* proceeds from the casting of the seed by the Supreme Lord. Brahmā is the chairperson or *adhyakṣa* of *Hiraṇyagarbha* and He is not different from God, the One and the only One Supreme Lord. When God assumes the role of creation, He becomes Brahmā who brings about the union of the field and the field-knower, the latter being associated with the adjuncts of nescience. Thereby the non-relational Field-Knower (*Brahman*) or the relational Field-Knower (God) becomes multiple field-knowers (*bhūtātmās*/*jīvātmās*). Evolution in insentient matter and energy (field) is not possible without the association of the the sentient field-knower. In our opinion, *Hiraṇyagarbha* is the Cosmic Egg and also Brahmā who presides over the Cosmic Egg. The context should determine one of the two meanings of the word, *hiraṇyagarbha* (either Brahmā, the *Hiraṇya-garbhātmā* or the Golden Embryo).

---

6. Swami Ranganathananda, 2003, vol. 3, p. 104.

> O son of Kuntī (Arjuna), whatever forms are produced in all wombs whatsoever, the Great *Mahat* (*Virāḍ, Buddhi*) is their womb and I am the seed-giving Father.[7]

This verse presents the common notion that a child has a father and a mother. Many religions speak of the Lord, the Father of the universe. They don't recognize anybody as the Mother of the universe. Most interpreters of even the Advaita Vedānta, being illusionists, use the term *Māyā* as "illusion." They do not consider Her as the Mother of the universe. The *BG*, in this verse, brings about a clear synthesis of the Advaita Vedānta, the Tantra and the Śākta philosophies. God (*Parameśvara*) is the Father of the universe. He is the seed-giver. *Māyā*, the *mūla-Prakṛti* is the Mother of the universe. She is the seed-receiver. *Mahat, Virāḍ*, or *Buddhi* is the uterus (*garbhāśaya*) of the universe. The Cosmic Egg (*CU*, III.19.1; *MS*, I.12) or the Golden Embryo is the *garbha* or *Hiraṇyagarbha*, from which all the entities of the universe of matter and energy have gradually evolved. The *Ṛgveda* and the *Śvetāśvatara Upaniṣad* use the word *Hiraṇyagarbha* for the presiding deity (chairperson) of the Golden Embryo.[8] He is Brahmā, God and only one God, the name being used when the Supreme Lord takes the role of creation. His Consort or Power is Mother Sarasvatī (Gāyatrī, Sāvitrī), a name used for one *Parameśvarī* when She plays the role of the Mother Creatrix.

### 14.03 : The Characteristics of the Three Guṇas

The three *guṇa*s — *sattva, rajas* and *tamas* — have already been introduced in topic 14.01. Their characteristics and functions will be described now. It may be noted here that, for the present purpose, *guṇa*s refer to attributes manifested in the created entities. On this topic, the Lord says :

> O Mighty-Armed (Arjuna), the *guṇas*, named as *sattva, rajas* and *tamas*, are produced by *Prakṛti* (*Māyā* or the *mūla-Prakṛti*). They

---

7. *BG*, XIV.4.

8. *ṚV*, X.121.1; *ŚU*, III.4.

bind the immutable, embodied spirit fast in the body.[9]

The three *guṇas*, mentioned in this verse, are *prakṛti-sambhavāḥ* (produced by *Prakṛti*). A number of interpreters are of the opinion that *Māyā* is constituted of these three *guṇas* and that the whole universe of matter and energy is constituted of these three *guṇas*. We do not agree to this view of Sāṅkhya origin. *Māyā* is *daivī* (divine). She is the power (*śakti*) of God. In our mundane language, She is the consort or feminine spouse of God. She is *guṇamayī*. The suffix *mayaṭ* is used in the sense of "full of." "A certain area of land is full of water." This statement does not say that the land is constituted of water. *Īśvara* is *saguṇa* (associated with attributes) and *Māyā* or *Īśvarī* is *saguṇā,* whereas *Brahman* is *nirguṇa* (without attributes). Both God and *Prakṛti* are associated with *guṇas*. *Māyā* is in posssession of *guṇas* or strings and is associated with the attributes of Her created entities. But it is not a fact that *Māyā* is made up of *guṇas*. *Īśvara* is associated with *guṇas*, but he is not in possession of *guṇas*. Verse 14.5 of the *BG* clearly states that the three *guṇas* are produced by *Prakṛti*. How are they produced? Mother Sarasvatī plays the three strings of the divine *vīṇā*. As a result, vibrations are produced, with innumerable musical notes. The vibrations are the virtual precursors of the virtual universe. Each and every entity of the universe is influenced by the vibrations to exhibit peculiar types of properties or attributes. Thus, the word *guṇa* in the Vedāntic concept has two meanings, namely, string and attribute. The former meaning has a direct reference to *Māyā*, whereas the latter meaning is applied to the created entities of the universe. But, in no case, attributes can be constituents of the created entities too.

Let us analyse the concept with one example. *Guṇas* (attributes, qualities, or properties) can never be the material cause of any effect. "Gold is yellow in colour and malleable." The precursor material of gold cannot be yellowness or malleability. The divine cosmic vibrations, resulting from the vibrations of the three subtle

9. *BG*, XIV.5.

strings, *sattva, rajas, tamas,* generate three modes of attributes that pertain to the manifested universe. These manifested attributes are also called *sattva, rajas* and *tamas.*

*Guṇa*s lead to *karma*s. *Karma*s leave latent karmic traces in the *antaḥkaraṇa.* These imprints are *saṁskāra*s of both *vāsanā* and non-*vāsanā* types. The *dehī* (*jīvātmā,* individual self) is bound to these *saṁskāra*s. A bound self, unless and until it is emancipated or released from this bondage, cannot be the Universal Self (*Brahman*). When the self is fully released from the bondage with the *karma-saṁskāra*s by emptying the *karmāśaya,* it attains liberation (*mokṣa*) and becomes *Brahman.* That is what the *BG* says B*rahma-nirvāṇa.*

Western psychology types personalities of human beings in a number of ways. Indian psychology, from the days of yore, has typed human personalities as *sāttvika, rājasika* and *tāmasika.* These are the main types of mental traits. But, in reality, the individual types are in legion. No single individual created being is purely in possession of *sattva, rajas* or *tamas.* We are all blends of different proportions. When we say, "Certain X is *sāttvika* in nature," we mean thereby that the *sattva guṇa* is dominant in X. There has been very little discussion on the personality-types in Indian psychology.

Now the Lord characterizes the three *guṇa*s (trait-types).

> Of these, *sattva,* being stainless, is luminous and free from evil. It binds, O sinless one (Arjuna), to clinging to happiness and to clinging to knowledge.[10]

The *sattva* trait-type imparts transparency to the *antaḥkaraṇa.* It is capable of revealing consciousness (*caitanya*). It is free from evil effects. Nevertheless, it has also some binding actions. It causes attachment to happiness (of benign type) and knowledge, and thereby virtually binds the self (*jīvātmā*).

> Know *rajas* to be of the nature of passion, and the source of thirst

10. *BG,* XIV.6.

> (craving) and attachment. O son of Kuntī (Arjuna), it fast binds the embodied self to attachment to actions.[11]
>
> But know *tamas* to be born of ignorance. It deludes all embodied selves. O Bhārata (Arjuna), it fast binds to error, indolence and sleepiness.[12]

*Tamas* is the trait-type of inertia. It renders a person inert. Error, indolence and sleep are the three main characteristics of *tamas.*

> O Bhārata, *sattva* attaches one to happiness and *rajas* to action, while *tamas,* verily shrouding knowledge, causes clinging to error.[13]

In verses 14.6 and 14.9, the word *sukha* has been used with reference to *sattva*. We have translated it as "happiness" rather than "pleasure" with the sole intention that "pleasure" may be misunderstood as "sensual and carnal pleasure."

Each of the three *guṇa*s predominates over the other two in every specific trait-type. This predominating effect is described in the next verse.

> O Bhārata, *sattva* arises, predominating over *rajas* and *tamas;* so also does *rajas* over *sattva* and *tamas,* and *tamas* over *sattva* and *rajas*.[14]

When one of the three *guṇa*s increases, it subjugates the other two and asserts its own nature. Thus, the asserting *guṇa* produces more of its effects.

### 14.04 : The Symptoms of the Guṇas

When a particular *guṇa* is predominant, its effects become spectacular. What are the indicatory marks by which the dominance of that particular *guṇa* can be known? The reply follows:

---

11. *BG*, XIV.7.
12. *BG*, XIV.8.
13. *BG*, XIV.9.
14. *BG*, XIV.10.

> When the light of wisdom beams through all the gateways (openings of the senses) in this body, then it may be known that *sattva* is predominant.[15]
>
> Greed, activity, commencement of works, restlessness, longing — these arise, O best of the Bhāratas, when *rajas* is predominant.[16]
>
> Gloom (darkness, absence of discrimination), inertness, error (heedlessness), and also delusion — these arise, O scion of Kuru, when *tamas* is predominant.[17]
>
> The embodied self, passing away (from the body) when the *sattva* dominates, attains the unstained worlds pertaining to those who know the highest.[18]

The uppermost in the mind at the time of leaving the body is the factor that decides the next birth of the self. Departing from the body at the time of *sattva*-dominance leads one to the highest (subtlest) world of *Brahmaloka* where the selves of the best spiritual persons reside. *Brahmaloka* is not contaminated with *rajas* and *tamas*. Nevertheless, residing in the *Brahmaloka* is not equivalent to liberation (*mokṣa*). Even the *sattva*-type of trait cannot yield *mokṣa*. The compound-word *uttamavidām* (of the knowers of the highest) does not mean "of the knowers and realizers of *Brahman*."

> Meeting death in *rajas*, one is born among those addicted to works. Likewise, dying in *tamas*, one is born in the wombs of the deluded.[19]

The word *mūḍha*, in this verse, literally means "deluded." Contextually, it means"irrational." One dying in *tamas* is born in the wombs of sub-human species in whom reason does not operate. Śaṅkara says : "*paśvādiyoniṣu jāyate*" (is born in the wombs of animals and so forth).

---

15. *BG*, XIV.11.
16. *BG*, XIV.12.
17. *BG*, XIV.13.
18. *BG*, XIV.14.
19. *BG*, XIV.15.

> They (the wise) say that the fruit of good action is *sāttvika* and pure; the fruit of *rajas* is pain, and the fruit of *tamas* is ignorance.[20]
>
> Knowledge is born of *sattva;* and greed from *rajas;* error, delusion and ignorance are born of *tamas.*[21]
>
> Those, fixed in *sattva,* go upwards; the *rājasika*s remain in the middle; and the *tāmasika*s, abiding in the function of the lowest *guṇa,* go downwards.[22]

Now we sum up the present section. Persons, steeped in *tamas,* wallow in the nether regions. They are ignorant, heedless, indolent, inert and sleepy. *Rājasika* persons are addicted to all types of works for getting more wealth, power, dominance, prestige and comforts. *Sāttvika* persons seek peace, benign happiness and knowledge. Persons of *sattva-guṇa* ascend the spiritual ladder; those of *rajas-guṇa* stay in the middle and get pain in life; while those of *tamas-guṇa* follow a downward path. The dominance of a *guṇa* at the time of death is the deciding factor of the nature of the future birth. The question is: Is it sufficient for a person to abide in *sattva* for getting release from the *saṁsāra* (metempsychosis)? The answer is "NO." For attaining liberation, one is to transcend even the *sattva.*

### 14.05 : Liberation by Transcending the Three Guṇas

In verse 2.45 of the *BG,* the Lord advises: "Transcend the *guṇa*s, O Arjuna (*nistraiguṇyo bhavārjuna*)." This idea has been elaborated in verses 19 and 20 of this chapter.

> When the seer perceives no agent other than the *guṇa*s and knows Him who is higher than the *guṇa*s attains to My Being.[23]

The seer (the person of enlighenment) has the ability to see what is correct and what is truth. He can distinguish right from wrong and good from bad. He beholds the *Puruṣa* as a non-doer (*akarttā*),

---

20. *BG,* XIV.16.
21. *BG,* XIV.17.
22. *BG,* XIV.18.
23. *BG,* XIV.19.

a chairperson (*adhyakṣa*) and witness (*sākṣī*) only. At the same time, he perceives the *Prakṛti* (the Mother Divine, *Māyā*, the *mūla-Prakṛti*) as the cosmic agent (*jagat-kartrī*); he also perceives Her *guṇa*s or strings that vibrate to produce cosmic entities, with *antaḥkaraṇa*s and attributes (*guṇa*s); he realizes that it is the *antaḥkaraṇa*, with a trait-type, that is the real agent of the individual actions.

"Such a seer attains My status (*madbhāvaṁ so 'dhigacchati*)." This sentence needs some clarification. The Lord says : "He attains My status as Vāsudeva, for, he sees that everything is Vāsudeva (vide *BG*, 7.19)." Alternatively, the meaning of the Lord's statement may be like this : "He realizes the Self (*Brahman/Īśvara*) as his self; that is, his identity with *Brahman* becomes manifest."

How does the seer attain to the Lord's status? It is being stated in the next verse:

> Having transcended these three *guṇa*s whence the body has sprung up, the embodied self is freed from birth, death, old age (decay) and pain, and attains to immortality.[24]

Śaṅkara says that the three *guṇa*s (*sattva, rajas* and *tamas*) are the *upādhi*s of *Māyā* (*māyopādhibhūtāḥ*). The first evolute, resulting from the disturbed equipoise of these *guṇa*s (strings) is *Virāḍ, Mahat, Buddhi,* the cosmic mind or the supermind. All manifested entities of the universe gradually and sequentially evolve from the cosmic intellect. The inner mental instrument (*antaḥkaraṇa* = *buddhi* + *ahaṅkāra* + *manas* + ten subtle *indriya*s) is the agent of actions of an individual created being (inanimate or animate). God or even His power (*Īśvara-Śakti* = *Māyā*) is not the agent of our actions (of any individual created being, inanimate or animate). Of course, *Māyā* or the Mother Divine is the executive agent of the creation, sustenance and dissolution of the universe. The maintenance of cosmic order is part of sustenance which is discharged by the Mother Divine.

We do not agree with Śaṅkara to his point that the three *guṇa*s are the *upādhi*s of *Māyā*. We have already clarified the distinction

24. *BG*, XIV.20.

between the string-*guṇa* and the attribute-*guṇa*, the latter being the trait-type of the created entities of the universe. However, we infer from Śaṅkara's statement that *guṇa*s are not the constituents of *Māyā*, that is, She is not made up of *guṇa*s. One is apt to be confused with the difference between the superstring *guṇa* and the attribute or quality *guṇa*. The vibrations of the superstring *guṇa*s produce innumerable entities of the virtual universe, possessing the attribute *guṇa*s. Both *Parameśvara* and *Parameśvarī* (*Māyā*) are associated with the virtual attribute *guṇa*s. And, hence, are they *saguṇa*s (with attributes).

What has been described in verse 14.20 of the *BG* relates to a *jīvanmukta* (one who is released albeit still living). He identifies himself with the Supreme Self rather than with his body. He is free from body-consciousness even though he dwells in his body. He attains to immortality even while still alive. This does not mean that a *jīvanmukta* does not die or does not depart from his body. After departing from the body, he re-establishes his identity with *Brahman* and is not born again.

### 14.06 : The Characteristics of One Who Has Transcended the Guṇas

After listening to the instructions of the Lord, stated in section 14.05, Arjuna got an occasion for further questioning. He asked three questions to clarify his doubts.

> What are the marks (characteristics), O Lord, of him who has transcended these three *guṇa*s? How does he behave? And how does he go beyond these three *guṇa*s?[25]

Arjuna's three questions are linked together. The Lord replies through several verses.

> O Pāṇḍava (Arjuna), he hates not light, activity and delusion, when present, nor longs for them, when absent.[26]

*Prakāśa* or the light of knowledge and happiness are the effects of *sattva*. *Pravṛtti* or activity is the effect of *rajas*. *Moha* or delusion is

25. *BG*, XIV.21.

26. *BG*, XIV.22.

the effect of *tamas*. The sage who has transcended these three *guṇa*s does not hate these when they spring up; nor does he desire them when they disappear.

> He who is seated as if indifferent, is not disturbed by the *guṇa*s, and does not move but remains firm, knowing that the *guṇa*s operate; to whom pain and pleasure are the same, who abides in the Self, who treats alike a clod of earth, a stone and gold, to whom the pleasant and the unpleasant are alike, who is calm, to whom censure and praise are alike, who is the same in honour and dishonour, and equal toward friends and foes, who relinquishes the initiation of all actions, is said to have gone beyond the *guṇa*s.[27]

Four verses have characterized a sage who is *guṇātīta* (risen above the *guṇa*s and liberated albeit still living). Such a *jīvanmukta* person maintains equanimity in opposite conditions and does not bother about the presence or absence of *guṇa*s.

There may be a dispute over the statement, "He relinquishes all undertakings (*sarvārambhaparityāgī*)." Does the *BG* preach inaction? Had it been so, Lord Vāsudeva would not have instructed Arjuna to fight. What is true for a normal man, living in a society and a household, is not so for a *guṇātīta, jīvanmukta* and *saṁnyāsī*. In that state of spiritual ascension, he renounces all sorts of actions except those for the mere maintenance of the body.

### 14.07 : How Does One Transcend the Three Guṇas?

In section 14.06, the characteristics of a person who has transcended the three *guṇa*s have been described. But Arjuna has also asked a question in verse 14.21. How does one pass beyond these three *guṇa*s? Now the Lord answers to this question.

> And he, who serves Me with unwavering (unswerving) *yoga* of devotion, transcends these *guṇa*s and is fitted for becoming *Brahman*.[28]

It is not so easy to become *guṇātīta* (one who has transcended the

27. *BG*, XIV.23.

28. *BG*, XIV.26.

three *guṇas*). Nor is it impossible too. The ascetic (*karma-saṁnyāsī*) gets liberation by transcending the three *guṇas* in the present life and, thus, he becomes a *jīvanmukta* (released while still living). Here, in the non-dualistic sense, liberation means "becoming *Brahman*", "the self merging in the Self and becoming the Self, without maintaining any separate identity."

Devotion (*bhakti*) is the only means to go beyond the *guṇas*. God (*Īśvara, Nārāyaṇa*) resides in the hearts of all beings. Being all-pervasive, He is inside and outside all created beings, both inanimate and animate. There is no need of searching for Him, because He is everywhere. The devotee cognizes Nārāyaṇa (God) everywhere, both within and without. He has to incessantly contemplate the Lord, without allowing the mind to be distracted otherwise. If that is done, the Lord's grace showers on the devotee. As a result, he gets *buddhi-yoga*. As darkness disappears with the appearance of light, so do the three *guṇas* disappear with the advent of Plenary Knowledge (*Brahma-jñāna* which is *Pūrṇa Jñāna*). With the dawn of *Brahma-jñāna*, the devotee becomes *Brahman*, while still alive. It is a case of the harmonization of devotion (*bhakti*) and knowledge (*jñāna*).

Ācārya Śaṅkara, in interpreting verse 14.26 of the *BG*, has translated the expression *avyabhicāreṇa bhakiyogen* as "by unwavering (*avicalita*) *yoga* of devotion." We accept this interpretation. However, we have an additional interpretation too. The word *vyabhicāra* means "transgression" or "offence." Anyone who indulges in immoral activities is a *vyabhicārī*. The absence of *vyabhicāra* is *avyabhicāra*. For some religious persons, no evil actions are bad, provided they can deceive God by praying and superficial, ritual worshipping. This verse of the *BG* expresses disapproval of formal devotion with simultaneous indulgence in vices. Virtuous conduct and purity in benevolent actions — mental, verbal and physical — must be inseparable with devotion to God. And so do the scriptures say: *ācārahīnaṁ na punanti vedāḥ*. (The Vedas do not purify a person devoid of ethical and moral conduct.)

The Lord expounds the rationale of what has been said in

verse 14.26 in the next verse which is the concluding one of chapter 14 of the *BG*.

> For I am the ground of *Brahman*, the Immortal and the Immutable, as also of the Eternal Righteousness and the Absolute (Unfailing) Bliss.[29]

We have gone through the interpretation of this verse, made by several learned scholars. With all humility, we say that we are unable to agree with them. Here we put forth our own interpretatation that may be judged by our readers and other critical scholars.

In the Vedānta, at least in the Advaita Vedānta, *Brahman* is the Absolute Reality. *Brahman*, with *Māyā* as the *upādhi*, is *Parameśvara* (the Supreme God). Both *Brahman* and *Parameśvara* are one and the same, except the fact that the former is attributeless (*nirguṇa*) and the latter is associated with attributes (*saguṇa*). A number of interpreters say that God (*Parameśvara*) is the abode (*pratiṣṭhā*) of *Brahman* and that He is the base or the support of *Brahman*. Such a concept seems to be incongruous.

The verse says that *Brahman* is Immortal, Immutable, *Sanātana Dharma* (Eternal Righteousness) and Absolute Bliss. There is no dispute over this statement. *Brahman*, being birthless and deathless, continues to stay as Consciousness only. It is changeless or unmodifiable, and, hence, is called *avyaya*. It has no properties and no functions. It is *Dharma*, because it holds (the verb-root *dhṛ* means "to hold") the universe by virtue of its being the substratum (*adhiṣṭhāna*). It is Absolute Bliss, without the admixture of joyfulness and sorrowfulness. These statements necessarily go with the concept of *Brahman*. Having accepted these statements and the implied concept, we cannot say that *Brahman* becomes graceful in helping the devotee go beyond the three *guṇa*s. And verse 14.26 does not say anything from which we can derive such a meaning. It refers to Lord Vāsudeva (Nārāyaṇa, *Parameśvara*, or God) who bestows grace on the devotee.

29. *BG*, XIV.27.

The puzzle is solved by correctly interpreting the word *pratiṣṭhā* in verse 14.27. God is the ground of *Brahman*. On this ground does the tree of the universe sprout, grow, decay and finally dissolve. The three processes of creation, sustenance and dissolution move in cycles, without beginning and end.

God is a non-doer (*akarttā*), a chairperson (*adhyakṣa*) and a witness (*sākṣī*). The devotee becomes *nistraiguṇya* (free from the three *guṇas*) and a *jīvanmukta* (liberated albeit living with a body) by the grace of God. Now we have apparent contradictions and confusions. How does God, being a non-doer, perform actions? Whatever God desires is executed by His power (*Māyā,* the *mūla-Prakṛti,* the Mother Divine). She is the executive agent on behalf of God. But we have to remember that the power (*śakti*) and the possessor of power (*śaktimān*) are not two different entities. They constitute the bipolar Reality.

The next chapter starts with the tree of the *saṁsāra* (metempsychosis). The universe is rooted in *Māyā,* the *Īśvara-Śakti* (the power of God). God, as the chairperson, superintends the mundane existence (*saṁsāra*). In reality, the universe is rooted in God. It is God who is the support of the *saṁsāra*.

God cannot be the support of *Brahman*. The word *pratiṣṭhā* may mean "support." It may also mean "ground." The simile of the ground, supporting shrubs and trees, holds good for *Īśvara* (God) and the *saṁsāra*. It may not be correct to say that the non-relational, *nirguṇa Brahman* is the support of the *saṁsāra*. Neither is it correct to say that *Īśvara* is the support of *Brahman*. It is God (the *saguṇa* aspect of the *nirguṇa Brahman*) who works as the ground of the universe. The expression "of *Brahman, brahmaṇaḥ*" in the last verse of chapter 14 of the *BG* has to be understood by the way of conceptual analysis. The Lord says : "I, of *Brahman,* am the support or ground (for the universe)." The expression "for the universe" has been understood in the verse. Moreover, the first three verses of the next chapter corroborate the meaning we have given here.

# 15

## Puruṣottama Yogaḥ
## (The Yoga of the Supreme Spirit)

### 15.01: The Inverted Pīpal Tree

A *karma-yogī* gets the fruits of his detached actions through the grace of God. A *jñāna-yogī* gets the fruits of his *Brahma-jñāna* through the grace of God. He goes beyond the *guṇas* by getting the grace of God (the Supreme Self). *Jñāna-yoga* bears fruit, which is nothing other than liberation (*mokṣa*), only when God bestows grace on the *yogī* who thereby transcends the three *guṇas*. *Bhakti-yoga* (the Yoga of devotion) is the only medium through which *karma* and *jñāna* fructify.

A *bhakti-yogī* should thoroughly understand the true nature of the Self (the Supreme Spirit = God) and also the nature of *saṁsāra* (transmigratory existence, mundane existence). The *saṁsāra* is spoken of as a *pīpal* tree, with roots above and branches below. First, the Lord explains the metaphor of the *pīpal* tree.

> They speak of the eternal *pīpal* tree, with roots above and branches below. Its leaves are the Vedic hymns. He who knows it is the knower of the Vedas.[1]

This metaphor of the *pīpal* tree, with roots above and branches below, has also been stated in the *Kaṭhopaniṣad*[2] and the *Mahābhārata*.[3] The *Brahma*-tree, as upside down, has also been

1. *BG*, XV.1.
2. *KTU*, II.3.1.
3. *MBhā*, Aśvamedha-parva, 35.20-22; 47.12-15.

illustrated in other Upaniṣads.[4] *Brahman* abides in the tree of *saṁsāra* as the essence (*sāra-bhūtam*) of the latter. It is *Brahman* alone that appears as the virtual universe, owing to *avidyā* (nescience). *Brahman* also transcends the universe. It is the support of the tree of *saṁsāra*. But *Brahman*, the Immutable (*kūṭastha*), cannot by itself be the cause. Its power (*śakti*), the *avyakta* (unmanifest) or *Māyā* (the Mother Divine) is the source from which the eternal tree of the *saṁsāra* has sprung up. The tree has also developed by getting nourishment from the same *avyakta*. God presides over the tree, superintends it and pervades it. But it is the Mother Divine (*Māyā*) that causes the seed to sprout. The tree of *saṁsāra* is eternal in a special sense. Although the universe has a beginning and an end, its manifestation, sustenance and dissolution move in cycles, with infinite numbers in the past and infinite numbers in the future. *Virāḍ* (*Mahat*, *Buddhi* or the cosmic intellect or the supermind) is the first evolute from which the universe serially evolves. In the final process of dissolution, the universe, in the reverse path, dissolves serially to finally become *Virāḍ*. As a crystal of salt dissolves in water and again recrystallizes from water, so also does *Virāḍ* dissolve in the Mother Divine (*Māyā*) and again manifest from the same Mother Divine. The latter process is known as creation and the former as dissolution. If we consider the unending cosmic cycles, as described here, we have to admit that the *saṁsāra* is eternal in a special sense.

*Aśvattha* (*Ficus religiosa*) is a tree. The selection of the name of the tree has etymological and metaphysical significance. The word *śvaḥ*, means "tomorrow." *Aśvattha* signifies "that which is not today as it was yesterday and will not be tomorrow as it is today." It is a befitting metaphor for the *jagat* (*gam* + *kvip*; the universe that constantly changes, that is in constant motion) of virtual and phenomenal existence.

The leaves of the inverted *pīpal* tree are the Vedic chants. Here a contextual reference to the ritual part (*karmakāṇḍa*) of the Vedas

4. *ŚU*, III.9; *MTU*, VI.4.

has been made. Vedic rituals, in the Pūrva Mīmāṁsā system, are meant for worldly prosperity and comforts.

The Lord continues to describe the parts of the inverted *pīpal* tree in the following verse:

> Below and above spread its branches, nourished by the *guṇa*s. Sense-objects are its buds. Below in the world of men, stretch forth the roots that link up actions.[5]

The branches of the cosmic tree spread profusely above and below. The branches grow above, that is, they grow up to the *Brahmaloka*. They spread downwards; that is, they grow in a downward direction to the regions of men and other inferior beings. The nature of works decides the upward or downward growth. The latent impressions (*vāsanā*s) produced by attachment, aversion and such other afflictions are stored in the karmic reservoir of the subtle and causal bodies. The results of good or evil actions engender latent karmic impressions. Good *karma*s make the branches grow upwards; bad *karma*s make the branches grow downwards.

The three *guṇa*s function to supply the required sap. The branches get nourishment from this sap. The senses feast on the sense-organs and thereby put forth the buds and twigs. The sprouting, leafing and thriving of the cosmic tree continue so long as the *guṇa*s supply the sap.

More is told regarding the tree of *saṁsāra* (metempsychosis, mundane, transmigratory existence) in the next verse.

> Its form here is not perceived as such, neither its end, nor its beginning, nor its existence. Having cut asunder this firm-rooted *aśvattha* with the strong weapon of non-attachment, contemplating the idea "I seek refuge in that Primeval *Puruṣa* whence streamed forth the ancient activity," then one is to laboriously seek after that goal, going whither, they do not return again.[6]

---

5. *BG*, XV.2.

6. *BG*, XV.3-4.

A modern man of science, with a good grasp of Heisenberg's Principle of Indeterminacy (Heisenberg's *Uncertainty Principle*), will be able to comprehend the first half of verse 15.3. Here we may quote an English translation of Śaṅkara's interpretation:

> Its form, as described, is not known for certain here at all; for it is like a dream, water of the mirage or a city in the sky. It is fugitive. Therefore, it has no end, fixity or conclusion. Similarly it has no beginning. None knows it as having a firm existence or a middle state.[7]

The cosmic tree is phenomenal rather than noumenal. Its existence, appearance and functioning are purely virtual. We cannot know all its phenomenal characteristics with certainty. Once we approach the precision of one aspect, the other aspect becomes indeterminable. This virtual universe is fugitive. We cannot say "It exists." Neither can we say "It does not exist." It is totally illusory; but is still not nothing.

Our goal is to reach the Supreme Spirit (*Puruṣottama*). We can reach Him by cutting the tree of transmigratory existence with the sword of non-attachment.

The second line of verse 15.4 of the *BG* contains the expression *yataḥ pravṛttiḥ prasṛtā purāṇī*. The literal meaning of this statement is: "From whom streamed forth the ancient activity." A clarification of this statement is necessary. "From that Pimeval Spirit alone sprang the beginningless and endless cyclic processes of the creation, sustenance and dissolution of the eternal cosmic tree."

In verse 15.1, the inverted *pīpal* tree has been said to be *avyayam* (indestructible, imperishable, eternal; that cannot be spent and reduced). The universe has a beginning and an end. How is it eternal then? The process of creation, sustenance and dissolution of the universe is cyclic, without a beginning and an end. The whole universe, in its phase of involution, finally becomes *Virāḍ*, *Mahat*, or *Buddhi* (the cosmic intellect). This *Virāḍ* may be compared

---

7. A.G.K. Warrier, 1983, p. 494.

with the hard disc of a computer. It contains all the latent impressions of the universe. The *bindu* or singularity finally dissolves in the power of God (*Śakti* or *Māyā*, the Mother Divine). This is the process of the total dissolution. In the first phase of the next cycle, what we call "creation" is really the emanation or manifestation of *Virāḍ* from *Māyā*. *Virāḍ* is the first evolute and the last involute. The Vedāntic process of creation is not a *de novo* creation of something out of nothing, but is manifestation out of the unmanifest (*avyakta* becoming *vyakta*). If one considers the two phases (the expanding phase which is the phase of evolution and the contracting phase which is the phase of involution) and three types of activities (creation, sustenance and dissolution) of each cosmic cycle, repeating *ad infinitum*, one has to say that the tree of the universe is imperishable.

But, for a liberated self, the tree of the universe perishes so far as that self is concerned. Its firm roots can be cut asunder with the strong axe of non-attachment (verse 15.3). The self, free from bondage, is released. A released self is not different from the Supreme Self which is Pure Consciousness.

### 15.02 : Persons Competent to Reach the Supreme Goal

The supreme goal is God (*Parameśvara*, the Supreme *Puruṣa*). One reaches that goal after severing the link with the cosmic tree. Many interpreters of the *BG* have followed the Sāṅkhya concept of liberation (*kaivalya*), according to which the individual self (*jīva* = *puruṣa*) becomes isolated from *Prakṛti* to live blissfully in an isolated state. The Sāṅkhya does not recognize the Supreme Self and His power (*Śakti*), the Mother Divine (*Māyā* or the *mūla-Prakṛti*). The *BG* recommends to cut the *pīpal* tree of *saṁsāra* through non-attachment. It does not recommend the weaning of the *jīvātmā* from the *mūla-Prakṛti*, severing the link with the Mother Divine. The Father Divine and the Mother Divine are inseparable. We have to extricate ourselves from the cobweb of Sāṅkhya in order to interpret the Advaita Vedānta correctly.

Which persons are capable of cutting the tree of *saṁsāra?* The *BG* contains two verses to answer this question.

> Free from pride and delusion, having conquered the flaws of attachment, always remaining firm in spirituality, with desires completely receded, released from pairs of opposites called pleasures and pains, the undeluded reach that Imperishable Goal.[8]

In the following verse, that very goal is further distinguished:

> The sun does not illumine that, neither does the moon nor does the fire. That is My Supreme Abode, after reaching which they return not.[9]

Darkness is removed by light. In fact, the absence of light is darkness, the latter being a mental construct only. Light from the source of the sun, moon, or fire renders the material world visible. But *Brahman* is not material. It is spaceless, timeless and causeless. It is Pure Consciousness and all-pervading. Thus, the *dhāma* (abode) of Viṣṇu (God) is not a higher region in space. It is neither heaven nor *Vaikuṇṭha*. The abode of Viṣṇu/*Brahman* is the entire universe. Again, the abode is not limited to the universe only. It also transcends the universe. If we use the word "light" in a spiritual sense for the Fundamental Consciousness (*Brahman*), this light illumines all created beings, including the sun, moon and fire. However, the reverse is not the case.

On entering the sea, a river gets merged in it. After the merger, the river loses its individuality and becomes the vast ocean. So is the case with the individual self that, merging in *Brahman,* becomes *Brahman* (the Ocean of Pure Consciousness). This is the concept of liberation (*mokṣa*) in the philosophy of non-dualism. This is what the *BG* calls *Brahma-nirvāṇa*. Some other schools of philosophy such as the dualistic Vedānta claim that the released self maintains its individual existence. Such a concept holds true for the non-

---

8. *BG*, XV.5.

9. *BG*, XV.6.

released (*baddha* = bound) self, but not for the released (*mukta*) one. The bound self, with karmic *saṁskāras*, comes back, that is, it is reborn. The self, freed from the karmic *saṁskāras*, does not come back after becoming Pure Consciousness. Śrī Aurobindo holds the opinion that all supramental released selves do maintain their individual existence as gnostic beings. And these gnostic beings would also be *Saccidānanda* (*sat* = existence; *cit* = consciousness; *ānanda* = bliss). He further upholds a concept of a linear universe and the conversion of the earth into eternal heaven. The eternally cyclical go of the *saṁsāra* is not found in his philosophy. The existence of multiple *Brahmans* or multiple Gods would not be philosophically sound. Moreover, our sun and its earth are impermanent, with birth and death. Geocentrism and anthropocentrism are not parts of the Vedāntic philosophy. Even the whole universe cannot be eternal. It has repeated births and deaths in cycles, without beginning and end. The *BG* says that the repetitions of the *saṁsāra* are eternal phenomena.

### 15.03: The Jīvātmā and the Paramātmā

All individual selves (*jīvātmās*) and the Supreme Self (*Paramātmā*) are identical. Still, before the liberation, an embodied, bound self is conceptually different. The identity of a self and the Self and the separateness of a self from the Self are explained in the verses to follow.

> An eternal portion of Myself alone, having the *jīva* in the world of living beings, draws the (five) senses, together with mind as the sixth, abiding in *Prakṛti*.[10]

The Supreme Spirit is partless, indivisible and an unbroken whole. That being so, the question of its portion (*aṁśa*) does not arise. The non-dualist philosopher solves this problem by saying that the portion is only imagined as such due to limitations imposed by nescience. We may consider *Ākāśa* (*Mahākāśa*, cosmic space) and *ākāśa* in many pots (*ghaṭākāśas*). The pots are limiting adjuncts

10. *BG*, XV.7.

(*upādhis*) only. After breaking a pot, space in it is no longer limited and separated from *Mahākāśa* (great space). As a pot serves as an *upādhi* for space (*ākāśa*), so does an individual body for the *jīvātmā*. We may take a second example. Water of an ocean and water present in all aquatic animals and plants living inside the ocean are different and non-different. Water in a crab's blood and that in a snake's blood, living in the same ocean, acquire different properties.

In verse 15.7, *Prakṛti* means "manifested or created *aparā prakṛti*" (AP-M). The *avyakta (Māyā* or the *mūla-Prakṛti* or the *Īśvara-Śakti*) is also *aparā prakṛti* (AP-UM), but ever unmanifest (*avyakta*). It is *Māyā* that unfolds the universe out of the universe infolded in *Virāḍ* and dissolved in *Māyā*, subsequent to a dissolution. Her action of projection of the universe out of Her supermind is a creative evolution; it is not a mechanical repetition, although many cosmic phenomena in the total painting of the Divine Painter do repeat.

> When the Lord obtains a body and when He leaves it, He takes these (subtle sense-organs) just as wind carries scents from their sources.[11]

The word *Īśvara* (Lord) has been used for the *jīva* (individual self) in verse 15.8. The *jīva*, in truth, is not a portion of the Supreme Self. Divested of the *karma-saṁskāras*, the *jīva* and Śiva (the Supreme Self) are identical. When the *jīva* enters into a fresh body at the time of conception, or leaves the body at the time of death, it carries the causal body in which the subtle body has been dissolved. The subtle sense-organs are component parts of the subtle body. It is only the gross body that the *jīva* leaves at the time of death.

> Presiding over the subtle sense-organs of the ear, the eye, the touch, the taste, the smell, as also the mind, he experiences objects.[12]

---

11. *BG*, XV.8.
12. *BG*, XV.9.

In the analogy of a pot serving as a limiting adjunct of Great Space (*Mahākāśa*), and space inside the pot (*ghaṭākāśa*) becoming empirically distinct from the former, the Supreme Self becomes individual selves (*jīvas*) in individual bodies. In the case of the *jīva*, it is something more than what has been said in the simile. The internal instrument (*antaḥkaraṇa*) stays in the subtle body as intellect (*buddhi*), ego (*ahaṅkāra*), mind (*manas*) and the ten subtle sensory and motor organs (*jñānendriyāṇi* 5 + *karmendriyāṇi* 5). The self presides over these subtle structures and, being associated with the *guṇas*, experiences the objects of the senses. In this process, the self is bonded with the *karma-saṁskāras* that are imprinted in the *antaḥkaraṇa*. Thus, the individual self is bound (*baddha*) until the time of its release (*mukti, mokṣa*). The body (gross, subtle, causal) functions as a limiting adjunct (*upādhi*) of the self. In addition, the *karma-bandhana* is a major distinguishing feature of the *jīva*.

## 15.04: The Divine Eye of Wisdom

The individual self resides in the body, presides over the subtle organs of perception and action, experiences the sense-objects while being united with the *guṇas*, and leaves the body while carrying the *antaḥkaraṇa* and the *karma-saṁskāras* imprinted therein. The existence and the functioning of the body are not possible without the *jīva* (self), the substratum (*adhiṣṭhāna*) of the living body. In spite of these facts, we cannot take it for granted that everybody cognizes the *jīva*. The Buddhist philosophy adheres to its doctrine of no-self (*anātma-vāda*). The British empiricists and the logical positivists do not recognize the soul. (We use the word "soul" in the sense of the Vedāntic "self," although they are not identical nor similar in meanings. According to Christianity, God creates a soul for a newly formed zygote in the mother's womb out of nothing at the time of conception. The soul has a birth, but no death. After the Day of Judgement, God sends the soul to the heaven or the hell for eternal bliss in the former and for eternal damnation in the latter. In contrast, the Vedāntic "self" is God

Himself or *Brahman* Itself. The self is birthless and deathless). So also is the case with the Marxists and other atheists who refuse to recognize both the soul and the self.

In this section, we will quote two verses of the *BG* and interpret them wherever necessary.

> The deluded do not perceive him who departs, resides and experiences through association with the *guṇas*. Only those who have the eye of wisdom perceive him.[13]

The Cārvākas, the atheists, the agnostics and the empiricists recognize the existence of only that which is perceived by the senses (which is sense-perceptible). They do not consider the basic fact that sense-perception is possible through the light of the self. All sense-organs are material and all material objects are insentient (*jaḍa*). Consciousness is induced in the material objects through the reflection of the light of the self which is nothing else but the Fundamental Consciousness (*Brahman*).

The eye of wisdom is the third eye at the eyebrow centre in the subtle body. Informational knowledge on matter and energy and their evolutes would not help for cognizing the self. Intuitive knowledge is necessary for this purpose. Revealed knowledge in a state of meditational ecstasy is more dependable than even intuitive knowledge.

The question is: How can one obtain the eye of wisdom? How can one develop the intuitive faculty? How is knowledge to be revealed to someone? Can one get the eye of wisdom by self-efforts?

> Those who strive, endued with Yoga, behold him (the self or *jīva*) dwelling in themselves (in their subtle and causal bodies). But the unrefined and unintelligent, though striving, see him not.[14]

For the second group of persons, the *BG* has used the words

---

13. *BG*, XV.10.

14. *BG*, XV.11.

*akṛtātmanaḥ* and *acetasaḥ*. These two words have been translated as "unrefined" and "unintelligent," respectively. It is to be admitted that the translations are inexact. By the practice of yoga, one has to purify his *buddhi* and *citta*. Without *citta-śuddhi* and with an opaque *buddhi*, one cannot gain the eye of wisdom. Further, one has to erase the mental imprints (*karma-saṁskāras*). Thereby one frees the self from the *bandhana* (bondage). One who has done this is a *kṛtātmanaḥ*.

By means of the practice of yoga, one has to link his self with the Supreme Self. Without this linking, one cannot realize *Brahman* or the *Paramātman*. In the state of *samādhi*, one merges in *Brahman* and, at that time, one loses one's individual identity. One becomes the ocean of Cosmic Consciousness. That type of realization is the same as "beholding the Supreme Self." To behold the Supreme Self, yoga must open the third eye, and that is the correct striving. Any amount of striving for seeing the self/Self through the ordinary sense-perception shall bear no fruit.

### 15.05: The Immanence of the Supreme Self

In this section, we shall quote four verses of the *BG*. All of them are on the immanence of God, the Supreme Self. God is both immanent and transcendent. Here we shall deal with the former aspect.

> That luminous energy, residing in the sun, illumines the entire world; that which is in the moon and fire — know that radiance to be Mine.[15]

This verse perhaps does not refer directly to the light or radiant energy of the sun, moon and fire. *Brahman* is *Cit* (Consciousness). *Brahman* and Viṣṇu (The verb-root *viś* means "to pervade" or "to enter"; thus, Viṣṇu means "All-Pervading God"), being identical, except the fact that the former is without attributes and the latter is associated with attributes, the light of Consciousness of Viṣṇu or the Supreme Self uniformly pervades in all created beings, both

15. *BG*, XV.12.

inanimate and animate. The sun, the moon and fire are brilliantly radiant and, hence, are mentioned here as illustrations. The focal point is this: cosmic consciousness is ubiquitous due to the immanence of the Supreme Self.

> Entering into the material bodies of the universe, with (My) potency (force), I support all (created) beings; becoming the sapid *soma*, I nourish all herbs.[16]

The first part of the verse refers to the gravitational force. For this force only, all celestial bodies and material entities in the stars, planets and satellites are held in their relative positions and their constituent units are held together. In this connection, reference may be made to the Vedic chants.[17]

Most interpreters have taken the word *soma*, given in the second part of the verse, as the moon. However, we have a different opinion. It is the *soma-rasa*, the divine, nourishing sap.

> Dwelling in the bodies of living beings and becoming *Vaiśvānara*, associated with the *prāṇa* and the *apāna* (*vāyus*), I digest the fourfold food.[18]

The fourfold food includes *bhojyam* (food eaten by mastication), *bhakṣyam* (food eaten by swallowing), *coṣyam* (food eaten by sucking) and *lehyam* (food eaten by licking). In the present context, *Vaiśvānara* is the fire of digestion.[19] The *prāṇa* is the Prāṇic force associated with inhalation and absorption of nutrients, and the *apāna* is that associated with exhalation and the excretion of catabolic products.

> I am seated in the hearts of all; from Me (spring) memory, knowledge and forgetfulness (the absence or loss of memory). I am verily that which is to be known by means of all the Vedas. I am indeed the Author of the Vedānta and the Knower of the

---

16. *BG*, XV.13.
17. *R̥V*, X.121.1 & 5; *TS*, IV.1.8.
18. *BG*, XV.14.
19. *BU*, V.9.1.

Vedas.[20]

To sum up this section, the existence and functions of all created beings are due to the immanence of the Supreme Self. This immanence is not limited to human beings only. It holds good for the entire universe and individual entities of the universe, both inanimate and animate.

### 15.06: The Three Categories of Puruṣa

The concluding section of chapter 15 of the *BG* contains five verses that present a description of three categories of *Puruṣa*. Let us know what the Lord says on these three categories.

> There are two *Puruṣa*s in the world — the Perishable (*Kṣara*) and the Imperishable (*Akṣara*). The Perishable consists of all beings. The *Kūṭastha* (Immutable) is said to be the Imperishable.[21]

The universe of matter and energy is the manifested *aparā-prakṛti* (AP-M). The gross body, the subtle body and the causal body of an individual belong to this manifested *aparā-prakṛti*. The manifested *aparā-prakṛti* is perishable. The *BG* unusually uses the word *Puruṣa* for this perishable nature. It is a virtual manifestation of *Brahman*. The inverted tree which is simply phenomenal is rooted in *Brahman*. The tree does not exist without *Brahman*; but the reverse is not true. The *Māyā-Śakti* of the Lord brings about the birth of the perishable universe. In a special sense, the manifested *aparā-prakṛti* which is perishable (*kṣara*) is termed as one category of the *Puruṣa* in conformity with the Puruṣa-Sūkta of the *Ṛgveda* (X.90.2).

Many interpreters of the *BG* have considered the *jīvātmā*s as the imperishable *Puruṣa*s. We don't agree with them. No distinction has been maintained by the *BG* between the *Paramātmā* and the *jīvātmā*s in the present verse. We have a full agreement with Ācārya Śaṅkara. According to him, *Māyā*, the *mūla-Prakṛti* or

20. *BG*, XV.15.

21. *BG*, XV.16.

the unmanifested *aparā-Prakṛti* is a second category of *Puruṣa*. She is imperishable (*akṣara*) and *kūṭastha*. The word *kūṭa* has two meanings. It means "a heap." One is *kūṭastha* when one is immovable like a heap. A second meaning of *kūṭa* is *māyā*, carrying the concept of "illusion," "deception," "falsity," "tortuousness." *Kūṭastha* is the *mūla-Prakṛti* or *Māyā*, because She has the power of creating illusion and creating an illusory universe. She, being co-eternal with *Īśvara/Brahman*, is imperishable (*akṣara*). Both the *aparā-prakṛtis*, manifested and unmanifested, have been categorized as *Puruṣas*. This is in conformity with the Puruṣa-Sūkta of the *Ṛgveda* (X.90.2) that declares: All this is verily *Brahman* (*puruṣa evedaṁ sarvam*).

We are apt to confuse if we do not maintain caution in taking the contextual meanings of words used in the *BG*, or, for this purpose, any other scripture. The *BG* uses the word *kūṭastha* (12.3) and *akṣara* (8.4) for the Supreme Self (*Paramātmā*). In the present verse (15.16), it uses both the words for the *mūla-Prakṛti* or *Māyā*. The philosophical foundation of the *BG* is non-dualism. It does not uphold the dualistic doctrine. When everything is *Brahman*, the use of words does not become specific in all occasions. Hence, we have to consider the contextual meanings.

The next verse mentions the third category of *Puruṣa*, the Supreme Self (*Puruṣottama* or God).

> But distinct is the Supreme *Puruṣa*, known as the Supernal Self. He is the Immutable Lord who, pervading the three worlds, sustains them.[22]

The third category of *Puruṣa* is God Himself. He is the Supreme Self. He pervades the three worlds (*bhūḥ, bhuvaḥ, svaḥ*) and sustains them.

The three worlds are present here, there and everywhere. They vary in grossness and subtlety. They also have varying number of dimensions. The gross world is *bhūḥ*. The subtlest

22. *BG*, XV.17.

world, among the three, is *svaḥ*. The world, intermediate between *bhūḥ* and *svaḥ*, is *bhuvaḥ*.

> Since I transcend the Perishable and am even above the Imperishable, both in common speech and in the Vedas, I am celebrated as the Supreme Spirit (*Puruṣottama*).[23]

> He who, undeluded, knows Me as the Supreme Spirit is all-knowing. He adores Me, O Bhārata (Arjuna), in all possible moods.[24]

> Thus, O sinless one, has this most occult scripture been described by Me. Knowing this, one becomes wise, O Bhārata, and all his duties are accomplished.[25]

The scripture known as the *BG*, in its entirety, is known as the *śāstra* (scriptural science). Nevertheless, chapter 15 of the *BG* is declared here as the most occult scripture, knowing which one accomplishes all his duties.

---

23. *BG*, XV.18.
24. *BG*, XV.19.
25. *BG*, XV.20.

# 16

## Daivāsura-Sampad-Vibhāga-Yogaḥ
## (The Mode of Dividing Traits into Divine and Demoniac)

### 16.01 : The Divine Traits

IN verses 12 and 13 of chapter 9 of the *BG*, indications have been given about the divine, demoniac and devilish natures belonging to sentient beings. The present chapter explains them in greater detail. It divides human nature into two main types, namely, divine (*daiva*) and demoniac (*āsura*). The first three verses of chapter 16 depict the divine traits.

> Fearlessness, purity of mind, steadfastness in the *yoga* of knowledge (*jñāna-yoga* = the *yoga* of the knowledge of *Brahman*), charity, sense-control (self-restraint), sacrifice, study of scriptures, austerity (penance), uprightness (straightforwardness), non-violence, truthfulness, freedom from wrath, renunciation, serenity (tranquillity), absence of envy, compassion to living beings, non-covetousness, gentleness, modesty, absence of fickleness, splendour, forgiveness, fortitude (patience), purity (cleanliness), absence of hatred, non-haughtiness (absence of pride) — these pertain to one born for a lot of divine traits, O Bhārata.[1]

The divine (*daiva*) trait-group is constituted by a number of properties. They are the symptoms exhibited when the *sattva-guṇa* is dominant. No religion is necessary if a person sticks to these divine properties.

1. *BG*, XVI.1-3.

Fear is the root of many types of immorality. One has to be fearless in order to be ethical. There is one exception, however. God is benevolent and never malevolent. But the divine laws do take cognizance of one's bad actions. Nobody can escape from the fruits of his *karma*, either in this life or in the lives to come. Hence, be God-fearing. In the real sense, don't fear God, because He never causes harm to anybody. Be devoted to Him with love and respect. But, fear Him when you plan to indulge in unethical and immoral activities.

One should have *citta-śuddhi*. One cannot be good with dirty ideas in the mind. A dirty mirror can poorly reflect or cannot reflect at all. So does the *buddhi* (intellect) that has been rendered translucent or opaque with mental dirt. The *buddhi* is to be rid of impurities and should always be transparent and clean. What *buddhi* is may be clarified here. It is not "intelligence" or "intellect," as in common use. It is a subtle psycho-organ located in the subtle body and is an important component of the *antaḥkaraṇa*.

All the divine properties, listed in verses 16.1-3, can hardly be acquired without *Brahma-jñāna*. Everything is permissible if there is no God. An atheist or an agnostic may live an ethical life in ordinary situations. But, in some critical juncture in which his own interests are jeopardized, he would deviate from the moral path. Without a comprehensive knowledge on *Brahman*, *Īśvara* (God or the Supreme Self), the *jīvātmā* (the individual self) and the nature of the virtual universe (*jagat*), a person is likely to be unable to distinguish the ethical from the non-ethical. His religious rituals may end in superstition, if he is bankrupt of spiritual knowledge and wisdom.

*Svādhyāya* (the study of really spiritual scriptures) helps a person be a *jñāna-yogī*. No scripture has been written by God, although He is the source of all our revelations. Intuition has very little meaning in the absence of the hypothetical non-existence of God. But we have no guarantee to the effect that an author of a scripture has been able to get all correct revelations. Due to this fact of human error, no scripture is inviolable and incorrigible. No word is the final word. With reference to *svādhyāya*, especially to God's authorship of scriptures, we would indicate a note of caution so that one would avoid fundamentalism and fanaticism.

Regarding *śauca* (cleanliness), we have to clarify the meaning of this word. It is not restricted to physical cleanliness only. One's mind (thought) and speech should also be clean. Thus, one should have *kāyika śauca* (bodily cleanliness), *mānasika śauca* (mental cleanliness) and *vācanika śauca* (verbal cleanliness).

We have translated the Sanskrit word *dhṛtiḥ* as "fortitude" or "patience" (*dhairya*). It is courage in pain or adversity. There is hardly any life bereft of pain and adversity. A *sāttvika* person bears the painful and adverse situations with inexhaustible patience.

The other divine characteristics, mentioned in the three verses, do not need elaboration. Their actual practice makes a person noble. If one acquires these qualities, one may not embrace any religion and does not need other sermons for the ascent of man from animality to humanity and from humanity to divinity. The divine traits, listed in the three verses, make a full package for spiritual transformation. Once that happens, one will be free from the three *guṇa*s. The *sattva-guṇa* serves as a ladder to ascend and reach the roof. Once one reaches the roof, the ladder is no longer necessary. In the state of freedom from the three *guṇa*s, one is liberated. One merges in *Brahman*. One loses one's individual identity and becomes *Brahman*. That's the liberation or *Brahma-nirvāṇa* of non-dualism.

After enumerating all the virtues belonging to the divine trait in the quoted three stanzas, the Lord wanted to present the contrasting demoniac traits. He briefly mentioned some vices belonging to the demoniac trait. Then He told the effects of these two traits.

> Ostentation (religious hypocrisy), arrogance, excessive vanity, anger, harshness and ignorance belong to one who is born, O

Pārtha (son of Pṛthā = Arjuna), for a lot of demoniac traits.[2]

The word *dambhaḥ* means "ostentatious religiousity." Arrogance (*darpaḥ*) is the bad quality of presuming oneself as superior to others. An arrogant person is elated due to his knowledge, wealth, power and relations of higher status. *Abhimānaḥ* or *atimānitā* is excessive vanity or self-conceit. A person of this type prides himself on being educated, moneyed and high-born. Wrath is a demoniac attribute. *Pāruṣyam* is harshness exhibited by a demoniac person. It is a special type of harshness. It is a sadistic, cruel satire. It is blunt speech for hurting others such as describing a blind man as one with bright eyes, an ugly person as being handsome, a person of low birth as one of high lineage, and so on. Ignorance is non-discriminating cognition. An ignorant person has erroneous notions about his duties and actions. He lacks in his judgement. He does not know what ought to be done and what ought not to be done. He evinces his wrong judgement by holding unrighteousness as righteousness.

Verse 16.5 points out the effects of the divine and the demoniac traits.

> The divine state is deemed to conduce to liberation; the demoniac to bondage. Grieve not, O Pāṇḍava (Arjuna); you are born for a state of divine traits.[3]

Both the divine and the demoniac traits are inborn qualities, shaped by the *karma-saṁskāras* of one's past lives. The former trait leads to the path of liberation and the latter to that of bondage. Of course, all persons in the world cannot be placed in these two clear groups. There are many blends of different combinations and permutations. The two traits, instead of forming two discrete groups, make a continuous series by a mixture of the two. The Lord assures Arjuna that the latter has been born with a divine trait-type.

2. *BG*, XVI.4.

3. *BG*, XVI.5.

## 16.02: The Detailed Description of the Demoniacal Traits

A brief description of the demoniacal traits has already been given in verse 16.4. Now a detailed description will be made in a number of verses. The Lord says:

> There are two types of beings in this world, the divine and the demoniac. The divine has been described at length. Hear from Me, O Pārtha, of the demoniac.[4]

About the two types of persons created by Prajāpati (Brahmā = Creator God of the Hindu Trinity; one and only one God, assuming the role of creation), reference may also be made to the Upaniṣads.[5]

In modern Western psychology, personality-types are described. Indian psychology has typed human beings as *daiva* and *āsura*, or alternatively, as *sāttvika*, *rājasika* and *tāmasika*. This fact has been mostly ignored in the subject of psychology.

Verses 16.7-18 describe the demoniac attributes that are vividly pictured so that they may be eschewed.

> The demoniac men do not know action and inaction. Neither cleanliness nor right conduct nor truth is found in them.[6]

Here the word *pravṛtti* means "action in which one should be engaged" and *nivṛtti* means "action from which one should abstain." In this regard, we may quote Śaṅkara's own language in defining *pravṛtti* and *nivṛtti*: *pravṛttiṁ ca pravartanaṁ, yasmin puruṣārthasādhane kartavye pravṛttiḥ tāṁ, nivṛttiṁ ca etadviparītaṁ, yasmāt anarthahetoḥ nivartitavyaṁ sā nivṛttiḥ* . . . . "*pravṛtti* is that action in which one should be engaged, as being the means of achieving the ends of human life, that is, *puruṣārtha*. Its opposite is that action which is productive of harm and from which one should desist").

In the present context, we accept the meanings of the two

---

4. *BG*, XVI.6.
5. *BU*, I.3.1.
6. *BG*, XVI.7.

words, as expounded by Ācārya Śaṅkara. But, here we want to pinpoint the significance of these two words, as used in the verse of the *BG*. *Pravṛtti* is the action of being engaged in activities that are good and noble and *nivṛtti* is the action of being refrained from activities that are bad and ignoble. The demoniac persons are unable to distinguish good and desirable activities from bad and undesirable ones. They are ignorant of what to do and what not to do. They are physically, mentally and verbally unclean. Their conduct is bad. They are untruthful, deceptive and hypocrites.

> They say, "The universe is without truth, without a basis, without a God, and is born of mutual union, with lust for its cause; what else?"[7]

The demoniac have a distorted view of the universe. They say: "The entire universe is false; righteousness and unrighteousness are not its foundation, that is, it has no moral ground; there is no God to rule over this universe; it is a product of lustful, sexual indulgence. Carnal gratification is the only cause to produce living beings. Persons of *āsura* (demoniac) nature are materialists (*lokāyatika*s) and atheists (*nāstika*s). Such are their views:

> Holding this view, these ruined souls of little wit and fierce deeds rise as the enemies of the universe for its destruction.[8]
>
> Resorting to insatiable lust, possessed of hypocrisy, pride and arrogance, clinging to dogmas through delusion, they work with unclean resolve.[9]
>
> Beset with endless speculations (always full of anxiety) till death, regarding gratification of lust as the highest, and feeling sure that this is all, bound by a hundred ties of hopes, given up to lust and wrath, they strive to secure by unjust means hoards of wealth for sensual enjoyment.[10]

---

7. *BG*, XVI.8.
8. *BG*, XVI.9.
9. *BG*, XVI.10.
10. *BG*, XVI.11-12.

> Today I have gained this; I shall fulfil this desire; (now) this is mine; this wealth also shall be mine again (in future).[11]

> That enemy I have slain; and I shall slay others too; I am the mighty lord, the enjoyer. I am successful, powerful and happy.[12]

> I am rich and well-born. Who else is equal to me? I will perform fire-ritual (*yajña*); I will give alms; I will make merry. Thus deluded by ignorance, bewildered by many a fancy, enmeshed in the snare of delusion, addicted to the gratification of lust, they fall into an unclean hell.[13]

> Self-exalted, stubborn, conceited and arrogant on account of wealth, they hypocritically offer nominal worship out of ostentation, defying scriptural ordinances.[14]

> Given over to egoism, power, insolence, lust and wrath, these malicious people hate Me in their own bodies and in the bodies of others.[15]

For a detailed description of the demoniac traits, we have translated the relevant verses. The verses are self-explanatory. Hence, we do not feel the need for their interpretation.

### 16.03: The Downfall of the Demoniac

Chapter 16 of the *BG* classifies the nature of people as *daiva* (divine) and *āsura* (demoniac). Verse 16.5 states that the divine trait is for liberation and the demoniac trait for bondage. Now the Lord speaks out the fall of the demoniac.

> Those cruel haters, vilest among men in the transmigratory life, impious evil-doers — I perpetually hurl (them) into demoniac wombs only.[16]

The word "perpetually" in this verse should mean "continually."

---

11. *BG*, XVI.13.
12. *BG*, XVI.14.
13. *BG*, XVI.15-16.
14. *BG*, XVI.17.
15. *BG*, XVI.18.
16. *BG*, XVI.19.

God does not whimsically decree a fate to anybody. An individual earns it by virtue of his/her *karma*. God is a non-doer (*akarttā*). But, He, through His Power, *Māyā*, selects a suitable womb, at the time of conception, for the *jīva* in accordance with the past *karma* of the individual. The *daiva jīva*s go on rising and the demoniac ones go on falling. The fall is not confined to the human species only. The demoniac *jīva* may get a womb of a sub-human species and sub-human cruel species.

> Entering into demoniac wombs, the deluded ones, in birth after birth, without ever reaching Me, O son of Kuntī (Arjuna), fall into a condition still lower than that.[17]
>
> Threefold is this gate of hell, destructive of the self — lust, wrath and greed. Therefore, one should abandon these three.[18]
>
> A man, released from these three doors of darkness, O son of Kuntī (Arjuna), practises what is good for him; thus, he proceeds to the Supreme Goal.[19]
>
> Rejecting the prescription of the scripture, he, who acts under the impulse of desire, does not achieve perfection, happiness and the Supreme Goal.[20]
>
> Therefore, let the scripture be your authority in deciding what ought to be done and what ought not to be done. Knowing the work prescribed by the scripture, you ought to perform it here.[21]

We conclude this chapter by commenting on the two types of human personality, namely, *daiva* (divine) and *āsura* (demoniac). Indian psychology has so far been neglected. It types human personality in two or three groups. The first typing refers to *daiva* and *āsura*. The second typing refers to *sāttvika, rājasika* and *tāmasika*. Both the *daiva* and the *sāttvika* pertain to one type of trait. The

---

17. *BG*, XVI.20.
18. *BG*, XVI.21.
19. *BG*, XVI.22.
20. *BG*, XVI.23.
21. *BG*, XVI.24.

*āsura* trait is a broad one that includes the *rājasika* and the *tāmasika* natures, with a preponderance of the latter.

People in general, barring some spiritually accomplished ones, have innumerable sub-types of human traits. The number increases because of the mixture of two or three of the *guṇa*s in different proportions. Mathematically speaking, the three *guṇa*s do not constitute individual discrete series; they are rather continuous in the spectrum of traits.

The basis of the classification of human traits, done by the *BG*, is the presence of the *guṇa*s in varying proportions through many permutations and combinations. To precisely quantify the exact proportions of the *guṇa*s in an individual human being is a difficult task. However, it is not an impossible job. Methods may be found in future to determine working sub-types.

# 17

## Śraddhātrayavibhāgayogaḥ
## (The Yoga of Threefold Faith)

### 17.01: Three Grades of Śraddhā

THE last verse of chapter 16 (16.24) says: "The scripture shall be your guide." This point prompted Arjuna to make a query. He put a question to the Lord with a view to knowing the fate of believers who are not acquainted with the scriptures.

> What, O Kṛṣṇa, is the nature of the devotion of those who perform sacrifice with *śraddhā*, while ignoring the injunction of the scriptures? Is it one of *sattva, rajas* or *tamas?*[1]

The word *śraddhā* has been mostly translated as "faith." It is not exactly faith or belief. There is no proper equivalent word in English to express the meaning of *śraddhā*. It connotes "disposition or tendency, mixed with liking or devotion and faith." We will use the word *śraddhā* as such in the present chapter.

There are many common people who are not acquainted with any specific procedure described in the Śruti (Vedas) or Smṛti (post-Vedic, Purāṇic scriptures). Being endued with *śraddhā*, they worship God, gods or others. "Is the *śraddhā* of such persons *sāttvika, rājasika* or *tāmasika?* To what category does their worship belong?" This was the query of Arjuna.

To clarify the doubt of Arjuna, the Lord first gives a description of the three types of *śraddhā*.

> Threefold is the *śraddhā* of the embodied, born of their nature. It

1. *BG*, XVII.1.

> may be *sāttvika, rājasika* or *tāmasika*. Listen to it.[2]

What the *śraddhā* would be is inherent in each individual human being. It is *svabhāvajā* (inherent in nature). The latent impressions, recorded in the *karmāśaya* of the subtle body, are the resultants of actions, good or bad, done in the previous lives. *Śraddhā* is what is born of these resultants.

> The *śraddhā* of every person, O Bhārata (Arjuna), conforms to his natural disposition. A person is of the nature of his *śraddhā*. He is verily what his *śraddhā* is.[3]

The *karma-saṁskāras*, imprinted in the *antaḥkaraṇa* (inner instrument), give a shape to the nature, tendencies and disposition of a person. In other words, we may say that the *karma*, performed in previous lives, decides the type of the *śraddhā* which a person would possess. The type of one's *śraddhā* has to be inferred from the characteristic mark exhibited.

> *Sāttvika* persons offer sacrifice to the gods; *rājasika* persons to supernatural beings (the *yakṣa*s) and monsters (the *rākṣasa*s); and others, the *tāmasika* persons, offer sacrifice to ancestral spirits (*preta*s) and hosts of ghosts (*bhūta*s).[4]

> Those persons who practise severe austerity, unordained by the scriptures, moved by hypocricy and egoism, impelled by the force of lust and attachment; enfeebling all the organs of the body, and Me too, who dwells within the body, know such senseless fools to be demoniacally resolved.[5]

Persons, with *āsurika śraddhā*, practise austerities that are harmful to the body and mind. Bare-bodied they lie on spikes. They walk on fire. Keeping one hand lifted up, they stand on one leg only under the scorching sun. They gaze at the midday sun constantly for hours together, without knowing the injuries caused to the

2. *BG*, XVII.2.
3. *BG*, XVII.3.
4. *BG*, XVII.4.
5. *BG*, XVII.5-6.

eyes. They stand in neck-deep chilling water in a pond at midnight in the extreme winter season. They pierce their tongues or cheeks with nails. These and such other practices are made to acquire mystic powers. Really such notions are erroneous. All good scriptures do not approve of such practices.

The Lord now introduces the idea of the threefold division of food, sacrifice, penance and charity.

> The food also that is dear to all is of three kinds. So are the sacrifice, penance and charity. Listen to their distinctions.[6]

### 17.02: The Three Kinds of Food

The *BG* nowhere says: "Eat this and don't eat that." It divides food into three categories and describes the characteristic of each one.

> Foods, promoting longevity, augmenting energy and vigour, conducive to health, comfort and pleasure, which are rich in nutrients, are non-irritants, are firm and appetising, are liked by persons of *sāttvika* temperament.[7]

The word *sthira* (firm) in this verse has a special meaning. Some foods deteriorate quickly. Some nutrients of such foods are not stable. They are lost in the cooking process. The keeping quality of some foods is not good. The loss of their nutrients is fast. Such foods are not stable or firm.

> The foods that are bitter, sour, saltish, over-hot, pungent, harsh and burning are liked by persons of *rājasika* temperament. They cause pain, grief and ill health.[8]
>
> The food dear to the persons of *tāmasika* temperament is stale, ill-cooked with loss of nutrients, putrid, rotten, refuse and impure.[9]

---

6. *BG*, XVII.7.
7. *BG*, XVII.8.
8. *BG*, XVII.9.
9. *BG*, XVII.10.

The literal meaning of *yātayāma* is "cooked three hours ago." Contextually, it means "not fresh, stale." Some interpreters have translated the word *gatarasam* as "tasteless." *Tāmasika* persons, on many occasions, eat "tasteful" food, tasty to the mouth, but injurious to health. Literally, the word, *gatarasam*, means "that from which juice has been lost." Its contextual meaning is "food that has lost its nutrients due to ill-cooking, overcooking and such other processing."

Man cannot live without eating food. It is necessary for the maintenance and growth of the body. Food has also favourable or unfavourable influence on the mind. The three *guṇa*s, namely, *sattva, rajas* and *tamas*, exert determining effects on the nature of food a person likes. These *guṇa*s (attributes) are decided by the *karma-saṁskāra*s, acquired during the past lives. But the interaction of the *guṇa*s with the type of the food is reversible. *Guṇa*s influence the liking of persons for one of the three kinds of foods. On the other hand, the kind of food influences the attribute of a person. By the exercise of free will, one can change one's liking for a kind of food that promotes physical, mental and spiritual health.

If one resolves to live a spiritual life, one has to develop a *sāttvika* temperament for eating food of *sāttvika* kind.

### 17.03: Three Types of Worship

Three verses (17.11-13) of the *BG* describe three sorts of worship. The *BG* uses the word *yajña* for the purpose of worshipping. The word *yajña* has been derived from the verb-root *yaj*, meaning "to worship, adore, honour, especially with fire-sacrifice or oblations." Many interpreters have translated the word *yajñaḥ* as "sacrifice." It is not a befitting translation, however. The Vedic Aryans were worshipping God mainly through offering oblations to fire. In the post-Vedic period, worship was diversified. For a general purpose, we take the meaning of *yajñaḥ* as "worship, devotion, prayer."

There are three kinds of worship, namely, *sāttvika, rājasika* and *tāmasika*. Depending upon the *karma-saṁskāras* of the past lives, an individual person possesses anyone of the three temperaments for worshipping. The Lord describes these three types in three verses (17.11-13) of the *BG*.

> *Sāttvika* is that *yajña* which is performed without desire for its fruit, as prescribed by scriptures, with the mind fixed on the thought that the *yajña* should be offered.[10]

What we call *niṣkāma upāsanā* (worship without any desire for fruits and expectation of rewards) has been described in verse 17.11. The devotee finds satisfaction in the worship only. In adoring God, he expects nothing in return. Moreover, his adoration is quite in tune with scriptural prescriptions. All forms of adorations of a *sāttvika* person are done with unshakable faith in the Almighty. The *sāttvika* person worships the Almighty, only because He should be worshipped.

> But, O best of the Bhāratas (Arjuna), know that *yajña,* performed in expectation of fruits and for ostentation (for a pretentious and vulgar display; for self-glorification), to be *rājasika*.[11]

Persons born with *rājasika* disposition do everything in a bartering spirit. They apply that spirit too to their spiritual work. They pray to God, adore Him and offer oblations to Him in the expectation of getting material gain, higher power, more fame and social prestige, cure of diseases and many other gains. There are other *rājasika* persons who offer worship for a pompous show, self-advertisement or self-glorification.

> The *yajña*, which is not scripturally enjoined, in which no food (*naivedya*) is offered, which is done without *mantra* (sacred chants) and without giving *dakṣiṇā* (honorarium or reverent gifts to the priest) and which is uninspired by faith, is declared as *tāmasika*.[12]

10. *BG*, XVII.11.
11. *BG*, XVII.12.
12. *BG*, XVII.13.

Persons born with *tāmasika* nature very often perform *pūjā* (worship) too. But they do not care for scriptural prescriptions. They do not offer *naivedyam* (food-articles meant for God). If they do, they offer impure and unholy food such as meat, fish, liquor, et cetera. They do not feed brāhmaṇas (spiritual persons who have *Brahma*-realization) and *daridra-nārāyaṇa*s (poor persons, respectfully deemed as gods). They do not chant holy hymns with appropriate metres and proper accents. They do not satisfy the priests by offering reverent gifts in cash and/or kind. They do not have faith and devotion in spite of the fact that they appear to worship God. This type of worship is *tāmasika*.

Some interpreters of the *BG* have condemned both *rājasika* and *tāmasika* worships and have recommended the *sāttvika* worship only. Without ifs and buts, we recommend the *sāttvika* worship and condemn the *tāmasika* one. But we realize that most persons (except the highly spiritual ones) cannot do desireless worship (*niṣkāma pūjā*). We do condemn the *rājasika* worship for ostentation (*dambha*). But we do not condemn all sorts of worships with desire for fruits (*sakāma pūjā*). Seeking for fruits, with never unquenched thirst for wealth, power, sensual gratification and such other things cannot be supported. At the same time, worshipping God for getting divine mercy to get relief from poverty, calamity, diseases, for protection from evil forces and all sorts of dangers should not be condemned for persons living worldly lives. If a distressed person is prohibited from begging divine mercy, whom will he approach for getting protection and redemption then? What is the meaning of desireless worship for a suffering person? Persons would rarely worship if *sakāma pūjā* of benign type is condemned.

### 17.04: The Threefold Penance

Purposeless torturing of the body cannot be supported. In spite of this statement, austerity or penance is a holy means for man to ascend the ladder from humanity to divinity. The characteristics of austerity (*tapaḥ*) have been described in verses 17.14-19 of the *BG*.

> Worship of God (Brahmā, Viṣṇu, Rudra, or God with any other name, with or without form), of the twice-born, of the *gurus* and of the wise, cleanliness (of the body, mind and speech), uprightness, continence and non-violence — these are said to be the austerity of the body.[13]

The literal meaning of the word *tapaḥ* is "heat." For any type of spiritual *tapaḥ* (austerity, penance), a person opts for undergoing some suffering for purifying himself in the analogy of gold being purified by the heat of fire.

The word *deva* (divine being) should not be understood in a parochial sense. It means God of any religion, with any name. It should also mean "the Power of God" (*Īśvara-Śakti*), the Mother Divine.

The word *dvija* literally means "twice-born." When a person is born, he has still animality and, hence, is still an animal (*jantu*). With proper and adequate spiritual education, he gets a second birth (at the mental level) to forsake his animality and to take a vow for living a dedicated spiritual life.

A *guru* is a preceptor for humanizing and spiritualizing a person. He is a venerable person. The mother, the father, the teacher and the spiritual preceptor are the *gurus*. Among them, the spiritual preceptor, with proper spiritual realization, noble conduct, competence for imparting spiritual training, and ability to transform a person of animality to that of humanity, divinity and *Brahman*-hood in upward sequence, is the super-*guru*.

The *prājña* is the wise man who is awakened to the state of *Brahman*-hood (*Brahmāvasthā*).

The word *brahmacarya* means "sex-abstinence" in the traditional sense. However, its etymological meaning is different. A *Brahma*-realized person, living a divine life with noble conduct (*divyācaraṇa*) is a *brahmacārī*. We are of the opinion that the traditional meaning should not be applied to all circumstances. Ancient Indian seers

---

13. *BG*, XVII.14.

(*ṛṣis*) were mostly married and had children. But they had sex-restraint, had restricted marital sex, and had no extra-marital sex relationship at all. A householder may marry and may have moderate marital (not pre-marital and extra-marital) sex. A *saṁnyāsī* (one who has renounced the worldly life) who dedicates his full life to higher level of spirituality should not marry and should refrain from sexual activity (mentally, verbally and physically). A householder has the duty to spend much time for the family. A person, with a highly spiritual, noble end in life, cannot afford to spend that much of time for family affairs. Hence, he may avoid a family life in order to devote his full time to spirituality. Moreover, sexual indulgence is contradictory to a perfectly holy, spiritual life. In this regard, one should understand that what is true for a *saṁnyāsī* is not so for a householder.

> A speech that does not offend and that is truthful, pleasant and beneficial and also the habitual reading of scriptures are said to constitute verbal penance.[14]

One's speech should not be *udvegakaram*. There are different translations for this Sanskrit word. Some say: "The speech should not cause excitement." Others say: "The speech should not offend." We express it by using a group of statements. "The speech should not hurt and offend; it should not cause worries and tension; and it should not cause mental distress and disturbance."

One's speech should contain truth; it should be pleasing; it should be beneficial too. One should apply one's discretion in combining these three criteria of speech. The fulfilment of all these three conditions is the best one. However, on some occasions, it is not possible to meet all these three requirements. Speech may be truthful and beneficial, but may not be very pleasant. In that situation, one may try to make the speech less unpleasant as much as possible.

On some less common occasions, one's speech may be untrue for a greater benefit. Spirituality allows such benign untruth. Here

---

14. *BG*, XVII.15.

we may cite an example to remove misunderstanding. A young lady runs in distress and enters into the hermitage of a sage. A robust man, cruel, uncultured and immoral in nature, chases the lady for raping her. He asks the sage: "In which direction did the woman run away? Did she hide herself somewhere here?" The noble sage answers: "She has run away to the north and entered into the deep forest." Plainly speaking, the sage told a lie. But, let us consider it. Is it not a benign lie? Is it not a moral lie? Is it benevolent or not? Is it compassionate or not? On some occasions, benign lies must be the better choice than plain truth.

*Svādhyāyābhyasanam* means "habitual reading or chanting with proper intonation of good scriptures." The word good is to be emphasized. No scripture, without a single exception, is written by God, or even dictated by God. No scripture is the final truth. No scripture is incorrigible and inviolable. Intuition, revelation and linking the mind of the author with the Supermind (the Divine Mind) do play major roles in the textual truth of the scripture. But there is no guarantee that the linking of the human mind with the Supermind has been flawless and perfect. The acceptance of scriptural evidence should be based on harmony with empirical evidences and all sources of human knowledge. It should be provisional, subject to revision, correction, partial rejection, or complete rejection, if future facts and evidences do demand.

> Serenity of mind, gentleness (good-heartedness), silence, self-control and purity of thought — this is called the mental austerity.[15]

When a person eschews mental conflicts and confusions and becomes established in a blissful calmness, he has serenity of mind (*manaḥ prasādaḥ*). Being kindly disposed towards all is *saumyatvam*. In the present verse, *maunam* has a special meaning. In the process of keeping all mentation in a state of equilibrium, one gets restraint of speech, which is "silence" in the present context. Silence, in its literal sense, is "abstinence from speech." Periodical silence of

15. *BG*, XVII.16.

this latter type is also necessary for spiritual persons to link the self with the Supreme Self. Self-control (*ātmavinigrahaḥ*) is an all-round and general control of the mind. Full purification of thoughts (*bhāva-saṁśuddhi*) or purity of disposition is attained when the heart becomes altruistic, with the absence of malice, perniciousness and hypocrisy, with the presence of honesty of motive and with the fullness of spiritual thinking.

So far have we described the austerity of the body, of speech and of mind. Next, we shall associate the austerity with the three *guṇas*, namely, *sattva, rajas* and *tamas*.

> They declare that this threefold austerity practised by steadfast men with great *śraddhā*, desiring no fruit, is *sāttvika*.[16]

Here we highlight three characteristics of a *sāttvika* person. He is unaffected in success and failure, that is, he is steadfast. He practises the threefold austerity with great *śraddhā*. Such a person has unwavering faith in the existence of God and in lives after death (unless one is liberated). Thirdly, he must not desire fruits for his threefold austerity.

> Austerity performed with ostentation with the object of gaining respect, honour and reverence is said here to be *rājasika*. It is unstable and uncertain.[17]

The word *dambha* has been translated here as "ostentation." It is hypocrisy. The person has no sincere belief. He practises austerity for mere show.

> That austerity which is performed obstinately out of foolish notion, involving self-torture, or for the purpose of ruining others, is declared to be *tāmasika*.[18]

There are dullards who practise austerity without proper understanding. They commit self-immolation by fasting up to

---

16. *BG*, XVII.17.
17. *BG*, XVII.18.
18. *BG*, XVII.19.

death, burning their bodies and doing such other deeds. They torture their bodies by lying on nails, piercing their tongues with nails, exposing their bodies to the scorching heat of the sun, walking on fire, dipping themselves in cold water of ponds and rivers in the extreme cold winter and doing many such other things. If they happen to gain some psychic power, they utilize it for hurting, wrecking and ruining others. This type of austerity is *tāmasika* and is to be condemned.

### 17.05: The Threefold Gift

Gifts are threefold in nature, depending upon the three types of *guṇa*s, namely, *sattva, rajas* and *tamas*. The *BG* describes the three sorts of gifts in three verses, 17.20-22.

> That gift which is made with the thought that it is one's duty to give, made to one from whom no service in return is expected, and made at the right place, right time and to a worthy person is held to be *sāttvika*.[19]

One should not cherish any motive for making gifts. One should feel that it is one's duty to give and so does he give. Gifts should not be motivated investments. If a gift is made with the expectation that something in return, such as favour, financial gain, fulfilment of lustful desire and any other reward, would be made available, it is not *sāttvika*. A *sāttvika* gift is that which is offered as a duty without expecting anything in return. The gift should be made to the right recipient. He needs it; he is worthy of it. He should be a person who would well spend the gift on worthy causes. The bestowing ought to be made at a proper time when it is needed and at a proper place where it is needed.

> But that gift which is given with a view to receiving a return, or looking for the fruit, or again grudgingly (reluctantly) is held to be *rājasika*.[20]

The *rājaṣika* person gives only when he expects multiple gains and

19. *BG*, XVII.20.

20. *BG*, XVII.21.

benefits from the recipients. He gives with the hope that his gift would produce some favourable results. And he makes the gift regretfully, accompanied by mental distress. He is reluctant to part with his possessions and still circumstances compel him to give.

> The gift that is given at a wrong place or time, to unworthy persons, without respect and with insult is declared to be *tāmasika*.[21]

*Tāmasika* persons do not consider the right place, the right time and the deserving recipient while they give gifts. The unworthy recipients may utilize the gifts for destructive and immoral purposes. A gift should be given with respect for the recipient. But it is not the case with a *tāmasika* gift. A *tāmasika* person behaves with the recipient of the gift disrespectfully and insolently. When he doles out, he does with abuses and scoldings.

Persons very often claim that they do charity by contributing to public causes. If they do so due to pressure exerted by Government officers and politicians in power, such a charity cannot be said to be *sāttvika*. Very often bribes are given in the guise of voluntary contribution for noble causes. In fact, these gifts are base in nature and are *tāmasika*.

### 17.06: The Way of Turning Demerits into Merits

*Yajña* (worship in general and fire-sacrifice in particular), *dāna* (charity, gift), and *tapas* (austerity, penance) of *sāttvika*, *rājasika* and *tāmasika* types have been described in the present chapter. Even the holiest type of these actions may degenerate and become defective due to carelessness. The *BG* lays down instructions to rectify the defects.

> "*Om tat sat*," this has been declared to be the triple designation of *Brahman*. Thus of yore were fashioned the *Brāhmaṇas*, the Vedas and the *Yajñas*.[22]

---

21. *BG*, XVII.22.
22. *BG*, XVII.23.

*Om, tat* and *sat* traditionally constitute the threefold designation of *Brahman*. In this connection, reference may be made to the Upaniṣads.[23] *Brahman* is referred to by the utterance of *om*. It is devoid of form, attributes and functions. Hence, no language can be used to describe it. It can be indicated by the Sanskrit word, *tat* (the English word, "That"). It is Existence (*Sat*, derived from the verb-root, *as*, meaning "to exist"). It is the only Existence and nothing else exists. It exists eternally and timelessly without changes and modifications. It is timeless (*akālam*), spaceless (*anākāśam*), acausal and constant (*dhruva*). It has no birth, no growth, no decay and no death. It is imperishable (*avyaya, akṣaya*).

The cosmos, including its associated chaos, is not nihil, however. It is phenomenal and virtual. *Brahman, B*, appears as $J_1$, $J_2$, $J_3$....., $J_n$...., $J_{inf}$ (J standing for *jagat*, a Sanskrit word for the universe, meaning "that which is in motion," "that which constantly changes").

*Brahman*, associated with its power (*Śakti, Māyā-Śakti*) is *Īśvara* (God). The former is attributeless (*nirguṇa*) whereas the latter is associated with attributes (*saguṇa*). The power of *Brahman/Īśvara* is *Māyā*. The Power and the possessor of power are not two different Beings, Being being one and non-dual only. When God desires to have a universe, *Māyā*, the executive agent of God, projects a universe, which is not nothing, but which is the reflective manifestation of *Brahman* (one and the only one non-dual Being, timelessly non-becoming, appears as the multiplicity of the universe). If we properly comprehend this fact, we would not be wrong to say that the cosmos is the virtual, phenomenal manifestation of *Brahman*.

When God desires to have a universe, Mother Sarasvatī, the creative aspect of *Māyā*, the *mūla-Prakṛti*, plays Her *vīṇā* (a special, divine, musical string instrument with three strings — *sattva, rajas,* and *tamas*). The vibrations of these strings disturb their equipoise (*sāmyāvasthā*) and generate *om* (not the *oṅkāra dhvani* or sound

23. *CU*, VI.2.1; VI.8.7; *TU*, I.8.1.

transmitted in the medium of air, absent in the beginning of creation and still absent in many parts of the universe), a set of vibrations equivalent to the sound vibrations of *om,* chanted by the human vocal organ in the modern world. The primal universe did not possess the physical conditions to produce sound vibrations to be propagated in air. Through a number of cosmogonical steps, *Virāḍ* or *Mahat* that first manifests from *Māyā* produces a cosmic egg that stays for one year of Brahmā and then explodes. The universe evolves and is still evolving. The evolution in the expanding phase and the involution in the contracting phase of the universe continue as a result of the continuing vibrations of the strings. Subsequent to the total dissolution of the universe in *Māyā*, the three strings of the *vīṇā* of Mother Sarasvatī go back to the equipoised state.

Who is this Mother Sarasvatī? The universe has one Divine Father and one Divine Mother only. God, the one Divine Father, takes the role of three fathers, namely, Brahmā, Viṣṇu and Rudra. They have their consorts, Sarasvatī, Lakṣmī, Kālī (Gaurī, Pārvatī), respectively. *Māyā* or the *mūla-Prakṛti* (the primordial, unmanifested nature) is the power (*śakti*) of *Brahman/Īśvara* (God). She is one only. She is the mother of the universe. She assumes the role of three mothers, as already named. God is the presiding (*adhyakṣa*) Being. His executive is the Mother Divine. It may not be misunderstood, however, that the Hindu trinity speaks of three Gods. The Hindu metaphysics is strictly monotheistic. Secondly, the power (*śakti*) and the possesser of power (*śaktimān*) constitute a bipolar Reality; they are One and the same. They are not two Beings.

The universe is not a hallucination, but an illusion. It is not nothing. It does exist, in an uncertain manner, phenomenally and virtually. It constitutes the virtual becomings of the non-dual Being. It is a superficial reflection of the underlying Reality. The substratum (*adhiṣṭhāna*) of the becoming universe is *Brahman* in the analogy of a rope apparently perceived as a snake. The whole universe is the sportive play (*līlā*) of God. Had there been absence of the two players (Father Divine and Mother Divine), no play and no universe at all could have been the outcome.

Incidentally, we would like to mention the *nāda-brahma* here. It is also a subject matter of the *BG*. The initial vibrations (*nāda, spanda, kampana*) of the three strings (*guṇas*) of the *vīṇā* of Mother Sarasvatī generate a subtle sound *OM* (*AUM*). This *OM* is otherwise known as *praṇava*. It causes the manifestation of *Virāḍ* (*Mahat* or *Buddhi*), which is the cosmic mind or the supermind, the mind of *Māyā*. The subsequent stepwise evolution of the cosmos is brought about by the innumerable notes generated out of the *OM*. The generation of *OM* is a continuous process so long as the phenomenal universe continues to stay and function. Mother Sarasvatī is the divine, musical, creative artist who continues to play Her *vīṇā* from the beginning of time to the end of time in every cosmic cycle. She also plays Her *vīṇā* in the absence of the manifested universe. The *līlā* of the divine couple is *sanātana*. But, in the acosmic state, the divine music, being equipoised, is not productive of manifestation.

*Āpaḥ* evolves from *Virāḍ*. *Prāṇa* evolves from *Āpaḥ*. *Ākāśa* evolves from *Prāṇa*. The superheated *Ākāśa* is the source of all micro-particles and particles. Subsequent to the evolution of *Ākāśa* (Space), the subtle, divine *nāda* (*anāhata-dhvani* = unbeaten sound), the manifestation of the primeval *oṅkāra dhvani*, is propagated through the all-pervading *Ākāśa*. All of us can listen to it when we enter into the deep state of *dhyāna* or into the yogic state of *samādhi*. This *nāda-brahma* or *anāhata-dhvani* is transmitted in any of the three subtle media, namely, *Āpaḥ, Prāṇa,* or *Ākāśa*.

The *nāda-brahma* is interpreted by many as real *Brahman*. It is, however, not a fact. No product, subtle or gross, is *Brahman*, since *Brahman* is an immutable Existence as Consciousness only. The whole phenomenal or virtual universe is a reflection of *Brahman* as an appearance. In that sense, it may not be wrong to say that the universe is *Brahman*. As a matter of fact, it has been said so in the Vedas and in many Vedāntic scriptures. In the same analogy, we would not be wrong to say that the *nāda-brahma* is *Brahman*. But, in a strict metaphysical sense, we would commit a mistake by equating *Brahman* with *nāda-brahma* or *śabda-brahma*.

The Vedas, the Brāhmaṇas (post-Vedic scriptures such as the *Śatapatha-Brāhmaṇa* and others) and the *yajña*s (the Vedic rituals given in the *karma-kāṇḍa* scriptures, providing details of fire-sacrifice and other methods of worship) evolved in conformity with the *praṇava*. These three occupy the foremost place in the *nāda-brahma*.

> Therefore, the followers of the Vedas always undertake the acts of sacrifice, gift and austerity, as enjoined in the scriptures, with the utterance of *OM*.[24]
>
> No *mantra* is sanctified unless it begins with *OM*. The act may be fire-sacrifice, gift-giving, or austerity; its relevant *mantra* must be chanted by beginning with *OM*.
>
> Without aiming at the fruits, after uttering *TAT*, various rites of sacrifice, gift-giving and austerity are performed by the seekers of liberation (*mokṣa*).[25]

*TAT* (that) is a designation of *Brahman*. The inexpressible Reality cannot be expressed by the use of any language. Language describes the form, attributes, functions and relations of any entity. *Brahman*, being devoid of all these, cannot be described by language. *TAT* is a symbolic indication to point out *Brahman*. It is uttered before the act of sacrifice, gift and penance.

> The word *SAT* is used to denote Existence (Reality, *Brahman*) and righteousness. O Pārtha (Arjuna), the word *SAT* is also used in the sense of an auspicious act.[26]
>
> Steadfastness in sacrifice, austerity and gift is also called *sat*; and action for the sake of God is called *sat*.[27]

---

24. *BG*, XVII.24.
25. *BG*, XVII.25.
26. *BG*, XVII.26.
27. *BG*, XVII.27.

God has no needs. The devotee does not do any action to serve the needs of God. Then what is the meaning of *tadarthīyam* (for the sake of That, the Supreme Reality)? It means "good work done for the creation of God."

> Whatever is sacrificed, given as a gift, performed as an austerity, or done, without *śraddhā* (faith, love and devotion) is said, O Pārtha (Arjuna), to be *asat* (not *sat*). It is not effective neither here nor hereafter.[28]

The word *hutam* means "sacrificed." It is not "sacrificed" in a general sense. It refers to oblation of dehydrated, clarified butter in a fire-sacrifice (*yajña, havana*) which was the main Vedic ritual in vogue for worshipping God in ancient Vedic India. For the modern world, we may use the word *yajña* for *havana*, worship and prayer in general. The word *iha* literally means "here." In this verse, it means "in this life or in this world." The word *pretya* means "hereafter" or "after death."

Worship, charity and penance, performed without faith, love and devotion (*śraddhā*), is futile in this life and in the lives to come. The blemish may be overcome by uttering *om tat sat* at the commencement of every spiritual undertaking. Mechanical utterance does not serve any purpose. The mind must be attuned to the idea (*bhāva*) conveyed by the triple designation of *Brahman*.

In this connection of the emphasis on the *bhāva*, we would quote a Sanskrit verse here: *na kāṣṭhe vidyate devo na pāṣāṇe na mṛṇmaye; bhāve hi vidyate devastasmād bhāvo hi kāraṇam*. The deity does not exist in the wood (in the wooden idol); neither in the stone (stone-icon) nor in the earthen idol. The deity verily stays in the idea; hence, it is the idea which is the cause. This verse has been written in connection with image-worship *versus* formless worship. It is also applicable with reference to mechanical, ritual worship *versus* meditative, sincere worship.

---

28. *BG*, XVII.28.

# 18

## Mokṣa-Saṁnyāsa-Yogaḥ
## (The Yoga of Liberation by Renunciation)

### 18.01: Saṁnyāsa and Tyāga Explained

THIS concluding chapter sums up the import of the entire *BG* and that of the Vedas. The chapter starts with the question of Arjuna who seeks to know the distinction between renunciation (*saṁnyāsa*) and relinquishment (*tyāga* or sacrifice).

> O Mighty-Armed, O Hṛṣīkeśa, O slayer of Keśi, I desire to know the distinction between the truth of renunciation (*saṁnyāsa*) and that of relinquishment (*tyāga*).[1]

After hearing this question, Lord Vāsudeva addresses Arjuna.

> Seers (sages) know renunciation (*saṁnyāsa*) to be the rejection of desireful actions (*kāmya karmas*). The wise declare the abandonment of the fruits of all works as relinquishment (*tyāga*).[2]

*Kāmya karma* is that action which is prompted by desire for their fruits. Actions are divided into three classes, namely, *nitya* (daily obligatory ones), *naimitya* (occasional specific ones) and *kāmya* (desireful ones). In the third category are included those actions connected with hankering after wealth, power, progeny, name, fame, social status and such other things. The *kāmya karmas* create new bondages leading to rebirths.

> Some intellectuals declare that all actions, being faulty or evil, should be abandoned, while others maintain that *yajña* (ritual

1. *BG*, XVIII.1.
2. *BG*, XVIII.2.

> fire-sacrifice, worship), gift (*dāna*), and austerity (penance, *tapaḥ*) ought not to be relinquished.[3]
>
> O best of the Bhāratas (Arjuna), in this connection of abandonment, listen to my decision. Abandonment (*tyāgaḥ*), O hero, has been verily declared to be of three kinds.[4]
>
> The work of *yajña,* gift and austerity should not be relinquished. It must necessarily be performed; for, *yajña,* gift, and also austerity are purifying to the wise.[5]
>
> But even these works, O Pārtha (Arjuna), should be performed, giving up attachment and the fruits. This is my firm and best decision.[6]

### 18.02: Tyāga of Three Kinds

Sacrifice (*tyāga*) is of three kinds, namely, *sāttvika, rājasika* and *tāmasika*. Verses 18.7 and 18.8 describe the *tāmasika* variety and the *rājasika* variety, respectively. Verses 18.9-12 describe the sacrifice of the *sāttvikka* variety. The Lord continues to explain:

> Verily, it is improper to renounce obligatory work. Its abandonment, due to delusion, is declared to be *tāmasika.*[7]

Bathing, eating, sleeping, doing some work for earning (for livelihood) and such other works, necessary for the body and living, are obligatory works. The body is to be taken care of for higher spiritual purposes. Hence, the obligatory duties are to be discharged as long as the body lasts. The idea of the abandonment of the obligatory works is born of a *tāmasika* disposition.

> He who, from fear of discomfort, abandons action, because it is painful to the body, performs a *rājasika* relinquishment. He shall not, indeed, obtain the fruit of relinquishment.[8]

---

3. *BG*, XVIII.3.
4. *BG*, XVIII.4.
5. *BG*, XVIII.5.
6. *BG*, XVIII.6.
7. *BG*, XVIII.7.
8. *BG*, XVIII.8.

No earthly existence is free from bodily pain. Here "earthly" should mean "pertaining to the universe of matter and energy." The possession of a body necessarily involves the experience of pain. The pain of life is to be borne and, at the same time, work must be done. If one fears the pain of life and tries to escape from the world by embracing *saṁyama*, one does not obtain the benefit of this type of *rājasika tyāga*. To become a *tyāgī*, one must not live a life of ease and comfort. The obligatory duty must be performed even if bodily pain accompanies the discharge of duties.

Next, the Lord explains the *tyāga* of *sāttvika* nature and urges that the *sāttvika tyāga* is indispensable for ascending the ladder leading to liberation.

> Whatever obligatory work is done, O Arjuna, merely because it ought to be done, abandoning attachment and also fruits, is a *tyāga* that is deemed to be *sāttvika*.[9]

Regarding performing obligatory work, the verse lays emphasis on three points, namely, the abandonment of attachment, the abandonment of fruits, and doing the work merely because it ought to be done. If these three conditions are fulfilled, the work is *sāttvika*.

> The relinquisher, imbued with *sattva*, intelligent and rid of doubts, neither hates a disagreeable work nor clings to an agreeable one.[10]

This verse teaches the purpose served by *karma-yoga*. The *yogī* hates not a disagreeable work such as a *kāmya-karma* (desireful action) which is the cause of transmigratory existence; nor is he attached to an agreeable one, such as the obligatory action (*nitya-karma*), which is the means to liberation (*mokṣa*) by purifying the *sattva* (the *antaḥkaraṇa*, the inner instrument). Briefly speaking, he is neutral to both situations.

It is indeed impossible for an embodied being to relinquish

9. *BG*, XVIII.9.
10. *BG*, XVIII.10.

> actions entirely; but he who relinquishes the fruits of action is said to be the relinquisher.[11]

The *BG* recognizes the fact that the relinquishment of all actions is not a feasible proposition. Who is a *tyāgī* (relinquisher) then? He who, while performing the obligatory works, relinquishes the thought of the fruits of action, is verily called a relinquisher.

What purpose is served by relinquishing all actions? This question is answered by the following verse:

> The threefold fruit of action — evil, good and mixed — accrues to the non-relinquishers (*atyāgī*s), after death, but never to the renouncers (*saṁnyāsī*s).[12]

This verse reaffirms the doctrine of reincarnation (*punarjanma-vāda*) and the doctrine of *karma* (*karma-vāda*). The fruits of good actions are good. The fruits of bad actions are evil. The fruits of good and bad actions are mixed. Non-relinquishers of actions get these results after their death (in the next birth). This is, however, not the case with the *saṁnyāsī*s (the renouncers). The seers of the Supreme Reality (*Brahman*) renounce all actions completely. Hence, the question of the fruits of action, accruing to them, after their death, does not arise.

### 18.03: The Components of Karma

The Lord has described the components of *karma* in four verses (*BG*, 18.13-16). Here we deal with them one by one.

> O mighty-armed (Arjuna), learn from Me these five causes, declared in the Sāṅkhya, which is the end of action, for the accomplishment of all works.[13]

The word "Sāṅkhya" in this verse must not be misunderstood. It does not refer to Kapila's Sāṅkhya system of philosophy. Here "Sāṅkhya" stands for *jñāna-yoga*, as declared in the Upaniṣads.

---

11. *BG*, XVIII.11.
12. *BG*, XVIII.12.
13. *BG*, XVIII.13.

The word *kṛtānta* means "the end of all actions." It qualifies "Sāṅkhya" (*jñāna-yoga*) in this verse. In this connection, reference may be made to the verses 2.46 and 4.33 of the *BG*.

The five factors for the accomplishment of all works are expounded in the next verse.

> (These are) the seat (the ground or the body), the doer (agent), various instruments (*indriyas*), different functions of various kinds, and also the presiding deity, the fifth one here.[14]

The ground is the assembled body. *Ahaṅkāra* (ego) is the agent or the doer (*karttā*). The five subtle organs of perception and the five subtle organs of action are the ten *indriyas* or *karaṇas*. The five *prāṇa-vāyus* (the prāṇic force with its five sub-types, namely, *prāṇa, apāna, udāna, vyāna* and *samāna*) perform different functions of various kinds. The individual self (the *jīvātmā*) is the presiding deity whose light of consciousness, being reflected on the other four factors, makes them work.

> These five are the causes of whatever work a person performs with his body, speech, or mind, whether right or the reverse.[15]
>
> That being so, the man of perverse mind, who, due to lack of correct understanding, looks upon the Pure Self (*Paramātmā*) as the agent, does not see at all.[16]

We uphold the view that the Great Self (*Paramātmā*) and the individual self (*jīvātmā*) are not intrinsically different. Hence, the Self is not the agent (*karttā*); neither is the self. To substantiate our view, we have to resolve the apparently contradictory notion expressed in verse 18.14. Ācārya Śaṅkara has explained the *daiva*, the fifth factor, differently. We may give the English rendering of his language: "The supernatural element is the fifth in this list; it is the solar deity, et cetera, superintending and guiding the functions of the sense-organs such as the eye." We cannot accept

---

14. *BG*, XVIII.14.

15. *BG*, XVIII.15.

16. *BG*, XVIII.16.

this explanation of Śaṅkara. Swāmī Cidbhāvānanda of the Ramakrishna Mission says: "The *jīvātman* is the presiding deity manipulating all these instruments."[17] We agree to this view, with some qualification, of course.

We have already said in the foregoing paragraph that the individual self (*jīvātmā*) is not the doer or agent. We have to resolve this seeming contradiction. The Advaita Vedānta has a doctrine of reflection (*ābhāsa-vāda*). Nothing in the body, including the *antaḥkaraṇa* (internal instrument), can work without *cidābhāsa*. The Self is Pure Consciousness; the self is also Pure Consciousness (*Viśuddha Cit*), both being one and the same. The light of the *cit* of the *jīvātmā* is reflected on the material body, the subtle organs of perception and action, the five *prāṇa-vāyus*, the *buddhi* (intellect), the ego (*ahaṅkāra*) and the mind (*manas*), all these being insentient (*jaḍa*). What is potentially insentient is rendered functionally sentient due to the reflection of Consciousness. But, in this action, the *jīvātmā* (individual self) does not really become an agent (*karttā*) of actions.

After saying that the Self or the self is not the doer of actions, the Lord tries to convince Arjuna that the Self (self) kills not.

### 18.04: When a Killer is not a Killer

The present section will be limited to one verse (18.17) only of the *BG*. The reader should properly assimilate the true significance of this verse. Otherwise, his idea of spirituality would perform a somersault. A sacred spiritual scripture like the *BG* is not expected to preach violence. Nevertheless, it preaches non-violence in unequivocal language. Does it give vent to an unparalleled concept such as non-violent killing? This idea of non-violent killing must be properly understood. If misunderstood, the reading of the *BG*, the perennial philosophy of the world in the language of Aldous Huxley, would be utterly futile. Let the English rendering of the verse be presented first.

---

17. Swami Chidbhavananda, 1971, p. 864.

> He who is free from the notion of egoism (who is completely I-less) and whose intellect is untainted, even after slaying all these people, neither slays nor is bound.[18]

Lord Vāsudeva does not persuade Arjuna to be a killer, a murderer. Killing is a violence, one of the worst types of violence. A spiritual scripture like the *BG*, spoken by the Lord of the universe Himself, cannot instruct Arjuna to commit violence. What is the meaning of this verse then?

Before the Mahābhārata War began, all efforts had been made by the Lord Himself to avert the War. But His efforts became futile due to the bad nature of Duryodhana and the evil manoeuvres of mischievous, sly Śakuni. For re-establishing *dharma* (righteousness), the War became inevitable. In such an unfortunate situation, the bodies of the evil-doers and those of virtuous persons such as Bhīṣma and Droṇa who, under compulsive circumstances, fought for Duryodhana, had to be killed. However, nobody could kill their selves (*ātmās*).

The Lord lays down two conditions so that killing would be non-violent. Firstly, the killer should be I-less. No selfish interest shall be involved in the killing. Secondly, the subtle organ of intellect in the *antaḥkaraṇa* of the subtle body must not be tainted. It should be transparent like a perfectly clean mirror. It should be as pure as possible. With love for the foes, without hatred, ill-will and malice, a virtuous war is to be fought. If these two conditions are fulfilled, killing would be non-violent.

The self does not kill the bodies of living beings, since it is not the doer of actions. It is the *prakṛti* that acts. In the present context, the *antaḥkaraṇa* of an individual person is his *prakṛti*. The self of an egoless person, without tainted intellect, cannot be bound, since impressions (*karma-saṁskāras*) are not formed to be printed on the intellect (on the *karmāśaya*, the reservoir of *karmas*).

---

18. *BG*, XVIII.17.

### 18.05: The Threefold Impetus and the Threefold Summary of Work

It has already been told that the self is not the doer and that it is the *prakṛti* (nature) that is the doer of actions. Let us know what the Lord says on this topic.

> Knowledge, the knowable (the object of knowledge) and the knower form the threefold impulse to action. The instrument, the work and the agent (doer, *karttā*) constitute the threefold summary of work.[19]

Before interpreting verse 18.18 of the *BG*, we feel the necessity of clarifying some words and concepts that are too technical in the Vedānta. The literal meaning of the word *karaṇam* is "an instrument," "something by which work is done." The living human body has two types of *karaṇa*, namely, *antaḥkaraṇa* (internal instrument) and *bahiḥkaraṇa* (external instrument). The former, located in the subtle body (*sūkṣma śarīra*), is in possession of three main components, *buddhi* (intellect), *ahaṅkāra* (ego) and *manas* (the subtle organ of mentation). In addition, it contains five subtle organs of cognition (*pañca-jñānendriyāṇi*) and five subtle organs of action (*pañca-karmendriyāṇi*). The five subtle sensory organs are visual, auditory, olfactory, gustatory, and tactile. The five subtle motor organs are prehensive, locomotive, phonatory, excretory and reproductive. The Sanskrit word *indriya* is used for all these ten subtle organs, and is sometimes used for the *manas* too. Each internal *indriya* has a corresponding external *indriya*, the former in the subtle body and the latter in the gross (*sthūla*) body. We may use the compound word "mind-complex" for the *antaḥkaraṇa*. It utilizes the brain and the other components of the nervous system as its apparatus.

The Vedānta holds that *Brahman* only is Consciousness (*Cit*) and all others in the universe are insentient (*jaḍa*). Accordingly, the *antaḥkaraṇa* or the mind-complex is insentient. Any insentient entity cannot function at all. We better do not raise the issue of

19. *BG*, XVIII.18.

purposeful, co-ordinated functioning on the part of an unconscious entity. We accept this doctrine of the Vedānta. But we have to explain the functioning of all the created entities. There is a doctrine of reflection (*ābhāsa-vāda*). This phenomenon is known as *cidābhāsa* in the Vedānta. *Brahman*, the Fundamental Consciousness, is reflected on everything of the universe and thereby the insentient are rendered sentient. It is a case of induction of consciousness. Because of the reflection of the *jīvātmā* on the *antaḥkaraṇa* or the mind-complex, the latter is rendered conscious.

*karmacodanā* means "incitement to action," "impulse to work." In Śaṅkara's language, it is *sarvakarmaṇāṁ pravarttikā*, the inducer or inspirer of all actions. The word *jñātā* means "knower." The word *parijñātā* means "knower" when referred to the self (*jīvātmā*). Śaṅkara says: *parijñātā upādhilakṣaṇo avidyākalpito bhoktā* (the self becomes the apparent experiencer, being associated with the body as the *upādhi*).

*Jñānam* is the act of knowing. *Jñeyam* is that which is known. A person gets knowledge by two methods, namely, (1) innate knowledge, acquired directly, without the help of sense-experience, and (2) empirical knowledge, received through the organs of perception and processed by the internal instrument. His internal instrument is the knower or *jñātā*. In both cases, the self or the *parijñātā* is indispensable. The triad of knowledge becomes an impulse to action. It is what arises in the mind first before doing the action. Thus it plays the role of an inducing agent.

The knowledge, the knowable and the knower form a triad (*tripuṭi*). They necessarily go together for the purpose of knowing.

The instrument, the object and the agent form a second triad through which actions, both desirable and undesirable, are performed. Physical functions, mental functions and verbal functions are the actions (*karma*). The *jīvātmā* (self), being the fundamental Consciousness, is reflected on the ten subtle organs of cognition and action. Because of this reflection and the proximity of the self, the instruments or *indriya*s are able to function. If we consider this role of the self in the functioning of the instruments, we think that the self is a doer, although in reality it is a non-doer. The real doer in the second triad (*tripuṭi*) is the *antaḥkaraṇa* (internal instrument).

### 18.06: The Threefold Knowledge according to Guṇas

The threefold distinction of knowledge, action and the agent is based on the three *guṇa*s. Thus, the present topic is introduced by verse 18.19 in the following manner:

> Knowledge, action and doer are declared in the science of *guṇa*s to be of three kinds only, in accordance with the distinction of *guṇa*s. Hear of them also as they are.[20]

The word *guṇasaṅkhyāne* means "in the science of *guṇa*s." Ordinarily, Sāṅkhya refers to Kapila's Sāṅkhya philosophy. But, in the *BG*, the Lord uses the term "Sāṅkhya" in a different sense. It denotes Vedānta philosophy, with special reference to its path of knowledge (*jñāna-yoga*). Śaṅkara interprets *guṇasaṅkhyāne* as *Kāpile śāstre* (in Kapila's scripture). We cannot agree with Śaṅkara on this point. However, we are pleased to know that this great philosopher does point out the fundamental difference between the Sāṅkhya and the Advaita Vedānta. He says: *tadapi guṇasaṅkhyānaṁ śāstraṁ guṇabhoktṛviṣaye pramāṇameva paramārthabrahmaikatvaviṣaye virudhyate.* (Although the Sāṅkhya refutes the non-duality of *Brahman*, it provides evidences in favour of the *jīva* experiencing the *guṇa*s).

> Know that knowledge to be *sāttvika* by which one sees in all beings the One Immutable Reality, undivided in the divided.[21]

The unmanifested *Prakṛti* (the *mūla-Prakṛti,* the Primordial Nature, *Māyā*, the Mother Divine) has projected the virtual universe (the manifested *prakṛti*) in multitudinous forms with diversity of properties. The manifested *prakṛti* is divided into manifold units.

---

20. *BG*, XVIII.19.

21. *BG*, XVIII.20.

But the Imperishable and Immutable Reality (the Being without becoming, *Brahman*) is One only, an Unbroken Whole, an undivided One, a continuous, homogeneous Consciousness that supports the divided universe as the substratum (*adhiṣṭhāna*) of the latter.

> But know as *rājasika* that knowledge by which one sees in all beings manifold entities of distinct kinds, varying from one another.[22]

The Supreme Self (*Paramātmā*) and all the individual selves (*bhūtātmā*s in non-living entities and *jīvātmā*s in living beings — plants, animal and humans) are not different. The Self (*Ātmā*) is One and Non-Dual. Only One *Ātmā* seems to be many and different due to the limiting adjuncts (*upādhi*s). Persons with *rājasika* knowledge see diversity in the selves. The universe is pluralistic, inhomogeneous and discontinuous. The underlying Reality that appears as the multitudinous universe is One only, non-dual, an Unbroken Whole and homogeneous. The person, with *rājasika* knowledge, sees the pluralistic surface, but does not see the underlying, unitary substratum (*adhiṣṭhāna*).

> That is said to be *tāmasika* knowledge, which unreasonably clings to one trivial single effect (object) as if it were the whole, without foundation in truth.[23]

A person, with *tāmasika* knowledge, knows that an image is the all of divinity, that this much is God and that there is no Self beyond this image. Someones hold that the *jīva* residing in the body is of the size of the body. Some others believe that God is simply a statue or idol made of stone, wood, or metal. These are a few examples only out of many. *Tāmasika* persons stick to such trifling subject matter for getting petty results. They are not logical in their approach. They are superficial and are not interested in searching for the fundamental truth.

---

22. *BG*, XVIII.21.
23. *BG*, XVIII.22.

## 18.07: The Threefold Action according to Guṇas

In the previous section, we have discussed the threefold knowledge according to *guṇas*. The present section will throw light on the threefold nature of action influenced by the three *guṇas*.

> *Sāttvika* is said to be the work that is obligatory and that is performed by one without attachment, passion and aversion, and without hankering after its fruit.[24]

Obligatory work (*nitya karma*) needs an explanation. Everyone has to do some work like breathing, eating, sleeping, et cetera, unavoidable for life. Such work is obligatory. The normal duty of a person, according to his station in life and his attainments, is obligatory for him. The duties of Arjuna, being a warrior (kṣatriya), are to wage righteous (not religious) wars to protect the weak, to punish the wicked and to prevent or fight injustice. These duties are his obligatory works.

> But that action done with craving for desires, or again with egoism, or with much troublesome effort, is said to be *rājasika*.[25]

There are two kinds of desires. One type of desire promotes ethical and spiritual progress. Such desire is fit to be fostered. The second type of desire entails unceasing craving for more and more wealth, power, name and fame and sensual gratification. Such desire is *rājasika* in nature and is to be eschewed.

The *rājasika* person does his work with pride and egotism. He thinks that he is superior to others and that's why he is able to get his work done. He demands more comforts and more dominance for his superiority.

Nothing good can be achieved without efforts. Hence, efforts, as such, should not be condemned. But the *rājasika* person makes all types of efforts, scrupulous or unscrupulous, to get his work

---

24. *BG*, XVIII.23.

25. *BG*, XVIII.24.

done. He does care for the end, but not for the means. Sometimes, he makes meaningless efforts too.

> That action which is undertaken due to delusion, without heed to the consequence, loss, violence involved and competence is said to be *tāmasika*.[26]

A *tāmasika* person is deluded. He lacks in judgement. He is not able to discern whether his undertaking is good or bad. He does not bother about pondering over the probable consequences of his action, the loss of his property, energy and time, the loss of others' property and lives, and the injury to others. He does not estimate his ability and competence before he undertakes a work.

### 18.08: The Threefold Doer (Agent) according to Guṇas

The Lord has dilated on threefold knowledge and threefold action in section 18.06 and 18.07, respectively. Now He sets forth the three different kinds of agents according to the three *guṇas*.

> An agent (doer, *karttā*) who is free from attachment, non-egoistic, endued with firmness and enthusiasm and changeless (unaffected) in success and failure is said to be *sāttvika*.[27]

A *sāttvika* person performs actions without attachment to the fruits thereof. He works with conviction and zeal. He does not vacillate in his decisions and judgements. He is not affected at all by success or failure.

> The agent who is passionate, seeker of the fruits of works, greedy, violent, unclean, glad and sad (affected by elation and dejection) is said to be *rājasika*.[28]

A *rājasika* agent works, being impelled by passion. He has a hankering for the fruits of action. He accumulates wealth by any means, fair or foul. He resorts to violence for getting his work done. His body, mind and speech are unclean. He is moved by

26. *BG*, XVIII.25.
27. *BG*, XVIII.26.
28. *BG*, XVIII.27.

joy and sorrow (*rājasika* agony and ecstasy).

> Unconcentrated, uncultured, stubborn (arrogant, stiff like a stick), deceitful, maliceous, indolent, despondent and procrastinating is the *tāmasika* agent.[29]

The *tāmasika* person is alien to self-control, self-discipline and self-dedication. He exhibits signs of vulgarity. He is unbending like a stick and refuses to pay homage to anybody, even to great men worthy of reverence. He hides his own real capacity and deceives all. He envies and undermines others. He neglects his duties and idles away time. Being pessimistic in outlook, he suffers from despondency. He has the habit of procrastination. He drags on a work that is to be urgently undertaken.

With this, we finish three sections (18.06 to 08) on the effects of the three *guṇa*s on knowledge, work and the agent. The *BG* gives a clear exposition on human traits, influenced by the three *guṇa*s — *sattva, rajas* and *tamas*. Modern psychology deals with types of human personality. It is unfortunate that Indian psychology which is ancient and very much advanced in quality has been almost ignored. We expect that psychologists should pay attention to what the Sāṅkhya, Vedānta, Yoga and Tantra systems say on personality types and many other aspects of fundamental and applied psychology.

## 18.09: The Threefold Intellect according to Guṇas

Our intellect (*buddhi*) and firmness (*dhṛti*) have gradations. Their types are three in number according to the *guṇa*s. This section will present the details of their threefold distinction.

> Also listen, O Dhanañjaya (Arjuna), to the threefold variety of intellect and of fortitude (resolve), according to the *guṇa*s, as elucidated exhaustively and distinctly.[30]

The word, *buddhi*, used in this verse and in many other places of

---

29. *BG*, XVIII.28.

30. *BG*, XVIII.29.

the *BG*, does not mean "intelligence." In Indian psychology (in the Sāṅkhya and the Vedānta), it is a subtle organ in the subtle body and is one of the three main components (*buddhi, ahaṅkāra, manas*) of the *antaḥkaraṇa* (internal instrument). It is located at the *ājñā-cakra* (the eyebrow centre). It is the faculty of distinguishing between the good and the bad, between the right and the wrong. *Buddhi* is a subtle anatomical organ whose functionality is expressed by the word "conscience."

The word *dhr̥ti* denotes "firmness of mind and resolve." A person of firm resolve does not slacken or waver in the execution of a work. It also means "patience (*dhairya*)."

> O Pārtha (Arjuna), that intellect which knows the path of worldly involvement (that entangles and binds) and that of renunciation (leading to liberation), duty and non-duty, fear and fearlessness, and bondage and liberation is *sāttvika*.[31]

*Pravr̥tti-marga* is the path of work involving indulgence and sensual gratification. It is the path of entanglement in earthly life. In contrast, *nivr̥tti-marga* is the path of renunciation, the path that leads to liberation or emancipation from the wheel of transmigratory existence. What has been stated here has been briefly expressed by Śaṅkara like this: *pravr̥ttiḥ pravartanaṁ bandhahetuḥ karmamārgaḥ; nivr̥ttiḥ mokṣahetuḥ saṁnyāsamārgaḥ*.

*Kārya* is the right action that ought to be done. It is the work that promotes social welfare and spiritual progress. *Akārya* is the wrong action that ought to be abandoned. It is detrimental to the person, family, society, country, the world and the universe. It is malignantly detrimental to spiritual progress.

In verse 1 of chapter 16, the *BG* eulogizes fearlessness (*abhaya*). With reference to that, we have to explain "fear and fearlessness," stated in the present verse. A person, with *sāttvika* intellect fears and fears not. If you are on the right path, if your actions are good and ethical, you must not fear anybody. Stay in *Brahman*

31. *BG*, XVIII.30.

(*brāhmī-sthiti*), dedicate your actions to God and surrender to Him (*Īśvara-praṇidhāna*). If you follow this path of righteousness, you will have fearlessness. If you are doing wrong actions detrimental to you, your family, your society, your country, the world, or the universe, you must be afraid of your bad actions. You are the person who will get the bad results of your bad actions in this life or the lives to come. The law of *karma* operates without any exception. Unrighteousness pulls you down and creates a hell for you in the present life and the future ones. On the other hand, righteousness promotes your spiritual ascent, finally leading to liberation. Fear your unethical actions. Don't fear the Father Divine and the Mother Divine. They are always benevolent (Śiva and Śivā) and never malevolent. They always love you. You are not different from them, except your alienated state of ignorance. Be devoted to them and love them.

A person of *sāttvika* intellect should be able to discriminate bondage (*bandha*) and liberation (*mokṣa*). Righteousness leads to liberation; unrighteousness leads to bondage.

> O Pārtha (Arjuna), *rājasika* is the intellect that wrongly (in a distorted way) understands righteousness (*dharma*) and unrighteousness (*adharma*), duty (what ought to be done) and non-duty (what ought not to be done).[32]

A person endowed with *rājasika* intellect can never be idle. He is capable of turning out an enormous quantity of work. But his evil nature always views the actions in a perverted way. His understanding is tainted. He erroneously makes a distortion of *dharma* (righteousness) and *adharma* (unrighteousness) and of duty (*kārya*) and non-duty (*akārya*).

> O Pārtha, *tāmasika* is that intellect, enveloped in darkness (in *tamas* or ignorance), which regards *adharma* (unrighteousness) as *dharma* (righteousness) and all kinds of things contrariwise.[33]

---

32. *BG*, XVIII.31.

33. *BG*, XVIII.32.

A person endowed with *tāmasika* intellect is perverted. He regards the good as bad and the bad as good. Darkness covers his intellect which becomes totally opaque. The light of the consciousness of the self (*ātmā*) is not reflected on his opaque *buddhi*. And, hence, does he contrarily view all things.

### 18.10: The Threefold Firmness according to Guṇas

The word *dhṛti* means "firmness," "fortitude," "resolve," or "patience." It is an indispensable and invaluable quality in ethical and spiritual life. By virtue of fortitude, the diverging beams are made to converge. Yoga fosters *dhṛti*. In this section, we shall present three types of *dhṛti*, as influenced by the three *guṇas*.

> O Pārtha, the firmness, being unfaltered through *yoga*, by which the functions of the mind, the *Prāṇa* and the senses are maintained is *sāttvika*.[34]

Firmness becomes unswerving when it is directed to the Lord in the analogy of the needle of a compass always pointing to the north. The mind, the prāṇic force and the senses of a *sāttvika* person do not falter, do not diverge, and they actually converge on one point, the Supreme Reality. *Sāttvika* resolve leads to liberation (*mokṣa*).

> But the resolve, O Arjuna, by which one holds fast to *dharma, kāma* and *artha*, desirous of the fruit of each on its occasion, is *rājasika*.[35]

*Puruṣārtha* in life is four-phased. The phases are *dharma, artha, kāma* and *mokṣa*. *Dharma* literally means righteousness. A *rājasika* person practises righteousness solely for getting good fruits. He conforms to the law of life to make an investment. He performs some good actions with the expectation that he will get good returns in the present life and the lives to come. The *dharma*, practised by a *sāttvika* person, has no ulterior motive. It is practised for its own

34. *BG*, XVIII.33.

35. *BG*, XVIII.34.

sake, without attachment to fruits. On the other hand, a *rājasika* person practises *dharma* with attachment to fruits.

*Kāma* is desire for pleasure, for enjoyment in life and for achieving worldly prosperity such as more wealth, power, name and fame. A *rājasika* person is in search of joy and pleasure. He clings to the earthly life for deriving enjoyment. He is very much attached to sex and all other types of worldly pleasures. The *dhṛti* of the *sāttvika* person leads to *śreyas*, culminating in liberation (*mokṣa*). On the other hand, the *dhṛti* of the *rājasika* person is primarily meant for *preyas*, to have his worldly desires fulfilled through more of *kāma* and *artha*.

In the present context, *artha* means "wealth." The *rājasika* person has an intense love of property. With firmness, he grabs wealth and holds on to it. He seeks property and sensual pleasure. His thirst for them remains ever unquenched.

> O Pārtha, that fortitude, by which a stupid man does not give up sleep, fear, grief, dejection (despair) and also conceit, is *tāmasika*.[36]

*Tamas* and ignorance are interrelated. A *tāmasika* person is stupid (*durmedhā*). He clings to sleep, fear, grief, dejection and conceit. Dhṛtarāṣṭra and Duryodhana are examples of *tāmasika* firmness. The number of such persons is not low in the society.

### 18.11: The Threefold Pleasure according to Guṇas

It is a universal truth that man seeks pleasure. Types of pleasure are varied. When *Brahman* itself is Pure Bliss (*Śuddhānanda*), it is natural for a spiritually enlightened *sādhaka* to be in search of *ānanda* (bliss). To avoid pain and to search for pleasure are the common attempts of living beings. But there are low grades of pleasure too. In this section, we shall dilate the threefold pleasure, as influenced by the three *guṇa*s. Now let us know what the Lord says to Arjuna on this topic:

> And now hear from Me, O Best of Bhāratas (Arjuna), the threefold

---

36. BG, XVIII.35.

> pleasure. That in which, through practice, one delights, reaching the end of pain, which, in the beginning, is like poison, but, at the end, is like nectar (ambrosia), is declared to be *sāttvika,* born of the transparency of one's own intellect.[37]

Long and sustained practice of *yoga* and other techniques of spirituality imparts transparency to the intellect (*buddhi*) of a *sāttvika* person. He realizes the Self and thereby he reaches the end of his pain and he rejoices. In the beginning, the practice is arduous and seems to be like poison. But, in the end, the seeming poison really becomes ambrosia. This consequence of spiritual practice is brought about by the purification of the intellect. An opaque intellect, due to deposition of dirt on it, becomes harmful to the person. A transparent intellect is better than an opaque one. A *sāttvika* person, by his sustained practice of spirituality, removes all the dirt from his intellect and makes it transparent. Transparency of the intellect is a prerequisite for the realization of the Self. And a Self-realized person rejoices bliss.

> It is held that *rājasika* is the pleasure which arises from the contact of the senses and their objects and which is like nectar in the beginning, but like poison at the end.[38]

The *rājasika* pleasure is sensual. It arises from the contact of the senses with their objects. A *rājasika* person craves for sensual gratification. In the beginning, he enjoys sensual pleasure and becomes happy. But what seems to him as nectar in the beginning proves to be poison at the end. The final results of sensuality are always harmful.

> *Tāmasika* is declared to be that pleasure which, in the beginning and at the end, deludes the self and springs from sleep, sloth and miscomprehension.[39]

The person of *tāmasika* nature also gets pleasure. But his pleasure,

---

37. *BG,* XVIII.36-37.

38. *BG,* XVIII.38.

39. *BG,* XVIII.39.

in the beginning and in the sequel, is delusive. It confuses the self. It arises from sleep, indolence and misconception.

The following verse concludes the current section:

> There is no being on earth or again in heaven among the gods (*devas*), that is free from these three *guṇas*, born of *Prakṛti*.[40]

The three *guṇas* of *Māyā* have already been dealt with in the *BG* in the seventh chapter (7.13-14). In the present verse (18.40), it is emphasized that none is an exception in being influenced by the *guṇas*. The verse says that even gods are not exceptions. We will apply this principle even to God who is not an exception. Only *Brahman*, being *nirguṇa* (attributeless), is an exception. Of course, a clarification must be tagged to the statement that even God is not an exception. Although God is *saguṇa* (with *guṇa*), He is not made up of *guṇas* and not in possession of *guṇas*. *Māyā* being His own Power, He is associated with Her three strings and also with the three attributes of the cosmic entities, created by Her. Thus, He is *sambandhī* (relational) whereas *Brahman* is *asambandhī* (non-relational). *Māyā* is under the control of God, and the reverse statement is not true. *Guṇas* cannot impel God to do this thing or that; and they cannot influence Him in any way whatsoever. If *guṇas* were to control God, He could not be the Supreme Controller of the universe. It is also a fact that *Māyā* controls the *guṇas*, without being controlled by the latter. This divine *Śakti* creates, sustains and dissolves the universe under God's chairpersonship.

The text of the verse says that the three *guṇas* are born of *Prakṛti*. From this, we understand that *Prakṛti* virtually and phenomenally generates these *guṇas* through Her creative power. She does this generation of the *guṇas* through the mechanism of the vibrations of Her three strings — *sattva, rajas* and *tamas*. However, it should not be logically inferred that *Prakṛti* is made up of the three *guṇas*. Neither should it be understood that *Prakṛti*

40. *BG*, XVIII.40.

gives birth to the three *guṇa*s as a mother giving birth to a child.

In the details of the interpretation of the three *guṇa*s of *Māyā*, we have some disagreement with other commentators. Some hold the opinion that *Māyā* is constituted of three *guṇa*s. We differ on this point. *Māyā* or the *mūla-Prakṛti* is undifferentiated (*avyākṛtā*). Whereas the Sāṅkhya *Prakṛti* is matter, the Vedānta *Prakṛti* or *Māyā* is neither matter nor energy. She is *avastu* (not an object, not a substance). That being so, the three *guṇa*s cannot be the constituents of *Māyā*. She supramentally generates Her *vīṇā*, with three divine strings. She Herself plays the instrumental music. The vibrations of the strings generate all entities of the universe, carrying three trait-types, namely, *rajas, sattva, tamas*. No created beings — inanimate, animate, *deva*s (divine beings) — are free from attributes, without a single exception.

With this much commentary on the *guṇa-traya*, we conclude this section after answering a probable question. Taken it for granted that the intrinsic *guṇa*-blend of a person has already been determined, he seems to have been doomed. Has he *puruṣārtha* to gain a control over the *guṇa*s? The answer is affirmative. By the spiritual practice of *yoga*, one can change the *guṇa*-type and can ascend in the upward path from *tāmasika* to *rājasika*, from *rājasika* to *sāttvika*, and finally he can transcend all the three *guṇa*s (becomes *nistraiguṇya*). That is the stage of becoming a *jīvanmukta* (released albeit still living). A person, with an *antaḥkaraṇa* having zero *karma-saṁskāras*, is liberated. When we say "One is liberated," thereby we mean "One becomes *Brahman*." In that state, *guṇa*s cannot affect the *nirguṇa Brahman*.

### 18.12: The Fourfold Nature of Human Beings

Eight verses of the *BG* (18.41-48) describe the fourfold nature of human beings. One is apt to misunderstand these verses if one mistakenly identifies them with the caste-system, presently in vogue in the Hindu society of India. The *BG* (4.13) clearly says that persons are classified as brāhmaṇas, kṣatriyas, vaiśyas and śūdras according to their *guṇa* (trait) and *karma* (action). In this classification, birth in a family does not become the criterion of the fixation of caste. Throughout the world, irrespective of religions, persons are in possession of one of these four traits. Now let us know what these traits are:

> O scourge of foes (Arjuna), the works of brāhmaṇas, kṣatriyas, vaiśyas, as also those of the śūdras are described according to the qualities born of their own nature.[41]

Śaṅkara has equated *svabhāva* with *Prakṛti*, the *Māyā-Śakti* of *Īśvara* (*svabhāvaḥ īśvarasya prakṛtiḥ triguṇātmikā māyā*). Contextually, however, it is not so. It is the trait-type inherent in an individual person. We have already interpreted a number of verses of the *BG* on the topic of *guṇa* and *Prakṛti* or *Māyā*. We have said that *guṇa* has at least two meanings. It means "string" with reference to the three strings of the *vīṇā* of Mother Sarasvatī, the Mother Creatrix. It also means "attribute" or "quality" or "trait" with reference to the cosmic entities, phenomenalized by the vibrations of the strings of *Māyā*. We do not accept the common interpretation that *Prakṛti* or *Māyā* is constituted of (is made up of) three *guṇa*s or attributes. This point has already been elaborately explained in our previous discussions.

Still we have to answer a pertinent question. What is the cause of the differences among the tendencies or trait-types? The *karma-saṁskāra*s, especially the *vāsanā-saṁskāra*s (latent impressions in the *antaḥkaraṇa*) determine the qualities of an individual person. Finally speaking, the inherent qualities of an individual person are in conformity with his karmic impressions. In our opinion, *svabhāva* in the present verse means "the *karma-saṁskāra*s in the *antaḥkaraṇa*."

> Serenity (tranquillity), self-restraint, austerity (penance), purity (cleanliness of body, speech and mind), forgiveness, and also uprightness, knowledge, realization (of *Brahman*), belief in the existence of God — these are the works of Brāhmaṇas, born of their own nature (their latent karmic impressions).[42]

---

41. *BG*, XVIII.41.

42. *BG*, XVIII.42.

It may be mentioned here that brāhmaṇas exist in all religions, societies, geographical locations and ages. They will continue to exist so long as the human species is not extinct. But the present caste-system in Hindu society, based on one's birth in a certain family, shall and should dwindle away.

That person is a brāhmaṇa who possesses the qualities mentioned in verse 18.42 of the *BG*. He is tranquil in all circumstances. He exercises restraint on his senses and mind. He is always ready to undergo all types of suffering (*tapaḥ*, literally meaning "heat") for a noble cause in the service of the creation of God. He is clean physically, verbally and mentally. He is glad to forgive others. He is upright. His thought, words and actions are in perfect unison. He is a man of knowledge and wisdom. He has realization of *Brahman*. He is not an atheist. He believes in the existence of God. Any person in this world or extra-terrestrial worlds, conforming to these standards, is a brāhmaṇa.

> Heroism, vigour, firmness, dexterity, and also non-flight from battle, generosity, and lordliness are the works of a kṣatriya, born of his own nature (his latent karmic impressions).[43]

This paragraph is self-explanatory. On one point only shall we focus here. A kṣatriya is not only a warrior, but also a ruler. One who is a king, an emperor, a president, a prime minister, an administrator, a general, a commander, or a soldier is a kṣatriya. Everywhere and always is the necessity of kṣatriyas. A person, with an aptitude of a brāhmaṇa, a vaiśya, or a śūdra cannot successfully discharge the duties of a kṣatriya.

> Agriculture, cattle-rearing and trade are the works of a vaiśya, born of his own nature (his latent karmic impressions). And action consisting of physical service is the work of a śūdra, born of his own nature.[44]

The word "agriculture (*kr̥ṣi*)" in the verse refers to farming for

43. *BG*, XVIII.43.

44. *BG*, XVIII.44.

the production of crops on the land. The compound-word "cattle-rearing (*gaurakṣya*)" should extend its meaning to animal-husbandry in general. Trade or business includes a long range of commercial activities. The vaiśyas engage themselves in the production of food and other commodities for the society. In addition to production, they also do purchase and sale. Without the appropriate temperament of a vaiśya, one is not likely to get success in business. The production and trading of wealth are very important activities for the welfare of any society.

A *paricāraka* (*paricārikā* in feminine gender) is one who serves. His/her service is mostly manual. One cannot be a successful śūdra, without a service-mentality. Unfortunately, the word śūdra has become derogatory and been associated with disrespect and contempt. We may substitute this word with any other one. But the fact remains that all societies in the world need manual services. One may be a farm-labourer, a factory-labourer, a household-worker or worker of any other type. The dignity of the dirty hand must be recognized in order that a society improves and humanity is respected. We should see that the labour-class must not be exploited. Their socio-economic conditions must be improved. All efforts must be done to treat labourers as respectable human beings. But any hollow, political slogan can never get rid of a labour-class in a society.

In verses 18.41-44, the *BG* has described four types of persons (not by virtue of their family-lineage, but of their aptitudes and temperaments, born of their karmic impressions). It may be emphasized here that all these four types are vitally important for the holistic progress of any society. No work is to be looked down upon. No work is contemptible. Social discords are bound to creep in whenever this fact is ignored or distorted due to political or any other parochial selfish gains.

Each individual person is born of his own nature (karmic impressions). He cannot change his inherent nature in this life. Whatever has been his inherent nature, he can perform his duties sincerely in conformity with his nature and thereby attain liberation. On this aspect of the topic, the Lord declares:

> Man attains his highest perfection through devotion to his duties. How he attains perfection by being engaged in his own duty, that do you know.[45]
>
> A man attains perfection by worshipping Him (God) with his own duty. From Him (God), all beings have proceeded and, by Him, all this has been pervaded.[46]

The above-mentioned two verses lay emphasis on the fact that "Work is worship." Do your duty sincerely in conformity with your inherent nature. You can attain liberation (*mokṣa*) by worshipping God with the sincere performance of your duties.

It is God from whom all things have proceeded and it is He by whom everything has been pervaded. There is a special significance of this statement in verse 18.46 of the *BG*. All persons belonging to all professions and vocations should be equally respected as human beings. A śūdra, because of the nature of his physical and manual work and service to the society, should not be considered inferior in the creation of God. All persons have proceeded from God. The Lord is the source of all. He pervades all. His presence inside a brāhmaṇa and a śūdra is in no way different.

> Better is one's own *dharma*, albeit defective, than that of another well-performed. One incurs no sin by doing the duty ordained by one's own nature.[47]

The word *svabhāva* (own nature) means "one's own trait-type moulded by one's karmic impressions." The *svabhāva* of a person may not be perfect unlike that of another. Notwithstanding this fact, it is better for one to perform one's duties ordained by one's own nature. The word *dharma* in this verse does not mean

---

45. *BG*, XVIII.45.
46. *BG*, XVIII.46.
47. *BG*, XVIII.47.

"religion." What is *svadharma* then? The word *sva* means "own." *Svadharma* is the duty that is in tune with a person's disposition. The Lord further elaborates the *sahaja karma*.

> O son of Kuntī (Arjuna), work determined by the inborn nature, though defective, should not be abandoned; for all undertakings are enveloped by flaws, as fire by smoke.[48]

The word *sahajam* has been analysed by Śaṅkara as *saha janmanā eva utpannam* (produced with the birth). Every person has been born due to his *karma-saṁskāra*s. One's *saṁskāra*s (karmic impressions) mould a trait-type, and that is his *svabhāva* (own nature). Every *sahaja karma* is *triguṇātmaka* (one that partakes of the three *guṇa*s). And anything, partaking of the three *guṇa*s, cannot be altogether free from flaws. Having accepted this fact, we have to admit that all undertakings are shrouded in flaws, as fire by smoke.

Even though all works are shrouded in flaws, one should not abandon work. The work in unison with *svadharma* and *svabhāva*, albeit with more flaws in comparison with that of another person, should not be abandoned.

Lord Vāsudeva persuades Arjuna to do the duties of a kṣatriya. The kṣatriya-*dharma* may be inferior to the *dharma* of a brāhmaṇa or a recluse. Still Arjuna should do his duties ordained by his inborn dispositions.

### 18.13: Karma-Yoga is Karma-Saṁnyāsa

In this section, we will discuss nine verses (18.49-57) of the *BG*. These verses will highlight the method of converting the *yoga* of action into the *yoga* of renunciation of action.

> He whose intellect is unattached everywhere, who has subdued his self and from whom desires have departed, attains the supreme perfection of worklessness by means of renunciation.[49]

48. *BG*, XVIII.48.

49. *BG*, XVIII.49.

This verse pinpoints three characteristics of the *karma-yogī*. He engages himself in actions, being an *asaktabuddhiḥ*. Śaṅkara defines this word like this: *asaktā saṅgarahitā buddhiḥ antaḥkaraṇaṁ yasya sa asaktabuddhiḥ*. (He whose intellect or *antaḥkaraṇam* or inner instrument is unattached to objects like children, wife, wealth, power, fame and so forth is a person of unattached intellect). The second condition is: He subdues his self; he becomes a *jītātmā*. In the compound-word *jītātmā*, *ātmā* does not mean "the *jīvātmā*." The question of subduing the *jīvātmā* does not carry any meaning. In Śaṅkara's language, one who has subdued his *antaḥkaraṇa* (inner instrument) is a *jītātmā* (*jītaḥ vaśīkṛtaḥ ātmā antaḥkaraṇaṁ yasya sa jītātmā*). In the ordinary people, thoughts and feelings rise in the mind like waves on the sea. They generate karmic impressions. But the mind of the *yogī* maintains a placid state in the analogy of a waveless sea. In that mental state, the *yogī* is a *jītātmā*. The third condition is *vigataspṛhaḥ*. Śaṅkara analyses this word like this: *vigatā spṛhā tṛṣṇā dehajīvitabhogeṣu yasmāt sa vigataspṛhaḥ*. A *vigataspṛhaḥ* is he whose clinging to body, life and enjoyments has departed. Such a Self-knower wins the status of a total renouncer, although he does not renounce actions.

> O son of Kuntī (Arjuna), learn from Me, in brief, how one, attaining such perfection (*siddhi*), reaches *Brahman*, the supreme consummation of knowledge.[50]

The practice of *yoga* chisels the mind of all its angularities. It shapes it into perfection. A *siddha* is one who purges all of the defects from his mind. When this state of a purified mind is attained, it is the initial *siddhi*. Such a *siddha* person becomes fit for getting *Brahma-jñāna*. Reference has been made to *jñāna-niṣṭhā*. Here *niṣṭhā* means "consummation," "perfection," "the termination," "the final stage." The Lord instructs Arjuna to learn from Him the procedure for the attainment of *jñāna-niṣṭhā*. A mind, purified through the practice of *yoga*, becomes fit for attaining *Brahma-jñāna*. This is the highest perfection to be attained.

---

50. *BG*, XVIII.50.

> Endued with a purified intellect, restraining the self with firmness, rejecting sense-objects like sound and abandoning attraction (passion) and aversion, dwelling in solitude, eating lightly, controlling speech, body and mind, always engaged in the *yoga* of meditation, resorting to dispassion, renouncing egoism, force, pride (arrogance), lustful desires, wrath and possession (accumulation) of property, becoming my-less (being free from the notion of "mine") and being tranquil, one is fit for becoming *Brahman*.[51]

In verse 18.51, "restraining the self with firmness (*dhṛtyā 'tmānaṁ niyamya)*" is one of the conditions for becoming *Brahman*. Here "self" does not mean the *jīvātmā*, "the individual self." The Supreme Self and the individual self are identical. There is no need for restraining the self. And, both the Self and the self being identical, who will restrain the self? What is the true significance of this condition then? In the present context, it means "restraining the intellect and the psycho-physical organism." The first condition in the said verse is "being united with the intellect, the faculty of decision, that has been purged of all guile." "Rejecting objects like objects seen and sounds heard" means "not seeking sense-pleasure in sense-objects."

In verse 18.53 of the *BG*, two out of many conditions are abandoning egoism (*ahaṅkāra*) and becoming my-less (*nirmama*). The word *kāma* is hankering after sense-pleasure. One must give it up in order to ascend the spiritual ladder and reach the peak. The word *bala* literally means "force." It contextually means "violence." The word *parigraha* needs a clarification. It should not strictly mean "non-possession of property." Some minimum amount of property is indispensable for the sustenance of the body and for the needs of life. It really means "non-accumulation of property," "non-exploitation," "non-acceptance of unearned property," "non-covetousness for more and more wealth" and "pleasure in giving up." A *yogī* must not possess property more than his bare needs.

---

51. *BG*, XVIII.51-53.

The other conditions to be fulfilled for attaining to *Brahman*-hood do not need further elucidation.

> Becoming *Brahman*, with tranquillized mind, he neither grieves nor desires. The same towards all beings, he obtains supreme devotion to Me.[52]

In this verse, the difference between knowledge and devotion has been obliterated. Having risen to the status of *Brahman*, the *yogī* obtains serenity of mind. He does not feel distressed when something, unfavourable for him, happens. When he has already become a *Brahman*-knower, he seeks nothing and does not desire any ungained object. The *yogī* becomes the same towards all beings. This statement has a special meaning here. It does not mean "the perception of the One Self, the same in all," a concept stated in the next verse. It has a reference to verse 6.32 of the *BG*. The *yogī* looks upon the pleasure and the pain of all beings by the same standard as for himself.

This verse brings about a confluence of devotion (*bhakti*) and knowledge (*jñāna*). *Bhakti* is involved in *jñāna* and vice versa. A *brahma-jñānī* has the realization of the concept "He is I" (*so 'ham*) and simultaneously he is a staunch devotee of God. He is the realized person who has the highest devotion to the Supreme Lord. His is the devotion which comes out of conviction and realization. Reference may be made to verse 7.16 of the *BG* that describes the fourth kind of devotees.

> By devotion, he comprehends Me, what and who I am. Then, having known Me in reality, he forthwith enters into Me.[53]

The *jñānī-bhakta* (knower of *Brahman* and devotee of God) gets a good comprehension of the Supreme Lord by means of his devotion. He knows what God is, that is, he knows God's extent, the vast multiplicity caused by the limiting adjuncts (*upādhi*s). He also knows who the Supreme Spirit is. The Spirit is in truth devoid

---

52. *BG*, XVIII.54.

53. *BG*, XVIII.55.

of all the multiplicity caused by the *upādhis*. He is the non-dual One whose sole essence is Consciousness (*Cit*).

The knower of *Brahman* becomes *Brahman*. After truly knowing what and who the Supreme Spirit is, the *yogī* immediately enters into *Brahman*; or, in other words, he immediately becomes *Brahman*.

The *BG* unambiguously supports non-dualism. This verse and some other ones speak of *Brahma-nirvāṇa*. On attaining liberation (*mokṣa*), one enters into or merges in *Brahman*. The individuality, preceding liberation, is lost consequent upon the attainment of liberation. In the concept of *Brahma-nirvāṇa*, something does not become nihil (*śūnya*) unlike the corresponding Buddhistic doctrine. That something becomes Plenum or Full (*pūrṇa*); when the river-water becomes the ocean-water, there is no annihilation of the former. The dualistic schools of Indian philosophy claim that the *jīvātmā* still retains its individuality subsequent to its liberation. They vehemently antagonize the idea that the individual self can become the Supreme Self. They also interpret the *BG* in their favour. But they thereby try to distort what has been truly given in the *BG*. It is also a fact that religions born in countries outside India reject the concept of souls becoming God. They do not have any provision of reincarnation. On the Day of Judgement, God sends the souls either to the heaven or the hell, depending upon the actions of the individual. And the stay in the heaven or the hell is permanent and irrevocable.

> Even performing all works continually, taking refuge in Me, by My grace, one reaches the eternal, undecaying (immutable) Abode.[54]

In the highest state of *sādhanā*, knowledge (*jñāna*) and devotion (*bhakti*) are the same for the *sādhaka*. In the climax of *sādhanā*, *jñāna* and *karma* (action) are also the same for him. If he takes refuge in God, if he surrenders his ego to God, even though he works always, he gets divine grace. Due to the grace of God, the *sādhaka*

---

54. *BG*, XVIII.56.

who is the *jñānī* (knower), the *bhakta* (devotee) and the *karmī* (worker) becomes Pure Consciousness (*Brahman*). Here the differences among knowledge, devotion and action are totally obliterated. For achieving liberation, one must take refuge in God; then only does he obtain divine grace. Once one gets God's grace, one is emancipated.

> Mentally resigning all works to Me, regarding Me as the Supreme, resorting to *buddhi-yoga*, always fix your mind on Me.[55]

Śaṅkara defines *buddhi-yoga* as "resorting to concentrated understanding (*samāhitabuddhitvaṁ buddhiyogaḥ*)." However, our meaning of *buddhi-yogaḥ* is different. It is equanimity of mind over success or failure of actions, although rightly and sincerely performed (vide *BG*, 2.48-51).

In different schools of Indian philosophy, divergent views appear on the topic of liberation. Some say: Knowledge (plenary knowledge on *Brahman*) is the only means for attaining liberation. Some others say that devotion is the only means for attaining liberation. It is a general trend to denounce action as a means to liberation. But, here in the *BG*, the three have been nicely blended together.

### 18.14: The Harmful Effects of Ego and the Role of Innate Tendencies

In the last part of chapter 18 of the *BG*, utmost emphasis has been laid on total surrender to God. That is the culmination of *bhakti-yoga*. In our opinion, total surrender to God is the culmination of yoga as a whole.

A person, with ego being forceful, cannot really surrender to God. A person, without plenary knowledge on *Brahman*, cannot surrender to God. A person, without devotional attitude, cannot surrender to God. A person who cannot offer (*samarpaṇa*) all his works to God cannot surrender to Him. Ego is the main obstacle

55. *BG*, XVIII.57.

to total surrender. In this section, the Lord elaborates the harmful effects of ego.

> With your mind fixed on Me, you shall overcome all obstacles by My grace; but if, due to egoism, you do not hear (Me), you shall perish.[56]

At the conclusive part of the *BG*, the scripture is converging on devotion (*bhakti*). Focusing the mind on God and surrendering to Him are the means for getting His grace. When God's grace is obtained, all difficulties and obstacles shall be overcome. Without trying to get the grace of God, if one works egoistically, one shall perish. The Lord further explains the harm created by egoism.

> Having taken refuge in egoism, if you think "I will not fight," vain is this, your resolve. Your nature will constrain you.[57]

In this verse, the word *prakṛti* means neither the primordial nature (*Māyā* or *Īśvara-Śakti*) nor the created nature of matter and energy. It refers to the kṣatriya (warrior-class) temperament of Arjuna. The inborn nature of every individual is shaped by his cumulative karmic impressions (*karma-saṁskāra*s) of previous births. This nature compels a person to do this or that. The inborn nature (innate tendency), supplemented with the nurture, works synergistically.

> O son of Kuntī (Arjuna), bound by your own action, born of (your) nature, helplessly against your will, you shall also do what you do not wish to do due to delusion.[58]

While interpreting the previous verse, the word "nature" (*prakṛti, svabhāva*) has already been explained. One's action is born of one's *svabhāva* (innate tendencies). As the dream of a person takes its form from his disposition, so is the action of a person bound to be in conformity with his nature. A bad *svabhāva* generates delusion that compels the person to act as the *svabhāva* dictates. The *svabhāva*,

56. *BG*, XVIII.58.

57. *BG*, XVIII.59.

58. *BG*, XVIII.60.

carrying the meaning of "innate tendencies," is shaped by the *karma-saṁskāras*, cumulatively stored due to actions done in the past lives.

### 18.15: Total Surrender to God

Verse 18.61 of the *BG* introduces the topic of "total surrender to God" and verse 18.66 pinnacles the *yoga* of devotion (*bhakti-yoga*). All the teachings of the *Gītā* culminate in the latter verse.

> O Arjuna, God dwells in the hearts of all beings. By His *Māyā*, He causes all beings to revolve as though they are mounted on a machine.[59]

The whole *saṁsāra* (cyclic universe of matter and energy in co-ordinated motion) is compared with a machine. All created beings are mounted on it. This is a revolving machine which constantly whirls. God desires it to be in whirling motion and so does He accomplish it through His *Māyā-Śakti*.

*Īśvara* is He who rules over all. The Sanskrit verb-root *īś* means "to rule" or "to control." He is the Lord; He is God, in whatever religion or whatever language we name Him. He dwells in the hearts of all. Being all-pervasive, He is present everywhere, inside and outside all inanimate and animate beings. It is not a fact that God dwells in a certain locality called "heaven."

Śaṅkara, while giving his commentary on the quoted verse, has given a reference to the *Ṛgveda*.[60] (*ahaśca kṛṣṇamahararjuna ca* — the day is black and the day is white). The literal meaning of the word *arjuna* is "white (*śukla*)." The person Arjuna in the *Gītā* is *śuklāntarātmasvabhāvaḥ* (with white inner self). His inner instrument (*antaḥkaraṇa*) is extremely pure. This Vedic allusion has no relevance to the said verse of the *Gītā*. It is not understood why Śaṅkara thought it proper to quote the Vedas.

We are great admirers of Śaṅkara, the philosopher genius of

59. *BG*, XVIII.61.

60. *ṚV*, VI.9.1.

India and the world. At the same time, we are sometimes very critical of his over-emphasis on his doctrine of illusion. He interprets the word *māyayā* in this verse as *chadmanā* (through illusion). We take *Māyā* as *Īśvara-Śakti* (the Power of God, the Mother of the universe) and not as illusion. Of course, She has the power to create illusion by her concealing power (*āvaraṇa-śakti*) and projecting power (*vikṣepa-śakti*). Most often Śaṅkara correctly interprets *Māyā* as *Īśvara-Śakti* (the Power of God) who creates, sustains and dissolves the virtual universe under the chairpersonship of God. Nevertheless, he sometimes becomes an illusionist perhaps due to the influence of his grandteacher, Gauḍapāda.

> O scion of Bharata (Arjuna), seek refuge in Him alone with all your heart. By His grace you will win supreme peace and the eternal Abode.[61]

To be emancipated from the whirling motion of the *saṁsāra*, there is one way only. And that is taking refuge in God. The Lord says: Take refuge in God wholeheartedly (*sarvabhāvena*) and not half-heartedly. Thereby we gain divine grace. Only by gaining the grace of God, we can escape from the whirling machine of *saṁsāra*, get supreme peace and get the eternal status of Viṣṇu (All-Pervading God).

In verse 18.62, the word *sthānam* has been translated as "abode." It does not really mean a place like heaven or *Vaikuṇṭha* where Lord Nārāyaṇa (*nāra* = subtle Cosmic Plasma = subtle waters = *Āpaḥ*; God reclines on the *Āpaḥ* and, hence, is known as Nārāyaṇa) dwells. God is all-pervasive and is omnipresent; He does not reside in a certain locality in the universe. He is immanent in the universe; He is transcendent to the universe. The expression "the eternal Abode" (*śāśvataṁ sthānam*) means "the Supreme State of Viṣṇu or Nārāyaṇa."

> Again listen to My supreme word, the most secret of all. You are

61. *BG*, XVIII.62.

> dear to Me and steadfastly (consistently) close to Me. Therefore I will speak what is good for you.[62]

> Fix your mind on Me; be devoted to Me; sacrifice unto Me; prostrate before Me; you will surely come to Me. Truly do I promise you, for you are dear to Me.[63]

The Lord transmits some important techniques of the *yoga* of devotion to Arjuna. "With mind fixed on Me (*manmanāḥ*), be devoted to Me." The verb-root *yaj* means "oblation," "to offer dehydrated and clarified butter (*ghr̥tam*) to God." Its general and popular meaning is "to worship." The expression *bhava madyājī* means "Worship Me." In *bhakti-yoga*, prostration is a mark of subordinating one's individuality to Almighty God. This is a physical symptom of surrender. Lord Vāsudeva says to Arjuna: "I am promising you. Through wholehearted devotion to Me, you shall come to Me."

Now the Lord reveals the quintessence of yoga and that of the *BG*.

> Giving up all *dharma*s, take refuge in Me alone. I will liberate you from all sins; grieve not.[64]

The literal meaning of *dharma* is "act of righteousness." The literal meaning of *adharma* is "act of unrighteousness." How can the *BG* teach to renounce all acts of righteousness? If we understand this verse in such a literal sense, it would be better not to read the *BG* and not to act according to its prescriptions and proscriptions.

Śaṅkara says: *Dharma* here includes *adharma* also. What is sought to be conveyed is the idea of freedom from all works (*dharmaśabdena atra adharmaḥ api gr̥hyate, naiṣkarmyasya vivikṣitatvāt*). Śaṅkara steadfastly holds that by nothing else other than the knowledge of *Brahman* can liberation (*mokṣa*) be attained.

We do not agree with Śaṅkara on his interpretation of verse

62. *BG*, XVIII.64.

63. *BG*, XVIII.65.

64. *BG*, XVIII.66.

18.66 of the *BG*. To harp on knowledge alone is an extreme view. It does not truly present what the *BG* instructs. Nowhere in the *BG* is *naiṣkarmya* (freedom from all actions) prescribed. For all practical purposes, this verse is the last one in the *BG* that could transform Arjuna from a person of agony, dejection and escapism from work to one of optimism and dedication to unattached action. In the first chapter of the *Gītā*, he renounced action and expressed his determined view not to fight the war. In the last chapter of the *Gītā*, especially after listening to the present verse, he regained the conviction to fight the war. In such a context, we cannot accept the *naiṣkarmya*-doctrine of Śaṅkara.

Verse 18.66 and the ones immediately preceding it lay importance on the *yoga* of devotion. Many verses in the beginning of chapter 18 of the *BG* present a confluence of *jñāna* (knowledge), *karma* (action) and *bhakti* (devotion). In the first chapter of the *BG*, Arjuna renounced action in a dejected mood. He listened to the Lord's instructions in the whole of the *BG*. This unparalleled scripture nowhere denounced the triad of action, knowledge and devotion in their proper perspective. It is an integral, perennial philosophy for humankind. It laid stress on unattached action; but it denounced inaction. It emphasized devotion; but did emphasize devotion backed up by knowledge. Chapter 11 of the *BG* gives a description of the Cosmic Image of the Lord. This vision of the Cosmic Image (*viśva-rūpa-darśana*) could dispel all doubts from the mind of Arjuna who could be convinced of the fact that the Lord himself was imparting instructions to him. Verse 18.66 is the quintessence of the *yoga* of devotion. Taking all these facts into consideration, we are unable to accept the *naiṣkarmya*-doctrine of Śaṅkara.

Some religions of the world and some sects of Hinduism itself lay over-emphasis on blind devotion at the cost of ethicality and morality in actions and they give hardly any importance on knowledge. They hold the view: "Do any work irrespective of considering it of being virtuous or sinful, righteous or unrighteous.

Pray to God; repent for your sins; beg for forgiveness. You will get salvation." Some interpreters of verse 18.66 of the *BG*, especially those of the dualistic school of philosophy, speak in favour of what has been said here. We reject this view outright.

We have not yet said how we interpret this verse. We must perform our duties without attachment to the fruits of our actions, although we do not plead for the rejection of the fruits of actions whatever they may be. We offer our work (*karma-samarpaṇa*) to God. We should be conscious of the fact that *Brahman* is the only non-dual Reality. Without *brahma-jñāna* (right knowledge on *Brahman*) and *brahmānubhūti* (realization of *Brahman*), our work may be unrighteous (*adharma*). Having performed unrighteous work, we shall distance ourselves from the *summum bonum* of our life, that is, from the goal of liberation (*mokṣa*). We need the grace of God for treading on the right path, ascending the rungs of the spiritual ladder, leading to the final goal, the attainment of *Brahman*-hood. For this, total surrender to God is the inevitable condition. It is the climax of *bhakti-yoga*.

Whenever and whatever we work, we may be confused about its rightness and wrongness. Most or all works are not totally free from evil. We very often meet with the crisis of *dharmādharma* (*dharma* and *adharma*, righteousness and unrighteousness). This situation is otherwise known as *dharma-saṅkaṭa* (*saṅkaṭa* = crisis, inability in deciding what to do and what not to do). The Lord says in verse 18.66 of the *BG*: "Give up all your crises of deciding righteousness and unrighteousness. Fully surrender to Me. I will liberate you from all sins; grieve not."

Here we may spell out the mechanism of liberation. A person, fully surrendered to God, gets *buddhi-yoga*. He becomes neutral to success and failure. He becomes free from attachment. Such a person does not accumulate new mental impressions (*karma-saṁskāras*). God, through the agency of His *Māyā* (*Īśvara-Śakti*, the Power of God, the Mother of the universe), erases the already accumulated *karma* (*sañcita karma*) and the already initiated *karma* (*prārabdha karma*). Thus, the *buddhi* (intellect) of the internal instrument (*antaḥkaraṇa*) is fully erased. When the devotee attains to this status, he is liberated. His self becomes the Self; his *jīvātmā* becomes the *Paramātmā*.

What has been said here seems to contradict the doctrine of *karma* (*karma-vāda*). What seems is not really so. To fully surrender to God is also a *karma* (action) and it is the peak action in the *yoga* of devotion. This action, instead of generating *saṁskāras*, cleanses the *buddhi* of all accumulated *saṁskāras* and prevents any further accumulation. This process is in the ambit of *buddhi-yoga* and in conformity with *karma-vāda*.

*Īśvara* (God) is *akarttā* (a non-doer). This statement is correct. But, if not properly understood, it makes the concept of *Īśvara* topsy-turvy. Whatever God desires, He gets it done through the agency of His Power, *Māyā*. He directly does not work. From this concept of non-doership, we must not infer that He is an impotent onlooker of all sorts of happenings, virtues or vices.

An impotent onlooker cannot be the Supreme Ruler of the universe. The word *Īśvara* has been derived from the verb-root *īś*, meaning "to rule," "to control." Not only is He the Ruler, but also is the Supreme Ruler (*Parameśvara*). There is no other ruler above Him. Being a mere witness (*sākṣī*) and without being omnipresent, omniscient and omnipotent, one cannot be the Ruler of the universe. God, not directly being a Ruler, works indirectly through His own power (*Śakti*). The *Śakti* and the *Śaktimān* (the possessor of power), being inseparable, we have to comprehend this issue in its proper perspective in order to dispel any misconception.

Some religious books and preachers distort the true meaning of total surrender to God. They say: "Do whatever you like. Pray to God. Worship Him. All your sins will be washed away." This is a pernicious and mischievous concept. Once you realize God and fully surrender to Him, you should avoid evils and vices and adhere to virtues and righteousness. You see God in all and all in God Who is immanent and transcendent. When you reach this state of spiritual summit, you cannot do any injury to anybody. Ritual prayers and worship, without spiritual transformation, shall not give *mokṣa* (liberation) to anybody. You must come out of the mud and wash your feet. You must not enter into the mud again. Annihilate your ego. Instead of being an individual self, become the Universal Self and that is the hidden meaning of "the annihilation of yourself." This transformation is possible by means of *karma-yoga, jñāna-yoga* or *bhakti-yoga,* or a blend of any two or all the three. In verse 18.66 of the *BG*, the Lord emphatically says that Arjuna (the algebraic *X*) can transform himself by surrendering to God. Once you surrender to the Supreme Self, being merciful, He will extend His hands to lift you even from the abyss to the topmost state. He will pull you into Himself. You will merge in Him. After being merged, you will not be nihil; you will be the Plenum. You will not be a helpless creature; you will become God, the non-dual *Brahman*.

This is the concept of *mokṣa* in the Advaita Vedānta. In no other religious scripture or philosophy do we find such highest level of optimism. It is you to make yourself a demon; it is you who can make yourself God.

**18.16: Free Will**

On this topic, two schools of thought prevail in philosophy. One pleads for determinism and the other for indeterminism. According to the former school, everything has been predetermined and there is no scope at all for free will. This is a rigid type of determinism. The latter school rejects the concept of determinism and speaks in favour of indeterminism. It holds the concept of chance, randomness and chaos. According to indeterminism, no certainty can be predicted except the probability and an event becomes an event only after its occurrence.

There is a school of deterministic philosophy that accepts predetermination without recognizing a predeterminer. It is an atheistic school that seems to be irrational. What is the mechanism of predeterminism in the absence of a predeterminer? This question is avoided and remains unanswered.

There is a sub-school of determinism that is theistic, that discards free will, speaks in favour of predeterminism and throws all blames on the shoulders of God. It apparently eulogizes God and does not blame Him. "I do and make others do. There is no doer other than I alone." "I know what *dharma* (righteousness) is. I do not have tendencies to act righteously. I know what *adharma* (unrighteousness) is. I do not have tendencies to refrain from the acts of unrighteousness. O Hṛṣīkeśa (Vāsudeva, God), I act in whatever way you, dwelling in my heart, engage me." (Quoted from the *Pāṇḍava-Gītā*).

There is a travesty of truth in the two quotations given in the foregoing paragraph. If these ideas are accepted, religions, agnostic ethics and theistic moral philosophy lose their relevance. There must be accountability in religions, agnosticism and secularism. Everyone is accountable for his/her actions. If the murderer, robber or rapist says that God has engaged him to do what he has done, religions, secular ethics and State laws become irrelevant and the concepts of virtues and vices become meaningless.

Let us know what the Lord says in the *BG* on this important philosophical issue.

> Thus has wisdom, more secret than all that is secret, been declared to you by Me. Reflecting over it fully, do as you wish.[65]

In this verse, the Lord gives His verdict in favour of free will. He puts two conditions: Before exercising one's free will in correct perspective, one should be aware of the pros and cons of the issue, with full knowledge on the subject. Secondly, one should analyse the facts, think over them, scrutinize them fully and comprehensively, and then only should one take a decision as one wishes.

The *BG* has nowhere declared commandments of do's and

---

65. *BG*, XVIII.63.

don't s. It throws light on the subject matter. It gives full freedom to the doer of the actions in taking decisions.

There have been references to the *prakṛti* or *svabhāva* (individual innate tendencies), born of the *karma-saṁskāras*, that impels a person to go on the path of *pravṛtti* or *nivṛtti*.[66] And it is said that a person cannot avoid the compelling urge of the *svabhāva*.[67] The question is: Can free will and the impelling *svabhāva* go together?

Both the concepts of *svabhāva* (*prakṛti*) and free will are correct. They seem to be incompatible, although not really so. Free will and *puruṣakāra* (individual efforts) are closely linked. An intellect (*buddhi*), rid of dirt and enlightened by the self, with strong determination, can counteract the impelling forces of *svabhāva* and even can annul the latter.

"An individual person has no free will. He is compelled by his *prakṛti* (nature), born of his *karma-saṁskāras*." If we accept this idea *in toto*, we cannot successfully explain accountability and cannot think of conscious efforts for ascending the ladder of spirituality to reach the apex point, the status of *Brahman*-hood. Secondly, if we accept the notion that God impels one to do or not to do every action, we cannot logically hold one responsible for one's good or bad actions.

We do accept the fact of a cosmic design. Derivatively, we have to accept a default blueprint. The acceptance of this fact gives a recognition to determinism. But this determinism is not rigid. A rigid determinism cannot allow creative evolution. Mother Sarasvatī has full freedom for playing Her *vīṇā* to generate musical notes; She is a creative artist. Every individual created being can customize the default settings by exercising his free will. We plead for a doctrine of elastic determinism. We cannot amend the fundamental features of the cosmic Constitution. We are to act without violating the cosmic laws. We cannot upset the cosmic

---

66. *BG*, V.14; XVII.2; XVIII.41-44; 47; 60.

67. *BG*, XVIII.59.

balance. Subject to these limitations, we can exercise our free will to change the blueprint of our building while we are in the constructing process.

### 18.17: The Gītā-Svādhyāya as a Jñāna-Yajña and Benefits Therefrom

The *BG* completes its main teaching with the declaration of verse 18.66. There are still some more verses after it. In the present section, we discuss those verses that describe the *Gītā-svādhyāya* as a *jñāna-yajña* and the benefits obtained therefrom.

Before we discuss the individual verses, we would give the meanings of three words stated in the caption. These words are: *svādhyāya, jñāna* and *yajña*. Originally, *svādhyāya* means "the study of the Vedas." But its meaning is more extensive and expansive than this specific one. It means "the study of any good scripture that promotes the understanding of the Reality, of spirituality in general, of ethical values, and of self-transformation from animality to humanity, from humanity to divinity, leading finally to the apex state of Godhead." The word *jñāna* literally means "knowledge." But, in the Vedānta, unless otherwise stated, it means "knowledge on *Brahman*." The verb-root *yaj* means "to adore or honour with oblation," "to worship," "to sacrifice." The word *yajña*, derived from the verb-root *yaj*, means "oblation," "worship," "prayer," "devotion," "offering," "giving away for the satisfaction or welfare of others at the cost of even one's own comforts." The last meaning is otherwise stated as "sacrifice (*tyāga*)." One must not misunderstand "sacrifice" as "killing birds, animals, or even human beings and offering their flesh and blood to a so-called deity." Such inhuman, cruel and ignorant superstition is known as *vali*. Of course, this word is also used for self-sacrifice for a good cause. Spiritual scriptures like the Vedas, the Upaniṣads and the *BG* are against violence and cannot preach in favour of animal- or human-sacrifice.

The first verse in this section (18.67) declares the incompetence of some persons for *jñāna-yajña*.

> This (scripture) which has been taught to you is never to be told to one who is devoid of austerities, nor to a non-devotee, nor to one who desires not to listen, nor to one who reviles Me.[68]

This verse directly focuses the non-eligibility of persons for the study of the *BG*. It also indirectly gives a description of the eligibility. Next are set forth the benefits accruing to one who propagates the Lord's teachings in the *BG*.

> He who, nurturing utmost devotion to Me, will teach this supreme secret to My devotees shall doubtlessly come to Me alone.[69]

The person who propagates the profound philosophy of the *BG* must be an unsverving devotee of the Lord. And he should hand over this knowledge to devotees only. Such a devotee who carries this spiritual message to devotees desirous of learning it attains liberation.

> None among men, other than he, does a dearer service to Me, nor shall there be another on the earth dearer to Me than he.[70]

Verses 18.68-69 eulogize a devotee who does *jñāna-yajña* by imparting the knowledge of the *BG* to spiritually inclined persons. Such a devotee is the dearest one to the Lord and he goes to the Lord alone.

Now the benefits accrued to the reader of the *BG* are described by the Lord.

> He who will study this righteous dialogue between us will worship Me by *jñāna-yajña*; this is My view.[71]

There may be some others who are unable to study the *BG*. They should hear the *BG* for their emancipation.

> The person who, full of faith and free from malice, even listens

---

68. *BG*, XVIII.67.
69. *BG*, XVIII.68.
70. *BG*, XVIII.69.
71. *BG*, XVIII.70.

> to the *Gītā*, also being liberated, shall attain to the auspicious realms reserved for persons of righteous deeds.[72]

This section deals with *jñana-yajña*, with special reference to the *svādhyāya* of the *Gītā*. Those who teach the message of the *Gītā*, who read this sacred scripture and who listen to it perform *jñāna-yajña*. Any person belonging to any of these three categories attains liberation (*mokṣa*).

What is the mechanism of being liberated by doing *jñāna-yajña*? The knowledge of the message of the *Gītā* helps a person in a number of ways. He gets *jñana* (knowledge) on *Brahman*, on what it is, on the nature of the universe and on all spiritual matters. This knowledge helps him work without attachment. He becomes a staunch devotee of God. He surrenders to God. And what else shall be the final outcome other than liberation or emancipation?

### 18.18: Arjuna's Delusion Destroyed

Some pseudo-pundits misinterpret the *BG*, especially its eleventh chapter. They have no competence for the study of this scripture. Being spiritually bankrupt, none can understand the higher philosophical message of this sacred scripture. These pseudo-pundits say that Śrīkṛṣṇa stupefied Arjuna by exhibiting some black magic, vividly narrated in the eleventh chapter of the *BG*. The sceptics say: "Arjuna, after being hypnotized and stunned with astonishment, mechanically obeyed what Śrīkṛṣṇa commanded."

God is formless. He is immanent in the universe. He is also transcendent to the universe. How can one see formless God in a form by one's naked eyes? The true divine vision must be the Cosmic Vision. And the Cosmic Vision is not common place. A perfected *yogī* can have that vision. A person, with divine compassion and blessings, can have that vision too. Cosmic Vision is not a figment of imagination. It is a fact for some deserving, blessed ones. Even without attaining to that state, a spiritually

72. *BG*, XVIII.71.

poetic vision is the Cosmic Vision, at a lower level, of course. When you cannot see the formless Reality, you can see the manifestations of that Reality in forms of the created universe if and only if you ascend to the higher spiritual level, or you get divine compassion. A perfected *yogī* can see the *viśva-rūpa;* a perfected *bhakta* (devotee) can have a vision of the *viśva-rūpa.* After listening to the *Bhagavad-Gītā* from the mouth of the Lord, Arjuna became a perfected *bhakta.* He became deserving for getting the compassion of the Lord.

The Cosmic Vision of Arjuna served as an eye-opener and removed his veil of ignorance. The *BG* has not ended in the eleventh chapter. Seven more chapters follow the eleventh one. Nowhere in the *BG,* has the Lord commanded Arjuna. Nowhere in the *BG,* are do's and don'ts, prescriptions and proscriptions recorded. The pages of ignorance and wisdom have been objectively unfolded. Arjuna had the full freedom of questioning the Lord and getting his doubts clarified. Finally, in verse 18.63, the Lord advises: "Thus, has wisdom been declared to you by Me. Consider it critically and scrutinize it thoroughly. Take your own decision. Do as you wish."

Where are the alleged commandments? A good teacher, after finishing his teaching, asks the pupil: "Are your doubts clarified? Have you any more questions?" So does the Lord ask the following questions:

> Has this been heard by you, O Pārtha, with one-pointed concentration (with attentive mind)? O Wealth-Winner (Arjuna), has your delusion, wrought by ignorance, been dispelled?[73]

Arjuna answers to the questions of the Lord:

> O Acyuta (Kṛṣṇa, God), destroyed is (my) delusion. I have regained memory (knowledge) through Your grace. I am firm, with doubts gone. I will act according to your word.[74]

---

73. *BG,* XVIII.72.

74. *BG,* XVIII.73.

**18.19: Sañjaya's Conclusive Statements**

The teaching of the *BG* is practically over with the completion of the verse 18.73. In order to connect with the main story of the *Mahābhārata*, Sañjaya presents his concluding statements.

> Thus have I listened to this wonderful dialogue between Vāsudeva and the great-souled Pārtha (Arjuna), causing my hair to stand on end.[75]
>
> Due to the grace of Vyāsa, I have heard this most secret and supreme Yoga, directly from Kṛṣṇa, the Lord of Yoga, Himself declaring it.[76]

Due to the favour of Vyāsa, Sañjaya got the power of clairvoyance and clairaudience. It was, therefore, possible for him to see what happened in the battlefield, to hear the dialogue between Kṛṣṇa and Arjuna and to learn yoga from the Lord of Yoga who Himself declared it.

Vyāsa has portrayed Śrīkṛṣṇa as God (*Bhagavān*) in the *BG*. One has the liberty to accept Śrīkṛṣṇa as God or to accept Him as a man. Some Vedic organizations, very secretively, misinterpret the word *yogeśvara*. According to them, *yogeśvara* means "a master *yogī*." They do not give recognition to *avatāras*. They steadfastly hold the opinion that God who is formless does never take a form, human or otherwise. It is not argued here whether they are right or wrong. But it is a fact that Vyāsa's Śrīkṛṣṇa is the Lord of the universe (*jagadīśvara*) and that He was not a master *yogī*. In Śaṅkara's language, Śrīkṛṣṇa is the Lord of all *yogas* (*sarvayogānām īśvaraḥ*). The *yogīs*, in meditation, link their selves (*ātmās*) with this *Yogeśvara* who is *Parameśvara, Paramātmā, Bhagavān* (God). We are firm about the notion that God is formless and unborn. At the same time, we do not consider the body of Śrīkṛṣṇa as a normal human body. The whole universe is virtual and phenomenal. Our human bodies, being material, are empirical and phenomenal. In

75. *BG*, XVIII.74.

76. *BG*, XVIII.75.

contrast, the body of *Yogeśvara* is illusory, conjured by His power, *Māyā*, as desired by the Lord. Through the agency of the power of God, the whole universe has been created. Can't She create an illusory body for Her Lord?

Sañjaya continues further in his concluding statements:

> O king, as I recall again and again this wonderful and holy dialogue between Keśava (Śrīkṛṣṇa) and Arjuna, I repeatedly rejoice.[77]

> Repeatedly calling to mind the most wonderful form of Hari (Kṛṣṇa), great is my amazement, O king, and I rejoice again and again.[78]

> Wherever is Kṛṣṇa, the Lord of Yoga, wherever is Pārtha (Arjuna), the wielder of the bow (the archer), there dwell prosperity, victory, happiness and sound policy; such is my conviction.[79]

Arjuna, the archer, symbolizes a person with the four types of *puruṣārtha*s, namely, *dharma, artha, kāma*, and *mokṣa*. Not a single item of these four can be achieved without the mercy of God. On the other hand, God does not directly act. Had it been the case, Śrīkṛṣṇa would have fought the war instead of Arjuna. Both God's grace and human endeavour combinedly bring success. The human endeavour must be in tune with the will of the Almighty and in conformity with cosmic laws. Then only does divine grace shower. This ideal condition prevailed in favour of the Pāṇḍavas.

In this last verse of the *BG*, Sañjaya foretold the inevitable consequence of the Mahābhārata War. He indirectly, but without ambiguity, told the blind king, Dhṛtarāṣṭra, that the Kauravas would be defeated and all the sons of Dhṛtarāṣṭra would be killed in the War. After hearing what Sañjaya told, deluded Dhṛtarāṣṭra should have changed his stubborn attitude. But his *putra-moha* (deluded attachment to his sons) and *rāṣṭra-moha* (deluded

77. *BG*, XVIII.76.
78. *BG*, XVIII.77.
79. *BG*, XVIII.78.

attachment to the kingdom and throne) impelled him not to change his mind and decision. A man convinced against his will is of the same opinion still. The result was the total disaster and ruination of the Kaurava family and the intolerable agony of the blind king and his queen, Gāndhārī. In conformity with cosmic laws, the end was the victory of *dharma* (righteousness) and the defeat of *adharma* (unrighteousness).

# Original Text and Transliteration

## 1. अर्जुनविषादयोगः

**धृतराष्ट्र उवाच —**

धर्मक्षेत्रे कुरुक्षेत्रे समवेता युयुत्सवः ।
मामकाः पाण्डवाश्चैव किमकुर्वत सञ्जय ॥१॥

***dhṛtarāṣṭra uvāca —***

*dharma-kṣetre kurukṣetre samavetā yuyutsavaḥ,*
*māmakāḥ pāṇḍavāś caiva kim akurvata sañjaya* ॥1 ॥

**सञ्जय उवाच —**

दृष्ट्वा तु पाण्डवानीकं व्यूढं दुर्योधनस्तदा ।
आचार्यमुपसङ्गम्य राजा वचनमब्रवीत् ॥२॥

***sañjaya uvāca —***

*dṛṣṭvā tu pāṇḍavānīkaṁ vyūḍhaṁ duryodhanas tadā* ।
*ācāryam upasaṅgamya rājā vacanam abravīt* ॥2 ॥

पश्यैतां पाण्डुपुत्राणामाचार्य महतीं चमूम् ।
व्यूढां द्रुपदपुत्रेण तव शिष्येण धीमता ॥३॥

*paśyaitāṁ pāṇḍu-putrāṇām ācārya mahatīṁ camūm* ।
*vyūḍhāṁ drupada-putreṇa tava śiṣyeṇa dhīmatā* ॥3 ॥

अत्र शूरा महेष्वासा भीमार्जुनसमा युधि ।
युयुधानो विराटश्च द्रुपदश्च महारथः ॥४॥

*atra śūrā maheṣvāsā bhīmārjunasamā yudhi* ।
*yuyudhāno virāṭaś ca drupadaś ca mahārathaḥ* ॥4 ॥

धृष्टकेतुश्चेकितानः काशिराजश्च वीर्यवान् ।
पुरुजित्कुन्तिभोजश्च शैब्यश्च नरपुङ्गवः ॥५॥

*dhṛṣṭaketuś cekitānaḥ kāśirājaś ca vīryavān* ।
*purujit kuntibhojaś ca śaibyaś ca narapuṅgavaḥ* ॥5 ॥

युधामन्युश्च विक्रान्त उत्तमौजाश्च वीर्यवान् ।
सौभद्रो द्रौपदेयाश्च सर्व एव महारथाः ॥६॥

*yudhāmanyuś ca vikrānta uttamaujāś ca vīryavān* ।
*saubhadro draupadeyāś ca sarva eva mahārathāḥ* ॥6 ॥

अस्माकं तु विशिष्टा ये तान्निबोध द्विजोत्तम ।
नायका मम सैन्यस्य संज्ञार्थं तान्ब्रवीमि ते ॥७॥

*asmākaṁ tu viśiṣṭā ye tān nibodha dvijottama* ।
*nāyakā mama sainyasya saṁjñārthaṁ tān bravīmi te* ॥7 ॥

भवान्भीष्मश्च कर्णश्च कृपश्च समितिञ्जयः ।
अश्वत्थामा विकर्णश्च सौमदत्तिस्तथैव च ॥८॥

*bhavān bhīṣmaś ca karṇaś ca kṛpaś ca samitiñjayaḥ* ।
*aśvatthāmā vikarṇaś ca saumadattis tathaiva ca* ॥8 ॥

अन्ये च बहवः शूरा मदर्थे त्यक्तजीविताः ।
नानाशस्त्रप्रहरणाः सर्वे युद्धविशारदाः ॥९॥

*anye ca bahavaḥ śūrā mad-arthe tyakta-jīvitāḥ* ।
*nānā-śastra-praharanāḥ sarve yuddha-viśāradāḥ* ॥9 ॥

अपर्याप्तं तदस्माकं बलं भीष्माभिरक्षितम् ।
पर्याप्तं त्विदमेतेषां बलं भीमाभिरक्षितम् ॥१०॥

*aparyāptaṁ tad asmākaṁ balaṁ bhīṣmābhirakṣitam* ।
*paryāptaṁ tvidam eteṣāṁ balaṁ bhīmābhirakṣitam* ॥10 ॥

अयनेषु च सर्वेषु यथाभागमवस्थिताः ।
भीष्ममेवाभिरक्षन्तु भवन्तः सर्व एव हि ॥११॥

*ayaneṣu ca sarveṣu yathā-bhāgam avasthitāḥ* ।
*bhīṣmam evābhirakṣantu bhavantaḥ sarva eva hi* ॥11 ॥

तस्य सञ्जनयन्हर्षं कुरुवृद्धः पितामहः ।
सिंहनादं विनद्योच्चैः शङ्खं दध्मौ प्रतापवान् ॥१२॥

*tasya sañjanayan harṣaṁ kuru-vṛddhaḥ pitāmahaḥ* ।
*siṁhanādaṁ vinadyoccaiḥ śaṅkhaṁ dadhmau pratāpavān* ॥12 ॥

ततः शङ्खाश्च भेर्यश्च पणवानकगोमुखाः ।
सहसैवाभ्यहन्यन्त स शब्दस्तुमुलोऽभवत् ॥१३॥

*tataḥ śaṅkhāś ca bheryaś ca paṇavānaka-gomukhāḥ* ।
*sahasaivābhyahanyanta sa śabdas tumulo 'bhavat* ॥13 ॥

ततः श्वेतैर्हयैर्युक्ते महति स्यन्दने स्थितौ ।
माधवः पाण्डवश्चैव दिव्यौ शङ्खौ प्रदध्मतुः ॥१४॥

*tataḥ śvetair hayair yukte mahati syandane sthitau* ।
*mādhavaḥ pāṇḍavaś caiva divyau śaṅkhau pradadhmatuḥ* ॥14 ॥

पाञ्चजन्यं हृषीकेशो देवदत्तं धनञ्जयः ।
पौण्ड्रं दध्मौ महाशङ्खं भीमकर्मा वृकोदरः ॥१५॥

*pāñcajanyaṁ hṛṣīkeśo devadattaṁ dhanañjayaḥ* ।
*pauṇḍraṁ dadhmau mahā-śaṅkhaṁ bhīma-karmā vṛkodaraḥ* ॥15 ॥

अनन्तविजयं राजा कुन्तीपुत्रो युधिष्ठिरः ।
नकुलः सहदेवश्च सुघोषमणिपुष्पकौ ॥१६॥

*anantavijayaṁ rājā kuntī-putro yudhiṣṭhiraḥ* ।
*nakulaḥ sahadevaś ca sughoṣa-maṇipuṣpakau* ॥16 ॥

काश्यश्च परमेष्वासः शिखण्डी च महारथः ।
धृष्टद्युम्नो विराटश्च सात्यकिश्चापराजितः ॥१७॥

*kāśyaś ca parameṣvāsaḥ śikhaṇḍī ca mahārathaḥ* ।
*dhṛṣṭadyumno virāṭaś ca sātyakiś cāparājitaḥ* ॥17 ॥

द्रुपदो द्रौपदेयाश्च सर्वशः पृथिवीपते ।
सौभद्रश्च महाबाहुः शङ्खान्दध्मुः पृथक्पृथक् ॥१८॥

*drupado draupadeyāś ca sarvaśaḥ pṛthivīpate* ।
*saubhadraś ca mahābāhuḥ śaṅkhān dadhmuḥ pṛthakpṛthak* ॥18 ॥

स घोषो धार्तराष्ट्राणां हृदयानि व्यदारयत् ।
नभश्च पृथिवीं चैव तुमुलो व्यनुनादयन् ॥१९॥

*sa ghoṣo dhārtarāṣṭrāṇāṁ hṛdayāni vyadārayat* ।
*nabhaś ca pṛthivīṁ caiva tumulo vyanunādayan* ॥19 ॥

अथ व्यवस्थितान्दृष्ट्वा धार्तराष्ट्रान्कपिध्वजः ।
प्रवृत्ते शस्त्रसंपाते धनुरुद्यम्य पाण्डवः ॥२०॥

हृषीकेशं तदा वाक्यमिदमाह महीपते ।

*atha vyavasthitān dṛṣṭvā dhārtarāṣṭrān kapidhvajaḥ* ।
*pravṛtte śastra-saṁpāte dhanur udyamya pāṇḍavaḥ* ॥20 ॥

*hṛṣīkeśaṁ tadā vākyam idam āha mahīpate* ।

**अर्जुन उवाच —**

सेनयोरुभयोर्मध्ये रथं स्थापय मेऽच्युत ॥२१॥

***arjuna uvāca —***

*senayor ubhayor madhye rathaṁ sthāpaya me 'cyuta* ॥21 ॥

यावदेतान्निरीक्षेऽहं योद्धुकामानवस्थितान् ।
कैर्मया सह योद्धव्यमस्मिन्रणसमुद्यमे ॥२२॥

*yāvad etān nirīkṣe 'haṁ yoddhu-kāmān avasthitān* ।
*kair mayā saha yoddhavyam asmin raṇa-samudyame* ॥22 ॥

योत्स्यमानानवेक्षेऽहं य एतेऽत्र समागताः ।
धार्तराष्ट्रस्य दुर्बुद्धेर्युद्धे प्रियचिकीर्षवः ॥२३॥

*yotsyamānān avekṣe 'haṁ ya ete 'tra samāgatāḥ* ।
*dhārtarāṣṭrasya durbuddher yuddhe priyacikīrṣavaḥ* ॥23 ॥

**सञ्जय उवाच —**

एवमुक्तो हृषीकेशो गुडाकेशेन भारत ।
सेनयोरुभयोर्मध्ये स्थापयित्वा रथोत्तमम् ॥२४॥

***sañjaya uvāca —***

*evam ukto hṛṣīkeśo guḍākeśena bhārata* ।
*senayor ubhayor madhye sthāpayitvā rathottamam* ॥24 ॥

भीष्मद्रोणप्रमुखतः सर्वेषां च महीक्षिताम् ।
उवाच पार्थ पश्यैतान् समवेतान्कुरूनिति ॥२५॥

*bhīṣma-droṇa-pramukhataḥ sarveṣāṁ ca mahīkṣitām* ।
*uvāca pārtha paśyaitān samavetān kurūn iti* ॥25 ॥

तत्रापश्यत्स्थितान् पार्थः पितृनथ पितामहान् ।
आचार्यान्मातुलान्भ्रातृन्पुत्रान्पौत्रान्सखींस्तथा ॥२६॥

*tatrāpaśyat sthitān pārthaḥ pitṝn atha pitāmahān* ।
*ācāryān mātulān bhrātṝn putrān pautrān sakhīṁs tathā* ॥26 ॥

श्वशुरान् सुहृदश्चैव सेनयोरुभयोरपि ।
तान्समीक्ष्य स कौन्तेयः सर्वान् बन्धूनवस्थितान् ॥२७॥
कृपया परयाविष्टो विषीदन्निदमब्रवीत् ।

*śvaśurān suhṛdaś caiva senayor ubhayor api* ।
*tān samīkṣya sa kaunteyaḥ sarvān bandhūn avasthitān* ॥27 ॥
*kṛpayā parayāviṣṭo viṣīdann idam abravīt* ।

**अर्जुन उवाच —**

दृष्ट्वेमं स्वजनं कृष्ण युयुत्सुं समुपस्थितम् ॥२८॥

***arjuna uvāca —***

*dṛṣṭvemaṁ svajanaṁ kṛṣṇa yuyutsuṁ samupasthitam* ॥28 ॥

सीदन्ति मम गात्राणि मुखं च परिशुष्यति ।
वेपथुश्च शरीरे मे रोमहर्षश्च जायते ॥२९॥

*sīdanti mama gātrāṇi mukhaṁ ca pariśuṣyati* ।
*vepathuś ca śarīre me roma-harṣaś ca jāyate* ॥29 ॥

गाण्डीवं स्रंसते हस्तात्त्वक्चैव परिदह्यते ।
न च शक्नोम्यवस्थातुं भ्रमतीव च मे मनः ॥३०॥

*gāṇḍīvaṁ sraṁsate hastāt tvak caiva paridahyate* ।
*na ca śaknomy avasthātuṁ bhramatīva ca me manaḥ* ॥30 ॥

निमित्तानि च पश्यामि विपरीतानि केशव ।
न च श्रेयोऽनुपश्यामि हत्वा स्वजनमाहवे ॥३१॥

*nimittāni ca paśyāmi viparītāni keśava* ।
*na ca śreyo 'nupaśyāmi hatvā svajanam āhave* ॥31 ॥

न कांक्षे विजयं कृष्ण न च राज्यं सुखानि च ।
किं नो राज्येन गोविन्द किं भोगैर्जीवितेन वा ॥३२॥

*na kāṅkṣe vijayaṁ kṛṣṇa na ca rājyaṁ sukhāni ca* ।
*kiṁ no rājyena govinda kiṁ bhogair jīvitena vā* ॥32 ॥

येषामर्थे काङ्क्षितं नो राज्यं भोगाः सुखानि च ।
त इमेऽवस्थिता युद्धे प्राणांस्त्यक्त्वा धनानि च ॥३३॥

*yeṣām arthe kāṅkṣitaṁ no rājyaṁ bhogāḥ sukhāni ca* ।
*ta ime 'vasthitā yuddhe prāṇāṁs tyaktvā dhanāni ca* ॥33 ॥

आचार्याः पितरः पुत्रास्तथैव च पितामहाः ।
मातुलाः श्वसुराः पौत्राः श्यालाः सम्बन्धिनस्तथा ॥३४॥

*ācāryāḥ pitaraḥ putrās tathaiva ca pitāmahāḥ* ।
*mātulāḥ śvasurāḥ pautrāḥ śyālāḥ sambandhinas tathā* ॥34 ॥

एतान्न हन्तुमिच्छामि घ्नतोऽपि मधुसूदन ।
अपि त्रैलोक्यराज्यस्य हेतोः किं नु महीकृते ॥३५॥

*etān na hantum icchāmi ghnato 'pi madhusūdana* ।
*api trailokya-rājyasya hetoḥ kiṁ nu mahīkṛte* ॥35 ॥

निहत्य धार्तराष्ट्रान्नः का प्रीतिः स्याज्जनार्दन ।
पापमेवाश्रयेदस्मान्हत्वैतानाततायिनः ॥३६॥

*nihatya dhārtarāṣṭrān naḥ kā prītiḥ syāj janārdana* ।
*pāpam evāśrayed asmān hatvaitān ātatāyinaḥ* ॥36 ॥

तस्मान्नार्हा वयं हन्तुं धार्तराष्ट्रान् स्वबान्धवान् ।
स्वजनं हि कथं हत्वा सुखिनः स्याम माधव ॥३७॥

*tasmān nārhā vayaṁ hantuṁ dhārtarāṣṭrān svabāndhavān* ।
*svajanaṁ hi kathaṁ hatvā sukhinaḥ syāma mādhava* ॥37 ॥

यद्यप्येते न पश्यन्ति लोभोपहतचेतसः
कुलक्षयकृतं दोषं मित्रद्रोहे च पातकम् ॥३८॥

*yady apy ete na paśyanti lobhopahata-cetasaḥ* ।
*kula-kṣaya-kṛtaṁ doṣaṁ mitra-drohe ca pātakam* ॥38 ॥

कथं न ज्ञेयमस्माभिः पापादस्मान्निवर्तितुम् ।
कुलक्षयकृतं दोषं प्रपश्यद्भिर्जनार्दन ॥३९॥

*kathaṁ na jñeyam asmābhiḥ pāpād asmān nivartitum* ।
*kula-kṣaya-kṛtaṁ doṣaṁ prapaśyadbhir janārdana* ॥39 ॥

कुलक्षये प्रणश्यन्ति कुलधर्माः सनातनाः ।
धर्मे नष्टे कुलं कृत्स्नमधर्मोऽभिभवत्युत ॥४०॥

*kula-kṣaye praṇaśyanti kula-dharmāḥ sanātanāḥ* ।
*dharme naṣṭe kulaṁ kṛtsnam adharmo 'bhibhavaty uta* ॥40 ॥

अधर्माभिभवात्कृष्ण प्रदुष्यन्ति कुलस्त्रियः ।
स्त्रीषु दुष्टासु वार्ष्णेय जायते वर्णसङ्करः ॥४१॥

*adharmābhibhavāt kṛṣṇa praduṣyanti kula-striyaḥ* ।
*strīṣu duṣṭāsu vārṣṇeya jāyate varṇa-saṅkaraḥ* ॥41 ॥

सङ्करो नरकायैव कुलघ्नानां कुलस्य च ।
पतन्ति पितरो ह्येषां लुप्तपिण्डोदकक्रियाः ॥४२॥

*saṅkaro narakāyaiva kulaghnānāṁ kulasya ca* ।
*patanti pitaro hy eṣāṁ lupta-piṇḍodaka-kriyaḥ* ॥42 ॥

दोषैरेतैः कुलघ्नानां वर्णसङ्करकारकैः ।
उत्साद्यन्ते जातिधर्माः कुलधर्माश्च शाश्वताः ॥४३॥

*doṣair etaiḥ kulaghnānāṁ varṇa-saṅkara-kārakaiḥ* ।
*utsādyante jāti-dharmāḥ kula-dharmāś ca śāśvatāḥ* ॥43 ॥

उत्सन्नकुलधर्माणां मनुष्याणां जनार्दन ।
नरकेऽनियतं वासो भवतीत्यनुशुश्रुम ॥४४॥

*utsanna-kula-dharmāṇāṁ manuṣyāṇāṁ janārdana* ।
*narake 'niyataṁ vāso bhavatīty anuśuśruma* ॥44 ॥

अहो बत महत्पापं कर्तुं व्यवसिता वयम् ।
यद्राज्यसुखलोभेन हन्तुं स्वजनमुद्यताः ॥४५॥

*aho bata mahat pāpaṁ kartuṁ vyavasitā vayam* ।
*yad rājya-sukha-lobhena hantuṁ svajanam udyatāḥ* ॥45 ॥

यदि मामप्रतीकारमशस्त्रं शस्त्रपाणयः ।
धार्तराष्ट्रा रणे हन्युस्तन्मे क्षेमतरं भवेत् ॥४६॥

*yadi mām apratīkāram aśastraṁ śastra-pāṇayaḥ* ।
*dhārtarāṣṭrā raṇe hanyus tan me kṣemataraṁ bhavet* ॥46 ॥

**सञ्जय उवाच —**

एवमुक्त्वार्जुनः सङ्ख्ये रथोपस्थ उपाविशत् ।
विसृज्य सशरं चापं शोकसंविग्नमानसः ॥४७॥

***sañjaya uvāca —***

*evam uktvārjunaḥ saṅkhye rathopastha upāviśat* ।
*visṛjya saśaraṁ cāpaṁ śoka-saṁvigna-mānasaḥ* ॥47 ॥

# 2. सांख्ययोगः

**सञ्जय उवाच —**

तं तथा कृपयाविष्टमश्रुपूर्णाकुलेक्षणम् ।
विषीदन्तमिदं वाक्यमुवाच मधुसूदनः ।।१।।

***sañjaya uvāca —***

*taṁ tathā kr̥payāviṣṭam aśrupūrṇākulekṣaṇam ।*
*viṣīdantam idaṁ vākyam uvāca madhusūdanaḥ* ॥1 ॥

**श्रीभगवानुवाच —**

कुतस्त्वा कश्मलमिदं विषमे समुपस्थितम् ।
अनार्यजुष्टमस्वर्ग्यमकीर्तिकरमर्जुन ।।२।।

***śrī bhagavān uvāca —***

*kutas tvā kaśmalam idaṁ viṣame samupasthitam ।*
*anārya-juṣṭam asvargyam akīrtikaram arjuna* ॥2 ॥

क्लैब्यं मा स्म गमः पार्थ नैतत्त्वय्युपपद्यते ।
क्षुद्रं हृदयदौर्बल्यं त्यक्त्वोत्तिष्ठ परन्तप ।।३।।

*klaibyaṁ mā sma gamaḥ pārtha naitat tvayy upapadyate ।*
*kṣudraṁ hr̥daya-daurbalyaṁ tyaktvottiṣṭha parantapa* ॥3 ॥

**अर्जुन उवाच —**

कथं भीष्ममहं सङ्ख्ये द्रोणं च मधुसूदन ।
इषुभिः प्रतियोत्स्यामि पूजार्हावरिसूदन ।।४।।

***arjuna uvāca —***

*kathaṁ bhīṣmam aham saṅkhye droṇaṁ ca madhusūdana ।*
*iṣubhiḥ pratiyotsyāmi pujārhāvarisūdana* ॥4 ॥

गुरूनहत्वा हि महानुभावान् श्रेयो भोक्तुं भैक्ष्यमपीह लोके ।
हत्वार्थकामांस्तु गुरूनिहैव भुञ्जीय भोगान् रुधिरप्रदिग्धान् ।।५।।

*gurūn ahatvā hi mahānubhāvān śreyo bhoktuṁ bhaikṣyam apīha loke ।*
*hatvārtha-kāmāṁs tu gurūn ihaiva bhuñjīya bhogān rudhira-pradigdhān* ॥5 ॥

न चैतद्विद्मः कतरन्नो गरीयो यद्वा जयेम यदि वा नो जयेयुः ।
यानेव हत्वा न जिजीविषामस्तेऽवस्थिताः प्रमुखे धार्तराष्ट्राः ॥६॥

*na caitad vidmaḥ kataran no garīyo yad vā jayema yadi vā no jayeyuḥ ।*
*yān eva hatvā na jijīviṣāmas te 'vasthitāḥ pramukhe dhārtarāṣṭrāḥ* ॥6॥

कार्पण्यदोषोपहतस्वभावः पृच्छामि त्वां धर्मसम्मूढचेताः ।
यच्छ्रेयः स्यान्निश्चितं ब्रूहि तन्मे शिष्यस्तेऽहं शाधि मां त्वां प्रपन्नम् ॥७॥

*kārpaṇya-doṣopahata-svabhāvaḥ pṛcchāmi tvāṁ dharma-sammūḍhacetāḥ ।*
*yac chreyaḥ syān niścitaṁ brūhi tan me śiṣyas te 'haṁ śādhi māṁ tvāṁ prapannam* ॥7॥

न हि प्रपश्यामि ममापनुद्याद् यच्छोकमुच्छोषणमिन्द्रियाणाम् ।
अवाप्य भूमावसपत्नमृद्धं राज्यं सुराणामपि चाधिपत्यम् ॥८॥

*na hi prapaśyāmi mamāpanudyād yac chokam ucchoṣaṇam indriyāṇām ।*
*avāpya bhūmāv asapatnam ṛddhaṁ rājyaṁ surāṇām api cādhipatyam* ॥8॥

**सञ्जय उवाच —**

एवमुक्त्वा हृषीकेशं गुडाकेशः परन्तप ।
न योत्स्य इति गोविन्दमुक्त्वा तूष्णीं बभूव ह ॥९॥

***sañjaya uvāca —***

*evam uktvā hṛṣīkeśaṁ guḍākeśaḥ parantapa ।*
*na yotsya iti govindam uktvā tūṣṇīṁ babhūva ha* ॥9॥

तमुवाच हृषीकेशः प्रहसन्निव भारत ।
सेनयोरुभयोर्मध्ये विषीदन्तमिदं वचः ॥१०॥

*tam uvāca hṛṣīkeśaḥ prahasann iva bhārata ।*
*senayor ubhayor madhye viṣīdan tam idaṁ vacaḥ* ॥10॥

**श्रीभगवानुवाच —**

अशोच्यानन्वशोचस्त्वं प्रज्ञावादांश्च भाषसे ।
गतासूनगतासूंश्च नानुशोचन्ति पण्डिताः ॥११॥

**śrī bhagavān uvāca —**

*aśocyān anvaśocas tvaṁ prajñā-vādāṁś ca bhāṣase* ।
*gatāsūn agatāsūṁś ca nānuśocanti paṇḍitāḥ* ॥11 ॥

न त्वेवाहं जातु नासं न त्वं नेमे जनाधिपाः ।
न चैव न भविष्यामः सर्वे वयमतः परम् ॥१२॥

*na tvevāhaṁ jātu nāsaṁ na tvaṁ neme janādhipāḥ* ।
*na caiva na bhaviṣyāmaḥ sarve vayam ataḥ param* ॥12 ॥

देहिनोऽस्मिन्यथा देहे कौमारं यौवनं जरा ।
तथा देहान्तरप्राप्तिर्धीरस्तत्र न मुह्यति ॥१३॥

*dehino 'smin yathā dehe kaumāraṁ yauvanaṁ jarā* ।
*tathā dehā 'ntara-prāptir dhīras tatra na muhyati* ॥13 ॥

मात्रास्पर्शास्तु कौन्तेय शीतोष्णसुखदुःखदाः ।
आगमापायिनोऽनित्यास्तांस्तितिक्षस्व भारत ॥१४॥

*mātrā-sparśās tu kaunteya śītoṣṇa-sukha-duḥkhadāḥ* ।
*āgamāpāyino 'nityās tāṁs titikṣasva bhārata* ॥14 ॥

यं हि न व्यथयन्त्येते पुरुषं पुरुषर्षभ ।
समदुःखसुखं धीरं सोऽमृतत्वाय कल्पते ॥१५॥

*yaṁ hi na vyathayanty ete puruṣaṁ puruṣarṣabha* ।
*sama-duḥkha-sukhaṁ dhīraṁ so 'mṛtatvāya kalpate* ॥15 ॥

नासतो विद्यते भावो नाभावो विद्यते सतः ।
उभयोरपि दृष्टोऽन्तस्त्वनयोस्तत्त्वदर्शिभिः ॥१६॥

*nāsato vidyate bhāvo nābhāvo vidyate sataḥ* ।
*ubhayor api dṛṣṭo 'ntas-tv anayos tattva-darśibhiḥ* ॥16 ॥

अविनाशि तु तद्विद्धि येन सर्वमिदं ततम् ।
विनाशमव्ययस्यास्य न कश्चित्कर्तुमर्हति ॥१७॥

*avināśi tu tad viddhi yena sarvam idaṁ tatam* ।
*vināśam avyayasyāsya na kaścit kartum arhati* ॥17 ॥

अन्तवन्त इमे देहा नित्यस्योक्ताः शरीरिणः ।
अनाशिनोऽप्रमेयस्य तस्माद्युध्यस्व भारत ॥१८॥

*antavanta ime dehā nityasyoktāḥ śarīriṇaḥ* ।
*anāśino 'prameyasya tasmād yudhyasva bhārata* ॥18 ॥

य एनं वेत्ति हन्तारं यश्चैनं मन्यते हतम् ।
उभौ तौ न विजानीतो नायं हन्ति न हन्यते ॥१९॥

*ya enaṁ vetti hantāraṁ yaś cainaṁ manyate hatam* ।
*ubhau tau na vijānīto nāyaṁ hanti na hanyate* ॥19 ॥

न जायते म्रियते वा कदाचिन्नायं भूत्वा भविता वा न भूयः ।
अजो नित्यः शाश्वतोऽयं पुराणो न हन्यते हन्यमाने शरीरे ॥२०॥

*na jāyate mriyate vā kadācin nāyaṁ bhūtvā bhavitā vā na bhūyaḥ* ।
*ajo nityaḥ śāśvato 'yaṁ purāṇo na hanyate hanyamāne śarīre* ॥20 ॥

वेदाविनाशिनं नित्यं य एनमजमव्ययम् ।
कथं स पुरुषः पार्थ कं घातयति हन्ति कम् ॥२१॥

*vedāvināśinaṁ nityaṁ ya enam ajam avyayam* ।
*kathaṁ sa puruṣaḥ pārtha kaṁ ghātayati hanti kam* ॥21 ॥

वासांसि जीर्णानि यथा विहाय नवानि गृह्णाति नरोऽपराणि ।
तथा शरीराणि विहाय जीर्णान्यन्यानि संयाति नवानि देही ॥२२॥

*vāsāṁsi jīrṇāni yathā vihāya navāni gṛhṇāti naro 'parāṇi* ।
*tathā śarīrāṇi vihāya jīrṇāny-anyāni saṁyāti navāni dehī* ॥22 ॥

नैनं छिन्दन्ति शस्त्राणि नैनं दहति पावकः ।
न चैनं क्लेदयन्त्यापो न शोषयति मारुतः ॥२३॥

*nainaṁ chindanti śastrāṇi nainaṁ dahati pāvakaḥ* ।
*na cainaṁ kledayanty āpo na śoṣayati mārutaḥ* ॥23 ॥

अच्छेद्योऽयमदाह्योऽयमक्लेद्योऽशोष्य एव च ।
नित्यः सर्वगतः स्थाणुरचलोऽयं सनातनः ॥२४॥

*acchedyo 'yam adāhyo 'yam akledyo 'śoṣya eva ca* ।
*nityaḥ sarvagataḥ sthāṇuı acalo 'yaṁ sanātanaḥ* ॥24 ॥

अव्यक्तोऽयमचिन्त्योऽयमविकार्योऽयमुच्यते ।
तस्मादेवं विदित्वैनं नानुशोचितुमर्हसि ॥२५॥

*avyakto 'yam acintyo 'yam avikāryo 'yam ucyate* ।
*tasmād evaṁ viditvainaṁ nānuśocitum arhasi* ॥25 ॥

अथ चैनं नित्यजातं नित्यं वा मन्यसे मृतम् ।
तथापि त्वं महाबाहो नैवं शोचितुमर्हसि ॥२६॥

*atha cainaṁ nitya-jātaṁ nityaṁ vā manyase mṛtam* ।
*tathāpi tvaṁ mahābāho naivaṁ śocitum arhasi* ॥26 ॥

जातस्य हि ध्रुवो मृत्युर्ध्रुवं जन्म मृतस्य च ।
तस्मादपरिहार्येऽर्थे न त्वं शोचितुमर्हसि ॥२७॥

*jātasya hi dhruvo mṛtyur dhruvaṁ janma mṛtasya ca* ।
*tasmād aparihārye 'rthe na tvaṁ śocitum arhasi* ॥27 ॥

अव्यक्तादीनि भूतानि व्यक्तमध्यानि भारत ।
अव्यक्तनिधनान्येव तत्र का परिदेवना ॥२८॥

*avyaktādīni bhūtāni vyakta-madhyāni bhārata* ।
*avyakta-nidhanāny eva tatra kā paridevanā* ॥28 ॥

आश्चर्यवत्पश्यति कश्चिदेनमाश्चर्यवद्वदति तथैव चान्यः ।
आश्चर्यवच्चैनमन्यः शृणोति श्रुत्वाप्येनं वेद न चैव कश्चित् ॥२९॥

*āścaryavat paśyati kaścid enam āścaryavad vadati tathaiva cānyaḥ* ।
*āścaryavac cainam anyaḥ śṛṇoti śrutvāpy enaṁ veda na caiva*
*kaścit* ॥29 ॥

देही नित्यमवध्योऽयं देहे सर्वस्य भारत ।
तस्मात्सर्वाणि भूतानि न त्वं शोचितुमर्हसि ॥३०॥

*dehī nityam avadhyo 'yaṁ dehe sarvasya bhārata* ।
*tasmāt sarvāṇi bhūtāni na tvaṁ śocitum arhasi* ॥30 ॥

स्वधर्ममपि चावेक्ष्य न विकम्पितुमर्हसि ।
धर्म्याद्धि युद्धाच्छ्रेयोऽन्यत्क्षत्रियस्य न विद्यते ॥३१॥

*svadharmam api cāvekṣya na vikampitum arhasi* ।
*dharmyād dhi yuddhācchreyo 'nyat kṣatriyasya na vidyate* ॥31 ॥

यदृच्छया चोपपन्नं स्वर्गद्वारमपावृतम् ।
सुखिनः क्षत्रियाः पार्थ लभन्ते युद्धमीदृशम् ॥३२॥

*yadṛcchayā copapannaṁ svarga-dvāram apāvṛtam* ।
*sukhinaḥ kṣatriyāḥ pārtha labhante yuddham īdṛśam* ॥32 ॥

अथ चेत्त्वमिमं धर्म्यं सङ्ग्रामं न करिष्यसि ।
ततः स्वधर्मं कीर्तिं च हित्वा पापमवाप्स्यसि ॥३३॥

*atha cet tvam imaṁ dharmyaṁ saṅgrāmaṁ na kariṣyasi* ।
*tataḥ svadharmaṁ kīrtiṁ ca hitvā pāpam avāpsyasi* ॥33 ॥

अकीर्तिं चापि भूतानि कथयिष्यन्तितेऽव्ययाम् ।
सम्भावितस्य चाकीर्तिर्मरणादतिरिच्यते ।।३४।।

*akīrtiṁ cāpi bhūtāni kathayiṣyantite 'vyayām* ।
*sambhāvitasya cākīrtir maraṇād atiricyate* ॥34 ॥

भयाद्रणादुपरतं मंस्यन्ते त्वां महारथाः ।
येषां च त्वं बहुमतो भूत्वा यास्यसि लाघवम् ।।३५।।

*bhayād raṇād uparataṁ maṁsyante tvāṁ mahārathāḥ* ।
*yeṣāṁ ca tvaṁ bahumato bhūtvā yāsyasi lāghavam* ॥35 ॥

अवाच्यवादांश्च बहून्वदिष्यन्ति तवाहिताः ।
निन्दन्तस्तव सामर्थ्यं ततो दुःखतरं नु किम् ।।३६।।

*avācya-vādāṁś ca bahūn vadiṣyanti tavāhitāḥ* ।
*nindantas tava sāmarthyaṁ tato duḥkhataraṁ nu kim* ॥36 ॥

हतो वा प्राप्स्यसि स्वर्गं जित्वा वा भोक्ष्यसे महीम् ।
तस्मादुत्तिष्ठ कौन्तेय युद्धाय कृतनिश्चयः ।।३७।।

*hato vā prāpsyasi svargaṁ jitvā vā bhokṣyase mahīm* ।
*tasmād uttiṣṭha kaunteya yuddhāya kṛta-niścayaḥ* ॥37 ॥

सुखदुःखे समे कृत्वा लाभालाभौ जयाजयौ ।
ततो युद्धाय युज्यस्व नैवं पापमवाप्स्यसि ।।३८।।

*sukha-duḥkhe same kṛtvā lābhālābhau jayājayau* ।
*tato yuddhāya yujyasva naivaṁ pāpam avāpsyasi* ॥38 ॥

एषा तेऽभिहिता साङ्ख्ये बुद्धिर्योगे त्विमां शृणु ।
बुद्ध्या युक्तो यया पार्थ कर्मबन्धं प्रहास्यसि ।।३९।।

*eṣā te 'bhihitā sāṅkhye buddhir yoge tvimāṁ śṛṇu* ।
*buddhyā yukto yayā pārtha karma-bandhaṁ prahāsyasi* ॥39 ॥

नेहाभिक्रमनाशोऽस्ति प्रत्यवायो न विद्यते ।
स्वल्पमप्यस्य धर्मस्य त्रायते महतो भयात् ।।४०।।

*nehābhikrama-nāśo 'sti pratyavāyo na vidyate* ।
*svalpam apy asya dharmasya trāyate mahato bhayāt* ॥40 ॥

व्यवसायात्मिका बुद्धिरेकेह कुरुनन्दन ।
बहुशाखा ह्यनन्ताश्च बुद्धयोऽव्यवसायिनाम् ।।४१।।

*vyavasāyātmikā buddhir ekeha kuru-nandana* ।
*bahu-śākhā hy anantāś ca buddhayo 'vyavasāyinām* ॥41 ॥

यामिमां पुष्पितां वाचं प्रवदन्त्यविपश्चितः ।
वेदवादरताः पार्थ नान्यदस्तीति वादिनः ॥४२॥

*yām imāṁ puṣpitāṁ vācaṁ pravadanty avipaścitaḥ* ।
*vedavāda-ratāḥ pārtha nānyad astīti vādinaḥ* ॥42 ॥

कामात्मानः स्वर्गपरा जन्मकर्मफलप्रदाम् ।
क्रियाविशेषबहुलां भोगैश्वर्यगतिं प्रति ॥४३॥

*kāmātmānaḥ svarga-parā janma-karma-phala-pradām* ।
*kriyā-viśeṣa-bahulāṁ bhogaiśvarya-gatiṁ prati* ॥43 ॥

भोगैश्वर्यप्रसक्तानां तयापहृतचेतसाम् ।
व्यवसायात्मिका बुद्धिः समाधौ न विधीयते ॥४४॥

*bhogaiśvarya-prasaktānāṁ tayāpahṛta-cetasām* ।
*vyavasāyātmikā buddhiḥ samādhau na vidhīyate* ॥44 ॥

त्रैगुण्यविषया वेदा निस्त्रैगुण्यो भवार्जुन ।
निर्द्वन्द्वो नित्यसत्त्वस्थो निर्योगक्षेम आत्मवान् ॥४५॥

*traiguṇya-viṣayā vedā nistraiguṇyo bhavārjuna* ।
*nirdvandvo nitya-sattvastho niryogakṣema ātmavān* ॥45 ॥

यावानर्थ उदपाने सर्वतः सम्प्लुतोदके ।
तावान्सर्वेषु वेदेषु ब्राह्मणस्य विजानतः ॥४६॥

*yāvān artha udapāne sarvataḥ samplutodake* ।
*tāvān sarveṣu vedeṣu brāhmaṇasya vijānataḥ* ॥46 ॥

कर्मण्येवाधिकारस्ते मा फलेषु कदाचन ।
मा कर्मफलहेतुर्भूर्मा ते सङ्गोऽस्त्वकर्मणि ॥४७॥

*karmaṇy evādhikāras te mā phaleṣu kadācana* ।
*mā karma-phala-hetur bhūr mā te saṅgo 'stv akarmaṇi* ॥47 ॥

योगस्थः कुरु कर्माणि सङ्गं त्यक्त्वा धनञ्जय ।
सिद्ध्यसिद्ध्योः समो भूत्वा समत्वं योग उच्यते ॥४८॥

*yogasthaḥ kuru karmāṇi saṅgaṁ tyaktvā dhanañjaya* ।
*siddhy-asiddhyoḥ samo bhūtvā samatvaṁ yoga ucyate* ॥48 ॥

दूरेण ह्यवरं कर्म बुद्धियोगाद्धनञ्जय ।
बुद्धौ शरणमन्विच्छ कृपणाः फलहेतवः ।।४९।।

*dūreṇa hy avaraṁ karma buddhi-yogād dhanañjaya* ।
*buddhau śaraṇam anviccha kṛpaṇāḥ phala-hetavaḥ* ॥49 ॥

बुद्धियुक्तो जहातीह उभे सुकृतदुष्कृते ।
तस्माद्योगाय युज्यस्व योगः कर्मसु कौशलम् ।।५०।।

*buddhi-yukto jahātīha ubhe sukṛta-duṣkṛte* ।
*tasmād yogāya yujyasva yogaḥ karmasu kauśalam* ॥50 ॥

कर्मजं बुद्धियुक्ता हि फलं त्यक्त्वा मनीषिणः ।
जन्मबन्धविनिर्मुक्ताः पदं गच्छन्त्यनामयम् ।।५१।।

*karmajaṁ buddhi-yuktā hi phalaṁ tyaktvā manīṣiṇaḥ* ।
*janma-bandha-vinirmuktāḥ padaṁ gacchanty anāmayam* ॥51 ॥

यदा ते मोहकलिलं बुद्धिर्व्यतितरिष्यति ।
तदा गन्तासि निर्वेदं श्रोतव्यस्य श्रुतस्य च ।।५२।।

*yadā te moha-kalilaṁ buddhir vyatitariṣyati* ।
*tadā gantāsi nirvedaṁ śrotavyasya śrutasya ca* ॥52 ॥

श्रुतिविप्रतिपन्ना ते यदा स्थास्यति निश्चला ।
समाधावचला बुद्धिस्तदा योगमवाप्स्यसि ।।५३।।

*śruti-vipratipannā te yadā sthāsyati niścalā* ।
*samādhāv acalā buddhis tadā yogam avāpsyasi* ॥53 ॥

**अर्जुन उवाच —**

स्थितप्रज्ञस्य का भाषा समाधिस्थस्य केशव ।
स्थितधीः किं प्रभाषेत किमासीत व्रजेत किम् ।।५४।।

***arjuna uvāca —***

*sthita-prajñasya kā bhāṣā samādhisthasya keśava* ।
*sthita-dhīḥ kiṁ prabhāṣeta kim āsīta vrajeta kim* ॥54 ॥

**श्रीभगवानुवाच —**

प्रजहाति यदा कामान्सर्वान्पार्थ मनोगतान् ।
आत्मन्येवात्मना तुष्टः स्थितप्रज्ञस्तदोच्यते ।।५५।।

***śrī bhagavān uvāca —***

*prajahāti yadā kāmān sarvān pārtha mano-gatān* ।
*ātmany-evātmanā tuṣṭaḥ sthita-prajñas tadocyate* ॥55 ॥

दुःखेष्वनुद्विग्नमनाः सुखेषु विगतस्पृहः ।
वीतरागभयक्रोधः स्थितधीर्मुनिरुच्यते ॥५६॥

*duḥkheṣv anudvigna-manāḥ sukheṣu vigata-spṛhaḥ* ।
*vīta-rāga-bhaya-krodhaḥ sthita-dhīr munir ucyate* ॥56 ॥

यः सर्वत्रानभिस्नेहस्तत्तत्प्राप्य शुभाशुभम् ।
नाभिनन्दति न द्वेष्टि तस्य प्रज्ञा प्रतिष्ठिता ॥५७॥

*yaḥ sarvatrānabhisnehas tat-tat prāpya śubhāśubham* ।
*nābhinandati na dveṣṭi tasya prajñā pratiṣṭhitā* ॥57 ॥

यदा संहरते चायं कूर्मोऽङ्गानीव सर्वशः ।
इन्द्रियाणीन्द्रियार्थेभ्यस्तस्य प्रज्ञा प्रतिष्ठिता ॥५८॥

*yadā saṁharate cāyaṁ kūrmo 'ṅgānīva sarvaśaḥ* ।
*indriyāṇīndriyārthebhyas tasya prajñā pratiṣṭhitā* ॥58 ॥

विषया विनिवर्तन्ते निराहारस्य देहिनः ।
रसवर्जं रसोऽप्यस्य परं दृष्ट्वा निवर्तते ॥५९॥

*viṣayā vinivartante nirāhārasya dehinaḥ* ।
*rasa-varjaṁ raso 'pyasya paraṁ dṛṣṭvā nivartate* ॥59 ॥

यततो ह्यपि कौन्तेय पुरुषस्य विपश्चितः ।
इन्द्रियाणि प्रमाथीनि हरन्ति प्रसभं मनः ॥६०॥

*yatato hy api kaunteya puruṣasya vipaścitaḥ* ।
*indriyāṇi pramāthīni haranti prasabhaṁ manaḥ* ॥60 ॥

तानि सर्वाणि संयम्य युक्त आसीत मत्परः ।
वशे हि यस्येन्द्रियाणि तस्य प्रज्ञा प्रतिष्ठिता ॥६१॥

*tāni sarvāṇi saṁyamya yukta āsīta mat-paraḥ* ।
*vaśe hi yasyendriyāṇi tasya prajñā pratiṣṭhitā* ॥61 ॥

ध्यायतो विषयान्पुंसः सङ्गस्तेषूपजायते ।
सङ्गात्सञ्जायते कामः कामात्क्रोधोऽभिजायते ॥६२॥

*dhyāyato viṣayān puṁsaḥ saṅgas teṣūpajāyate* ।
*saṅgāt sañjāyate kāmaḥ kāmāt krodho 'bhijāyate* ॥62 ॥

क्रोधाद्भवति सम्मोहः सम्मोहात्स्मृतिविभ्रमः ।
स्मृतिभ्रंशाद् बुद्धिनाशो बुद्धिनाशात्प्रणश्यति ।।६३।।

*krodhād bhavati sammohaḥ sammohāt smṛti-vibhramaḥ* ।
*smṛti-bhraṁśād buddhi-nāśo buddhi-nāśāt praṇaśyati* ॥63 ॥

रागद्वेषवियुक्तैस्तु विषयानिन्द्रियैश्चरन् ।
आत्मवश्यैर्विधेयात्मा प्रसादमधिगच्छति ।।६४।।

*rāga-dveṣa-viyuktais tu viṣayān indriyaiś caran* ।
*ātma-vaśyair vidheyātmā prasādam adhigacchati* ॥64 ॥

प्रसादे सर्वदुःखानां हानिरस्योपजायते ।
प्रसन्नचेतसो ह्याशु बुद्धिः पर्यवतिष्ठते ।।६५।।

*prasāde sarva-duḥkhānāṁ hānir asyopajāyate* ।
*prasanna-cetaso hy āśu buddhiḥ paryavatiṣṭhate* ॥65 ॥

नास्ति बुद्धिरयुक्तस्य न चायुक्तस्य भावना ।
न चाभावयतः शान्तिरशान्तस्य कुतः सुखम् ।।६६।।

*nāsti buddhir ayuktasya na cāyuktasya bhāvanā* ।
*na cābhāvayataḥ śāntir aśāntasya kutaḥ sukham* ॥66 ॥

इन्द्रियाणां हि चरतां यन्मनोऽनुविधीयते ।
तदस्य हरति प्रज्ञां वायुर्नावमिवाम्भसि ।।६७।।

*indriyāṇāṁ hi caratāṁ yan mano 'nuvidhīyate* ।
*tad asya harati prajñāṁ vāyur nāvam ivāmbhasi* ॥67 ॥

तस्माद्यस्य महाबाहो निगृहीतानि सर्वशः ।
इन्द्रियाणीन्द्रियार्थेभ्यस्तस्य प्रज्ञा प्रतिष्ठिता ।।६८।।

*tasmād yasya mahābāho nigṛhītāni sarvaśaḥ* ।
*indriyāṇīndriyārthebhyas-tasya prajñā pratiṣṭhitā* ॥68 ॥

या निशा सर्वभूतानां तस्यां जागर्ति संयमी ।
यस्यां जाग्रति भूतानि सा निशा पश्यतो मुनेः ।।६९।।

*yā niśā sarva-bhūtānāṁ tasyāṁ jāgarti saṁyamī* ।
*yasyāṁ jāgrati bhūtāni sā niśā paśyato muneḥ* ॥69 ॥

आपूर्यमाणमचलप्रतिष्ठं समुद्रमापः प्रविशन्ति यद्वत् ।
तद्वत्कामा यं प्रविशन्ति सर्वे स शान्तिमाप्नोति न कामकामी ।।७०।।

*āpūryamāṇam acala-pratiṣṭhaṁ samudram āpaḥ praviśanti yadvat* ।
*tadvat kāmā yaṁ praviśanti sarve sa śāntim āpnoti na kāma-kāmī* ॥70 ॥

विहाय कामान्यः सर्वान्पुमांश्चरति निःस्पृहः ।
निर्ममो निरहङ्कारः स शान्तिमधिगच्छति ॥७१॥

*vihāya kāmān yaḥ sarvān pumāṁś carati niḥspṛhaḥ* ।
*nirmamo nirahaṅkāraḥ sa śāntim adhigacchati* ॥71 ॥

एषा ब्राह्मी स्थितिः पार्थ नैनां प्राप्य विमुह्यति ।
स्थित्वास्यामन्तकालेऽपि ब्रह्मनिर्वाणमृच्छति ॥७२॥

*eṣā brāhmī sthitiḥ pārtha naināṁ prāpya vimuhyati* ।
*sthitvāsyām antakāle 'pi brahma-nirvāṇam ṛcchati* ॥72 ॥

## 3. कर्मयोगः

**अर्जुन उवाच —**

ज्यायसी चेत्कर्मणस्ते मता बुद्धिर्जनार्दन ।
तत्किं कर्मणि घोरे मां नियोजयसि केशव ॥१॥

***arjuna uvāca —***

*jyāyasī cet karmaṇas te matā buddhir janārdana* ।
*tat kiṁ karmaṇi ghore māṁ niyojayasi keśava* ॥1 ॥

व्यामिश्रेणेव वाक्येन बुद्धिं मोहयसीव मे ।
तदेकं वद निश्चित्य येन श्रेयोऽहमाप्नुयाम् ॥२॥

*vyāmiśreṇeva vākyena buddhiṁ mohayasīva me* ।
*tad ekaṁ vada niścitya yena śreyo 'ham āpnuyām* ॥2 ॥

**श्रीभगवानुवाच —**

लोकेऽस्मिन्द्विविधा निष्ठा पुरा प्रोक्ता मयानघ ।
ज्ञानयोगेन साङ्ख्यानां कर्मयोगेन योगिनाम् ॥३॥

***śrībhagavān uvāca —***

*loke 'smin dvividhā niṣṭhā purā proktā mayānagha* ।
*jñāna-yogena sāṅkhyānāṁ karma-yogena yoginām* ॥3 ॥

न कर्मणामनारम्भान्नैष्कर्म्यं पुरुषोऽश्नुते ।
न च सन्न्यसनादेव सिद्धिं समधिगच्छति ॥४॥

*na karmaṇām anārambhān naiṣkarmyaṁ puruṣo 'śnute* ।
*na ca sannyasanād eva siddhiṁ samadhigacchati* ॥4 ॥

न हि कश्चित्क्षणमपि जातु तिष्ठत्यकर्मकृत् ।
कार्यते ह्यवशः कर्म सर्वः प्रकृतिजैर्गुणैः ॥५॥

*na hi kaścit kṣaṇam api jātu tiṣṭhaty akarma-kṛt* ।
*kāryate hy avaśaḥ karma sarvaḥ prakṛtijair guṇaiḥ* ॥5 ॥

कर्मेन्द्रियाणि संयम्य य आस्ते मनसा स्मरन् ।
इन्द्रियार्थान्विमूढात्मा मिथ्याचारः स उच्यते ॥६॥

*karmendriyāṇi saṁyamya ya āste manasā smaran* ।
*indriyārthān vimūḍhātmā mithyācāraḥ sa ucyate* ॥6 ॥

यस्त्विन्द्रियाणि मनसा नियम्यारभतेऽर्जुन ।
कर्मेन्द्रियैः कर्मयोगमसक्तः स विशिष्यते ॥७॥

*yas tv indriyāṇi manasā niyamyārabhate 'rjuna* ।
*karmendriyaiḥ karma-yogam asaktaḥ sa viśiṣyate* ॥7 ॥

नियतं कुरु कर्म त्वं कर्म ज्यायो ह्यकर्मणः ।
शरीरयात्रापि च ते न प्रसिद्ध्येदकर्मणः ॥८॥

*niyataṁ kuru karma tvaṁ karma jyāyo hy akarmaṇaḥ* ।
*śarīra-yātrāpi ca te na prasiddhyed akarmaṇaḥ* ॥8 ॥

यज्ञार्थात्कर्मणोऽन्यत्र लोकोऽयं कर्मबन्धनः ।
तदर्थं कर्म कौन्तेय मुक्तसङ्गः समाचर ॥९॥

*yajñārthāt karmaṇo 'nyatra loko 'yaṁ karma-bandhanaḥ* ।
*tad arthaṁ karma kaunteya mukta-saṅgaḥ samācara* ॥9 ॥

सहयज्ञाः प्रजाः सृष्ट्वा पुरोवाच प्रजापतिः ।
अनेन प्रसविष्यध्वमेष वोऽस्त्विष्टकामधुक् ॥१०॥

*saha-yajñāḥ prajāḥ sṛṣṭvā purovāca prajāpatiḥ* ।
*anena prasaviṣyadhvam eṣa vo 'stv iṣṭa-kāmadhuk* ॥10 ॥

देवान्भावयतानेन ते देवा भावयन्तु वः ।
परस्परं भावयन्तः श्रेयः परमवाप्स्यथ ॥११॥

*devān bhāvayatānena te devā bhāvayantu vaḥ* ।
*parasparaṁ bhāvayantaḥ śreyaḥ param avāpsyatha* ॥11 ॥

इष्टान्भोगान्हि वो देवा दास्यन्ते यज्ञभाविताः ।
तैर्दत्तानप्रदायैभ्यो यो भुङ्क्ते स्तेन एव सः ॥१२॥

*iṣṭān bhogān hi vo devā dāsyante yajña-bhāvitāḥ* ।
*tair dattān apradāyaibhyo yo bhuṅkte stena eva saḥ* ॥12 ॥

यज्ञशिष्टाशिनः सन्तो मुच्यन्ते सर्वकिल्बिषैः ।
भुञ्जते ते त्वघं पापा ये पचन्त्यात्मकारणात् ॥१३॥

*yajña-śiṣṭāśinaḥ santo mucyante sarva-kilbiṣaiḥ* ।
*bhuñjate te tv aghaṁ pāpā ye pacanty ātma-kāraṇāt* ॥13 ॥

अन्नाद्भवन्ति भूतानि पर्जन्यादन्नसम्भवः ।
यज्ञाद्भवति पर्जन्यो यज्ञः कर्मसमुद्भवः ॥१४॥

*annād bhavanti bhūtāni parjanyād anna-sambhavaḥ* ।
*yajñād bhavati parjanyo yajñaḥ karma-samudbhavaḥ* ॥14 ॥

कर्म ब्रह्मोद्भवं विद्धि ब्रह्माक्षरसमुद्भवम् ।
तस्मात्सर्वगतं ब्रह्म नित्यं यज्ञे प्रतिष्ठितम् ॥१५॥

*karma brahmodbhavaṁ viddhi brahmā 'kṣara-samudbhavam* ।
*tasmāt sarvagataṁ brahma nityaṁ yajñe pratiṣṭhitam* ॥15 ॥

एवं प्रवर्तितं चक्रं नानुवर्तयतीह यः ।
अघायुरिन्द्रियारामो मोघं पार्थ स जीवति ॥१६॥

*evaṁ pravartitaṁ cakraṁ nānuvartayatīha yaḥ* ।
*aghāyur indriyārāmo moghaṁ pārtha sa jīvati* ॥16 ॥

यस्त्वात्मरतिरेव स्यादात्मतृप्तश्च मानवः ।
आत्मन्येव च सन्तुष्टस्तस्य कार्यं न विद्यते ॥१७॥

*yas tvātma-ratir eva syād ātma-tṛptaś ca mānavaḥ* ।
*ātmany eva ca saṁtuṣṭas tasya kāryaṁ na vidyate* ॥17 ॥

नैव तस्य कृतेनार्थो नाकृतेनेह कश्चन ।
न चास्य सर्वभूतेषु कश्चिदर्थव्यपाश्रयः ॥१८॥

*naiva tasya kṛtenārtho nākṛteneha kaścana* ।
*na cāsya sarva-bhūteṣu kaścid artha-vyapāśrayaḥ* ॥18 ॥

तस्मादसक्तः सततं कार्यं कर्म समाचर ।
असक्तो ह्याचरन्कर्म परमाप्नोति पूरुषः ॥१९॥

*tasmād asaktaḥ satataṁ kāryaṁ karma samācara ।*
*asakto hyācaran karma param āpnoti pūruṣaḥ* ॥19 ॥

कर्मणैव हि संसिद्धिमास्थिता जनकादयः ।
लोकसङ्ग्रहमेवापि सम्पश्यन्कर्तुमर्हसि ॥२०॥

*karmaṇaiva hi saṁsiddhim āsthitā janakādayaḥ ।*
*loka-saṁgraham evāpi saṁpaśyan kartum arhasi* ॥20 ॥

यद्यदाचरति श्रेष्ठस्तत्तदेवेतरो जनः ।
स यत्प्रमाणं कुरुते लोकस्तदनुवर्तते ॥२१॥

*yad yad ācarati śreṣṭhas tat tad evetaro janaḥ ।*
*sa yat pramāṇaṁ kurute lokas tad anuvartate* ॥21 ॥

न मे पार्थास्ति कर्तव्यं त्रिषु लोकेषु किञ्चन ।
नानवाप्तमवाप्तव्यं वर्त एव च कर्मणि ॥२२॥

*na me pārthāsti kartavyaṁ triṣu lokeṣu kiñcana ।*
*nānavāptam avāptavyaṁ varta eva ca karmaṇi* ॥22 ॥

यदि ह्यहं न वर्तेयं जातु कर्मण्यतन्द्रितः ।
मम वर्त्मानुवर्तन्ते मनुष्याः पार्थ सर्वशः ॥२३॥

*yadi hy ahaṁ na varteyaṁ jātu karmaṇy atandritaḥ ।*
*mama vartmānuvartante manuṣyāḥ pārtha sarvaśaḥ* ॥23 ॥

उत्सीदेयुरिमे लोका न कुर्यां कर्म चेदहम् ।
सङ्करस्य च कर्ता स्यामुपहन्यामिमाः प्रजाः ॥२४॥

*utsīdeyur ime lokā na kuryāṁ karma ced aham ।*
*saṅkarasya ca kartā syām upahanyām imāḥ prajāḥ* ॥24 ॥

सक्ताः कर्मण्यविद्वांसो यथा कुर्वन्ति भारत ।
कुर्याद्विद्वांस्तथासक्तश्चिकीर्षुर्लोकसङ्ग्रहम् ॥२५॥

*saktāḥ karmaṇy avidvāṁso yathā kurvanti bhārata ।*
*kuryād vidvāṁs tathāsaktaś cikīrṣur lokasaṅgraham* ॥25 ॥

न बुद्धिभेदं जनयेदज्ञानां कर्मसङ्गिनाम् ।
जोषयेत्सर्वकर्माणि विद्वान्युक्तः समाचरन् ॥२६॥

*na buddhi-bhedaṁ janayed ajñānāṁ karma-saṅginām* ।
*joṣayet sarva-karmāṇi vidvān yuktaḥ samācaran* ॥26 ॥

प्रकृतेः क्रियमाणानि गुणैः कर्माणि सर्वशः ।
अहङ्कारविमूढात्मा कर्ताहमिति मन्यते ॥२७॥

*prakṛteḥ kriyamāṇāni guṇaiḥ karmāṇi sarvaśaḥ* ।
*ahaṅkāra-vimūḍhātmā kartāham iti manyate* ॥27 ॥

तत्त्ववित्तु महाबाहो गुणकर्मविभागयोः ।
गुणा गुणेषु वर्तन्त इति मत्वा न सज्जते ॥२८॥

*tattva-vit tu mahā-bāho guṇa-karma-vibhāgayoḥ* ।
*guṇā guṇeṣu vartanta iti matvā na sajjate* ॥28 ॥

प्रकृतेर्गुणसम्मूढाः सज्जन्ते गुणकर्मसु ।
तानकृत्स्नविदो मन्दान्कृत्स्नविन्न विचालयेत् ॥२९॥

*prakṛter guṇa-sammūḍhāḥ sajjante guṇa-karmasu* ।
*tān akṛtsna-vido mandān kṛtsna-vin na vicālayet* ॥29 ॥

मयि सर्वाणि कर्माणि संन्यस्याध्यात्मचेतसा ।
निराशीर्निर्ममो भूत्वा युध्यस्व विगतज्वरः ॥३०॥

*mayi sarvāṇi karmāṇi saṁnyasyādhyātma-cetasā* ।
*nirāśīr nirmamo bhūtvā yudhyasva vigata-jvaraḥ* ॥30 ॥

ये मे मतमिदं नित्यमनुतिष्ठन्ति मानवाः ।
श्रद्धावन्तोऽनसूयन्तो मुच्यन्ते तेऽपि कर्मभिः ॥३१॥

*ye me matam idaṁ nityam anutiṣṭhanti mānavāḥ* ।
*śraddhāvanto 'nasūyanto mucyante te 'pi karmabhiḥ* ॥31 ॥

ये त्वेतदभ्यसूयन्तो नानुतिष्ठन्ति मे मतम् ।
सर्वज्ञानविमूढांस्तान्विद्धि नष्टानचेतसः ॥३२॥

*ye tv etad abhyasūyanto nānutiṣṭhanti me matam* ।
*sarva-jñāna-vimūḍhāṁs tān viddhi naṣṭān acetasaḥ* ॥32 ॥

सदृशं चेष्टते स्वस्याः प्रकृतेर्ज्ञानवानपि ।
प्रकृतिं यान्ति भूतानि निग्रहः किं करिष्यति ॥३३॥

*sadṛśaṁ ceṣṭate svasyāḥ prakṛter jñānavān api* ।
*prakṛtiṁ yānti bhūtāni nigrahaḥ kiṁ kariṣyati* ॥33 ॥

इन्द्रियस्येन्द्रियस्यार्थे रागद्वेषौ व्यवस्थितौ ।
तयोर्न वशमागच्छेत्तौ ह्यस्य परिपन्थिनौ ॥३४॥

*indriyasyendriyasyārthe rāga-dveṣau vyavasthitau* ।
*tayor na vaśam āgacchet tau hy asya paripanthinau* ॥34 ॥

श्रेयान्स्वधर्मो विगुणः परधर्मात्स्वनुष्ठितात् ।
स्वधर्मे निधनं श्रेयः परधर्मो भयावहः ॥३५॥

*śreyān svadharmo viguṇaḥ para-dharmāt svanuṣṭhitāt* ।
*svadharme nidhanaṁ śreyaḥ para-dharmo bhayāvahaḥ* ॥35 ॥

**अर्जुन उवाच —**

अथ केन प्रयुक्तोऽयं पापं चरति पूरुषः ।
अनिच्छन्नपि वार्ष्णेय बलादिव नियोजितः ॥३६॥

***arjuna uvāca —***

*atha kena prayukto 'yaṁ pāpaṁ carati pūruṣaḥ* ।
*anicchann api vārṣṇeya balād iva niyojitaḥ* ॥36 ॥

**श्रीभगवानुवाच —**

काम एष क्रोध एष रजोगुणसमुद्भवः ।
महाशनो महापाप्मा विद्ध्येनमिह वैरिणम् ॥३७॥

***śrī bhagavān uvāca —***

*kāma eṣa krodha eṣa rajo-guṇa-samudbhavaḥ* ।
*mahāśano mahā-pāpmā viddhy enam iha vairiṇam* ॥37 ॥

धूमेनाव्रियते वह्निर्यथादर्शो मलेन च ।
यथोल्बेनावृतो गर्भस्तथा तेनेदमावृतम् ॥३८॥

*dhūmenāvriyate vahnir yathā'darśo malena ca* ।
*yatholbenāvṛto garbhas tathā tenedam āvṛtam* ॥38 ॥

आवृतं ज्ञानमेतेन ज्ञानिनो नित्यवैरिणा ।
कामरूपेण कौन्तेय दुष्पूरेणानलेन च ॥३९॥

*āvṛtaṁ jñānam etena jñānino nitya-vairiṇā* ।
*kāma-rūpeṇa kaunteya duṣpūreṇānalena ca* ॥39 ॥

इन्द्रियाणि मनो बुद्धिरस्याधिष्ठानमुच्यते ।
एतैर्विमोहयत्येष ज्ञानमावृत्य देहिनम् ॥४०॥

*indriyāṇi mano buddhir asyādhiṣṭhānam ucyate* ।
*etair vimohayaty eṣa jñānam āvṛtya dehinam* ॥40 ॥

तस्मात्त्वमिन्द्रियाण्यादौ नियम्य भरतर्षभ ।
पाप्मानं प्रजहि ह्येनं ज्ञानविज्ञाननाशनम् ॥४१॥

*tasmāt tvam indriyāṇy ādau niyamya bharatarṣabha* ।
*pāpmānaṁ prajahi hy enaṁ jñāna-vijñāna-nāśanam* ॥41 ॥

इन्द्रियाणि पराण्याहुरिन्द्रियेभ्यः परं मनः ।
मनसस्तु परा बुद्धिर्यो बुद्धेः परतस्तु सः ॥४२॥

*indriyāṇi parāṇy āhur indriyebhyaḥ paraṁ manaḥ* ।
*manasas tu parā buddhir yo buddheḥ paratas tu saḥ* ॥42 ॥

एवं बुद्धेः परं बुद्ध्वा संस्तभ्यात्मानमात्मना ।
जहि शत्रुं महाबाहो कामरूपं दुरासदम् ॥४३॥

*evaṁ buddheḥ paraṁ buddhvā saṁstabhyātmānamātmanā* ।
*jahi śatruṁ mahā-bāho kāma-rūpaṁ durāsadam* ॥43 ॥

# 4. ज्ञान-कर्म-संन्यास-योगः

**श्रीभगवानुवाच —**

इमं विवस्वते योगं प्रोक्तवानहमव्ययम् ।
विवस्वान्मनवे प्राह मनुरिक्ष्वाकवेऽब्रवीत् ॥१॥

***śrī bhagavān uvāca —***

*imaṁ vivasvate yogaṁ proktavān aham avyayam* ।
*vivasvān manave prāha manur ikṣvākave 'bravīt* ॥1 ॥

एवं परम्पराप्राप्तमिमं राजर्षयो विदुः ।
स कालेनेह महता योगो नष्टः परन्तप ॥२॥

*evaṁ paramparā-prāptam imaṁ rājarṣayo viduḥ* ।
*sa kāleneha mahatā yogo naṣṭaḥ parantapa* ॥2 ॥

स एवायं मया तेऽद्य योगः प्रोक्तः पुरातनः ।
भक्तोऽसि मे सखा चेति रहस्यं ह्येतदुत्तमम् ॥३॥

*sa evāyaṁ mayā te 'dya yogaḥ proktaḥ purātanaḥ* ।
*bhakto 'si me sakhā ceti rahasyaṁ hy etad uttamam* ॥3 ॥

**अर्जुन उवाच —**

अपरं भवतो जन्म परं जन्म विवस्वतः ।
कथमेतद्विजानीयां त्वमादौ प्रोक्तवानिति ।।४।।

***arjuna uvāca —***

*aparaṁ bhavato janma paraṁ janma vivasvataḥ* ।
*katham etad vijānīyāṁ tvam ādau proktavān iti* ॥4 ॥

**श्रीभगवानुवाच —**

बहूनि मे व्यतीतानि जन्मानि तव चार्जुन ।
तान्यहं वेद सर्वाणि न त्वं वेत्थ परन्तप ।।५।।

***śrī bhagavān uvāca —***

*bahūni me vyatītāni janmāni tava cārjuna* ।
*tāny ahaṁ veda sarvāṇi na tvaṁ vettha parantapa* ॥5 ॥

अजोऽपि सन्नव्ययात्मा भूतानामीश्वरोऽपि सन् ।
प्रकृतिं स्वामधिष्ठाय सम्भवाम्यात्ममायया ।।६।।

*ajo 'pi sann avyayātmā bhūtānām īśvaro 'pi san* ।
*prakṛtiṁ svām adhiṣṭhāya sambhavāmy ātma-māyayā* ॥6 ॥

यदा यदा हि धर्मस्य ग्लानिर्भवति भारत ।
अभ्युत्थानमधर्मस्य तदात्मानं सृजाम्यहम् ।।७।।

*yadā yadā hi dharmasya glānir bhavati bhārata* ।
*abhyutthānam adharmasya tadātmānaṁ sṛjāmy aham* ॥7 ॥

परित्राणाय साधूनां विनाशाय च दुष्कृताम् ।
धर्मसंस्थापनार्थाय सम्भवामि युगे युगे ।।८।।

*paritrāṇāya sādhūnāṁ vināśāya ca duṣkṛtām* ।
*dharma-saṁsthāpanārthāya sambhavāmi yuge yuge* ॥8 ॥

जन्म कर्म च मे दिव्यमेवं यो वेत्ति तत्त्वतः ।
त्यक्त्वा देहं पुनर्जन्म नैति मामेति सोऽर्जुन ।।९।।

*janma karma ca me divyam evaṁ yo vetti tattvataḥ* ।
*tyaktvā dehaṁ punar-janma naiti mām eti so 'rjuna* ॥9 ॥

वीतरागभयक्रोधा मन्मया मामुपाश्रिताः ।
बहवो ज्ञानतपसा पूता मद्भावमागताः ।।१०।।

*vīta-rāga-bhaya-krodhā manmayā mām upāśritāḥ* ।
*bahavo jñāna-tapasā pūtā mad bhāvam āgatāḥ* ॥10 ॥

ये यथा मां प्रपद्यन्ते तांस्तथैव भजाम्यहम् ।
मम वर्त्मानुवर्तन्ते मनुष्याः पार्थ सर्वशः ॥११॥

*ye yathā māṁ prapadyante tāṁs tathaiva bhajāmy aham* ।
*mama vartmānuvartante manuṣyāḥ pārtha sarvaśaḥ* ॥11 ॥

काङ्क्षन्तः कर्मणां सिद्धिं यजन्त इह देवताः ।
क्षिप्रं हि मानुषे लोके सिद्धिर्भवति कर्मजा ॥१२॥

*kāṅkṣantaḥ karmaṇāṁ siddhiṁ yajanta iha devatāḥ* ।
*kṣipraṁ hi mānuṣe loke siddhir bhavati karmajā* ॥12 ॥

चातुर्वर्ण्यं मया सृष्टं गुणकर्मविभागशः ।
तस्य कर्तारमपि मां विद्ध्यकर्तारमव्ययम् ॥१३॥

*cāturvarṇyaṁ mayā sṛṣṭaṁ guṇa-karma-vibhāgaśaḥ* ।
*tasya kartāram api māṁ viddhy akartāram avyayam* ॥13 ॥

न मां कर्माणि लिम्पन्ति न मे कर्मफले स्पृहा ।
इति मां योऽभिजानाति कर्मभिर्न स बध्यते ॥१४॥

*na māṁ karmāṇi limpanti na me karma-phale spṛhā* ।
*iti māṁ yo 'bhijānāti karmabhir na sa badhyate* ॥14 ॥

एवं ज्ञात्वा कृतं कर्म पूर्वैरपि मुमुक्षुभिः ।
कुरु कर्मैव तस्मात्त्वं पूर्वैः पूर्वतरं कृतम् ॥१५॥

*evaṁ jñātvā kṛtaṁ karma pūrvair api mumukṣubhiḥ* ।
*kuru karmaiva tasmāt tvaṁ pūrvaiḥ pūrvataraṁ kṛtam* ॥15 ॥

किं कर्म किमकर्मेति कवयोऽप्यत्र मोहिताः ।
तत्ते कर्म प्रवक्ष्यामि यज्ज्ञात्वा मोक्ष्यसेऽशुभात् ॥१६॥

*kiṁ karma kim akarmeti kavayo 'py atra mohitāḥ* ।
*tat te karma pravakṣyāmi yaj jñātvā mokṣyase 'śubhāt* ॥16 ॥

कर्मणो ह्यपि बोद्धव्यं बोद्धव्यं च विकर्मणः ।
अकर्मणश्च बोद्धव्यं गहना कर्मणो गतिः ॥१७॥

*karmaṇo hy api boddhavyaṁ boddhavyaṁ ca vikarmaṇaḥ* ।
*akarmaṇaś ca boddhavyaṁ gahanā karmaṇo gatiḥ* ॥17 ॥

कर्मण्यकर्म यः पश्येदकर्मणि च कर्म यः ।
स बुद्धिमान्मनुष्येषु स युक्तः कृत्स्नकर्मकृत् ॥१८॥

*karmaṇy akarma yaḥ paśyed akarmaṇi ca karma yaḥ* ।
*sa buddhimān manuṣyeṣu sa yuktaḥ kṛtsna-karma-kṛt* ॥18 ॥

यस्य सर्वे समारम्भाः कामसङ्कल्पवर्जिताः ।
ज्ञानाग्निदग्धकर्माणं तमाहुः पण्डितं बुधाः ॥१९॥

*yasya sarve samārambhāḥ kāma-saṅkalpa-varjitāḥ* ।
*jñānāgni-dagdha-karmāṇaṁ tam āhuḥ paṇḍitaṁ budhāḥ* ॥19 ॥

त्यक्त्वा कर्मफलासङ्गं नित्यतृप्तो निराश्रयः ।
कर्मण्यभिप्रवृत्तोऽपि नैव किञ्चित्करोति सः ॥२०॥

*tyaktvā karma-phalāsaṅgaṁ nitya-tṛpto nirāśrayaḥ* ।
*karmaṇy abhipravṛtto 'pi naiva kiñcit karoti saḥ* ॥20 ॥

निराशीर्यतचित्तात्मा त्यक्तसर्वपरिग्रहः ।
शारीरं केवलं कर्म कुर्वन्नाप्नोति किल्बिषम् ॥२१॥

*nirāśīr yata-cittātmā tyakta-sarva-parigrahaḥ* ।
*śārīraṁ kevalaṁ karma kurvan nāpnoti kilbiṣam* ॥21 ॥

यदृच्छालाभसंतुष्टो द्वन्द्वातीतो विमत्सरः ।
समः सिद्धावसिद्धौ च कृत्वापि न निबध्यते ॥२२॥

*yadṛcchā-lābha-saṁtuṣṭo dvandvātīto vimatsaraḥ* ।
*samaḥ siddhāv asiddhau ca kṛtvā 'pi na nibadhyate* ॥22 ॥

गतसङ्गस्य मुक्तस्य ज्ञानावस्थितचेतसः ।
यज्ञायाचरतः कर्म समग्रं प्रविलीयते ॥२३॥

*gata-saṅgasya muktasya jñānāvasthita-cetasaḥ* ।
*yajñāyācarataḥ karma samagraṁ pravilīyate* ॥23 ॥

ब्रह्मार्पणं ब्रह्म हविर्ब्रह्माग्नौ ब्रह्मणा हुतम् ।
ब्रह्मैव तेन गन्तव्यं ब्रह्मकर्मसमाधिना ॥२४॥

*brahmārpaṇaṁ brahma havir brahmāgnau brahmaṇā hutam* ।
*brahmaiva tena gantavyaṁ brahma-karma-samādhinā* ॥24 ॥

दैवमेवापरे यज्ञं योगिनः पर्युपासते ।
ब्रह्माग्नावपरे यज्ञं यज्ञेनैवोपजुह्वति ॥२५॥

*daivam evāpare yajñaṁ yoginaḥ paryupāsate* ।
*brahmāgnau apare yajñaṁ yajñenaivopajuhvati* ॥25 ॥

श्रोत्रादीनीन्द्रियाण्यन्ये संयमाग्निषु जुह्वति ।
शब्दादीन्विषयानन्य इन्द्रियाग्निषु जुह्वति ॥२६॥

*śrotrādīnīndriyāṇy anye saṁyamāgniṣu juhvati* ।
*śabdādīn viṣayān anya indriyāgniṣu juhvati* ॥26 ॥

सर्वाणीन्द्रियकर्माणि प्राणकर्माणि चापरे ।
आत्मसंयमयोगाग्नौ जुह्वति ज्ञानदीपिते ॥२७॥

*sarvāṇīndriya-karmāṇi prāṇa-karmāṇi cāpare* ।
*ātma-saṁyama-yogāgnau juhvati jñāna-dīpite* ॥27 ॥

द्रव्ययज्ञास्तपोयज्ञा योगयज्ञास्तथापरे ।
स्वाध्यायज्ञानयज्ञाश्च यतयः संशितव्रताः ॥२८॥

*dravya-yajñas tapo-yajñā yoga-yajñas tathapare* ।
*svādhyāya-jñāna-yajñaś ca yatayaḥ saṁśita-vratāḥ* ॥28 ॥

अपाने जुह्वति प्राणं प्राणेऽपानं तथापरे ।
प्राणापानगती रुद्ध्वा प्राणायामपरायणाः ॥२९॥

*apāne juhvati prāṇaṁ prāṇe 'pānaṁ tathāpare* ।
*prāṇāpāna-gatī ruddhvā prāṇāyāma-parāyanāḥ* ॥29 ॥

अपरे नियताहाराः प्राणान्प्राणेषु जुह्वति ।
सर्वेऽप्येते यज्ञविदो यज्ञक्षपितकल्मषाः ॥३०॥

*apare niyatāhārāḥ prāṇān prāṇeṣu juhvati* ।
*sarve 'py ete yajña-vido yajña-kṣapita-kalmaṣāḥ* ॥30 ॥

यज्ञशिष्टामृतभुजो यान्ति ब्रह्म सनातनम् ।
नायं लोकोऽस्त्ययज्ञस्य कुतोऽन्यः कुरुसत्तम ॥३१॥

*yajña-śiṣṭāmṛta-bhujo yānti brahma sanātanam* ।
*nāyaṁ loko 'sty ayajñasya kuto 'nyaḥ kuru-sattama* ॥31 ॥

एवं बहुविधा यज्ञा वितता ब्रह्मणो मुखे ।
कर्मजान्विद्धि तान्सर्वानेवं ज्ञात्वा विमोक्ष्यसे ॥३२॥

*evaṁ bahuvidhā yajñā vitatā brahmaṇo mukhe* ।
*karmajān viddhi tān sarvān evaṁ jñātvā vimokṣyase* ॥32 ॥

श्रेयान्द्रव्यमयाद्यज्ञाज्ज्ञानयज्ञः परन्तप ।
सर्वं कर्माखिलं पार्थ ज्ञाने परिसमाप्यते ॥३३॥

*śreyān dravya-mayād yajñāj jñāna-yajñaḥ parantapa* ।
*sarvaṁ karmā 'khilaṁ pārtha jñāne parisamāpyate* ॥33 ॥

तद्विद्धि प्रणिपातेन परिप्रश्नेन सेवया ।
उपदेक्ष्यन्ति ते ज्ञानं ज्ञानिनस्तत्त्वदर्शिनः ॥३४॥

*tad viddhi praṇipātena paripraśnena sevayā* ।
*upadekṣyanti te jñānaṁ jñāninas tattva-darśinaḥ* ॥34 ॥

यज्ज्ञात्वा न पुनर्मोहमेवं यास्यसि पाण्डव ।
येन भूतान्यशेषेण द्रक्ष्यस्यात्मन्यथो मयि ॥३५॥

*yaj jñātvā na punar moham evaṁ yāsyasi pāṇḍava* ।
*yena bhūtāny aśeṣena drakṣyasy ātmany atho mayi* ॥35 ॥

अपि चेदसि पापेभ्यः सर्वेभ्यः पापकृत्तमः ।
सर्वं ज्ञानप्लवेनैव वृजिनं सन्तरिष्यसि ॥३६॥

*api ced asi pāpebhyaḥ sarvebhyaḥ pāpa-kṛttamaḥ* ।
*sarvaṁ jñāna-plavenaiva vṛjinaṁ santariṣyasi* ॥36 ॥

यथैधांसि समिद्धोऽग्निर्भस्मसात्कुरुतेऽर्जुन ।
ज्ञानाग्निः सर्वकर्माणि भस्मसात्कुरुते तथा ॥३७॥

*yathaidhāṁsi samiddho 'gnir bhasmasāt kurute 'rjuna* ।
*jñānāgniḥ sarva-karmāṇi bhasmasāt kurute tathā* ॥37 ॥

न हि ज्ञानेन सदृशं पवित्रमिह विद्यते ।
तत्स्वयं योगसंसिद्धः कालेनात्मनि विन्दति ॥३८॥

*na hi jñānena sadṛśaṁ pavitram iha vidyate* ।
*tat svayaṁ yoga-saṁsiddhaḥ kālenātmani vindati* ॥38 ॥

श्रद्धावाँल्लभते ज्ञानं तत्परः संयतेन्द्रियः ।
ज्ञानं लब्ध्वा परां शान्तिमचिरेणाधिगच्छति ॥३९॥

*śraddhāvāṁ llabhate jñānaṁ tat-paraḥ saṁyatendriyaḥ* ।
*jñānaṁ labdhvā parāṁ śāntim acireṇādhigacchati* ॥39 ॥

अज्ञश्चाश्रद्दधानश्च संशयात्मा विनश्यति ।
नायं लोकोऽस्ति न परो न सुखं संशयात्मनः ॥४०॥

*ajñaś cāśraddadhānaś ca saṁśayātmā vinaśyati* ।
*nāyaṁ loko 'sti na paro na sukhaṁ saṁśayātmanaḥ* ॥40 ॥

योगसन्न्यस्तकर्माणं ज्ञानसञ्छिन्नसंशयम् ।
आत्मवन्तं न कर्माणि निबध्नन्ति धनञ्जय ॥४१॥

*yoga-saṁnyasta-karmāṇam jñāna-sañchinna-saṁśayam* ।
*ātmavantaṁ na karmāṇi nibadhnanti dhanañjaya* ॥41 ॥

तस्मादज्ञानसम्भूतं हृत्स्थं ज्ञानासिनात्मनः ।
छित्त्वैनं संशयं योगमातिष्ठोत्तिष्ठ भारत ॥४२॥

*tasmād ajñāna-sambhūtaṁ hṛtsthaṁ jñānāsinātmanaḥ* ।
*chittvainaṁ saṁśayaṁ yogam ātiṣṭhottiṣṭha bhārata* ॥42 ॥

# 5. कर्मसंन्यासयोगः

**अर्जुन उवाच —**

संन्यासं कर्मणां कृष्ण पुनर्योगं च शंससि ।
यच्छ्रेय एतयोरेकं तन्मे ब्रूहि सुनिश्चितम् ॥१॥

***arjuna uvāca —***

*saṁnyāsaṁ karmaṇāṁ kṛṣṇa punar yogaṁ ca śaṁsasi* ।
*yac chreya etayor ekaṁ tan me brūhi suniścitam* ॥1 ॥

**श्रीभगवानुवाच —**

संन्यासः कर्मयोगश्च निःश्रेयसकरावुभौ ।
तयोस्तु कर्मसंन्यासात्कर्मयोगो विशिष्यते ॥२॥

***śrī bhagavān uvāca —***

*saṁnyāsaḥ karma-yogaś ca niḥśreyasakarāv ubhau* ।
*tayos tu karma-saṁnyāsāt karma-yogo viśiṣyate* ॥2 ॥

ज्ञेयः स नित्यसंन्यासी यो न द्वेष्टि न काङ्क्षति ।
निर्द्वन्द्वो हि महाबाहो सुखं बन्धात्प्रमुच्यते ॥३॥

*jñeyaḥ sa nitya-saṁnyāsī yo na dveṣṭi na kāṅkṣati* ।
*nirdvandvo hi mahā-bāho sukhaṁ bandhāt pramucyate* ॥3 ॥

साङ्ख्ययोगौ पृथग्बालाः प्रवदन्ति न पण्डिताः ।
एकमप्यास्थितः सम्यगुभयोर्विन्दते फलम् ॥४॥

*sāṅkhya-yogau pṛthag bālāḥ pravadanti na paṇḍitāḥ* ।
*ekam apy āsthitaḥ samyag ubhayor vindate phalam* ॥4 ॥

यत्साङ्ख्यैः प्राप्यते स्थानं तद्योगैरपि गम्यते ।
एकं साङ्ख्यं च योगं च यः पश्यति स पश्यति ॥५॥

*yat sāṅkhyaiḥ prāpyate sthānaṁ tad yogair api gamyate* ।
*ekaṁ sāṅkhyaṁ ca yogaṁ ca yaḥ paśyati sa paśyati* ॥5 ॥

संन्यासस्तु महाबाहो दुःखमाप्तुमयोगतः ।
योगयुक्तो मुनिर्ब्रह्म नचिरेणाधिगच्छति ॥६॥

*saṁnyāsas tu mahā-bāho duḥkham āptum ayogataḥ* ।
*yoga-yukto munir brahma nacireṇādhigacchati* ॥6 ॥

योगयुक्तो विशुद्धात्मा विजितात्मा जितेन्द्रियः ।
सर्वभूतात्मभूतात्मा कुर्वन्नपि न लिप्यते ॥७॥

*yoga-yukto viśuddhātmā vijitātmā jitendriyaḥ* ।
*sarva-bhūtātma-bhūtātmā kurvann api na lipyate* ॥7 ॥

नैव किञ्चित्करोमीति युक्तो मन्येत तत्त्ववित् ।
पश्यञ्शृण्वन्स्पृशञ्जिघ्रन्नश्नन्गच्छन्स्वपञ्श्वसन् ॥८॥

*naiva kiñcit karomīti yukto manyeta tattva-vit* ।
*paśyañ śṛṇvan spṛśañ jighrann aśnan gacchan svapañ śvasan* ॥8 ॥

प्रलपन्विसृजन्गृह्णन्नुन्मिषन्निमिषन्नपि ।
इन्द्रियाणीन्द्रियार्थेषु वर्तन्त इति धारयन् ॥९॥

*pralapan visṛjan gṛhṇann unmiṣan nimiṣann api* ।
*indriyāṇīndriyārtheṣu vartanta iti dhārayan* ॥9 ॥

ब्रह्मण्याधाय कर्माणि सङ्गं त्यक्त्वा करोति यः ।
लिप्यते न स पापेन पद्मपत्रमिवाम्भसा ॥१०॥

*brahmaṇy ādhāya karmāṇi saṅgaṁ tyaktvā karoti yaḥ* ।
*lipyate na sa pāpena padma-patram ivāmbhasā* ॥10 ॥

कायेन मनसा बुद्ध्या केवलैरिन्द्रियैरपि ।
योगिनः कर्म कुर्वन्ति सङ्गं त्यक्त्वात्मशुद्धये ॥११॥

*kāyena manasā buddhyā kevalair indriyair api* ।
*yoginaḥ karma kurvanti saṅgaṁ tyaktvātma-śuddhaye* ॥11 ॥

युक्तः कर्मफलं त्यक्त्वा शान्तिमाप्नोति नैष्ठिकीम् ।
अयुक्तः कामकारेण फले सक्तो निबध्यते ॥१२॥

*yuktaḥ karma-phalaṁ tyaktvā śāntim āpnoti naiṣṭhikīm* ।
*ayuktaḥ kāma-kāreṇa phale sakto nibadhyate* ॥12॥

सर्वकर्माणि मनसा संन्यस्यास्ते सुखं वशी ।
नवद्वारे पुरे देही नैव कुर्वन्न कारयन् ॥१३॥

*sarva-karmāṇi manasā saṁnyasyāste sukhaṁ vaśī* ।
*nava-dvāre pure dehī naiva kurvan na kārayan* ॥13॥

न कर्तृत्वं न कर्माणि लोकस्य सृजति प्रभुः ।
न कर्मफलसंयोगं स्वभावस्तु प्रवर्तते ॥१४॥

*na kartṛtvaṁ na karmāṇi lokasya sṛjati prabhuḥ* ।
*na karma-phala-saṁyogaṁ svabhāvas tu pravartate* ॥14॥

नादत्ते कस्यचित्पापं न चैव सुकृतं विभुः ।
अज्ञानेनावृतं ज्ञानं तेन मुह्यन्ति जन्तवः ॥१५॥

*nādatte kasyacit pāpaṁ na caiva sukṛtaṁ vibhuḥ* ।
*ajñānenāvṛtaṁ jñānaṁ tena muhyanti jantavaḥ* ॥15॥

ज्ञानेन तु तदज्ञानं येषां नाशितमात्मनः ।
तेषामादित्यवज्ज्ञानं प्रकाशयति तत्परम् ॥१६॥

*jñānena tu tad ajñānaṁ yeṣāṁ nāśitam ātmanaḥ* ।
*teṣām ādityavaj jñānaṁ prakāśayati tat param* ॥16॥

तद्बुद्धयस्तदात्मानस्तन्निष्ठास्तत्परायणाः ।
गच्छन्त्यपुनरावृत्तिं ज्ञाननिर्धूतकल्मषाः ॥१७॥

*tad-buddhayas tad-ātmānas tan-niṣṭhās tat-parāyaṇāḥ* ।
*gacchanty apunar-āvṛttiṁ jñāna-nirdhūta-kalmaṣāḥ* ॥17॥

विद्याविनयसंपन्ने ब्राह्मणे गवि हस्तिनि ।
शुनि चैव श्वपाके च पण्डिताः समदर्शिनः ॥१८॥

*vidyā-vinaya-saṁpanne brāhmaṇe gavi hastini* ।
*śuni caiva śvapāke ca paṇḍitāḥ sama-darśinaḥ* ॥18॥

इहैव तैर्जितः सर्गो येषां साम्ये स्थितं मनः ।
निर्दोषं हि समं ब्रह्म तस्माद् ब्रह्मणि ते स्थिताः ॥१९॥

*ihaiva tair jitaḥ sargo yeṣām sāmye sthitaṁ manaḥ* ।
*nirdoṣaṁ hi samaṁ brahma tasmād brahmaṇi te sthitāḥ* ॥19 ॥

न प्रहृष्येत्प्रियं प्राप्य नोद्विजेत्प्राप्य चाप्रियम् ।
स्थिरबुद्धिरसम्मूढो ब्रह्मविद् ब्रह्मणि स्थितः ॥२०॥

*na prahṛṣyet priyaṁ prāpya nodvijet prāpya cāpriyam* ।
*sthira-buddhir asammūḍho brahma-vid brahmaṇi sthitaḥ* ॥20 ॥

बाह्यस्पर्शेष्वसक्तात्मा विन्दत्यात्मनि यत्सुखम् ।
स ब्रह्मयोगयुक्तात्मा सुखमक्षयमश्नुते ॥२१॥

*bāhya-sparśeṣv asaktātmā vindaty ātmani yat sukham* ।
*sa brahma-yoga-yuktātmā sukham akṣayam aśnute* ॥21 ॥

ये हि संस्पर्शजा भोगा दुःखयोनय एव ते ।
आद्यन्तवन्तः कौन्तेय न तेषु रमते बुधः ॥२२॥

*ye hi saṁsparśajā bhogā duḥkha-yonaya eva te* ।
*ādyantavantaḥ kaunteya na teṣu ramate budhaḥ* ॥22 ॥

शक्नोतीहैव यः सोढुं प्राक्शरीरविमोक्षणात् ।
कामक्रोधोद्भवं वेगं स युक्तः स सुखी नरः ॥२३॥

*śaknotīhaiva yaḥ soḍhuṁ prāk-śarīra-vimokṣaṇāt* ।
*kāma-krodhodbhavaṁ vegaṁ sa yuktaḥ sa sukhī naraḥ* ॥23 ॥

योऽन्तःसुखोऽन्तरारामस्तथान्तर्ज्योतिरेव यः ।
स योगी ब्रह्मनिर्वाणं ब्रह्मभूतोऽधिगच्छति ॥२४॥

*yo 'ntaḥ-sukho 'ntar-ārāmas tathāntar-jyotir eva yaḥ* ।
*sa yogī brahma-nirvāṇaṁ brahma-bhūto 'dhigacchati* ॥24 ॥

लभन्ते ब्रह्मनिर्वाणमृषयः क्षीणकल्मषाः ।
छिन्नद्वैधा यतात्मानः सर्वभूतहिते रताः ॥२५॥

*labhante brahma-nirvāṇam ṛṣayaḥ kṣīṇa-kalmaṣāḥ* ।
*chinna-dvaidhā yatātmānaḥ sarva-bhūta-hite ratāḥ* ॥25 ॥

कामक्रोधवियुक्तानां यतीनां यतचेतसाम् ।
अभितो ब्रह्मनिर्वाणं वर्तते विदितात्मनाम् ॥२६॥

*kāma-krodha-viyuktānāṁ yatīnāṁ yata-cetasām* ।
*abhito brahma-nirvāṇaṁ vartate viditātmanām* ॥26 ॥

स्पर्शान्कृत्वा बहिर्बाह्यांश्चक्षुश्चैवान्तरे भ्रुवोः ।
प्राणापानौ समौ कृत्वा नासाभ्यन्तरचारिणौ ॥२७॥

*sparśān kṛtvā bahir bāhyāṁś cakṣuś caivāntare bhruvoḥ ।*
*prāṇāpānau samau kṛtvā nāsābhyantara-cāriṇau* ॥27 ॥

यतेन्द्रियमनोबुद्धिर्मुनिर्मोक्षपरायणः ।
विगतेच्छाभयक्रोधो यः सदा मुक्त एव सः ॥२८॥

*yatendriya-mano-buddhir munir mokṣa-parāyaṇaḥ ।*
*vigatecchā-bhaya-krodho yaḥ sadā mukta eva saḥ* ॥28 ॥

भोक्तारं यज्ञतपसां सर्वलोकमहेश्वरम् ।
सुहृदं सर्वभूतानां ज्ञात्वा मां शान्तिमृच्छति ॥२९॥

*bhoktāraṁ yajña-tapasāṁ sarva-loka-maheśvaram ।*
*suhṛdaṁ sarva-bhūtānāṁ jñātvā māṁ śāntim ṛcchati* ॥29 ॥

## 6. ध्यानयोगः

**श्रीभगवानुवाच —**

अनाश्रितः कर्मफलं कार्यं कर्म करोति यः ।
स संन्यासी च योगी च न निरग्निर्न चाक्रियः ॥१॥

***śrī bhagavān uvāca —***

*anāśritaḥ karma-phalaṁ kāryaṁ karma karoti yaḥ ।*
*sa saṁnyāsī ca yogī ca na niragnir na cākriyaḥ* ॥1 ॥

यं संन्यासमिति प्राहुर्योगं तं विद्धि पाण्डव ।
न ह्यसंन्यस्तसङ्कल्पो योगी भवति कश्चन ॥२॥

*yaṁ saṁnyāsam iti prāhur yogaṁ taṁ viddhi pāṇḍava ।*
*na hy asaṁnyasta-saṅkalpo yogī bhavati kaścana* ॥2 ॥

आरुरुक्षोर्मुनेर्योगं कर्म कारणमुच्यते ।
योगारूढस्य तस्यैव शमः कारणमुच्यते ॥३॥

*ārurukṣor muner yogaṁ karma kāraṇam ucyate ।*
*yogārūḍhasya tasyaiva śamaḥ kāraṇam ucyate* ॥3 ॥

यदा हि नेन्द्रियार्थेषु न कर्मस्वनुषज्जते ।
सर्वसङ्कल्पसंन्यासी योगारूढस्तदोच्यते ॥४॥

*yadā hi nendriyārtheṣu na karmasv anuṣajjate* ।
*sarva-saṅkalpa-saṁnyāsī yogārūḍhas tadocyate* ॥4 ॥

उद्धरेदात्मनात्मानं नात्मानमवसादयेत् ।
आत्मैव ह्यात्मनो बन्धुरात्मैव रिपुरात्मनः ॥५॥

*uddhared ātmanātmānaṁ nātmānam avasādayet* ।
*ātmaiva hy ātmano bandhur ātmaiva ripur ātmanaḥ* ॥5 ॥

बन्धुरात्मात्मनस्तस्य येनात्मैवात्मना जितः ।
अनात्मनस्तु शत्रुत्वे वर्तेतात्मैव शत्रुवत् ॥६॥

*bandhur ātmātmanas tasya yenātmaivātmanā jitaḥ* ।
*anātmanas tu śatrutve vartetātmaiva śatruvat* ॥6 ॥

जितात्मनः प्रशान्तस्य परमात्मा समाहितः ।
शीतोष्णसुखदुःखेषु तथा मानापमानयोः ॥७॥

*jitātmanaḥ praśāntasya paramātmā samāhitaḥ* ।
*śītoṣṇa-sukha-duḥkheṣu tathā mānāpamānayoḥ* ॥7 ॥

ज्ञानविज्ञानतृप्तात्मा कूटस्थो विजितेन्द्रियः ।
युक्त इत्युच्यते योगी समलोष्टाश्मकाञ्चनः ॥८॥

*jñāna-vijñāna-tṛptātmā kūṭastho vijitendriyaḥ* ।
*yukta ity ucyate yogī sama-loṣṭāśma-kāñcanaḥ* ॥8 ॥

सुहृन्मित्रार्युदासीनमध्यस्थद्वेष्यबन्धुषु ।
साधुष्वपि च पापेषु समबुद्धिर्विशिष्यते ॥९॥

*suhṛn-mitrāry-udāsīna-madhyastha-dveṣya-bandhuṣu* ।
*sādhuṣv api ca pāpeṣu sama-buddhir viśiṣyate* ॥9 ॥

योगी युञ्जीत सततमात्मानं रहसि स्थितः ।
एकाकी यतचित्तात्मा निराशीरपरिग्रहः ॥१०॥

*yogī yuñjīta satatam ātmānaṁ rahasi sthitaḥ* ।
*ekākī yata-cittātmā nirāśīr aparigrahaḥ* ॥10 ॥

शुचौ देशे प्रतिष्ठाप्य स्थिरमासनमात्मनः ।
नात्युच्छ्रितं नातिनीचं चैलाजिनकुशोत्तरम् ॥११॥

*śucau deśe pratiṣṭhāpya sthiram āsanam ātmanaḥ* ।
*nātyucchritaṁ nāti-nīcaṁ cailājina-kuśottaram* ॥11 ॥

तत्रैकाग्रं मनः कृत्वा यतचित्तेन्द्रियक्रियः ।
उपविश्यासने युञ्ज्याद्योगमात्मविशुद्धये ॥१२॥

*tatraikāgraṁ manaḥ kṛtvā yata-cittendriya-kriyaḥ* ।
*upaviśy āsane yuñjyād yogam ātma-viśuddhaye* ॥12 ॥

समं कायशिरोग्रीवं धारयन्नचलं स्थिरः ।
सम्प्रेक्ष्य नासिकाग्रं स्वं दिशश्चानवलोकयन् ॥१३॥

*samaṁ kāya-śiro-grīvaṁ dhārayann acalaṁ sthiraḥ* ।
*samprekṣya nāsikāgraṁ svaṁ diśaś cānavalokayan* ॥13 ॥

प्रशान्तात्मा विगतभीर्ब्रह्मचारिव्रते स्थितः ।
मनः संयम्य मच्चित्तो युक्त आसीत मत्परः ॥१४॥

*praśāntātmā vigatabhīr brahmacāri-vrate sthitaḥ* ।
*manaḥ saṁyamya maccitto yukta āsīta matparaḥ* ॥14 ॥

युञ्जन्नेवं सदात्मानं योगी नियतमानसः ।
शान्तिं निर्वाणपरमां मत्संस्थामधिगच्छति ॥१५॥

*yuñjann evaṁ sadātmānaṁ yogī niyata-mānasaḥ* ।
*śāntiṁ nirvāṇa-paramāṁ mat-saṁsthām adhigacchati* ॥15 ॥

नात्यश्नतस्तु योगोऽस्ति न चैकान्तमनश्नतः ।
न चातिस्वप्नशीलस्य जाग्रतो नैव चार्जुन ॥१६॥

*nātyaśnatas tu yogo 'sti na caikāntam anaśnataḥ* ।
*na cāti-svapna-śīlasya jāgrato naiva cārjuna* ॥16 ॥

युक्ताहारविहारस्य युक्तचेष्टस्य कर्मसु ।
युक्तस्वप्नावबोधस्य योगो भवति दुःखहा ॥१७॥

*yuktāhāra-vihārasya yukta-ceṣṭasya karmasu* ।
*yukta-svapnāvabodhasya yogo bhavati duḥkhahā* ॥17 ॥

यदा विनियतं चित्तमात्मन्येवावतिष्ठते ।
निःस्पृहः सर्वकामेभ्यो युक्त इत्युच्यते तदा ॥१८॥

*yadā viniyataṁ cittam ātmany evāvatiṣṭhate* ।
*niḥspṛhaḥ sarva-kāmebhyo yukta ity ucyate tadā* ॥18 ॥

यथा दीपो निवातस्थो नेङ्गते सोपमा स्मृता ।
योगिनो यतचित्तस्य युञ्जतो योगमात्मनः ॥१९॥

*yathā dīpo nivātastho neṅgate sopamā smṛtā* ।
*yogino yata-cittasya yuñjato yogam ātmanaḥ* ॥19 ॥

यत्रोपरमते चित्तं निरुद्धं योगसेवया ।
यत्र चैवात्मनात्मानं पश्यन्नात्मनि तुष्यति ॥२०॥

*yatroparamate cittaṁ niruddhaṁ yoga-sevayā* ।
*yatra caivātmanātmānaṁ paśyann ātmani tuṣyati* ॥20 ॥

सुखमात्यन्तिकं यत्तद्बुद्धिग्राह्यमतीन्द्रियम् ।
वेत्ति यत्र न चैवायं स्थितश्चलति तत्त्वतः ॥२१॥

*sukham ātyantikaṁ yat tad buddhi-grāhyam atīndriyam* ।
*vetti yatra na caivāyaṁ sthitaś calati tattvataḥ* ॥21 ॥

यं लब्ध्वा चापरं लाभं मन्यते नाधिकं ततः ।
यस्मिन्स्थितो न दुःखेन गुरुणापि विचाल्यते ॥२२॥

*yaṁ labdhvā cāparaṁ lābhaṁ manyate nādhikaṁ tataḥ* ।
*yasminsthito na duḥkhena guruṇāpi vicālyate* ॥22 ॥

तं विद्याद् दुःखसंयोगवियोगं योगसञ्ज्ञितम् ।
स निश्चयेन योक्तव्यो योगोऽनिर्विण्णचेतसा ॥२३॥

*taṁ vidyād duḥkha-saṁyoga-viyogaṁ yoga-sañjñitam* ।
*sa niścayena yoktavyo yogo 'nirviṇṇa-cetasā* ॥23 ॥

सङ्कल्पप्रभवान्कामांस्त्यक्त्वा सर्वानशेषतः ।
मनसैवेन्द्रियग्रामं विनियम्य समन्ततः ॥२४॥

*saṅkalpa-prabhavān kāmāṁs tyaktvā sarvān aśeṣataḥ* ।
*manasaivendriya-grāmaṁ viniyamya samantataḥ* ॥24 ॥

शनैः शनैरुपरमेद्बुद्ध्या धृतिगृहीतया ।
आत्मसंस्थं मनः कृत्वा न किञ्चिदपि चिन्तयेत् ॥२५॥

*śanaiḥ-śanair uparamed buddhyā dhṛti-gṛhītayā* ।
*ātma-saṁsthaṁ manaḥ kṛtvā na kiñcid api cintayet* ॥25 ॥

यतो यतो निश्चरति मनश्चञ्चलमस्थिरम् ।
ततस्ततो नियम्यैतदात्मन्येव वशं नयेत् ॥२६॥

*yato-yato niścarati manaś cañcalam asthiram* ।
*tatas-tato niyamyaitad ātmany eva vaśaṁ nayet* ॥26 ॥

प्रशान्तमनसं ह्येनं योगिनं सुखमुत्तमम् ।
उपैति शान्तरजसं ब्रह्मभूतमकल्मषम् ।।२७।।

*praśānta-manasaṁ hy enaṁ yoginaṁ sukham uttamam* ।
*upaiti śānta-rajasaṁ brahma-bhūtam akalmaṣam* ॥27 ॥

युञ्जन्नेवं सदात्मानं योगी विगतकल्मषः ।
सुखेन ब्रह्मसंस्पर्शमत्यन्तं सुखमश्नुते ।।२८।।

*yuñjann evaṁ sadātmānaṁ yogī vigata-kalmaṣaḥ* ।
*sukhena brahma-saṁsparśam atyantaṁ sukham aśnute* ॥28 ॥

सर्वभूतस्थमात्मानं सर्वभूतानि चात्मनि ।
ईक्षते योगयुक्तात्मा सर्वत्र समदर्शनः ।।२९।।

*sarva-bhūtastham ātmānaṁ sarva-bhūtāni cātmani* ।
*īkṣate yoga-yuktātmā sarvatra sama-darśanaḥ* ॥29 ॥

यो मां पश्यति सर्वत्र सर्वं च मयि पश्यति ।
तस्याहं न प्रणश्यामि स च मे न प्रणश्यति ।।३०।।

*yo māṁ paśyati sarvatra sarvaṁ ca mayi paśyati* ।
*tasyāhaṁ na praṇaśyāmi sa ca me na praṇaśyati* ॥30 ॥

सर्वभूतस्थितं यो मां भजत्येकत्वमास्थितः ।
सर्वथा वर्तमानोऽपि स योगी मयि वर्तते ।।३१।।

*sarvabhūtasthitaṁ yo māṁ bhajaty ekatvam āsthitaḥ* ।
*sarvathā vartamāno 'pi sa yogī mayi vartate* ॥31 ॥

आत्मौपम्येन सर्वत्र समं पश्यति योऽर्जुन ।
सुखं वा यदि वा दुःखं स योगी परमो मतः ।।३२।।

*ātmaupamyena sarvatra samaṁ paśyati yo 'rjuna* ।
*sukhaṁ vā yadi vā duḥkhaṁ sa yogī paramo mataḥ* ॥32 ॥

**अर्जुन उवाच —**

योऽयं योगस्त्वया प्रोक्तः साम्येन मधुसूदन ।
एतस्याहं न पश्यामि चञ्चलत्वात्स्थितिं स्थिराम् ।।३३।।

***arjuna uvāca —***

*yo 'yaṁ yogas tvayā proktaḥ sāmyena madhusūdana* ।
*etasyāhaṁ na paśyāmi cañcalatvāt sthitiṁ sthirām* ॥33 ॥

चञ्चलं हि मनः कृष्ण प्रमाथि बलवद्दृढम् ।
तस्याहं निग्रहं मन्ये वायोरिव सुदुष्करम् ॥३४॥

*cañcalaṁ hi manaḥ kṛṣṇa pramāthi balavaddṛḍham ।*
*tasyāhaṁ nigrahaṁ manye vāyor iva suduṣkaram* ॥34॥

**श्रीभगवानुवाच —**

असंशयं महाबाहो मनो दुर्निग्रहं चलम् ।
अभ्यासेन तु कौन्तेय वैराग्येण च गृह्यते ॥३५॥

***śrī bhagavān uvāca —***

*asaṁśayaṁ mahābāho mano durnigrahaṁ calam ।*
*abhyāsena tu kaunteya vairāgyeṇa ca gṛhyate* ॥35॥

असंयतात्मना योगो दुष्प्राप इति मे मतिः ।
वश्यात्मना तु यतता शक्योऽवाप्तुमुपायतः ॥३६॥

*asaṁyatātmanā yogo duṣprāpa iti me matiḥ ।*
*vaśyātmanā tu yatatā śakyo 'vāptum upāyataḥ* ॥36॥

**अर्जुन उवाच —**

अयतिः श्रद्धयोपेतो योगाच्चलितमानसः ।
अप्राप्य योगसंसिद्धिं कां गतिं कृष्ण गच्छति ॥३७॥

***arjuna uvāca —***

*ayatiḥ śraddhayopeto yogāc calita-mānasaḥ ।*
*aprāpya yoga-saṁsiddhiṁ kāṁ gatiṁ kṛṣṇa gacchati* ॥37॥

कच्चिन्नोभयविभ्रष्टश्छिन्नाभ्रमिव नश्यति ।
अप्रतिष्ठो महाबाहो विमूढो ब्रह्मणः पथि ॥३८॥

*kaccinnobhaya-vibhraṣṭaś chinnābhram iva naśyati ।*
*apratiṣṭho mahā-bāho vimūḍho brahmaṇaḥ pathi* ॥38॥

एतन्मे संशयं कृष्ण छेत्तुमर्हस्यशेषतः ।
त्वदन्यः संशयस्यास्य छेत्ता न ह्युपपद्यते ॥३९॥

*etan me saṁśayaṁ kṛṣṇa chettum arhasy aśeṣataḥ ।*
*tvad-anyaḥ saṁśayasyāsya chettā na hy upapadyate* ॥39॥

**श्रीभगवानुवाच —**

पार्थ नैवेह नामुत्र विनाशस्तस्य विद्यते ।
न हि कल्याणकृत्कश्चिद्दुर्गतिं तात गच्छति ।।४०।।

***śrī bhagavān uvāca —***

*pārtha naiveha nāmutra vināśas tasya vidyate* ।
*na hi kalyāṇa-kṛt kaścid durgatiṁ tāta gacchati* ॥40 ॥

प्राप्य पुण्यकृतां लोकानुषित्वा शाश्वतीः समाः ।
शुचीनां श्रीमतां गेहे योगभ्रष्टोऽभिजायते ।।४१।।

*prāpya puṇya-kṛtāṁ lokān uṣitvā śāśvatīḥ samāḥ* ।
*śucīnāṁ śrīmatāṁ gehe yoga-bhraṣṭo 'bhijāyate* ॥41 ॥

अथवा योगिनामेव कुले भवति धीमताम् ।
एतद्धि दुर्लभतरं लोके जन्म यदीदृशम् ।।४२।।

*athavā yogināṁ eva kule bhavati dhīmatām* ।
*etaddhi durlabhataraṁ loke janma yad īdṛśam* ॥42 ॥

तत्र तं बुद्धिसंयोगं लभते पौर्वदेहिकम् ।
यतते च ततो भूयः संसिद्धौ कुरुनन्दन ।।४३।।

*tatra taṁ buddhi-saṁyogaṁ labhate paurva-dehikam* ।
*yatate ca tato bhūyaḥ saṁsiddhau kuru-nandana* ॥43 ॥

पूर्वाभ्यासेन तेनैव ह्रियते ह्यवशोऽपि सः ।
जिज्ञासुरपि योगस्य शब्दब्रह्मातिवर्तते ।।४४।।

*pūrvābhyāsena tenaiva hriyate hy avaśo 'pi saḥ* ।
*jijñāsur api yogasya śabda-brahmātivartate* ॥44 ॥

प्रयत्नाद्यतमानस्तु योगी संशुद्धकिल्बिषः ।
अनेकजन्मसंसिद्धस्ततो याति परां गतिम् ।।४५।।

*prayatnād yatamānas tu yogī saṁśuddha-kilbiṣaḥ* ।
*aneka-janma-saṁsiddhas tato yāti parāṁ gatim* ॥45 ॥

तपस्विभ्योऽधिको योगी ज्ञानिभ्योऽपि मतोऽधिकः ।
कर्मिभ्यश्चाधिको योगी तस्माद्योगी भवार्जुन ।।४६।।

*tapasvibhyo 'dhiko yogī jñānibhyo 'pi mato 'dhikaḥ* ।
*karmibhyaś cādhiko yogī tasmād yogī bhavārjuna* ॥46 ॥

योगिनामपि सर्वेषां मद्गतेनान्तरात्मना ।
श्रद्धावान्भजते यो मां स मे युक्ततमो मतः ।।४७।।

*yoginām api sarveṣāṁ mad-gatenāntarātmanā* ।
*śraddhāvān bhajate yo māṁ sa me yuktatamo mataḥ* ॥47 ॥

# 7. ज्ञानविज्ञानयोगः

**श्रीभगवानुवाच —**

मय्यासक्तमनाः पार्थ योगं युञ्जन्मदाश्रयः ।
असंशयं समग्रं मां यथा ज्ञास्यसि तच्छृणु ।।१।।

***śrī bhagavān uvāca —***

*mayy āsakta-manāḥ pārtha yogaṁ yuñjan mad-āśrayaḥ* ।
*asaṁśayaṁ samagraṁ māṁ yathā jñāsyasi tac chṛṇu* ॥1 ॥

ज्ञानं तेऽहं सविज्ञानमिदं वक्ष्याम्यशेषतः ।
यज्ज्ञात्वा नेह भूयोऽन्यज्ज्ञातव्यमवशिष्यते ।।२।।

*jñānam te 'haṁ savijñānam idaṁ vakṣyāmy aśeṣataḥ* ।
*yaj jñātvā neha bhūyo 'nyaj-jñātavyam avaśiṣyate* ॥2 ॥

मनुष्याणां सहस्रेषु कश्चिद्यतति सिद्धये ।
यततामपि सिद्धानां कश्चिन्मां वेत्ति तत्त्वतः ।।३।।

*manuṣyāṇāṁ sahasreṣu kaścid yatati siddhaye* ।
*yatatām api siddhānāṁ kaścin māṁ vetti tattvataḥ* ॥3 ॥

भूमिरापोऽनलो वायुः खं मनो बुद्धिरेव च ।
अहङ्कार इतीयं मे भिन्ना प्रकृतिरष्टधा ।।४।।

*bhūmir āpo 'nalo vāyuḥ khaṁ mano buddhir eva ca* ।
*ahaṅkāra itīyaṁ me bhinnā prakṛtir aṣṭadhā* ॥4 ॥

अपरेयमितस्त्वन्यां प्रकृतिं विद्धि मे पराम् ।
जीवभूतां महाबाहो ययेदं धार्यते जगत् ।।५।।

*apareyam itas tv anyāṁ prakṛtiṁ viddhi me parām* ।
*jīva-bhūtāṁ mahā-bāho yayedaṁ dhāryate jagat* ॥5 ॥

एतद्योनीनि भूतानि सर्वाणीत्युपधारय ।
अहं कृत्स्नस्य जगतः प्रभवः प्रलयस्तथा ।।६।।

*etad-yonīni bhūtāni sarvāṇīty upadhāraya* ।
*ahaṁ kṛtsnasya jagataḥ prabhavaḥ pralayas tathā* ॥6 ॥

मत्तः परतरं नान्यत्किञ्चिदस्ति धनञ्जय ।
मयि सर्वमिदं प्रोतं सूत्रे मणिगणा इव ॥७॥

*mattaḥ parataraṁ nānyat kiñcid asti dhanañjaya* ।
*mayi sarvam idaṁ protaṁ sūtre maṇi-gaṇā iva* ॥7 ॥

रसोऽहमप्सु कौन्तेय प्रभास्मि शशिसूर्ययोः ।
प्रणवः सर्ववेदेषु शब्दः खे पौरुषं नृषु ॥८॥

*raso 'ham apsu kaunteya prabhāsmi śaśi-sūryayoḥ* ।
*praṇavaḥ sarva-vedeṣu śabdaḥ khe pauruṣaṁ nṛṣu* ॥8 ॥

पुण्यो गन्धः पृथिव्यां च तेजश्चास्मि विभावसौ ।
जीवनं सर्वभूतेषु तपश्चास्मि तपस्विषु ॥९॥

*puṇyo gandhaḥ pṛthivyāṁ ca tejaś cāsmi vibhāvasau* ।
*jīvanaṁ sarva-bhūteṣu tapaś cāsmi tapasviṣu* ॥9 ॥

बीजं मां सर्वभूतानां विद्धि पार्थ सनातनम् ।
बुद्धिर्बुद्धिमतामस्मि तेजस्तेजस्विनामहम् ॥१०॥

*bījaṁ māṁ sarva-bhūtānāṁ viddhi pārtha sanātanam* ।
*buddhir buddhimatām asmi tejas tejasvinām aham* ॥10 ॥

बलं बलवतां चाहं कामरागविवर्जितम् ।
धर्माविरुद्धो भूतेषु कामोऽस्मि भरतर्षभ ॥११॥

*balaṁ balavatāṁ cāhaṁ kāma-rāga-vivarjitam* ।
*dharmāviruddho bhūteṣu kāmo 'smi bharatarṣabha* ॥11 ॥

ये चैव सात्त्विका भावा राजसास्तामसाश्च ये ।
मत्त एवेति तान्विद्धि न त्वहं तेषु ते मयि ॥१२॥

*ye caiva sāttvikā bhāvā rājasās tāmasāś ca ye* ।
*matta eveti tān viddhi na tvahaṁ teṣu te mayi* ॥12 ॥

त्रिभिर्गुणमयैर्भावैरेभिः सर्वमिदं जगत् ।
मोहितं नाभिजानाति मामेभ्यः परमव्ययम् ॥१३॥

*tribhir guṇamayair bhāvair ebhiḥ sarvam idaṁ jagat* ।
*mohitaṁ nābhijānāti mām ebhyaḥ param avyayam* ॥13 ॥

दैवी ह्येषा गुणमयी मम माया दुरत्यया ।
मामेव ये प्रपद्यन्ते मायामेतां तरन्ति ते ।।१४।।

*daivī hy eṣā guṇamayī mama māyā duratyayā* ।
*mām eva ye prapadyante māyām etāṁ taranti te* ॥14 ॥

न मां दुष्कृतिनो मूढाः प्रपद्यन्ते नराधमाः ।
माययापहृतज्ञाना आसुरं भावमाश्रिताः ।।१५।।

*na māṁ duṣkṛtino mūḍhāḥ prapadyante narādhamāḥ* ।
*māyayāpahṛta-jñānā āsuraṁ bhāvam āśritāḥ* ॥15 ॥

चतुर्विधा भजन्ते मां जनाः सुकृतिनोऽर्जुन ।
आर्तो जिज्ञासुरर्थार्थी ज्ञानी च भरतर्षभ ।।१६।।

*caturvidhā bhajante māṁ janāḥ sukṛtino 'rjuna* ।
*ārto jijñāsur arthārthī jñānī ca bharatarṣabha* ॥16 ॥

तेषां ज्ञानी नित्ययुक्त एकभक्तिर्विशिष्यते ।
प्रियो हि ज्ञानिनोऽत्यर्थमहं स च मम प्रियः ।।१७।।

*teṣām jñānī nitya-yukta eka-bhaktir viśiṣyate* ।
*priyo hi jñānino 'tyartham ahaṁ sa ca mama priyaḥ* ॥17 ॥

उदाराः सर्व एवैते ज्ञानी त्वात्मैव मे मतम् ।
आस्थितः स हि युक्तात्मा मामेवानुत्तमां गतिम् ।।१८।।

*udārāḥ sarva evaite jñānī tv ātmaiva me matam* ।
*āsthitaḥ sa hi yuktātmā mām evānuttamāṁ gatim* ॥18 ॥

बहूनां जन्मनामन्ते ज्ञानवान्मां प्रपद्यते ।
वासुदेवः सर्वमिति स महात्मा सुदुर्लभः ।।१९।।

*bahūnāṁ janmanām ante jñānavān māṁ prapadyate* ।
*vāsudevaḥ sarvam iti sa mahātmā sudurlabhaḥ* ॥19 ॥

कामैस्तैस्तैर्हृतज्ञानाः प्रपद्यन्तेऽन्यदेवताः ।
तं तं नियममास्थाय प्रकृत्या नियताः स्वया ।।२०।।

*kāmais tais tair hṛta-jñānāḥ prapadyante 'nya-devatāḥ* ।
*taṁ taṁ niyamam āsthāya prakṛtyā niyatāḥ svayā* ॥20 ॥

यो यो यां यां तनुं भक्तः श्रद्धयार्चितुमिच्छति ।
तस्य तस्याचलां श्रद्धां तामेव विदधाम्यहम् ।।२१।।

*yo yo yāṁ yāṁ tanuṁ bhaktaḥ śraddhayārcitum icchati* ।
*tasya-tasyācalāṁ śraddhāṁ tām eva vidadhāmy aham* ॥21 ॥

स तया श्रद्धया युक्तस्तस्याराधनमीहते ।
लभते च ततः कामान्मयैव विहितान्हि तान् ॥२२॥

*sa tayā śraddhayā yuktas tasyārādhanam īhate* ।
*labhate ca tataḥ kāmān mayaiva vihitān hi tān* ॥22 ॥

अन्तवत्तु फलं तेषां तद्भवत्यल्पमेधसाम् ।
देवान्देवयजो यान्ति मद्भक्ता यान्ति मामपि ॥२३॥

*antavat tu phalaṁ teṣāṁ tad bhavaty alpa-medhasām* ।
*devān deva-yajo yānti mad-bhaktā yānti mām api* ॥23 ॥

अव्यक्तं व्यक्तिमापन्नं मन्यन्ते मामबुद्धयः ।
परं भावमजानन्तो ममाव्ययमनुत्तमम् ॥२४॥

*avyaktaṁ vyaktim āpannaṁ manyante mām abuddhayaḥ* ।
*paraṁ bhāvam ajānanto mamāvyayam anuttamam* ॥24 ॥

नाहं प्रकाशः सर्वस्य योगमायासमावृतः ।
मूढोऽयं नाभिजानाति लोको मामजमव्ययम् ॥२५॥

*nāhaṁ prakāśaḥ sarvasya yoga-māyā samāvṛtaḥ* ।
*mūḍho 'yaṁ nābhijānāti loko mām ajam avyayam* ॥25 ॥

वेदाहं समतीतानि वर्तमानानि चार्जुन ।
भविष्याणि च भूतानि मां तु वेद न कश्चन ॥२६॥

*vedāhaṁ samatītāni vartamānāni cārjuna* ।
*bhaviṣyāṇi ca bhūtāni māṁ tu veda na kaścana* ॥26 ॥

इच्छाद्वेषसमुत्थेन द्वन्द्वमोहेन भारत ।
सर्वभूतानि सम्मोहं सर्गे यान्ति परन्तप ॥२७॥

*icchā-dveṣa-samutthena dvandva-mohena bhārata* ।
*sarva-bhūtāni sammohaṁ sarge yānti parantapa* ॥27 ॥

येषां त्वन्तगतं पापं जनानां पुण्यकर्मणाम् ।
ते द्वन्द्वमोहनिर्मुक्ता भजन्ते मां दृढव्रताः ॥२८॥

*yeṣām tv anta-gataṁ pāpaṁ janānāṁ puṇya-karmaṇām* ।
*te dvandva-moha-nirmuktā bhajante māṁ dṛḍha-vratāḥ* ॥28 ॥

जरामरणमोक्षाय मामाश्रित्य यतन्ति ये ।
ते ब्रह्म तद्विदुः कृत्स्नमध्यात्मं कर्म चाखिलम् ॥२९॥

*jarā-maraṇa-mokṣāya mām āśritya yatanti ye ।*
*te brahma tad viduḥ kṛtsnam adhyātmaṁ karma cākhilam ॥29 ॥*

साधिभूताधिदैवं मां साधियज्ञं च ये विदुः ।
प्रयाणकालेऽपि च मां ते विदुर्युक्तचेतसः ॥३०॥

*sādhibhūtādhidaivaṁ māṁ sādhiyajñaṁ ca ye viduḥ ।*
*prayāṇa-kāle 'pi ca māṁ te vidur yukta-cetasaḥ ॥30 ॥*

# 8. अक्षरब्रह्मयोगः

**अर्जुन उवाच —**

किं तद्ब्रह्म किमध्यात्मं किं कर्म पुरुषोत्तम ।
अधिभूतं च किं प्रोक्तमधिदैवं किमुच्यते ॥१॥

***arjuna uvāca —***

*kiṁ tad brahma kim adhyātmaṁ kiṁ karma puruṣottama ।*
*adhibhūtaṁ ca kiṁ proktam adhidaivaṁ kim ucyate ॥1 ॥*

अधियज्ञः कथं कोऽत्र देहेऽस्मिन्मधुसूदन ।
प्रयाणकाले च कथं ज्ञेयोऽसि नियतात्मभिः ॥२॥

*adhiyajñaḥ kathaṁ ko 'tra dehe 'smin madhusūdana ।*
*prayāṇa-kāle ca kathaṁ jñeyo 'si niyatātmabhiḥ ॥2 ॥*

**श्रीभगवानुवाच —**

अक्षरं ब्रह्म परमं स्वभावोऽध्यात्ममुच्यते ।
भूतभावोद्भवकरो विसर्गः कर्मसञ्ज्ञितः ॥३॥

***śrī bhagavān uvāca —***

*akṣaraṁ brahma paramaṁ svabhāvo 'dhyātmam ucyate ।*
*bhūta-bhāvodbhava-karo visargaḥ karma-saṁjñitaḥ ॥3 ॥*

अधिभूतं क्षरो भावः पुरुषश्चाधिदैवतम् ।
अधियज्ञोऽहमेवात्र देहे देहभृतां वर ॥४॥

*adhibhūtaṁ kṣaro bhāvaḥ puruṣaścādhidaivatam ।*
*adhiyajño 'ham evātra dehe deha-bhṛtāṁ vara ॥4 ॥*

अन्तकाले च मामेव स्मरन्मुक्त्वा कलेवरम् ।
यः प्रयाति स मद्भावं याति नास्त्यत्र संशयः ।।५।।

*anta-kāle ca mām eva smaran muktvā kalevaram* ।
*yaḥ prayāti sa mad-bhāvaṁ yāti nāsty atra saṁśayaḥ* ॥5 ॥

यं यं वापि स्मरन्भावं त्यजत्यन्ते कलेवरम् ।
तं तमेवैति कौन्तेय सदा तद्भावभावितः ।।६।।

*yaṁ yaṁ vāpi smaran bhāvaṁ tyajaty ante kalevaram* ।
*taṁ tam evaiti kaunteya sadā tad-bhāva-bhāvitaḥ* ॥6 ॥

तस्मात्सर्वेषु कालेषु मामनुस्मर युध्य च ।
मय्यर्पितमनोबुद्धिर्मामेवैष्यस्यसंशयः ।।७।।

*tasmāt sarveṣu kāleṣu mām anusmara yudhya ca* ।
*mayy arpita-mano-buddhir mām evaiṣyasy asaṁśyaḥ* ॥7 ॥

अभ्यासयोगयुक्तेन चेतसा नान्यगामिना ।
परमं पुरुषं दिव्यं याति पार्थानुचिन्तयन् ।।८।।

*abhyāsayoga-yuktena cetasā nānya-gāminā* ।
*paramaṁ puruṣaṁ divyaṁ yāti pārthānucintayan* ॥8 ॥

कविं पुराणमनुशासितारमणोरणीयांसमनुस्मरेद्यः ।
सर्वस्य धातारमचिन्त्यरूपमादित्यवर्णं तमसः परस्तात् ।।९।।

*kaviṁ purāṇam anuśāsitaram aṇor aṇīyāṁsam anusmared yaḥ* ।
*sarvasya dhātāram acintya-rūpam āditya-varṇaṁ tamasaḥ parastāt* ॥9 ॥

प्रयाणकाले मनसाचलेन भक्त्या युक्तो योगबलेन चैव ।
भ्रुवोर्मध्ये प्राणमावेश्य सम्यक् स तं परं पुरुषमुपैति दिव्यम् ।।१०।।

*prayāṇa-kāle manasācalena bhaktyā yukto yoga-balena caiva* ।
*bhruvor madhye prāṇam āveśya samyak sa taṁ paraṁ puruṣam upaiti divyam* ॥10 ॥

यदक्षरं वेदविदो वदन्ति विशन्ति यद्यतयो वीतरागाः ।
यदिच्छन्तो ब्रह्मचर्यं चरन्ति तत्ते पदं सङ्ग्रहेण प्रवक्ष्ये ।।११।।

*yad akṣaram veda-vido vadanti viśanti yad yatayo vīta-rāgāḥ* ।
*yad icchanto brahmacaryaṁ caranti tat te padaṁ saṅgraheṇa*

*pravakṣye* ||11 ||

सर्वद्वाराणि संयम्य मनो हृदि निरुध्य च ।
मूर्ध्न्याधायात्मनः प्राणमास्थितो योगधारणाम् ।।१२।।

*sarva-dvārāṇi saṁyamya mano hṛdi nirudhya ca* |
*mūrdhny ādhāyātmanaḥ prāṇam āsthito yoga-dhāraṇām* ||12 ||

ओमित्येकाक्षरं ब्रह्म व्याहरन्मामनुस्मरन् ।
यः प्रयाति त्यजन्देहं स याति परमां गतिम् ।।१३।।

*om ity ekākṣaraṁ brahma vyāharan mām anusmaran* |
*yaḥ prayāti tyajan dehaṁ sa yāti paramāṁ gatim* ||13 ||

अनन्यचेताः सततं यो मां स्मरति नित्यशः ।
तस्याहं सुलभः पार्थ नित्ययुक्तस्य योगिनः ।।१४।।

*ananya-cetāḥ satataṁ yo māṁ smarati nityaśaḥ* |
*tasyāhaṁ sulabhaḥ pārtha nitya-yuktasya yoginaḥ* ||14 ||

मामुपेत्य पुनर्जन्म दुःखालयमशाश्वतम् ।
नाप्नुवन्ति महात्मानः संसिद्धिं परमां गताः ।।१५।।

*mām upetya punar-janma duḥkhālayam aśāśvatam* |
*nāpnuvanti mahātmānaḥ saṁsiddhiṁ paramāṁ gatāḥ* ||15 ||

आब्रह्मभुवनाल्लोकाः पुनरावर्तिनोऽर्जुन ।
मामुपेत्य तु कौन्तेय पुनर्जन्म न विद्यते ।।१६।।

*ā-brahma-bhuvanāl lokāḥ punar-āvartino 'rjuna* |
*mām upetya tu kaunteya punar janma na vidyate* ||16 ||

सहस्रयुगपर्यन्तमहर्यद्ब्रह्मणो विदुः ।
रात्रिं युगसहस्रान्तां तेऽहोरात्रविदो जनाः ।।१७।।

*sahasra-yuga-paryantam ahar yad brahmaṇo viduḥ* |
*rātriṁ yuga-sahasrāntāṁ te 'ho-rātra-vido janāḥ* ||17 ||

अव्यक्ताद्व्यक्तयः सर्वाः प्रभवन्त्यहरागमे ।
रात्र्यागमे प्रलीयन्ते तत्रैवाव्यक्तसञ्ज्ञके ।।१८।।

*avyaktād vyaktayaḥ sarvāḥ prabhavanty aharāgame* |
*rātry-āgame pralīyante tatraiva 'vyakta sañjñake* ||18 ||

भूतग्रामः स एवायं भूत्वा भूत्वा प्रलीयते ।
रात्र्यागमेऽवशः पार्थ प्रभवत्यहरागमे ।।१९।।

*bhūta-grāmaḥ sa evāyaṁ bhūtvā bhūtvā pralīyate* ।
*rātry-āgame 'vaśaḥ pārtha prabhavaty ahar-āgame* ॥19 ॥

परस्तस्मात्तु भावोऽन्योऽव्यक्तोऽव्यक्तात्सनातनः ।
यः स सर्वेषु भूतेषु नश्यत्सु न विनश्यति ॥२०॥

*paras tasmāt tu bhāvo 'nyo 'vyakto 'vyaktāt sanātanaḥ* ।
*yaḥ sa sarveṣu bhūteṣu naśyatsu na vinaśyati* ॥20 ॥

अव्यक्तोऽक्षर इत्युक्तस्तमाहुः परमां गतिम् ।
यं प्राप्य न निवर्तन्ते तद्धाम परमं मम ॥२१॥

*avyakto 'kṣara ity uktas tam āhuḥ paramāṁ gatim* ।
*yaṁ prāpya na nivartante tad dhāma paramaṁ mama* ॥21 ॥

पुरुषः स परः पार्थ भक्त्या लभ्यस्त्वनन्यया ।
यस्यान्तःस्थानि भूतानि येन सर्वमिदं ततम् ॥२२॥

*puruṣaḥ sa paraḥ pārtha bhaktyā labhyas tv ananyayā* ।
*yasyāntaḥ sthāni bhūtāni yena sarvam idaṁ tatam* ॥22 ॥

यत्र काले त्वनावृत्तिमावृत्तिं चैव योगिनः ।
प्रयाता यान्ति तं कालं वक्ष्यामि भरतर्षभ ॥२३॥

*yatra kāle tv anāvṛttim āvṛttiṁ caiva yogīnaḥ* ।
*prayātā yānti taṁ kālaṁ vakṣyāmi bharatarṣabha* ॥23 ॥

अग्निर्ज्योतिरहः शुक्लः षण्मासा उत्तरायणम् ।
तत्र प्रयाता गच्छन्ति ब्रह्म ब्रह्मविदो जनाः ॥२४॥

*agnir jyotir ahaḥ śuklaḥ ṣaṇmāsā uttarāyaṇam* ।
*tatra prayātā gacchanti brahma brahma-vido janāḥ* ॥24 ॥

धूमो रात्रिस्तथा कृष्णः षण्मासा दक्षिणायनम् ।
तत्र चान्द्रमसं ज्योतिर्योगी प्राप्य निवर्तते ॥२५॥

*dhūmo rātris tathā kṛṣṇaḥ ṣaṇmāsā dakṣiṇāyanam* ।
*tatra cāndramasaṁ jyotir yogī prāpya nivartate* ॥25 ॥

शुक्लकृष्णे गती ह्येते जगतः शाश्वते मते ।
एकया यात्यनावृत्तिमन्ययावर्तते पुनः ॥२६॥

*śukla-kṛṣṇe gatī hy ete jagataḥ śāśvate mate* ।
*ekayā yāty anāvṛttim anyayā vartate punaḥ* ॥26 ॥

नैते सृती पार्थ जानन्योगी मुह्यति कश्चन ।
तस्मात्सर्वेषु कालेषु योगयुक्तो भवार्जुन ॥२७॥

*naite sṛtī pārtha jānan yogī muhyati kaścana* ।
*tasmāt sarveṣu kāleṣu yogayukto bhavārjuna* ॥27 ॥

वेदेषु यज्ञेषु तपःसु चैव दानेषु यत्पुण्यफलं प्रदिष्टम् ।
अत्येति तत्सर्वमिदं विदित्वा योगी परं स्थानमुपैति चाद्यम् ॥२८॥

*vedeṣu yajñeṣu tapaḥsu caiva dāneṣu yat puṇya-phalaṁ pradiṣṭam* ।
*atyeti tat sarvam idaṁ viditvā yogī paraṁ sthānam upaiti cādyam* ॥28 ॥

# 9. राजविद्याराजगुह्ययोगः

**श्रीभगवानुवाच —**

इदं तु ते गुह्यतमं प्रवक्ष्याम्यनसूयवे ।
ज्ञानं विज्ञानसहितं यज्ज्ञात्वा मोक्ष्यसेऽशुभात् ॥१॥

***śrī bhagavān uvāca —***

*idaṁ tu te guhyatamaṁ pravakṣyāmy anasūyave* ।
*jñānaṁ vijñāna-sahitaṁ yaj jñātvā mokṣyase 'śubhāt* ॥1 ॥

राजविद्या राजगुह्यं पवित्रमिदमुत्तमम् ।
प्रत्यक्षावगमं धर्म्यं सुसुखं कर्तुमव्ययम् ॥२॥

*rāja-vidyā rāja-guhyaṁ pavitram idam uttamam* ।
*pratyakṣāvagamaṁ dharmyaṁ susukhaṁ kartum avyayam* ॥2 ॥

अश्रद्दधानाः पुरुषा धर्मस्यास्य परन्तप ।
अप्राप्य मां निवर्तन्ते मृत्युसंसारवर्त्मनि ॥३॥

*aśraddadhānāḥ puruṣā dharmasyāsya parantapa* ।
*aprāpya māṁ nivartante mṛtyu-saṁsāra-vartmani* ॥3 ॥

मया ततमिदं सर्वं जगदव्यक्तमूर्तिना ।
मत्स्थानि सर्वभूतानि न चाहं तेष्ववस्थितः ॥४॥

*mayā tatam idaṁ sarvaṁ jagad avyakta-mūrtinā* ।
*mat-sthāni sarva-bhūtāni na cā 'haṁ teṣv avasthitaḥ* ॥4 ॥

न च मत्स्थानि भूतानि पश्य मे योगमैश्वरम् ।
भूतभृन्न च भूतस्थो ममात्मा भूतभावनः ॥५॥

*na ca mat-sthāni bhūtāni paśya me yogam aiśvaram* ।
*bhūta-bhṛn na ca bhūtastho mamā 'tmā bhūta-bhāvanaḥ* ॥5 ॥

यथाकाशस्थितो नित्यं वायुः सर्वत्रगो महान् ।
तथा सर्वाणि भूतानि मत्स्थानीत्युपधारय ॥६॥

*yathākāśa-sthito nityaṁ vāyuḥ sarvatrago mahān* ।
*tathā sarvāṇi bhūtāni mat sthānīty upadhāraya* ॥6 ॥

सर्वभूतानि कौन्तेय प्रकृतिं यान्ति मामिकाम् ।
कल्पक्षये पुनस्तानि कल्पादौ विसृजाम्यहम् ॥७॥

*sarva-bhūtāni kaunteya prakṛtiṁ yānti māmikāṁ* ।
*kalpa-kṣaye punas tāni kalpādau visṛjāmy ahaṁ* ॥7 ॥

प्रकृतिं स्वामवष्टभ्य विसृजामि पुनः पुनः ।
भूतग्राममिमं कृत्स्नमवशं प्रकृतेर्वशात् ॥८॥

*prakṛtiṁ svām avaṣṭabhya viṣrjāmi punaḥ-punaḥ* ।
*bhūta-grāmam imaṁ kṛtsnam avaśaṁ prakṛter vaśāt* ॥8 ॥

न च मां तानि कर्माणि निबध्नन्ति धनञ्जय ।
उदासीनवदासीनमसक्तं तेषु कर्मसु ॥९॥

*na ca māṁ tāni karmāṇi nibadhnanti dhanañjaya* ।
*udāsīnavad āsīnam asaktaṁ teṣu karmasu* ॥9 ॥

मयाध्यक्षेण प्रकृतिः सूयते सचराचरम् ।
हेतुनानेन कौन्तेय जगद्विपरिवर्तते ॥१०॥

*mayādhyakṣena prakṛtiḥ sūyate sacarācaram* ।
*heturānena kaunteya jagad viparivartate* ॥10 ॥

अवजानन्ति मां मूढा मानुषीं तनुमाश्रितम् ।
परं भावमजानन्तो मम भूतमहेश्वरम् ॥११॥

*avajānanti māṁ mūḍhā mānuṣīṁ tanum āśritam* ।
*paraṁ bhāvam ajānanto mama bhūta-maheśvaram* ॥11 ॥

मोघाशा मोघकर्माणो मोघज्ञाना विचेतसः ।
राक्षसीमासुरीं चैव प्रकृतिं मोहिनीं श्रिताः ॥१२॥

*moghāśā mogha-karmāṇo mogha-jñāna vicetasaḥ* ।
*rākṣasīm āsurīṁ caiva prakṛtiṁ mohinīṁ śritāḥ* ॥12 ॥

महात्मानस्तु मां पार्थ दैवीं प्रकृतिमाश्रिताः ।
भजन्त्यनन्यमनसो ज्ञात्वा भूतादिमव्ययम् ॥१३॥

*mahātmānas tu māṁ pārtha daivīṁ prakṛtim aśritāḥ* ।
*bhajanty ananya-manaso jñātvā bhūtādim avyayaṁ* ॥13 ॥

सततं कीर्तयन्तो मां यतन्तश्च दृढव्रताः ।
नमस्यन्तश्च मां भक्त्या नित्ययुक्ता उपासते ॥१४॥

*satataṁ kīrtayanto māṁ yatantaś ca dṛḍha-vratāḥ* ।
*namasyantaś ca māṁ bhaktyā nitya-yuktā upāsate* ॥14 ॥

ज्ञानयज्ञेन चाप्यन्ये यजन्तो मामुपासते ।
एकत्वेन पृथक्त्वेन बहुधा विश्वतोमुखम् ॥१५॥

*jñāna-yajñena cāpy anye yajanto mām upāsate* ।
*ekatvena pṛthaktvena bahudhā viśvato-mukham* ॥15 ॥

अहं क्रतुरहं यज्ञः स्वधाहमहमौषधम् ।
मन्त्रोऽहमहमेवाज्यमहमग्निरहं हुतम् ॥१६॥

*ahaṁ kratur ahaṁ yajñaḥ svadhāham aham auṣadhaṁ* ।
*mantro 'ham aham evājyam aham agnir ahaṁ hutaṁ* ॥16 ॥

पिताहमस्य जगतो माता धाता पितामहः ।
वेद्यं पवित्रमोङ्कार ऋक्साम यजुरेव च ॥१७॥

*pitāham asya jagato mātā dhātā pitāmahaḥ* ।
*vedyaṁ pavitram oṅ-kāra ṛk sāma yajur eva ca* ॥17 ॥

गतिर्भर्ता प्रभुः साक्षी निवासः शरणं सुहृत् ।
प्रभवः प्रलयः स्थानं निधानं बीजमव्ययम् ॥१८॥

*gatīr bhartā pabhuḥ sākṣī nivāsaḥ śaranaṁ suhṛt* ।
*prabhavaḥ pralayaḥ sthānaṁ nidhānaṁ bījam avyayam* ॥18 ॥

तपाम्यहमहं वर्षं निगृह्णाम्युत्सृजामि च ।
अमृतं चैव मृत्युश्च सदसच्चाहमर्जुन ॥१९॥

*tapāmy aham ahaṁ varsaṁ nigṛhṇāmy utsṛjāmi ca* ।
*amṛtaṁ caiva mṛtyuś ca sad asac cāham arjuna* ॥19 ॥

त्रैविद्या मां सोमपाः पूतपापा यज्ञैरिष्ट्वा स्वर्गतिं प्रार्थयन्ते ।
ते पुण्यमासाद्य सुरेन्द्रलोकमश्नन्ति दिव्यान्दिवि देवभोगान् ॥२०॥

*traividyā māṁ soma-pāḥ pūta-pāpā yajñair iṣṭvā svar-gatiṁ prārthayante* ।
*te puṇyam āsādya surendra-lokam aśnanti divyān divi deva-bhogān* ॥20॥

ते तं भुक्त्वा स्वर्गलोकं विशालं क्षीणे पुण्ये मर्त्यलोकं विशन्ति ।
एवं त्रयीधर्ममनुप्रपन्ना गतागतं कामकामा लभन्ते ॥२१॥

*te taṁ bhuktvā svarga-lokaṁ viśālaṁ kṣīṇe puṇye martya-lokaṁ viśanti* ।
*evaṁ trayī-dharmam anuprapannā gatāgataṁ kāma-kāmā labhante* ॥21॥

अनन्याश्चिन्तयन्तो मां ये जनाः पर्युपासते ।
तेषां नित्याभियुक्तानां योगक्षेमं वहाम्यहम् ॥२२॥

*ananyāś cintayanto māṁ ye janāḥ paryupāsate* ।
*teṣāṁ nityābhiyuktānāṁ yoga-kṣemaṁ vahāmy aham* ॥22॥

येऽप्यन्यदेवता भक्ता यजन्ते श्रद्धयान्विताः ।
तेऽपि मामेव कौन्तेय यजन्त्यविधिपूर्वकम् ॥२३॥

*ye 'py anya-devatā bhaktā yajante śraddhayānvitāḥ* ।
*te 'pi mām eva kaunteya yajanty avidhi-pūrvakam* ॥23॥

अहं हि सर्वयज्ञानां भोक्ता च प्रभुरेव च ।
न तु मामभिजानन्ति तत्त्वेनातश्च्यवन्ति ते ॥२४॥

*ahaṁ hi sarva-yajñānāṁ bhoktā ca prabhur eva ca* ।
*na tu mām abhijānanti tattvenātaś cyavanti te* ॥24॥

यान्ति देवव्रता देवान्पितॄन्यान्ति पितृव्रताः ।
भूतानि यान्ति भूतेज्या यान्ति मद्याजिनोऽपि माम् ॥२५॥

*yānti deva-vratā devān pitṝn yānti pitṛ-vratāḥ* ।
*bhūtāni yānti bhūtejyā yānti mad-yājino 'pi mām* ॥25॥

पत्रं पुष्पं फलं तोयं यो मे भक्त्या प्रयच्छति ।
तदहं भक्त्युपहृतमश्नामि प्रयतात्मनः ॥२६॥

*patraṁ puṣpaṁ phalaṁ toyaṁ yo me bhaktyā prayacchati* ।
*tad ahaṁ bhakty-upahṛtam aśnāmi prayatātmanaḥ* ॥26॥

यत्करोषि यदश्नासि यज्जुहोषि ददासि यत् ।
यत्तपस्यसि कौन्तेय तत्कुरुष्व मदर्पणम् ॥२७॥

*yat karoṣi yad aśnāsi yaj juhoṣi dadāsi yat* ।
*yat tapasyasi kaunteya tat kuruṣva mad-arpaṇam* ॥27 ॥

शुभाशुभफलैरेवं मोक्ष्यसे कर्मबन्धनैः ।
संन्यासयोगयुक्तात्मा विमुक्तो मामुपैष्यसि ॥२८॥

*śubhāśubha-phalair evaṁ mokṣyase karma-bandhanaiḥ* ।
*saṁnyāsa-yoga-yuktātmā vimukto mām upaiṣyasi* ॥28 ॥

समोऽहं सर्वभूतेषु न मे द्वेष्योऽस्ति न प्रियः ।
ये भजन्ति तु मां भक्त्या मयि ते तेषु चाप्यहम् ॥२९॥

*samo 'haṁ sarvabhūteṣu na me dveṣyo 'sti na priyaḥ* ।
*ye bhajanti tu māṁ bhaktyā mayi te teṣu cāpy aham* ॥29 ॥

अपि चेत्सुदुराचारो भजते मामनन्यभाक् ।
साधुरेव स मन्तव्यः सम्यग्व्यवसितो हि सः ॥३०॥

*api cet sudurācāro bhajate mām ananya-bhāk* ।
*sādhur eva sa mantavyaḥ samyag vyavasito hi saḥ* ॥30 ॥

क्षिप्रं भवति धर्मात्मा शश्वच्छान्तिं निगच्छति ।
कौन्तेय प्रति जानीहि न मे भक्तः प्रणश्यति ॥३१॥

*kṣipraṁ bhavati dharmātmā śaśvac-chāntiṁ nigacchati* ।
*kaunteya prati jānīhi na me bhaktaḥ praṇaśyati* ॥31 ॥

मां हि पार्थ व्यपाश्रित्य येऽपि स्युः पापयोनयः ।
स्त्रियो वैश्यास्तथा शूद्रास्तेऽपि यान्ति परां गतिम् ॥३२॥

*māṁ hi pārtha vyapāśritya ye 'pi syuḥ pāpa-yonayaḥ* ।
*striyo vaiśyās tathā śūdrās te 'pi yānti parāṁ gatīm* ॥32 ॥

किं पुनर्ब्राह्मणाः पुण्या भक्ता राजर्षयस्तथा ।
अनित्यमसुखं लोकमिमं प्राप्य भजस्व माम् ॥३३॥

*kiṁ punar brāhmaṇāḥ puṇyā bhaktā rājarṣayas tathā* ।
*anityam asukhaṁ lokam imaṁ prāpya bhajasva mām* ॥33 ॥

मन्मना भव मद्भक्तो मद्याजी मां नमस्कुरु ।
मामेवैष्यसि युक्त्वैवमात्मानं मत्परायणः ॥३४॥

*manmanā bhava mad-bhakto mad-yājī māṁ namas-kuru* ।
*mām evaiṣyasi yuktvaivam ātmānaṁ mat-parāyaṇaḥ* ॥34 ॥

# 10. विभूतियोगः

**श्रीभगवानुवाच —**

भूय एव महाबाहो शृणु मे परमं वचः ।
यत्तेऽहं प्रीयमाणाय वक्ष्यामि हितकाम्यया ॥१॥

***śrī bhagavān uvāca —***

*bhūya eva mahā-bāho śṛṇu me paramaṁ vacaḥ* ।
*yat te 'haṁ prīyamāṇāya vakṣyāmi hita-kāmyayā* ॥1 ॥

न मे विदुः सुरगणाः प्रभवं न महर्षयः ।
अहमादिर्हि देवानां महर्षीणां च सर्वशः ॥२॥

*na me viduḥ sura-gaṇāḥ prabhavaṁ na maharṣayaḥ* ।
*aham ādir hi devānāṁ maharṣīṇāṁ ca sarvaśaḥ* ॥2 ॥

यो मामजमनादिं च वेत्ति लोकमहेश्वरम् ।
असम्मूढः स मर्त्येषु सर्वपापैः प्रमुच्यते ॥३॥

*yo mām ajam anādiṁ ca vetti loka-maheśvaram* ।
*asammūḍhaḥ sa martyeṣu sarvapāpaiḥ pramucyate* ॥3 ॥

बुद्धिर्ज्ञानमसम्मोहः क्षमा सत्यं दमः शमः ।
सुखं दुःखं भवोऽभावो भयं चाभयमेव च ॥४॥

*buddhir jñānam asammohaḥ kṣamā satyaṁ damaḥ śamaḥ,*
*sukhaṁ duḥkaṁ bhavo 'bhāvo bhayaṁ cābhayam eva ca* ॥4 ॥

अहिंसा समता तुष्टिस्तपो दानं यशोऽयशः ।
भवन्ति भावा भूतानां मत्त एव पृथग्विधाः ॥५॥

*ahiṁsā samatā tuṣṭis tapo dānaṁ yaśo 'yaśaḥ* ।
*bhavanti bhāvā bhūtānāṁ matta eva pṛthag-vidhāḥ* ॥5 ॥

महर्षयः सप्त पूर्वे चत्वारो मनवस्तथा ।
मद्भावा मानसा जाता येषां लोक इमाः प्रजाः ॥६॥

*maharṣayaḥ sapta pūrve catvāro manavas tathā* ।
*mad-bhāvā mānasā jātā yeṣāṁ loka imāḥ prajāḥ* ॥6॥

एतां विभूतिं योगं च मम यो वेत्ति तत्त्वतः ।
सोऽविकम्पेन योगेन युज्यते नात्र संशयः ॥७॥

*etāṁ vibhūtiṁ yogaṁ ca mama yo vetti tattvataḥ* ।
*so 'vikampena yogena yujyate nātra saṁśayaḥ* ॥7॥

अहं सर्वस्य प्रभवो मत्तः सर्वं प्रवर्तते ।
इति मत्वा भजन्ते मां बुधा भावसमन्विताः ॥८॥

*ahaṁ sarvasya prabhavo mattaḥ sarvaṁ pravartate* ।
*iti matvā bhajante māṁ budhā bhāva-samanvitāḥ* ॥8॥

मच्चित्ता मद्गतप्राणा बोधयन्तः परस्परम् ।
कथयन्तश्च मां नित्यं तुष्यन्ति च रमन्ति च ॥९॥

*mac-cittā mad-gata-prāṇā bodhayantaḥ parasparam* ।
*kathayantaś ca māṁ nityaṁ tuṣyanti ca ramanti ca* ॥9॥

तेषां सततयुक्तानां भजतां प्रीतिपूर्वकम् ।
ददामि बुद्धियोगं तं येन मामुपयान्ति ते ॥१०॥

*teṣāṁ satata-yuktānāṁ bhajatāṁ prīti-pūrvakam* ।
*dadāmi buddhi-yogaṁ taṁ yena mām upayānti te* ॥10॥

तेषामेवानुकम्पार्थमहमज्ञानजं तमः ।
नाशयाम्यात्मभावस्थो ज्ञानदीपेन भास्वता ॥११॥

*teṣām evānukampārtham aham ajñānajaṁ tamaḥ* ।
*nāśayāmy ātmabhāvastho jñāna-dīpena bhāsvatā* ॥11॥

**अर्जुन उवाच —**

परं ब्रह्म परं धाम पवित्रं परमं भवान् ।
पुरुषं शाश्वतं दिव्यमादिदेवमजं विभुम् ॥१२॥

***arjuna uvāca —***

*paraṁ brahma paraṁ dhāma pavitraṁ paramaṁ bhavān* ।
*puruṣaṁ śāśvataṁ divyam ādi-devam ajaṁ vibhum* ॥12॥

आहुस्त्वामृषयः सर्वे देवर्षिर्नारदस्तथा ।
असितो देवलो व्यासः स्वयं चैव ब्रवीषि मे ॥१३॥

*āhus tvām ṛṣayaḥ sarve devarṣir nāradas tathā* ।
*asito devalo vyāsaḥ svayaṁ caiva bravīṣi me* ॥13 ॥

सर्वमेतदृतं मन्ये यन्मां वदसि केशव ।
न हि ते भगवन्व्यक्तिं विदुर्देवा न दानवाः ॥१४॥

*sarvam etad ṛtaṁ manye yan māṁ vadasi keśava* ।
*na hi te bhagavan vyaktiṁ vidur devā na dānavāḥ* ॥14 ॥

स्वयमेवात्मनात्मानं वेत्थ त्वं पुरुषोत्तम ।
भूतभावन भूतेश देवदेव जगत्पते ॥१५॥

*svayam evātmanātmānaṁ vettha tvaṁ puruṣottama* ।
*bhūta-bhāvana bhūteśa deva-deva jagat pate* ॥15 ॥

वक्तुमर्हस्यशेषेण दिव्या ह्यात्मविभूतयः ।
याभिर्विभूतिभिर्लोकानिमांस्त्वं व्याप्य तिष्ठसि ॥१६॥

*vaktum arhasy aśeṣeṇa divyā hy ātma-vibhūtayaḥ* ।
*yābhir vibhūtibhir lokān imāṁs tvaṁ vyāpya tiṣṭhasi* ॥16 ॥

कथं विद्यामहं योगिंस्त्वां सदा परिचिन्तयन् ।
केषु केषु च भावेषु चिन्त्योऽसि भगवन्मया ॥१७॥

*kathaṁ vidyām ahaṁ yogiṁs tvāṁ sadā paricintayan* ।
*keṣu keṣu ca bhāveṣu cintyo 'si bhagavan mayā* ॥17 ॥

विस्तरेणात्मनो योगं विभूतिं च जनार्दन ।
भूयः कथय तृप्तिर्हि शृण्वतो नास्ति मेऽमृतम् ॥१८॥

*vistareṇātmano yogaṁ vibhūtiṁ ca janārdana* ।
*bhūyaḥ kathaya tṛptir hi śṛṇvato nāsti me 'mṛtam* ॥18 ॥

**श्रीभगवानुवाच —**

हन्त ते कथयिष्यामि दिव्या ह्यात्मविभूतयः ।
प्राधान्यतः कुरुश्रेष्ठ नास्त्यन्तो विस्तरस्य मे ॥१९॥

***śrī bhagavān uvāca —***

*hanta te kathayiṣyāmi divyā hy ātma-vibhūtayaḥ* ।
*prādhānyataḥ kuru-śreṣṭha nāstyanto vistarasya me* ॥19 ॥

अहमात्मा गुडाकेश सर्वभूताशयस्थितः ।
अहमादिश्च मध्यं च भूतानामन्त एव च ॥२०॥

*aham ātmā guḍākeśa sarva-bhūtāśaya-sthitaḥ* ।
*aham ādiś ca madhyaṁ ca bhūtānām anta eva ca* ॥20 ॥

आदित्यानामहं विष्णुर्ज्योतिषां रविरंशुमान् ।
मरीचिर्मरुतामस्मि नक्षत्राणामहं शशी ॥२१॥

*ādityānām ahaṁ viṣṇur jyotiṣāṁ ravir aṁśumān* ।
*marīcir marutām asmi nakṣatrāṇām ahaṁ śasī* ॥21 ॥

वेदानां सामवेदोऽस्मि देवानामस्मि वासवः ।
इन्द्रियाणां मनश्चास्मि भूतानामस्मि चेतना ॥२२॥

*vedānāṁ sāma-vedo 'smi devānām asmi vāsavaḥ* ।
*indriyāṇāṁ manaś cāsmi bhūatānām asmi cetanā* ॥22 ॥

रुद्राणां शंकरश्चास्मि वित्तेशो यक्षरक्षसाम् ।
वसूनां पावकश्चास्मि मेरुः शिखरिणामहम् ॥२३॥

*rudrāṇāṁ śaṅkaraś cāsmi vitteśo yakṣa-rakṣasām* ।
*vasūnāṁ pāvakaś cāsmi meruḥ śikhariṇām aham* ॥23 ॥

पुरोधसां च मुख्यं मां विद्धि पार्थ बृहस्पतिम् ।
सेनानीनामहं स्कन्दः सरसामस्मि सागरः ॥२४॥

*purodhasāṁ ca mukhyaṁ māṁ viddhi pārtha bṛhaspatim* ।
*senānīnām ahaṁ skandaḥ sarasām asmi sāgaraḥ* ॥24 ॥

महर्षीणां भृगुरहं गिरामस्म्येकमक्षरम् ।
यज्ञानां जपयज्ञोऽस्मि स्थावराणां हिमालयः ॥२५॥

*maharṣīṇāṁ bhṛgur ahaṁ girām asmy ekam akṣaram* ।
*yajñānāṁ japa-yajño 'smi sthāvarāṇāṁ himālayaḥ* ॥25 ॥

अश्वत्थः सर्ववृक्षाणां देवर्षीणां च नारदः ।
गन्धर्वाणां चित्ररथः सिद्धानां कपिलो मुनिः ॥२६॥

*aśvatthaḥ sarva-vṛkṣāṇāṁ devarṣīṇāṁ ca nāradaḥ* ।
*gandharvāṇāṁ citrarathaḥ siddhānāṁ kapilo muniḥ* ॥26 ॥

उच्चैःश्रवसमश्वानां विद्धि माममृतोद्भवम् ।
ऐरावतं गजेन्द्राणां नराणां च नराधिपम् ॥२७॥

*uccaiḥśravasam aśvānāṁ viddhi mām amṛtodbhavam* ।
*airāvataṁ gajendrāṇāṁ narāṇāṁ ca narādhipam* ॥27 ॥

आयुधानामहं वज्रं धेनूनामस्मि कामधुक् ।
प्रजनश्चास्मि कन्दर्पः सर्पाणामस्मि वासुकिः ।।२८।।

*āyudhānām ahaṁ vajraṁ dhenūnām asmi kāma-dhuk* ।
*prajanaś cāsmi kandarpaḥ sarpāṇām asmi vāsukiḥ* ॥28 ॥

अनन्तश्चास्मि नागानां वरुणो यादसामहम् ।
पितॄणामर्यमा चास्मि यमः संयमतामहम् ।।२९।।

*anantaś cāsmi nāgānāṁ varuṇo yādasām aham* ।
*pitṝṇām aryamā cāsmi yamaḥ saṁyamatām aham* ॥29 ॥

प्रह्लादश्चास्मि दैत्यानां कालः कलयतामहम् ।
मृगाणां च मृगेन्द्रोऽहं वैनतेयश्च पक्षिणाम् ।।३०।।

*prahlādaś cāsmi daityānāṁ kālaḥ kalayatām aham* ।
*mṛgāṇāṁ ca mṛgendro 'haṁ vainateyaś ca pakṣiṇām* ॥30 ॥

पवनः पवतामस्मि रामः शस्त्रभृतामहम् ।
झषाणां मकरश्चास्मि स्रोतसामस्मि जाह्नवी ।।३१।।

*pavanaḥ pavatām asmi rāmaḥ śastra-bhṛtām aham* ।
*jhaṣāṇāṁ makaraś cāsmi śrotasām asmi jāhnavī* ॥31 ॥

सर्गाणामादिरन्तश्च मध्यं चैवाहमर्जुन ।
अध्यात्मविद्या विद्यानां वादः प्रवदतामहम् ।।३२।।

*sargāṇām ādir antaś ca madhyaṁ caivāham arjuna* ।
*adhyātma-vidyā vidyānāṁ vādaḥ pravadatām aham* ॥32 ॥

अक्षराणामकारोऽस्मि द्वन्द्वः सामासिकस्य च ।
अहमेवाक्षयः कालो धाताहं विश्वतोमुखः ।।३३।।

*akṣarāṇām akāro 'smi dvandvaḥ sāmāsikasya ca* ।
*aham evākṣayaḥ kālo dhātā 'haṁ viśvato-mukhaḥ* ॥33 ॥

मृत्युः सर्वहरश्चाहमुद्भवश्च भविष्यताम् ।
कीर्तिः श्रीर्वाक्च नारीणां स्मृतिर्मेधा धृतिः क्षमा ।।३४।।

*mṛtyuḥ sarva-haraś cāham udbhavaś ca bhaviṣyatām* ।
*kīrtiḥ śrīr vāk ca nārīṇāṁ smṛtir medhā dhṛtiḥ kṣamā* ॥34 ॥

बृहत्साम तथा साम्नां गायत्री छन्दसामहम् ।
मासानां मार्गशीर्षोऽहमृतूनां कुसुमाकरः ।।३५।।

*bṛhat-sāma tathā sāmnāṁ gāyatrī chandasām aham* ।
*māsānāṁ mārgaśīrṣo 'ham ṛtūnāṁ kusumākaraḥ* ॥35 ॥

द्यूतं छलयतामस्मि तेजस्तेजस्विनामहम् ।
जयोऽस्मि व्यवसायोऽस्मि सत्त्वं सत्त्ववतामहम् ॥३६॥

*dyūtaṁ chalayatām asmi tejas tejasvinām aham* ।
*jayo 'smi vyavasāyo 'smi sattvaṁ sattvavatām aham* ॥36 ॥

वृष्णीनां वासुदेवोऽस्मि पाण्डवानां धनञ्जयः ।
मुनीनामप्यहं व्यासः कवीनामुशना कविः ॥३७॥

*vṛṣṇīnāṁ vāsudevo 'smi pāṇḍavānāṁ dhanañjayaḥ* ।
*munīnām apy ahaṁ vyāsaḥ kavīnam uśanā kaviḥ* ॥37 ॥

दण्डो दमयतामस्मि नीतिरस्मि जिगीषताम् ।
मौनं चैवास्मि गुह्यानां ज्ञानं ज्ञानवतामहम् ॥३८॥

*daṇḍo damayatām asmi nītir asmi jigīṣatām* ।
*maunaṁ caivāsmi guhyānāṁ jñānaṁ jñānavatām aham* ॥38 ॥

यच्चापि सर्वभूतानां बीजं तदहमर्जुन ।
न तदस्ति विना यत्स्यान्मया भूतं चराचरम् ॥३९॥

*yac cāpi sarva-bhūtānāṁ bījaṁ tad aham arjuna* ।
*na tad asti vinā yat syān mayā bhūtaṁ carācaram* ॥39 ॥

नान्तोऽस्ति मम दिव्यानां विभूतीनां परन्तप ।
एष तूद्देशतः प्रोक्तो विभूतेर्विस्तरो मया ॥४०॥

*nānto 'sti mama divyānāṁ vibhūtīnāṁ parantapa* ।
*eṣa tūddeśataḥ prokto vibhūter vistaro mayā* ॥40 ॥

यद्यद्विभूतिमत्सत्त्वं श्रीमदूर्जितमेव वा ।
तत्तदेवावगच्छ त्वं मम तेजोंऽशसम्भवम् ॥४१॥

*yad-yad vibhūtimat sattvaṁ śrīmad ūrjitam eva vā* ।
*tat-tad evāvagaccha tvaṁ mama tejo 'ṁśa-sambhavam* ॥41 ॥

अथवा बहुनैतेन किं ज्ञातेन तवार्जुन ।
विष्टभ्याहमिदं कृत्स्नमेकांशेन स्थितो जगत् ॥४२॥

*athavā bahunaitena kiṁ jñātena tavārjuna* ।
*viṣṭabhyāham idaṁ kṛtsnam ekāṁśena sthito jagat* ॥42 ॥

# 11. विश्वरूपदर्शनयोगः

**अर्जुन उवाच —**

मदनुग्रहाय परमं गुह्यमध्यात्मसञ्ज्ञितम् ।
यत्त्वयोक्तं वचस्तेन मोहोऽयं विगतो मम ॥१॥

***arjuna uvāca —***

*mad-anugrahāya paramaṁ guhyam adhyātma sañjñitam* ।
*yat tvayoktaṁ vacas tena moho 'yaṁ vigato mama* ॥1॥

भवाप्ययौ हि भूतानां श्रुतौ विस्तरशो मया ।
त्वत्तः कमलपत्राक्ष माहात्म्यमपि चाव्ययम् ॥२॥

*bhavāpyayau hi bhūtānāṁ śrutau vistaraśo mayā* ।
*tvattaḥ kamala-patrākṣa māhātmyam api cāvyayam* ॥2॥

एवमेतद्यथात्थ त्वमात्मानं परमेश्वर ।
द्रष्टुमिच्छामि ते रूपमैश्वरं पुरुषोत्तम ॥३॥

*evam etad yathāttha tvam ātmānaṁ parameśvara* ।
*draṣṭum icchāmi te rūpam aiśvaraṁ puruṣottama* ॥3॥

मन्यसे यदि तच्छक्यं मया द्रष्टुमिति प्रभो ।
योगेश्वर ततो मे त्वं दर्शयात्मानमव्ययम् ॥४॥

*manyase yadi tac chakyaṁ mayā draṣṭum iti prabho* ।
*yogeśvara tato me tvaṁ darśayātmānam avyayam* ॥4॥

**श्रीभगवानुवाच —**

पश्य मे पार्थ रूपाणि शतशोऽथ सहस्रशः ।
नानाविधानि दिव्यानि नानावर्णाकृतीनि च ॥५॥

***śrī bhagavān uvāca —***

*paśya me pārtha rūpāṇi śataśo 'tha sahasraśaḥ* ।
*nānā-vidhāni divyāni nānā-varṇākṛtīni ca* ॥5॥

पश्यादित्यान्वसून्रुद्रानश्विनौ मरुतस्तथा ।
बहून्यदृष्टपूर्वाणि पश्याश्चर्याणि भारत ॥६॥

*paśyādityān vasūn rudrān aśvinau marutas tathā* ।
*bahūny adṛṣṭa-pūrvāṇi paśyāścaryāṇi bhārata* ॥6॥

इहैकस्थं जगत्कृत्स्नं पश्याद्य सचराचरम् ।
मम देहे गुडाकेश यच्चान्यद्द्रष्टुमिच्छसि ।।७।।

*ihaikasthaṁ jagat kṛtsnaṁ paśyādya sacarācaram* ।
*mama dehe guḍākeśa yac cānyad draṣṭum icchasi* ॥7 ॥

न तु मां शक्यसे द्रष्टुमनेनैव स्वचक्षुषा ।
दिव्यं ददामि ते चक्षुः पश्य मे योगमैश्वरम् ।।८।।

*na tu māṁ śakyase draṣṭum anenaiva svacakṣuṣā* ।
*divyaṁ dadāmi te cakṣuḥ paśya me yogam aiśvaram* ॥8 ॥

**सञ्जय उवाच —**

एवमुक्त्वा ततो राजन्महायोगेश्वरो हरिः ।
दर्शयामास पार्थाय परमं रूपमैश्वरम् ।।९।।

***sañjaya uvāca —***

*evam uktvā tato rājan mahā-yogeśvaro hariḥ* ।
*darśayāmāsa pārthāya paramaṁ rūpam aiśvaram* ॥9 ॥

अनेकवक्त्रनयनमनेकाद्भुतदर्शनम् ।
अनेकदिव्याभरणं दिव्यानेकोद्यतायुधम् ।।१०।।

*aneka-vaktra-nayanam anekādbhuta-darśanam* ।
*aneka-divyābharaṇaṁ divyānekodyatāyudham* ॥10 ॥

दिव्यमाल्याम्बरधरं दिव्यगन्धानुलेपनम् ।
सर्वाश्चर्यमयं देवमनन्तं विश्वतोमुखम् ।।११।।

*divya-mālyāmbara-dharaṁ divya-gandhānulepanam* ।
*sarvāścarya-mayaṁ devam anantaṁ viśvatomukham* ॥11 ॥

दिवि सूर्यसहस्रस्य भवेद्युगपदुत्थिता ।
यदि भाः सदृशी सा स्याद्भासस्तस्य महात्मनः ।।१२।।

*divi sūrya-sahasrasya bhaved yugapad utthitā* ।
*yadi bhāḥ sadṛśī sā syād bhāsas tasya mahātmanaḥ* ॥12 ॥

तत्रैकस्थं जगत्कृत्स्नं प्रविभक्तमनेकधा ।
अपश्यद्देवदेवस्य शरीरे पाण्डवस्तदा ।।१३।।

*tatraikasthaṁ jagatkṛtsnaṁ pravibhaktam anekadhā* ।
*apaśyad deva-devasya śarīre pāṇḍavas tadā* ॥13 ॥

ततः स विस्मयाविष्टो हृष्टरोमा धनञ्जयः ।
प्रणम्य शिरसा देवं कृताञ्जलिरभाषत ॥१४॥

*tataḥ sa vismayāviṣṭo hṛṣṭa-romā dhanañjayaḥ* ।
*praṇamya śirasā devaṁ kṛtāñjalir abhāṣata* ॥14 ॥

**अर्जुन उवाच —**

पश्यामि देवांस्तव देव देहे सर्वांस्तथा भूतविशेषसङ्घान् ।
ब्रह्माणमीशं कमलासनस्थमृषींश्च सर्वानुरगांश्च दिव्यान् ॥१५॥

***arjuna uvāca —***

*paśyāmi devāṁs tava deva dehe sarvāṁs tathā bhūta-viśeṣa-saṅghān* ।
*brahmāṇam īśaṁ kamalāsanastham ṛṣīṁś ca sarvān uragāṁś ca divyān* ॥15 ॥

अनेकबाहूदरवक्त्रनेत्रं पश्यामि त्वां सर्वतोऽनन्तरूपम् ।
नान्तं न मध्यं न पुनस्तवादिं पश्यामि विश्वेश्वर विश्वरूप ॥१६॥

*aneka-bāhūdara-vaktra-netraṁ paśyāmi tvāṁ sarvato 'nanta-rūpam* ।
*nāntaṁ na madhyaṁ na punas tavādiṁ paśyāmi viśveśvara viśva-rūpa* ॥16 ॥

किरीटिनं गदिनं चक्रिणं च तेजोराशिं सर्वतो दीप्तिमन्तम् ।
पश्यामि त्वां दुर्निरीक्ष्यं समन्ताद्दीप्तानलार्कद्युतिमप्रमेयम् ॥१७॥

*kirīṭinaṁ gadinaṁ cakriṇaṁ ca tejo-rāśiṁ sarvato dīptimantam*
*paśyāmi tvāṁ durnirīkṣyaṁ samantād dīptānalārka-dyutim aprameyam* ॥17 ॥

त्वमक्षरं परमं वेदितव्यं त्वमस्य विश्वस्य परं निधानम् ।
त्वमव्ययः शाश्वतधर्मगोप्ता सनातनस्त्वं पुरुषो मतो मे ॥१८॥

*tvam akṣaraṁ paramaṁ veditavyaṁ tvam asya viśvasya paraṁ nidhānam* ।
*tvam avyayaḥ śāśvata-dharma-goptā sanātanas tvaṁ puruṣo mato me* ॥18 ॥

अनादिमध्यान्तमनन्तवीर्यमनन्तबाहुं शशिसूर्यनेत्रम् ।
पश्यामि त्वां दीप्तहुताशवक्त्रं स्वतेजसा विश्वमिदं तपन्तम् ॥१९॥

*anādi-madhyāntam ananta-vīryam ananta-bāhuṁ śaśi-sūrya-netraṁ* ।
*paśyāmi tvāṁ dīpta-hutāśa-vaktraṁ sva-tejasā viśvam idaṁ tapantam* ॥19 ॥

द्यावापृथिव्योरिदमन्तरं हि व्याप्तं त्वयैकेन दिशश्च सर्वाः ।
दृष्ट्वाद्भुतं रूपमुग्रं तवेदं लोकत्रयं प्रव्यथितं महात्मन् ॥२०॥

*dyāvā-pṛthivyor idam antaraṁ hi vyāptaṁ tvay aikena diśaś ca sarvāḥ* ।
*dṛṣṭvādbhutam rūpam ugraṁ tavedaṁ loka-trayaṁ pravyathitaṁ mahātman* ॥20 ॥

अमी हि त्वां सुरसङ्घा विशन्ति केचिद्भीताः प्राञ्जलयो गृणन्ति ।
स्वस्तीत्युक्त्वा महर्षिसिद्धसङ्घाः स्तुवन्ति त्वां स्तुतिभिः पुष्कलाभिः ॥२१॥

*amī hi tvāṁ sura-saṅghā viśanti kecid bhītāḥ prāñjalayo gṛṇanti* ।
*svastīty uktvā maharṣi-siddha-saṅghā stuvanti tvāṁ stutibhiḥ puṣkalābhiḥ* ॥21 ॥

रुद्रादित्या वसवो ये च साध्या विश्वेऽश्विनौ मरुतश्चोष्मपाश्च ।
गन्धर्वयक्षासुरसिद्धसङ्घा वीक्षन्ते त्वां विस्मिताश्चैव सर्वे ॥२२॥

*rudrādityā-vasavo ye ca sādhyā viśve 'śvinau marutaś coṣmapāś ca* ।
*gandharva-yakṣāsura-siddha-saṅghā vīkṣante tvāṁ vismitāś caiva sarve* ॥22 ॥

रूपं महत्ते बहुवक्त्रनेत्रं महाबाहो बहुबाहूरुपादम् ।
बहूदरं बहुदंष्ट्राकरालं दृष्ट्वा लोकाः प्रव्यथितास्तथाहम् ॥२३॥

*rūpaṁ mahat te bahu-vaktra-netraṁ mahā-bāho bahu-bāhūru-pādam* ।
*bahūdaraṁ bahu-daṁṣṭrā-karālaṁ dṛṣṭvā lokāḥ pravyathitās tathāham* ॥23 ॥

नभःस्पृशं दीप्तमनेकवर्णं व्यात्ताननं दीप्तविशालनेत्रम् ।
दृष्ट्वा हि त्वां प्रव्यथितान्तरात्मा धृतिं न विन्दामि शमं च विष्णो ॥२४॥

*nabhaḥ-spṛśaṁ dīptam aneka varṇaṁ vyāttānanaṁ dīpta-viśāla-netram* ।
*dṛṣṭvā hi tvāṁ pravyathitāntarātmā dhṛtiṁ na vindāmi śamaṁ ca viṣṇo* ॥24 ॥

दंष्ट्राकरालानि च ते मुखानि दृष्ट्वैव कालानलसन्निभानि ।
दिशो न जाने न लभे च शर्म प्रसीद देवेश जगन्निवास ॥२५॥

*daṁṣṭrā-karālāni ca te mukhāni dṛṣṭvaiva kālānala-sannibhāni* ।
*diśo na jāne na labhe ca śarma prasīda deveśa jagan-nivāsa* ॥25 ॥

अमी च त्वां धृतराष्ट्रस्य पुत्राः सर्वे सहैवावनिपालसङ्घैः ।
भीष्मो द्रोणः सूतपुत्रस्तथासौ सहास्मदीयैरपि योधमुख्यैः ॥२६॥

*amī ca tvāṁ dhṛtarāṣṭrasya putrāḥ sarve sahaivāvani-pāla saṅghaiḥ* ।
*bhīṣmo droṇaḥ sūta-putras tathāsau sahāsmadīyair api yodha-mukhyaiḥ* ॥26 ॥

वक्त्राणि ते त्वरमाणा विशन्ति दंष्ट्राकरालानि भयानकानि ।
केचिद्विलग्ना दशनान्तरेषु सन्दृश्यन्ते चूर्णितैरुत्तमाङ्गैः ॥२७॥

*vaktrāṇi te tvaramāṇā viśanti daṁṣṭrā-karālāni bhayānakāni* ।
*kecid vilagnā daśanāntareṣu sandṛśyante cūrṇitair uttamāṅgaiḥ* ॥27 ॥

यथा नदीनां बहवोऽम्बुवेगाः समुद्रमेवाभिमुखा द्रवन्ति ।
तथा तवामी नरलोकवीरा विशन्ति वक्त्राण्यभिविज्वलन्ति ॥२८॥

*yathā nadīnāṁ bahavo 'mbu-vegāḥ samudram evābhimukhā dravanti* ।
*tathā tavāmī nara-loka-vīrā viśanti vaktrāṇy abhivijvalanti* ॥28 ॥

यथा प्रदीप्तं ज्वलनं पतङ्गा विशन्ति नाशाय समृद्धवेगाः ।
तथैव नाशाय विशन्ति लोकास्तवापि वक्त्राणि समृद्धवेगाः ॥२९॥

*yathā pradīptaṁ jvalanaṁ pataṅgā viśanti nāśāya samṛddha-vegāḥ* ।
*tathaiva nāśāya viśanti lokās tavāpi vaktrāṇi samṛddha-vegāḥ* ॥29 ॥

लेलिह्यसे ग्रसमानः समन्ताल्लोकान्समग्रान्वदनैर्ज्वलद्भिः ।
तेजोभिरापूर्य जगत्समग्रं भासस्तवोग्राः प्रतपन्ति विष्णो ॥३०॥

*lelihyase grasamānaḥ samantāl lokān samagrān vadanair jvaladbhiḥ* ।
*tejobhir āpūrya jagat samagraṁ bhāsas tavogrāḥ pratapanti viṣṇo* ॥30 ॥

आख्याहि मे को भवानुग्ररूपो नमोऽस्तु ते देववर प्रसीद ।
विज्ञातुमिच्छामि भवन्तमाद्यं न हि प्रजानामि तव प्रवृत्तिम् ॥३१॥

*ākhyā hi me ko bhavān ugra-rūpo namo 'stu te deva-vara prasīda* ।
*vijñātum icchāmi bhavantam ādyaṁ na hi prajānāmi tava pravṛttim* ॥31॥

**श्रीभगवानुवाच —**

कालोऽस्मि लोकक्षयकृत्प्रवृद्धो लोकान् समाहर्तुमिह प्रवृत्तः ।
ऋतेऽपि त्वां न भविष्यन्ति सर्वे येऽवस्थिताः प्रत्यनीकेषु योधाः ॥३२॥

***śri bhagavān uvāca —***

*kālo 'smi loka-kṣaya-kṛt pravṛddho lokān samāhartum iha pravṛttaḥ* ।
*ṛte 'pi tvāṁ na bhaviṣyanti sarve ye 'vasthitāḥ pratyanīkeṣu yodhāḥ* ॥32॥

तस्मात्त्वमुत्तिष्ठ यशो लभस्व जित्वा शत्रून् भुङ्क्ष्व राज्यं समृद्धम् ।
मयैवैते निहताः पूर्वमेव निमित्तमात्रं भव सव्यसाचिन् ॥३३॥

*tasmāt tvām uttiṣṭha yaśo labhasva jitvā śatrūn bhuṅkṣva rājyaṁ samṛddham* ।
*mayaivaite nihatāḥ pūrvam eva nimitta-mātraṁ bhava savyasācin* ॥33॥

द्रोणं च भीष्मं च जयद्रथं च कर्णं तथान्यानपि योधवीरान् ।
मया हतांस्त्वं जहि मा व्यथिष्ठा युध्यस्व जेतासि रणे सपत्नान् ॥३४॥

*droṇaṁ ca bhīṣmaṁ ca jayadrathaṁ ca karṇaṁ tathānyān api yodha-vīrān* ।
*mayā hatāṁs tvaṁ jahi mā vyathiṣṭhā yudhyasva jetāsi raṇe sapatnān* ॥34॥

**सञ्जय उवाच —**

एतच्छ्रुत्वा वचनं केशवस्य कृताञ्जलिर्वेपमानः किरीटी ।
नमस्कृत्वा भूय एवाह कृष्णं सगद्गदं भीतभीतः प्रणम्य ॥३५॥

***sañjaya uvāca —***

*etacchrutvā vacanaṁ keśavasya kṛtāñjalir vepamānaḥ kirīṭī* ।
*namas-kṛtvā bhūya evāha kṛṣṇaṁ sagadgadaṁ bhīta-bhītaḥ praṇamya* ॥35॥

**अर्जुन उवाच —**

स्थाने हृषीकेश तव प्रकीर्त्या जगत्प्रहृष्यत्यनुरज्यते च ।
रक्षांसि भीतानि दिशो द्रवन्ति सर्वे नमस्यन्ति च सिद्धसङ्घाः ।।३६।।

***arjuna uvāca —***

*sthāne hṛṣīkeśa tava prakīrtyā jagat prahṛṣyaty anurajyate ca ।*
*rakṣāṁsi bhītāni diśo dravanti sarve namasyanti ca siddha-saṅghāḥ* ॥36 ॥

कस्माच्च ते न नमेरन्महात्मन् गरीयसे ब्रह्मणोऽप्यादिकर्त्रे ।
अनन्त देवेश जगन्निवास त्वमक्षरं सदसत्तत्परं यत् ।।३७।।

*kasmāc ca te na nameran mahātman garīyase brahmaṇo 'py ādi kartre ।*
*ananta deveśa jagan-nivāsa tvam akṣaraṁ sad asat tat paraṁ yat* ॥37 ॥

त्वमादिदेवः पुरुषः पुराणस्त्वमस्य विश्वस्य परं निधानम् ।
वेत्तासि वेद्यं च परं च धाम त्वया ततं विश्वमनन्तरूप ।।३८।।

*tvam ādi-devaḥ puruṣaḥ purāṇas tvam asya viśvasya paraṁ nidhānam ।*
*vettā'si vedyaṁ ca paraṁ ca dhāma tvayā tataṁ viśvam anantarūpa* ॥38 ॥

वायुर्यमोऽग्निर्वरुणः शशाङ्कः प्रजापतिस्त्वं प्रपितामहश्च ।
नमो नमस्तेऽस्तु सहस्रकृत्वः पुनश्च भूयोऽपि नमो नमस्ते ।।३९।।

*vāyur yamo 'gnir varuṇaḥ śaśāṅkaḥ prajāpatis tvaṁ prapitāmahaś ca,*
*namo namas te 'stu sahasra-kṛtvaḥ punaś ca bhūyo 'pi namo namas te* ॥39 ॥

नमः पुरस्तादथ पृष्ठतस्ते नमोऽस्तु ते सर्वत एव सर्व ।
अनन्तवीर्यामितविक्रमस्त्वं सर्वं समाप्नोषि ततोऽसि सर्वः ।।४०।।

*namaḥ purastād atha pṛṣṭhatas te namo 'stu te sarvata eva sarva ।*
*ananta-vīryāmita-vikramas tvaṁ sarvaṁ samāpnoṣi tato 'si sarvaḥ* ॥40 ॥

सखेति मत्वा प्रसभं यदुक्तं हे कृष्ण हे यादव हे सखेति ।
अजानता महिमानं तवेदं मया प्रमादात्प्रणयेन वापि ।।४१।।

*sakheti matvā prasabhaṁ yad uktaṁ he kṛṣṇa he yādava he sakheti* ।
*ajānatā mahimānaṁ tavedaṁ mayā pramādāt praṇayena vāpi* ॥41 ॥

यच्चावहासार्थमसत्कृतोऽसि विहारशय्यासनभोजनेषु ।
एकोऽथवाप्यच्युत तत्समक्षं तत्क्षामये त्वामहमप्रमेयम् ॥४२॥

*yac cāvahāsārtham asat-kṛto 'si vihāra-śayyāsana-bhojaneṣu* ।
*eko 'thavāpy acyuta tat-samakṣaṁ tat kṣāmaye tvām aham aprameyam* ॥42 ॥

पितासि लोकस्य चराचरस्य त्वमस्य पूज्यश्च गुरुर्गरीयान् ।
न त्वत्समोऽस्त्यभ्यधिकः कुतोऽन्यो लोकत्रयेऽप्यप्रतिमप्रभाव ॥४३॥

*pitāsi lokasya carācarasya tvam asya pūjyasya gurur-garīyān* ।
*na tvat-samo 'sty abhyadhikaḥ kuto 'nyo loka-traye 'py apratima-prabhāva* ॥43 ॥

तस्मात्प्रणम्य प्रणिधाय कायं प्रसादये त्वामहमीशमीड्यम् ।
पितेव पुत्रस्य सखेव सख्युः प्रियः प्रियायार्हसि देव सोढुम् ॥४४॥

*tasmāt praṇamya praṇidhāya kāyaṁ prasādaye tvām aham īśam īḍyam* ।
*piteva putrasya sakheva sakhyuḥ priyaḥ priyāyārhasi deva soḍhum* ॥44 ॥

अदृष्टपूर्वं हृषितोऽस्मि दृष्ट्वा भयेन च प्रव्यथितं मनो मे ।
तदेव मे दर्शय देवरूपं प्रसीद देवेश जगन्निवास ॥४५॥

*adṛṣṭa-pūrvaṁ hṛṣito 'smi dṛṣṭvā bhayena ca pravyathitaṁ mano me* ।
*tad eva me darśaya devarūpaṁ prasīda deveśa jagan-nivāsa* ॥45 ॥

किरीटिनं गदिनं चक्रहस्तमिच्छामि त्वां द्रष्टुमहं तथैव ।
तेनैव रूपेण चतुर्भुजेन सहस्रबाहो भव विश्वमूर्ते ॥४६॥

*kirīṭinaṁ gadinaṁ cakra-hastam icchāmi tvāṁ draṣṭum ahaṁ tathaiva* ।
*tenaiva rūpeṇa catur-bhujena sahasra-bāho bhava viśva-mūrte* ॥46 ॥

**श्रीभगवानुवाच —**

मया प्रसन्नेन तवार्जुनेदं रूपं परं दर्शितमात्मयोगात् ।
तेजोमयं विश्वमनन्तमाद्यं यन्मे त्वदन्येन न दृष्टपूर्वम् ।।४७।।

***śrī bhagavān uvāca —***

*māyā prasannena tavārjunedaṁ rūpaṁ paraṁ darśitam ātmayogāt* ।
*tejomayaṁ viśvam anantam ādyaṁ yan me tvadanyena na dṛṣṭa-pūrvam* ॥47 ॥

न वेदयज्ञाध्ययनैर्न दानैर्न च क्रियाभिर्न तपोभिरुग्रैः ।
एवंरूपः शक्य अहं नृलोके द्रष्टुं त्वदन्येन कुरुप्रवीर ।।४८।।

*na veda-yajñādhyayanair na dānair na ca kriyābhir na tapobhir ugraiḥ* ।
*evaṁ-rūpaḥ śakya ahaṁ nṛ-loke draṣṭuṁ tvad-anyena kurupravīra* ॥48 ॥

मा ते व्यथा मा च विमूढभावो दृष्ट्वा रूपं घोरमीदृङ्ममेदम् ।
व्यपेतभीः प्रीतमनाः पुनस्त्वं तदेव मे रूपमिदं प्रपश्य ।।४९।।

*mā te vyathā mā ca vimūḍha-bhāvo dṛṣṭvā rūpaṁ ghoram īdṛṅ mamedam* ।
*vyapeta-bhīḥ prīta-manāḥ punastvaṁ tad eva me rūpam idaṁ prapaśya* ॥49 ॥

**सञ्जय उवाच —**

इत्यर्जुनं वासुदेवस्तथोक्त्वा स्वकं रूपं दर्शयामास भूयः ।
आश्वासयामास च भीतमेनं भूत्वा पुनः सौम्यवपुर्महात्मा ।।५०।।

***sañjaya uvāca —***

*ity arjunaṁ vāsudevas tathoktvā svakaṁ rūpaṁ darśayāmāsa bhūyaḥ* ।
*āśvāsayāmāsa ca bhītam enaṁ bhūtvā punaḥ saumya-vapur mahātmā* ॥50 ॥

**अर्जुन उवाच —**

दृष्ट्वेदं मानुषं रूपं तव सौम्यं जनार्दन ।
इदानीमस्मि संवृत्तः सचेताः प्रकृतिं गतः ।।५१।।

***arjuna uvāca —***

*dṛṣṭvedaṁ mānuṣaṁ rūpaṁ tava saumyaṁ janārdana ।*
*idanīm asmi saṁvṛttaḥ sacetāḥ prakṛtiṁ gataḥ* ॥51 ॥

**श्रीभगवानुवाच —**

सुदुर्दर्शमिदं रूपं दृष्टवानसि यन्मम ।
देवा अप्यस्य रूपस्य नित्यं दर्शनकाङ्क्षिणः ॥५२॥

***śrī bhagavān uvāca —***

*sudurdarśam idaṁ rūpaṁ dṛṣṭavān asi yan mama ।*
*devā apy asya rūpasya nityaṁ darśana-kāṅkṣiṇaḥ* ॥52 ॥

नाहं वेदैर्न तपसा न दानेन न चेज्यया ।
शक्य एवंविधो द्रष्टुं दृष्टवानसि मां यथा ॥५३॥

*nāhaṁ vedair na tapasā na dānena na cejyayā ।*
*śakya evaṁ-vidho draṣṭuṁ dṛṣṭavān asi māṁ yathā* ॥53 ॥

भक्त्या त्वनन्यया शक्य अहमेवंविधोऽर्जुन ।
ज्ञातुं द्रष्टुं च तत्त्वेन प्रवेष्टुं च परन्तप ॥५४॥

*bhaktyā tv-ananyayā śakya aham evaṁ-vidho 'rjuna ।*
*jñātuṁ draṣṭuṁ ca tattvena praveṣṭuṁ ca parantapa* ॥54 ॥

मत्कर्मकृन्मत्परमो सद्भक्तः सङ्गवर्जितः ।
निर्वैरः सर्वभूतेषु यः स मामेति पाण्डव ॥५५॥

*mat-karma-kṛn mat-paramo mad-bhaktaḥ saṅga-varjitaḥ ।*
*nirvairaḥ sarva-bhūteṣu yaḥ sa mām eti pāṇḍava* ॥55 ॥

# 12. भक्ति-योगः

**अर्जुन उवाच —**

एवं सततयुक्ता ये भक्तास्त्वां पर्युपासते ।
ये चाप्यक्षरमव्यक्तं तेषां के योगवित्तमाः ॥१॥

***arjuna uvāca —***

*evaṁ satata-yuktā ye bhaktās tvāṁ paryupāsate ।*
*ye cāpy akṣaram avyaktaṁ teṣāṁ ke yoga-vittamāḥ* ॥1 ॥

**श्रीभगवानुवाच —**

मय्यावेश्य मनो ये मां नित्ययुक्ता उपासते ।
श्रद्धया परयोपेतास्ते मे युक्ततमा मताः ॥२॥

***śrī bhagavān uvāca —***

*mayy āveśya mano ye māṁ nitya-yuktā upāsate,*
*śraddhayā parayopetās te me yukta-tamā matāḥ* ॥2 ॥

ये त्वक्षरमनिर्देश्यमव्यक्तं पर्युपासते ।
सर्वत्रगमचिन्त्यं च कूटस्थमचलं ध्रुवम् ॥३॥

*ye tv akṣaram anirdeśyam avyaktaṁ paryupāsate* ।
*sarvatragam acintyaṁ ca kūṭastham acalaṁ dhruvam* ॥3 ॥

सन्नियम्येन्द्रियग्रामं सर्वत्र समबुद्धयः ।
ते प्राप्नुवन्ति मामेव सर्वभूतहिते रताः ॥४॥

*sanniyamyendriya-grāmaṁ sarvatra sama-buddhayaḥ* ।
*te prāpnuvanti mām eva sarva-bhūta-hite ratāḥ* ॥4 ॥

क्लेशोऽधिकतरस्तेषामव्यक्तासक्तचेतसाम् ।
अव्यक्ता हि गतिर्दुःखं देहवद्भिरवाप्यते ॥५॥

*kleśo 'dhikataras teṣām avyaktāsakta-cetasām* ।
*avyaktā hi gatīr duḥkhaṁ dehavadbhir avāpyate* ॥5 ॥

ये तु सर्वाणि कर्माणि मयि संन्यस्य मत्पराः ।
अनन्येनैव योगेन मां ध्यायन्त उपासते ॥६॥

*ye tu sarvāṇī karmāṇi mayi saṁnyasya mat-parāḥ* ।
*ananyenaiva yogena māṁ dhyāyanta upāsate* ॥6 ॥

तेषामहं समुद्धर्ता मृत्युसंसारसागरात् ।
भवामि नचिरात्पार्थ मय्यावेशितचेतसाम् ॥७॥

*teṣām ahaṁ samuddhartā mṛtyu-saṁsāra-sāgarāt* ।
*bhavāmi nacirāt pārtha mayy āveśita-cetasām* ॥7 ॥

मय्येव मन आधत्स्व मयि बुद्धिं निवेशय ।
निवसिष्यसि मय्येव अत ऊर्ध्वं न संशयः ॥८॥

*mayy eva mana ādhatsva mayi buddhiṁ niveśaya* ।
*nivasiṣyasi mayy eva ata ūrdhvaṁ na saṁśayaḥ* ॥8 ॥

अथ चित्तं समाधातुं न शक्नोषि मयि स्थिरम् ।
अभ्यासयोगेन ततो मामिच्छाप्तुं धनञ्जय ॥९॥

*atha cittaṁ samādhātuṁ na śaknoṣi mayi sthiram* ।
*abhyāsa-yogena tato mām icchāptuṁ dhanañjaya* ॥9॥

अभ्यासेऽप्यसमर्थोऽसि मत्कर्मपरमो भव ।
मदर्थमपि कर्माणि कुर्वन्सिद्धिमवाप्स्यसि ॥१०॥

*abhyāse 'py asamartho 'si mat-karma-paramo bhava* ।
*mad-artham api karmāṇi kurvan siddhim avāpsyasi* ॥10॥

अथैतदप्यशक्तोऽसि कर्तुं मद्योगमाश्रितः ।
सर्वकर्मफलत्यागं ततः कुरु यतात्मवान् ॥११॥

*athaitad apy aśakto 'si kartuṁ mad-yogam āśritaḥ* ।
*sarva-karma-phala-tyāgaṁ tataḥ kuru yatātmavān* ॥11॥

श्रेयो हि ज्ञानमभ्यासाज्ज्ञानाद्ध्यानं विशिष्यते ।
ध्यानात्कर्मफलत्यागस्त्यागाच्छान्तिरनन्तरम् ॥१२॥

*śreyo hi jñānam abhyāsāj jñānād dhyānaṁ viśiṣyate* ।
*dhyānāt karma-phala-tyāgas tyāgāc chāntir anantaram* ॥12॥

अद्वेष्टा सर्वभूतानां मैत्रः करुण एव च ।
निर्ममो निरहङ्कारः समदुःखसुखः क्षमी ॥१३॥

*adveṣṭā sarva-bhūtānāṁ maitraḥ karuṇa eva ca* ।
*nirmamo nirahaṁkāraḥ sama-duḥkha-sukhaḥ kṣamī* ॥13॥

सन्तुष्टः सततं योगी यतात्मा दृढनिश्चयः ।
मय्यर्पितमनोबुद्धिर्यो मद्भक्तः स मे प्रियः ॥१४॥

*santuṣṭaḥ satataṁ yogī yatātmā dṛḍha-niścayaḥ* ।
*mayy arpita-mano-buddhir yo mad-bhaktaḥ sa me priyaḥ* ॥14॥

यस्मान्नोद्विजते लोको लोकान्नोद्विजते च यः ।
हर्षामर्षभयोद्वेगैर्मुक्तो यः स च मे प्रियः ॥१५॥

*yasmān nodvijate loko lokān nodvijate ca yaḥ* ।
*harṣāmarṣa-bhayodvegair mukto yaḥ sa ca me priyaḥ* ॥15॥

अनपेक्षः शुचिर्दक्ष उदासीनो गतव्यथः ।
सर्वारम्भपरित्यागी यो मद्भक्तः स मे प्रियः ॥१६॥

*anapekṣaḥ śucir dakṣa udāsīno gata-vyathaḥ* ।
*sarvārambha-parityāgī yo mad-bhaktaḥ sa me priyaḥ* ॥16॥

यो न हृष्यति न द्वेष्टि न शोचति न काङ्क्षति ।
शुभाशुभपरित्यागी भक्तिमान्यः स मे प्रियः ॥१७॥

*yo na hṛṣyati na dveṣṭi na śocati na kāṅkṣati* ।
*śubhāśubha-parityāgī bhaktimān yaḥ sa me priyaḥ* ॥17॥

समः शत्रौ च मित्रे च तथा मानापमानयोः ।
शीतोष्णसुखदुःखेषु समः सङ्गविवर्जितः ॥१८॥

*samaḥ śatrau ca mitre ca tathā mānāpamānayoḥ* ।
*śītoṣṇa-sukha-duḥkheṣu samaḥ saṅga-vivarjitaḥ* ॥18॥

तुल्यनिन्दास्तुतिर्मौनी संतुष्टो येन केनचित् ।
अनिकेतः स्थिरमतिर्भक्तिमान्मे प्रियो नरः ॥१९॥

*tulya-nindā-stutir maunī saṁtuṣṭo yena kenacit* ।
*aniketaḥ sthira-matir bhaktimān me priyo naraḥ* ॥19॥

ये तु धर्म्यामृतमिदं यथोक्तं पर्युपासते ।
श्रद्दधाना मत्परमा भक्तास्तेऽतीव मे प्रियाः ॥२०॥

*ye tu dharmyāmṛtam idaṁ yathoktaṁ paryupāsate* ।
*śraddadhānā mat-paramā bhaktās te 'tīva me priyāḥ* ॥20॥

# 13. क्षेत्र-क्षेत्रज्ञ-विभागयोगः

**श्रीभगवानुवाच —**

इदं शरीरं कौन्तेय क्षेत्रमित्यभिधीयते ।
एतद्यो वेत्ति तं प्राहुः क्षेत्रज्ञ इति तद्विदः ॥१॥

***śrī bhagavān uvāca —***

*idaṁ śarīraṁ kaunteya kṣetram ity abhidhīyate* ।
*etad yo vetti taṁ prāhuḥ kṣetrajña iti tad vidaḥ* ॥1॥

क्षेत्रज्ञं चापि मां विद्धि सर्वक्षेत्रेषु भारत ।
क्षेत्रक्षेत्रज्ञयोर्ज्ञानं यत्तज्ज्ञानं मतं मम ॥२॥

*kṣetrajñaṁ cāpi māṁ viddhi sarva-kṣetreṣu bhārata* ।
*kṣetra-kṣetrajñayor jñānaṁ yat taj jñānaṁ mataṁ mama* ॥2॥

तत्क्षेत्रं यच्च यादृक्च यद्विकारि यतश्च यत् ।
स च यो यत्प्रभावश्च तत्समासेन मे शृणु ।।३।।

*tat kṣetraṁ yac ca yādṛk ca yad vikāri yataś ca yat |*
*sa ca yo yat prabhāvaś ca tat samāsena me śṛṇu* ||3 ||

ऋषिभिर्बहुधा गीतं छन्दोभिर्विविधैः पृथक् ।
ब्रह्मसूत्रपदैश्चैव हेतुमद्भिर्विनिश्चितैः ।।४।।

*ṛṣibhir bahudhā gītaṁ chandobhir vividhaiḥ pṛthak |*
*brahma-sūtra-padaiś caiva hetumadbhir viniścitaiḥ* ||4 ||

महाभूतान्यहङ्कारो बुद्धिरव्यक्तमेव च ।
इन्द्रियाणि दशैकं च पञ्च चेन्द्रियगोचराः ।।५।।

*mahābhūtāny ahaṅkāro buddhir avyaktam eva ca |*
*indriyāṇi daśaikaṁ ca pañca cendriya-gocarāḥ* ||5 ||

इच्छा द्वेषः सुखं दुःखं सङ्घातश्चेतना धृतिः ।
एतत्क्षेत्रं समासेन सविकारमुदाहृतम् ।।६।।

*icchā dveṣaḥ sukhaṁ duḥkhaṁ saṁghātaś cetanā dhṛtiḥ |*
*etat kṣetraṁ samāsena savikāram udāhṛtam* ||6 ||

अमानित्वमदम्भित्वमहिंसा क्षान्तिरार्जवम् ।
आचार्योपासनं शौचं स्थैर्यमात्मविनिग्रहः ।।७।।

*amānitvam adambhitvam ahiṁsā kṣāntir ārjavam |*
*ācāryopāsanaṁ śaucaṁ sthairyam ātma-vinigrahaḥ* ||7 ||

इन्द्रियार्थेषु वैराग्यमनहङ्कार एव च ।
जन्ममृत्युजराव्याधिदुःखदोषानुदर्शनम् ।।८।।

*indriyārtheṣu vairāgyam anahaṅkāra eva ca |*
*janma-mṛtyu-jarā-vyādhi-duḥka-doṣānudarśanam* ||8 ||

असक्तिरनभिष्वङ्गः पुत्रदारगृहादिषु ।
नित्यं च समचित्तत्वमिष्टानिष्टोपपत्तिषु ।।९।।

*asaktir anabhiṣvaṅgaḥ putra-dāra-gṛhādiṣu |*
*nityaṁ ca sama-cittatvam iṣṭāniṣṭopapattiṣu* ||9 ||

मयि चानन्ययोगेन भक्तिरव्यभिचारिणी ।
विविक्तदेशसेवित्वमरतिर्जनसंसदि ।।१०।।

*mayi cānanya-yogena bhaktir avyabhicāriṇī* ।
*vivikta-deśa-sevitvam aratir jana-saṁsadi* ॥10 ॥

अध्यात्मज्ञाननित्यत्वं तत्त्वज्ञानार्थदर्शनम् ।
एतज्ज्ञानमिति प्रोक्तमज्ञानं यदतोऽन्यथा ॥११॥

*adhyātma-jñāna-nityatvaṁ tattva-jñānārtha-darśanam* ।
*etat jñānam iti proktam ajñānaṁ yad ato 'nyathā* ॥11 ॥

ज्ञेयं यत्तत्प्रवक्ष्यामि यज्ज्ञात्वामृतमश्नुते ।
अनादिमत्परं ब्रह्म न सत्तन्नासदुच्यते ॥१२॥

*jñeyaṁ yat tat pravakṣyāmi yaj jñātvā 'mṛtam aśnute* ।
*anādimat paraṁ brahma na sat tan nā 'sad ucyate* ॥12 ॥

सर्वतःपाणिपादं तत्सर्वतोऽक्षिशिरोमुखम् ।
सर्वतःश्रुतिमल्लोके सर्वमावृत्य तिष्ठति ॥१३॥

*sarvataḥ pāṇi-pādaṁ tat sarvato 'kṣi-śiro-mukham* ।
*sarvataḥśrutimal loke sarvam āvṛtya tiṣṭhati* ॥13 ॥

सर्वेन्द्रियगुणाभासं सर्वेन्द्रियविवर्जितम् ।
असक्तं सर्वभृच्चैव निर्गुणं गुणभोक्तृ च ॥१४॥

*sarvendriya-guṇābhāsaṁ sarvendriya-vivarjitam* ।
*asaktaṁ sarva-bhṛc caiva nirguṇaṁ guṇa-bhoktṛ ca* ॥14 ॥

बहिरन्तश्च भूतानामचरं चरमेव च ।
सूक्ष्मत्वात्तदविज्ञेयं दूरस्थं चान्तिके च तत् ॥१५॥

*bahir antaś ca bhūtānām acaraṁ caram eva ca* ।
*sūkṣmatvāt tad avijñeyaṁ dūrasthaṁ cāntike ca tat* ॥15 ॥

अविभक्तं च भूतेषु विभक्तमिव च स्थितम् ।
भूतभर्तृ च तज्ज्ञेयं ग्रसिष्णु प्रभविष्णु च ॥१६॥

*avibhaktaṁ ca bhūteṣu vibhaktam iva ca sthitam* ।
*bhūtabhartṛ ca taj jñeyaṁ grasiṣṇu prabhaviṣṇu ca* ॥16 ॥

ज्योतिषामपि तज्ज्योतिस्तमसः परमुच्यते ।
ज्ञानं ज्ञेयं ज्ञानगम्यं हृदि सर्वस्य विष्ठितम् ॥१७॥

*jyotiṣām api taj jyotis tamasaḥ param ucyate* ।
*jñānaṁ jñeyaṁ jñāna-gamyaṁ hṛdi sarvasya viṣṭhitam* ॥17 ॥

इति क्षेत्रं तथा ज्ञानं ज्ञेयं चोक्तं समासतः ।
मद्भक्त एतद्विज्ञाय मद्भावायोपपद्यते ॥१८॥

*iti kṣetraṁ tathā jñānaṁ jñeyaṁ coktaṁ samāsataḥ* ।
*mad bhakta etad vijñāya mad bhāvāyopapadyate* ॥18 ॥

प्रकृतिं पुरुषं चैव विद्ध्यनादी उभावपि ।
विकारांश्च गुणांश्चैव विद्धि प्रकृतिसम्भवान् ॥१९॥

*prakṛtiṁ puruṣaṁ caiva viddhy anādī ubhāvapi* ।
*vikārāṁś ca gunāṁś caiva viddhi prakṛti-saṁbhavān* ॥19 ॥

कार्यकारणकर्तृत्वे हेतुः प्रकृतिरुच्यते ।
पुरुषः सुखदुःखानां भोक्तृत्वे हेतुरुच्यते ॥२०॥

*kārya-kāraṇa-kartṛtve hetuḥ prakṛtir ucyate* ।
*puruṣaḥ sukha-duḥkhānāṁ bhoktṛtve hetur ucyate* ॥20 ॥

पुरुषः प्रकृतिस्थो हि भुङ्क्ते प्रकृतिजान्गुणान् ।
कारणं गुणसङ्गोऽस्य सदसद्योनिजन्मसु ॥२१॥

*puruṣaḥ prakṛtistho hi bhuṅkte prakṛtijān guṇān* ।
*kāraṇaṁ guṇasaṅgo 'sya-sad-asad-yoni-janmasu* ॥21 ॥

उपद्रष्टानुमन्ता च भर्ता भोक्ता महेश्वरः ।
परमात्मेति चाप्युक्तो देहेऽस्मिन्पुरुषः परः ॥२२॥

*upadraṣṭā 'numantā ca bhartā bhoktā maheśvaraḥ* ।
*paramātmeti cāpy ukto dehe 'smin puruṣaḥ paraḥ* ॥22 ॥

य एवं वेत्ति पुरुषं प्रकृतिं च गुणैः सह ।
सर्वथा वर्तमानोऽपि न स भूयोऽभिजायते ॥२३॥

*ya evaṁ vetti puruṣaṁ prakṛtiṁ ca guṇaiḥ saha* ।
*sarvathā vartamāno 'pi na sa bhūyo 'bhijāyate* ॥23 ॥

ध्यानेनात्मनि पश्यन्ति केचिदात्मानमात्मना ।
अन्ये साङ्ख्येन योगेन कर्मयोगेन चापरे ॥२४॥

*dhyānenātmani paśyanti kecid ātmānam ātmanā* ।
*anye sāṅkhyena yogena karma-yogena cāpare* ॥24 ॥

अन्ये त्वेवमजानन्तः श्रुत्वान्येभ्य उपासते ।
तेऽपि चातितरन्त्येव मृत्युं श्रुतिपरायणाः ॥२५॥

*anye tvevam ajānantaḥ śrutvā'nyebhya upāsate* ।
*te 'pi cātitaranty eva mṛtyuṁ śruti-parāyaṇāḥ* ॥25 ॥

यावत्सञ्जायते किञ्चित्सत्त्वं स्थावरजङ्गमम् ।
क्षेत्रक्षेत्रज्ञसंयोगात्तद्विद्धि भरतर्षभ ॥२६॥

*yāvat saṁjāyate kiñcit sattvaṁ sthāvara-jaṅgamam* ।
*kṣetra-kṣetrajña-saṁyogāt tad viddhi bharatarṣabha* ॥26 ॥

समं सर्वेषु भूतेषु तिष्ठन्तं परमेश्वरम्।
विनश्यत्स्वविनश्यन्तं यः पश्यति स पश्यति ॥२७॥

*samaṁ sarveṣu bhūteṣu tiṣṭhantaṁ parameśvaram* ।
*vinaśyatsv avinaśyantaṁ yaḥ paśyati sa paśyati* ॥27 ॥

समं पश्यन्हि सर्वत्र समवस्थितमीश्वरम् ।
न हिनस्त्यात्मनात्मानं ततो याति परां गतिम् ॥२८॥

*samaṁ paśyan hi sarvatra sam avasthitam īśvaram* ।
*na hinasty ātmanātmānaṁ tato yāti parāṁ gatīm* ॥28 ॥

प्रकृत्यैव च कर्माणि क्रियमाणानि सर्वशः ।
यः पश्यति तथात्मानमकर्तारं स पश्यति ॥२९॥

*prakṛtyaiva ca karmāṇi kriyamāṇāni sarvaśaḥ* ।
*yaḥ paśyati tathātmānam akartāraṁ sa paśyati* ॥29 ॥

यदा भूतपृथग्भावमेकस्थमनुपश्यति ।
तत एव च विस्तारं ब्रह्म सम्पद्यते तदा ॥३०॥

*yadā bhūta-pṛthag bhāvam ekastham anupaśyati* ।
*tata eva ca vistāraṁ brahma sampadyate tadā* ॥30 ॥

अनादित्वान्निर्गुणत्वात्परमात्मायमव्ययः ।
शरीरस्थोऽपि कौन्तेय न करोति न लिप्यते ॥३१॥

*anāditvān nirguṇatvāt paramātmāyam avyayaḥ* ।
*śarīrastho 'pi kaunteya na karoti na lipyate* ॥31 ॥

यथा सर्वगतं सौक्ष्म्यादाकाशं नोपलिप्यते ।
सर्वत्रावस्थितो देहे तथात्मा नोपलिप्यते ॥३२॥

*yathā sarva-gataṁ saukṣmyād ākāśaṁ nopalipyate* ।
*sarvatrāvasthito dehe tathātmā nopalipyate* ॥32 ॥

यथा प्रकाशयत्येकः कृत्स्नं लोकमिमं रविः ।
क्षेत्रं क्षेत्री तथा कृत्स्नं प्रकाशयति भारत ॥३३॥

*yathā prakāśayaty ekaḥ kṛtsnaṁ lokam imaṁ raviḥ* ।
*kṣetraṁ kṣetrī tathā kṛtsnaṁ prakāśayati bhārata* ॥33 ॥

क्षेत्रक्षेत्रज्ञयोरेवमन्तरं ज्ञानचक्षुषा ।
भूतप्रकृतिमोक्षं च ये विदुर्यान्ति ते परम् ॥३४॥

*kṣetra-kṣetrajñayor evam antaraṁ jñāna-cakṣuṣā* ।
*bhūta-prakṛti-mokṣaṁ ca ye vidur yānti te param* ॥34 ॥

# 14. गुण-त्रय-विभागयोगः

**श्रीभगवानुवाच —**

परं भूयः प्रवक्ष्यामि ज्ञानानां ज्ञानमुत्तमम् ।
यज्ज्ञात्वा मुनयः सर्वे परां सिद्धिमितो गताः ॥१॥

*śri bhagavān uvāca —*

*paraṁ bhūyaḥ pravakṣyāmi jñānānāṁ jñānam uttamam* ।
*yaj jñātvā munayaḥ sarve parāṁ siddhim ito gatāḥ* ॥1 ॥

इदं ज्ञानमुपाश्रित्य मम साधर्म्यमागताः ।
सर्गेऽपि नोपजायन्ते प्रलये न व्यथन्ति च ॥२॥

*idaṁ jñānam upāśritya mama sādharmyam āgatāḥ* ।
*sarge 'pi nopajāyante pralaye na vyathanti ca* ॥2 ॥

मम योनिर्महद्ब्रह्म तस्मिन्गर्भं दधाम्यहम् ।
संभवः सर्वभूतानां ततो भवति भारत ॥३॥

*mama yonir mahad brahma tasmin garbhaṁ dadhāmy ahaṁ* ।
*sambhavaḥ sarva-bhūtānāṁ tato bhavati bhārata* ॥3 ॥

सर्वयोनिषु कौन्तेय मूर्तयः सम्भवन्ति याः ।
तासां ब्रह्म महद्योनिरहं बीजप्रदः पिता ॥४॥

*sarva-yoniṣu kaunteya mūrtayaḥ saṁbhavanti yāḥ* ।
*tāsāṁ brahma mahad yonir ahaṁ bīja-pradaḥ pitā* ॥4 ॥

सत्त्वं रजस्तम इति गुणाः प्रकृतिसम्भवाः ।
निबध्नन्ति महाबाहो देहे देहिनमव्ययम् ॥५॥

*sattvaṁ rajas tama iti guṇāḥ prakṛti-saṁbhavāḥ* ।
*nibadhnanti mahā-bāho dehe dehinam avyayam* ॥5 ॥

तत्र सत्त्वं निर्मलत्वात्प्रकाशकमनामयम् ।
सुखसङ्गेन बध्नाति ज्ञानसङ्गेन चानघ ॥६॥

*tatra sattvaṁ nirmalatvāt prakāśakam anāmayam* ।
*sukha-saṅgena badhnāti jñāna-saṅgena cānagha* ॥6 ॥

रजो रागात्मकं विद्धि तृष्णासङ्गसमुद्भवम् ।
तन्निबध्नाति कौन्तेय कर्मसङ्गेन देहिनम् ॥७॥

*rajo rāgātmakaṁ viddhi tṛṣṇā-saṅga-samudbhavam* ।
*tan nibadhnāti kaunteya karma-saṅgena dehinam* ॥7 ॥

तमस्त्वज्ञानजं विद्धि मोहनं सर्वदेहिनाम् ।
प्रमादालस्यनिद्राभिस्तन्निबध्नाति भारत ॥८॥

*tamas tv ajñānajaṁ viddhi mohanaṁ sarva-dehinām* ।
*pramādālasya-nidrābhis tan nibadhnāti bhārata* ॥8 ॥

सत्त्वं सुखे सञ्जयति रजः कर्मणि भारत ।
ज्ञानमावृत्य तु तमः प्रमादे सञ्जयत्युत ॥९॥

*sattvaṁ sukhe sañjayati rajaḥ karmaṇi bhārata* ।
*jñānam āvṛtya tu tamaḥ pramāde sañjayaty uta* ॥9 ॥

रजस्तमश्चाभिभूय सत्त्वं भवति भारत ।
रजः सत्त्वं तमश्चैव तमः सत्त्वं रजस्तथा ॥१०॥

*rajas tamaś cābhibhūya sattvaṁ bhavati bhārata* ।
*rajaḥ sattvaṁ tamaś caiva tamaḥ sattvaṁ rajas tathā* ॥10 ॥

सर्वद्वारेषु देहेऽस्मिन्प्रकाश उपजायते ।
ज्ञानं यदा तदा विद्याद्विवृद्धं सत्त्वमित्युत ॥११॥

*sarva-dvāreṣu dehe 'smin prakāśa upajāyate* ।
*jñānaṁ yadā tadā vidyād vivṛddhaṁ sattvam ity uta* ॥11 ॥

लोभः प्रवृत्तिरारम्भः कर्मणामशमः स्पृहा ।
रजस्येतानि जायन्ते विवृद्धे भरतर्षभ ॥१२॥

*lobhaḥ pravṛttir ārambhaḥ karmaṇām aśamaḥ spṛhā* ।
*rajasy etāni jāyante vivṛddhe bharatarṣabha* ॥12 ॥

अप्रकाशोऽप्रवृत्तिश्च प्रमादो मोह एव च ।
तमस्येतानि जायन्ते विवृद्धे कुरुनन्दन ॥१३॥

*aprakāśo 'pravṛttiś ca pramādo moha eva ca* ।
*tamasy etāni jāyante vivṛddhe kuru-nandana* ॥13 ॥

यदा सत्त्वे प्रवृद्धे तु प्रलयं याति देहभृत् ।
तदोत्तमविदां लोकानमलान्प्रतिपद्यते ॥१४॥

*yadā sattve pravṛddhe tu pralayaṁ yāti deha-bhṛt* ।
*tadottama-vidāṁ lokān amalān pratipadyate* ॥14 ॥

रजसि प्रलयं गत्वा कर्मसङ्गिषु जायते ।
तथा प्रलीनस्तमसि मूढयोनिषु जायते ॥१५॥

*rajasi pralayaṁ gatvā karma-saṅgiṣu jāyate* ।
*tathā pralīnas tamasi mūḍha-yoniṣu jāyate* ॥15 ॥

कर्मणः सुकृतस्याहुः सात्त्विकं निर्मलं फलम् ।
रजसस्तु फलं दुःखमज्ञानं तमसः फलम् ॥१६॥

*karmaṇaḥ sukṛtasyāhuḥ sāttvikaṁ nirmalaṁ phalam* ।
*rajasas tu phalaṁ duḥkham ajñānaṁ tamasaḥ phalam* ॥16 ॥

सत्त्वात्सञ्जायते ज्ञानं रजसो लोभ एव च ।
प्रमादमोहौ तमसो भवतोऽज्ञानमेव च ॥१७॥

*sattvāt sañjāyate jñānaṁ rajaso lobha eva ca* ।
*pramāda-mohau tamaso bhavato 'jñānam eva ca* ॥17 ॥

ऊर्ध्वं गच्छन्ति सत्त्वस्था मध्ये तिष्ठन्ति राजसाः ।
जघन्यगुणवृत्तिस्था अधो गच्छन्ति तामसाः ॥१८॥

*ūrdhvaṁ gacchanti sattvasthā madhye tiṣṭhanti rājasāḥ* ।
*jaghanya-guṇa-vṛttisthā adho gacchanti tāmasāḥ* ॥18 ॥

नान्यं गुणेभ्यः कर्तारं यदा द्रष्टानुपश्यति ।
गुणेभ्यश्च परं वेत्ति मद्भावं सोऽधिगच्छति ॥१९॥

*nānyaṁ guṇebhyaḥ kartāraṁ yadā draṣṭānupaśyati* ।
*guṇebhyaś ca paraṁ vetti mad-bhāvaṁ so 'dhigacchati* ॥19 ॥

गुणानेतानतीत्य त्रीन्देही देहसमुद्भवान् ।
जन्ममृत्युजरादुःखैर्विमुक्तोऽमृतम श्नुते ॥२०॥

*guṇān etān atītya trīn dehī deha-samudbhavān* ।
*janma-mṛtyu-jarā-duḥkhair vimukto 'mṛtam aśnute* ॥20 ॥

**अर्जुन उवाच —**

कैर्लिङ्गैस्त्रीन्गुणानेतानतीतो भवति प्रभो ।
किमाचारः कथं चैतांस्त्रीन्गुणानतिवर्तते ॥२१॥

***Arjuna uvāca —***

*kair liṅgais trīn guṇān etān atīto bhavati prabho* ।
*kim ācāraḥ katham caitāṁs trīn guṇān ativartate* ॥21 ॥

**श्रीभगवानुवाच —**

प्रकाशं च प्रवृत्तिं च मोहमेव च पाण्डव ।
न द्वेष्टि सम्प्रवृत्तानि न निवृत्तानि काङ्क्षति ॥२२॥

***śrī bhagavān uvāca —***

*prakāśaṁ ca pravṛttiṁ ca moham eva ca pāṇḍava* ।
*na dveṣṭi saṁpravṛttāni na nivṛttāni kāṅkṣati* ॥22 ॥

उदासीनवदासीनो गुणैर्यो न विचाल्यते ।
गुणा वर्तन्त इत्येव योऽवतिष्ठति नेङ्गते ॥२३॥

*udāsīnavad āsīno guṇair yo na vicālyate* ।
*guṇā vartanta ity eva yo 'vatiṣṭhati neṅgate* ॥23 ॥

समदुःखसुखः स्वस्थः समलोष्टाश्मकाञ्चनः ।
तुल्यप्रियाप्रियो धीरस्तुल्यनिन्दात्मसंस्तुतिः ॥२४॥

*sama-duḥkha-sukhaḥ svasthaḥ sama-loṣṭāśma-kāñcanaḥ* ।
*tulya-prīyāpriyo dhīras tulya-nindātma-saṁstutiḥ* ॥24 ॥

मानापमानयोस्तुल्यस्तुल्यो मित्रारिपक्षयोः ।
सर्वारम्भपरित्यागी गुणातीतः स उच्यते ॥२५॥

*mānāpamānayos tulyas tulyo mitrāri-pakṣayoḥ* ।
*sarvārambha-parityāgī guṇātītaḥ sa ucyate* ॥25 ॥

मां च योऽव्यभिचारेण भक्तियोगेन सेवते ।
स गुणान्समतीत्यैतान्ब्रह्मभूयाय कल्पते ॥२६॥

*māṁ ca yo 'vyabhicāreṇa bhakti-yogena sevate* ।
*sa guṇān samatītyaitān brahma-bhūyāya kalpate* ॥26 ॥

ब्रह्मणो हि प्रतिष्ठाहममृतस्याव्ययस्य च ।
शाश्वतस्य च धर्मस्य सुखस्यैकान्तिकस्य च ।।२७।।

*brahmaṇo hi pratiṣṭhā 'ham amṛtasyāvyayasya ca* ।
*śāśvatasya ca dharmasya sukhasyaikāntikasya ca* ॥27 ॥

# 15. पुरुषोत्तमयोगः

**श्रीभगवानुवाच —**

ऊर्ध्वमूलमधःशाखमश्वत्थं प्राहुरव्ययम् ।
छन्दांसि यस्य पर्णानि यस्तं वेद स वेदवित् ।।१।।

***śrī bhagavān uvāca —***

*ūrdhva-mūlam adhaḥ śākham aśvatthaṁ prāhur avyayam* ।
*chandāṁsi yasya parṇāni yas taṁ veda sa veda-vit* ॥1 ॥

अधश्चोर्ध्वं प्रसृतास्तस्य शाखा गुणप्रवृद्धा विषयप्रवालाः ।
अधश्च मूलान्यनुसन्ततानि कर्मानुबन्धीनि मनुष्यलोके ।।२।।

*adhaś cordhvaṁ prasṛtās tasya śākhā guṇa-pravṛddhā viṣaya-pravālāḥ* ।
*adhaś ca mūlāny anusantatāni karmānubandhīni manuṣya-loke* ॥2 ॥

न रूपमस्येह तथोपलभ्यते नान्तो न चादिर्न च सम्प्रतिष्ठा ।
अश्वत्थमेनं सुविरूढमूलमसङ्गशस्त्रेण दृढेन छित्त्वा ।।३।।

*na rūpam asyeha tathopalabhyate nānto na cādir na ca sam-pratiṣṭhā* ।
*aśvattham enaṁ suvirūḍha-mūlam asaṅga-śastreṇa dṛḍhena chittvā* ॥3 ॥

ततः पदं तत्परिमार्गितव्यं यस्मिन्गता न निवर्तन्ति भूयः ।
तमेव चाद्यं पुरुषं प्रपद्ये यतः प्रवृत्तिः प्रसृता पुराणी ।।४।।

*tataḥ padaṁ tat parimārgitavyaṁ yasmin gatā na nivartanti bhūyaḥ* ।
*tam eva cādyaṁ puruṣaṁ prapadye yataḥ pravṛttiḥ prasṛtā pūrāṇī* ॥4 ॥

निर्मानमोहा जितसङ्गदोषा अध्यात्मनित्या विनिवृत्तकामाः ।
द्वन्द्वैर्विमुक्ताः सुखदुःखसञ्ज्ञैर्गच्छन्त्यमूढाः पदमव्ययं तत् ॥५॥

*nirmāna-mohā jita-saṅga-doṣā adhyātma-nityā vinivṛtta-kāmāḥ ।*
*dvandvair vimuktāḥ sukha-duḥkha-sañjñair gacchanty amūḍhāḥ padam avyayaṁ tat* ॥5 ॥

न तद्भासयते सूर्यो न शशाङ्को न पावकः ।
यद्गत्वा न निवर्तन्ते तद्धाम परमं मम ॥६॥

*na tad bhāsayate sūryo na śaśāṅko na pāvakaḥ ।*
*yad gatvā na nivartante tad dhāma paramaṁ mama* ॥6 ॥

ममैवांशो जीवलोके जीवभूतः सनातनः ।
मनःषष्ठानीन्द्रियाणि प्रकृतिस्थानि कर्षति ॥७॥

*mamaivāṁśo jīva-loke jīva-bhūtaḥ sanātanaḥ ।*
*manaḥ-ṣaṣṭhānīndriyāṇi prakṛti-sthāni karṣati* ॥7 ॥

शरीरं यदवाप्नोति यच्चाप्युत्क्रामतीश्वरः ।
गृहीत्वैतानि संयाति वायुर्गन्धानिवाशयात् ॥८॥

*śarīraṁ yad avāpnoti yac cāpy utkrāmatīśvaraḥ ।*
*gṛhītvaitāni saṁyāti vāyur gandhān ivāśayāt* ॥8 ॥

श्रोत्रं चक्षुः स्पर्शनं च रसनं घ्राणमेव च ।
अधिष्ठाय मनश्चायं विषयानुपसेवते ॥९॥

*śrotraṁ cakṣuḥ sparśanaṁ ca rasanaṁ ghrāṇam eva ca ।*
*adhiṣṭhāya manaś cāyaṁ viṣayān upasevate* ॥9 ॥

उत्क्रामन्तं स्थितं वापि भुञ्जानं वा गुणान्वितम् ।
विमूढा नानुपश्यन्ति पश्यन्ति ज्ञानचक्षुषः ॥१०॥

*utkrāmantaṁ sthitaṁ vāpi bhuñjānaṁ vā guṇānvitam ।*
*vimūḍhā nānupaśyanti paśyanti jñāna-cakṣuṣaḥ* ॥10 ॥

यतन्तो योगिनश्चैनं पश्यन्त्यात्मन्यवस्थितम् ।
यतन्तोऽप्यकृतात्मानो नैनं पश्यन्त्यचेतसः ॥११॥

*yatanto yoginaś cainaṁ paśyanty ātmany avasthitam ।*
*yatanto 'py akṛtātmāno nainaṁ paśyanty acetasāḥ* ॥11 ॥

यदादित्यगतं तेजो जगद्भासयतेऽखिलम् ।
यच्चन्द्रमसि यच्चाग्नौ तत्तेजो विद्धि मामकम् ॥१२॥

*yad āditya-gataṁ tejo jagad bhāsayate 'khilam* ।
*yac candramasi yac cāgnau tat tejo viddhi māmakam* ॥12॥

गामाविश्य च भूतानि धारयाम्यहमोजसा ।
पुष्णामि चौषधीः सर्वाः सोमो भूत्वा रसात्मकः ॥१३॥

*gām āviśya ca bhūtāni dhārayāmy aham ojasā* ।
*puṣṇāmi cauṣadhīḥ sarvāḥ somo bhūtvā rasātmakaḥ* ॥13॥

अहं वैश्वानरो भूत्वा प्राणिनां देहमाश्रितः ।
प्राणापानसमायुक्तः पचाम्यन्नं चतुर्विधम् ॥१४॥

*ahaṁ vaiśvānaro bhūtvā prāṇināṁ deham āśritaḥ* ।
*prāṇāpāna-samāyuktaḥ pacāmy annaṁ catur vidham* ॥14॥

सर्वस्य चाहं हृदि सन्निविष्टो मत्तः स्मृतिर्ज्ञानमपोहनं च ।
वेदैश्च सर्वैरहमेव वेद्यो वेदान्तकृद्वेदविदेव चाहम् ॥१५॥

*sarvasya cāhaṁ hṛdi sanniviṣṭo mattaḥ smṛtir jñānam apohanaṁ ca* ।
*vedaiś ca sarvair aham eva vedyo vedānta-kṛd veda-vid eva cāham* ॥15॥

द्वाविमौ पुरुषौ लोके क्षरश्चाक्षर एव च ।
क्षरः सर्वाणि भूतानि कूटस्थोऽक्षर उच्यते ॥१६॥

*dvāv imau puruṣau loke kṣaraś cākṣara eva ca* ।
*kṣaraḥ sarvāṇi bhūtāni kūṭastho 'kṣara ucyate* ॥16॥

उत्तमः पुरुषस्त्वन्यः परमात्मेत्युदाहृतः ।
यो लोकत्रयमाविश्य बिभर्त्यव्यय ईश्वरः ॥१७॥

*uttamaḥ puruṣas tv anyaḥ paramātmety udāhṛtaḥ* ।
*yo loka-trayam āviśya bibharty avyaya īśvaraḥ* ॥17॥

यस्मात्क्षरमतीतोऽहमक्षरादपि चोत्तमः ।
अतोऽस्मि लोके वेदे च प्रथितः पुरुषोत्तमः ॥१८॥

*yasmāt kṣaram atīto 'ham akṣarād api cottamaḥ* ।
*ato 'smi loke vede ca prathitaḥ puruṣottamaḥ* ॥18॥

यो मामेवमसम्मूढो जानाति पुरुषोत्तमम् ।
स सर्वविद्भजति मां सर्वभावेन भारत ॥१९॥

*yo mām evam asammūḍho jānāti puruṣottamam* ।
*sa sarvavid bhajati māṁ sarva bhāvena bhārata* ॥19 ॥

इति गुह्यतमं शास्त्रमिदमुक्तं मयानघ ।
एतद्बुद्ध्वा बुद्धिमान्स्यात्कृतकृत्यश्च भारत ॥२०॥

*iti guhyatamaṁ śāstram idaṁ uktaṁ mayānagha* ।
*etad buddhvā buddhimān syāt kr̥ta-kr̥tyaś ca bhārata* ॥20 ॥

# 16. दैवासुर-सम्पद्-विभागयोगः

**श्रीभगवानुवाच —**

अभयं सत्त्वसंशुद्धिर्ज्ञानयोगव्यवस्थितिः ।
दानं दमश्च यज्ञश्च स्वाध्यायस्तप आर्जवम् ॥१॥

***śrī bhagavān uvāca —***

*abhayaṁ sattva-saṁśuddhir jñāna-yoga-vyavasthitiḥ* ।
*dānaṁ damaś ca yajñaś ca svādhyāyas tapa ārjavam* ॥1 ॥

अहिंसा सत्यमक्रोधस्त्यागः शान्तिरपैशुनम् ।
दया भूतेष्वलोलुप्त्वं मार्दवं ह्रीरचापलम् ॥२॥

*ahiṁsā satyam akrodhas tyāgaḥ śāntir apaiśunam* ।
*dayā bhūteṣv aloluptvaṁ mārdavaṁ hrīr acāpalam* ॥2 ॥

तेजः क्षमा धृतिः शौचमद्रोहो नातिमानिता ।
भवन्ति संपदं दैवीमभिजातस्य भारत ॥३॥

*tejaḥ kṣamā dhr̥tiḥ śaucam adroho nātimānitā* ।
*bhavanti saṁpadaṁ daivīm abhijātasya bhārata* ॥3 ॥

दम्भो दर्पोऽभिमानश्च क्रोधः पारुष्यमेव च ।
अज्ञानं चाभिजातस्य पार्थ सम्पदमासुरीम् ॥४॥

*dambho darpo 'bhimānaś ca krodhaḥ pāruṣyam eva ca* ।
*ajñānaṁ cābhijātasya pārtha sampadam āsurīm* ॥4 ॥

दैवी सम्पद्विमोक्षाय निबन्धायासुरी मता ।
मा शुचः सम्पदं दैवीमभिजातोऽसि पाण्डव ॥५॥

*daivī sampad vimokṣāya nibandhāyāsurī matā* ।
*mā śucaḥ sampadaṁ daivīm abhijāto 'si pāṇḍava* ॥5 ॥

द्वौ भूतसर्गौ लोकेऽस्मिन्दैव आसुर एव च ।
दैवो विस्तरशः प्रोक्त आसुरं पार्थ मे शृणु ॥६॥

*dvau bhūta-sargau loke 'smin daiva āsura eva ca ।*
*daivo vistaraśaḥ prokta āsuraṁ pārtha me śṛṇu* ॥6 ॥

प्रवृत्तिं च निवृत्तिं च जना न विदुरासुराः ।
न शौचं नापि चाचारो न सत्यं तेषु विद्यते ॥७॥

*pravṛttiṁ ca nivṛttiṁ ca janā na vidur āsurāḥ ।*
*na śaucaṁ nāpi cācāro na satyaṁ teṣu vidyate* ॥7 ॥

असत्यमप्रतिष्ठं ते जगदाहुरनीश्वरम् ।
अपरस्परसम्भूतं किमन्यत्कामहैतुकम् ॥८॥

*asatyam apratiṣṭhaṁ te jagad āhur anīśvaram ।*
*aparaspara-sambhūtaṁ kim anyat kāma-haitukam* ॥8 ॥

एतां दृष्टिमवष्टभ्य नष्टात्मानोऽल्पबुद्धयः ।
प्रभवन्त्युग्रकर्माणः क्षयाय जगतोऽहिताः ॥९॥

*etāṁ dṛṣṭim avaṣṭabhya naṣṭātmāno 'lpa-buddhayaḥ ।*
*prabhavanty ugra-karmāṇaḥ kṣayāya jagato 'hitāḥ* ॥9 ॥

काममाश्रित्य दुष्पूरं दम्भमानमदान्विताः ।
मोहादृहीत्वासद्ग्राहान्प्रवर्तन्तेऽशुचिव्रताः ॥१०॥

*kāmam āśritya duṣpūraṁ daṁbha-māna-madānvitāḥ ।*
*mohād gṛhītvāsad-grāhān pravartante 'śuci-vratāḥ* ॥10 ॥

चिन्तामपरिमेयां च प्रलयान्तामुपाश्रिताः ।
कामोपभोगपरमा एतावदिति निश्चिताः ॥११॥

*cintām aparimeyāṁ ca pralayāntām upāśritāḥ ।*
*kāmopabhoga-paramā etāvad iti niścitāḥ* ॥11 ॥

आशापाशशतैर्बद्धाः कामक्रोधपरायणाः ।
ईहन्ते कामभोगार्थमन्यायेनार्थसञ्चयान् ॥१२॥

*āśā-pāśa-śatair baddhāḥ kāma-krodha-parāyaṇāḥ ।*
*īhante kāma-bhogārtham anyāyenārtha-sañcayān* ॥12 ॥

इदमद्य मया लब्धमिमं प्राप्स्ये मनोरथम् ।
इदमस्तीदमपि मे भविष्यति पुनर्धनम् ॥१३॥

*idam adya mayā labdham imaṁ prāpsye manoratham* ।
*idam astīdam api me bhaviṣyati punar dhanam* ॥13 ॥

असौ मया हतः शत्रुर्हनिष्ये चापरानपि ।
ईश्वरोऽहमहं भोगी सिद्धोऽहं बलवान्सुखी ॥१४॥

*asau mayā hataḥ śatrur haniṣye cāparān api* ।
*iśvaro 'ham ahaṁ bhogī siddho 'haṁ balavān sukhī* ॥14 ॥

आढ्योऽभिजनवानस्मि कोऽन्योऽस्ति सदृशो मया ।
यक्ष्ये दास्यामि मोदिष्य इत्यज्ञानविमोहिताः ॥१५॥

*āḍhyo 'bhijanavān asmi ko 'nyo 'sti sadṛśo mayā* ।
*yakṣye dāsyāmi modiṣya ity ajñāna-vimohitāḥ* ॥15 ॥

अनेकचित्तविभ्रान्ता मोहजालसमावृताः ।
प्रसक्ताः कामभोगेषु पतन्ति नरकेऽशुचौ ॥१६॥

*aneka-citta-vibhrāntā moha-jāla-samāvṛtāḥ* ।
*prasaktāḥ kāma-bhogeṣu patanti narake 'śucau* ॥16 ॥

आत्मसम्भाविताः स्तब्धा धनमानमदान्विताः ।
यजन्ते नामयज्ञैस्ते दम्भेनाविधिपूर्वकम् ॥१७॥

*ātma-sambhāvitāḥ stabdhā dhana-māna-madānvitāḥ* ।
*yajante nāmayajñais te dambhenāvidhi-pūrvakam* ॥17 ॥

अहङ्कारं बलं दर्पं कामं क्रोधं च संश्रिताः ।
मामात्मपरदेहेषु प्रद्विषन्तोऽभ्यसूयकाः ॥१८॥

*ahankāraṁ balaṁ darpaṁ kāmaṁ krodhaṁ ca saṁśritāḥ* ।
*mām ātma-para-deheṣu pradviṣanto 'bhyasūyakāḥ* ॥18 ॥

तानहं द्विषतः क्रूरान्संसारेषु नराधमान् ।
क्षिपाम्यजस्रमशुभानासुरीष्वेव योनिषु ॥१९॥

*tān ahaṁ dviṣataḥ krūrān saṁsāreṣu narādhamān* ।
*kṣipāmy ajasram aśubhān āsurīṣveva yoniṣu* ॥19 ॥

आसुरीं योनिमापन्ना मूढा जन्मनि जन्मनि ।
मामप्राप्यैव कौन्तेय ततो यान्त्यधमां गतिम् ॥२०॥

*āsurīṁ yonim āpannā mūḍhā janmani janmani* ।
*mām aprāpyaiva kaunteya tato yānty adhamāṁ gatim* ॥20 ॥

त्रिविधं नरकस्येदं द्वारं नाशनमात्मनः ।
कामः क्रोधस्तथा लोभस्तस्मादेतत्त्रयं त्यजेत् ॥२१॥

*tri-vidhaṁ narakasyedaṁ dvāraṁ nāśanam ātmanaḥ ।*
*kāmaḥ krodhas-tathā lobhas tasmād etat trayaṁ tyajet ॥21 ॥*

एतैर्विमुक्तः कौन्तेय तमोद्वारैस्त्रिभिर्नरः ।
आचरत्यात्मनः श्रेयस्ततो याति परां गतिम् ॥२२॥

*etair vimuktaḥ kaunteya tamo-dvārais tribhir naraḥ ।*
*ācaraty ātmanaḥ śreyas tato yāti parāṁ gatim ॥22 ॥*

यः शास्त्रविधिमुत्सृज्य वर्तते कामकारतः ।
न स सिद्धिमवाप्नोति न सुखं न परां गतिम् ॥२३॥

*yaḥ śāstra-vidhim utsṛjya vartate kāmakārataḥ ।*
*na sa siddhim avāpnoti na sukhaṁ na parāṁ gatim ॥23 ॥*

तस्माच्छास्त्रं प्रमाणं ते कार्याकार्यव्यवस्थितौ ।
ज्ञात्वा शास्त्रविधानोक्तं कर्म कर्तुमिहार्हसि ॥२४॥

*tasmāc chāstraṁ pramāṇaṁ te kāryākārya-vyavasthitau ।*
*jñātvā śāstra-vidhānoktaṁ karma kartum ihārhasi ॥24 ॥*

# 17. श्रद्धात्रय-विभागयोगः

**अर्जुन उवाच —**

ये शास्त्रविधिमुत्सृज्य यजन्ते श्रद्धयान्विताः ।
तेषां निष्ठा तु का कृष्ण सत्त्वमाहो रजस्तमः ॥१॥

***arjuna uvāca —***

*ye śāstra-vidhim utsṛjya yajante śraddhayānvitāḥ ।*
*teṣāṁ niṣṭhā tu kā kṛṣṇa sattvam āho rajas tamaḥ ॥1 ॥*

**श्रीभगवानुवाच —**

त्रिविधा भवति श्रद्धा देहिनां सा स्वभावजा ।
सात्त्विकी राजसी चैव तामसी चेति तां शृणु ॥२॥

***śrī bhagavān uvāca —***

*tri-vidhā bhavati śraddhā dehināṁ sā svabhāvajā ।*
*sāttvikī rājasī caiva tāmasī ceti tāṁ śṛṇu ॥2 ॥*

सत्त्वानुरूपा सर्वस्य श्रद्धा भवति भारत ।
श्रद्धामयोऽयं पुरुषो यो यच्छ्रद्धः स एव सः ॥३॥

*sattvānurūpā sarvasya śraddhā bhavati bhārata* ।
*śraddhāmayo 'yaṁ puruṣo yo yac-chraddhaḥ sa eva saḥ* ॥3 ॥

यजन्ते सात्त्विका देवान्यक्षरक्षांसि राजसाः ।
प्रेतान्भूतगणांश्चान्ये यजन्ते तामसा जनाः ॥४॥

*yajante sāttvikā devān yakṣa-rakṣāṁsi rājasāḥ* ।
*pretān bhūta-gaṇāṁś cānye yajante tāmasā janāḥ* ॥4 ॥

अशास्त्रविहितं घोरं तप्यन्ते ये तपो जनाः ।
दम्भाहङ्कारसंयुक्ताः कामरागबलान्विताः ॥५॥

*aśāstra-vihitaṁ ghoraṁ tapyante ye tapo janāḥ* ।
*dambhāhaṅkāra-saṁyuktāḥ kāma-rāga-balānvitāḥ* ॥5 ॥

कर्शयन्तः शरीरस्थं भूतग्राममचेतसः ।
मां चैवान्तःशरीरस्थं तान्विद्ध्यासुरनिश्चयान् ॥६॥

*karśayantaḥ śarīrasthaṁ bhūta-grāmam acetasaḥ* ।
*māṁ caivāntaḥ-śarīrasthaṁ tān viddhy āsura-niścayān* ॥6 ॥

आहारस्त्वपि सर्वस्य त्रिविधो भवति प्रियः ।
यज्ञस्तपस्तथा दानं तेषां भेदमिमं शृणु ॥७॥

*āhāras tvapi sarvasya trividho bhavati priyaḥ* ।
*yajñas-tapas-tathā dānaṁ teṣāṁ bhedam imaṁ śṛṇu* ॥7 ॥

आयुःसत्त्वबलारोग्यसुखप्रीतिविवर्धनाः ।
रस्याः स्निग्धाः स्थिरा हृद्या आहाराः सात्त्विकप्रियाः ॥८॥

*āyuḥ-sattva-balārogya-sukha-prīti-vivardhanāḥ* ।
*rasyāḥ snigdhāḥ sthirā hṛdyā āhārāḥ sāttvika-priyāḥ* ॥8 ॥

कट्वम्ललवणात्युष्णतीक्ष्णरूक्षविदाहिनः ।
आहारा राजसस्येष्टा दुःखशोकामयप्रदाः ॥९॥

*kaṭv-amla-lavaṇātyuṣṇa tīkṣṇa-rūkṣa-vidāhinaḥ* ।
*āhārā rājasasyeṣṭā duḥkha-śokāmaya-pradāḥ* ॥9 ॥

यातयामं गतरसं पूति पर्युषितं च यत् ।
उच्छिष्टमपि चामेध्यं भोजनं तामसप्रियम् ॥१०॥

*yāta-yāmaṁ gata-rasaṁ pūti paryuṣitaṁ ca yat* ।
*ucchiṣṭam api cāmedhyaṁ bhojanaṁ tāmasa-priyam* ॥10 ॥

अफलाकाङ्क्षिभिर्यज्ञो विधिदृष्टो य इज्यते ।
यष्टव्यमेवेति मनः समाधाय स सात्त्विकः ॥११॥

*aphalākāṅkṣibhir yajño vidhi-dṛṣṭo ya ijyate* ।
*yaṣṭavyam eveti manaḥ samādhāya sa sāttvikaḥ* ॥11 ॥

अभिसन्धाय तु फलं दम्भार्थमपि चैव यत् ।
इज्यते भरतश्रेष्ठ तं यज्ञं विद्धि राजसम् ॥१२॥

*abhisandhāya tu phalaṁ dambhārtham api caiva yat* ।
*ijyate bharata-śreṣṭha taṁ yajñaṁ viddhi rājasam* ॥12 ॥

विधिहीनमसृष्टान्नं मन्त्रहीनमदक्षिणम् ।
श्रद्धाविरहितं यज्ञं तामसं परिचक्षते ॥१३॥

*vidhihīnam asṛṣṭānnaṁ mantra-hīnam adakṣiṇam* ।
*śraddhā-virahitaṁ yajñaṁ tāmasaṁ paricakṣate* ॥13 ॥

देवद्विजगुरुप्राज्ञपूजनं शौचमार्जवम् ।
ब्रह्मचर्यमहिंसा च शारीरं तप उच्यते ॥१४॥

*deva-dvija-guru-prājña-pūjanaṁ śaucam ārjavam* ।
*brahmacaryam ahiṁsā ca śārīraṁ tapa ucyate* ॥14 ॥

अनुद्वेगकरं वाक्यं सत्यं प्रियहितं च यत् ।
स्वाध्यायाभ्यसनं चैव वाङ्मयं तप उच्यते ॥१५॥

*anudvega-karaṁ vākyaṁ satyaṁ priya-hitaṁ ca yat* ।
*svādhyāyābhyasanaṁ caiva vāṅmayaṁ tapa ucyate* ॥15 ॥

मनःप्रसादः सौम्यत्वं मौनमात्मविनिग्रहः ।
भावसंशुद्धिरित्येतत्तपो मानसमुच्यते ॥१६॥

*manaḥ-prasādaḥ saumyatvaṁ maunam ātma-vinigrahaḥ* ।
*bhāva-saṁśuddhir ity-etat tapo mānasam ucyate* ॥16 ॥

श्रद्धया परया तप्तं तपस्तत्त्रिविधं नरैः ।
अफलाकाङ्क्षिभिर्युक्तैः सात्त्विकं परिचक्षते ॥१७॥

*śraddhayā parayā taptaṁ tapas tat trividhaṁ naraiḥ* ।
*aphalākāṅkṣibhir-yuktaiḥ sāttvikaṁ paricakṣate* ॥17 ॥

सत्कारमानपूजार्थं तपो दम्भेन चैव यत् ।
क्रियते तदिह प्रोक्तं राजसं चलमध्रुवम् ॥१८॥

*satkāra-māna-pūjārthaṁ tapo dambhena caiva yat ।*
*kriyate tad iha proktaṁ rājasaṁ calam adhruvam* ॥18 ॥

मूढग्राहेणात्मनो यत्पीडया क्रियते तपः ।
परस्योत्सादनार्थं वा तत्तामसमुदाहृतम् ॥१९॥

*mūḍha-grāheṇātmano yat pīḍayā kriyate tapaḥ ।*
*parasyotsādanārthaṁ vā tat tāmasam udāhṛtam* ॥19 ॥

दातव्यमिति यद्दानं दीयतेऽनुपकारिणे ।
देशे काले च पात्रे च तद्दानं सात्त्विकं स्मृतम् ॥२०॥

*dātavyam iti yad dānaṁ dīyate 'nupakāriṇe ।*
*deśe kāle ca pātre ca tad dānaṁ sāttvikaṁ smṛtam* ॥20 ॥

यत्तु प्रत्युपकारार्थं फलमुद्दिश्य वा पुनः ।
दीयते च परिक्लिष्टं तद्दानं राजसं स्मृतम् ॥२१॥

*yat tu pratyupakārārthaṁ phalam uddiśya vā punaḥ ।*
*dīyate ca parikliṣṭam tad dānaṁ rājasaṁ smṛtam* ॥21 ॥

अदेशकाले यद्दानमपात्रेभ्यश्च दीयते ।
असत्कृतमवज्ञातं तत्तामसमुदाहृतम् ॥२२॥

*adeśa-kāle yad dānam apātrebhyaś ca dīyate ।*
*asatkṛtam avajñātaṁ tat tāmasam udāhṛtam* ॥22 ॥

ॐ तत्सदिति निर्देशो ब्रह्मणस्त्रिविधः स्मृतः ।
ब्राह्मणास्तेन वेदाश्च यज्ञाश्च विहिताः पुरा ॥२३॥

*om tat sad iti nirdeśo brahmaṇas-trividhaḥ smṛtaḥ ।*
*brāhmaṇās tena vedāś ca yajñāś ca vihitāḥ purā* ॥23 ॥

तस्मादोमित्युदाहृत्य यज्ञदानतमःक्रियाः ।
प्रवर्तन्ते विधानोक्ताः सततं ब्रह्मवादिनाम् ॥२४॥

*tasmād om ity udāhṛtya yajña-dāna-tapaḥ-kriyāḥ ।*
*pravartante vidhānoktāḥ satataṁ brahma-vādinām* ॥24 ॥

तदित्यनभिसन्धाय फलं यज्ञतपःक्रियाः ।
दानक्रियाश्च विविधाः क्रियन्ते मोक्षकाङ्क्षिभिः ॥२५॥

*tad ity anabhisandhāya phalaṁ yajña-tapaḥ-kriyāḥ* ।
*dāna-kriyāś ca vividhāḥ kriyante mokṣa-kāṅkṣibhiḥ* ॥25 ॥

सद्भावे साधुभावे च सदित्येतत्प्रयुज्यते ।
प्रशस्ते कर्मणि तथा सच्छब्दः पार्थ युज्यते ॥२६॥

*sad-bhāve sādhu-bhāve ca sad ity etat prayujyate* ।
*praśaste karmaṇi tathā sac-chabdaḥ pārtha yujyate* ॥26 ॥

यज्ञे तपसि दाने च स्थितिः सदिति चोच्यते ।
कर्म चैव तदर्थीयं सदित्येवाभिधीयते ॥२७॥

*yajñe tapasi dāne ca sthitiḥ sad iti cocyate* ।
*karma caiva tad-arthīyaṁ sad ity evābhidhīyate* ॥27 ॥

अश्रद्धया हुतं दत्तं तपस्तप्तं कृतं च यत् ।
असदित्युच्यते पार्थ न च तत्प्रेत्य नो इह ॥२८॥

*aśraddhayā hutaṁ dattaṁ tapas taptaṁ kṛtaṁ ca yat* ।
*asad ity ucyate pārtha na ca tat pretya no iha* ॥28 ॥

# 18. मोक्ष-संन्यासयोगः

**अर्जुन उवाच —**

संन्यासस्य महाबाहो तत्त्वमिच्छामि वेदितुम् ।
त्यागस्य च हृषीकेश पृथक्केशिनिषूदन ॥१॥

***arjuna uvāca —***

*saṁnyāsasya mahābāho tattvam icchāmi veditum* ।
*tyāgasya ca hṛṣīkeśa pṛthak keśi-niṣūdana* ॥1 ॥

**श्रीभगवानुवाच —**

काम्यानां कर्मणां न्यासं संन्यासं कवयो विदुः ।
सर्वकर्मफलत्यागं प्राहुस्त्यागं विचक्षणाः ॥२॥

***śrī bhagāvan uvāca —***

*kāmyānāṁ karmaṇāṁ nyāsaṁ saṁnyāsaṁ kavayo viduḥ* ।
*sarva-karma-phala-tyāgaṁ prāhus tyāgaṁ vicakṣaṇāḥ* ॥२ ॥

त्याज्यं दोषवदित्येके कर्म प्राहुर्मनीषिणः ।
यज्ञदानतपःकर्म न त्याज्यमिति चापरे ॥३॥

*tyājyaṁ doṣavad ity eke karma prāhur manīṣiṇaḥ* ।
*yajña-dāna-tapaḥ karma na tyājyam iti cāpare* ॥3 ॥

निश्चयं शृणु मे तत्र त्यागे भरतसत्तम ।
त्यागो हि पुरुषव्याघ्र त्रिविधः सम्प्रकीर्तितः ॥४॥

*niścayaṁ śṛṇu me tatra tyāge bharata-sattama* ।
*tyāgo hi puruṣa-vyāghra trividhaḥ saṁprakīrtitaḥ* ॥4 ॥

यज्ञदानतपःकर्म न त्याज्यं कार्यमेव तत् ।
यज्ञो दानं तपश्चैव पावनानि मनीषिणाम् ॥५॥

*yajña-dāna-tapaḥ-karma na tyājyaṁ kāryam eva tat* ।
*yajño dānaṁ tapaś caiva pāvanāni manīṣiṇām* ॥5 ॥

एतान्यपि तु कर्मणि सङ्गं त्यक्त्वा फलानि च ।
कर्तव्यानीति मे पार्थ निश्चितं मतमुत्तमम् ॥६॥

*etāny api tu karmāṇi saṅgaṁ tyaktvā phalāni ca* ।
*kartavyānīti me pārtha niścitaṁ matam uttamam* ॥6 ॥

नियतस्य तु संन्यासः कर्मणो नोपपद्यते ।
मोहात्तस्य परित्यागस्तामसः परिकीर्तितः ॥७॥

*niyatasya tu saṁnyāsaḥ karmaṇo nopapadyate* ।
*mohāt tasya parityāgas tāmasaḥ parikīrtitaḥ* ॥7 ॥

दुःखमित्येव यत्कर्म कायक्लेशभयात्त्यजेत् ।
स कृत्वा राजसं त्यागं नैव त्यागफलं लभेत् ॥८॥

*duḥkham ity eva yat karma kāya-kleśa-bhayāt tyajet* ।
*sa kṛtvā rājasaṁ tyāgaṁ naiva tyāga-phalaṁ labhet* ॥8 ॥

कार्यमित्येव यत्कर्म नियतं क्रियतेऽर्जुन ।
सङ्गं त्यक्त्वा फलं चैव स त्यागः सात्त्विको मतः ॥९॥

*kāryam ity eva yat karma niyataṁ kriyate 'rjuna* ।
*saṅgaṁ tyaktvā phalaṁ caiva sa tyāgaḥ sāttviko mataḥ* ॥9 ॥

न द्वेष्ट्यकुशलं कर्म कुशले नानुषज्जते ।
त्यागी सत्त्वसमाविष्टो मेधावी छिन्नसंशयः ॥१०॥

*na dveṣṭy akuśalaṁ karma kuśale nānuṣajjate* ।
*tyāgī sattva-samāviṣṭo medhāvī chinna-saṁśayaḥ* ॥10 ॥

न हि देहभृता शक्यं त्यक्तुं कर्माण्यशेषतः ।
यस्तु कर्मफलत्यागी स त्यागीत्यभिधीयते ॥११॥

*na hi deha-bhṛtā śakyaṁ tyaktuṁ karmāṇy aśeṣataḥ* ।
*yas tu karma-phala-tyāgī sa tyāgīty abdhidhīyate* ॥11 ॥

अनिष्टमिष्टं मिश्रं च त्रिविधं कर्मणः फलम् ।
भवत्यत्यागिनां प्रेत्य न तु संन्यासिनां क्वचित् ॥१२॥

*aniṣṭam iṣṭaṁ miśraṁ ca trividhaṁ karmaṇaḥ phalam* ।
*bhavaty atyāgināṁ pretya na tu saṁnyāsināṁ kvacit* ॥12 ॥

पञ्चैतानि महाबाहो कारणानि निबोध मे ।
सांख्ये कृतान्ते प्रोक्तानि सिद्धये सर्वकर्मणाम् ॥१३॥

*pañcaitāni mahā-bāho kāraṇāni nibodha me* ।
*sāṁkhye kṛtānte proktāni siddhaye sarva-karmaṇām* ॥13 ॥

अधिष्ठानं तथा कर्ता करणं च पृथग्विधम् ।
विविधाश्च पृथक्चेष्टा दैवं चैवात्र पञ्चमम् ॥१४॥

*adhiṣṭhānaṁ tathā kartā karaṇaṁ ca pṛthag-vidham* ।
*vividhāś ca prthak-ceṣṭā daivaṁ caiv ātra pañcamam* ॥14 ॥

शरीरवाङ्मनोभिर्यत्कर्म प्रारभते नरः ।
न्याय्यं वा विपरीतं वा पञ्चैते तस्य हेतवः ॥१५॥

*śarīra-vāṅ-manobhir yat karma prārabhate naraḥ* ।
*nyāyyaṁ vā viparītaṁ vā pañcaite tasya hetavaḥ* ॥15 ॥

तत्रैवं सति कर्तारमात्मानं केवलं तु यः ।
पश्यत्यकृतबुद्धित्वान्न स पश्यति दुर्मतिः ॥१६॥

*tatraivaṁ sati kartāram ātmānaṁ kevalaṁ tu yaḥ* ।
*paśyaty akṛta-buddhitvān na sa paśyati durmatiḥ* ॥16 ॥

यस्य नाहङ्कृतो भावो बुद्धिर्यस्य न लिप्यते ।
हत्वापि स इमाँल्लोकान्न हन्ति न निबध्यते ॥१७॥

*yasya nāhaṅkṛto bhāvo buddhir yasya na lipyate* ।
*hatvāpi sa imāṁllokānna hanti na nibadhyate* ॥17 ॥

ज्ञानं ज्ञेयं परिज्ञाता त्रिविधा कर्मचोदना ।
करणं कर्म कर्तेति त्रिविधः कर्मसङ्ग्रहः ॥१८॥

*jñānaṁ jñeyaṁ parijñātā trividhā karma-codanā ।*
*karaṇam karma karteti trividhaḥ karma-saṅgrahaḥ* ॥18 ॥

ज्ञानं कर्म च कर्ता च त्रिधैव गुणभेदतः ।
प्रोच्यते गुणसङ्ख्याने यथावच्छृणु तान्यपि ॥१९॥

*jñānaṁ karma ca kartā ca tridhaiva guṇa-bhedataḥ ।*
*procyate guṇa-saṅkhyāne yathāvāc chṛṇu tāny api* ॥19 ॥

सर्वभूतेषु येनैकं भावमव्ययमीक्षते ।
अविभक्तं विभक्तेषु तज्ज्ञानं विद्धि सात्त्विकम् ॥२०॥

*sarva-bhūteṣu yenaikaṁ bhāvam avyayam īkṣate ।*
*avibhaktaṁ vibhakteṣu taj jñānaṁ viddhi sāttvikam* ॥20 ॥

पृथक्त्वेन तु यज्ज्ञानं नानाभावान्पृथग्विधान् ।
वेत्ति सर्वेषु भूतेषु तज्ज्ञानं विद्धि राजसम् ॥२१॥

*pṛthaktvena tu yaj jñānaṁ nānā-bhāvān pṛthag-vidhān ।*
*vetti sarveṣu bhūteṣu taj jñānaṁ viddhi rājasam* ॥21 ॥

यत्तु कृत्स्नवदेकस्मिन्कार्ये सक्तमहैतुकम् ।
अतत्त्वार्थवदल्पं च तत्तामसमुदाहृतम् ॥२२॥

*yat tu kṛtsnavad ekasmin kārye saktam ahaitukam ।*
*atattvārthavad alpaṁ ca tat tāmasam udāhṛtam* ॥22 ॥

नियतं सङ्गरहितमरागद्वेषतः कृतम् ।
अफलप्रेप्सुना कर्म यत्तत्सात्त्विकमुच्यते ॥२३॥

*niyataṁ saṅga-rahitam arāga-dveṣataḥ kṛtam ।*
*aphala-prepsunā karma yat tat sāttvikam ucyate* ॥23 ॥

यत्तु कामेप्सुना कर्म साहङ्कारेण वा पुनः ।
क्रियते बहुलायासं तद्राजसमुदाहृतम् ॥२४॥

*yat tu kāmepsunā karma sāhaṁkāreṇa vā punaḥ ।*
*kriyate bahulāyāsaṁ tad rājasam udāhṛtam* ॥24 ॥

अनुबन्धं क्षयं हिंसामनवेक्ष्य च पौरुषम् ।
मोहादारभ्यते कर्म यत्तत्तामसमुच्यते ॥२५॥

*anubandhaṁ kṣayaṁ hiṁsām anavekṣya ca pauruṣam* ।
*mohād ārabhyate karma yat tat tāmasam ucyate* ॥25 ॥

मुक्तसङ्गोऽनहंवादी धृत्युत्साहसमन्वितः ।
सिद्ध्यसिद्ध्योर्निर्विकारः कर्ता सात्त्विक उच्यते ॥२६॥

*mukta-saṅgo 'nahaṁ-vādī dhṛty-utsāha-samanvitaḥ* ।
*siddhy-asiddhyor nirvikāraḥ kartā sāttvika ucyate* ॥26 ॥

रागी कर्मफलप्रेप्सुर्लुब्धो हिंसात्मकोऽशुचिः ।
हर्षशोकान्वितः कर्ता राजसः परिकीर्तितः ॥२७॥

*rāgī karma-phala-prepsur lubdho hiṁsātmako 'śuciḥ* ।
*harṣa-śokānvitaḥ kartā rājasaḥ parikīrtitaḥ* ॥27 ॥

अयुक्तः प्राकृतः स्तब्धः शठो नैकृतिकोऽलसः ।
विषादी दीर्घसूत्री च कर्ता तामस उच्यते ॥२८॥

*ayuktaḥ prākṛtaḥ stabdhaḥ śaṭho naikṛtiko 'lasaḥ* ।
*viṣādī dīrgha-sūtrī ca kartā tāmasa ucyate* ॥28 ॥

बुद्धेर्भेदं धृतेश्चैव गुणतस्त्रिविधं शृणु ।
प्रोच्यमानमशेषेण पृथक्त्वेन धनञ्जय ॥२९॥

*buddher bhedaṁ dhṛteś caiva guṇatas trividhaṁ śṛṇu* ।
*procyamānam aśeseṇa pṛthaktvena dhanañjaya* ॥29 ॥

प्रवृत्तिं च निवृत्तिं च कार्याकार्ये भयाभये ।
बन्धं मोक्षं च या वेत्ति बुद्धिः सा पार्थ सात्त्विकी ॥३०॥

*pravṛttiṁ ca nivṛttiṁ ca kāryākārye bhayābhaye* ।
*bandhaṁ mokṣaṁ ca yā vetti buddhiḥ sā pārtha sāttvikī* ॥30 ॥

यया धर्ममधर्मं च कार्यं चाकार्यमेव च ।
अयथावत्प्रजानाति बुद्धिः सा पार्थ राजसी ॥३१॥

*yayā dharmam adharmaṁ ca kāryaṁ cākāryam eva ca* ।
*ayathāvat prajānāti buddhiḥ sā pārtha rājasī* ॥31 ॥

अधर्मं धर्ममिति या मन्यते तमसावृता ।
सर्वार्थान्विपरीतांश्च बुद्धिः सा पार्थ तामसी ॥३२॥

*adharmaṁ dharmam iti yā manyate tamasāvṛtā* ।
*sarvārthān viparītāṁś ca buddhiḥ sā pārtha tāmasī* ॥32 ॥

धृत्या यया धारयते मनःप्राणेन्द्रियक्रियाः ।
योगेनाव्यभिचारिण्या धृतिः सा पार्थ सात्त्विकी ॥३३॥

*dhṛtyā yayā dhārayate manaḥ-prāṇendriya-kriyāḥ* ।
*yogenāvyabhicāriṇyā dhṛtiḥ sā pārtha sāttvikī* ॥33 ॥

यया तु धर्मकामार्थान्धृत्या धारयतेऽर्जुन ।
प्रसङ्गेन फलाकाङ्क्षी धृतिः सा पार्थ राजसी ॥३४॥

*yayā tu dharma-kāmārthān dhṛtyā dhārayate 'rjuna* ।
*prasaṅgena phalākāṅkṣī dhṛtiḥ sā pārtha rājasī* ॥34 ॥

यया स्वप्नं भयं शोकं विषादं मदमेव च ।
न विमुञ्चति दुर्मेधा धृतिः सा पार्थ तामसी ॥३५॥

*yayā svapnaṁ bhayaṁ śokaṁ viṣādaṁ madam eva ca* ।
*na vimuñcati durmedhā dhṛtiḥ sā pārtha tāmasī* ॥35 ॥

सुखं त्विदानीं त्रिविधं शृणु मे भरतर्षभ ।
अभ्यासाद्रमते यत्र दुःखान्तं च निगच्छति ॥३६॥

*sukhaṁ tv idānīṁ trividhaṁ śṛṇu me bharatarṣabha* ।
*abhyāsād ramate yatra duḥkhāntaṁ ca nigacchati* ॥36 ॥

यत्तदग्रे विषमिव परिणामेऽमृतोपमम् ।
तत्सुखं सात्त्विकं प्रोक्तमात्मबुद्धिप्रसादजम् ॥३७॥

*yat tad agre viṣam iva pariṇāme 'mṛtopamam* ।
*tat sukhaṁ sāttvikaṁ proktam ātma-buddhi-prasādajam* ॥37 ॥

विषयेन्द्रियसंयोगाद्यत्तदग्रेऽमृतोपमम् ।
परिणामे विषमिव तत्सुखं राजमं स्मृतम् ॥३८॥

*viṣayendriya-saṁyogād yat tad agre 'mṛtopamam* ।
*pariṇāme viṣam iva tat sukhaṁ rājasaṁ smṛtam* ॥38 ॥

यदग्रे चानुबन्धे च सुखं मोहनमात्मनः ।
निद्रालस्यप्रमादोत्थं तत्तामसमुदाहृतम् ॥३९॥

*yad agre cānubandhe ca sukhaṁ mohanam ātmanaḥ* ।
*nidrālasya-pramādotthaṁ tat tāmasam udāhṛtam* ॥39 ॥

न तदस्ति पृथिव्यां वा दिवि देवेषु वा पुनः ।
सत्त्वं प्रकृतिजैर्मुक्तं यदेभिः स्यात्त्रिभिर्गुणैः ॥४०॥

*na tad asti pṛthivyāṁ vā divi deveṣu vā punaḥ* ।
*sattvaṁ prakṛtijair muktaṁ yad ebhiḥ syāt tribhir guṇaiḥ* ॥40 ॥

ब्राह्मणक्षत्रियविशां शूद्राणां च परन्तप ।
कर्माणि प्रविभक्तानि स्वभावप्रभवैर्गुणैः ।।४१।।

*brāhmaṇa-kṣatriya-viśāṁ śūdrāṇāṁ ca parantapa* ।
*karmāṇi pravibhaktāni svabhāva-prabhāvair guṇaiḥ* ॥41 ॥

शमो दमस्तपः शौचं क्षान्तिरार्जवमेव च ।
ज्ञानं विज्ञानमास्तिक्यं ब्रह्मकर्म स्वभावजम् ।।४२।।

*śamo damas tapaḥ śaucaṁ kṣāntir ārjavam eva ca* ।
*jñānaṁ vijñānam āstikyaṁ brahma-karma svabhāvajam* ॥42 ॥

शौर्यं तेजो धृतिर्दाक्ष्यं युद्धे चाप्यपलायनम् ।
दानमीश्वरभावश्च क्षात्रं कर्म स्वभावजम् ।।४३।।

*śauryaṁ tejo dhṛtir dākṣyaṁ yaddhe cāpy apalāyanam* ।
*dānam īśvara-bhāvaś ca kṣātraṁ karma svabhāvajam* ।43 ॥

कृषिगौरक्ष्यवाणिज्यं वैश्यकर्म स्वभावजम् ।
परिचर्यात्मकं कर्म शूद्रस्यापि स्वभावजम् ।।४४।।

*kṛṣi-gaurakṣya-vāṇijyaṁ vaiśya-karma svabhāvajam* ।
*paricaryātmakaṁ karma śūdrasyāpi svabhāvajam* ॥44 ॥

स्वे स्वे कर्मण्यभिरतः संसिद्धिं लभते नरः ।
स्वकर्मनिरतः सिद्धिं यथा विन्दति तच्छृणु ।।४५।।

*sve sve karmaṇy abhirataḥ saṁsiddhiṁ labhate naraḥ* ।
*sva-karma-nirataḥ siddhiṁ yathā vindati tacchṛṇu* ॥45 ॥

यतः प्रवृत्तिर्भूतानां येन सर्वमिदं ततम् ।
स्वकर्मणा तमभ्यर्च्य सिद्धिं विन्दति मानवः ।।४६।।

*yataḥ pravṛttir bhūtānāṁ yena sarvam idaṁ tatam* ।
*sva-karmaṇā tam abhyarcya siddhiṁ vindati mānavaḥ* ॥46 ॥

श्रेयान्स्वधर्मो विगुणः परधर्मात्स्वनुष्ठितात् ।
स्वभावनियतं कर्म कुर्वन्नाप्नोति किल्बिषम् ।।४७।।

*śreyān svadharmo viguṇaḥ para-dharmāt svanuṣṭhitāt* ।
*svabhāva-niyataṁ karma kurvan nāpnoti kilbiṣam* ॥47 ॥

सहजं कर्म कौन्तेय सदोषमपि न त्यजेत् ।
सर्वारम्भा हि दोषेण धूमेनाग्निरिवावृताः ॥४८॥

*sahajaṁ karma kaunteya sadoṣam api na tyajet* ।
*sarvārambhā hi doṣeṇa dhūmenāgnir ivāvṛtāḥ* ॥48 ॥

असक्तबुद्धिः सर्वत्र जितात्मा विगतस्पृहः ।
नैष्कर्म्यसिद्धिं परमां संन्यासेनाधिगच्छति ॥४९॥

*asakta-buddhiḥ sarvatra jitātmā vigata-spṛhaḥ* ।
*naiṣkarmya-siddhiṁ paramāṁ saṁnyāsenādhigacchati* ॥49 ॥

सिद्धिं प्राप्तो यथा ब्रह्म तथाप्नोति निबोध मे ।
समासेनैव कौन्तेय निष्ठा ज्ञानस्य या परा ॥५०॥

*siddhiṁ prāpto yathā brahma tathāpnoti nibodha me* ।
*samāsenaiva kaunteya niṣṭhā jñānasya yā parā* ॥50 ॥

बुद्ध्या विशुद्धया युक्तो धृत्यात्मानं नियम्य च ।
शब्दादीन्विषयांस्त्यक्त्वा रागद्वेषौ व्युदस्य च ॥५१॥

*buddhyā viśuddhayā yukto dhṛtyātmānaṁ niyamya ca* ।
*śabdādīn viṣayāṁs tyaktvā rāga-dveṣau vyudasya ca* ॥51 ॥

विविक्तसेवी लघ्वाशी यतवाक्कायमानसः ।
ध्यानयोगपरो नित्यं वैराग्यं समुपाश्रितः ॥५२॥

*vivikta-sevī laghvāśī yata-vāk-kāya-mānasaḥ* ।
*dhyāna-yoga-paro nityaṁ vairāgyaṁ samupāśritaḥ* ॥52 ॥

अहङ्कारं बलं दर्पं कामं क्रोधं परिग्रहम् ।
विमुच्य निर्ममः शान्तो ब्रह्मभूयाय कल्पते ॥५३॥

*ahaṅkāraṁ balaṁ darpaṁ kāmaṁ krodhaṁ parigraham* ।
*vimucya nirmamaḥ śānto brahma-bhūyāya kalpate* ॥53 ॥

ब्रह्मभूतः प्रसन्नात्मा न शोचति न काङ्क्षति ।
समः सर्वेषु भूतेषु मद्भक्तिं लभते पराम् ॥५४॥

*brahma-bhūtaḥ prasannātmā na śocati na kāṅkṣati* ।
*samaḥ sarveṣu bhūteṣu mad-bhaktiṁ labhate parām* ॥54 ॥

भक्त्या मामभिजानाति यावान्यश्चास्मि तत्त्वतः ।
ततो मां तत्त्वतो ज्ञात्वा विशते तदनन्तरम् ॥५५॥

*bhaktyā mām abhijānāti yāvān yaś-cāsmi tattvataḥ* ।
*tato māṁ tattvato jñātvā viśate tad-anantaram* ॥55 ॥

सर्वकर्माण्यपि सदा कुर्वाणो मद्व्यपाश्रयः ।
मत्प्रसादादवाप्नोति शाश्वतं पदमव्ययम् ॥५६॥

*sarva-karmāny api sadā kurvāṇo mad-vyapāśrayaḥ* ।
*mat-prsādād avāpnoti śāśvataṁ padam avyayam* ॥56 ॥

चेतसा सर्वकर्माणि मयि संन्यस्य मत्परः ।
बुद्धियोगमुपाश्रित्य मच्चित्तः सततं भव ॥५७॥

*cetasā sarva-karmāṇi mayi saṁnyasya mat-paraḥ* ।
*buddhi-yogam upāśritya mac-cittaḥ satataṁ bhava* ॥57 ॥

मच्चित्तः सर्वदुर्गाणि मत्प्रसादात्तरिष्यसि ।
अथ चेत्त्वमहङ्कारान्न श्रोष्यसि विनङ्क्ष्यसि ॥५८॥

*maccittaḥ sarva-durgāṇi mat-prasādāt tariṣyasi* ।
*atha cet tvam ahaṅkārān na śroṣyasi vinaṅkṣyasi* ॥58 ॥

यदहङ्कारमाश्रित्य न योत्स्य इति मन्यसे ।
मिथ्यैष व्यवसायस्ते प्रकृतिस्त्वां नियोक्ष्यति ॥५९॥

*yad ahaṅkāram āśritya na yotsya iti manyase* ।
*mithyaiṣa vyavasāyas te prakṛtis tvāṁ niyokṣyati* ॥59 ॥

स्वभावजेन कौन्तेय निबद्धः स्वेन कर्मणा ।
कर्तुं नेच्छसि यन्मोहात्करिष्यस्यवशोऽपि तत् ॥६०॥

*svabhāvajena kaunteya nibaddhaḥ svena karmaṇā* ।
*kartuṁ necchasi yan mohāt kariṣyasy avaśo 'pi tat* ॥60 ॥

ईश्वरः सर्वभूतानां हृद्देशेऽर्जुन तिष्ठति ।
भ्रामयन्सर्वभूतानि यन्त्रारूढानि मायया ॥६१॥

*īśvaraḥ sarva-bhūtānāṁ hṛd-deśe 'rjuna tiṣṭhati* ।
*bhrāmayan sarva-bhūtāni yantrārūḍhāni māyayā* ॥61 ॥

तमेव शरणं गच्छ सर्वभावेन भारत ।
तत्प्रसादात्परां शान्तिं स्थानं प्राप्स्यसि शाश्वतम् ॥६२॥

*tam eva śaraṇam gaccha sarva-bhāvena bhārata* ।
*tat-prasādāt parāṁ śāntiṁ sthānaṁ prāpsyasi śāśvatam* ॥62 ॥

इति ते ज्ञानमाख्यातं गुह्याद्गुह्यतरं मया ।
विमृश्यैतदशेषेण यथेच्छसि तथा कुरु ॥६३॥

*iti te jñānam ākhyātaṁ guhyād guhyataraṁ mayā |*
*vimṛśyaitad aśeṣeṇa yathecchasi tathā kuru* ॥63॥

सर्वगुह्यतमं भूयः शृणु मे परमं वचः ।
इष्टोऽसि मे दृढमिति ततो वक्ष्यामि ते हितम् ॥६४॥

*sarva-guhyatamaṁ bhūyaḥ śṛṇu me paramaṁ vacaḥ |*
*iṣṭo 'si me dṛḍham iti tato vakṣyāmi te hitam* ॥64॥

मन्मना भव मद्भक्तो मद्याजी मां नमस्कुरु ।
मामेवैष्यसि सत्यं ते प्रतिजाने प्रियोऽसि मे ॥६५॥

*man-manā bhava mad-bhakto mad-yājī māṁ namas-kuru |*
*mām evaiṣyasi satyaṁ te pratijāne priyo 'si me* ॥65॥

सर्वधर्मान्परित्यज्य मामेकं शरणं व्रज ।
अहं त्वा सर्वपापेभ्यो मोक्षयिष्यामि मा शुचः ॥६६॥

*sarva-dharmān parityajya mām ekaṁ śaraṇaṁ vraja |*
*ahaṁ tvā sarva-pāpebhyo mokṣayiṣyāmi mā śucaḥ* ॥66॥

इदं ते नातपस्काय नाभक्ताय कदाचन ।
न चाशुश्रूषवे वाच्यं न च मां योऽभ्यसूयति ॥६७॥

*idaṁ te nātapaskāya nābhaktāya kadācana |*
*na cāśuśrūṣave vācyaṁ na ca māṁ yo 'bhyasūyati* ॥67॥

य इमं परमं गुह्यं मद्भक्तेष्वभिधास्यति ।
भक्तिं मयि परां कृत्वा मामेवैष्यत्यसंशयः ॥६८॥

*ya imaṁ paramaṁ guhyaṁ mad-bhakteṣv abhidhāsyati |*
*bhaktiṁ mayi parāṁ kṛtvā mām evaiṣyaty asaṁśayaḥ* ॥68॥

न च तस्मान्मनुष्येषु कश्चिन्मे प्रियकृत्तमः ।
भविता न च मे तस्मादन्यः प्रियतरो भुवि ॥६९॥

*na ca tasmān manuṣyeṣu kaścin me priya-kṛttamaḥ |*
*bhavitā na ca me tasmād anyaḥ priyataro bhuvi* ॥69॥

अध्येष्यते च य इमं धर्म्यं संवादमावयोः ।
ज्ञानयज्ञेन तेनाहमिष्टः स्यामिति मे मतिः ॥७०॥

*adhyeṣyate ca ya imaṁ dharmyaṁ saṁvādam āvayoḥ* ।
*jñāna-yajñena tenāham iṣṭaḥ syām iti me matiḥ* ॥70 ॥

श्रद्धावाननसूयश्च शृणुयादपि यो नरः ।
सोऽपि मुक्तः शुभाँल्लोकान्प्राप्नुयात्पुण्यकर्मणाम् ॥७१॥

*śraddhāvān anasūyaś ca śṛnuyād api yo naraḥ* ।
*so 'pi muktaḥ śubhāṁllokān prāpnuyāt puṇya-karmaṇām* ॥71 ॥

कच्चिदेतच्छ्रुतं पार्थ त्वयैकाग्रेण चेतसा ।
कच्चिदज्ञानसंमोहः प्रणष्टस्ते धनञ्जय ॥७२॥

*kaccid etac chrutaṁ pārtha tvayaikāgreṇa cetasā* ।
*kaccid ajñāna-saṁmohaḥ praṇaṣṭas te dhanañjaya* ॥72 ॥

**अर्जुन उवाच —**

नष्टो मोहः स्मृतिर्लब्धा त्वत्प्रसादान्मयाच्युत ।
स्थितोऽस्मि गतसन्देहः करिष्ये वचनं तव ॥७३॥

***arjuna uvāca —***

*naṣṭo mohaḥ smṛtir labdhā tvat-prasādān mayācyuta* ।
*sthito 'smi gata-sandehaḥ kariṣye vacanaṁ tava* ॥73 ॥

**सञ्जय उवाच —**

इत्यहं वासुदेवस्य पार्थस्य च महात्मनः ।
संवादमिममश्रौषमद्भुतं रोमहर्षणम् ॥७४॥

***sañjaya uvāca —***

*ity ahaṁ vāsudevasya pārthasya ca mahātmanaḥ* ।
*saṁvādam imam aśrauṣam adbhutaṁ roma-harṣaṇam* ॥74 ॥

व्यासप्रसादाच्छ्रुतवानेतद्गुह्यमहं परम् ।
योगं योगेश्वरात्कृष्णात्साक्षात्कथयतः स्वयम् ॥७५॥

*vyāsa-prasādāc chrutavān etad guhyaṁ ahaṁ param* ।
*yogaṁ yogeśvarāt kṛṣṇāt sākṣāt kathayataḥ svayam* ॥75 ॥

राजन्संस्मृत्य संस्मृत्य संवादमिममद्भुतम् ।
केशवार्जुनयोः पुण्यं हृष्यामि च मुहुर्मुहुः ॥७६॥

*rājan saṁsmṛtya saṁsmṛtya saṁvādam imam adbhutam* ।
*keśavārjunayoḥ puṇyaṁ hṛṣyāmi ca muhur muhuḥ* ॥76 ॥

तच्च संस्मृत्य संस्मृत्य रूपमत्यद्भुतं हरेः ।
विस्मयो मे महान् राजन्हृष्यामि च पुनः पुनः ॥७७॥

*tacca saṁsmṛtya saṁsmṛtya rūpam atyadbhutaṁ hareḥ* ।
*vismayo me mahān rājan hṛṣyāmi ca punaḥ punaḥ* ॥77 ॥

यत्र योगेश्वरः कृष्णो यत्र पार्थो धनुर्धरः ।
तत्र श्रीर्विजयो भूतिर्ध्रुवा नीतिर्मतिर्मम ॥७८॥

*yatra yogeśvaraḥ kṛṣṇo yatra pārtho dhanurdharaḥ* ।
*tatra śrīr vijayo bhūtir dhruvā nītir matir mama* ॥78 ॥

# Glossary

*a*: Not; non-

*ābhāsa*: Reflection.

*ābhāsa-vāda*: The doctrine of reflection.

*abhaya*: Fearlessness.

*abhimānaḥ*: Excessive vanity.

*abhiniveśaḥ*: Fear of death; tenacity of mundane existence; clinging to life.

*abhivyakti*: Manifestation; the act of being expressed.

*abhyāsa*: Regular, repeated practice.

*abhyāsa-yoga*: The *yoga* of repeated efforts.

*acalam*: Motionless; immovable.

*ācārahīna*: Unethical, immoral and unscrupulous in practices.

*ācārya*: A venerable teacher who imparts knowledge after experimenting and practising.

*acetana*: Devoid of consciousness; insentient.

*acetasaḥ*: Unintelligent.

*acintya*: Unthinkable; imponderable.

*ādhāra*: Container; holder.

*adharma*: Unrighteousness; not virtuous.

*ādheya*: Content; that which is held.

*ādibhautika*: Arising from external agents.

*Ādhibhūta*: 1. God's manifestation in matter and energy. 2. Perishable existence.

*Ādhidaiva*: God's manifestation in divinities. 2. God Himself.

*ādhidaivika*: Arising from the acts of gods, planets and *prārabdha karma* (already initiated karmic *saṁskāra*s).

*adhiṣṭhāna*: An all-pervasive One, homogeneously present inside and outside all created entities, holding and supporting the latter.

*Adhiyajña*: God's manifestation in worship, penances and sacrifices.

*Adhyakṣa* (*adhyakṣa*): Chairperson.

*adhyakṣatā*: Chairpersonship.

*adhyāropa*: Superimposition.

*adhyas*: To place over or upon.

*adhyāsa*: 1. Superimposition. 2. The phenomenon of *X* appearing as non-*X* in one form or in diversity.

*adhyāsa-vāda*: The doctrine of superimposition; the doctrine of *B* (*Brahman*) appearing in diversity as non-*B*.

*Adhyātma*: 1. The innate nature of the Supreme Self. 2. The inner self or *Brahman* residing in each body.

*adhyātma-vidyā*: Spiritual knowledge.

*ādhyātmika*: 1. Spiritual. 2. Arising in the body.

*ādi*: Beginning.

*advaita*: Non-dual.

*advaita-vāda*: The doctrine of non-dualism.

*āgāmī karma*: *Karma* done in the present life and saved for fructification in future lives.

*agnihotra*: Fire-sacrifices; fire-rituals; oblation in fire.

*ahaṅkāra*: Ego; egoity; the subtle psycho-structure that evolves from *buddhi* and is responsible for the I-sense.

*aja:* Birthless; unborn.

*ajaya*: Defeat; non-victory.

*ājñā-cakra*: The subtle vortex-organ, located on the spot between the two eyebrows.

*ajñaḥ*: Ignorant.

*ājyam*: Melted and clarified butter used for oblation.

*ajñānam*: Ignorance; nescience; insentience.

*akālam*: Timeless.

*akarma*: Inaction.

*akarttā*: A non-doer.

*akartavya*: Contrary duty; what should not be done.

*akārya*: An action that should not be performed.

*Ākāśa*: The totality of space, standing for *Mahākāśa*, written as "Space." *ākāśa*. The subtlest one among the five states of matter — solid, liquid, gaseous, energy and ākāsic. The so-called void (*ākāśa* or space) is really a plenum, pregnant with material particles and quanta.

*akhaṇḍa*: Unbroken whole; partless.

*akr̥tātmanaḥ*: Unrefined.

*akṣara*: Imperishable; one that does not wane, melt away or trickle.

*akṣaya*: Undecaying.

*alābha*: No gain; loss.

*amanāḥ*: Mindless.

*amara*: Deathless.

*amr̥tam*: 1. Immortality. 2. Ambrosia; nectar.

*aṁśa*: Part.

*anādi*: Beginningless.

*anākāśam*: Spaceless.

*Ānanda*: Bliss; when referred to *Brahman*, an ecstatic state, neutral to joyfulness and sorrowfulness.

*ānanda*: Joyfulness or ecstasy, referred to created entities.

*ānandamaya kośa*: The blissful sheath.

*ananta*: Endless.

*anāsakta*: Detached; unattached.

*anāśritaḥ*: Not sheltered in; without expectation in return.

*anātmajñaḥ*: Ignorant of the Self or the self.

*anātma-vāda*: The doctrine of no self.

*aṇḍa/āṇḍa*: An egg.

*andha*: Blind.

*anityam*: Impermanent; transient.

*annamaya kośa*: The material sheath.

*anta*: End.

*antaḥkaraṇa*: Internal instrument; a subtle, compound psycho-structure in the subtle body, consisting of three principal sub-structures, namely, *buddhi, ahaṅkāra, manas*.

*Antaryāmī*: God who is the inner controller, the inner ruler.

*anubhūti*: Experience.

*anucita*: Ought not.

*anumantā*: One who gives assent or approval to an action.

*Āpaḥ*: The Primordial Waters or the subtlest Cosmic Plasma; the first evolute from *Virāḍ* (*Virāṭ, Mahat, Buddhi*).

*apāna*: 1. The Out-breath. 2. The component of *Prāṇa* that causes excretion and expulsion.

*aparā*: Lower; inferior (in feminine gender).

*Aparā-Prakṛti*: Lower or Inferior Nature. *Māyā*, as *Aparā-Prakṛti*, is Unmanifest; the universe, as *Aparā-Prakṛti*, is Manifest.

*aparigraha*: Non-accumulation of property; non-exploitation; non-acceptance of unearned property; covetousness for more and more.

*aparokṣa*: Without mediation; direct.

*aparokṣānubhūti*: Direct experience without any mediation.

*ardha*: One-half.

*arjuna*: 1. White. 2. Free from dirt or blemishes.

*arpaṇa*: Offering.

*artha*: 1. Finance; wealth; money. 2. Material prosperity. 3. Meaning.

*arūpam*: Formless (in neuter gender).

*āsakta*: Attached.

*āsakta-buddhi*: One whose intellect is attached.

*asaktaḥ*: Unattached.

*āsakti*: Attachment.

*asambandhi*: Non-relational (in neuter gender).

*asat*: 1. That which does not exist. 2. A non-being.

*asiddhi*: Failure.

*āśīrmudrā*: Blessing gesture.

*asmitā*: I-centredness; ego-centricity (vide Pātañjala psychology).

*āśrama*: A hermitage.

*asukham*: Joyless; unhappiness.

*asura*: A demon.

*āsura*: Demoniac.

*āsurika*: Demoniac.

*asvatantrā*: Not independent (in feminine gender).

*Aśvattha*: *Ficus religiosa* tree; the *pīpal* tree.

*atimānaḥ*: Excessive vanity.

*atīndriya*: That which transcends the usual sense-experience.

*Ātmā*: Self; the Great Self; God or Īśvara; *Brahman*.

*ātmā*: 1. The self; the individual self; the individual spirit. 2. Oneself.

*ātmabhūtā*: That which has become from the self (in feminine gender).

*ātmaśuddhi*: The purification of the *antaḥkaraṇa* (*buddhi* + *ahaṅkāra* + *manas*).

*ātma-śuddhyartham*: For the purification of the self (here "self" means "the *antaḥkaraṇa*").

*ātmavān*: One who has mastered oneself.

*atyāgī*: A non-relinquisher.

*auṣadha*: 1. Herbs on which living beings feed, including rice, wheat, barley, etc. 2. Healing herbs.

*avaccheda-vāda*: The doctrine of limiting adjunct; the doctrine of delimitation.

*avadhya*: What cannot (should not) be killed or slain.

*āvaraṇa*: The act of covering, hiding or concealing.

*āvaraṇa-śakti*: Concealing power.

*avastu*: Not a substance made up of matter and energy.

*Avatāra/avatāra*: God born with an illusory, individual body of any living species, human or sub-human. The word literally means "descent."

*avatāra-vāda*: The doctrine of reincarnation.

*avidyā*: 1. Ignorance; nescience; insentience. 2. The Unconscious, as conceived by Patañjali in his depth-psychology.

*avikārya*: Unmodifiable; immutable; unchangeable.

*avikriya*: Changeless.

*avyākṛta*: Undifferentiated (in masculine gender).

*avyākṛtā*: Undifferentiated (in feminine gender).

*Avyakta*: The Unmanifest; the Unmanifest *Māyā*.

*avyakta*: Anything existing in an unmanifested state.

*Avyakta Prakṛti*: *Māyā*, the Mother Divine, the *Mūla-Prakṛti* or the Primordial Nature that ever remains in an unmanifested state. (This is the concept of the Advaita Vedānta in contrast with the Sāṅkhya.)

*avyaya*: Not liable to change; undecaying.

*avyayātmā*: The immutable Self/self.

*baddha*: Bound.

*bala*: 1. Force. 2. Violence.

*bala-śakti*: The power of force.

*bandhana*: Binding; bondage.

*Bhagavān*: God.

*bhakṣyam*: Food eaten by swallowing.

*bhakta*: A devotee.

*bhakti*: Devotion.

*bhakti-yoga*: The *yoga* of devotion.

*bharttā*: Supporter; maintainer; sustainer; nourisher.

*bhāvaḥ*: 1. Becoming something. 2. An idea; a thought.

*bhāvaśūnyāvasthā*: A state of thoughtlessness.

*bhāvātīta*: Beyond thoughts; transcending thoughts; the total absence of thoughts.

*bhojyam*: Food eaten by mastication.

*bhoktā*: 1. Experiencer. 2. Eater.

*bhrānti*: Illusion.

*Bhūḥ*: 1. The grossest *Lokaḥ* of the universe. 2. God presiding over *Bhūḥ*.

*Bhūrloka*: The gross and the first *Lokaḥ* of the universe.

*bhūta*: 1. A created entity; anything that has become, like *X* modified into *Y*.

*bhūtagrāmaḥ*: The multitude of beings, both inanimate and animate.

*bhūta-jaya*: Victory over the five material states of matter and energy.

*bhūtātmā*: The self in a non-living entity; all-pervasive *Brahman* inside a non-living entity, the latter serving as an *upādhi*.

*Bhuvaḥ*: 1. The second *lokaḥ*, subtler than the *Bhūḥ*. 2. God presiding over the *Bhuvaḥ*.

*bhuvanaḥ*: Any one of the seven *loka*s in the universe.

*Bhuvarlokaḥ*: The second *lokaḥ*, subtler than the *Bhūrlokaḥ*, but grosser than the *Svaḥ*.

*bīja*: 1. Seed. 2. A seed-syllable.

*Bīja-Śakti*: Seminal Power.

*bindu*: 1. A point. 2. The singularity of modern cosmology.

*Brahma* (*Brahman*): The fundamental Reality which is Pure Existence, Pure Consciousness and Pure Bliss; formless, functionless, attributeless, non-relational Being without becoming.

Brahmā: Only one God, taking the role of the Creator, is named as Brahmā.

*brahmacārī*: 1. One who practises celibacy. 2. One treading the divine path.

*brahmacarya*: 1. Sex-abstinence. 2. Regulated, moral sex-life.

*brahma-darśī*: A seer of *Brahman*; one who sees everything and everybody in *Brahman* and sees *Brahman* in everything and everybody.

*Brahma-jñāna*: Knowledge, with realization, on *Brahman*.

*Brahma-jñānī*: A knower of *Brahman*.

*Brahma-Loka*: The seventh and the subtlest *lokaḥ*, otherwise known as *Satya-Loka*.

*Brahman*: See *Brahma*.

*brāhmaṇa*: An enlightened person who knows and realizes *Brahman*; a Hindu priest.

*Brahma-nirvāṇa*: Merging in *Brahman*, with the concurrent loss of individual identity; liberation culminating in a total identification with *Brahman;* the self becoming the Self; the *jīvātmā* becoming the *Paramātmā*.

*Brahmānubhūti*: The experience of *Brahman*.

*brahma-randhra*: The subtle aperture as the terminal point of the *suṣumṇā* at the apex of the head.

*Brahmārpaṇam*: Offering to *Brahman*.

*Brahma-Śakti*: The Power of *Brahman; Māyā*.

*Brahmatva*: *Brahman*-hood.

*Brahmavid* (*Brahmavit*): The knower of *Brahman*.

*Brahma-yukta*: United with *Brahman*.

*Brāhmī-sthiti*: Stay in *Brahman*.

*Brahmopalabdhi*: The realization of *Brahman*.

*bṛhat*: Huge; very large; great.

*Buddhi*: The Cosmic Mind or Supermind; the Cosmic Intellect; the same as *Virāḍ* or *Mahat*; intellect inducted in *Māyā* due to the presence of *Brahman*.

*buddhi*: Individual intellect inducted in a created entity due to the presence of *Brahman*.

*buddhi-nāśa*: The loss of intelligence.

*buddhi-nirmāṇam*: Mental construct; mentally conceived and constructed.

*buddhi-yoga*: The *yoga* through which one unites one's intellect with God, dedicates one's actions to Him, abandons attachment to the fruits of actions, maintains equanimity of mind and remains unaffected with success or failure.

*buddhi-yogī*: A sincere practitioner of *buddhi-yoga*.

*caitanyam:* Consciousness.

*catuḥ*: Four.

*cāturvarṇyam*: Four types according to attributes and actions.

*cetanā*: Awareness.

*Cidābhāsa*: The reflection of Consciousness.

*Cit*: Consciousness, referred to *Brahman*, the Fundamental Consciousness.

*cit*: Consciousness, referred to induced consciousness in a created entity.

*citta*: The same as the *antaḥkaraṇa*, the internal instrument.

*citta-śuddhi*: The purification of the *citta*.

*citta-śuddhyartham*: For the purification of the *citta*.

*coṣyam*: Food eaten by sucking.

*daiva*: Divine (Masculine in gender).

*daivī*: Pertaining to *deva*; divine (feminine in gender).

*dakṣiṇā*: An honorarium or a reverent gift offered to a priest or a *guru*.

*dambhaḥ*: Ostentation, with hypocrisy.

*dāna*: A gift; a charity.

*dānava*: A demon.

*daridra-nārāyaṇa*: A poor person who is helped and served with respect as if he is God.

*darpaḥ*: The bad quality of presuming oneself as superior to others.

*darśana*: 1. Vision. 2. Philosophy.

*Dāsa*: 1. A servant. 2. Any aboriginal, non-Aryan tribe.

*deha*: The body.

*dehī*: The embodied self.

*deva*: 1. A divine being or a god (not God). 2. With lustre and virtues.

*deva-loka*: The world of gods; a celestial realm.

*devatā*: 1. God immanent in a large, created entity and chairing the latter that serves as an *upādhi*, acquires divine power and plays the role of a deity.

*devī*: The same as *deva*, but in feminine gender.

*dhairya*: Patience.

*dhāma*: Divine abode.

Dhanañjaya: 1. One who has conquered wealth. 2. One of the names of Arjuna.

*dhāraṇā*: Pin-pointed concentration on a specific spot or a location.

*dharma*: 1. Righteousness. 2. Innate properties. 3. Duties done for the sake of duties only.

*dharma-kṣetra*: A sacred field.

*dharma-saṅkaṭa*: Crisis in discriminating right from wrong and righteousness from unrighteousness.

*dharma-yuddha*: War for restoring righteousness.

*dhṛtiḥ*: 1. Fortitude; firmness. 2. Properties inherent or intrinsic in a created being.

*dhruva*: Constant; a certainty.

*dhvajā*: A flag.

*dhvani*: Sound in musical tuning.

*dhyāna*: Meditation; uninterrupted concentration on a single idea; focusing attention on a single idea that flows continuously without interruption.

*dhyāna-yoga*: The *yoga* of one-pointed concentration on God; the *yoga* of meditation.

*divyācaraṇa*: Living a noble life, with divine conduct.

*divya-dṛṣṭi*: Divine vision; clairvoyance.

*divya-śravaṇa*: Divine hearing; clairaudience.

*draṣṭā*: Seer.

*dravya*: A material substance.

*duḥkha*: Pain; suffering.

*durmedhā*: Stupid.

*dvandva*: 1. Oscillations between extreme opposites. 2. Additive compounds in grammar.

*dvāpara*: The aeon following *tretā*, having a duration of 864,000 earth-years.

*dveṣa*: Dispassion; aversion; aversion to already experienced pain; hostility; hatred; dislike.

*dvija*: Twice born; the first-time birth carries the usual sense; the second birth in the same life is the transformation of animality into humanity and higher.

*dvīpa*: An island.

*dyauḥ*: 1. Space. 2. The primeval field.

*gahana*: Difficult to be understood.

*gandha*: Odour.

*gatarasam*: 1. That from which juice has been lost. 2. Food that has lost its nutrients.

*gati*: Motion.

*gaurakṣya*: 1. Rearing and protecting cattle. 2. Animal husbandry.

Gāyatrī: Mother Sarasvatī; one who sings (plays musical instruments); one who generates the *oṅkāra-dhvani*. A Vedic metre. This word is in feminine gender.

*ghaṭa*: A pot.

*ghaṭākāśa*: Space inside a pot.

*gr̥hastha*: Householder.

*ghr̥tam*: Dehydrated, clarified butter.

*guḍākā*: Sleep.

*guhya*: Secret; mysterious.

*guṇa*: 1. Attribute; quality. 2. A string or a chord.

*guṇa-kṣobha*: A disturbance in an equilibrium.

*guṇamayī*: Full of *guṇas*; in possession of *guṇa*(s). This word is in feminine gender.

*guṇa-saṅkhyāna*: The science of *guṇas*.

*guṇātīta*: 1. One who has transcended the three attributes — *sattva, rajas, tamas*. 2. One who is not affected by the vibrations of the three strings of the *vīṇā* of Mother Sarasvatī.

*guṇa-traya*: The triad of strings/attributes.

*guru*: 1. A preceptor; a spiritual preceptor.

*havana*: Oblation; fire-sacrifice.

*Hiraṇyagarbha*: 1. The Golden Embryo; the Cosmic Egg. 2. Brahmā; God who presides the Cosmic Egg for the creation of the universe.

*homa*: Oblation.

*hṛdaya-puṇḍarīka*: The lotus of the heart.

*hutam*: Dehydrated, clarified butter used for oblation in a fire-sacrifice.

*icchā-śakti*: 1. The power of mentation. 2. Will-power.

*iha*: Literally means "here"; contextually means "in this life" or "in this world."

*indra-jāla*: Magical illusion.

*indriya*: Five subtle organs of perception and five subtle organs of action that utilize their corresponding gross organs for functioning.

*indriya-gocara*: sense-perceptible.

*indriya-gocarāḥ*: Objects of senses.

*īśaḥ*: Master; controller; controlling Lord.

*Īśvara*: The Supreme Ruler or Controller; the Lord of the universe; God; *Brahman*, with *Māyā*, as its *upādhi*.

*Īśvarādhīnā*: Under the control of God.

*Īśvara-praṇidhāna*: Surrender to God.

*Īśvara-Śakti*: The Power of God; *Māyā*.

*Īśvarāśrayā*: Dependent on God; sheltered in God.

*jaḍa*: Insentient.

*jagadīśvara*: The Lord of the universe.

*jagat*: That which is in motion; the universe; that which is ever changeable, with uncertain existence.

*jāgatika*; Pertaining to the universe.

*jagat-kartrī*: Cosmic Agent; the Executive of the universe, in feminine gender.

*jalpa*: Debating with an assertion of one's own opinion, while aggressively refuting opinions of adversaries.

*Janaḥ*: 1. The fifth *lokaḥ*, subtler than the *Mahaḥ*. 2. God presiding the

*Janaḥ*.

*jaṅgama*: Moving.

*janma*: Birth.

*jantu*: An animal.

*japa*: Repeated utterances of God's name and of *mantras*.

*jaya*: Victory.

*jītātmā*: One who has subdued his inner instrument (*antaḥkaraṇa*).

*jīva*: See *jīvātmā*.

*jīvana*: Life.

*jīvanmukta*: Liberated albeit still living with a body.

*jīvātmā*: An individual self; *Brahman*, with an individual body as its *upādhi*.

*jñāna*: 1. Knowledge. 2. Knowledge on *Brahman*, the Fundamental Being, the Reality.

*jñāna-kāṇḍa*: Subjects pertaining to knowledge on the Reality.

*jñāna-yoga*: The *yoga* that leads to knowledge on *Brahman* and the realization of *Brahman*.

*jñāna-yogī*: A person proficient in the *yoga* of knowledge.

*jñānendriya*: Sensory organs for perception, both subtle and gross.

*jñānī*: A person who has acquired knowledge. In some contexts in the *BG*, "knowledge" means "knowledge on *Brahman*."

*jñātā*: The knower.

*jñeyam*: The object of knowledge.

*jvara*: Fever.

*ka*: The primordial Casmic Plasma; *Āpaḥ*; the subtlest substance (Waters) evolved from *Virāḍ*.

*kaivalya*: Liberation according to the Sāṅkhya and the Yoga of Patañjali; the separation of the *puruṣa* (spirit) from the *prakṛti* (nature) and the isolated, blissful stay of the former.

*Kāla*: God conditioned by the power of destroying activities.

*kāla*: 1. Time. 2. Destroyer.

*Kālāgni*: All-consuming fire of Time at the dissolution of the universe.

*kalatra*: Spouse.

*kali*: The aeon of badness, conflict and social turbulence, following *dvāpara*, having a duration of 432,000 earth-years; the last one of the group of the four *yugas*.

Kālī: Mother Divine who is the Power and Consort of Lord Rudra-Śiva. She is full of *tamas*.

*kalpa*: One day of 12 hours of Brahmā (excluding His night) or 4.32 billion human years or earth-years. (One day of 24 hours in the *deva-loka* = one earth-year; one *deva*-year = 360 *deva*-days of 24 hours; one *caturyuga* = 12,000 *deva*-years; 1,000 *caturyugas* = one day, excluding the night, of Brahmā = one *kalpa*. The steps in the mathematical calculations are: $1{,}000 \times 12{,}000 \times 360 = 4320{,}000{,}000 = 4.32 \times 10^9$ = 4.32 billion.)

*kāma*: 1. Craving; a strong desire, a longing for sensual gratification, material gain, name, fame and power. 2. Yearning for emancipation.

*kāmanā*: A desire.

*kampana*: 1. Vibration. 2. The action of trembling.

*kāmya*: Desireful.

*kapi:* A monkey.

*karaṇa*: 1. An instrument. 2. The five subtle organs of perception and the five subtle organs of action.

*kāraṇa*: A cause.

*kāraṇa-śarīra*: The causal body.

*karma*: 1. Action. 2. The psychic impressions of actions recorded in the subtle-psycho-super-compacted disc (SPSCD) known as *karmāśaya* (reservoir of *karmas*) located in the subtle body.

*karma-bandhana*: The apparent binding of the *jīvātmā* to the karmic traces.

*karmaja*: Born of the karmic impressions; born of *karma-saṁskāras*.

*karmajā siddhi*: Success born of works.

*karma-kāṇḍa*: 1. Accessory Vedic scriptures for ritual observances. 2. Religious ritualism done for the fulfilment of desires.

*karma-kāṇḍī*: A person with strict observance of the rules and rituals of the *karma-kāṇḍa*.

*karma-saṁnyāsa*: The renunciation of work.

*karma-saṁnyāsī*: An ascetic; one who has renounced worldly activities.

*karma-saṁskāra*: Karmic traces imprinted in the *karmāśaya*, a subtle bio-disc in the subtle body.

*karmāśaya*: The reservoir of karmic impressions.

*karma-vāda*: The doctrine of *karma*.

*karma-yoga:* The *yoga* of detached action.

*karma-yogī*: A person who sincerely practises *karma-yoga*.

*karmendriya*: Motor instrumental organs for action, both subtle and gross.

*karttā*: Doer.

*kartavya*: Duty; what should be done.

*kartrī*: Doer, in feminine gender.

*kartṛka kāraṇa*: The subjective cause of an action.

*kārya*: 1. Effect. 2. Action. 3. An action that should be performed.

*kārya karma*: A deed (an action) which ought to be done.

*kāryānumeyā*: Inferable from the effect.

*kasturi*: Musk.

Kaunteya: Arjuna; the son of Kuntī.

*Kauravas*: The scions of Kuru.

*kauśalam*: Skill.

*kāyika*: Physical; pertaining to the body.

*kirīṭa*: A diadem.

*kleśa*: Affliction.

*kratu*: A type of Vedic sacrificial rite.

*kriyamāṇa karma*: Karmic impressions being imprinted in the present life; *karma* being done in the current life.

*kriyā-śakti*: Power of activity.

*krodha*: Anger; wrath.

*kṛṣi*; Agriculture.

*kṛṣṇa*: Black; dark.

*kṛtānta*: The end of all actions.

*kṛta-yuga*: See *satya-yuga*.

*kṛtsna*: The whole; the totality.

*kṛtsnavit*: The knower of the whole.

*kṣara*: Perishable.

kṣatriya: A person belonging to the warrior class among the Hindus; one who subdues the wicked, protects the weak and fights against injustice.

*kṣema*: 1. Security. 2. Preservation and protection of what has been acquired and achieved.

*kṣetra*: Field.

*kṣetrajña*: The field-knower.

*kṣobha*: Disturbance.

*kula*: Family.

*kula-dharma*: Family tradition of virtues and righteousness.

*kumbhaka*: The retention (holding) of *prāṇa* through the suspension of breath following inhalation.

*kūṭa*: 1. A heap. 2. Illusion, deception, falsity, tortuousness, diplomacy.

*kūṭastha*: Immutable.

*lābha*: Gain; profit.

Lakṣmī: Mother Divine who is the Power and Consort of Lord Viṣṇu and who sustains and supports the universe.

*laya*: Destruction; annihilation; dissolution.

*lehyam*: Food eaten by licking.

*līlā*: Sportive play; ecstatic play; play with an overwhelming feeling of joy or rapture.

*liṅga*: 1. Subtle. 2. Gender. 3. Symptom.

*liṅga-śarīra*: The subtle body.

*lipta*: Involved.

*lobha*: Covetousness; greed.

*Lokaḥ*: Any one of the seven realms of the universe.

*lokaḥ*: A person.

*loka-saṁgraha*: 1. The collection of the worlds. 2. All people.

*lokāyatika*: A materialist.

*mada*: Pride with arrogance.

*mahā*: Great.

*mahābhūta*: The great, basic material state of existence — solid, liquid, gaseous, energy, ākāśic; the field of each material state or particle.

*Mahaḥ*: 1. The fourth *Lokaḥ*, subtler than the *Svaḥ*. 2. God presiding the *Mahaḥ*.

*Mahākāśa*: Great Space; the so-called void which holds all objects and through which objects move. It is the subtlest positive substance rather than a vacuum.

*Mahāmāyā*: The great *Māyā;* the same as *Māyā*, the Mother of the universe, the Power of *Brahman/Īśvara*.

*mahā-pralaya*: Total dissolution at the termination of a Cosmic Cycle.

*Mahā-Rava*: The *Śaiva* and the *Tāntrika* term for the Big-Bang; a huge, roaring or exploding sound.

*Mahat*: The Sāṅkhya word for the Vedic *Virāḍ*, both literally meaning "great." It is the Cosmic Intellect or the Cosmic Mind (the Supermind) that serves as a Cosmic Super-Compacted Disc (CSCD). It is the first evolute in the beginning of a Cosmic Cycle.

*Maheśvara*: The Great Lord; the Supreme Ruler and Controller.

*manas*: A subtle psycho-organ in the subtle body, an evolute of *ahaṅkāra;* the organ for mentation and sensory and motor control of the *indriyas* (instruments).

*mānasa-pūjā*: Worshipping through mental offering.

*mānavatva*: Humanitarianism; the virtuous state with human values.

*mānasika*: Mental.

*manomaya kośa*: The mental sheath.

*mantra*: 1. A spell that serves as a thinking aid. 2. mystic syllable(s), word(s), sentence(s), chanted silently, whisperingly or loudly for self-purification or influencing other minds or matter. 3. A sacred text that is chanted while oblation is offered.

*maraṇa-trāsa*: The fear of death.

*mārga*: Path.

*mātsarya*: Envy; malice.

*Māyā*: The Power (*Śakti*) of *Brahman/Īśvara/*God; the Mother Divine; the Mother of the universe; the source and the final refuge of the universe; God's Power that can create illusion, that is the Mother Creatrix and that is the Executive under the Chairpersonship of God.

*māyā*: 1. Illusion. 2. Deceptive action. 3. Delusion with excessive attachment.

*māyāja*: An illusory form produced by *Māyā*.

*māyā-jāla*: Magical illusion.

*Māyā-Śakti*: The Power of *Brahman/Īśvara*, known as *Māyā* or *Mahāmāyā*.

*māyā-śarīra*: An illusory body.

*māyā-vāda*: The doctrine of illusionism.

*Mīmāṁsaka*: A lover and follower of the Mīmāṁsā school of philosophy.

*mithyā*: 1. A contrary term of *satya*; dependent and uncertain existence. 2. "False" is its popular meaning.

*mithyā-jñānam*: False knowledge; knowledge of *B* as non-*B*.

*moha*: Delusion with strong attachment.

*mohagrasta*: Seized with delusion.

*mokṣa:* Liberation; emancipation; salvation; release from the transmigratory existence of birth and death.

*mṛtyuḥ*: Death.

*mūḍha*: 1. Deluded. 2. Irrational.

*mukta*: Free; released; liberated.

*mukti*: Release; liberation.

*mūla*: Root; source; foundation; primordial; primeval.

*Mūla-Prakṛti*: The Primordial Nature, ever unmanifested, co-eternal with God; *Māyā,* the Power of *Brahman/Īśvara;* the Agency or the Executive of God for the creation, sustenance and dissolution of the universe.

*muni*: A sage who practises silence.

*mūrdhan*: 1. Apex; summit; roof. 2. The thousand-petalled lotus (*sahasrāra*).

*nāda*: Vibration.

*Nāda-Brahma*: The inequal vibrations of the three strings of the *vīṇā* of Mother Sarasvatī, generating *oṅkāra*-frequencies and thereby causing the manifestation of *Virāṭ* and its serial evolutes.

*nāḍī*: Subtle channels in the subtle body for the flow of *prāṇa*.

*naimitya*: Occasional.

*nairātmya-vāda*: The doctrine of no-self.

*naiṣkarmya*: Freedom from all actions.

*naivedyam*: Food-articles offered to a deity.

*Nāra*: The same as *Āpaḥ*. The primordial Cosmic Plasma on which Lord Nārāyaṇa reclines.

Nārāyaṇa: Lord Viṣṇu; God who pervades and sustains the universe; the Divine Being whose *ayana* (path, going) is *Nāra* (the primordial, subtle, Cosmic Plasma).

*nāstika*: An atheist.

*nidrā*: Sleep.

*nigrahaḥ*: Prohibition.

*nikṣema*: Free from the anxiety for the preservation of already acquired property or power.

*nimitta-kāraṇa*: A causal agent on behalf of which/whom something is caused.

*niraham*: I-less.

*nirahaṅkāra*: Free from egoity; one who has annihilated one's ego.

*nirāsakta*: Without attachment; unattached.

*nirāśī*: One who does not expect anything as fruits of one's actions; one who craves not.

*nirāśraya*: 1. Dependent on nothing. 2. Shelterless; helpless.

*nirātmakam*: Devoid of the Self.

*niravayava*: Impartite; devoid of component parts.

*nirdvandva*: Devoid of contradictions; free from the pairs of opposites.

*nirguṇa:* 1. Attributeless. 2. Without strings; devoid of cords.

*nirmama*: My-less.

*nirupādhikam*: Devoid of limiting adjunct (in neuter gender).

*nirvāṇa*: 1. The act of being extinguished. 2. Becoming nihil or nothing in Buddhist philosophy. 3. Becoming plenum or *Brahman* in the concept of the *BG*.

*niryoga*: Free from the anxiety for new acquisition.

*niṣkāma pūjā*: Worship without any desire for fruits.

*niṣkriya*: Functionless.

*niṣprapañca*: Beyond all phenomena; unconnected with the universe.

*niṣṭhā*: consummation, perfection, termination, final stage.

*nistraiguṇya*: A state of a complete void of the three attributes/strings — *sattva*, *rajas* and *tamas*.

*nīti-saṅkaṭa*: Moral crisis.

*nitya*: 1. Eternal. 2. Daily.

*nitya-mukta*: Ever-free.

*nivṛtti*: 1. Abstention from activity; the path of renunciation. 2. Activity from which one should abstain.

*nivṛtti-mārga*: The way of a recluse who abandons activities except the minimum ones essential for living.

*niyatam:* Obligatory and unavoidable; prescribed by scriptures.

*om*: The Vedic monosyllabic seed syllable, standing for *Brahman* or *Īśvara* (God), otherwise known as *Praṇava*.

*oṅkāra-dhvani*: The vibratory tuning of the monosyllable, *om*.

*pālaka*: Preserver; sustainer.

*pañca*: Five.

Pāṇḍavas: The sons of Pāṇḍu.

*paṇḍita*: A pundit; a well-informed, erudite scholar; a learned person.

*pāpa*: Vice; sin; evil work of demerits.

*para*: One Cosmic Period from $t_o$ (the beginning of time corresponding to the moment of the creation of the universe) to $t_m$ (the end of time corresponding to the total dissolution of the universe); one *para* = 311.04 trillion earth-years = the span of life of Brahmā; one day of Brahmā = 4.32 billion earth-years and night of Brahmā is the same period; one year of Brahmā = 8.64 × 360 = 3.1104 trillion earth-years; Brahmā lives for a period of 100 years of his time; thus, one *para* is equal to 311.04 trillion human or earth-years.

*parā*: Higher; superior (in feminine gender).

*param*: Supreme (in neuter gender).

*parama*: Supreme; the best.

*pāramārthika*: Absolute; in the sense of the highest Truth.

*pāramārthika satya*: The Absolute Reality.

*paramārthataḥ*: Metaphysically; in the supreme sense.

*Paramātmā*: The Supreme Self; the Great Self; God.

*paramātma-bhāva*: The state of abidance as the Supreme Self.

*Parameśvara*: The Supreme Controller; the Supreme Lord; God.

*Parameśvarāśrayā*: Dependent on the Supreme Lord; sheltered in the Supreme Lord.

*Parameśvarī*: Mother Goddess who is the Supreme Ruler or Controller; the Power or the *Śakti* of God; the Executive Agent of God; the Consort of God.

*Parā-Prakṛti*: Higher or Superior Nature; the *jīvātmā*.

*parārdha*: One-half of a *para*. The first *parārdha* is the period during which the universe expands. The second *parārdha* is the period during which the universe contracts.

*paricāraka*: A male person who manually serves; a male servant.

*paricārikā*: A maid-servant.

*parigraha*: The opposite of *aparigraha;* accumulation of property.

*parijñātā*: The knower.

*pariṇāma-vāda*: The doctrine of transformation, advocated by the Sāṅkhya.

*paripālana*: Sustenance; maintenance; support.

*pariprakāśa*: Manifestation.

*parityāgī*: One who relinquishes.

*parokṣa*: Indirect; through mediation.

Pārtha: The son of Pṛthā or Kuntī; Arjuna.

*pāruṣyam*: Harshness exhibited by a sadistic, cruel satire.

*parva*: A part of a scripture.

*paśutva*: Animality; bestiality.

Pātañjala: Pertaining to Patañjali, the seer and Yoga-philosopher.

*patnī*: 1. A female who governs or exercises power. 2. A wife.

*pippala*: The *pīpal* tree; *Ficus religiosa*.

*pitāmaha*: A grandfather.

*pracodaka kāraṇa*: Inspiring or inducing cause.

*pracodana*: Inspiration; induction.

*Pradhāna*: 1. Literally means "chief" or "principal." 2. A Sāṅkhya word as a synonym of *Prakṛti*. *Pradhāna* is unmanifest, insentient, active and independent of *puruṣas*.

Prajāpati: 1. The Lord of all created beings. 2. Brahmā, one and only one God when referred to His creative role.

*prajñā*: Wisdom.

*prājña*: A person who has acquired wisdom.

*prajñāvān*: A person in possession of *prajñā* or wisdom.

*prakāśa*: The light of knowledge.

*Prakṛti/prakṛti*: 1. The feminine component of the bipolar Reality; the unmanifested Primordial Nature or the *Mūla-Prakṛti;* the power of *Brahman/Īśvara*. 2. The created nature of matter and energy. 3. One's own innate nature, trait or *svabhāva;* mental impressions or *karma-*

*saṁskāras* imprinted and stored in the karmic reservoir located in the *buddhi*. 4. The insentient, active material Being of the Sāṅkhya.

*pralaya*: Dissolution.

*Prāṇa*: An evolute of *Āpaḥ*; the vitalizing entity that energizes everything, living and non-living; the super-unified, subtle substance from which the four fundamental forces and all types of energy spring.

*prāṇa*: 1. The in-breath. 2. One of the five components of the *Prāṇa* that causes intake and absorption.

*prāṇamaya kośa*: The vital sheath.

*Praṇava*: *OM*; the monosyllabic sound, *OM*, that is the designation of God.

*Prāṇa-vāyu*: Mechanical Forces, five in type, arising out of the Primordial *Prāṇa*.

*prāṇāyāma*: A yogic technique of breathing through which *prāṇa* from the cosmic source is collected and stored in the *cakra*s, the brain-cells and other body-cells get enough oxygen and impurities in gaseous form are efficiently expelled from the body.

*prārabdha karma*: Initiated karmic *saṁskāra*s.

*prātibhāsika*: phenomenal; reflected appearance.

*pratibimba-vāda*: The doctrine of imaging.

*pratijānīhi*: Know my certain proclamation; know my promise.

*pratijñā*: Certain proclamation; oath; promise.

*pratiṣṭhā*: Abode; foundation; base; ground.

*pratyagātman*: The directly experienced inner self.

*pratyakṣa:* Direct; without any mediation.

*pravartana-vāda*: The doctrine of induction.

*pravṛtti*: 1. Innate urge or intrinsic propensity for activity. 2. The path of action. 3. Passionate activities for sensuous pleasure and worldly gains.

*pravṛtti-mārga*: The way of being engaged in activity.

*preraṇa-vāda*: The doctrine of induction.

*preta*: 1. An ancestral spirit. 2. A bound *jīvātmā*, after leaving the gross body and before acquiring a fresh one.

*pretya*: Hereafter or after death.

*preyas*: Something that promotes pleasure.

Pṛthā: A name of Kuntī who had wide eyes. The word literally means "wide," "vast."

*pūjā*: Worship.

*punarjanma-vāda*: The doctrine of reincarnation.

*puṇya*: Virtue; good work of merits.

*pūraka*: The intake of *prāṇa* through inhalation.

*purī*: The city of the body.

*pūrṇa*: Full; the plenum.

*pūrṇa-vāda*: The doctrine of plenum or fullness.

*Puruṣa*: 1. *Brahman*. 2. The Supreme Lord, the Supreme Being or God; the Supreme Spirit. 3. The Pimeval Being or the Primeval Spirit.

*puruṣa*: 1. A male person. 2. The individual self or the *jīvātmā* in the Sāṅkhya; in this system, the *puruṣa*s are innumerable. 3. The individual self in the Vedānta. 4. That by which all is filled. 5. He who lies in the city of *Virāṭ* and all its evolutes.

*puruṣakāraḥ*: Individual initiative; individual determined effort to get something done; the same as *puruṣārtha*.

*puruṣārtha*: Personal endeavour with positive thought and firm determination.

*puruṣa-viśeṣaḥ*: A special self. It is used by Patañjali for *Īśvara* (God).

*Puruṣottama*: The best among the *puruṣa*s; Supreme Spirit; the Supreme Lord; God.

Pūrva-Mīmāṁsā: A school of ancient Indian philosophy that does not recognize a creator God, that upholds the doctrine of a steady-state universe and that adheres to Vedic ritualism.

*putra*: A son.

*putra-moha*: Deluded attachment for one's son.

*rāga*: Passion; attachment; hankering after pleasure.

*rāja-guhya*: Royal mystery; top secret.

*rajas*: 1. One of the three strings of the *vīṇā* of Mother Sarasvatī. 2. A name for a group of traits — passionate activity; propensity; strong desire and attachment; thirst for dominance, possesion, power and gratification.

*rājasabhā*: Royal Assembly.

*rājasika*: 1. Pertaining to the string or attribute of *rajas*. 2. One in possession of *rajas* as a dominant attribute.

*rāja-vidyā*: Royal knowledge; the supreme knowledge.

*rāja-yoga*: 1. The king of *yoga*s. 2. Patañjali's *yoga* of meditation.

*rākṣasa*: A monster; a crude and cruel being from whom protection is necessary.

*rāṣṭra-moha*: Delusion for the kingdom and throne.

*ratha*: A chariot.

*rathī*: The Lord of the chariot. God immanent in the body that is compared with a chariot.

*recaka*: Exhalation. The outgo of impurities through exhalation.

*ripu*: A foe or an enemy; something detrimental or malignant.

*ṛṣi*: A seer; a saint.

*ṛta*: Order; Cosmic Order.

Rudra: One and only one God, referred to the role in annihilation and His association with the attribute of *tamas*.

*rūpa*: Form; shape; appearance.

*sa*: Means "with," when prefixed.

*śabda*: 1. A word. 2. Sound.

*śabda-brahma*[1]: The same as *nāda-brahma*, the *oṅkāra* vibrations. It also includes its serial evolutes of the virtual universe which is nothing but the vibrations of the three superstrings.

*śabda-brahma*[2]: 1. As Śaṅkara says: The fruits of actions performed in conformity with whatever has been said in the Vedas. 2. The Veda considered as a revealed sound and identified with the Supreme.

*Saccidānanda*: *Sat* = Existence; *Cit* = Consciousness; *Ānanda* = Bliss. This compound word has a reference to *Brahman*.

*sadguru*: A spiritual preceptor, with high spiritual enlightenment, moral values and *Brahma*-realization.

*sādhaka*: A sincere, arduous practitioner of spiritual disciplines and techniques.

*sādhanā*: Sincere and sustained efforts to achieve something noble and attainable.

*saguṇa*: 1. With attributes. 2. In possession of strings; associated with strings.

*sahajam*: Produced with the birth.

*sahasrāra*: The thousand-petalled lotus.

*sakāma pūjā*: Worship with a desire to be fulfilled.

*sākṣāt*: Direct.

*sākṣī*: Witness.

*Śakti*: 1. Power. 2. Consort, with reference to God. 3. The Power of God/ *Brahman*. 4. God's Executive Agent. 5. The Mother of the universe.

*śakti*: Power.

*Śaktimān*: The possessor of power.

*śama*: Quiescence.

*samācara*: Perform.

*sama-darśana*: 1. The act of seeing *Brahman* in everything and everything in *Brahman*. 2. The same vision in the diversity of things. 3. Equal vision.

*samadarśī*: One who sees the same in all; one who sees *Brahman* everywhere and in everything.

*samādhi*: The highest yogic state of thoughtlessness, in which the individual self is fully absorbed in the Supreme Self; a state in which a complete identity of the individual self and the Supreme Self is established.

*samādhi-yoga*: The same as *dhyāna-yoga*; the *yoga* of meditation.

*samāhāra*: The process of reabsorption.

*samāna*: The component of *Prāṇa* that maintains an equilibrium between opposites and that induces the production of energy.

*samanvaya*: Harmony.

*samārambha*: Undertaking; initiative.

*samarpaṇa*: Offering with devotion.

*samaṣṭi*: Collective; aggregate.

*samaṣṭi-buddhi*: Aggregate intellect; The Vedic *Virāḍ* or the Sāṅkhya *Mahat*; the Cosmic Intellect; the Supermind.

*sambandhi*: Relational (in neuter gender).

*saṁhāra*: Destruction.

*saṁharttā*: Destroyer.

*saṁhitā*: Works collected and systematically compiled.

*sampad*: Wealth; good luck.

*saṁsāra*: 1. Metempsychosis. 2. The transmigratory world of repeated births and deaths. 3. The Cosmos in harmony and motion.

*saṁsaya*: Doubt.

*saṁskāra*: Psychic biodata stored in a subtle bio-disc known as *karmāśaya;* karmic impressions arising out of actions done.

*saṁskāraja*: Born of the karmic impressions.

*sāmyāvasthā*: A state of equipoise.

*sanātana*: Eternal and timeless; both cosmic and acosmic existence.

*sañcita karma*: Cumulative karmic impressions.

*saṅga*: Attachment.

*saṅgharṣa*: Struggle.

*saṅghāta*: 1. Compression, condensation, compactness, aggregate. 2. *Prāṇa,* the Super-Unified Force. It also includes the four fundamental forces serially separated from it.

*saṅgraha*: 1. Holding together. 2. A number of items held together. 3. Collection.

*saṅkalpa*: 1. The objective of worshipping expressed and addressed to a deity. 2. Definite plan and objective determined before initiating a project. 3. A strong determination for working out a comprehensively planned project. 4. Will; volition; mental resolve. 5. Determined purpose. 6. A solemn vow to perform an observance.

*saṅkara*: Hybrid; mixture.

*saṅkaṭa*: Crisis; inability in deciding what to do and what not to do.

Sāṅkhya: An ancient Indian dualistic school of philosophy, founded by Kapila.

Sāṅkhya-Yoga: This compound word is used in a special sense in the *BG*. It means *jñāna-yoga*, the *yoga* of knowledge on *Brahman*.

*saṁnyāsa*: Renunciation.

*saṁnyāsī*: One who has renounced the worldly life.

*sānnidhya-vāda*: The doctrine of vicinity or proximity.

*sannyāsa*: Renunciation. Alternatively written as *saṁnyāsa.*

*śānti*: Peace.

Sarasvatī: Mother Divine who is the Power and Consort of Lord Brahmā.

*sārathi*: Charioteer.

*sārthi*: A person born of a kṣatriya father and a brāhmaṇa mother.

*sarvabhāvena*: Fully and wholeheartedly.

*sarvagata*: All-pervasive.

*sarvahara*: One who carries all away; one in whom all dissolve.

*sarvārambha*: All undertakings.

*sarva-vyāpī*: All-pervasive.

*śāstra*: A scripture; a sacred book by which one is disciplined.

*śāstra-pramāṇam*: Scriptural evidence.

*śāśvata*: Eternal.

*Sat*: Existence, derived from the verb-root *as*; whatever exists as the fundamental Reality.

*sat*: That which exists.

*sattva*: 1. A group-name for noble traits — goodness, purity, righteousness, true knowledge. 2. One of the three strings of the *vīṇā* of Mother Sarasvatī.

*sattva-śuddhi*: Mental purification; purification of the *antaḥkaraṇa*.

*sāttvika*: 1. Pertaining to the attribute or the string of *sattva*;. 2. In posseession of *sattva* as a dominant attribute.

*Satya*: 1. The seventh *Lokaḥ*, subtler than the *Tapaḥ*; the subtlest one among the seven. 2. God presiding over the *Satya-Loka*.

*satya*: 1. That which exists. 2. Truth. 3. Existence. 4. Cosmic Law.

*Satya-Lokaḥ*: The seventh and the subtlest *Lokaḥ* of the universe; the *Lokaḥ* of Brahmā.

*satyaniṣṭha*: Committed to truth.

*satya-yuga*; An aeon, having a duration of 1,728,000 earth-years; the aeon of goodness, truth and honesty.

Sāvitrī: Mother Sarasvatī; one who generates, procreates, gives birth to (in feminine gender); the Mother Creatrix; the Consort of Lord Brahmā.

*siddha*: 1. Perfected. 2. One who purges all of one's defects from one's mind.

*siddhi*: 1. Success. 2. Perfection in *yoga* by which supernormal powers are acquired.

*siṁhāsana*: A throne.

*sammoha*: A potent delusion.

*śauca*: Physical, mental and verbal cleanliness.

Śiva: Auspicious; benign; good and benevolent. A name of God in Hinduism.

*śiva*: Benevolent (masculine in gender).

*śivā*: Benevolent (feminine in gender).

Smṛti: Post-Vedic Hindu Epic and Purāṇic scriptures.

*smṛti*: Memory.

*soma-rasa*: The juice of a herb (plant) known as *Soma*. This Vedic plant has not yet been identified. It cools the brain and gives strength to the body.

*spanda*: Vibration.

*spandana*: Vibration.

*śraddhā*: Firm faith, mixed with love, affection, respect and devotion.

*sraṣṭā*: Creator.

*śreyas*: Something that is good and attainable irrespective of its pleasantness or unpleasantness.

*śrī*: Revered; respected; prosperity; beauty; grace; splendour; lustre; virtue; excellence; affluence; wealth; the Goddess of Wealth — Mother Lakṣmī.

*sṛṣṭa*: Created (in masculine gender).

*sṛṣṭā*: Created (in feminine gender).

*sṛṣṭi*: Creation; emanation.

*śruti*: 1. The act of hearing. 2. The Vedas.

*śruti-pramāṇa*: Vedic evidence.

*sthānam*: 1. Place. 2. An abode.

*sthāṇu*: Stable; with stability and without movement.

*sthāvara*: Unmoving.

*sthira*: Firm; stable.

*sthiratā*: Steadfastness.

*sthitaprajña*: A person of stable wisdom.

*sthiti*: 1. Sustenance; maintenance. 2. Situation.

*sthūla*: Gross.

*sthūla-śarīra*: The gross body of matter and energy.

*śuddha*: Pure; free from contamination and admixture.

*Śuddhānanda*: Pure Bliss.

śūdra: A Hindu of the serving community.

*sukha*: Pleasure; happiness.

*śukla*: Bright; white.

*sūkṣma*: Subtle.

*sūkṣma-śarīra*: The subtle body, not ordinarily perceptible.

*sūkta*: A hymn.

*Sundara/sundara*: Beautiful.

*śūnya*: A void; a vacuum; empty.

*śūnya-vāda*: The doctrine of nihilism.

*suṣumṇā*: The central, subtle channel inside the spinal cord for the flow of *prāṇa*.

*sūtra*: An aphorism.

*svabhāva*: Own state; own nature; own traits born of own *karma-saṁskāras*; individual innate tendencies.

*svabhāvaja*: Born of own nature, of *karma-saṁskāra*s stored in one's *karmāśaya*.

*svabhūtā*: That which has become out of the self.

*svadhā*: 1. Offering of food, made to ancestral spirits. 2. The food of all living beings.

*svadharma*: 1. Own duty. 2. Own nature, in conformity with one's karmic impressions.

*svādhyāya*: The study of sacred scriptures like the Vedas, the Vedānta, the *Gītā*, the great epics and any piece of good literature. 2. The chanting of *OM*, with the realization of its meaning.

*svādhyābhyasanam*: Habitual reading or chanting, with proper intonation, of good scriptures.

*Svaḥ*: 1. The third *Lokaḥ*, subtler than the *Bhuvaḥ*. 2. God presiding the *svaḥ*.

*Svarlokaḥ*: The third *Lokaḥ*, subtler than the *Bhuvarlokaḥ*.

*svānubhūti*: The realization of the Self (self).

*svataḥsiddha*: Self-evidenced.

*tadarthīyam*: For the sake of THAT; for the Supreme Reality.

*tamas*: 1. One of the three strings of the *vīṇā* of Mother Sarasvatī. 2. The demoniac trait-type of ignorance, sloth, indolence, inertia and unrighteousness.

*tāmasika*: One in possession of *tamas* as a dominant attribute.

*tanhā*: A Pāli word for thirst (Sanskrit *tṛṣṇā*).

*Tapaḥ*: 1. The sixth *Lokaḥ*, subtler than the *Janaḥ*. 2. God presiding over the *Tapaḥ*.

*tapaḥ*: 1. Penance; austerities. 2. Literally means "heat."

*tapas*: The same as *tapaḥ*.

*tapasyā*: Austerities and asceticism.

*tāraka*: Saving.

*Tat/tat*: That; a word indicatory of *Brahman* that cannot be described by language.

*tāta*: Literally meaning "father"; affectionately used to address a son.

*traya*: Three; threefold; triplet; triad.

*tretā-yuga*: The aeon, following *satya*, having a duration of 1,296,000 earth-years.

*triguṇātmikā*: In possession of three strings/attributes (in feminine gender).

*tripuṭi*: Triad.

*tṛṣṇā*: 1. Thirst. 2. Passionate hankering.

*tucchya*: Practically nothing; really nihil.

*tyāga*: Relinquishment; sacrifice; abandoning the fruits of actions.

*ucita*: Ought; what should be done.

*udāna*: The component of *Prāṇa* that moves upwards.

*udbhava*: Source; origin.

*upādāna*: A material of which something is made.

*upādāna-kāraṇa*: Material cause.

*upādhi*: An *X* is an *upādhi* of omnipresent, immanent and transcendent *Brahman* by serving as a container or a limiting adjunct of the latter that induces consciousness in the former by virtue of proximity and reflection.

*upadraṣṭā*: Onlooker; one who stays near and looks on without being engaged in any activity.

*upalabdhi*: Realization.

*ūrjā*: Energy.

*uttamavidām*: Of the knowers of the highest.

*uttarāyaṇa*: The summer solstice.

*vācanika*: Verbal; vocal.

*vāda*: 1. Doctrine. 2. Discussion devoid of bias, with the sole object of arriving at the truth.

*Vaikuṇṭha*: Heaven; the abode of Nārāyaṇa or God in the Vaiṣṇavite tradition.

*vairāgya*: Detachment.

*Vaiśvānara*: 1. Fire; 2. God presiding over fire.

vaiśya: 1. A Hindu whose vocation is business, farming and animal husbandry. 2. A person of the business community.

*vajra*: 1. The name of Indra's weapon. 2. Extremely hard.

*varṇa*: 1. Colour. 2. Occupational class and aptitude-type in a special sense in the *BG*. 3. Race or caste. 4. A letter of the alphabet.

*varṇa-saṅkara*: Racial and cultural hybrid.

*vāsanā*: Potent karmic impressions recorded in the Unconscious. *Vāsanā-saṁskāra*s affect the psyche more forcefully than non-*vāsanā-saṁskāra*s.

*vāsanā-saṁskāra*: Karmic impressions, generated by *vāsanā*s and imprinted in the *karmāśaya*.

Vāyu: God immanent in the cosmic Mechanical Force.

*vāyu*: 1. Air. 2. Gas. 3. Any one of the five components of *Prāṇa*, namely, *prāṇa, apāna, vyāna, udāna, samāna*.

*veda*: Knowledge.

Veda: The original Hindu scripture comprising true knowledge on God, His creation and guidelines on ethical living.

*vibhāga*: Division.

*vibhūti*: 1. Divine, glorious manifestations. 2. Supernormal phenomena. 3. Miracles.

*vidyā*: Knowledge; knowledge on *Brahman*.

*vigata-jvara*: Free from mental agony.

*vigataspṛha*: One whose clinging to body, life and enjoyments has departed.

*vijayī*: Victorious.

*vijñāna*: 1. Knowledge on and realization of *Brahman*. 2. Realized, divine knowledge. 3. Science.

*vijñānamaya-kośa*: The intellectual sheath.

*vikalpa*: 1. Perceiving something that does not really exist; hallucination. 2. Alternative.

*vikāra*: Changes; modifications; transformations.

*vikarma*: Bad action.

*vikārya*: Modifiable; changeable.

*vikṛti*: Unnatural product.

*vikṣepa*: Projection; the projecting action.

*vikṣepa-śakti*: Projecting power; the power of projecting *B* as non-*B*.

*vilaya*: Complete destruction; annihilation; dissolution.

*vīṇā*: 1. An Indian musical string instrument. 2. The string instrument of Mother Sarasvatī.

*Virāḍ*: The Cosmic Supermind, the mind of *Māyā* or the *Mūla-Prakṛti*. The Fundamental Consciousness or *Brahman*, inducted in *Māyā*. The word literally means "Great."

*Virāḍātmā*: God presiding over *Virāḍ*; Brahmā.

*Virāṭ*: The nominative, singular form of *Virāḍ*. It is a Vedic word synonymous with *Buddhi*, the Cosmic Mind or the Supermind.

*viṣāda*: Agony.

*Viṣāda-Yoga*: The way of despondency or dejection.

*visargaḥ*: Emanation.

*viṣaya*: Sense-objects.

Viṣṇu: 1. God. 2. God who pervades all, everything and everybody. 3. God, with *sattva* attribute, who sustains and nourishes the universe.

*viṣṇu*: All-pervading.

*viśuddha*: Pure; free from contamination and impurity.

*viśva*: 1. All. 2. The universe.

*viśva-rūpa*: The world-image; the cosmic form.

*viśva-rūpa-darśana*: The vision of the Cosmic Image of God.

*vitaṇḍā*: Carping at the arguments of opponents, with disregard of logical refutation.

*vivartta*: The phenomenon of an illusory appearance in the analogy of a rope appearing as a snake.

*vivartta-vāda*: The doctrine of illusory appearance.

*viveka*: Conscience; the faculty of judgement of good and bad and right and wrong.

*vyakta*: Manifested; expressed.

*vyakta-prakṛti*: The manifested nature of matter and energy; the universe.

*vyāna*: The component of *Prāṇa* that circulates prāṇic energy in all directions of the body.

*vyaṣṭi*: Individual.

*vyaṣṭi-buddhi*: Cosmic *Buddhi* inside an individual entity; individual intellect which is a subtle psycho-organ in the subtle body. It is a special concept in Indian psychology.

*vyāvahārika*: Virtual; usable; empirical.

*vyāvahārika satya*: Virtual existence; empirical existence; usable, but not real, substance.

*vyavasāya*: Resolve.

*Yajña* (*yajña*): 1. Sacrifice. 2. Fire-sacrifice. 3. God, the embodiment of sacrifices.

*yakṣa*: A type of supernatural being.

*yātayāma*: Not fresh; stale; food cooked three hours ago.

Yoga: Patañjali's system of philosophy, comprising metaphysical theories and spiritual practices.

*yoga*[1]: It literally means "union," "the act of uniting." Spiritual techniques that help unite the individual self with the Supreme Self; it also has mechanical techniques that improve physical health and meditational techniques that improve mental as well as spiritual health.

*yoga*[2]: 1. What has already been gained and aquired. 2. Prosperity.

*yogaja saṁskāra*: Mental impress produced by the practice of *yoga*.

*Yoga-Māyā*: The Power of God personified as a deity; the same as *Māyā*.

*yogārūḍha*: One who has ascended the ladder of *yoga* and reached its peak; stationed on the summit of *yoga*.

*yogasthaḥ*: While the intellect is united with God.

*yogeśvara*: The Lord of all *yoga*s; the Supreme Self with whom *yogī*s try to unite their individual selves; God.

*yogī*: A person, competent in the science and practice of *yoga*.

*yoni*: 1. Source. 2. The female genital-organ.

*yuddha*: Battle; war.

*yuga*: An epoch; a very long era; aeon.

*yukta*: United.

# Bibliography


Aiyar, C.V. Ramachandra (tr.), 1988, *Sri Sankara's Gita Bhashya*, Mumbai: Bharatiya Vidya Bhavan.

*Atharvaveda-Saṁhitā, The*, with *Sāyaṇa-Bhāṣyam*, Varanasi: Chaukhamba Vidyabhawan, 1997.

*Bhagavad-Gītā, Śrīmad*, with *Śāṅkara-Bhāṣyam*, Sanskrit text with Hindi trans., Gorakhpur (U.P., India): Gita Press, 1988.

*Bhāgavatam, The* (*Śrimad-Bhāgavata-Mahāpurāṇa*), vol. 1 & 2, Gorakhpur (U.P., India): Gita Press.

Chinmayananda, Swami (comm.), *The Holy Geeta*, Mumbai: Central Chinmaya Mission Trust.

Desai, Mahadev (tr. & comm.), 1956 (1st publ. 1946), *The Gospel of Selfless Action* or *The Gita According to Gandhi*, Ahmedabad: Navajivan Publishing House.

*Devī-Bhāgavatam, Sabhāṣāṭīkam*, part 1 & 2, Mumbai: Venkateshwar Press.

Goyandka, Sri Harikrishnadas, *saṁ.* 2053, *The Bhagavad-Gītā*, (*Śrīmad-Bhagavad-Gītā* with *Śāṅkara-Bhāṣyam* and Hindi trans.), Gorakhpur (U.P., India): Gita Press.

Gupta, Srimunilal (tr.), 1990, *Śrīśrīviṣṇupurāṇa* (original Sanskrit text, with Hindi trans.), Gorakhpur (U.P., India): Gita Press.

Joshi, K.L. (ed.), 1982 (1st publ. 1981), *The Brahma-Sūtra* (*The Brahma-Sūtra Śāṅkara Bhāṣya*), vol. 1 & 2, Delhi: Parimal Publications.

Panda, N.C., 1996, *Mind and Supermind*, vol. 1 & 2, New Delhi: D.K. Printworld.

———, 2000, (1st publ. 1995), *The Vibrating Universe*, 2nd edn., Delhi: Motilal Banarsidass.

———, 2002, *Cyclic Universe*, vol. 1 & 2, New Delhi: D.K. Printworld.

———, 2008 (1st publ. 1991), *Māyā in Physics*, 5th rpt. edn., Delhi: Motilal Banarsidass.

Paṇsīkar, W.L.S. (ed), 1992, *Bhagavad-Gītā, Śrīmad*, with the commentaries of *ācāryas*, Delhi: Chaukhamba Sanskrit Pratisthan.

Poddar, Hanumanaprasad (Hindi trans.), *Śrīmadbhāgavatamahāpurāṇa*, vol. 1 & 2, Gorakhpur (U.P., India): Gita Press.

Radhakrishnan, S. (ed), 1960, *The Brahma-Sūtra*, London: George Allen & Unwin.

———, (ed.), 1967 (1st publ. 1948), *The Bhagavadgītā*, London: George Allen & Unwin.

———, 1969 (1st publ. 1953), *The Principal Upaniṣads*, London: George Allen & Unwin.

Ranganathananda, Swami, 2003 (1st publ. 2001), *Universal Message of The Bhagavadgītā: an Exposition of the Gītā in the Light of Modern Thought and Modern Needs*, vol. 1, 2 and 3, Kolkata: Advaita Ashrama.

*R̥gveda Saṁhitā, The*, with *Sāyaṇa Bhāṣyam*, Varanasi: Chaukhamba Vidyabhawan, 1991.

Śaṅkarācārya, *The Saundaryalaharī*, ed. V.K. Subramaniyam, Delhi: Motilal Banarsidass, 1990 (1st edn. 1977).

Sankaranarayanan, P. (tr.), 1988 (1st publ. 1973), *Vivekacūḍāmaṇi of Śaṅkarācārya*, Mumbai: Bharatiya Vidya Bhavan.

*Sāṅkhya-Kārikā*, See Nandalal Sinha, 1979.

*Sāṅkhya-Pravacana-Sūtra*, See Nandalal Sinha, 1979.

Shastri, G.D. (ed.), 1990, *Yoga-Darśanam of Patañjali: Sāṅkhya-Yoga-Darśanam*, with classical commentaries, Varanasi: Chaukhamba Sanskrit Samsthan.

Shastri, J.L. (ed.), 1984 (1st publ. 1970), *Upaniṣatsaṁgrahaḥ*, Delhi: Motilal Banarsidass.

Sinha, Nandalal, 1979 (1st publ. 1915), *The Sāṅkhya Philosophy*, New Delhi: Munshiram Manoharlal.

Sri Aurobindo, 1989 (1st publ. 1916-20 in the monthly review *Ārya*), *Essays on the Gita*, Pondicherry: Sri Aurobindo Ashram.

Swami Chidbhavananda (tr. & comm.), 1971, *The Bhagavadgītā*, Tiruchirappali (Tamil Nadu): Sri Ramakrishna Tapovanam.

Swami Omananda Tirtha (comm.), *saṁ.* 2053, *Yoga-Darśanam of Patañjali: Pātañjala Yoga-Pradīpa*, 14th edn., Gorakhpur (U.P., India): Gita Press.

Tagare, G.V. (tr.), 1976-78, *Bhāgavata Purāṇa*, vol. 1-5, rev. edn., Delhi: Motilal Banarsidass.

Tilak, Bal Gangadhar (comm.), 1971, *Srimad Bhagavadgita-Rahasya* or *Karma-Yoga-Sastra*, 3rd edn., Pune: Tilak Brothers.

Warrier, A.G.K. (tr.), 1983, *The Bhagavad-Gītā (Śrimad Bhagavad-Gītā Bhāṣya of Śrī Śaṅkarācārya)*, Chennai: Sri Ramakrishna Math.

*Yajurveda, The* (*Śukla-Yajurveda-Saṁhitā*, with the commentaries of Uvaṭa and Mahīdhara), 1st publ. 1971, reprint 1987, ed. Pandit Jagadishlal Shastri, Delhi: Motilal Banarsidass.

Yardi, M.R. (tr. from Marathi), 1991, *Shri Jnanadeva's Bhavartha Dipika (Jnaneshwari)*, Pune: Bharatiya Vidya Bhavan.

*Yoga-Darśanam of Patañjali: Pātañjala Yoga-Darśana* with *Vyāsa Bhāṣya*, Varanasi: Chaukhamba Sanskrit Samsthan, 1990.

# अनुक्रमणिका

**प**

## ह

# Index